AIRCRAFT GAS TURBINE POWERPLANTS
TEXTBOOK

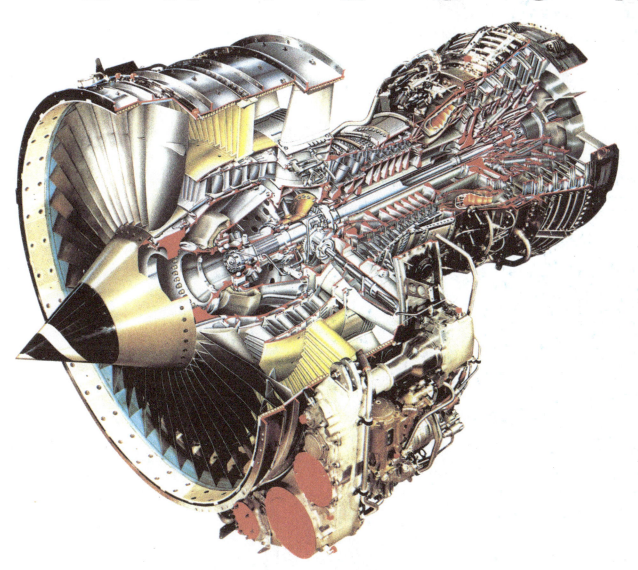

Charles E. Otis   **Peter A. Vosbury**

Library of Congress Cataloging-in-Publication Number 91-14478

Copyright © 1997, 2001, 2002, 2010 by Charles E. Otis, M. Ed. and Peter A. Vosbury, M. Ed.
Published by Aircraft Technical Book Company.
All Rights Reserved.

No part of this publication may be reproduced, stored in a retrieval system, transmitted in any form or by any means, electronic, mechanical, photocopying, recording or otherwise, without the prior written permission of the publisher.

ISBN 978-1941144695

Table of Contents

Preface viii
Introduction ix

CHAPTER 1
History of Turbine Engine Development 1-1
Hero's Aeolipile 1-1
Chinese Rocket 1-1
Branca's Turbine Device 1-1
Newton's Horseless Carriage 1-2
Moss Turbo-Supercharger 1-2
Sir Frank Whittle, British Development 1-2
German and Italian Developments 1-5
Early American Gas Turbine Development 1-6
Commercial Aircraft Development 1-6
Commuter and Business Jets 1-8
Other Developments 1-8

CHAPTER 2
Jet Propulsion Theory 2-1
Four Types of Jet Engines 2-1
Powerplant Selection 2-2
Turbine Engine Types 2-5
Physics of the Gas Turbine Engine 2-10
Potential and Kinetic Energy 2-14
Bernoulli's Principle 2-14
The Brayton Cycle 2-16
Newton's Laws and the Gas Turbine 2-18
Thrust and SHP Calculations 2-20
Gas Turbine Engine Performance Curves 2-29
RPM Limits Imposed on Turbine Engines 2-37
Why the Turbofan is Replacing the Turbojet 2-38

CHAPTER 3
Turbine Engine Design and Construction 3-1
Turbine Engine Entrance Ducts 3-1
Accessory Section 3-6
Compressor Section 3-9
Compressor-Diffuser Section 3-29
Combustion Section 3-29
Turbine Section 3-36
Exhaust Section 3-45
Thrust Reversers 3-51
Noise Suppression 3-54
Engine Compartment Ventilation and Cooling 3-58
Engine Mounts 3-58
Bearings 3-58
Construction Materials 3-58
Engine Stations 3-63
Directional References 3-63

CHAPTER 4
Engine Familiarization 4-1
The Pratt & Whitney JT8D Turbofan Engine 4-1
Familiarization with the Rolls-Royce Allison Model 250 Turboshaft Engine 4-12
Familiarization with the Pratt & Whitney Pt6 Turboprop Engine 4-24
Familiarization with the GE/Snecma, CFM56 Turbofan Engine 4-34
Engine Data Sheets 4-48

CHAPTER 5
Inspection and Maintenance 5-1
Line Maintenance 5-1
Shop Maintenance 5-8
Nondestructive Inspections and Repairs 5-12
Cold Section Inspection and Repair 5-17
Hot Section Inspection and Repair 5-25
Main Bearings and Seals 5-33
Torque Wrench Use 5-42
Locking Methods for Engine Fasteners 5-44
Test Cell Maintenance 5-46
Engine Time Change and On-Condition Maintenance Concepts 5-50
Troubleshooting — Aircraft Ground Operation 5-51
Troubleshooting Aircraft In-Flight Data 5-54
Inspection and Troubleshooting Terms 5-58
Technical Data Standards 5-60

CHAPTER 6
Lubrication Systems 6-1
Principles of Engine Lubrication 6-1
Requirements of Turbine Engine Lubricants 6-1
Oil Sampling 6-3
Synthetic Lubricants 6-5
Servicing 6-7
Wet Sump Lubrication Systems 6-8
Dry Sump Systems 6-9
Small Engine Lubrication System — General Electric CJ610 Turbojet 6-23
Small Engine Lubrication System — Pratt & Whitney PT6 Turboprop 6-31
Large Engine Lubrication System — Pratt & Whitney JT8D Turbofan 6-33
Large Engine Lubrication System — CFM56-7B Turbofan 6-35
Hot Tank Versus Cold Tank Systems 6-38
Troubleshooting Lubrication Systems 6-39

CHAPTER 7
Fuel Systems 7-1
Principles of Fuel Systems 7-1
Fuel Controlling Systems 7-7
Fuel Control Signals 7-8
Simplified Fuel Control Schematic (Hydro-Mechanical Unit) 7-8
Hydro-Pneumatic Fuel Control System, PT6 Turboprop (Bendix Fuel Control) 7-11
Bendix Dp-L2® Fuel Control (Hydro-Pneumatic Unit) 7-16
Electronic Fuel Scheduling Systems 7-18
Auxiliary Power Unit Fuel Controlling System 7-28
Fuel Control Adjustments, Main Engines 7-30
Water Injection Thrust Augmentation 7-43
Fuel System Components and Accessories 7-48

Example of a Corporate Engine Fuel System 7-65
Example of a Commercial Engine Fuel System (Pratt & Whitney Jt8d) 7-65
Example of a Commercial Engine Fuel System (G.E./Snecma CFM56) 7-65
Troubleshooting Fuel Systems 7-68

CHAPTER 8
Compressor Anti-Stall Systems 8-1

Variable Angle Compressor Stator Vane System (Large Engine) 8-1
Variable Angle Compressor Vane System with Fadec Interface (General Electric CFM56 Turbofan) 8-4
Variable Angle Inlet Guide Vane System (Small Engine) 8-5
Troubleshooting the Variable Vane System 8-6
Compressor Anti-Stall Bleed Systems 8-6
Troubleshooting Compressor Bleed Systems 8-14

CHAPTER 9
Anti-Icing Systems 9-1

System Operation 9-3
Cockpit Controls and Anti-Ice Valve Operation 9-4
Anti-Icing Interface with an Electronic Engine Control and FADEC 9-5
Electro-Thermal Anti-Icing System 9-5
Troubleshooting the Anti-Icing System 9-5

CHAPTER 10
Starter Systems 10-1

Electric Starters 10-3
Starter-Generator, Small Engines 10-3
Large Engine Starter-Generators 10-4
Pneumatic (Air Turbine) Starter 10-6
Other Starting Systems 10-14
Troubleshooting the Starter System 10-18

CHAPTER 11
Ignition Systems 11-1

Main Ignition System 11-1
Special Handling 11-4
Joule Ratings 11-5
Types of Ignition Systems 11-5
Igniter Plugs 11-11
Complete Engine Ignition System — G.E./Snecma CFM56 11-16
Troubleshooting the Ignition System 11-19

CHAPTER 12
Engine Instrument Systems 12-1

Exhaust Temperature Indicating Systems 12-4
Troubleshooting the EGT/ITT Indicating System 12-11
Troubleshooting the Engine with the EGT/ITT Indicating System 12-11
Tachometer Percent RPM Indicating Systems 12-12
Troubleshooting the Tachometer Percent RPM Indicating System 12-16
Troubleshooting the Engine with the Tachometer Percent RPM Indicating System 12-17
Engine Pressure Ratio System 12-17

Troubleshooting the EPR Indicating System ... 12-18
Troubleshooting the Engine with the EPR Indicating System ... 12-19
Torque Indicating System ... 12-19
Troubleshooting the Torque Indicating System ... 12-24
Troubleshooting the Engine with the Torque Indicating System ... 12-24
Fuel Flow Indicating System ... 12-24
Troubleshooting the Fuel Flow Indicating System ... 12-27
Troubleshooting the Engine with the Fuel Flow Indicating System ... 12-27
Oil System Indicators ... 12-28
Troubleshooting the Oil Indicating System ... 12-31
Troubleshooting the Engine with Oil System Indicators ... 12-32
Marking of Powerplant Instruments ... 12-32

CHAPTER 13
Fire/Overheat Detection and Extinguishing Systems for Turbine Engines ... 13-1

Single-Wire Thermal Fire/Overheat Detection Switch ... 13-1
Two-Wire Thermal Fire/Overheat Detection Switch ... 13-1
Continuous Loop Fire/Overheat Detection System ... 13-2
Pneumatic Fire/Overheat Detection System ... 13-3
Other Fire Detection Systems ... 13-6
Fire Extinguishing ... 13-6
Cleaning the Engine After Use of Extinguishing Agents ... 13-8
Pneumatic Fire/Overheat Detection and Fire Extinguishing System ... 13-8

CHAPTER 14
Engine Operation ... 14-1

Safety Precautions ... 14-1
Turbojet and Turbofan Engine Run-Up ... 14-1
Engine Operation with FADEC Capabilities ... 14-2
Emergency Operating Procedures ... 14-4
Engine Runup of Turboprop Engines (Fixed Turbine Engine) ... 14-5
FAA Engine Power Ratings ... 14-9
Typical Operating Cautions for All Turbine-Powered Aircraft ... 14-9

Appendix 1	Type Certificate Data Sheet No. E1GL	A1-1
Appendix 2	Type Certificate Data Sheet No. E23EA	A2-1
Appendix 3	Decimal Equivalents, Drill Sizes/Decimal Equivalents, Temperature Conversions, Conversion Factors	A3-1
Appendix 4	Gas Turbine-Powered Aircraft Familiarization	A4-1
Appendix 5	Common Hand Signals	A5-1
Appendix 6	Local Speed of Sound (Cs) Chart	A6-1
Appendix 7	U.S. Standard Atmosphere, 1962 (Geopotential Altitude)	A7-1
Appendix 8	Other Useful Formulae and Standard Information	A8-1
Appendix 9	Pressure Correction Factors, Temperature Correction Factors	A9-1
Appendix 10	Ground Vs. Flight Performance Data	A10-1
Glossary		G-1
Answers to Study Questions		Q-1
Index		I-1

Preface

The *Aircraft Gas Turbine Powerplants* textbook belongs to a family of classroom and self-study texts from Aircraft Technical Book Company, a long-time leader in aviation technical training materials. In this textbook you will find comprehensive information about the historical development and theory of gas turbine engines as well as specific technical aspects regarding their application in a variety of aircraft including helicopters, turboprops, and jet airplanes up to the largest transport-category airliners.

The goal of Aircraft Technical Book Companies training manuals is to improve the quality of education for aviation maintenance and flight personnel as well as aviation enthusiasts throughout the world. Bear in mind that you should always obtain specific repair and application information directly from the manufacturer and follow all manufacturers' procedures in detail.

The Aircraft Gas Turbine Powerplants textbook includes a series of carefully prepared study questions at the end of each chapter. These questions (supported by an answer key at the back of the book) emphasize key elements and enable you to continually check your understanding and retain information as you navigate through the material.

ACKNOWLEDGEMENTS

The authors would like to extend special thanks to the following manufacturers and organizations for their help in providing key information. Without their help, this book would not have been possible.

- Aircraft Technical Book Company
- The Boeing Company
- General Electric Aircraft Engine Company
- Honeywell Aerospace
- Kidde Aerospace and Fenwal Safety Systems
- Pratt & Whitney, a United Technologies Company
- Rolls-Royce Group plc
- Hamilton Sundstrand
- Unison Industries
- U.S. Air Force Training
- U.S. Navy Training

THE AUTHORS

Charles E. Otis is a Professor Emeritus at Embry-Riddle Aeronautical University

Peter A. Vosbury, Professor of Aeronautical Science, ERAU

Charles E. Otis Biography

CHARLES E. OTIS

Charles E. Otis grew up in Rhode Island during World War II. While quite young, he developed a strong interest in aircraft and spent many hours collecting scrapbook pictures of aircraft and making models of aircraft from different materials. Much of his leisure time, while in high school, was spent at the local airports spotting and identifying aircraft for his personal logbook.

Shortly after graduation from high school he enlisted in the Air Force and applied for the Aircraft and Engine training course at Sheppard Air Force Base in Wichita Falls, Texas. After going to school, Charles started his Air Force career by performing flight-line maintenance on a variety of military transport aircraft. His career progressed and he moved on to supervise personnel performing these same tasks. As a supervisor of aircraft maintenance, he attended many conferences with aircraft and engine manufacturers, assisting in the upgrading of technical data essential to aircraft performance and safety.

During his twenty-one year military career, Charles attended Federal Aviation Administration classroom courses and workshops and ended up receiving an FAA Airframe and Powerplant certification. He also enrolled in university extension courses offered by the University of Maryland, Boston University, and the University of West Florida (UWF). He later attended UWF full time and graduated with a baccalaureate degree in education.

When his twenty-one year military career ended, Charles attended the University of Central Florida in Orlando and received a Masters in Education. He then took a position at Embry-Riddle Aeronautical University (ERAU) in Daytona Beach, Florida. His classroom and laboratory duties included curriculum development, instructing students in the history, design and maintenance of the gas turbine engine, and the numerous FAA regulations applicable to aircraft maintenance. He also became the course monitor for the Gas Turbine Engine courses, teaching both the classroom material and the associated laboratory hands-on instruction. The laboratory instruction included the disassembly, inspection, repair and performance testing of the gas turbine engines that were part of the student's training.

Eventually he received a full professorship at ERAU. Charles continued to teach both American and international students who were interested in receiving their FAA Airframe and Powerplant certification. Many of his students went on to complete a two-year associate degree or a baccalaureate degree at ERAU. Charles is now retired from Embry-Riddle, with the honorary academic rank of Professor Emeritus.

Charles is the co-author of this textbook and its companion workbook, and he is also the co-author of The Encyclopedia of Jet Aircraft Engines. He has written numerous published magazine articles in his field. He was a contract person for Technical Advisory Service for Attorneys (TASA) in Washington, D.C., performing research on FAA safety regulations as they applied to aircraft litigation cases. He also served as a consultant to the turbine engine industry.

In his retirement Charles has been busy volunteering his time at a facility that provides housing to the homeless. As a result of his volunteer work, he was given a United Way Volunteer of the Year Award as well as being a national Point of Light recipient. He resides in Port Orange, Florida with his wife.

Peter A. Vosbury Biography

PETER A. VOSBURY

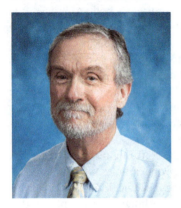

Peter A. Vosbury grew up in South Florida in the 1950s and early 60s. His first exposure to aviation was through his step-father, who was the Director of Personnel for Pan American World Airways. He spent time at the airport, watching airplanes take off and land, and was always asking questions about what made them fly and how all the parts and pieces worked. He always had an interest in technology, and enjoyed taking things apart, figuring out what made them work, and then putting them back together.

After graduating from high school, Peter had an opportunity to attend a liberal arts college in Winter Park, Florida. After one semester, he knew that was not the type of education he was looking for. He was interested in aviation and technology, and he learned about a school in Daytona Beach known as Embry-Riddle Aeronautical Institute (now University). He attended Embry-Riddle, graduating from the Airframe and Powerplant technical program.

After graduating from Embry-Riddle, he worked in General Aviation at an airport in Saint Petersburg, Florida, before joining the U.S. Navy in 1969. In the Navy he worked as an Aviation Machinist Mate Jet (ADJ), maintaining the powerplants on a squadron of airplanes known as the E-2 Hawkeye. He served on the aircraft carrier USS Forrestal, deploying to the Mediterranean four times between 1970 and 1973. When the squadron was not deployed, Peter had a chance to work in a propeller overhaul facility, and to have some flight engineer time in the C-130.

When Peter got out of the Navy in 1973, he went back to school, completing his graduate degree in education at the University of Central Florida. In 1976 he had an opportunity to become a member of the faculty at Embry-Riddle Aeronautical University, where he has been teaching ever since. He spent his first 25 years at Embry-Riddle teaching in the Aviation Maintenance Science Department, specializing in the math, physics, regulations and turbine engine courses. He is currently a professor in the Aeronautical Science Department, where he teaches the Aircraft Systems course and the Gas Turbine Engines course.

Peter is a published author, with articles appearing in the Aviation Mechanics Journal, chapters written for the FAA General Mechanics Handbook, and three published books to his credit. He is the co-author of this book on Aircraft Gas Turbine Powerplants, which is used in the turbines courses at Embry-Riddle, and at many other universities and collegiate programs. He is also the co-author of the Encyclopedia of Jet Aircraft and Engines. His most recent book, written in the last two years, is the Aircraft Systems For Professional Pilots textbook. This new book is used for the pilot systems courses at Embry-Riddle, and has also been adopted by more than ten other collegiate aviation programs. For International Aviation Publishers, Peter also wrote the answers and explanations text for the FAA General, Airframe and Powerplant written exams.

The success that Peter has had in the aviation industry can be credited primarily to three things. First and foremost is the love and support that his wife Linda has provided. Second is the work ethic and the desire to learn that his mother, Salley, instilled in him. Third is the kick start to his aviation education that Embry-Riddle provided, especially Professor Frank Moran, who mentored him when he was a student, and eventually hired him when he came back to be a member of the faculty.

Introduction

The first historical application of the jet propulsion principle occurred when a steam-driven toy was demonstrated in Egypt before the Common Era. For nearly twenty centuries, the idea of jet propulsion evolved slowly. It wasn't until the early 20th century that Sir Frank Whittle, an English inventor, first described the possibility of using a gas turbine device as a means of jet propulsion for aircraft. From this modest idea, jet aircraft use has grown into the large multinational industry we know today. Whittle, the "father of the modern gas turbine engine," remained active in gas turbine engine design well into his 70s. He died at the age of 89 in 1996.

To meet the growing demands of modern aircraft, gas turbine engine designs have become increasingly complex and powerful, and the technical tasks required to maintain them have become more and more demanding. It is no longer possible for technicians to gain expertise based on *hands-on* experience alone. Today's complex turbine engines and systems require expert technical training. This textbook serves as a starting point for this training process. It is intended both for those just beginning to explore the world of gas turbine engines and for experienced technicians and flight personnel who are exploring new directions and opportunities within the aviation industry.

Whether you proceed through this book in a formal classroom setting or as an independent student, the material in this textbook provides a sound foundation of the principles of gas turbine engine theory, design, maintenance, and troubleshooting.

Every successful technical educational endeavor begins by providing learners with solid entry-level knowledge. The proven way to acquire this knowledge is to read the material carefully, answer the questions at the end of each chapter, review and research the text, and finally reinforce this knowledge by applying it in actual work experience.

CHAPTER 1
History of Turbine Engine Development

The terms jet engine and gas turbine engine, although sometimes used synonymously to describe aircraft engines, represent substantially different engine designs. Therefore, these terms are carefully defined and used in this book.

The jet engine family includes the rocket jet, ramjet, pulsejet, and gas turbine-powered jet. The gas turbine-powered jet is further broken down into the turbojet, turbopropeller, turboshaft, and turbofan types. These four types of engines are the ones most commonly used in today's aircraft.

All of these engines have evolved for their own purposes. This book first explores the historical development of jet and gas turbine engines and then, in subsequent chapters, concentrates on the types of gas turbine powerplants used for aircraft propulsion.

HERO'S AEOLIPILE

Today's modern turbine engine is based on a centuries-old concept—the reaction principle.

One of the earliest accounts of the use of the reaction principle describes an Egyptian mathematician and philosopher named Heron, or Hero, who invented a device called an aeolipile that converted steam pressure to mechanical power. Current historians date this invention between 100 and 200 B.C. By heating water in a closed vessel and by supplying steam to opposing nozzles mounted on a rotating sphere, Hero was able to successfully demonstrate the reaction principle. Whether he put his aeolipile to practical use remains unknown.

Figure 1-1 shows an artist's rendition of Hero's aeolipole, but the actual device might have looked quite differently.

CHINESE ROCKET

Another early application of the reaction principle occurred in rocket development as early as 1200 A.D. By using black powder, a mixture of charcoal, sulfur, and saltpeter (potassium nitrate), the Chinese were able to construct a solid-fuel rocket. Some historical sources cite a reference to a battle that took place about 1230 A.D. in which the Chinese recorded the use of the rocket as a military weapon. [Figure 1-2]

BRANCA'S TURBINE DEVICE

The first gas turbine device came into use in 1629 when the Italian engineer, Giovanni Branca, produced a steam-driven impulse turbine. Branca's design was a closed, water-filled vessel with one exhaust nozzle aimed at a turbine or impulse wheel. Solid fuel heated the vessel, and the system directed the resulting steam onto the impulse wheel. The rotating wheel then drove a crude cogwheel reduction-gear system. This mechanism, now on display in the British Museum, is said to be the forerunner of the modern turbosupercharger used on reciprocating engines. [Figure 1-3]

Figure 1-1. Hero's aeolipile.

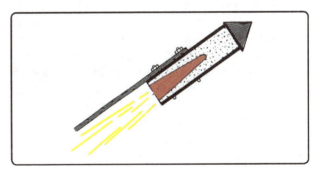

Figure 1-2. Chinese rocket.

Figure 1-3. Branca's turbine.

NEWTON'S HORSELESS CARRIAGE

In 1687, Sir Isaac Newton recognized the principle of jet propulsion and published his third law of motion, which states that every acting force has a reacting force equal in magnitude and opposite in direction. Later a British scientist named Gravensade designed and produced a model of a steam-powered vehicle based on Newton's third law. Unknown is whether he had an actual sketch made by Newton, but he nonetheless received credit for constructing a jet-powered vehicle based on Newton's principle. By mounting a watertight sphere on a four-wheeled carriage and heating the water to steam, he proposed to eject the hot exhaust rearward, thus propelling the vehicle forward. Although a thrust propelling force would be created in this manner, the vehicle would obviously be grossly overweight and underpowered. No record of successful operation of this vehicle exists. [Figure 1-4]

Figure 1-4. Newton's horseless carriage.

MOSS TURBO-SUPERCHARGER

In 1900, while studying for an advanced engineering degree, Dr. Sanford A. Moss published a thesis on the gas turbine engine. He used this early work years later when he developed the first gas turbine device for aircraft application. In 1918, as a General Electric Company engineer, he supervised the production of the gas turbine-driven turbo-supercharger for reciprocating engines. This early work fostered the development of many new low-weight, high-temperature, high-strength materials needed for industrial gas turbine experimentation, which was occurring in both Europe and the United States. [Figure 1-5]

SIR FRANK WHITTLE, BRITISH DEVELOPMENT

Frank Whittle, while a cadet in the British Royal Air College, wrote a thesis advocating use of the gas turbine engine for aircraft propulsion. He was aware of developing industrial uses of ground installation turbine engines and felt that, if an engine could be made light enough in weight, the ram effect of the incoming air in flight would provide sufficient power to make it an effective aircraft powerplant. In 1930, he patented the first turbojet aircraft engine, based on the ideas of his original

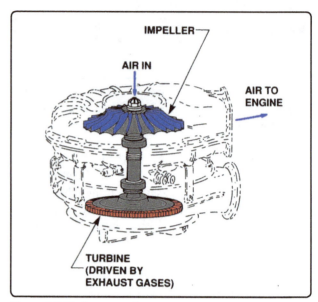

Figure 1-5. Turbo-supercharger.

thesis. His engine was to use a compressor impeller similar to that of Dr. Moss, driven by a turbine wheel.

During the early thirties, Whittle served as a regular officer in the Royal Air Force where he was a design engineer and test pilot of aircraft powered by reciprocating engines. Although reciprocating engines were then undergoing rapid development, Whittle was dissatisfied with what he felt were their obvious limitations—altitude and top speed.

Between 1930 and 1935, Whittle began work on his turbojet engine, but was unsuccessful in obtaining sufficient government or private support to continue development. The prevailing opinion at the time was that his engine was as impractical for business as it was for flight. Discouraged, he put his idea aside, failing even to renew his patent. However, military buildup and political unrest in Europe in 1936 prompted some of Whittle's friends to approach him about forming a private company to start development of a prototype engine. This led to the formation of Power Jets, Ltd., financed entirely by private funds.

The engine Power Jets developed was a pure reaction turbojet—that is, its total thrust came from reaction to the hot gas stream emitted from a propelling nozzle. The engine featured an impeller-type compressor, a multiple-can combustion chamber, and a single stage turbine wheel.

Today, the gas turbine engine receives its name from this design, wherein flowing gas drives the turbine wheel, which is attached to, and drives, the compressor impeller.

On April 12, 1937, Whittle's prototype engine was the first gas turbine engine intended for flight to run successfully on a test stand; the engine eventually produced about 3,000 shaft horsepower on the test stand. (A simi-

Figure 1-6. W-IX, first experimental turbojet demonstrator engine run, April 12, 1937.

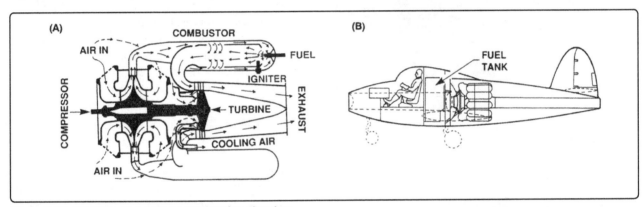

Figure 1-7A. Whittle's reverse-flow combustion chamber.
Figure 1-7B. The first British jet aircraft to fly, the Gloster E28/39 experimental airplane.

lar engine being concurrently developed by the Germans had not reached Whittle's stage of development.) In 1939, Power Jets, Ltd. received an Air Ministry contract to produce a flight engine. [Figure 1-6]

Whittle relates in his 1953 book, Jet - The Story of a Pioneer, that one of the biggest obstacles he had to overcome was obtaining the high-strength, high-temperature metals necessary for the combustion and turbine sections. The first combustor capable of withstanding the demands of flight took Whittle three years of repeated testing to produce. It had ten separate combustion chambers.

In May, 1941, the Whittle W-1 was installed in the Gloster Aircraft Company's newly prepared Model E28/39 aircraft. The aircraft, one of only three built, made its initial test flight at its design speed of 400 m.p.h. without complication. Its gas turbine powerplant produced 1,000 pounds of thrust. [Figure 1-7A and 1-7B, Figure 1-8, Figure 1-9]

Development was immediately started on the W-2, an engine of similar design but with more thrust, which in 1943 would power the twin-engine Meteor aircraft. The

Figure 1-8. Whittle W-1 turbojet engine.

Meteor later successfully engaged the German V1 pulse-jet-powered buzz bomb in the only jet-versus-jet confrontation of World War II. [Figure 1-10, Figure 1-11]

While working on his production engine, Whittle also experimented on several other engine types. In 1936, he patented the first turbofan engine, wrote proposals for use of the gas turbine to drive a propeller, and developed a prototype supersonic flight engine with an axial compressor. He did not have the funding or gov-

Figure 1-9. Gloster Meteor.

Figure 1-10. Whittle W2/700 turbojet engine.

Figure 1-11. Frank Whittle and the Whittle W-2/200 turbojet engine.

ernmental support to proceed with these projects and he eventually stopped his work on these new engine types. However, they were all later developed as practical engines, but only after Whittle had quit developing gas turbine engines.

In 1945, Frank Whittle wrote the following passages, which revealed his profound foresight regarding the potential of the gas turbine engine:

"The aircraft gas turbine has undoubtedly come to stay. In the space of a few years I expect to see it displace the reciprocating engine in all aircraft except possibly the light types. I make the reservation about light aircraft because at present it seems more difficult to design for lower powers than for much higher powers than we use at present, but it is possible that the gas turbine will invade the light aircraft field also.

"For very high speeds and moderate range the turbojet is the appropriate application but for lower speeds and long range the gas turbine driving a propeller will be used. Personally I think there is a strong case for the use of a gas turbine driving a ducted fan for moderate speeds. Although no strong claims can be made for it on the basis of fuel consumption, it has important advantages in respect to noise reduction and absence of vibration when compared with a turbine-airscrew combination (turboprop). Further, for civil aircraft the elimination of visible 'whirling lumps' is not an inconsiderable psychological factor in its favour.

"The speed possibilities inherent in gas turbines have been clearly shown by the establishment of the World's Air Speed Record at over 600 mph. Much higher speeds will undoubtedly be achieved in the fairly near future. There is no speed limit imposed by the powerplant. In fact, the higher the speed the greater the efficiency and power. The attainment of higher speeds therefore depends more upon the aircraft designer than on the turbine designer, though powerplant developments will naturally play their part. I do not think that we shall have to wait very long before aerodynamic developments make possible the attainment of supersonic speeds.

"If long range is to be combined with high speed, flight at great heights will be necessary, and hence the development of the pressure cabin is of great importance. In the not very distant future I expect to see passenger aircraft covering long distances at speeds of approximately 500 mph at altitudes of the order of 40,000 ft., as a result of the parallel development of the gas turbine, the aircraft, the pressure cabin, and radio and radar aids to navigation.

"The advent of the aircraft gas turbine makes necessary some important changes of outlook on the part of the designers. Hitherto it has been the practice to develop engines and aircraft virtually independently of each other, but this procedure will not do if we are to get the best out of gas turbine-powered aircraft. The performance of the turbine is very dependent upon its installation in the aeroplane and the installation has a very large influence on aircraft drag characteristics. It follows that powerplant and airframe must each be 'tailor-made' to suit the other. The short development time required for gas turbines should make this procedure easy to follow, more especially as the nature of the engine is such that any successful basic design can be scaled up or down without introducing a host of fresh development troubles. This indeed is a very valuable characteristic.

"We are as yet only at the beginning of this field of engineering and immense possibilities lie before us. The variations possible with a reciprocating engine are limited by the fact that the processes of compression, combustion and expansion take place in the same organ, the cylinder. In the gas turbine these processes take place in separate components. We can perform the compression process with axial flow compressors, centrifugal compressors, or combinations of these. The combustion chamber can take one of several forms, and there are a large number of variations possible in the turbine. There are many ways in which the major component units can be arranged in combination, and in addition there are the possibilities involved in the use of ducted fans, heat exchangers, after-burning, and other developments.

"Up to the present two clear lines of development have been apparent in aircraft gas turbines, characterized by the use of either centrifugal compressor or the axial flow compressor. I am frequently asked whether one or the other will be ultimately dominant. My view is that there is a field for both, and that there will be many types in which both will be used in combination.

"Much has been said about the high fuel consumption of turbojet units. It is true that they use a lot of fuel, but that is because they develop a lot of power. In fact, at speeds of the order of 600 mph, the fuel consumption in proportion to effective thrust horsepower is less than it would be for the piston engine and propeller combination at that speed. It is true, however, that at much lower speeds the turbo-jet unit compares very unfavourably with the conventional powerplant in respect of fuel consumption, but the gas turbine/propeller combination does not suffer from this disadvantage to anything like the same extent. In whatever form the gas turbine is used, the very low powerplant weight is an important compensating factor. Very low fuel consumption can be shown for complex engines, i.e., combinations of reciprocating engines and turbines. Though I have been amongst those who have proposed such schemes, I am doubtful whether the low fuel consumption is a sufficient compensation for the increased weight, complexity, long development time, and difficulty of installation, etc., except possibly for certain very specialized purposes."

Whittle did not enjoy the personal success or recognition in the gas turbine industry as did his engine. During the war years, 1939-1945, the government absorbed more and more control over his patents, allocating them to large manufacturers and diminishing Whittle's role. By the time he retired as an Air Commodore in 1948, he was no longer working in the gas turbine engine field.

GERMAN AND ITALIAN DEVELOPMENTS

While Whittle was struggling for governmental support, a German engineer named Hans Von Ohain, in 1936, had successfully demonstrated a model of the gas turbine engine to his government and was given practically unlimited funding for research and development. Working with the Heinkel Company, Von Ohain patented and designed the powerplant for the single engine He-178 aircraft, which, in August, 1939, made the first purely jet-propelled flight in history. Only one aircraft was built, and it flew a total of three times. [Figure 1-12]

The Heinkel He-178 was powered by a centrifugal flow turbojet engine, the HeS-3B, which produced approximately 1,100 pounds of thrust. Von Ohain's engine was produced by completely independent development. He used none of Whittle's early work in producing this first centrifugal compressor type engine. Von Ohain later went on to design the axial flow engine, which has become the standard today for all large gas turbine engines. [Figure 1-13]

In 1942 the Germans flew the two-engine Me-262 aircraft with axial flow turbojet engines made by the Junker Company. The BMW Company later produced a similar engine for this aircraft. Both had a takeoff

Figure 1-12. German Heinkle He-178, first flown on August 27, 1939.

Figure 1-13. Hans von Ohain next to his original flight engine, the HeS-3b, which powered the first turbojet powered plane.

thrust of approximately 2,000 pounds and were capable of propelling this aircraft at speeds up to 500 m.p.h. [Figure 1-14, Figure 1-15]

The hot section (combustor and turbine) of these engines was not as highly developed as its British counterpart, the Whittle W-1 Turbojet, and had to be disassembled for inspection and replacement of parts every 10 to 15 flight hours.

The Italian Caproni Company and its design engineer, Secundo Campini, worked on producing a jet-powered aircraft during the German and British developmental period. However, their designs were along the lines of earlier experimenters who advocated driving the compressor with a liquid-cooled reciprocating engine rather than by driving the compressor from a turbine wheel in the hot gas path, as described in Whittle's first patent. Their aircraft flew in late 1939 with a maximum speed of 205 m.p.h. The limitations placed on the engine by the piston powerplant driving the compressor were the same as those that Whittle had described in his 1929 thesis and, consequently, this design was abandoned with the Caproni-Campini jet aircraft of that era. [Figure 1-16]

EARLY AMERICAN GAS TURBINE DEVELOPMENT

While in England in 1941, General H.H. Hap Arnold was impressed by the progress being made with gas turbine-powered aircraft as a tactical weapon. He procured a Whittle engine and was instrumental in securing an Air Force contract with General Electric for research and development. Between October 1, 1941, and April 2, 1942, General Electric had a redesigned engine running on a test cell.

General Electric was chosen because it had developed many of the necessary high temperature metals for its turbo-supercharger production and because some of its affiliate companies had been supporting Whittle's work in Britain. GE went on to develop the first American prototype turbojet, the GE- I-A.

The Bell Aircraft Company of Buffalo, New York, was chosen to construct the first jet airplane. The urgency to support the nation's war effort precipitated Bell's rapid progress in designing an aircraft for General Electric's engine. In October, 1942, at Muroc Field, California, the Bell XP-59 (Airacomet) was test flown, powered by two General Electric GE-I-A engines, each producing 1,250 pounds of thrust. The Airacomet was never used in combat due to its limited flight time of 30 minutes. It did, however, become a valuable trainer for the later P-80 aircraft. A total of thirty XP-59A aircraft were built. [Figure 1-17, Figure 1-18]

Although the United States did not use the jet airplane in World War II, it did go on to use the basic work of Whittle and General Electric for future military, commercial, and industrial gas turbine development.

Figure 1-14. The first operational jet fighter, the Messerschmidt Me 262 Schwalbe (Swallow), first flown on July 18, 1942, and initially introduced as a bomber interceptor.

Figure 1-16. The Caproni-Campini "jet propelled" monoplane, which used an Isotta Franschini radial piston engine to power a ducted fan-type ramjet.

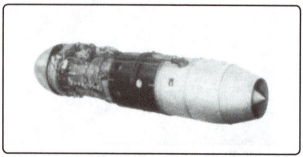

Figure 1-15. Junkers Jumo 004 turbojet engine, two of which powered the Me 262.

Figure 1-17. The Bell Airacomet, a twin turbojet fighter powered by two Whittle-type G.E. gas turbines.

History of Turbine Engine Development

Figure 1-18. The General Electric I-16 (J-31-GE-1 military designation) production model of the GE-1-A turbojet, which produced 1,650 lbs. of thrust at a rated 16,500 r.p.m.

COMMERCIAL AIRCRAFT DEVELOPMENT

The British tested the first turboprop powered passenger liner in 1948, the Vickers Viscount. This aircraft is still in service today. The British also tested the first turbojet-powered airliner, the DeHavilland Comet, in 1949. This four-engine airliner, placed in service in 1952, experienced structural fatigue cracking, resulting in high-altitude decompression. Because of catastrophic crashes that occurred from this new phenomenon, the Comet was grounded in 1954 for extensive testing. It was later reintroduced into airline service and remained in service for many years. [Figure 1-19]

During this period, the Boeing Company of Seattle, Washington, made a pioneering move to bring the United States into the commercial jet aircraft field. Using Pratt & Whitney engines developed for the military, Boeing invested approximately one-fourth of their net worth in what some considered to be one of the most notable business gambles ever taken in the aviation industry. The result was the world renowned Boeing 707, which, after years of testing, went into service in 1958. Boeing currently produces one narrow-body airliner, the B-737, and many wide-body airliners, like the B-747 (Figure 1-20B), B-777 and B-787.

In 1966 the Boeing Company tried to introduce supersonic airline service to the United States with their Boeing 2707, a Mach 2.8 airspeed, 300-passenger aircraft powered by four General Electric GE-4 turbojet engines, each capable of producing 68,000 pounds of thrust. Congress voted to stop funding for this program in the late 1960s primarily because of pressure from environmentalists. The theory at that time was that high flight (that is, in the 60,000-foot altitude range) would negatively affect the earth's ozone layer. In 1971 Boeing stopped work on the project. [Figure 1-21]

In 1976 the British, in partnership with the French, built and placed into service sixteen smaller supersonic jetliners named the Concorde. Powered by Rolls-Royce

Figure 1-19A. Vickers Viscount, the first commercial turboprop transport, placed in service in 1950.
Figure 1-19B. The first commercial jet transport, the de Havilland DH 106 Comet 1, which began passenger service in 1952.

Figure 1-20A. An early Boeing 707.
Figure 1-20B. Boeing 747.

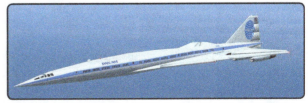

Figure 1-21. The American SST design, Boeing 2707-300.

Olympus turbojet engines, the Concorde could carry 100 passengers at speeds of 2.2 times the speed of sound. In actual service, its cruising speed was reduced closer to Mach 2.0 to reduce the additional stresses imposed on the airframe at higher airspeeds. [Figure 1-22]

Figure 1-22. The British-French Concorde SST.

Many researchers currently consider aircraft such as the Concorde and other high-flying military aircraft to have only a negligible impact on the ozone layer and theorize that the atmosphere readily repairs itself in the presence of high-flying aircraft. Current research seems to indicate that ozone depletion occurs primarily from industrial and agricultural pollution. The British/French Concorde was first flight tested in 1969 and was removed from service in 2003.

Two recent advancements in gas turbine development are worthy of mention. The first is the Europrop International Corporation's TP 400, an advanced, swept-back, eight-bladed turboprop (or propfan) capable of producing 11,000 shaft horsepower, making it the largest turboprop built to date. [Figure 1-23A] The second is the General Electric unducted fan engine (UDF), currently under development, which is designed to replace the mid-range thrust engines of present narrow-bodied airliners. [Figure 1-23B]

The aviation industry, however, must search for methods of complying with new and more stringent regulations issued by the Environmental Protection Agency (EPA) and the Federal Aviation Administration (FAA) concerning noise and exhaust pollution. Although only the future can reveal the ways in which the industry will solve these problems and take the next step forward in supersonic aviation, with history as a yardstick, the aviation industry will undoubtedly find the necessary solutions.

COMMUTER AND BUSINESS JETS

The use of the gas turbine engine in commuter aircraft, business jets, and even general aviation aircraft, has expanded greatly since the 1970s and the trend continues into the 21st century.

Although the commuter airline industry (also known as regional carriers) was once dominated by the small turboprop airplane, much of the industry is switching to turbofan-powered airplanes, known as regional jets. These airplanes, powered by high-bypass fan engines and capable of seating from 50 to 100 passengers, are selling briskly to meet demand.

Business jets, also with high-bypass fan engines, continue to increase in popularity and are no longer the sole domain of Fortune 50 or Fortune 100 companies.

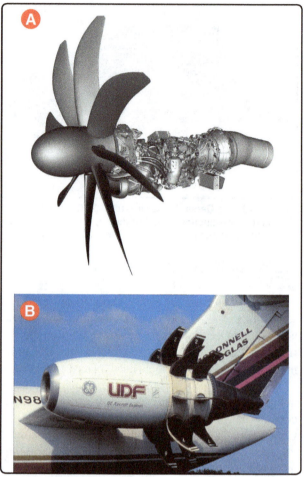

Figure 1-23A. Advanced swept-back eight-bladed turboprop (Propfan) on a test stand.
Figure 1-23B. General Electric unducted fan engine on an MD-80 testbed aircraft.

Many smaller companies now have business jets at their disposal, often by way of fractional ownership.

Some companies currently produce and sell what is sometimes referred to as the affordable jet. Also known as very light jets (VLJs), affordable jets were initially intended to sell for around 1 million dollars, but that price has now increased to 2 to 5 million dollars. The current VLJs have two small turbofan engines, seat 4 to 6 people, and cruise at 400 to 500 m.p.h. Each engine produces between 800 and 1,500 pounds of thrust, and weighs between 100 and 200 pounds. Some companies are also developing a single-engine VLJ.

A variety of U.S. and International companies now produce the bulk of gas turbine engines used in fixed-wing and rotary-wing aircraft common to commercial, commuter, business, and military aviation. Companies based in the United States include:
- United Technologies (Pratt & Whitney)
- General Electric Engines
- Honeywell-Lycoming
- Teledyne
- Williams International

International companies include:
- Rolls-Royce, Great Britain
- CFM International (General Electric, USA and Snecma, France)
- Europrop International, France
- International Aero Engines (Pratt & Whitney, Rolls-Royce, MTU Germany)
- Klimov, Russia
- Safran-Turbomeca, France.

These companies and others have all capitalized on earlier technological discoveries and developments for military and commercial engines to produce a more reliable powerplant for the turbine powered aircraft of today. The turbine engine-powered aircraft has become very popular, in part, because of its superior reliability and commercial airline type speed.

Much of the early technology base applied to the development of civil aviation was an outgrowth of work done for the military, sponsored with governmental funding. Today, throughout the world, research and development for new commercial and business aviation engines is carried out mostly with private investment.

OTHER DEVELOPMENTS

Some notable firsts in the evolution of the gas turbine engine in civil aviation include:
- First flight test of a commercial turboprop-powered aircraft—British Viscount, 1948.
- First flight test of a commercial turbojet-powered aircraft—British Comet, 1949.
- First flight test of a commercial turbofan-powered aircraft—British VC.10, 1959.
- First flight test of a supersonic commercial turbojet-powered airliner—USSR TU-144, 1968.
- First flight test of a commercial propfan engine in a Boeing 727 test aircraft—GE-36, unducted fan engine (UDF), 1986.
- First propfan in service—Progress-27, in a Russian Antonov AN-70, first test-flown in 1994.

QUESTIONS:

1. What is the earliest indication, in history, of the presence of a jet propulsion device?

2. Whose first patent for a jet propulsion flight engine causes him to be recognized today as the father of the jet engine?

3. Which aircraft made the first purely jet propelled flight?

4. Name America's first gas turbine powered commercial airliner.

5. Name the western world's only supersonic transport.

6. What purpose did the reciprocating engine serve in the Italian Caproni-Campini jet-propelled airplane?

7. What type of gas turbine was used to power the Vickers Viscount aircraft?

8. What was the designation of the first jet-propelled fighter aircraft?

9. What was the name of the first American jet-propelled fighter aircraft?

10. What was the designation of the Russian supersonic passenger liner comparable to the British/French Concorde?

CHAPTER 2
Jet Propulsion Theory

Jet propulsion is the reacting force produced by the acceleration of air, gas, or liquid through a nozzle.

FOUR TYPES OF JET ENGINES

The four common types of jet engines, the rocket jet, the ramjet, the pulsejet, and the turbine jet, are propelled by the emission of a gaseous fluid.

The rocket jet is a non–air-breathing engine. This means it does not use atmospheric air to support combustion but carries its own oxidizer and fuel in a solid or liquid form. Combustion transforms solids or liquids of small volume into gases of large volume that escape through an exhaust nozzle at an extremely high velocity. The reaction of the exhaust gases creates thrust that drives the rocket at very high supersonic speeds and completely out of the earth's atmosphere. [Figures 2-1 and 2-2]

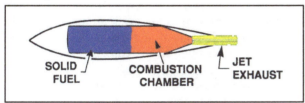

Figure 2-1. Solid fuel rocket

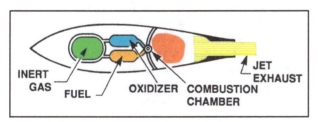

Figure 2-2. Liquid fuel rocket

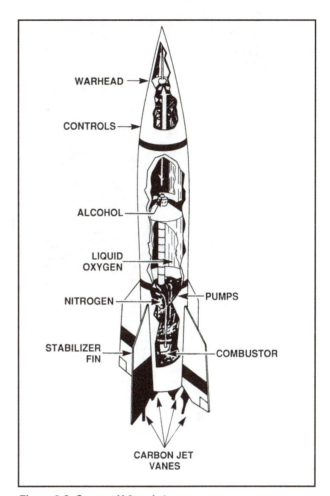

Figure 2-3. German V-2 rocket

The German V-2 rocket jet of World War II was propelled by the combustion of a mixture of alcohol as the fuel and liquid oxygen as the oxidizer and produced 52,000 pounds of thrust. The V-2 was capable of reaching Mach 3. [Figure 2-3]

The liquid hydrogen fuel of the space shuttle supplies each of the three main engines with approximately 400,000 pounds of thrust. The main engines and the solid fuel rocket boosters fire during takeoff. The boosters each produce approximately three million pounds of thrust and are jettisoned after takeoff. [Figure 2-4]

The athodyd (aero-thermodynamic duct), or ramjet, is the simplest of all powerplants. The ramjet uses the atmosphere to support combustion. It is essentially a duct with few component parts, which receives inlet air and changes its velocity to static pressure. The ramjet system adds fuel, typically of hydrocarbon base, to the compressed air, and the resultant combustion and expansion of gases causes the mass airflow to exit the engine. The rapid change in the velocity of entering and departing air results in reactive thrust. Currently, many pilotless weapons delivery vehicles use the ramjet. [Figures 2-5 and 2-6]

There is an application for a hypersonic (above Mach 6.0) engine undergoing testing that functions as a turbojet at lower speed flight and as a type of ramjet at very high speeds. This new engine type is called a scramjet because the airflow would be allowed to reach supersonic speeds during combustion, hence the term supersonic combustion-ramjet (scramjet). This engine will have to use a more exotic fuel than kerosene, perhaps hydrogen, in order to support combustion at high airflow velocities. Many aeronautical engineers believe that the scramjet

Figure 2-4. Space shuttle and rocket booster

has the potential to power future high-speed transports at velocities up to Mach 20.

The pulsejet is similar to a ramjet except that the pulsejet inlet is fitted with a system of air inlet flapper valves. Closed during combustion, these valves provide a moderate static thrust that the ramjet does not have. However, this thrust is insufficient to enable a pulsejet to take off under its own power, so it must be rocket boosted for initial flight. Major development of the pulsejet seems to have ceased with the German V-1 rocket of World War II. The V-1 was powered by a rocket-assisted pulsejet engine that could propel it to approximately 400 m.p.h.

The flapper valves in the V-1 engine automatically opened and closed approximately 40 times per second. Each time fuel pulsed into the combustion chamber, combustion backpressure closed the valves, and ram inlet air pressure reopened them after combustion. This intermittent combustion was, in effect, a series of rapid backfires or pulses of force that created forward thrust of approximately 600 pounds. A single electrical spark igniter was used for initial starting. Subsequent ignition occurred from internal residual heat. [Figure 2-7] Development of the pulsejet ceased in the late 1940s due to the poor performance of this engine design.

The aircraft gas turbine is a heat engine that uses air as a working fluid. In its most basic form, it consists of an air compressor, a combustion chamber, and a turbine that extracts energy from the high-velocity exhaust gases. Some of the energy in the hot gases drives the compressor and accessories; the remainder produces power or thrust. The turbine jet, specifically the gas turbine engine, is a name given to a family of engines based on the Whittle design, which include the turbojet, turboprop, turboshaft, and turbofan. These four gas turbines are discussed in detail throughout this chapter.

POWERPLANT SELECTION

Selection of a particular type of powerplant usually depends on the cruising speed requirements or the specialized use of the aircraft.

RECIPROCATING ENGINE — TURBOSHAFT ENGINE

Today's light aircraft, with a cruising speed of under 250 m.p.h., most commonly use a reciprocating engine because of its low initial and operating costs, while a rotorcraft is more likely to use a turboshaft engine for its low weight-to-power ratio.

A turboshaft engine of comparable power has an advantage of five to eight times less weight than a piston engine. Fuel consumption levels are about the same. The Honeywell (formerly Lycoming) T-55 Turboshaft engine used in the Chinook helicopter produces 4,800 shaft horsepower with a weight of 832 pounds, giving a 5.7:1 power-to-weight ratio. This excellent ratio surpasses even the turboprop engine due to the absence of a bulky propeller reduction gearing system. In helicopters, the major portion of the reduction gearing occurs in the aircraft transmission.

TURBOPROP ENGINE

Turboprop engine performance and economy are best in the 250 to 450 m.p.h. range because, like the turboshaft, it produces more power per pound of weight than does the reciprocating engine. For example, one

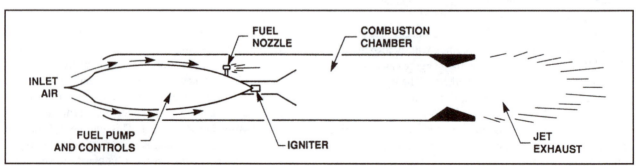

Figure 2-5. Ramjet engine

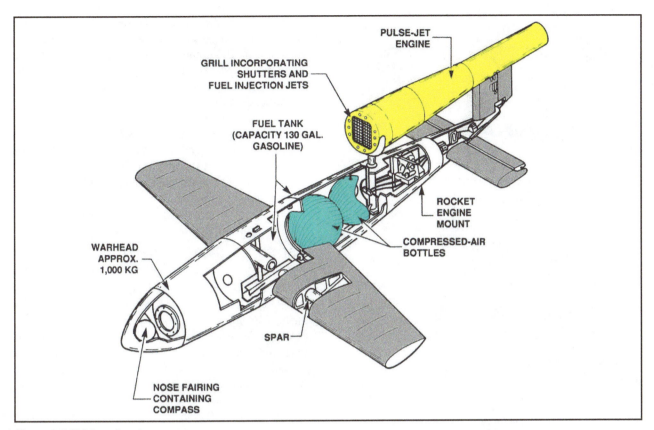

Figure 2-6. V-1 buzz bomb

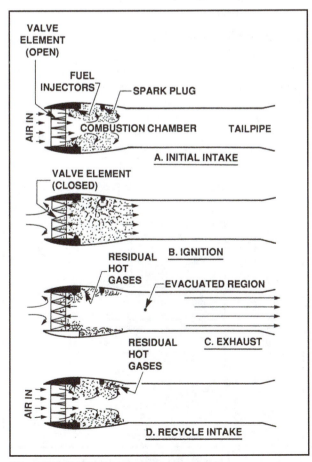

Figure 2-7. Pulsejet engine operating cycle

model developed by the Honeywell Company (formerly Garrett), the TPE 331 turboprop, weighs 360 pounds and produces 1,040 SHP with a resultant power-to-weight ratio in excess of 2.8 to 1. The best reciprocating engine/propeller combination would have a power-to-weight ratio of slightly less than 1:1. However, the turboprop aircraft, like a piston engine aircraft, rapidly loses its power due to increased drag at higher airspeeds.

TURBOFAN (TURBOJET)

The turbofan, or turbojet, is the most widely used engine in aircraft that cruise at speeds in excess of 450 m.p.h. [Figure 2-8] The turbofan is newer and has become the most popular powerplant for commercial and business jets because it produces the most propulsive power at higher subsonic cruising speeds. The turbofan engine permits higher turbine temperatures without a corresponding increase in jet velocity because a high jet velocity is inefficient for subsonic flight.

Today some large turbojets remain in use in military aviation. Low-bypass turbofan engines power all current military supersonic aircraft, like the B-1 bomber or F-22 advanced tactical fighter.

RATING THE POWER OUTPUT OF A GAS TURBINE ENGINE

The gas turbine engine produces power by reactive force. This thrust force is expressed in pounds, and the jet engine power output is rated in pounds of thrust. The manufacturer usually determines this rating by operating

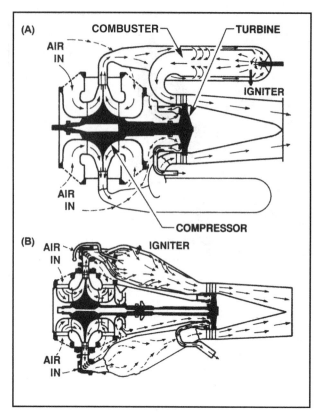

Figure 2-8A. Early Whittle turbojet with reverse-flow combustor

Figure 2-8B. Whittle turbojet with flow-through combustor

the engine in a special test cell where the thrust output can be measured accurately.

Because a jet engine is rated in pounds of thrust, and a conventional reciprocating engine is rated in brake horsepower (bhp), no direct comparison can be made between the two. However, the brake horsepower of a reciprocating engine is converted into thrust by the propeller, so the thrust from the jet engine can be compared with the thrust from the propeller of the reciprocating engine.

The graph in Figure 2-9 compares the thrust developed by four types of engines as airspeed increases. The four engine types are the reciprocating type driving a propeller (P), the jet turboprop engine driving a propeller (TP), the turbofan jet engine (TF), and the turbojet engine (TJ). The performance curve for each engine shows how thrust varies with airspeed, and the aircraft drag curve shows how maximum aircraft speed varies by engine type. Because the graph only compares relative performance, the exact thrust, aircraft speed, and drag have no numerical values.

When the thrust generated by these four powerplants is compared, certain things become evident. In the speed range shown to the left of Line A, the reciprocating engine (P) outperforms the other three types. The turboprop (TP) outperforms the turbofan (TF) in the range to the left of line C. The turbofan engine outperforms the turbojet (TJ) in the range to the left of Line F. The turbofan engine outperforms the conventional engine to the right of Line B and the turboprop to the right of Line C. The turbojet outperforms the conventional engine to the right of Line D, the turboprop to the right of Line E, and the turbofan to the right of Line F.

The intersections of the drag and thrust curves represent the maximum aircraft speeds. If a perpendicular line connected each point to the baseline of the graph, it would be evident that the turbojet aircraft can attain a higher maximum speed than aircraft equipped with the other types of engines. Aircraft equipped with the turbofan engine will attain a higher maximum speed than aircraft equipped with a turboprop or reciprocating engine.

LARGE VS. SMALL GAS TURBINE ENGINES

When comparing large and small gas turbine engines, it is apparent that an engine that is twice as large generates considerably more than twice as much thrust. This is because engine mass airflow in the gas turbine engine is approximately proportional to the square of the engine diameter. For example, a 48,000 lb. thrust engine will not be 16 times larger in physical size than a 3,000 lb. thrust engine; it will only be 4 times larger. If the diameter of the engine with 3,000 lbs. of thrust is 2 feet, the diameter of the engine with 48,000 lbs. of thrust will be 8 feet (4 times bigger in diameter, and 4 squared equals 16 times more mass airflow).

TURBINE VS. PISTON

Sometimes different types or sizes of powerplants are compared in terms of fuel consumption because large turbine engines are known to consume large amounts of fuel while reciprocating engines appear to be more fuel conscious. This is misleading. Comparison of the ton/miles of useful payload or of the passenger/miles per

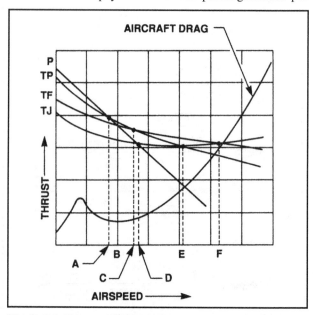

Figure 2-9. Thrust and airspeed in jet engines

fuel consumed methods is a more realistic way of determining which powerplant to select under a given set of circumstances.

A jumbo jet, for instance, can move more payload than the largest piston aircraft. If the B-747 could somehow be fitted with piston engines capable of providing the same aircraft performance, fuel consumption would be much higher. This increased fuel consumption would be the result of factors such as increased engine weight, size, drag, and propeller efficiency losses.

Today, the reciprocating engine is relegated to light, low performance aircraft because of design limitations. For instance, the compression, combustion, and expansion processes all occur in one location: the cylinder. In the gas turbine engine, there is a separate location for each process and many variations of design are possible for flexibility of performance and application. While it appears the reciprocating engine cannot grow much further, the gas turbine seems to have no limit.

An interesting comparison can be made between one of the largest piston engines ever produced, the R-4360, a 28-cylinder radial that developed 4,000 shp, and the JT9D engine that powers the Boeing 747. Using the generally accepted conversion of 2.5 pounds of thrust per shp, the propeller static thrust of R-4360 would be approximately 10,000 pounds (neglecting propeller efficiency losses). The Boeing 747 would need 23 R-4360 engines to produce the 230,000 lb. static thrust currently produced by its four JT9D turbofan engines.

Figure 2-10 and Figure 2-11 show two operational advantages of altitude and airspeed. Other advantages turbine engines have compared to reciprocating engines include:

- Development time is drastically reduced. A turbine unit can be designed, built, and brought to the stage of practical operation in ¼ the time usually necessary for a piston engine.
- Production is simpler and speedier. A turbine unit has only about ¼ the number of parts required for a comparable piston engine.
- Because turbine components each perform one specific function, a proven turbine unit can readily be scaled up or down to meet power requirements.
- Turbines produce power continuously instead of intermittently. Consequently, working pressures are low and the structure, casings, and ducting are of light construction and weight.
- The exclusive use of rotating components virtually eliminates turbine engine vibration, saving weight in the airframe.
- Absence of reciprocating parts enables higher operating speeds. Reduced frontal area and space improve the power/weight ratio. A turbine-jet unit is about ¼ the weight of a comparable piston engine and is more compact, resulting in a significant weight reduction in the aircraft structure.

- A turbine engine operates more efficiently at high altitude than at sea level. Therefore, it needs no complicated supercharging system to maintain power at altitude.
- When compared to the piston engine, the higher the aircraft speed (ram), the more efficiently the turbine engine functions. This is because ram pressure increases its mass airflow and exhaust velocity.

TURBINE ENGINE TYPES

There are two types of gas turbine engines: thrust producing engines and torque producing engines.

There are two classifications of thrust producing turbine engines (turbojet and turbofan) and two classifications of torque producing turbine engines (turboprop and turboshaft).

TURBOJET ENGINES

The turbojet, first patented by Sir Frank Whittle, had an impeller compressor, annular combustor, and a single stage turbine. Many varieties of turbojet engine designs exist today, but the basic components are still the compressor, combustor, and turbine. [Figure 2-12]

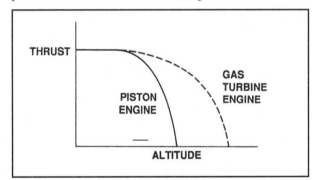

Figure 2-10. Thrust vs. altitude

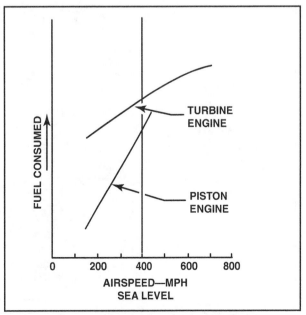

Figure 2-11. Fuel to airspeed engine comparison

The turbojet gets its propulsive power from reaction to the flow of hot gases. The compressor increases the pressure of the air entering the inlet. Fuel is added to the compressed air in the combustor and the expansion created by the heat of combustion rotates the turbine wheel. The turbine drives the compressor. The remaining energy downstream of the turbine accelerates into the atmosphere and creates thrust.

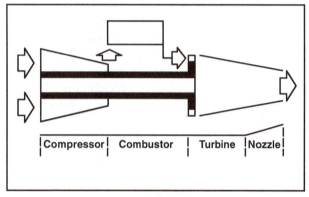

Figure 2-12. Turbojet

TURBOSHAFT ENGINES

A gas turbine engine that delivers power through a shaft to operate something other than a propeller is referred to as a turboshaft. Turboshaft engines are widely used in other industries as well as aviation.

The power output shaft in early turboshaft engines was coupled directly to the gas generator turbine wheel. Today, a separate turbine wheel drives the output shaft. This latter design is referred to as the free power turbine. Figures 2-13A and B show the free power turbine in both the front and rear power output shaft configurations. The figures also show that turboshaft engines are divided into two major sections: the gas generator section and the power turbine section.

The gas generator produces the energy required to drive the free power turbine system. The gas generator extracts about $2/3$ of the combustion energy, leaving approximately $1/3$ to drive the free power turbine, which, in turn, drives the aircraft transmission. The transmission is a high ratio reduction gearbox. Occasionally, a turboshaft engine for use in a helicopter is designed to produce some hot exhaust thrust (up to 10 percent). One consideration in this design is whether the rotor alone will produce the desired airspeed, while another is whether the helicopter can satisfactorily hover with an ongoing, constant forward thrust.

TURBOPROP ENGINES

The turboprop is similar in design to the turboshaft, except that the reduction gearbox is usually on the turboprop inlet. The turboprop is an application of the gas turbine engine with a propeller.

A turboprop propeller is driven by means of either a fixed or a free power turbine. [Figure 2-14] The fixed tur-

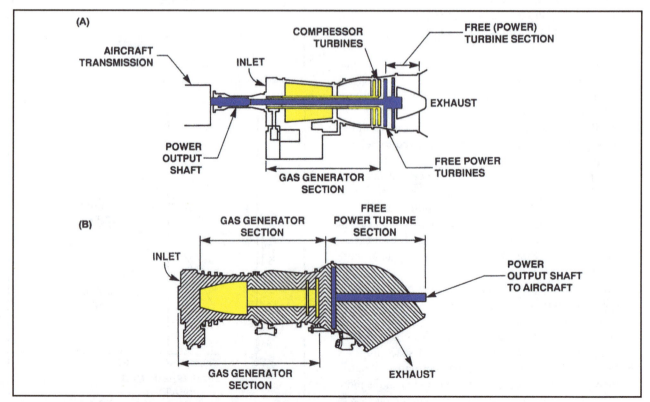

Figure 2-13A. General Electric T-64 turboshaft (front power output shaft)
Figure 2-13B. General Electric T-58 turboshaft (rear power output shaft)

bine connects directly to the compressor, reduction gearbox, and propeller shaft. The free power turbine connects only to the gearbox and propeller shaft. This arrangement allows the free power turbine to seek its optimum design speed while the compressor speed is set at its design point (point of best compression).

The advantages of the free turbine include:

- The propeller can be held at very low r.p.m. during taxiing, with low noise and low blade erosion.
- The engine is easier to start, especially in cold weather.
- The propeller and its gearbox do not directly transmit vibrations into the gas generator.
- A rotor brake can stop propeller movement during aircraft loading when engine shutdown is not desired.

One major difference between the turboprop engine and the basic gas turbine engine is that the turboprop needs more turbine stages to drive the output reduction gearbox and the propeller. The total power of the turboprop is the sum of propeller thrust and exhaust nozzle thrust, with the exhaust thrust contributing 5 to 25 percent.

The exact amount of hot thrust is a function of best fuel economy at cruise speed. Unlike the turboshaft, the turboprop generally has some hot thrust because the higher flight speeds and ram compression add to the propulsive efficiency of the engine. Propulsive efficiency will be defined later in this chapter.

A turboprop engine is only about $2/3$ the physical size of a turbojet of comparable thrust output because the mass airflow for thrust is handled by the propeller rather than the core portion of the engine.

The fuel consumption of the turboprop will be slightly less because of its higher propulsive efficiency at lower airspeeds.

ULTRA HIGH-BYPASS PROPFAN/UNDUCTED FAN ENGINES

Some present day designers feel that recent developments in propeller blade aerodynamics will result in dramatically increased use of a new version of the turboprop. Recent developments in blade materials of higher strength, blade weight reductions, and blade design improvements provide for increased propulsive efficiency and decreased fuel consumption.

The conventional propeller is presently capable of attaining a pressure ratio of approximately 1.05:1, while the propfan is capable of a 1.2:1 ratio. Contra-rotating (counter-rotating) propellers have demonstrated even higher ratios and may be in popular use in the near future. In present day propellers, the outward swirl imparted to airflow by a propeller is a loss of energy. Contra-rotation reduces the swirl losses by capturing the energy in the swirl of the first blade with the second blade and straightening it to a more nearly axial flow. [Figure 2-14E]

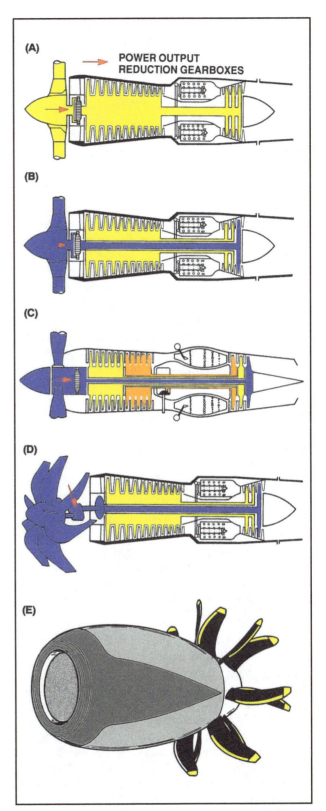

Figure 2-14A. Single axial flow compressor, direct drive turboprop

Figure 2-14B. Single axial flow compressor, free power turbine drive

Figure 2-14C. Dual compressor three-shaft turboprop with free power turbine drive to propeller

Figure 2-14D. Front propfan

Figure 2-14E. Rear propfan, counter-rotating blades

The propfan, sometimes called an open high-bypass fan, does not look like a conventional turboprop. It is fitted with a propeller of six to ten highly loaded, swept-back, and curved blades. This design was made possible by development in titanium, lightweight stainless steel, and composite materials. Conventional propeller designs of three or four blades of the same power would require larger blade diameter and result in a prohibitive loading factor and tip-generated noises. [Figure 2-14D]

This new powerplant is in the 10,000 to 15,000 horsepower class, which is two to three times the power of current turboprops. New engines, therefore, will have to be developed to accommodate the new propeller designs. The new propfan will power yet-to-be-produced, 150-200 passenger size aircraft at current airliner speeds of Mach 0.8. Some designers propose placing the fan in front. Others will locate the fan on the rear of the engine. Additional designs include encasing the propfan in a conventional cowled inlet to achieve speeds of Mach 0.9. These engines are known as ducted ultra high-bypass engines. Of the several varieties of turbofan engine, they are known as the most fuel conscious gas turbine in service, 15 to 20 percent more fuel efficient than the high-bypass turbofan. The Airbus A400 military transport is an example of this new design. This engine attains a higher fuel economy because hot combustion discharge gases are more efficient when they perform the internal mechanical work of driving a propeller shaft than when they are simply discharged from a tailpipe to create thrust.

Pure reactive thrust, by comparison, is decreased because some of the hot gas expands radially into the atmosphere, losing a good portion of its energy. In addition, the higher comparative thrust at low speeds associated with variable pitch propellers will decrease climbout time to cruise altitude and save even more fuel.

The propfan's required high-bypass ratio (the ratio of air passing outside versus air passing through the engine) ranging from 30:1 to a high of 100:1 will come from single or dual, 12- to 15-foot diameter propellers with higher tip speeds than propellers now in use. In order to propel an aircraft at Mach 0.8, the propeller tips may at times have to travel at supersonic speeds. During takeoff, this tip speed could be reduced to subsonic speed, but noise generated reportedly may still be in the 130 to 140 decibel range, which is 30 to 40 decibels higher than a turbofan of comparable size. Current development aims at reducing the negative aspects of high ground and cabin noise and to save 30 percent in fuel consumption.

Aircraft in the 400-passenger class will probably not convert to unducted designs because in order to generate the required 60,000 pounds of thrust (or more) they would need 25-foot diameter propfans, which does not seem practical at this time.

TURBOFAN ENGINES

The turbofan is a ducted propeller with 20 to 40 fixed-pitch blades driven by a gas turbine engine. This fan produces a pressure ratio of 2:1, or two atmospheres of compression. Turbofan ducted engine design incorporates the best features of the turbojet and the turboprop. The turbofan has turbojet cruise speed capability and yet retains some of the short field takeoff capability of the turboprop.

By comparison, the fan diameter of a turbofan engine is much less than that of the propeller on a turboprop engine, but it contains many more blades and moves the air with a greater velocity from its convergent exhaust nozzle.

Fan installation arrangements include:

- Bolting the fan directly to the front compressor, where the blades travel at the same r.p.m. [Figure 2-15A]
- Driving the fan by a separate turbine wheel to rotate independently of the compressor [Figure 2-15B]
- Locating the fan in the turbine section as an extension of the turbine wheel blades [Figure 2-15C]

The aft-fan is not a popular design today because the fan does not contribute to the engine compressor pressure ratio. The compressor of the aft-fan is also more susceptible to serious damage from ingested materials than the forward fan, which tends to throw these materials out-

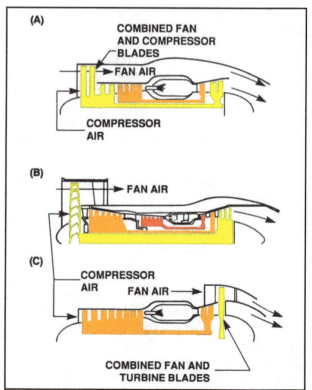

Figure 2-15A. Dual axial flow compressor, forward fan engine with mixed exhaust

Figure 2-15B. Triple-spool front fan engine with unmixed exhaust

Figure 2-15C. Turbofan engine with an aft-fan and unmixed exhaust

ward and through the fan exhaust, with damage usually limited to the fan.

Turbofan engines in civilian and military aircraft are generally divided into five classifications: ultra low-bypass, low-bypass, medium-bypass, high-bypass, and ultra high-bypass. Bypass refers to the quantity of air moved by the fan that does not enter the compressor, combustor, or turbine sections of the engine. The bypass of an engine is given as a ratio, such as 4:1, which, in this case, would indicate that 4 units of air exit the fan duct for every 1 unit that goes through the engine core.

Engines in the ultra low-bypass classification have less air exiting the fan duct than entering the core of the engine. These engines have fans that are not much larger in diameter than the engine core, and they would typically have a bypass ratio of 0.5:1. In other words, 0.5 pounds of air exit the fan duct for every 1 pound of air that goes through the core of the engine. This type of fan engine is typically used on military fighter airplanes, like the Navy F-18 or Air Force F-22, where a larger diameter fan would produce a prohibitive amount of drag.

The low-bypass classification indicates that the fan and the compressor sections use approximately the same mass airflow. They have a bypass ratio of 1:1. The fan discharge may be slightly higher or slightly lower. Keep in mind that the bypass ratio concerns airflow mass. The fan discharge air is ducted along the entire length of the engine from what is called a full fan duct. The end of the duct is configured with a converging discharge nozzle to produce a velocity increase and reactive thrust.

In the fully ducted fan engine shown in Figure 2-16, the hot and cold streams mix before being discharged to the atmosphere, which results in a reduction in the aerodynamic drag associated with short-ducted turbofans. Air passing over the core engine outer surfaces has much less skin friction if the air remains in the fan duct until it leaves the engine. With the full duct, there is gain of mass-airflow and thrust implied when drag is reduced. This design also has a noise attenuating quality as hot gas becomes diluted by fan air in the common exhaust duct.

Early turbofan powered airplanes like the Boeing 707 and 727 and the Douglas DC-9 used low-bypass engines. Newer airplanes manufactured by large airliner manufacturers such as Boeing and Airbus, as well as many other regional jet aircraft manufacturers, have engines with a much higher bypass ratio that makes them much more fuel efficient and quieter. Consequently, new airplanes will unlikely use engines with the low-bypass design.

The turbofan core engine compresses, ignites, and discharges air in the same manner as a turbojet engine. The thrust of each gas stream of the fully ducted engine shown in Figure 2-16 has approximately equal airflow, and each delivers approximately the same thrust.

Medium- or intermediate-bypass engines have a mass airflow ratio of 2:1 or 3:1, with a thrust ratio in approximate proportion to the bypass ratio. The fan will be slightly larger in diameter than a low-bypass fan of comparable engine power, and its diameter will determine both the bypass ratio and thrust output of the fan versus the core of the engine.

The high-bypass turbofan engine, with fan ratios of 4:1 to 9:1, have even wider diameter fans in order to move more air. Figure 2-17 shows the design features of current high-bypass turbofans produced by Pratt & Whitney, General Electric, and Rolls-Royce with fans over 100 inches in diameter and representing the current state-of-the-art large engine designs for jumbo-jet aircraft.

Ultra high-bypass turbofan engines with fan ratios of 10:1 and higher are beginning to emerge. One of the engine choices for the latest Boeing airliner, the B787, will have a bypass ratio of 11:1, and over time, even higher bypasses will be developed. There is a limit, of course, on how high the bypass ratio can go. It is not possible to send all the air out the fan duct because there would be no air in the core to support combustion and to drive the turbines.

High-bypass and ultra high-bypass engines boast the lowest fuel consumption of the various turbofan engines because of the smaller percentage of air that supports combustion in the core portion of the engine. For example, the Pratt & Whitney PW4000 series turbofans currently have a 5:1 to 9:1 bypass ratio engine with approximately 80 percent of the thrust produced by the fan and 20 percent by the core engine. The thrust percentages vary from engine to engine and are determined by such considerations as fuel economy at altitude, cruise speed, and propulsive efficiency for a particular aircraft design. For these higher bypass engines, the amount of air going out the fan duct falls between 80 and 92 percent of the total mass airflow.

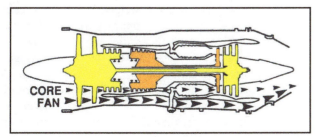

Figure 2-16. Fully ducted low- and medium-bypass turbofan design

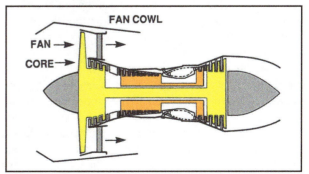

Figure 2-17. High-bypass ratio turbofan

In the past, the fan duct on high-bypass engines typically extended aft only $1/3$ to $1/2$ of the engine's length, unlike low-bypass engines that typically had full-length fan ducts. Even though the full-length duct provides thrust and drag advantages, the additional weight was a problem for the high-bypass engines. By using lower weight, high strength composites for the fan duct, it is now more common to extend the duct farther aft, and on some airplanes, to use a full-length duct.

Today's high-bypass fan engine has become the most widely used engine type for medium to large aircraft because it offers the best fuel economy by increasing the total mass airflow and decreasing the hot exhaust wake velocity. This conservation of energy keeps more power within the engine to drive the fan and leads to a considerable increase in propulsive and thermal efficiency.

In fact, the trend in the aviation industry today is toward the various fan engines and away from turbojet engines for high performance business, commercial, and military aircraft.

ULTRA HIGH-BYPASS TURBOFAN ENGINES (DUCTED, VARIABLE PITCH)

Another development in turbofans is the variable pitch (variable-bypass ratio) model, which, as of this writing, is being tested for certification. This model is predicted to have the lowest fuel consumption rate per thrust ratio of any turbofan currently in service. It is also expected to have much of the same flexibility of operation that the turboprops enjoy, and it will still be capable of the high subsonic cruising speeds that elude the conventional turboprop. Its bypass ratio will fall somewhere between the high-bypass turbofan and the propfan, and it will likely be fitted with a variable exhaust nozzle. [Figure 2-18]

PHYSICS OF THE GAS TURBINE ENGINE

A clear understanding of jet propulsion requires understanding the principles of physics that govern the action of mass or matter. The physics described in this section present the basic ideas necessary for understanding the physical relationships of gases and the turbo-machinery within a gas turbine engine.

In a discussion of turbine engines, we are concerned with the mass-flow of atmospheric air, which is compressed and accelerated to create useful work at the turbine wheel and, ultimately, thrust. The thrust is created from either pure reaction to the flowing gases or from a propeller or fan driven by a turbine.

Some of the most important physical properties that apply to the gas turbine engine are weight, density, temperature, pressure, and mass. These properties are useful when applied to formulas such as force, work, acceleration, thrust, and others that measure certain valuable performance factors. These properties will be described by formula in English Units throughout this text, for example, pounds instead of kilograms.

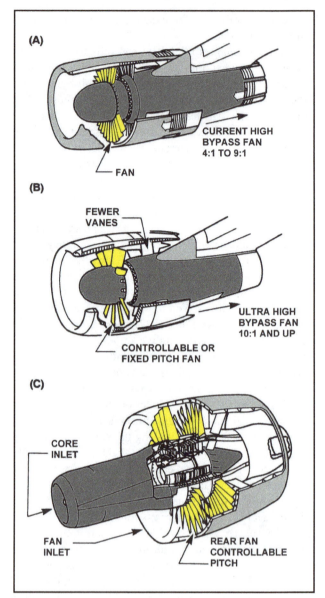

Figure 2-18A. Current technology turbofan engine
Figure 2-18B. Variable pitch front turbofan engine
Figure 2-18C. Variable pitch rear turbofan engine

Weight has direction and quantity and is measured in pounds of force. Figure 2-19A shows that weight is one-directional, toward the center of the earth, regardless of the type of material.

Density is the amount of material per unit volume. Figure 2-19B illustrates how two containers with identical contents will have different weights if the contents are packed closer together. The compressor of a gas turbine engine uses this principle by packing more molecules of air into a given space to increase the density and weight of the airflow to create thrust.

For example, at standard day condition the weight of air is 0.076475 pounds/cubic foot. In an engine with an overall compressor pressure ratio of 30:1, the weight of air per cubic foot will be 30 times 0.076475, or 2.295 pounds/cubic foot.

Jet Propulsion Theory

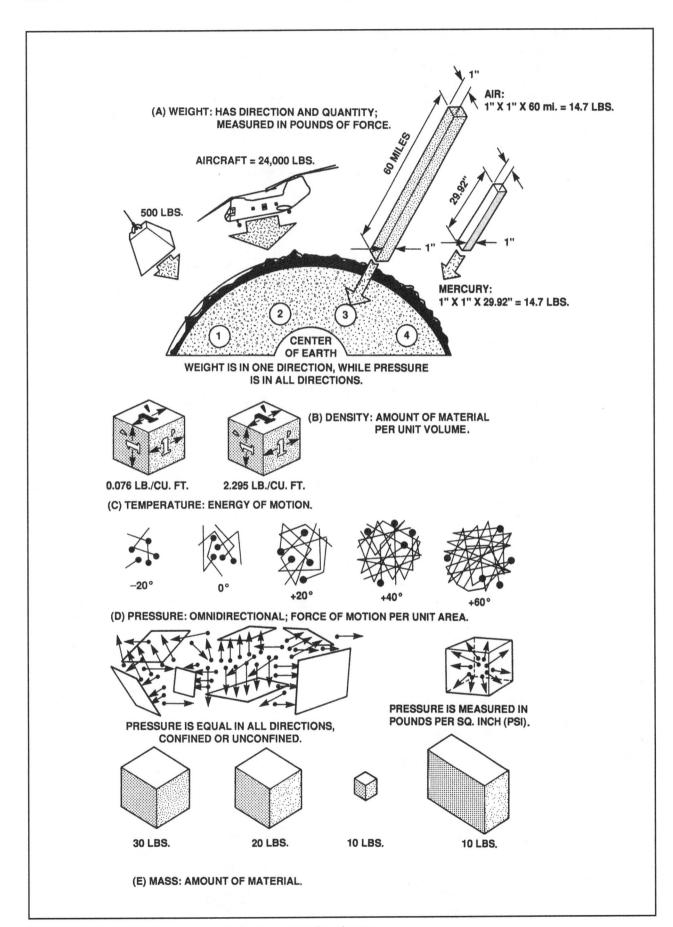

Figure 2-19A, B, C, D, E. Some important physical properties of matter

Figure 2-19C illustrates that temperature is the molecular energy of motion due to heat. Molecular motion is low at low temperature, but it increases at higher temperatures. This creates a problem in the compressor of a gas turbine engine because it requires more and more work in terms of compressor speed and fuel consumption to increase density if the air temperature increases.

Pressure is an omni-directional force of motion per unit area. [Figure 2-19D] Air molecules inside a container will rebound off the inner walls with such great rapidity that an essentially even pressure is exerted over all of the inner surfaces. If a pressure gauge were inserted into the closed container, it would produce a steady reading in pounds per square inch.

Figure 2-19E illustrates that mass is the amount of material a body contains. In this respect, it is similar to the description of density. Within a gas turbine engine, the denser the air per unit volume, the more weight it has and the more mass.

FORCE

Force is the capacity to do work or the tendency to produce work. It is also a vector quantity that tends to produce acceleration of a body in the direction of its application. It can be measured in pounds.

The formula for force is:

Force = Pressure × Area, or $F = P \times A$

Where: F = Force in pounds

P = Pressure in pounds per square inch (psi)

A = Area in square inches

EXAMPLE: The pressure across the opening of a jet tailpipe (exhaust nozzle) is 6 psi above ambient, and the opening is 300 square inches. What is the force present in pounds?

$F = P \times A$

$F = 6 \times 300$

$F = 1,800$ Pounds

The force mentioned here is present in addition to reactive thrust in most gas turbine engine designs.

WORK

Mechanical work is present when force acting on a body causes it to move through a distance. Work is described as useful motion. A force can act on an object vertically (opposite the effect of gravity), horizontally (90 degrees to the effect of gravity), or somewhere in between. A force can also act on an object in a downward direction, in which case it would be assisted by gravity. The typical units for work are inch-pounds and foot-pounds.

The formula for work is:

Work = Force × Distance, or $W = F \times D$

Where: W = Work in foot-pounds

F = Force in pounds

D = Distance in feet

EXAMPLE: How much work, in foot-pounds, is performed by a device that lifts a 2,500 pound engine a height of 9 feet?

$W = F \times D$

$W = 2,500 \times 9$

$W = 22,500$ foot-pounds

Because the engine is being lifted vertically, the applied force must be equal to the force of gravity, which is what causes the engine to weigh 2,500 pounds. If the same engine were moved nine feet horizontally along a hangar floor in a transport cart, it would not involve nearly as much work. Moving the engine horizontally only requires that a certain amount of friction be overcome.

POWER

The definition of work makes no mention of time. Whether it takes five seconds or five hours to move an object, the same amount of work would be accomplished. Power, by comparison, does take time into account. To lift a 10-pound object 15 feet off the floor in 5 seconds requires significantly more power than to lift it in 5 hours. Work performed per unit of time is power. Power is measured in units of foot-pounds per second, foot-pounds per minute, or mile-pounds per hour.

The formula for power is:

$$\text{Power} = \frac{\text{Force} \times \text{Distance}}{\text{time}}, \text{ or } P = \frac{F \times D}{t}$$

Where: P = Power in foot pounds per minute

D = Distance in feet

t = Time in minutes

EXAMPLE: How much power is required to hoist a 2,500 pound engine a height of 9 feet in 2 minutes?

$P = \dfrac{F \times D}{t}$

$P = \dfrac{2,500 \times 9}{2}$

$P = 11,250$ ft-lbs./min.

HORSEPOWER

Horsepower is a more common and useful measure of electrical power. Years ago using the multiplier of 1.5 times a strong horse's ability to do useful work, it was determined that 33,000 pounds of weight lifted 1 foot in 1 minute would be the standard in the English system. If power is in foot-pounds per minute, it can be divided by 33,000 to convert to horsepower. Mathematically, the units of foot-pounds per minute will cancel each other out, leaving only the number. Horsepower does not have units, since horsepower is the unit. If power is being dealt with in units of foot-pounds per second, 550 is the conversion number. If power is in mile-pounds per hour, 375 is the conversion number.

The formula for converting to horsepower is:

$$Hp = \frac{Power\ (ft.\ lbs./min.)}{33,000}$$

EXAMPLE: How much horsepower is required to hoist a 2,500 pound engine a height of 9 feet in 2 minutes? [Figure 2-20] (The previous example required 11,250 ft. lbs./min of power.)

$$Hp = \frac{Power}{33,000}$$

$$Hp = \frac{11,250}{33,000}$$

Hp = 0.34 or approximately 1/3 Hp

VELOCITY

Velocity describes how far an object moves, what direction it moves, and how long it takes to move that far. Velocity is expressed in the same units as speed, typically feet per second (f.p.s.) or miles per hour (m.p.h.). The difference is that speed does not have a particular direction associated with it. Velocity is identified as being a vector quantity, while speed is a scalar quantity.

The formula for velocity is:

Velocity = Distance ÷ time, or V = D ÷ t

EXAMPLE: Gas flows through a gas turbine engine tailpipe a distance of 5 feet in 0.003 seconds. What is its velocity in feet per second?

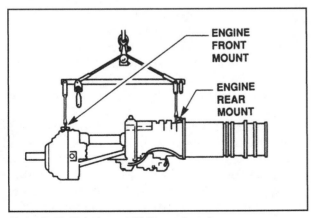

Figure 2-20. Hoisting a 2,500-pound engine

V = D ÷ t

V = 5 ÷ 0.003

V = 1,667 feet per second

To convert the velocity in feet per second to a value in miles per hour, divide the feet per second by 1.467. This conversion factor is the number of feet in a mile, 5280, divided by the number of seconds in an hour, 3600.

Velocity in f.p.s. ÷ 1.467 = m.p.h.

1,667 f.p.s. ÷ 1.467 = 1,136.3 m.p.h.

ACCELERATION

In physics, acceleration is defined as a change in velocity with respect to time. Distance traveled is not considered, only loss or gain of velocity with time. The units for acceleration are feet per second/second (fps/s), usually referred to as feet per second squared (fps^2), and miles per hour/second (mph/s).

The formula for calculating acceleration is:

$$Acceleration = \frac{Velocity\ Final - Velocity\ Initial}{time}$$

$$A = \frac{V_2 - V_1}{t}$$

EXAMPLE 1: For the Concorde SST in flight, the air enters the engine with a velocity of 500 feet per second. It exits the engine 1 second later with a velocity of 2,200 feet per second. What is the acceleration rate for the air?

$$A = \frac{V_2 - V_1}{t}$$

$$A = \frac{2,200\ f.p.s. - 500\ f.p.s.}{1\ second}$$

A = 1,700 fps^2

EXAMPLE 2: A military fighter going 300 m.p.h. goes into full afterburner, and after 10 seconds has accelerated to 1,200 m.p.h. What is the average acceleration in mph/s and in fps^2?

$$A = \frac{V_2 - V_1}{t}$$

$$A = \frac{1,200\ m.p.h. - 300\ m.p.h.}{10\ seconds}$$

A = 90 mph/s × 1.467 = 132 fps^2

When an object is in free fall with no drag, the acceleration rate due to gravity is 32.2 fps^2. [Figure 2-21] When an object accelerates at this rate, it is experiencing what

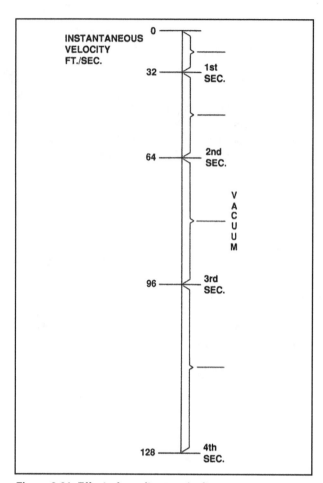

Figure 2-21. Effect of gravity on velocity

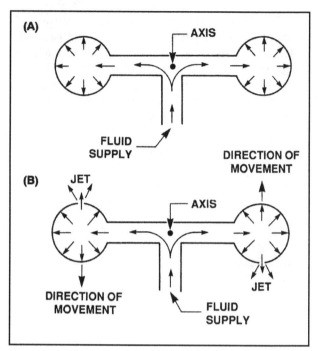

Figure 2-22A. Potential energy
Figure 2-22B. Kinetic energy

is known as a force of 1G. If we divided the acceleration rate for the example fighter airplane by 32.2, we would discover how many G forces it is experiencing (132 ÷ 32.2 = 4.1 G).

POTENTIAL AND KINETIC ENERGY

Energy is used to perform useful work. In the gas turbine engine this means producing motion and heat. The two forms of energy that best describe the propulsive power of the jet engine are potential and kinetic.

In Figure 2-22A, pressure is equal in all parts of the sprinkler head and no motive power is present. The energy in the sprinkler is potential, or stored, energy. In Figure 2-22B, two openings or jet nozzles are arranged 180 degrees apart in each sprinkler head. Opening the nozzles creates kinetic energy. At the points of exit, there is a reduced pressure as the fluid escapes from the nozzle. This creates a relatively higher pressure on the inside wall directly opposite the opening and causes the sprinkler head to rotate on its axis as a result of this motive power.

Rotation created by potential energy being converted to kinetic energy is clearly the result of a force within the device and not the force of the fluid pushing on the atmosphere. In fact, the rotation would be more rapid if the sprinkler were placed in a vacuum, which would remove atmospheric backpressure on the nozzle. Later, we will discuss how thrust is similarly created within the gas turbine engine.

BERNOULLI'S PRINCIPLE

Bernoulli's principle deals with pressure of gases. Pressure can be changed in the gas turbine engine by adding or removing heat, changing the number of molecules present, or changing the volume in which the gas is contained.

Changing the volume of a container is of immediate importance to the understanding of the gas cycle of the turbine engine because it is the basis of Bernoulli's principle. [Figure 2-23]

Bernoulli discovered that air behaves the way an incompressible fluid would behave when flowing at subsonic flow rates. That is, when a fluid or gas is supplied at a constant flow rate through a duct, the sum of pressure (potential) energy and velocity (kinetic) energy is constant. In other words, when static pressure increases, velocity (ram) pressure decreases. If static pressure decreases, velocity (ram) pressure increases, meaning that velocity pressure will change in relation to any change in static pressure.

To understand this, consider that air flowing through a duct has both internal (molecular motion) energy and kinetic energy. It can also be thought of as static pressure energy and kinetic (ram) pressure energy. If air is flowing through a straight section of ducting which then changes to a divergent shape, its kinetic energy in the axial direction will decrease as the air spreads out radially, and, because the total energy at constant flow rate of the air is

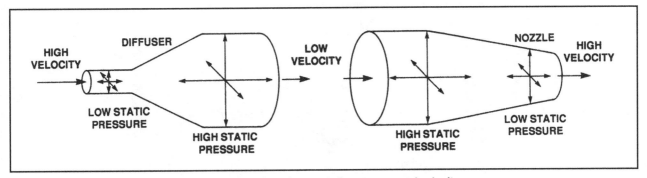

Figure 2-23. Diffuser and nozzle shaped ducts used to change static pressure and velocity

unchanged, the potential energy must increase in relation to the kinetic energy decrease.

Now the molecules of air are more numerous at a gauge opening in the divergent portion of the duct than at a similar opening in the straight portion. This is because of the increased time available for the molecules to bounce or expand into the opening. The molecular force within the gauge is read as pressure in pounds per square inch. Conversely, if the shape of the duct converges, an air stream at constant flow rate must speed up. That is, the kinetic energy of the air stream increases as its potential (static pressure) energy proportionally decreases.

At a gauge opening in the convergent portion of the duct, there will be fewer molecules from the air stream's potential energy because of the shorter time available in the faster moving air stream. As a result, a gauge will read out as a lower static pressure.

For a further understanding of the concept of static pressure, consider that internal (molecular) energy is present whether the gas is flowing or not, and that it is quite separate from the kinetic energy of flow. Static pressure occurs when molecules inside a gauge mechanism repeatedly rebound off the container walls so that it appears that they are exerting a steady push or pressure.

Total Pressure is the sum of static pressure plus ram pressure and is often described as the pressure required from the opposite direction to stop the flow.

In Figure 2-24, we must assume the flow rate in pounds per second is constant through the duct at points A, B, and C. Because B is smaller, it follows that the flowing gas will have to speed up with respect to A. The static pressure at B will be lower than at A.

This occurs because at the given gauge opening, with respect to time, fewer air molecules are present in duct B as the air stream velocity is increased. C will have a higher static pressure than B as the gas seeks the shape of its larger container by expanding outward and slowing down. The duct at A-B is described as a converging duct and at B-C as a diverging duct.

The diagram also illustrates that total pressure remains constant throughout the duct. A specially shaped probe measures both static and ram pressure components of total pressure. The total pressure can then be compared to the static pressure at the same point in the duct.

NOTE: To calculate ram pressure and total pressure if you know velocity and density, use Formulas 14 and 15 in Appendix 8.

MEASURING STATIC PRESSURE

Static pressure is the pressure of the air or fluid exerted at right angles to the direction of flow.

Suppose that an air stream is flowing through a duct [Figure 2-25], and a U-type water manometer is connected to the duct as shown at A. The pressure on the gauge tube will read the static pressure of the air inside the duct, indicated in inches of water.

If atmospheric air was not pressing on the water column in the right-hand leg of the gauge tube with a (normal) weight of 14.7 lb. per square inch, the water would be forced out of the gauge tube. The difference between the two levels in the water manometer is the pressure difference between atmospheric pressure and the pressure of the air motion inside the duct.

This difference is the measurement of static pressure inside the duct (expressed in inches of water) above atmospheric pressure.

MEASURING TOTAL PRESSURE

Total pressure is the force exerted by an air stream moving perpendicular to the plane of the duct. A water gauge connected to the duct at C measures this motion. The gauge tube penetrates to the center of the duct, and the open end bends into the air stream at 90 degrees.

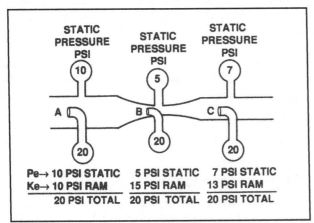

Figure 2-24. Application of Bernoulli's principle

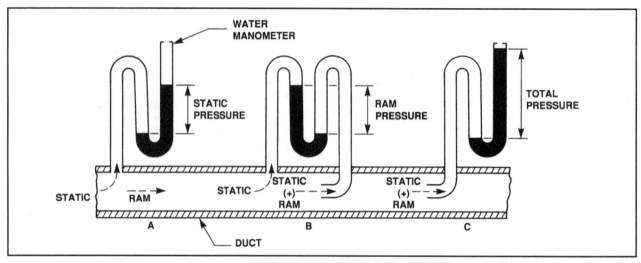

Figure 2-25. Measuring air pressure

The water column climbs higher than with the arrangement shown at A because of the greater pressure that the airflow exerts on the water column.

MEASURING RAM PRESSURE

Section A measures static pressure only; section B measures total pressure. Another force determines the speed of air motion, and that's ram pressure, which is total pressure minus the static pressure.

Notice that both inlets of the water gauge connect to the duct at B. The left inlet is connected the same as the left end of the gauge at A, measuring static pressure. The right end of the gauge at B connects in the same way as the inlet at C.

In arrangement B, the left leg of the gauge is the static tube and the other leg is the impact tube. Both static and ram forces act on the water column, and the difference between the fluid levels in the gauge tube in inches is the measurement of the ram pressure.

In the B arrangement, where ends of the gauge tube are open to the duct and neither has access to atmospheric pressure, the distance between the water levels in the two columns represents ram pressure.

PRESSURE-VELOCITY THROUGH THE ENGINE

Figure 2-26A illustrates the function of Bernoulli's principle where velocity rises as pressure drops in an open duct as seen on the pressure and velocity curves of a turbojet at points A, B, and C. C to D indicates pressure increasing rapidly under the influence of work done by the compressor. Velocity is also increasing slightly in the convergent duct formed by the compressor and its outer case. Points D to D show a slight pressure rise/velocity decrease, which is the effect of air passing through the divergent shaped diffuser.

Combustion occurs between D and E with pressure drop controlled by the diminishing flow area at the turbine section E to F. Pressure rapidly changes to velocity to drive the turbine wheel at E to F, and then pressure and velocity stabilize as the gas moves between the stator and rotor; then, both pressure and velocity drop across the turbine wheel. Velocity drops here because the gas is losing axial velocity as the wheel throws the gas in a tangential direction. There is another rise in axial velocity between F and G, but not to the same value as at the turbine nozzle.

The temperature difference with both velocities being choked (gas in motion at the speed of sound) causes the exhaust velocity to be lower than the velocity at the turbine nozzle because, at the turbine nozzle, temperature is higher, and therefore, the speed of sound is also higher.

Finally, pressure drops to a value slightly above ambient if the nozzle is choked or to ambient if it is not choked.

Figure 2-26B shows the pressure, temperature, and velocity of a dual compressor turbofan engine. This figure also includes a velocity curve of the fan bypass airflow. Notice that fan air branches off from inlet airflow and decreases in value as it expands through the bypass duct. In this duct, pressure would typically increase 1.5 or even 2.0 times the ambient pressure. The velocity curve rises sharply in the area of the exhaust as bypass air is expanded from its exhaust nozzle to mix with the core engine exhaust gases.

The velocities dealt with in this discussion are Mach 1 or less, which would normally be found throughout the typical gas turbine engine.

For a more in-depth understanding of the internal cycle of events of the gas turbine, consult texts in the field of thermodynamics and aerodynamic design of gas turbine engines.

THE BRAYTON CYCLE

The continuous thermodynamic cycle is called the Brayton cycle after George Brayton (October 3, 1830 –

Jet Propulsion Theory

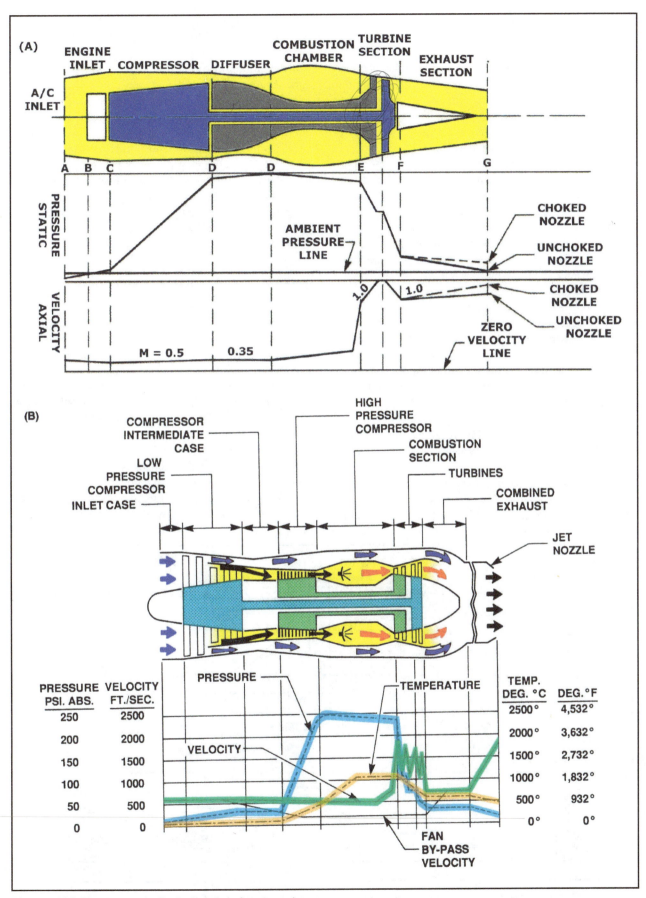

Figure 2-26A. Pressure, velocity (turbojet) during ground runup
Figure 2-26B. Pressure, velocity, temperature (turbofan) during ground runup

December 17, 1892), the Boston engineer who described the continuous combustion cycle of the gas turbine engine in the latter part of the 19th century.

The Brayton cycle is known as a constant pressure cycle because pressure is fairly constant across the combustion section of the gas turbine engine as volume increases and gas velocities increase. The cycle consists of four continuous events: intake, compression, expansion (power), and exhaust. [Figure 2-27A]

A to B indicates air entering the engine at below ambient pressure due to suction and increasing volume due to the divergent shape of the duct in the direction of flow. B to C shows air pressure returning to ambient and volume decreasing.

C to D shows compression occurring as volume is decreasing. D to E indicates a slight drop in pressure, approximately three percent, through the combustion section and an increasing volume. This pressure drop occurs as a result of combustion heat, and the carefully sized exhaust nozzle opening controls it. Recall that there is a basic gas law that states that gas will tend to flow from a point of high pressure to a point of low pressure.

The pressure drop in the combustor ensures the correct direction of gas flow through the engine from compressor to combustor. The air rushing in also cools and protects the metal by centering the flame.

E to F shows a pressure drop resulting from increasing velocity as the gas accelerates through the turbine section.

F to G shows the volume (expansion) increase, which causes this acceleration. G completes the cycle as gas pressure returns to ambient, or higher than ambient at the nozzle if it is choked.

The internal temperature graph (Figure 2-27B) can be interpreted as follows: During ground run-up, the temperature will drop slightly at points A, B, and C due to the chilling effect of fast moving air. C to D shows the temperature rise due to air compression. In very large engines, this rise can be as much as 1,000 degrees Fahrenheit. Points D to D show a slight rise in temperature to correspond with a slight pressure rise. Points D to E show combustor temperature peaking and then dropping off as cooling air enters the rear section of the combustor. The temperature continues to drop through sections F and G as the volumes (flow area within the engine) increase. Finally, the gas leaves the engine at a temperature much higher than ambient.

NEWTON'S LAWS AND THE GAS TURBINE

One principle of operation of the turbojet engine is based on Newton's first law of motion: "A body at rest tends to remain at rest, and a body in motion tends to remain in motion." This law states that a force is required to accelerate a mass; therefore, if an engine accelerates a mass of air rearward, the mass-flow of air will contain a reactive force within the engine that will apply a reactive force on the aircraft by way of its engine mounts.

In this respect, the propeller and the turbojet are closely related. The propeller generates thrust by a relatively small acceleration to a large amount of air. The turbojet and turbofan achieve thrust by imparting a greater acceleration to a smaller quantity of air. [Figure 2-28]

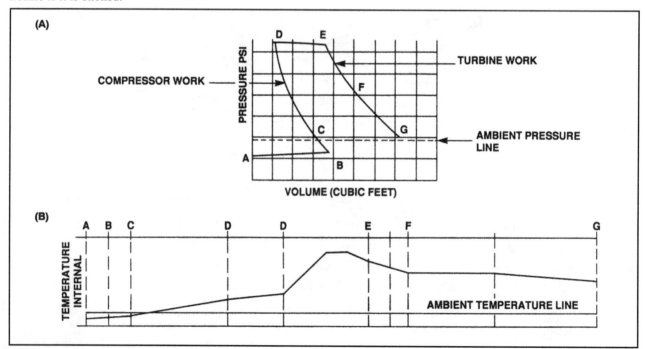

Figure 2-27A. Pressure-volume continuous combustion (Brayton cycle)
Figure 2-27B. Temperature graph

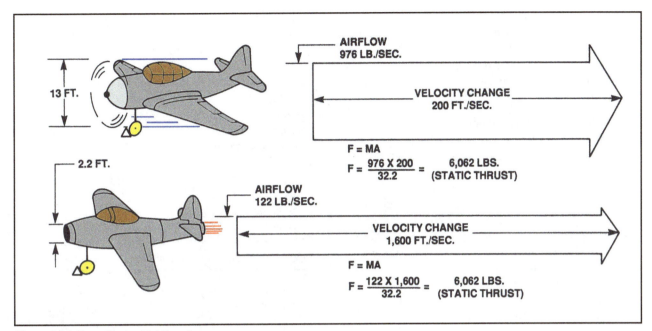

Figure 2-28. Propeller and jet thrust

NEWTON'S SECOND LAW

Newton's second law states that force is proportional to the product of mass and acceleration. As a formula, Newton's second law is expressed as:

Force = Mass × Acceleration, or F = MA

Where: F = Force in pounds
M = Mass in lbs/fps^2
A = Acceleration in fps^2

Mass units are difficult to use mathematically, so consider that mass and weight are similar quantities when an object is in the earth's gravitational field. Weight exists because of the force of gravity acting on a unit of mass, or mathematically stated:

Weight = Mass × gravity

This formula can be transposed to solve for mass, like this:

Mass = Weight / gravity

By using the formula for acceleration learned earlier in this chapter, and the formula for mass shown above, the formula for Newton's second law is expressed as:

Force = (Weight / gravity) × (Velocity Final − Velocity Initial) / time

$$F = \frac{W}{g} \times \frac{V_2 - V_1}{t}$$

Where: F = Force in pounds
W = Weight in pounds
g = Acceleration due to gravity in fps^2
V_2 = Exit velocity in f.p.s.
V_1 = Entry velocity in f.p.s.
t = Time in seconds

This formula is the foundation for calculating the reactive thrust of a gas turbine engine, such as a turbojet or turbofan. The force in pounds would be the thrust, the weight would be the pounds of air going through the engine every second, V_2 would be the velocity of the air leaving the engine, and V_1 would be the velocity of the air as it enters the engine.

COMPARISON: PROPELLER TO TURBOJET EXHAUST THRUST

Figure 2-28 compares the thrust of the two propulsion systems using the expanded F = MA formula. Although both methods are valid, this section uses Newton's Second Law rather than Bernoulli's Principle to explain propeller thrust.

In this example, the airplane is powered by a piston engine and propeller moving 976 pounds of air a second and accelerating it at 200 fps^2, and the turbojet powered airplane is moving 122 pounds of air a second and accelerating it at 1,600 fps^2. Calculating the thrust for both, the solutions are:

Piston Engine/Prop

$$F = \frac{W}{g} \times \frac{V_2 - V_1}{t}$$

$$F = \frac{976}{32.2} \times \frac{200 - 0}{1}$$

F = 6,062 lbs.

Turbojet

$$F = \frac{W}{g} \times \frac{V_2 - V_1}{t}$$

$$F = \frac{122}{32.2} \times \frac{1,600 - 0}{1}$$

F = 6,062 lbs.

These equations show that different types of propulsion systems provide different mass airflows and flow velocities. It is possible to have quite different mass and acceleration values and still have the same thrust, whether the engine is a piston and propeller combination, a turbo-propeller, a turbojet, or a turbofan.

NEWTON'S THIRD LAW

Newton's third law is the commonly stated theorem: "For every acting force there is an equal and opposite reacting force."

Figure 2-29 shows a balloon containing pressurized air. As the air is released, the "acting force" creates an "equal and opposite reacting force" on the forward wall inside the balloon. The same idea applies for the gun analogy. The air discharge and the bullet leaving the gun do not create reactive power by exerting a pushing force on the outside air. Rather, their acting forces create a reacting force within the device. In fact, if the air or bullet were to exit into a vacuum as rockets do in space, the exiting velocities would be greater and the resultant thrust would be greater.

A continuous flow cycle creates the acting force within a turbine engine. Ambient air enters the inlet diffuser, where it is subjected to changes in pressure, velocity, and temperature. It then passes through the compressor that mechanically increases the pressure, or potential energy. The air continues at constant pressure to the combustion section where its temperature and volume are greatly increased by the addition of fuel. Here, potential energy is converted to kinetic energy. The hot gases expand through an exhaust nozzle and create the necessary action to give the reacting thrust.

Figure 2-30 illustrates a different explanation of the creation of the acting force. The gas turbine engine operates on a principle of continuous combustion, or one unit of mass airflow in and one unit of mass airflow out. Because the unit trying to exit has been increased in size (volume), it will have to accelerate greatly to leave the exhaust nozzle as the new unit enters the inlet.

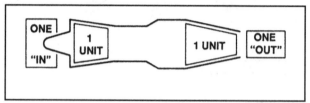

Figure 2-30. One-in, one-out theory

THRUST AND SHP CALCULATIONS

The engine mounts transmit thrust to the aircraft. It is not easy to identify all the points of thrust created within the engine, but variations in pressures within the engine exert forces all along its length, from the airframe inlet to the exhaust. A simple explanation of the operation of a gas turbine turbojet is that it is a device that increases potential energy and then converts it to kinetic energy. Some of this energy performs work at the turbine, while the remainder exits the engine in the form of thrust. These events are explained by Newton's laws. Newton's third law describes how thrust is created, but it does not allow for a mathematical solution. However, his first and second laws provide the mathematical formulas to measure the reaction mentioned in the third law.

The formula $F = MA$ can be expanded from the calculations in previous paragraphs to its final useful form for calculating thrust.

GROSS THRUST (STATIC)

Gross thrust (F_g) is computed when the airplane is at rest. The acceleration of the gas within the engine ($V_2 - V_1$) is the difference in velocities between a unit of air entering the engine and a unit of air exiting at the exhaust nozzle. When the engine is at rest, the value of V_1 will be zero because the air has no initial velocity before the engine starts working on it. The value of V_1 will be greater than zero when the engine (aircraft) is moving.

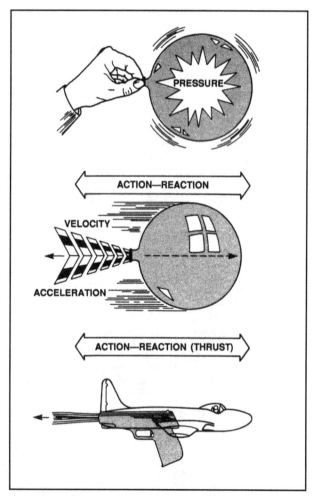

Figure 2-29. Jet propulsion principle (Newton's third law)

Using "Ms" for mass or weight of airflow per second through an engine, the formula for gross thrust is:

$$F_g = \frac{M_s(V_2 - V_1)}{g}$$

Where:
F_g = Gross thrust in lbs.
M_s = Weight of airflow in lbs/sec
V_2 = Exhaust velocity in f.p.s.
V_1 = Inlet velocity in f.p.s.
g = Gravity acceleration 32.2 fps^2

It appears that the time factor in the acceleration formula has disappeared, but it is included in the Ms value, which is pounds of airflow per second. Because the time is one second, there is no need to include its value in the calculation because dividing by one does not change the answer.

Think about the mass of airflow through the engine every second as air entering what is essentially a round engine inlet and moving at a certain number of feet per second. Imagine the air is moving at 200 feet per second, and the diameter of the engine inlet is 4 feet, then a column (cylinder) of air 200 feet long and 4 feet in diameter enters the engine every second. The question now becomes, how much does the air in that cylinder weigh? To answer the question, find out how many cubic feet of air the cylinder contains and then multiply by the weight of one cubic foot of air.

This is how you calculate a standard day weight of airflow in pounds per second:

Volume of a cylinder $(V) = \pi(r^2)(h)$

Where:
V = Cubic feet of space
π = 3.1416
r = Radius of the circle
h = Height of the cylinder (column of air)

One cubic foot of air, under standard day conditions, weighs 0.07647 lbs/ft^3. The volume of the cylinder, which is one second's worth of airflow, can be multiplied by this number to obtain the mass airflow in pounds per second.

Here are two examples:

If the diameter of an engine's inlet is 4 feet and its flow velocity is 400 feet per second, what is its mass airflow in pounds per second at standard day conditions?

Mass airflow (lbs./sec.) = $\pi(r^2)(h)(0.07647)$
= $3.1416(2^2)(400)(0.07647)$
= 384.4 lbs/sec

If a twin-engine, turbojet-powered business jet is at rest and preparing for takeoff, each engine's mass airflow at takeoff power is 60 pounds per second and the exhaust velocity is 1,300 feet per second. What gross thrust does each engine produce?

$$F_g = \frac{M_s(V_2 - V_1)}{g}$$

$$F_g = \frac{60(1,300 - 0)}{32.2}$$

F_g = 2,422.4 lbs.

Where:
F_g = Static thrust in pounds
M_s = 60 lbs/sec
V_2 = 1,300 f.p.s.
V_1 = 0 f.p.s.
g = 32.2 fps^2

It is helpful to note that velocity of air within the inlet is not V_1, which is defined as aircraft speed. The velocity of air in the inlet is the value of (h) in the $V = \pi(r^2)(h)$ formula, where $\pi(r^2)$ represents the effective flow area of the inlet and (h) represents the height or length of a cylinder that allows you to compute the flow velocity in feet per second in the inlet. You can use this value to compute the mass airflow in pounds per second.

You might have calculated the mass airflow of 60 pounds per second in the previous example as in the following example.

If the diameter of the inlet is 1.42 feet and the velocity of airflow within the inlet at takeoff r.p.m. is 496 feet per second:

Mass airflow (lbs/sec) = $\pi(r^2)(h)(0.07647)$
= $3.1416(0.71^2)(496)(0.07647)$
= 60.0 lbs/sec

NET THRUST

When an aircraft is flying, any unit of mass airflow has initial momentum at the engine inlet. Its velocity change across the engine will be greatly reduced as compared to an engine at rest. When an aircraft is in flight, the engine output is referred to as net thrust, versus gross or static thrust when the aircraft is stationary.

The aircraft speed effect is called ram drag, or inlet momentum drag. The net thrust of the engine is the difference between the static thrust and the ram drag. When expressed as a formula, it looks like this:

$F_n = F_g - F_d$

Where:
Fn = Net thrust in pounds
Fg = Gross thrust in pounds
Fd = Ram drag in pounds

The previous example of calculating gross thrust multiplied the mass airflow by the exhaust velocity and then divided by gravity. Nothing was done with the inlet velocity value because it was zero. The formula is:

$$Fg = \frac{Ms(V_2)}{g}$$

The formula for ram drag is:

$$Fd = \frac{Ms(V_1)}{g}$$

When ram drag is subtracted from gross thrust and the values are combined, the formula becomes the same one that was developed for the earlier examples:

$$Fn = \frac{Ms(V_2 - V_1)}{g}$$

For example, suppose the same business jet as in the gross thrust example is now flying at 400 m.p.h. (587 f.p.s.) near sea level. What is its net thrust if the mass airflow is still 60 lbs/sec and the exhaust velocity is still 1300 f.p.s.?

$$Fn = \frac{60(1,300 - 587)}{32.2}$$

Fn = 1,328.6 lbs.

THRUST WITH A CHOKED NOZZLE

Most gas turbine engines are fitted with a device called a choked exhaust nozzle, or jet nozzle. [Figure 2-31] From cruise to takeoff power, pressure in the exhaust duct is pushing the gas with such force that the gas velocity reaches the speed of sound. Pressure at the nozzle opening does not return to ambient with a choked nozzle but stays somewhere in excess of ambient. This pressure across the exhaust nozzle opening creates additional thrust by the principle of F = P × A, or force equals pressure times area.

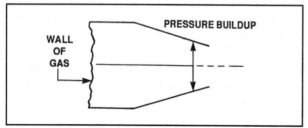

Figure 2-31. Wall of gas concept

According to Bernoulli's Principle, total pressure is the sum of static pressure and pressure due to flow and, if a gas is accelerated, its static pressure will decrease. If energy is added to accelerate the gas, it can only do so up to the speed of sound. So if the jet nozzle is choked, there are two types of energy in the tailpipe, energy of flow (rearward) and energy from internal pressure (in all directions).

As choking (gas flowing at the speed of sound) occurs, pressure starts to build in the tailpipe between the wall of flowing gases in the front section and the constricting exhaust nozzle opening at the rear. Pressure building above ambient pressure across the opening creates a forward push. [Figure 2-32]

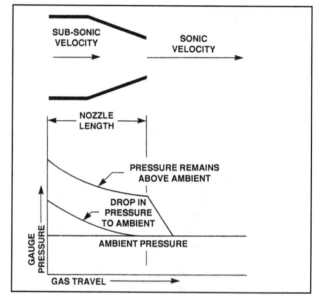

Figure 2-32. Choked-unchoked pressure curves

The total thrust of the engine is now the sum of what would be called the "reaction thrust" and the "pressure thrust." The formula for calculating this thrust is:

$$Fn = \frac{Ms(V_2 - V_1)}{g} + [A_j(P_j - P_{am})]$$

Where:
Fn = Net thrust in lbs.
Ms = Mass airflow in lbs/sec
V_2 = Exhaust velocity in f.p.s.
V_1 = Inlet velocity in f.p.s.
g = Gravity acceleration in fps^2
A_j = Area of jet nozzle in.^{2}
P_j = Pressure at jet nozzle in p.s.i.
Pam = Pressure ambient

When the flow is unchoked, only the flow energy of the gas is creating thrust because pressure energy is decreasing in proportion to velocity increase and has returned to ambient pressure at the jet nozzle opening.

Jet Propulsion Theory

Suppose the same aircraft as in the net thrust example now has a speed of 550 m.p.h. (807 f.p.s.), an Ms that is 50 percent of sea level value, and an exhaust velocity of 1,500 f.p.s. The pressure at the exhaust nozzle is 11.5 psi, the area of the exhaust nozzle is 50 square inches, and the ambient pressure is 5.5 psi. What is the net thrust?

$$Fn = \frac{Ms(V_2 - V_1)}{g} + [A_j(P_j - P_{am})]$$

$$Fn = \frac{30(1500 - 807)}{32.2} + [50(11.5 - 5.5)]$$

$$Fn = 646 + 300$$

$$Fn = 946 \text{ lbs.}$$

THRUST DISTRIBUTION

To calculate the rated thrust of an engine, find the sum of forward forces within the engine and subtract the sum of the rearward forces within the engine. The compressor, combustor, and the exit areas of the exhaust cones exert forward forces; the turbine and tailpipe exit areas exert a rearward force.

When the outlet of a particular section exerts more force than is present at the inlet of that section, there is a forward pushing force. When the inlet of a section, which is also the exit of the preceding section, exerts more force than is present at the exit, there is a rearward pushing force.

Figure 2-33 shows that the compressor section exerts a forward force. This occurs because the compressor discharge area has a much greater pressure force than the compressor inlet, which has zero force. A forward force or thrust is then exerted on the blades, vanes, and outer cases by internal gas pressure buildup at the compressor discharge area.

Mathematically this can be expressed as:

$$Fg = (A \times P) + \frac{Ms(V)}{g} - i$$

Where:
- Fg = Section gross thrust in lbs.
- A = Area in.^{2}
- P = Pressure in p.s.i.g.
- Ms = Mass airflow in lbs/sec
- V = Velocity in f.p.s.
- i = Initial force in lbs.
- g = 32.2 fps^2

The following examples should help explain thrust distribution within an engine.

AT THE COMPRESSOR OUTLET

The thrust-related data of our hypothetical turbojet engine is:

Compressor outlet area:	60 sq. in.
Pressure at outlet:	55 p.s.i.g.
Mass airflow:	30 lbs/sec
Velocity at outlet:	400 f.p.s.
Initial force at inlet:	0 lbs.
Gravity:	32.2 fps^2

$$Fg = (A \times P) + \frac{Ms(V)}{g} - i$$

$$Fg = (60 \times 55) + \frac{30 \times 400}{32.2} - 0$$

$$Fg = 3,300 + 373$$

$$Fg = 3,673 \text{ lbs. (forward thrust)}$$

The engine has a net forward thrust of 3,673 pounds because the compressor outlet creates 3,673 pounds of

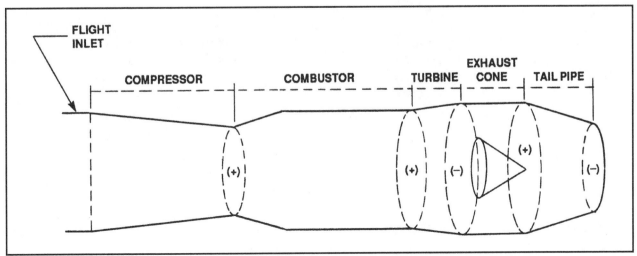

Figure 2-33. Thrust distribution

thrust or force, and the inlet of the compressor creates zero thrust.

Notice the similarity between this formula and the choked nozzle thrust formula; that is, thrust equals mass times acceleration, plus area times pressure. Its use here is possible because the pressure factor is always above ambient within the engine, just as it is when the jet nozzle is choked.

AT THE COMBUSTOR OUTLET

The force present at the combustor inlet is the same as the compressor outlet, 3,673 pounds. The thrust-related data is:

Combustor outlet area:	157 in.^{2}
Pressure at outlet:	53 p.s.i.g.
Mass airflow:	30 lbs/sec
Velocity at outlet:	1,055 f.p.s.
Initial force at inlet:	3,673 lbs.
Gravity:	32.2 fps^2

$$Fg = (A \times P) + \frac{Ms(V)}{g} - i$$

$$Fg = (157 \times 53) + \frac{30 \times 1,055}{32.2} - 3,673$$

$$Fg = 8,321 + 983 - 3,673$$

$$Fg = 5,631 \text{ lbs. (forward thrust)}$$

The net forward thrust of the combustor is 5,631 pounds. You arrive at this value by subtracting the thrust value at the combustor inlet from the thrust value at the combustor outlet.

AT THE TURBINE OUTLET

The force present at the turbine inlet is the same as the combustor outlet, 5,631 lbs. + 3,673 lbs., or a total of 9,304 pounds of thrust. The thrust related data is:

Turbine outlet area:	170 in.^{2}
Pressure at outlet:	11 p.s.i.g.
Mass airflow:	30 lbs/sec
Velocity at outlet:	605.7 f.p.s.
Initial force at inlet:	9,304 lbs.
Gravity:	32.2 fps^2

$$Fg = (A \times P) + \frac{Ms(V)}{g} - i$$

$$Fg = (170 \times 11) + \frac{30 \times 605.7}{32.2} - 9,304$$

$$Fg = 1,870 + 564.3 - 9,304$$

$$Fg = -6,869.7 \text{ lbs. (rearward thrust)}$$

The net rearward thrust of –6,869.7 pounds occurs because the turbine is creating only 2,434.3 pounds of thrust or force, and the total force measured at the combustor outlet is 9,304 pounds. This results from a change in direction of gas flow from axial to tangential (in the direction of the turbine blade rotation). Normally, we think of a pressure drop (53 dropping to 11) as creating a great velocity increase, but as the gas accelerates at an angle the effect of pressure drop to induce axial velocity change is lost. That is, a substantial pressure drop has actually resulted in an axial velocity decrease of 1,055 f.p.s. to 605.7 f.p.s.

AT THE EXHAUST CONE OUTLET

The force present at the inlet of the exhaust cone is the same as the turbine outlet, 2,434.3 pounds. The thrust related data is:

Exhaust cone outlet area:	202 in.^{2}
Pressure at outlet:	12 p.s.i.g.
Mass airflow:	30 lbs/sec
Velocity at outlet:	593.4 f.p.s.
Initial force at inlet:	2,434.3 lbs.
Gravity:	32.2 fps^2

$$Fg = (A \times P) + \frac{Ms(V)}{g} - i$$

$$Fg = (202 \times 12) + \frac{30 \times 593.4}{32.2} - 2,434.3$$

$$Fg = 2,424 + 552.8 - 2,434.3$$

$$Fg = 542.5 \text{ lbs. (forward thrust)}$$

The net forward thrust of 542.5 pounds occurs here because the exhaust cone outlet area and the inner section (tailpipe) form a divergent duct that has a thrust or force of 2,976.8 pounds. This is 542.5 pounds more than the exhaust cone inlet area (same as turbine outlet) of 2,434.3 pounds.

AT THE TAILPIPE (WITH ITS JET NOZZLE IN A CHOKED CONDITION)

Note that the positive side of the formula is the net thrust of the engine when the calculations are complete. The thrust related data is:

Jet nozzle outlet area:	105 in.^{2}
Pressure at outlet:	5 p.s.i.g.
Mass airflow:	30 lbs./sec
Velocity at outlet:	1,900 f.p.s.
Initial force at inlet:	2,976.8 lbs.
Gravity:	32.2 fps^2

$$Fg = (A \times P) + \frac{Ms(V)}{g} - i$$

$$Fg = (105 \times 5) + \frac{30 \times 1,900}{32.2} - 2,976.8$$

$$Fg = 525 + 1,770.2 - 2,976.8$$

$$Fg = -81.6 \text{ lbs. (rearward thrust)}$$

The rearward thrust of –681.6 pounds occurs because the constriction of flow within the tailpipe creates velocity at the expense of pressure. The tailpipe outlet force (thrust) is 2,295.2 pounds, but at the exhaust cone outlet (same as tailpipe inlet), the thrust is 2,976.8 pounds. This leaves –681.6 pounds of thrust or force. Note that the net thrust here (–681.6) is not the choked nozzle thrust, which is +525.

The sum of the rearward thrust or force values equals –7,551.3 pounds, and the sum of the forward thrust values equals 9,846.5. The difference between the two is a forward thrust of 2,295.2 lbs.

A comparison of the thrust distribution formula to the conventional choked nozzle thrust formula makes it clear that the final answer to a thrust calculation will be the same. The engine in the thrust distribution examples has a mass airflow of 30 pounds per second, a V_2 of 1,900 feet per second, a V_1 of zero feet per second, a pressure at the jet nozzle of 5 psig above ambient, and a jet nozzle area of 105 sq. in. If you apply these numbers to the choked nozzle thrust formula, the answer is 2,295.2 pounds.

FAN ENGINE THRUST (UNMIXED EXHAUST)

You can calculate the thrust of a fan engine in the same way as for the turbojet, except that you figure the values of the hot and cold stream nozzle thrust separately and then add them.

For example, suppose a business jet has turbofan engines with unmixed exhaust. The mass airflow of the engine core and the fan are both 60 lbs./sec. The velocity of the fan discharge air is 800 f.p.s. and the core velocity is 1,000 f.p.s. What is the total gross (static) thrust produced by the engine?

$$\text{Core Thrust } Fg = \frac{60(1000 - 0)}{32.2}$$

$$Fg = 1,863.4 \text{ lbs.}$$

$$\text{Fan Thrust } Fg = \frac{60(800 - 0)}{32.2}$$

$$Fg = 1,490.7 \text{ lbs.}$$

Total Thrust = 1,863.4 + 1,490.7 = 3,354.1 lbs.

Note that this example does not take into account how humidity influences thrust. The National Advisory Committee of Aeronautics (NACA) Standard Day conditions are 59°F (15°C), 14.7 psi (29.92 in. Hg), and zero percent humidity at 40° latitude. However, an engine is seldom operated at zero percent humidity. The reason for not considering humidity in thrust calculations is that 65% to 75% of the mass airflow through all types of gas turbine engines is used for cooling the combustion mixture, and the moisture suspended in the atmosphere has a negligible effect on either the cooling process or the remaining 25% to 35% of mass airflow used for combustion.

THRUST HORSEPOWER (THP) IN TURBOJET AND TURBOFAN ENGINES

Piston engines in airplanes are typically rated for the horsepower they create; turboprop engines are also rated in horsepower. However, the horsepower of an engine is not what propels the airplane. These engines drive a propeller, and the propeller converts horsepower to a force in pounds known as thrust. Because horsepower and thrust are not similar units, the concept of thrust horsepower allows a conversion of turbojet and turbofan engine output into units that are the same as those used for piston and turboprop engines.

Thrust-producing engines such as turbojets and turbofans create sufficient power for very high speed flight. It is possible to determine how much horsepower it would take to propel an aircraft at the same speeds using horsepower as a measurement instead of thrust. Thrust horsepower also allows comparison of fuel consumption rates between gas turbine engines. An example in Chapter 7 compares the fuel consumption per thrust horsepower of the Concorde Supersonic Aircraft with the DC-10 Subsonic Airliner.

Use this formula to convert gas turbine engine thrust to thrust horsepower:

$$Thp = \frac{Fn \times \text{aircraft speed}}{375 \text{ mile lbs. per hour}}$$

The value 375 mile-pounds per hour is derived from the basic horsepower formula as follows:

1 Horsepower = 33,000 ft. lbs/min.

33,000 × 60 = 1,980,000 ft. lbs/hour

$$\frac{1,980,000 \text{ ft. lbs/hour}}{5,280 \text{ ft./mile}} = 375 \text{ mile lbs/hour}$$

If aircraft speed is expressed in feet per second, the following formula applies:

$$Thp = \frac{Fn \times V_1}{550}$$

Where V_1 = Aircraft speed in feet per second (f.p.s.)

As the formula indicates, thrust horsepower can only be calculated in flight, so the use of the symbol Fn for thrust applies. The reasoning is that while the aircraft is stationary, no energy is expended for propulsion, and in the formula V_1 (f.p.s.) is zero.

EXAMPLE 1: At very high aircraft speeds, the thrust horsepower of a gas turbine engine can be considerable. For example, the now decommissioned Concorde SST, flying at 1,200 m.p.h., had a thrust horsepower factor of 1200 ÷ 375, or 3.2 times its net thrust output. On one model, thrust per engine at cruise is 10,000 lbs., so Thp = 3.2 x 10,000, or 32,000 thrust horsepower.

The graph in Figure 2-34 illustrates the relationship between thrust horsepower and aircraft speed (V_1) for the Concorde engine.

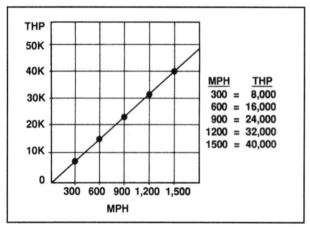

Figure 2-34. Thrust horsepower vs. airspeed for Concorde engine

This aircraft would not actually fly at all cruise speeds plotted on the graph at rated cruise thrust; rather, the graph indicates the faster the design speed for a given thrust, the greater the thrust horsepower. At 375 m.p.h., one pound of thrust is equal to one horsepower. At 1,200 m.p.h., one pound of thrust is equal to 3.2 horsepower.

As you can see, turbine engine development had to wait for faster aircraft to be designed before it could fulfill its role as an effective powerplant for high-speed flight. If the Concorde, for instance, were limited to a speed of 750 m.p.h., its per engine thrust horsepower in cruise would only be 20,000 (10,000 × 750 ÷ 375). Supersonic military aircraft today fulfill this role by using engines of very high thrust horsepower.

EXAMPLE 2: A gas turbine engine produces 3,230 pounds of thrust while the aircraft is flying at 500 miles per hour. What is the thrust horsepower?

$$Thp = \frac{Fn \times \text{aircraft speed}}{375 \text{ mile lbs. per hour}}$$

$$Thp = \frac{3,230 \times 500}{375}$$

$$Thp = 4,307$$

Note that thrust horsepower is not a means of measuring power of a turboshaft engine. Turboshaft engines and reciprocating engines are rated in shaft horsepower (shp), measured directly at the output shaft with a dynamometer.

PROPELLER (TURBOPROP) THRUST

In the thrust horsepower formula, we arrived at a shaft horsepower value for a given thrust and speed of a turbojet and turbofan. By rearranging this formula, we can arrive at a net thrust (Fn) value for a turboprop engine in straight and level flight.

If:

$$Thp = \frac{Fn \times mph}{375}$$

Then:

$$Fn = \frac{Thp \times 375}{mph}$$

If we substitute shaft horsepower (Shp) for thrust horsepower (Thp) and use the conventional 80 percent efficiency factor for a propeller (Fp), the formula for the force (thrust) generated by a propeller becomes:

$$Fp = \frac{Shp \times 375 \times 0.80}{mph}$$

If the propeller is 90 percent efficient, as compared to 80 percent, multiply by 0.90 instead of the 0.80 in the top line of the formula. Theoretically, the propeller could be 100 percent efficient if it had no friction or aerodynamic losses and converted all the power provided to it into thrust.

EXAMPLE: A turboprop engine produces 1,150 shp. How much propeller thrust does that equal if the aircraft is flying at 445 m.p.h. and the propeller efficiency is 100 percent?

$$Fp = \frac{Shp \times 375 \times 1.0}{mph}$$

$$Fp = \frac{1{,}150 \times 375 \times 1.0}{445}$$

$$Fp = 969.1\, lbs.$$

When calculating propeller thrust in a static condition (operating without moving forward), use a conversion factor of 2.5. In a static condition, one shaft horsepower equals 2.5 pounds of thrust, so an engine with 1,150 shaft horsepower equals 2,875 pounds of thrust in a static condition. If you compare the turboprop above to a turbofan of similar size, you find that the turbofan would also be in the range of 2,500 to 3,000 pounds of thrust at sea level.

To find the total thrust of the turboprop, add the hot exhaust thrust (Fn) to the propeller thrust (Fp).

Use Figure 2-35 to calculate thrust when the shaft horsepower of a turboprop is known. The shaft horsepower of a turboprop will be indicated directly by a cockpit thrust horsepower instrument, or the shaft horsepower can be calculated by formula from a torque gauge in the cockpit using a torque to shaft horsepower conversion factor supplied by the manufacturer.

Figure 2-35 shows that at 275 m.p.h. and 80 percent propeller efficiency, the Fp to shaft horsepower ratio is 1.1:1. Recall that in a static condition it was 2.5:1.

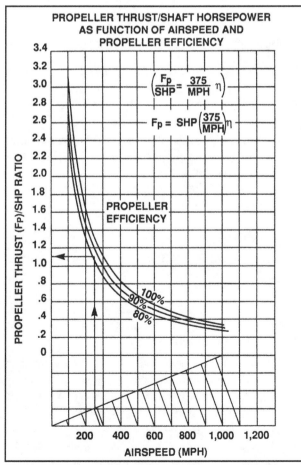

Figure 2-35. Propeller thrust per shaft horsepower

Now use Figure 2-35 to determine the propeller thrust if an engine is producing 525 shaft horsepower at 275 m.p.h. and the prop is 80 percent efficient.

$$Fp = Shp \times Conversion\ Factor$$

The plot for 275 m.p.h. and 80 percent intersects on the left of the chart at a ratio of 1.1.

$$Fp = 525 \times 1.1$$

$$Fp = 578\ lbs.$$

Confirm the 578 pounds of thrust calculation by applying the following formula:

$$Fp = \frac{Shp \times 375 \times 0.80}{mph}$$

$$Fp = \frac{525 \times 0375 \times 0.80}{275}$$

$$Fp = 573$$

This answer is only five pounds different from the previous answer of 578 pounds. The answer derived mathematically is the most accurate.

EQUIVALENT SHAFT HORSEPOWER (TURBOPROP GROUND RUNUP)

Another useful calculation usually included in a discussion of gas turbine theory is how to determine the power of a turboprop by converting the exhaust thrust to shaft horsepower and adding it to the shaft horsepower obtained from a dynamometer check. The sum is known as equivalent shaft horsepower (Eshp). Under static conditions, one shaft horsepower is equal to approximately 2.5 pounds of thrust. The formulas are as follows:

$$Eshp = Shp\ (dynamometer) + Hp\ (jet\ thrust)$$

$$Hp\ (jet\ thrust) = \frac{Jet\ Thrust\ (Fg)}{2.5}$$

Here is an example problem. The Garrett turboprop model TPE-331 produces 187.5 pounds of jet thrust, with a rating of 680 shaft horsepower. What is its equivalent shaft horsepower rating?

$$Hp\ (jet\ thrust) = \frac{Jet\ Thrust\ (Fg)}{2.5}$$

$$Hp\ (jet\ thrust) = \frac{187.5}{2.5}$$

$$Hp\ (jet\ thrust) = 75$$

$$Eshp = Shp\ (dynamometer) + Hp\ (jet\ thrust)$$

$$Eshp = 680 + 75$$

$$Eshp = 755$$

EQUIVALENT SHAFT HORSEPOWER (TURBOPROP IN FLIGHT)

Calculate the equivalent shaft horsepower in flight by introducing the variable of propeller efficiency. If thrust horsepower represents the shaft horsepower that a turbojet or turbofan has as useful power in flight, then shaft horsepower times horsepower will equal the useful power available to a turboprop in flight.

The following is the standard formula for computing thrust horsepower.

$$Thp = \frac{Fn \times V_1}{375}$$

$$Shp = Thp \div \eta p$$

$$Shp = \frac{Fn \times V_1}{375} \div \eta p$$

Where:

Fn = Net Thrust
V_1 = Aircraft Speed (m.p.h.)
375 = Conversion of power to Hp
ηp = Efficiency (propeller)

Because equivalent shaft horsepower (Eshp) equals the engine's shaft horsepower plus the shaft horsepower equivalent of the jet thrust, use the following formula to calculate Eshp in flight:

$$Eshp\,(flight) = Shp + \frac{Fn \times V_1}{\eta p \times 375}$$

Apply this formula to the following set of conditions to determine equivalent shaft horsepower. The cockpit power gauge of a turboprop aircraft operating in flight indicates 500 shaft horsepower. The aircraft speed is 275 m.p.h., there is 200 pounds of exhaust hot thrust present, and the industry-accepted propeller efficiency is 80 percent. What is the engine equivalent shaft horsepower?

$$Eshp\,(flight) = Shp + \frac{Fn \times V_1}{\eta p \times 375}$$

$$Eshp\,(flight) = 500 + \frac{200 \times 275}{0.80 \times 375}$$

$$Eshp\,(flight) = 683$$

It would take 683 Shp to produce the same airspeed as the present 500 Shp and 200 pounds of thrust.

HORSEPOWER REQUIREMENT TO DRIVE THE COMPRESSOR

The turbine drives the compressor by extracting power from the flowing gas. The compression process expends power to produce a pressure rise. If you know the temperature rise above ambient across compression and the engine mass airflow in pounds per second, you can use the following formula to calculate the horsepower required to produce that temperature rise.

$$Hp(compressor) = Tr \times Cp \times Ms \times 778 \div 550$$

Where:
Tr = Temperature rise (°F)
Cp = 0.24 BTU /lb/°F
Ms = Mass airflow in lbs/sec
778 = ft. lbs. in 1 BTU
550 = ft. lbs/sec in 1 Hp

It takes 0.24 BTU/lb to raise one pound of air one degree Fahrenheit. By comparison, it takes 1 BTU to raise a pound of water one degree Fahrenheit.

If there are 778 foot-pounds of work in one BTU, multiplying $Tr \times Cp \times Ms \times 778$ will give the power required to heat the air. Dividing power by the conversion factor of 550 foot-pounds/second will then give horsepower.

EXAMPLE 1: If the engine in the thrust distribution example covered earlier has an inlet temperature of 60°F, a compressor discharge temperature of 270°F, and a mass airflow of 30 pounds/second, what horsepower is required to drive its compressor?

$$Hp(compressor) = Tr \times Cp \times Ms \times 778 \div 550$$

$$Hp(compressor) = 210 \times 0.24 \times 30 \times 778 \div 550$$

$$Hp(compressor) = 2{,}138.8 \text{ Hp extracted by turbine}$$

On large, powerful engines, the horsepower extracted at the turbine is very high because both mass airflow (Ms) and temperature rise (Tr) are high due to high compression loads.

EXAMPLE 2: The Rolls-Royce Olympus 593 turbojet, in the Concorde aircraft, has a mass airflow of 415 pounds per second and a temperature rise across compression of 900°F above ambient. What horsepower is the turbine system extracting?

$$Hp(compressor) = Tr \times Cp \times Ms \times 778 \div 550$$

$$Hp(compressor) = 900 \times 0.24 \times 415 \times 778 \div 550$$

$$Hp(compressor) = 126{,}800$$

This represents only the power required to drive the compressor. The engine will also have to provide additional power to create thrust.

EXAMPLE 3: One model of the Pratt & Whitney JT8D dual spool turbofan is operating on a 59°F day and has the following operational parameters. What is the horsepower required to drive the compressor?

Fan Ms = 164 lbs/sec, fan discharge temp. = 214°F
N_1 Ms = 160 lbs/sec, N_1 discharge temp. = 380°F
N_2 Ms = 160 lbs/sec, N_2 discharge temp. = 820°F

(Continued on next page)

$Hp = Tr \times Cp \times Ms \times 778 \div 550$

$Hp(fan) = (214 - 59) \times 0.24 \times 164 \times 778 \div 550$

$Hp(fan) = 8{,}630$

$Hp(N_1) = (380 - 59) \times 0.24 \times 160 \times 778 \div 550$

$Hp(N_1) = 17{,}436$

$Hp(N_2) = (820 - 380) \times 0.24 \times 160 \times 778 \div 550$

$Hp(N_2) = 23{,}900$

OTHER SIGNIFICANT HORSEPOWER TERMS

Thermodynamic Horsepower. This value represents the total available horsepower of a turboprop or turboshaft engine as measured on a dynamometer. Many gas turbine engines are not used to their full potential (thermodynamic horsepower) because the aircraft does not require that amount of power. The reason for this is that there are more aircraft models and not as many engine choices; therefore, the aircraft manufacturer is forced to choose an engine of higher power than actually required. When this is the case, the engine is re-rated to a lower maximum horsepower, and the new power rating is given as the shaft horsepower rating of the engine.

Isentropic Gas Horsepower. This value represents the total potential work available in the exhaust gases leaving the gas generator portion of a free turbine turboprop or turboshaft engine. The gases then enter the power turbine and expand to turn it, producing work. The shaft horsepower rating of such an engine is obtained by multiplying the isentropic horsepower by the percentage of power turbine efficiency.

Ram Shaft Horsepower. This value represents the total equivalent shaft horsepower available to a turboprop engine at the point of takeoff. At this time, ram air compression in the engine inlet boosts the static rated takeoff equivalent shaft horsepower one to two percent.

GAS TURBINE ENGINE PERFORMANCE CURVES

The efficiency levels of gas turbine engines are best explained by graphs (curves) and formulas to show how propulsive efficiency and thermal efficiency interact to result in an overall efficiency rating of a particular engine.

PROPULSIVE EFFICIENCY

In Figure 2-36, the curves depict graphically how propulsive efficiency varies with aircraft speed, an important difference between turbine and reciprocating engines. The thrust of the turbine is fairly constant, but the thrust of reciprocating engines drops off rapidly as speed increases. The turbine engine performs better than a reciprocating engine under high-speed conditions because it uses the increased inlet air mass and the air pressure that results from the ram effect to maintain thrust.

Propulsive efficiency is the external powerplant efficiency, or a measure of the effectiveness with which a powerplant converts kinetic energy to useful work for propelling the aircraft. It can also be described as a comparison of the engine's propelling exhaust velocity (jet wake or prop wake) versus aircraft speed. The graph reveals how propeller-driven aircraft gain their efficiency first at low airspeeds because the controllable pitch propeller is capable of moving large mass airflows. The curves all peak out as soon as more fuel energy is introduced to create an exhaust velocity increase, which produces work in the form of increased aircraft speed.

The curves can be interpreted as follows:

- The aircraft (either piston or turbine driven) peaks out slightly above 85 percent, after which the propeller loses efficiency. Although its exhaust wake velocity continues to increase from added fuel energy, aircraft speed does not increase proportionally. After reaching approximately 375 m.p.h., propulsive efficiency starts

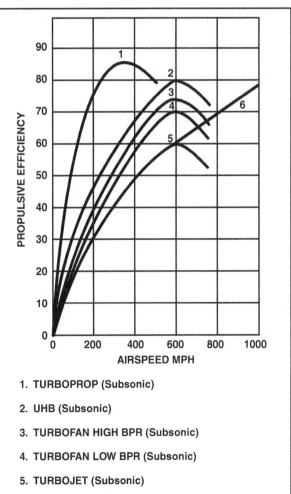

1. TURBOPROP (Subsonic)
2. UHB (Subsonic)
3. TURBOFAN HIGH BPR (Subsonic)
4. TURBOFAN LOW BPR (Subsonic)
5. TURBOJET (Subsonic)
6. TURBOFAN LOW BPR & TURBOJET (Supersonic)

Figure 2-36. Propulsive efficiency

to decrease. Aerodynamic drag and tip shock stall are involved here, and by 500 m.p.h. efficiency decreases to 65 percent.

- The ultra-high-bypass turbofan curve peaks at approximately 560 m.p.h. (Mach 0.85), after which the fan suffers the same losses in drag and tip speed as the propeller. In order to go 700 m.p.h. (aircraft speed), the exhaust velocity has to be increased to an uneconomical level.
- The high-bypass turbofan is the most widely used engine today in both large and small aircraft. Its propulsive efficiency curve peaks out slightly lower than the UHB engine but at approximately the same airspeed.
- Subsonic aircraft with low and medium-bypass turbofans all operate in the 500 to 600 m.p.h. range. Note that the curve shows a lower efficiency value than a high-bypass engine in that range. Because of this, high-bypass engines are rapidly replacing low- and medium-bypass engines in many aircraft.
- The supersonic low-bypass turbofan and turbojet have a theoretical propulsive efficiency peak limit in the 2,000 to 3,000 m.p.h. range. Their narrow, low-drag profile allows this range. Any additional energy added (in the form of fuel) to increase speed would raise the internal engine temperatures to unacceptable levels. The graph in Figure 2-37 can be defined mathematically for engines with a single exhaust, as follows:

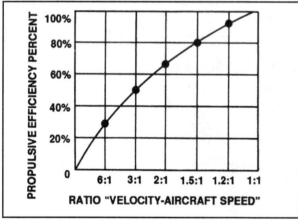

Figure 2-37. Exhaust velocity to aircraft speed ratio and propulsive efficiency

$$Peff = \frac{2}{1 + \frac{V_f}{V_i}}$$

Where: Peff = Propulsive efficiency
         V_f = Exhaust velocity (final)
         V_i = Aircraft speed (initial)

The propulsive efficiency formula is derived by manipulating the familiar kinetic energy formula, $Ke = 1/2mV^2$. Consider that there is a great deal of energy wasted or left behind the engine in its prop or jet wake. Calculating the energy wasted reveals the operating conditions that waste the least energy. In doing so, we can also find the conditions of highest propulsive efficiency. In the kinetic energy formula, "m" is airflow through the engine and "V" is the velocity change of that mass airflow as it moves through the engine.

The propulsive efficiency formula (Peff), as shown in the text above, is relatively simple to use and apply, but its derivation a complex process, as you can see from the following text. [Figure 2-38]

EXAMPLE 1: The propeller aircraft in the graph in Figure 2-36, which seems to have approximately 87 percent propulsive efficiency at 375 m.p.h., would also have a prop wake (V_f) of 490 m.p.h. as follows:

$$Peff = \frac{2}{1 + \frac{V_f}{V_i}}$$

$$Peff = \frac{2}{1 + \frac{490}{375}}$$

$$Peff = \frac{2}{2.3}$$

$$Peff = 0.87$$

$$Peff = 87\%$$

$$P_{eff} = \frac{\text{Thrust Power}}{\text{Thrust Power} + \text{Kinetic Energy Wasted}}$$

$$P_{eff} = \frac{\text{Thrust} \times V_i}{\text{Thrust} \times V_i + 1/2 M V^2}$$

$$P_{eff} = \frac{M(V_f - V_i)V_i}{M(V_f - V_i)V_i + 1/2M(V_f - V_i)^2}$$

$$P_{eff} = \frac{MV_f V_i - MV_i^2}{MV_f V_i - MV_i^2 + [1/2M(V_f^2 + V_i^2 - 2V_f V_i)]}$$

$$P_{eff} = \frac{M(V_f V_i - V_i^2)}{MV_f V_i - MV_i^2 + \frac{MV_f^2}{2} + \frac{MV_i^2}{2} - MV_f V_i}$$

$$P_{eff} = \frac{M(V_f V_i - V_i^2)}{M\left(\frac{V_i^2}{2} + \frac{V_f^2}{2} - V_i^2\right)}$$

$$P_{eff} = \frac{V_f V_i - V_i^2}{\frac{V_i^2}{2} + \frac{V_f^2}{2} - \frac{V_i^2}{1}}$$

$$P_{eff} = \frac{V_f V_i - V_i^2}{\frac{V_f^2 - V_i^2}{2}}$$

$$P_{eff} = V_f V_i - V_i^2 \div \left(\frac{V_f^2 - V_i^2}{2}\right)$$

$$P_{eff} = V_f V_i - V_i^2 \times \frac{2}{V_f^2 - V_i^2}$$

$$P_{eff} = \frac{2V_f V_i - 2V_i^2}{V_f^2 - V_i^2}$$

$$P_{eff} = \frac{2V_i(V_f - V_i)}{(V_f - V_i)(V_f + V_i)}$$

$$P_{eff} = \frac{2V_i}{V_f + V_i} = 2 \div \frac{V_f + V_i}{V_i}$$

$$P_{eff} = \frac{2}{\frac{V_f + V_i}{V_i}} = \frac{2}{\frac{V_i}{V_i} + \frac{V_f}{V_i}}$$

$$P_{eff} = \frac{2}{1 + \frac{V_f}{V_i}}$$

Figure 2-38. Derivation of the propulsive efficiency formula

EXAMPLE 2: A turbofan aircraft with a mixed exhaust is operating at cruise power. Its speed is 550 m.p.h. (807 f.p.s.). Velocity from the mixed exhaust is 1,348 f.p.s. What is the propulsive efficiency?

NOTE: This calculation is made in f.p.s. and works equally as well as calculations made in m.p.h.

$$P_{eff} = \frac{2}{1 + \frac{1,348}{807}}$$

$$P_{eff} = \frac{2}{2.67}$$

$$P_{eff} = 0.75$$

$$P_{eff} = 75\%$$

EXAMPLE 3: The turbofan aircraft in example 2 has just taken off and is climbing out. Its speed is 200 m.p.h. (293.4 f.p.s.) and the velocity of its exhaust is 1,650 f.p.s. What is the propulsive efficiency?

$$P_{eff} = \frac{2}{1 + \frac{1,650}{293.4}}$$

$$P_{eff} = \frac{2}{6.62}$$

$$P_{eff} = 0.30$$

$$P_{eff} = 30\%$$

NOTE: The low efficiency results from high exhaust velocity relative to aircraft speed.

The propulsive efficiency formula for a turbofan engine with an unmixed exhaust, which is the case with most high-bypass engines, is based on the kinetic energy being wasted by the hot stream gases and by the fan discharge gases. The complete formula, from which the simplified propulsive efficiency is derived, would be used. It would be necessary, however, to calculate for both gas streams.

EXAMPLE 4: A high-bypass turbofan is at cruise altitude, with a flight speed of 532 m.p.h. (780 f.p.s.). Its fan exhaust velocity is 995 f.p.s.; core engine exhaust velocity is 1,450 f.p.s.; fan mass airflow is 550 lb/sec; core engine mass airflow is 110 lb/sec. What is its propulsive efficiency? (See Figure 2-39).

> **FORMULA A**
>
> $$P_{eff} = \frac{M_1 V_i(V_{2f} - V_i) + M_2 V_i(V_{2j} - V_i)}{[M_1 V_i(V_{2f} - V_i)] + [M_2 V_i(V_{2j} - V_i)] + [1/2 M_1(V_{2f} - V_i)^2] + [1/2 M_2(V_{2j} - V_i)^2]}$$
>
> Where:
>
> M_1 = Mass airflow of the fan
>
> M_2 = Mass airflow of the core engine
>
> V_i = Aircraft speed
>
> V_{2f} = Exhaust velocity of the fan
>
> V_{2j} = Exhaust velocity of the core
>
> $$P_{eff} = \frac{550 \times 780 (995 - 780) + 110 \times 780 (1{,}450 - 780)}{[550 \times 780 (995 - 780)] + [110 \times 780 (1{,}450 - 780)] + [1/2 \times 550 (995 - 780)^2] + [1/2 \times 110 (1{,}450 - 780)^2]}$$
>
> $P_{eff} = 0.080 = 80\%$

Figure 2-40. Example of propulsive efficiency calculation

Conclusion: The closer the aircraft speed comes to exhaust velocity, the higher the propulsive efficiency. The ideal propulsive efficiency would appear to be reached by the aircraft traveling at the same speed as its prop wake or exhaust velocity; in other words, 100 percent. This, of course, is not possible in a practical sense because no momentum change would occur with regard to mass airflow and no reactive thrust would result.

THERMAL EFFICIENCY

Thermal efficiency, one of the prime factors in gas turbine performance, is the ratio of the net work produced by the engine to the fuel energy input. In the aircraft, thermal efficiency cannot be measured directly but could, if desired, be calculated by utilizing a cockpit fuel-flow indication.

$$\text{Thermal Efficiency} = \frac{\text{Hp output of engine}}{\text{Hp value of fuel consumed}}$$

EXAMPLE 1: A turboshaft engine produces 725 shaft horsepower. Its fuel consumption is 300 pounds/hour, and its fuel contains 18,730 BTU/pound. Each BTU can produce 778 ft. lbs. of work. What is the engine's thermal efficiency?

Fuel consumed per minute = 5 lbs. (300 ÷ 60)

BTU in 5 lbs. of fuel = 93,650

Power in 5 lbs. of fuel = 72,859,700 ft. lbs./min.

$$Hp = \frac{72{,}859{,}700 \text{ ft. lbs./min.}}{33{,}000 \text{ ft. lbs./min.}}$$

Hp = 2,208

$$\text{Thermal Efficiency} = \frac{725 \text{ engine Hp}}{2{,}208 \text{ fuel Hp}} = 32.8\%$$

Note that the other 67.2 percent is lost due to friction of the rotors (approximately 17 percent) and heat given up to the atmosphere (approximately 50 percent).

EXAMPLE 2: A turbofan engine produces 11,000 pounds of net thrust in flight at 561 m.p.h. Its fuel consumption is 7,500 pounds per hour. Its fuel contains 18,730 BTU/pound, and each BTU equals 778 ft. lbs. of work. What is its thermal efficiency?

Jet Propulsion Theory

Fuel consumed per minute = 125 lbs. (7,500 ÷ 60)

BTU in 125 lbs. of fuel = 2,341,250 BTU

Power in 125 lbs. of fuel = 1,821,492,500 ft. lbs./min

$$Hp = \frac{1,821,492,500 \text{ ft. lbs./min}}{33,000 \text{ ft. lbs./min}}$$

Hp = 55,197

Engine Thp = 11,000 × 561 ÷ 375 = 16,456

$$\text{Thermal Efficiency} = \frac{16,456 \text{ engine Hp}}{55,197 \text{ fuel Hp}} = 29.8\%$$

OVERALL EFFICIENCY

Selection of the exact designs of gas turbine engines for a particular aircraft is a process of numerous compromises. Physical features, such as weight, size, and shape are only a few of the considerations. Discovering just the right performance factors also figures heavily into the final design of any engine.

The propulsive efficiency idea previously discussed is one measure of an engine's performance, another concerns thermal efficiency. The engine designer carefully considers these two factors, called overall efficiency, in combination. [Figure 2-40]

Overall Efficiency = Pe% × Te%

EXAMPLE: A turbofan engine has a propulsive efficiency (Pe) of 80 percent and a thermal efficiency (Te) of 29.8 percent. What is its overall efficiency?

Overall Efficiency = 80% × 29.8% = 23.8%

Figure 2-40 illustrates three things:

- Propulsive efficiency increases as airspeed approaches exhaust velocity values.
- Thermal efficiency decreases due to added fuel needs at higher airspeeds.
- Overall efficiency increases as airspeed increases because propulsive efficiency increases more than thermal efficiency decreases.

THERMAL EFFICIENCY CURVES

The three most important factors affecting thermal efficiency are turbine inlet temperature (TIT), compressor pressure ratio, and component efficiencies of the compressor and turbine.

Figure 2-41 shows the effect that changing compressor pressure ratio has on thermal efficiency. The ideal cycle on the graph would result if compressor and turbine efficiencies were at 100 percent and all air turbulence within the engine was eliminated. The ideal curve would eventually peak out at approximately 70 percent and is of theoretical value only. The best thermal efficiency realized by aircraft today at cruise altitude is in the 45 to 50 percent range. This is seen in very large engines which have a 30:1 (or higher) overall compressor pressure ratio and turbine inlet temperatures of 2,500 to 3,000°F. The ideal situation on the graph in Figure 2-41 is 3,000°F, with a 32:1 compressor pressure ratio. This occurs because the greatest expansion in the combustion and turbine sections occurs in a combination of high pressure and high heat.

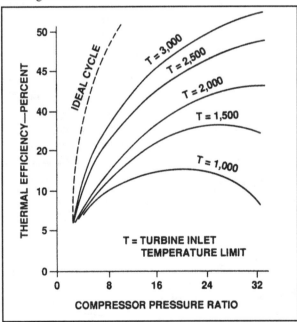

Figure 2-41. Compression ratio and thermal efficiency

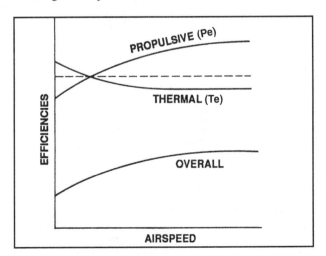

Figure 2-40. Example of propulsive efficiency calculation

High TIT is an indicator of high thermal efficiency. If a particular engine has higher heat-strength parts, it requires less cooling air. In turn, the compressor can be scaled down and the turbine wheel set to extract a corresponding lower amount of energy. This increases the thermal efficiency because for a particular fuel flow, more gas energy is present in the tailpipe for thrust or more energy is available to drive a turbine connected to a fan or propeller.

In all turbine engines, heat energy (fuel) accelerates the gases in the combustor. The designer tries to prevent the heated gas from directly touching the metal by providing a film of cooling air. This is not so easily done at the turbine section of the engine, and in older designs the heated gases did touch some of the metal and more cooling air had to be added to decrease turbine inlet temperatures, resulting in lower thermal efficiency.

The curve also shows that if a limit of only 1,000°F (TIT value) is set, the benefit of producing a high compressor pressure ratio is lost. That is, fuel consumption increases faster than horsepower production increases.

The compressor and turbine sections of a gas turbine engine are most energy efficient at low compression temperatures because low compressor temperatures allow greater temperature rise and gas expansion in the combustor.

Large modern engines have compressor and turbine efficiency percentages in the mid- to high-eighties. Because of scale effect, smaller engines will have a lower efficiency percentage, which means that small engines cannot withstand the same pressures and temperatures as larger ones. When compared to larger engines, smaller ones require that rotor blade tip clearances be a larger percentage of the blade length, resulting in a relatively greater tip leakage and a loss in efficiency.

Figure 2-42 illustrates that with 80 to 90 percent compressor and turbine efficiencies, thermal efficiency rises as compressor pressure ratio rises. In other words, the ideal compressor efficiency (adiabatic compression) occurs when the compressor produces the maximum pressure with the least temperature rise, and the ideal turbine extracts the most work for the least fuel consumption.

As engines build service time, a loss of compressor and turbine efficiency occurs for a couple of reasons. First, as higher temperatures appear during compression, more energy is required to raise temperatures still further in combustion for the purpose of gas expansion and power. Therefore, the combustor will require more BTU (fuel) per pound of air to raise air temperature when the compressor delivers warmer air to the combustor. This affects the overall thermal efficiency of the engine.

Second, ideal turbine efficiency exists when the turbine wheel performs the most work by rotating at high speeds with the least extraction of energy from the flowing gases. This is more attainable today than in the past because of lightweight materials, more advanced designs made possible by new manufacturing methods, and closer production tolerances in manufacture.

Referring to the graph in Figure 2-42, it follows that heat from compression is excessive below 60 percent efficiency, the compressor is dirty or damaged, or fuel flow is excessive because of damage to components in the turbine area.

FACTORS THAT AFFECT THRUST

Four factors affect inlet air density and affect gas turbine engine thrust: Ambient temperature, altitude, airspeed, and engine r.p.m.

Figure 2-43 shows changing ambient temperature affects net thrust if altitude, r.p.m., and airspeed are constant. This curve would equally apply to ground level (gross) thrust.

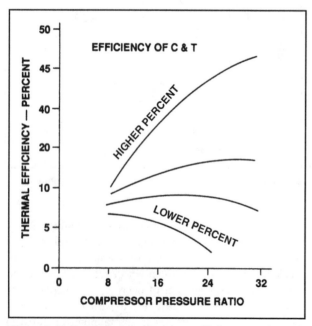

Figure 2-42. Turbine and compressor efficiency vs. thermal efficiency

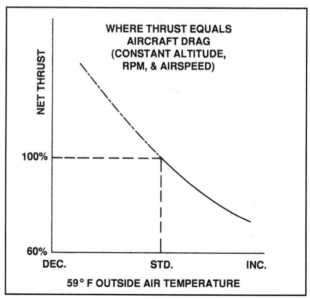

Figure 2-43. Effect of OAT on thrust output

Observe that as the temperature falls below the engine's rated outside air temperature (OAT), net thrust available at the base line increases over the 100 percent line to the left. Although sometimes desirable, such as in an emergency, it could quickly cause excessively high internal engine temperatures. For this reason, thrust above 100 percent rated power is rarely used.

Pilots usually apply power only to the minimum required for satisfactory operation of the aircraft in the interests of engine service life and fuel conservation.

The increased thrust on the graph due to low ambient temperatures is the result of two factors. First, the energy extracted at the turbine to drive the compressor(s) varies directly with air temperature. Cool air compresses more easily than warm air, and more energy is left in the engine to accelerate the airflow to create thrust. Second, cool air is denser, which increases the mass airflow, which in turn increases thrust.

As shown in Figure 2-44, increasing altitude has conflicting influences on thrust. Although the volume of flow into the engine for a given speed remains unchanged, mass airflow decreases. The altitude effect on thrust can best be discussed as a result of ambient temperature change and density pressure change. In this case, an increase in altitude causes a decrease in both pressure and temperature. Since the temperature lapse rate is less than the pressure lapse rate, a net decrease in density will result as altitude is increased.

As an aircraft gains altitude to 36,000 feet, its thrust decreases at a lower rate than it does above 36,000 feet. This is a result of the combined effects of temperature and pressure lapse rates previously mentioned. However, at 36,000 feet and above the ambient temperature remains constant (see Appendix 7 for Atmospheric Chart), while the barometric pressure continues to drop. This atmospheric phenomenon results in the more pronounced rate of decrease in thrust, as can be seen on the curve above 36,000 feet.

Another way to think about thrust is to observe the effect that ambient temperature and runway altitude have on takeoff thrust. Figure 2-45 shows an engine with 15,500 pounds of thrust at 59°F at sea level. This drops to 9,500 pounds of thrust at 59°F and 14,000 feet elevation. If the pilot were to add fuel to make up for deteriorating thrust, internal engine temperatures would reach prohibitively high levels long before achieving 15,500 pounds of thrust.

Also, notice that starting at the 2,000 feet line, the curves drop off in steps. This is to accommodate the aircraft's need for thrust, but at the expense of engine hot section life.

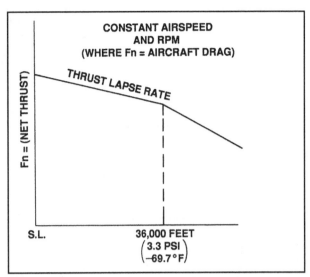

Figure 2-44. Effect of altitude on net thrust

Note that on this graph the full rated thrust of 15,500 pounds can only be attained up to 84°F (28.9°C), after which the pilot uses only the lesser corresponding thrust on the chart. The full rated thrust being available to a temperature higher than standard day is referred to as flat rating, a topic discussed in detail in Chapter 7.

When engine power is increased to a higher constant value, the aircraft flies faster and thrust is affected as shown in Figure 2-46.

Curve A indicates that net thrust will tend to increase as airspeed increases, due to ram air compression in the engine inlet.

Curve B shows the reverse occurring and the net thrust tendency decreasing due to the reduced velocity change of mass airflow through the engine.

Curve C represents curves A and B combined, and has an initial decrease in net thrust (point C_1). This can be interpreted as the effect of minimal help from ram compression, which occurs at low airspeed, at a time when thrust decreased from reduced velocity change within the engine is more immediate. The net result is an initially diminished thrust situation, a condition which eventually corrects itself as the aircraft approaches its design speed.

In actual figures, the point at which thrust in Curve C starts to recover in the average turbojet or turbofan engine is between 300 and 350 m.p.h., and the point at which thrust is recovered completely is between 500 and 600 m.p.h. (point C_2). This is because ram pressure in the inlet increases thrust at a faster rate than aircraft speed diminishes thrust.

Aircraft designed for subsonic cruise speeds, when moving from ground level to altitude, will eventually

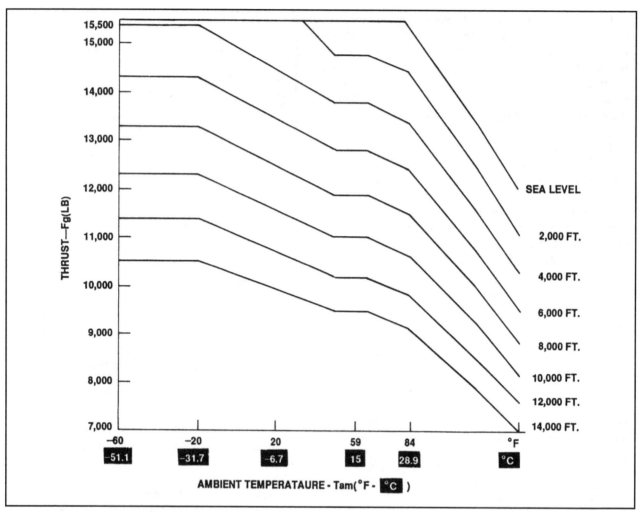

Figure 2-45. Effect of runway altitude on thrust

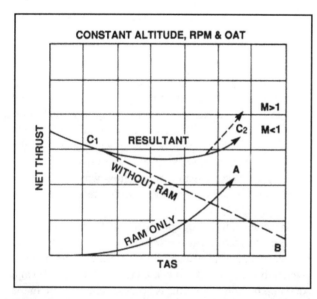

Figure 2-46. Effect of airspeed on net thrust

experience a decrease in net thrust due to altitude effect. With less drag on the aircraft at higher altitudes, the loss of thrust will not be as detrimental to the cruise capability of the aircraft.

In supersonic flight, one would see Curve C_2 turn upward very sharply as ram compression greatly increases mass airflow into the engine inlet. During supersonic flight in some aircraft, inlet pressure, due to ram compression, can be as much as 30:1, and net thrust will increase because of the increased forward speed.

Figure 2-47 shows the general effect that r.p.m. has on thrust. As r.p.m. increases thrust also increases because more mass airflow and velocity changes occur within the engine.

Some early turbojet engines had a close linear relationship between compressor speed and engine thrust that the operator could set engine power output [Figure 2-48] using the throttle and the percent r.p.m. cockpit indicator. The power available was dependent on outside air temperature and could be adjusted accordingly by the operator using standard r.p.m. to temperature charts.

Jet Propulsion Theory

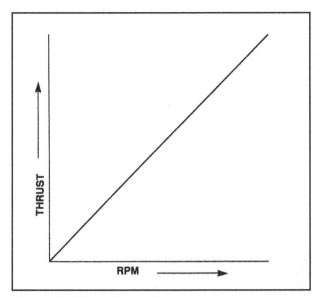

Figure 2-47. Effect of revolutions per minute on thrust

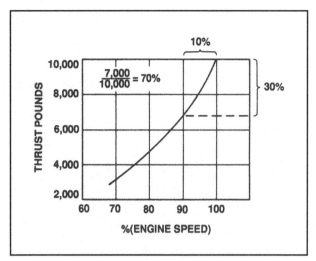

Figure 2-49. Revolutions per minute effect on thrust (dual-spool compressor)

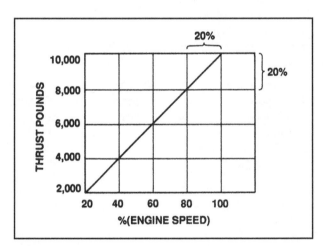

Figure 2-48. Revolutions per minute effect

Many modern turbofan engines also use fan speed (percent r.p.m.) as a means of setting engine thrust. [Figure 2-49] However, the relationship between fan speed and thrust must be computed by sophisticated electronic fuel scheduling systems and not by a simple temperature chart. Therefore the majority of dual- and triple-spool, thrust-producing engines use the compressor percent r.p.m. indicator only as an engine condition gauge and not as an indication of engine power. This is required because of the nonlinear relationship that exists between compressor speed and engine thrust. If a thrust producing engine does not use fan speed as a power performance cockpit indicator, it will use an engine pressure ratio (EPR) indicating system to show engine power.

RPM LIMITS IMPOSED ON TURBINE ENGINES

Serious limits are imposed on the compressor diameter and compressor r.p.m. because of the effect they have on compressor blade tip speed in feet per second and consequently Mach number. The imposed limits minimize airflow separation over airfoils from shock wave formation.

AXIAL FLOW COMPRESSORS

It might seem that increasing r.p.m. to higher values will negate or reverse the effects of atmospheric changes on thrust, but this is not the case because there is a definite r.p.m. limit in the form of tip speed limitations. The speed at the tips of all rotating airfoils within the engine is carefully governed to keep the airflow over any part of the airfoils from creating shock waves. Until recently, compressor designs permitted airflow only at subsonic values, and compression values were much lower for a given number of compression stages. Tip-flow limits today are much higher (in the low supersonic range), but definite limits are still imposed to prevent excessive shock stall and loss of component efficiency.

As a result, the diameter of the rotor itself is its own r.p.m. limiting factor. A look at the operational parameters of any small diameter turbine engine reveals that its rotational speed at full power is very high, perhaps as high as 50,000 revolutions per minute. Conversely, rotational speed of a large diameter engine would be much lower. For example, a Boeing 747 fan speed is only 3,000 revolutions per minute at full power.

Tip speed formulas:

Tip Speed (Ts) = π × diameter × r.p.m. ÷ 60

Mach Number (M) = Ts ÷ local speed of sound (Cs)

Where:

π = 3.1416
60 = conversion to revolutions per second
Dia. = value in feet
Cs (fps) = 49.022 √°Rankine
°Rankine = °Fahrenheit + 460

EXAMPLE 1: Use the above formulas to calculate the tip speed in feet per second and Mach number of the first compressor stage. The compressor diameter, blade tip to blade tip, is 1.8 feet. Rated speed is 16,500 revolutions per minute and temperature is 59°F.

Ts = π × diameter × r.p.m. ÷ 60
Ts = 3.1416 × 1.8 × 16,500 ÷ 60
Ts = 1,555.1 fps
M = Ts ÷ (Cs)
M = $\frac{1,555.1}{1,116.8}$ = 1.39

Where:

π = 3.1416
R.p.m. = 16,500
Dia. = 1.8 feet
Cs = 49.022 √519 = 1,116.8
°R = 59 + 460 = 519

In the rear stages of the compressor, the local speed of sound changes because of the change in temperature. As temperature increases, the speed of sound in air increases. Because the temperature in the rear stages of the compressor may be many hundreds of degrees higher than in the front stages, the same tip speed will be a substantially lower Mach number.

EXAMPLE 2: Calculate the tip speed of a 2.5-foot diameter turbine wheel rotating at 16,500 revolutions per minute when turbine gas temperature is 1,400°R.

Ts = 3.1416 × 2.5 × 16,500 ÷ 60
Ts = 2,159.9 f.p.s.
M = $\frac{2,159.9}{1,834.2}$
M = 1.18
Cs = 49.022 √1,400
Cs = 1,834.2 f.p.s.

CENTRIFUGAL FLOW COMPRESSORS

The centrifugal flow compressor also has r.p.m. limitations. Tip speeds of centrifugal compressors are generally in the range of Mach 1.2 to Mach 1.3. The compressor and diffuser design control the resulting minor shock waves and prevent loss of compressor aerodynamics. Centrifugal flow compressors are discussed in detail in Chapter 3.

SPEED OF SOUND

The speed of sound in air is solely dependent on temperature change and not change in pressure. These two changes continually take place in airflow within the engine.

Air temperature influences Mach number because the local speed of sound in air is dependent on both elasticity and density changes that take place in air. Observe the formula:

Cs = $\sqrt{\frac{\text{Elasticity of air}}{\text{Density of air}}}$

As temperature goes up, density of the air goes down, but elasticity remains constant. So, according to the Cs formula, a density decrease will cause a speed of sound increase.

Also, as pressure goes up, density and elasticity both go up proportionally. When computing with the (Cs) speed of sound formula, no change in the speed of sound will occur.

The two basic components that govern the speed of sound are density and elasticity. To see how this situation occurs within a gas turbine engine, consider that during compression both pressure and temperature are increasing, but only the air temperature increase affects the local speed of sound.

WHY THE TURBOFAN IS REPLACING THE TURBOJET

The turbofan has replaced the turbojet in most airliners and is now replacing them in business jets because the turbofan is as much as 30 to 40 percent more fuel efficient than turbojet engines. [Figure 2-50]

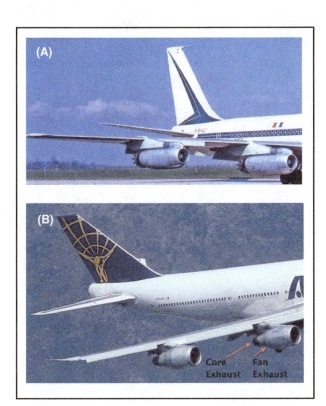

Figure 2-50A. Early turbojet powered airliner with narrow inlet and single exhaust

Figure 2-50B. Modern turbofan airliner showing wide inlet and dual (fan and core) exhaust

A turbofan will burn less fuel than a turbojet of the same rated thrust for a couple of reasons.

First, the lower amount of kinetic energy wasted from the turbofan exhaust makes it more propulsively efficient. That is, its average fan/core exhaust velocity (V_2) is closer to aircraft speed (V_1). Second, the amount of kinetic energy left in the atmosphere after the aircraft has passed by is less with the turbofan than with the turbojet.

EXAMPLE: An aircraft turbine engine expels 10 mass units of air from its exhaust (322 lb. divided by gravity constant), and its exhaust velocity is 1,000 f.p.s. faster than the aircraft speed. How much kinetic energy is being wasted?

$$\text{Kinetic Energy} = 1/2 \times M \times V^2$$

$$Ke = 1/2 \times 10 \times 1,000^2$$

$$Ke = 5,000,000 \text{ ft. lbs.}$$

Where:

$M = 10$ lbs/ft/sec^2

$V = 1,000$ f.p.s.

Realizing that thrust equals mass times acceleration (F = MA), it at first appears that either M or A can be doubled to get the same resulting doubling of thrust. That is true, but in terms of energy wasted, it is inefficient to increase the amount of acceleration unless the aircraft is going to fly at a very high speed. It is more efficient to increase thrust by increasing the amount of mass airflow and keeping the exhaust velocity as close as possible to the aircraft speed.

In the previous example, if the mass airflow were to be increased to 20 units, and the velocity increase reduced to 500 ft/sec, the engine thrust would be the same, but the engine would be much more fuel efficient.

Conclusion: The maximum thrust for the least fuel flow can be obtained by giving the smallest acceleration to the largest possible mass airflow. The high-bypass turbofan does just that. It also proves that high exhaust velocity at low aircraft speed is an inefficient operating condition.

QUESTIONS

1. Which of the four types of gas turbine engines (turbojet, turboshaft, turboprop, turbofan) would most likely be installed in a late model business jet of the 500 m.p.h. class?

2. What type of gas turbine engine does a helicopter use?

3. What type of compressor unit was in the gas turbine developed by Whittle?

4. Name the type of gas turbine most similar in design to the turboshaft engine.

5. Which of the two forms of energy (potential and kinetic) is energy of motion?

6. Considering the formulas for work, force, power, horsepower, velocity, and acceleration, which three formulas are expressed in units with respect to time?

7. Which of Newton's laws states the principle of "action-reaction"?

8. What type of thermodynamic cycle of events is known as the Brayton cycle?

9. Bernoulli's principle describes the relationship between the velocity pressure and the static pressure of a fluid moving through a duct. Is this relationship direct or inverse?

10. Is thrust calculated when an aircraft is in flight referred to as gross thrust or net thrust?

11. Does a choked nozzle add additional supersonic velocity or additional thrust?

12. What are the three most important factors that affect the thrust of a gas turbine engine during operation?

13. Would a turboprop engine be rated in thrust horsepower or equivalent shaft horsepower?

14. Which part of a compressor blade is speed-limited, and what occurs if this part of the blade exceeds the limiting speed by too high a value?

15. Thermal efficiency is a function of component efficiencies, turbine inlet temperature, and what other factor?

CHAPTER 3
Turbine Engine Design and Construction

The design features of gas turbine engines are varied, and engines in the same power classification often seem to have little or no resemblance to each other. Determining which design is optimal for a particular application or why an engine looks the way it does is sometimes difficult for the following reasons:

- Many engine designs are proprietary, and manufacturers are often reluctant to provide specific information about their engines.

- Many designs that do not appear to be the optimal are in fact best-suited for the engine and the aircraft on which it is intended to be installed. A compromise of designs for operation over a wide range of altitudes and power factors is common.

- Many designs depend on the prior experience of the manufacturer. Manufacturers might remain committed to their proven developments rather than changing to newer ones.

TURBINE ENGINE ENTRANCE DUCTS

The flight inlet duct (the point where atmospheric air enters the aircraft) is normally considered a part of the airframe, not of the engine. Nevertheless, it is usually identified as engine station number one. Understanding the function of the flight inlet duct and its importance to engine performance is a necessary part of any discussion on gas turbine engine design and construction. Figure 3-1 shows a variety of aircraft flight inlet ducts at different locations.

PRINCIPLES OF OPERATION

The flight inlet duct of a turbine engine must furnish a uniform supply of air to the compressor for the engine to enjoy stall-free compressor performance. The flight inlet duct must also create as little drag as possible. Even a small discontinuity of airflow can cause significant efficiency loss, as well as many otherwise inexplicable engine performance problems. To ensure that the flight inlet duct delivers air with minimum turbulence, it must

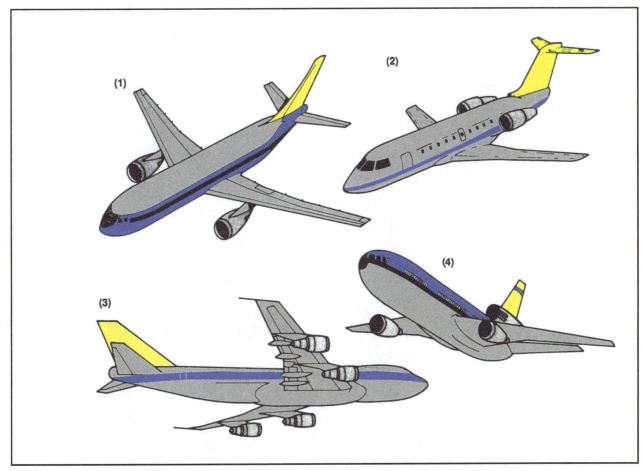

Figure 3-1. Common engine inlet location

be maintained in as close to new condition as possible. If repairs to this component are necessary, expertly installed flush patches are mandatory to prevent drag. Moreover, the use of an inlet cover should be used to promote cleanliness and to prevent corrosion and abrasion.

SUBSONIC FLIGHT INLET DUCTS

Subsonic flight inlet ducts, such as those found on business and commercial jet aircraft, are of fixed geometry and have a divergent shape. A diverging duct progressively increases in diameter from front to back, as shown in Figure 3-2. This duct is sometimes referred to as an inlet diffuser because of its effect on pressure. Air enters the aerodynamically contoured inlet at ambient pressure and starts to diffuse, arriving at the compressor at a slightly increased static pressure. Usually, the air is permitted to diffuse (increase in static pressure) in the front portion of the duct and to progress at a fairly constant pressure past the engine inlet fairing (also called the inlet center body) to the compressor. In this manner, the engine receives its air with minimal turbulence and at a more uniform pressure.

As the aircraft approaches its desired cruising speed, the increased inlet pressure adds significantly to the mass airflow. At cruising speed, the compressor reaches its aerodynamic design point and produces its optimum compression and best fuel economy. At this point, the flight inlet, compressor, combustor, turbine, and tailpipe are designed to work in concert with each other. If any section does not match the others (for example, because of damage, contamination, or ambient conditions), engine performance will be affected.

The turbofan inlet is similar in design to the turbojet inlet, except that only a portion of the air it provides to the fan is sent into the core of the engine, with the remainder being accelerated out of the fan discharge duct.

Figure 3-3 shows two common airflow arrangements. Figure 3-3A is a full duct design utilized on low- and medium-bypass engines, and the other, Figure 3-3B, is the short duct design of a high-bypass turbofan. The long ducting configuration in Figure 3-3A reduces surface

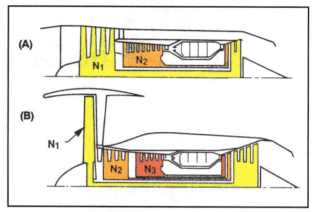

Figure 3-3A. Turbofan low- and medium-bypass ratio
Figure 3-3B. Turbofan high-bypass ratio

drag of the fan discharge air and enhances thrust. Many of the older high-bypass engines cannot take advantage of this drag reduction concept because of the excessive weight associated with the wide diameter of a long duct. With the emergence of new lightweight materials and designs, however, newer generation engines can take advantage of this drag reduction concept.

RAM PRESSURE RECOVERY

As mentioned in Chapter 2, when a gas turbine engine is operated in place on the ground, it has a negative pressure within its inlet because of the high velocity airflow. As the aircraft moves forward, a condition known as ram pressure recovery takes place. This is the point at which pressure inside the inlet returns to ambient value. Ram compression is the result of ram velocity and diffusion of the airflow. That is, as air spreads out radially, it slows down axially, and pressure increases accordingly.

The aircraft inlet, while stationary, will not generally achieve 100 percent duct recovery, which means the air pressure leaving the inlet will be lower than the air pressure entering. If ambient pressure is 14.7 pounds per square inch absolute (p.s.i.a.), pressure at the compressor inlet will be slightly less than 14.7 p.s.i.a. However, as the aircraft moves forward on the ground for takeoff, ram

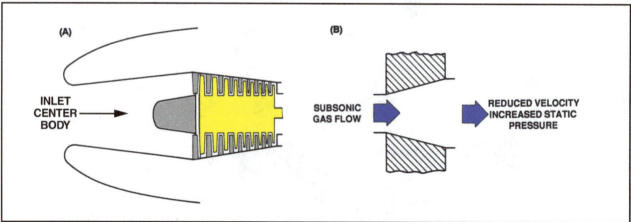

Figure 3-2A. Divergent subsonic inlet duct
Figure 3-2B. Divergent duct effect on airflow

Turbine Engine Design and Construction

compression occurs and the pressure at the compressor inlet will eventually return to ambient value. This point is generally reached in the average inlet duct at an aircraft speed of Mach 0.1 to Mach 0.2.

In Figure 3-4, note the gauge readings changing from a negative to a positive value as the aircraft goes from ground static condition to flight condition. As the aircraft moves faster in flight, the inlet produces more and more ram compression. The engine takes advantage of this condition by a corresponding increase in compressor pressure ratio, creating greater thrust with less fuel.

Use the following formula to calculate ram compression (ram pressure ratio) at any flight mach number:

$$\frac{P_t}{P_s} = \left[1 + \left(\frac{\gamma - 1}{2} \times M^2\right)\right]^{\frac{\gamma}{\gamma - 1}}$$

Where: γ(gamma) = 1.4 (specific heat)

M = Mach number

γ, 1, 2 = Constants

$$\frac{P_t}{P_s} = \frac{P_{t2}}{P_{am}}$$

$$\frac{\gamma}{\gamma - 1} = \frac{C_p}{C_p - C_v} \quad \text{(See Appendix 8)}$$

For example, consider a business jet that is traveling at Mach 0.8 flight speed at an altitude of 31,000 feet. Use the formula to calculate the pressure ratio of engine inlet pressure to ambient pressure.

$$\frac{Pt}{Ps} = \left[1 + \left(\frac{1.4 - 1}{2} \times 0.8^2\right)\right]^{\frac{1.4}{1.4 - 1}}$$

$$\frac{Pt}{Ps} = [1 + (0.2 \times 0.64)]^{3.5}$$

$$\frac{Pt}{Ps} = 1.524$$

This calculation makes obvious that very high-speed aircraft create significant inlet ram compression. For example, the supersonic Concorde airliner, at a cruise speed of Mach 2.2, produced a ram compression of 10.7 to 1.

The reasoning underlying the use of the Pt/Ps formula is as follows:

In actuality, the Pt/Ps formula represents Pt2/Pam, which is the pressure total at the engine face divided by pressure ambient, to give the inlet compression ratio. The formula becomes applicable because Pt2 is essentially the same value as Pt1, pressure total at the lip of the flight inlet, which is expressed in the formula as Pt.

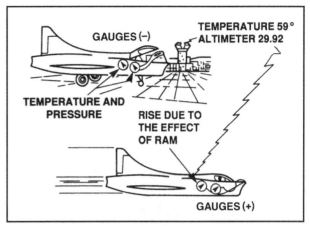

Figure 3-4. Ram pressure recovery

As air moves down the inlet, assuming 100 percent efficiency, the total pressure at which the air entered does not change. The changes occur in the static pressure and ram pressure components of total pressure—as the air moves through the inlet diffuser toward the engine, static pressure increases and ram pressure decreases, but total pressure remains the same.

When density in pounds per cubic foot and velocity in feet per second are known, calculate the total pressure in the inlet as follows:

Total pressure = Ram pressure (Q) + Static pressure (p)

Pt = Q + p

Pt = $1/2\, \rho V^2$ (flow density $\frac{w}{g}$) + p

Where:

Q = $1/2\, \rho V^2$ (flow density $\frac{w}{g}$)

ρ = lbs/ft^3 / gravity constant

V = ft/sec (in the inlet)

p = lbs/in^2 (static pressure)

For example, consider an airplane at an altitude of 25,000 feet that is cruising at 550 miles per hour (806 feet per second). The static pressure in the flight inlet is 5.454 pounds per square inch and the density, derived from a standard altitude chart (see Appendix 7), is .034267 pound per cubic foot.

1. What is the total pressure (Pt) in the inlet?
2. What is the inlet pressure ratio (Cr)?

Solution to question 1:

$$Q = 1/2\, \rho V^2 \text{ (flow density } \frac{w}{g}\text{)}$$

$$Q = 1/2 \left(\frac{0.034267 \text{ lbs/ft}^3}{32.16 \text{ ft/sec}^2}\right)\left(\frac{806 \text{ ft}}{\text{sec}}\right)^2$$

$$Q = 1/2\, \frac{0.034267 \text{ lbs.}}{\text{ft.}^3} \times \frac{\text{sec.}^2}{32.16 \text{ ft.}} \times \frac{806^2 \text{ ft.}^2}{\text{sec.}^2}$$

(Continued on next page)

Q = 346 lbs/ft^2

Q = 2.40 lbs/in^2

Pt = $Q + p$

Pt = 2.40 + 5.454

Pt = 7.85 lbs/in^2 (psi)

Solution to question 2:

Cr = 7.85 ÷ 5.454

Cr = 1.44 to 1 (inlet pressure ratio)

SUPERSONIC INLET DUCTS

All supersonic aircraft require a convergent-divergent inlet duct—either fixed or variable. A supersonic transport, for example, is configured with an inlet that slows the airflow to subsonic speed at the face of the engine, regardless of aircraft speed. Subsonic airflow into the compressor is required if the rotating airfoils are to remain free of shock wave accumulation, which is detrimental to the compression process.

To vary the geometry, or shape, of the inlet a movable restrictor is often employed to form a convergent-divergent (C-D) configuration of variable proportion. The C-D shaped duct becomes necessary in reducing supersonic airflow to subsonic speeds. Bear in mind that at subsonic flow rates, air flowing in a duct acts as an incompressible liquid, but at supersonic flow rates air is compressed to the point of creating the familiar shock wave phenomenon.

Figure 3-5 depicts a fixed geometry (nonadjustable) C-D duct in which supersonic airflow is slowed by air compression and shock formation at its throat area. After its speed is reduced to Mach-1, the airflow enters the subsonic diffuser section where velocity is further reduced and its pressure increased before entering the engine compressor. Some military aircraft, designed to fly as fast as Mach-2, use this type of inlet. However, a fixed geometry inlet is not always operationally feasible for a variety of reasons associated with the stagnation pressure effect of supersonic inlets, but a full discussion of that is beyond the scope of this book.

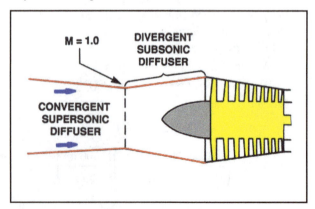

Figure 3-5. Supersonic convergent-divergent inlet

An inlet shock wave is similar to shock waves common to aircraft wings and other airfoils. A shock wave is an accumulation of sound wave energy, or pressure, developed when the wave, trying to move away from an object, is held stationary by the oncoming flow of air. One useful aspect of a shock wave is that airflow passing through the high-pressure shock region slows down. [Figure 3-6]

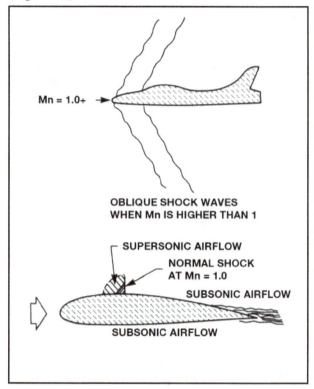

Figure 3-6. Shock wave formation

Figure 3-7 shows an example of a supersonic diffuser type of inlet, which provides a means of creating both a shock wave formation to reduce air velocity and a vari-

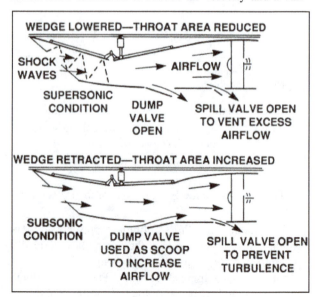

Figure 3-7. Supersonic airplane movable wedge inlet

able convergent-divergent shape to meet various flight conditions from takeoff to cruise. Air velocity drops to approximately Mach 0.8 in back of the final shock wave, and then to approximately Mach 0.5 by diffusion (spreading out radially). In high-speed flight (for example, Mach 2 to Mach 2.5), multiple shock waves form as the air flows through the inlet duct. The shock waves that form in the front part of the inlet are known as oblique, and although they slow the air velocity down, the velocity is still supersonic. Where the inlet changes shape from convergent to divergent (in an area known as the throat or waist), a final normal shock wave forms, which lowers the air velocity to subsonic. The diverging part of the inlet duct then acts as a typical subsonic diffuser.

The movable wedge design shown in Figure 3-7 shows the various wedge positions and functions of convergence, divergence, and shock wave formation. It also shows a spill valve used to control inlet air at high speed versus low speed. Many high-performance aircraft have either an excess or a deficiency of mass flow in various engine operating environments, and they require an onboard computer that monitors the inlet conditions and manages the position of the inlet's movable components.

BELLMOUTH COMPRESSOR INLETS

Bellmouth inlets, which are used primarily on helicopters, are converging in shape and provide very thin boundary layers and correspondingly low losses in pressure. This type of inlet produces a large drag factor, but its low speed drag is outweighed by the high degree of aerodynamic efficiency it provides.

During calibration, engines on ground test stands also use a bellmouth inlet, sometimes fitted with an anti-ingestion screen. Duct loss is so slight in this design that it is considered to be zero. Engine performance data, such as engine trimming for rated thrust, are obtained while using a bellmouth compressor inlet. [Figure 3-8]

Aerodynamic efficiency and duct loss are illustrated in Figure 3-9. Notice that a rounded leading edge [Figure

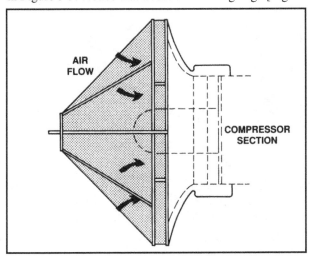

Figure 3-8. Bellmouth compressor inlet (with screen)

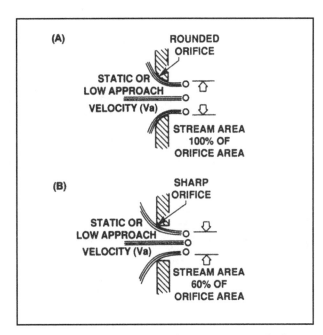

Figure 3-9A. Low-velocity entry flow through round-edge orifice

Figure 3-9B. Low-velocity entry flow through sharp-edge orifice

3-9A] enables the airstream to use the total inlet cross-section while a sharp-edged orifice [Figure 3-9B] greatly reduces the effective diameter.

COMPRESSOR INLET SCREENS, SAND, AND ICE SEPARATORS

The use of compressor inlet screens is usually limited to rotorcraft, turboprops, and ground turbine installations. This might seem peculiar given the appetite of all gas turbines for debris such as nuts, bolts, stones, and so on. Screens have been tried in high subsonic flight engines in the past, but icing and screen fatigue failure caused so many maintenance problems that the use of inlet screens has for the most part been abandoned.

When aircraft are fitted with inlet screens for protection against foreign object ingestion, they can be located internally or externally at either the inlet duct or the engine compressor inlet. [Figure 3-10A and 3-10B] Often these separators are removable at the discretion of the operator. In the sand separator shown in Figure 3-10B, inlet suction causes particles of sand and other small debris to be directed by centrifugal loading into a sediment trap.

Some sand and ice separators employ a movable vane that can be extended into the inlet airstream. This causes a sudden turn in the engine inlet air, and sand or ice particles continue out undeflected because of their greater momentum. The movable vane in this installation is operated by the pilot through a control handle in the cockpit. [Figure 3-10C]

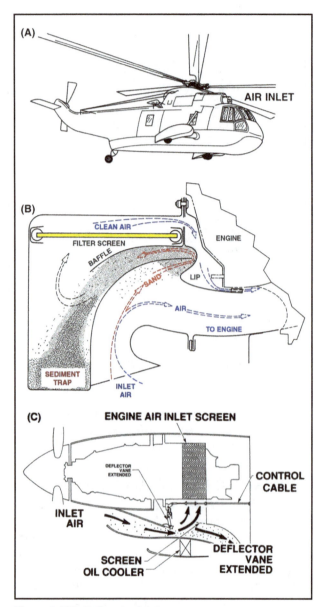

Figure 3-10A. Helicopter inlet
Figure 3-10B. Sand and ice separator
Figure 3-10C. Sand and ice separator (inertial)

ENGINE INLETS AND GROUND EFFECT

Some gas turbine engine inlets have a tendency to form a vortex between the ground and the flight inlet. The suction creating the vortex is strong enough to lift water and debris, such as sand, small stones, nuts, and bolts, from the ground and direct it into the engine, causing serious compressor erosion or damage. [Figure 3-11] This is especially true on wing pod-installed engines that are mounted with low ground clearance, as seen on many of the newer high-bypass turbofan-powered aircraft. To alleviate this problem, some inlets have been redesigned to be slightly out-of-round or flattened at the bottom to reduce ground effect.

Earlier aircraft used a vortex dissipator (also known as a blow-away jet). To dissipate the vortex, a small jet of

Figure 3-11. Water vortex during test cell run up

compressor discharge air is directed at the ground under the inlet from a discharge nozzle located in the lower part of the engine flight cowl. The system is generally activated by a landing gear switch, which opens a valve in the line between the engine compressor bleed port and the dissipator nozzle whenever the engine is operating and weight is on the main landing gear. [Figure 3-12]

ACCESSORY SECTION

The engine-driven external gearbox is the main unit of the accessory section. Accessory units essential to the operation of the engine, such as the fuel pump, oil pump, fuel control, and starter, and components such as hydraulic pumps and generators, are mounted on the main accessory gearbox. The accessory section is typically located below the compressor section or at the rear of the engine. [Figure 3-13A and B]

The gearbox is often driven by a radial drive shaft that connects the main or auxiliary gearbox to a bevel gear

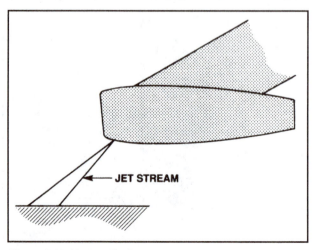

Figure 3-12. Vortex dissipater

Turbine Engine Design and Construction

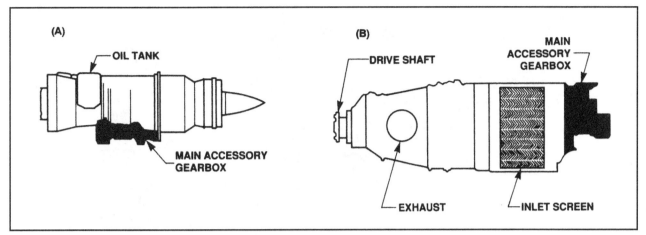

Figure 3-13A. Accessory gearbox location—six o'clock position
Figure 3-13B. Accessory gearbox location—rear

system driven by the main rotor shaft. On some installations, an auxiliary gearbox is employed to drive the main gearbox. This arrangement permits the gearbox to be placed so that the envelope size of the engine can be kept to a minimum. [Figure 3-14A] The main gearbox can also be located at the front or rear of the engine if the inlet or exhaust locations accommodate it. In rare instances, the main gearbox is located at the top of the engine in the area of the compressor. Some models of the CFM56 turbofan engine have the gearbox mounted on the side.

Each accessory and component drive pad is designed to provide a gear reduction from compressor speed, as needed. [Figures 3-14B]

The system of seal drain tubes shown in Figure 3-15A connects to each drive pad and is normally routed to the bottom of the engine cowling to drain away fluids that present a fire hazard. The leakage is generally minute and presents little problem as it leaves the drain point into the atmosphere. Each individual drive pad is a point of potential oil leakage. These fluids are classed as waste fluids and include fuel from the fuel control or fuel pump, engine oil from the main oil pump or scavenge oil pump, and hydraulic oil from the hydraulic pump. Oil can also leak from the gearbox through drive shaft seals of the components mentioned above and into the drain tubes. The allowable leakage rate of the various fluids is listed in the manufacturers' maintenance instructions and is typically in the range of 5 to 20 drops per minute, depending on the source of the leak.

Figure 3-15B shows the speed of each accessory. The direction that each accessory rotates is determined by the number of teeth on the gears and whether they mesh outside-to-outside or inside-to-outside. When a large gear drives a small gear, the small one turns faster and experiences a loss in torque. If the teeth mesh outside-to-outside, the direction of rotation is reversed. In Figure 3-15B, for example, the compressor bevel gear with 47 teeth drives the radial bevel gear with 35 teeth. The radial bevel gear turns in the opposite direction and faster by a

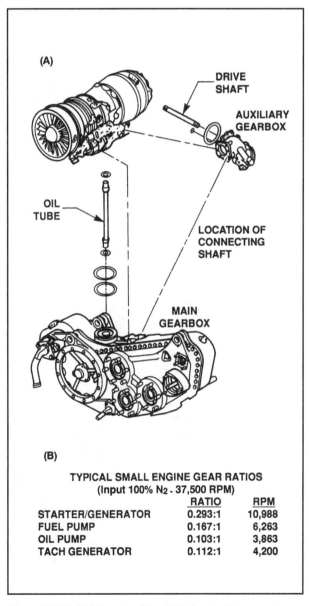

Figure 3-14A. Main and auxiliary gearbox arrangement
Figure 3-14B. Typical small-engine gear ratios

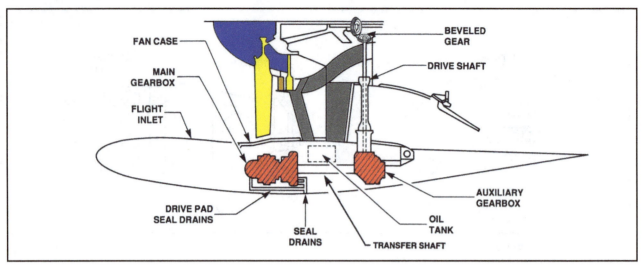

Figure 3-15A. Main accessory gearbox location

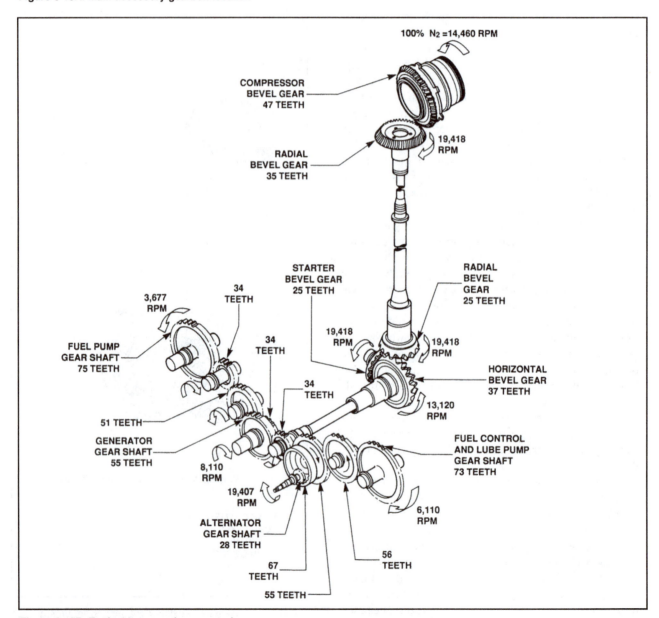

Figure 3-15B. Typical large-engine gear train

factor of 47/35. The alternator gear shaft turns the same direction as the gear driving it because it is meshing outside teeth to inside teeth. It also turns faster by a factor of 67/28 because it has 28 teeth and the gear driving it has 67 teeth.

A secondary function of many main gearboxes is to provide a collection point for scavenged oil before being pumped back to the oil tank. This arrangement permits splash-type lubrication of many internal gears and bearings inside the gearbox. However, modern engines do not typically locate the main oil supply in the accessory gearbox. Instead, a separate oil tank is normally used.

COMPRESSOR SECTION

The compressor section houses the compressor rotor and works to supply air in sufficient quantity to satisfy the needs of the combustor. Compression results when fuel energy of combustion and mechanical work of the compressor and turbine are converted into potential energy. Compressors operate on the principle of acceleration of a working fluid followed by diffusion to convert the acquired kinetic energy to a rise in pressure. The primary purpose of the compressor is to increase the pressure of the air mass entering the engine inlet and discharge it to the diffuser and then to the combustor section at the correct velocity, temperature, and pressure. [Figure 3-16] The problems associated with these requirements are evident when considering that some compressors must increase air flow to a velocity of 400 to 500 feet per second and raise its static pressure perhaps 20 to 30 times in the space of only a few feet of engine length.

In early compressors, which were less efficient than current technology, a given amount of work input produced air at a lower pressure and at a higher temperature. To improve on laminar air flow over hundreds of small airfoils at high velocity and pressure, compressors have undergone constant development through the years to achieve optimum efficiency. Currently, efficiency is said to be in the 85 to 90 percent range. As outlined in Chapter 2, compressor efficiency is based on the principle of maximum compression with the least temperature rise. Laminar flow minimizes friction-induced heat in the air.

A secondary purpose of the compressor section is to supply engine bleed air to cool hot section parts, pressurize bearing seals, and supply heated air for inlet anti-icing and fuel system heat for deicing. [Figure 3-17] Another secondary purpose is to extract clean pressurized air for aircraft uses unrelated to engine operating requirements. This air is usually referred to as customer service bleed air, and common uses for it include aircraft cabin pressurization, air conditioning systems, and pneumatic starting. Customer service bleed air can be shut off for a "No Bleed" takeoff on some aircraft, with the bleed air that the aircraft needs being drawn from the auxiliary power unit. This enables the aircraft's main engines to produce more thrust during takeoff because bleeding air from the engines robs them of power. On some newer aircraft such as the Boeing 787, customer service bleed air is not drawn from the engine. Instead, standalone compressors driven by electric motors provide the necessary air. The aircraft's engines must still provide power to drive the electric motors, because the electricity comes from the engine-driven generators, but this method is potentially a more efficient source of power.

CENTRIFUGAL FLOW COMPRESSORS

The centrifugal flow compressor, sometimes referred to as a radial outflow compressor, is the oldest compressor design but is still in use today. Many smaller engines,

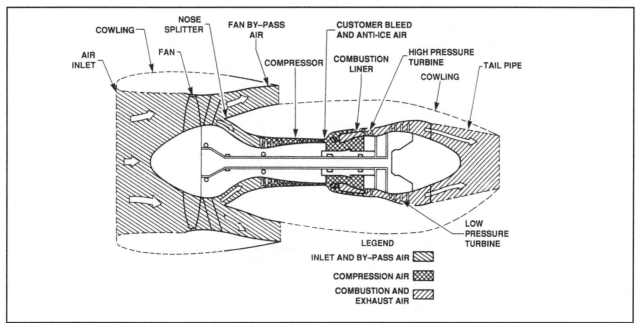

Figure 3-16. General Electric CF-34 airflow diagram

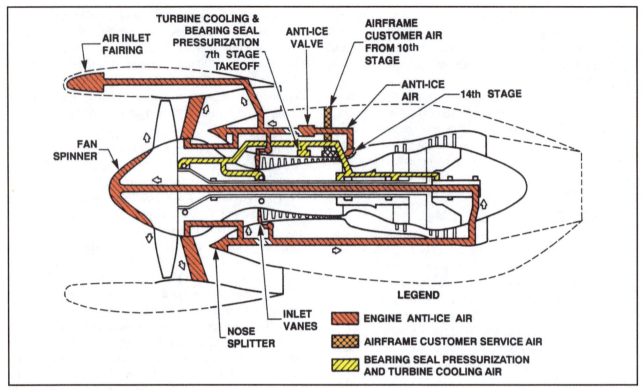

Figure 3-17. Bleed air distribution

as well as the majority of auxiliary gas turbine powerplants, use this design.

In a centrifugal flow engine, the compressor receives air at the center of the impeller in an axial direction and accelerates the air outward by centrifugal reaction to its rotational speed. The air then expands into a divergent duct—formed by the shape of the diffuser vanes—called a diffuser, and, acting in accord with Bernoulli's Principle, as the air spreads out, its speed slows, which causes the static pressure to build. [Figure 3-18A] The pressure and velocity graph in Figure 3-18B shows that velocity changes from an increasing to a decreasing value as pressure rises to its designed level at the exit of the diffuser vanes. The compressor efficiency graph in Figure 3-18D shows that in a centrifugal flow compressor, efficiency drops off after approximately 15:1 pressure ratio, but the axial flow compressor maintains its efficiency to a much higher level of pressure ratios. So as pressure ratio relates to mass airflow and thrust of a turbojet or turbofan engine (or horsepower of a turboprop or turboshaft engine), the axial flow compressor is required where higher power is needed for larger or faster aircraft.

The primary components in a centrifugal flow compressor assembly are the impeller rotor, the diffuser, and the manifold. [Figure 3-19] The impeller is usually made from an aluminum or titanium alloy and can be either single- or dual-sided. The diffuser provides a divergent duct in which the air spreads out, slows down, and increases in static pressure. The compressor manifold distributes the air in a turbulent-free condition to the combustion section.

The single-sided impeller shown in Figure 3-20A benefits from ram effect and less turbulent air entry, making it well-suited to many aircraft applications. The single-stage, dual-sided impeller design in Figure 3-20B results in a narrower overall engine diameter and high mass airflow, making it a favored design in many flight engines in the past. However, this design does not take advantage of the full benefit from ram effect because the air has to turn radially inward from a plenum chamber into the center of the impellers.

Attainable compressor pressure ratios are about the same for both types of single-stage impeller types. However, as seen in Figure 3-21, having more than two stages of single-entry type is considered impractical. The energy loss to the airflow that must slow when making the turns from one impeller to the next, the added weight, and the drive shaft power extraction all offset the benefit of additional compression with more than two stages.

The most common centrifugal compressor in use is the single-sided type in either one or two stages. It is most often used in small turboshaft, turboprop, and turbofan engines. It is not used in large gas turbine engines because it imposes a significant limitation on mass airflow. For example, the Pratt and Whitney 100 series turboprop has two separately rotating centrifugal compressors plus a power turbine and is described as a three-shaft, two-spool engine.

Centrifugal compressors have gained a resurgence of use, and recent developments have produced compressor pressure ratios as high as 10:1 from a single centrifugal

Turbine Engine Design and Construction

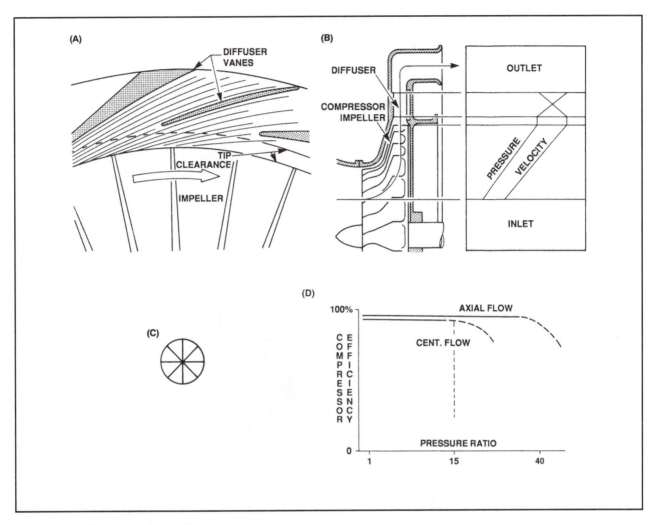

Figure 3-18A. Airflow at entry to diffuser
Figure 3-18B. Pressure and velocity changes through a centrifugal compressor
Figure 3-18C. Spoke theory of accelerating air
Figure 3-18D. Compressor pressure ratio versus efficiency

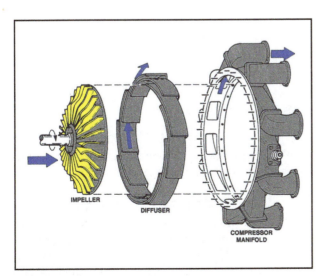

Figure 3-19. Components of a centrifugal flow compressor

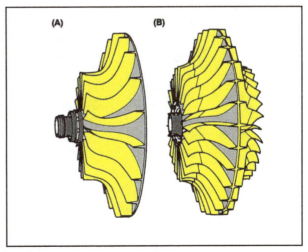

Figure 3-20A. Single-entry, single-stage impeller
Figure 3-20B. Dual-entry, single-stage impeller

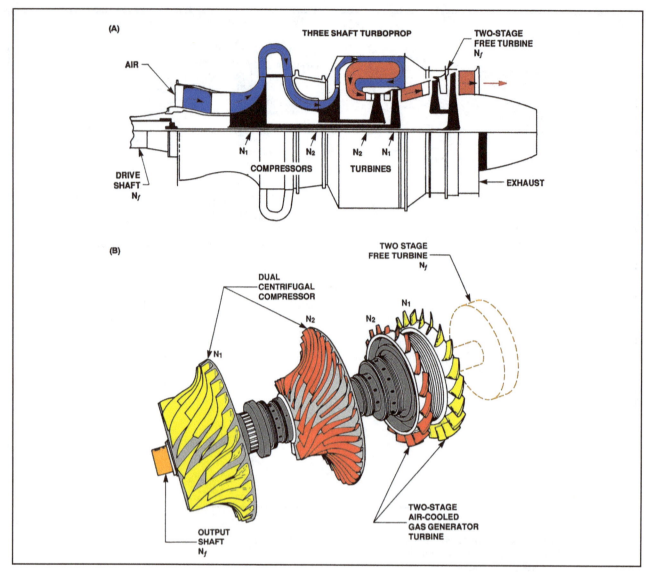

Figure 3-21A. Single-entry, two-stage, dual-centrifugal flow compressor arrangement—PW-120 turboprop
Figure 3-21B. Compressor and turbines of PW-120 turboprop

compressor. Previously, only axial flow compressors could attain this level of compression. The main advantage of a centrifugal compressor over its axial counterpart is its shorter length.

The tip speed of centrifugal impellers reaches approximately Mach 1.3. Radial airflow, however, remains subsonic. The pressure within the compressor casing is capable of preventing airflow separation at low supersonic rotor speeds and causing a high energy transfer to the airflow.

The advantages of the centrifugal flow compressor over the axial flow compressor are as follows:

- High pressure rise per stage—up to 10:1 for a single-stage and 15:1 for a dual-stage

- Good efficiency (compression) over a wide rotational speed range from idle to full power

- Simplicity of manufacture and low cost
- Low weight
- Low starting power requirements

Disadvantages are as follows:

- Large frontal area for a given mass airflow
- Impracticality of more than two stages because of the energy losses between stages

AXIAL FLOW COMPRESSORS AND FANS

The axial flow compressor is so named because airflow and compression occur parallel to the rotational axis of the compressor. Axial compressors are classified by the number of rotating sections, called spools. At one time, the word *spool* was used only when describing an axial flow compressor, but many manufacturers currently use spool when describing a centrifugal flow compressor as well.

TYPES

The three types of axial flow compressors are single-spool, dual-spool, and triple-spool. Smaller engines tend to use a single-spool compressor, and larger engines use dual- and triple-spool compressors because the additional spools deliver higher compression and mass airflow. The single-spool compressor was common in the past for small and large engines, but today it is typically found only in small turboshaft and turboprop engines. The dual-spool compressor is the most common design currently being used in large turbofan and turboprop engines. The triple-spool compressor, a more recent technological development, is used on some medium and large turbofan engines.

Figure 3-22A illustrates a single-spool axial compressor. This design was the first type of axial compressor developed for the gas turbine engine and is still seen in some contemporary aircraft. It has only one rotating mass. The compressor, shaft, and turbine all rotate as a single unit.

Figures 3-22B, 3-22C, and 3-22D show how, in multispool engines, the turbine shafts attach to their compressors by fitting coaxially—that is, how one shaft fits within the other. In Figure 3-22B, the front compressor is referred to as the low-pressure, or N_1, compressor. The rear compressor is referred to as the high-pressure, or N_2, compressor. In Figure 3-22C, the rotor arrangement is such that the fan is referred to as the N_1 (low-pressure) compressor, the compressor next in line is referred to as the N_2 (intermediate) compressor, and the innermost compressor is referred to as the N_3 (high-pressure) compressor.

Figure 3-22D shows a geared, fan-type, dual-spool engine. It was developed first for smaller engines so that higher turbine speeds could be converted to torque to drive the fan. The geared fan does not need a separate turbine to turn at a different speed from the compressor. For example, the Garrett TFE-731 turbofan has a fan gearbox ratio of 0.496:1. When its turbine is turning at 10,000 r.p.m., the fan is rotating only at 4,960 r.p.m. Because the fan is not attached directly to the compressor, the compressor speed is not limited to fan speed. Development is currently underway for geared fan engines in the 20,000-pound thrust range as a replacement for many midsized commercial aircraft. The advantages of the geared fan engine are potentially better efficiency and better fuel economy; its disadvantages are increased complexity and weight.

In many turbofan engines, blade tip speeds of the fan are permitted to exceed Mach 1 at high power settings. The pressure within the fan duct tends to retard airflow separation from the blades at speeds over Mach 1, resulting in a good energy transfer to the air, good pressure rise, and little aerodynamic disturbance from shock formation.

REASONS FOR MULTISPOOL DESIGNS

Dual- and triple-spool axial compressors were developed to provide operational flexibility to the engine in the form of high compressor pressure ratios, quick acceleration, and better control of stall characteristics. This

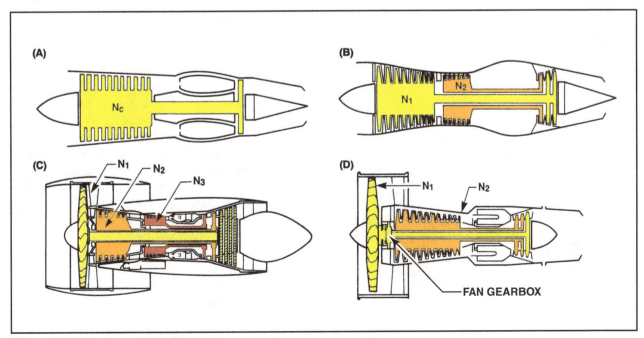

Figure 3-22A. Single-spool compressor
Figure 3-22B. Dual-spool compressor
Figure 3-22C. Triple-spool rotor arrangement
Figure 3-22D. Dual-spool engine (geared-fan)

operational flexibility is not possible with single-spool, axial flow engines.

For any given power lever setting, the high-pressure compressor speed is held fairly constant by a fuel control governor. Assuming that a near-constant energy level is available at the turbine, the speed of the low-pressure compressor increases and slows with changes in aircraft inlet conditions that result from atmospheric changes or flight maneuvers. The varying low-pressure compressor output, therefore, provides the high-pressure compressor with the best inlet condition within the limits of its design. That is, the N_1 compressor tries to supply the N_2 compressor with a fairly constant air pressure for a given power setting. [Figure 3-23]

To better understand the conditions under which the low-pressure compressor speeds up and slows down, consider that when ambient temperature increases, the air's molecular motion increases. To continue to collect air molecules at the same rate as the temperature increases, the compressor would have to change either its blade angles, which it cannot do, or its speed, which it can. Additionally, the speed of the low-pressure compressor increases with altitude as the atmosphere rarefies from barometric pressure density loss. Conversely, as the aircraft descends, the speed of the low-pressure compressor decreases as the air becomes more dense and easier to compress. Figure 3-24 shows the dual-shaft arrangement wherein the low-pressure compressor drive shaft that is driven by its low-pressure turbine is concentric with the high-pressure compressor drive shaft.

Figure 3-25A shows that as ambient temperature increases, N_2 speed increases. This is necessary to maintain the compressor pressure ratio and mass airflow until the compressor reaches a speed limit set by the fuel scheduling system.

Considering that the effect of ambient pressure change predominates over the effect of temperature change on density, Figure 3-25B shows that, as the altitude increases, N_1 speed also increases. The overall effect is similar to supercharging the N_2 system and results from the reduction in drag on the N_1 compressor in the rarefied air at altitude. With a fairly constant energy level, the N_1's turbine will rotate the N_1 system faster. In fact, the operator might need to prevent the N_1 system from exceeding its maximum speed by retarding the power lever.

Figure 3-25C shows that as N_2 rotor speed increases, N_1 also increases, but not in direct proportion. Although the rotors are not mechanically connected, they are linked by an aerodynamic couple.

Figure 3-25D shows the way in which N_2 speed is nonlinear to engine thrust (Fg). For example, at 90 percent N_2 speed, the available thrust is not necessarily 90 percent. Because of this, N_2 percent is not used as a power indicator in the cockpit.

Figure 3-25E shows that N_1 compressor speed of a turbojet or N_1 fan speed of a turbofan engine is linear to thrust. As a result, the N_1 tachometer indicator in the cockpit is often used as an indication of thrust.

Some dual- or triple-spool compressors have a counter-rotating component. Although not common, one spool can be made to rotate in the opposite direction of the other spools. This is done for aerodynamic reasons to dampen vibration along the compressor and turbine rotor shafts in turbofan and turboprop engines and also to improve efficiency of airflow, especially at the turbines that drive the compressors.

BLADES AND VANES

An axial flow compressor has two main components—the rotor and the stator. A rotor and the stator that is located immediately rearward make up a single stage, and several stages (depending on the design and the manufacturer) combine to make up the complete compressor. Each rotor consists of a set of blades fitted into a disk, which move air rearward through each stage.

The speed of the rotor determines the velocity in each stage. As the velocity increases, kinetic energy is transferred to the air. The stator vanes are placed behind the rotor blades to receive the high-velocity air and to act as a diffuser, changing kinetic energy to potential energy (pressure). The stators also direct airflow to the next stage of compression at the appropriate angle.

Compressor blades are constructed with a varying angle of incidence, or twist, similar to that of a propeller. This design feature compensates for the effect on airflow caused by differences in airflow over the different stations of each blade from the base to the tip.

The blades also become smaller from the first stage to the last to accommodate the converging or tapering shape of the compressor housing in which they are rotating. [Figure 3-26] The need for a converging duct within the compressor is explained in a subsequent section entitled "Compressor Taper Design." Regarding the shapes of compressor airfoils, the length, chord, thickness, and aspect ratio (ratio of length to width) are calculated to suit the performance factors required for a particular engine and aircraft combination.

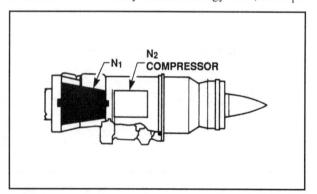

Figure 3-23. Location of dual-spool compressor within the engine

Turbine Engine Design and Construction

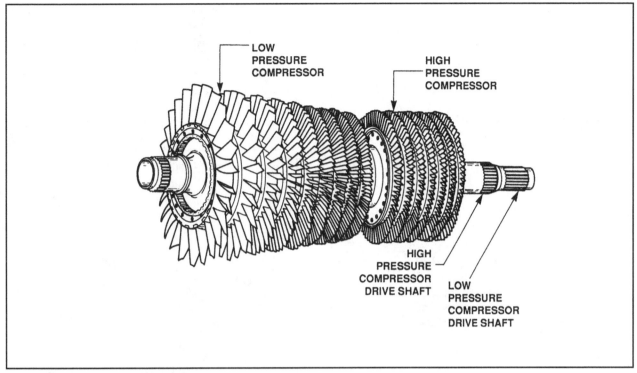

Figure 3-24. Dual-spool compressor

Some design aspects common to both compressor and fan blades are:

- A twist is present (called a stagger angle) from base to tip to maintain exit velocity of airflow at the same value along the blade length.

- The base area has more camber than the tip area to increase axial velocity of airflow and to maintain base-to-tip exit velocity.

- The trailing edge is knife-edge thin to minimize turbulence and to provide the best aerodynamic efficiency.

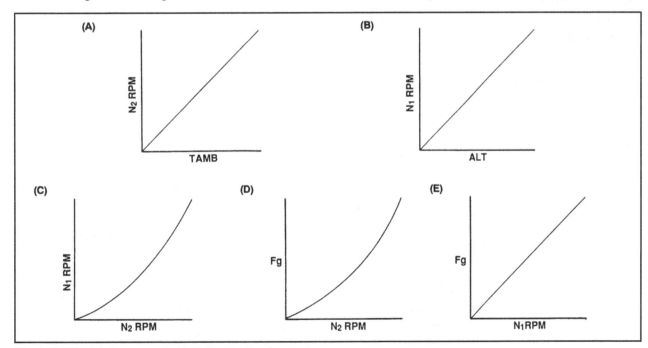

Figure 3-25A. N_2 increase vs. ambient temperature increase
Figure 3-25B. N_1 increase vs. altitude increase
Figure 3-25C. N_2 increase vs. N_1 increase
Figure 3-25D. N_2 increase vs. thrust (Fg) increase
Figure 3-25E. N_1 increase vs. thrust (Fg) increase

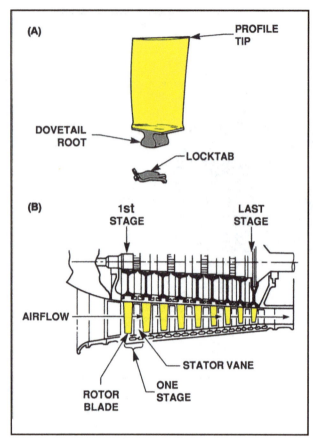

Figure 3-26A. Blade attachment and retention
Figure 3-26B. Identification of one stage (rotor blade followed by stator vane)

TIPS AND ROOTS

Axial compressors typically have from 10 to 18 stages of compression. The blades of each stage are usually dovetail-fitted into the disk and secured with a pin, locktab, or lock wire, as shown in Figure 3-26A.

As previously mentioned, the fan blade is considered the first stage of compression. The span-shroud, shown in Figure 3-27, is fitted to each blade. When all blades in the first stage are in place, their shrouds form a circular ring that supports the blades against the bending forces from the airstream. The shrouds, however, block some of the airflow and cause aerodynamic drag, which tends to reduce efficiency. As newer and stronger composite materials come under development, these older shrouds are being phased out.

The area from approximately the span-shrouds to the root acts as the core engine compressor blade section. The root of the blade is sometimes loosely fitted into the compressor disk for ease of blade assembly and the vibration damping effect that a loose fit provides. As the compressor rotates, centrifugal loading locks the blade in its correct position, and the airstream over the airfoil provides a shock mounting or cushioning effect.

Some blades are cut off square at the tip and are referred to as flat-machine tips, while some blades have a reduced thickness at the tips and are referred to as having a profile, or squealer tip. The following factors bear on the design of squealer tips:

- **Vibration** — All rotating machinery has a tendency to vibrate. One way to reduce the tendency of blades to vibrate is to increase the natural frequency of the blade beyond the frequency of rotation of the engine. Profiling is one means of increasing the natural frequency of blades—a process called frequency tuning. For blades without profiles, frequency tuning is done

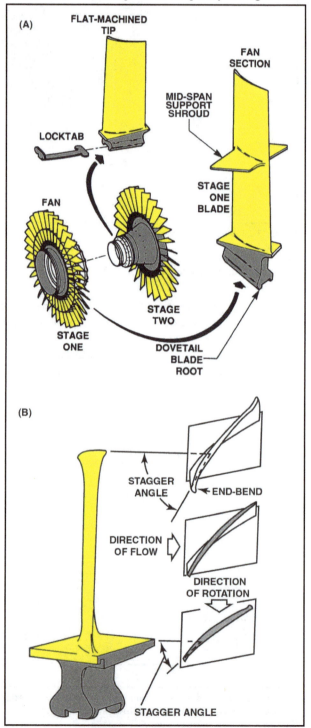

Figure 3-27A. Compressor blade and fan blade
Figure 3-27B. End-bend blade

by other aerodynamic designs. Tip vibration of blades is closely controlled because it causes blade root galling and even fatigue fractures, problems common to all types of rotating airfoils.

- **Tip Leakage** — The profile mentioned above is also designed as a vortex tip. The thin trailing edge section causes a vortex that increases air velocity and ensures minimum tip leakage and a smooth axial airflow.
- **Tip Clearance** — On some newer engines, the tips are designed with tight running clearances and rotate within a shroud strip of abradable material. This strip abrades (wears away) with no loss of blade length if contact loading takes place. The shroud strip is later replaced at overhaul. The term *squealer tip* comes from the fact that during coastdown, if a blade tip contacts the shroud strip, it generates a high-pitched squealing noise.
- **Tip Shock** — Some high-performance compressors need a means of controlling tip shock wave intensity. Profiling in this case changes the aerodynamics at the tip to facilitate smooth axial airflow even though the tip rotates at speeds beyond the speed of sound and flow separation starts to occur.

One tip design that departs from the traditional fan tip design is the shrouded tip fan blade similar to shrouded tip turbine blades. The shrouded tips are fitted with thin metal seals, called knife-edge seals, that can be fitted to the shroud outer surface with the knife-edge running close to the fan case. This design permits tighter operating clearances than possible with open tip blades. The advantages are a reduction in air turbulence and air leakage in this area and a gain in mass airflow.

Figure 3-27B shows another advanced tip design. It is called an end-bend blade due to its radical stagger angle at the base and tip. The aerodynamic effect of added twist and swirl counteracts the tendency of slow or stagnant airflow to occur in boundary layers at the blade base and in the area of the tip clearance. This design provides minimal airflow separation from the blade surfaces that are under high swirl conditions and results in a higher compression per stage.

INLET GUIDE VANES

Stator vanes can be either of two types, stationary or variable angle. Figure 3-28 shows the vane locations. This illustration also shows the location of the inlet guide vanes in front of the rotor blades. These vanes can also be of stationary or variable design. Their function is to direct airflow into the rotor at the most desirable angle. Similar vanes, called exit guide vanes, are placed at the compressor exit to remove the rotational moment imparted to the air during compression.

COMPRESSOR PRESSURE RATIO

Compressor pressure ratio of a gas turbine engine is an important design consideration. In general, the higher the pressure rise, the greater the thermal efficiency of

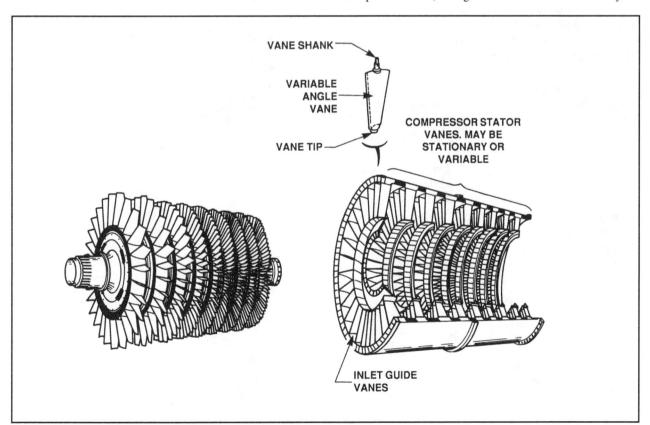

Figure 3-28. Compressor blade and vane arrangement

the engine. Designers strive to achieve the highest possible compressor pressure ratio (Cr) and the lowest mass airflow (Ms) and yet obtain the desired engine power output. The ideal combination produces an engine with the least flow area, smallest physical size, and lowest weight-to-power ratio.

In practice, the greater the pressure ratio for a given mass airflow and thrust, the lower the fuel consumption. If both pressure ratio and mass increase, thrust will increase. But engine weight also increases due to the increased weight of the stronger materials that the designs require.

Achieving very high pressure ratios incurs considerable expense due to the cost of the exotic construction materials required to produce the required compressor strength. Keeping in mind that a higher pressure ratio benefits the engine most when turbine inlet temperature is also high, additional expense is also incurred in the use of higher heat strength super alloys in the engine combustor and turbine areas.

A gas turbine engine in a business jet has a compressor pressure ratio of about 6:1 in older models and up to 24:1 in newer designs. By comparison, engines in a modern wide-body jumbo jet compress the air up to 40 to 50 atmospheres, or 40:1 to 50:1. The moderate compression pressure ratios used in modern compressors for business jets translate to a lower manufacturing cost. Although the manufacture of very high compression engines used in airline transport aircraft is very expensive, the success of the aircraft depends on the lowest operating expense over many thousands of operating hours.

Compressor pressure ratio is determined by measuring the total pressure, after the last stage of compression, and dividing it by compressor inlet total pressure. Assuming no velocity change between the two points, static pressures could be used to calculate compressor pressure ratio.

If ambient pressure is 14.7 p.s.i.a. and the inlet has 100 percent duct recovery, compressor inlet pressure total (Pt) will also be 14.7 p.s.i.a. Assuming an inlet air velocity of 500 feet per second at sea-level-rated power, ram pressure is calculated by formula at 2.06 psi, and the resultant static pressure will be 12.64 psi, giving a total pressure of 14.7 p.s.i.a.

Perform this calculation by using Formula 14 in Appendix 8, and the sea level density figure from Appendix 7.

$$Pt = 1/2\, \rho\, V^2 \text{ (flow density)} + p$$

$$Pt = \left(1/2 \frac{0.076474}{32.16} \times 500^2\right) + p$$

$$Pt = 297.24 \text{ lbs./ft}^2 + p$$

$$Pt = 2.06 \text{ lbs./in}^2 + p$$

$$Pt = 2.06 + 12.64$$

$$Pt = 14.7 \text{ psi}$$

Where:

$$\rho = \frac{\text{Specific weight of air}}{\text{Atmospheric standard for gravity}}$$

$$\rho = 0.076474 \text{ lb/cu.ft} \div 32.16 \text{ ft/sec}^2$$

Observe that when compressor inlet total pressure is 14.7 p.s.i.a. and compressor discharge total pressure is 97.0 p.s.i.a., the compressor pressure ratio is expressed as 97 divided by 14.7, or 6.6 to 1, as indicated in Figure 3-29. The expression "compression ratio" is not used when discussing the gas turbine engine. This is because compression ratio, by definition in many disciplines, is a ratio of air density or air volume rather than air pressure.

Pressure Rise Per Stage

The compressor pressure ratio of a compressor is also described in terms of pressure ratio per stage. For example, assume that a particular business jet has a small turbofan with an overall pressure rise of 6.6:1 over eight stages. The 8th root of 6.6 is 1.266, which equates to a pressure ratio per stage equal to 1.266:1. The fan, if it is a single stage, would probably have a pressure ratio between 1.5:1 and 1.7:1. Toward the hub, where the fan blades become the first stage compressor blades, compression would be 1.266:1. The twist in the blades accomplishes this change in the pressure ratio.

The pressure rise per stage throughout compression is an average. Compressors are not designed for constant pressure rise per stage but rather for constant efficiency per stage. To achieve this end, as many as 50 different blade designs might be used within the same compressor. To calculate compression at each stage, the standard day pressure rise would occur as follows:

Stage	P1	Cr	Exit Pressure
1	14.7	1.266	18.61
2	18.61	1.266	23.56
3	23.56	1.266	29.83
4	29.83	1.266	37.76
5	37.76	1.266	47.81
6	47.81	1.266	60.53
7	60.53	1.266	76.63
8	76.63	1.266	97.01

For dual-spool engines, compressor pressure ratio is normally given for each compressor as follows in this typical example:

N_1 compressor = 3:1

N_2 compressor = 7:1

Total compressor pressure ratio = 21:1

Note that the ratio of one compressor is multiplied by the other to calculate the total compressor pressure ratio. The N_2 compressor, because of its smaller diameter, is able to turn at a higher speed and therefore generate more compression than the N_1 compressor. The N_2 compressor is also able to generate more pressure rise per stage than the N_1 compressor because it is working with the higher pressures supplied to it by the N_1 compressor. Thus, a dual compressor of ten stages would have a higher compressor pressure ratio than a single compressor of ten stages. This is one of the principal advantages of the dual-spool compressor. The ability of the N_1 compressor to increase speed in flight results in a higher compressor pressure ratio than can be attained by a single-spool compressor of the same size and weight.

Cycle Pressure Ratio

The cycle pressure ratio of a gas turbine engine is calculated using flight conditions at full aircraft speed. It is calculated by multiplying the compressor pressure ratio by the inlet compression due to ram. If the compressor pressure ratio is 10:1 for a particular engine, and inlet conditions change from 14.7 pounds per square inch to 16 pounds per square inch as the aircraft speed increases, then the compressor discharge pressure will be 160 pounds per square inch instead of the original 147.

An engine's compressor pressure ratio is essentially the same at all flight altitudes. However, the cycle pressure ratio is not the same at all flight altitudes because of the aerodynamic changes that occur in the engine inlet. If the engine shown in Figure 3-29 were in an aircraft flying at Mach 0.8, with an inlet compression of 1.524 to 1, the cycle pressure ratio would be 10.06 to 1 (1.524 times 6.6).

Increasing inlet compression also affects mass airflow. If the mass airflow rating of an engine is 50 pounds per second at sea level, with standard day conditions at full power, as the aircraft moves forward, mass airflow increases with an increase in compressor discharge pressure. In fact, the mass airflow change that occurs after takeoff will require the pilot to reduce power to keep from overboosting the engine.

At altitudes where ambient pressure is only about 25 percent that of sea level value, ram compression created in the engine inlet helps to alleviate the diminishing mass airflow condition.

Fan Pressure Ratio

Fan pressure ratios for single low-bypass fans are approximately 1.5:1 and for high-bypass fans as high as 1.7:1. Some high-bypass engines (those with fan bypass ratios of 4:1 and above) are designed with high aspect ratio blades. That is, they are long with a narrow chord. [Figure 3-30]

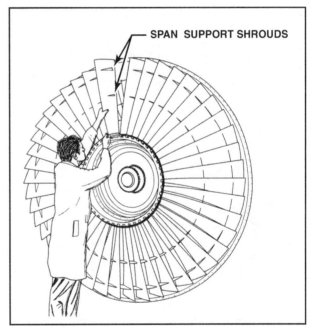

Figure 3-30. High-bypass fan with high aspect ratio blades

Low aspect ratio (wide-chord) blades are becoming more common because of their greater resistance to damage from foreign objects, especially bird strike damage. In the past, designers avoided using low aspect ratio blades because of their high weight. Recently, however, hollow titanium blades with composite inner reinforcement materials, as well as composite carbon-carbon blades (carbon fibers imbedded into a carbon base) have been developed. These blades have no span support shrouds and thus produce more mass airflow because of the greater flow area. Fan diameters range from 100 to 155 inches in this turbofan design for high-thrust engines. [Figure 3-31]

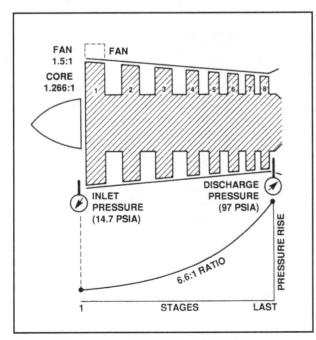

Figure 3-29. Compressor pressure ratio graph

Figure 3-31. High-bypass fan with low aspect ratio blades

Fan Bypass Ratio

Fan bypass ratio is the ratio of the mass airflow that flows through the fan duct divided by the mass airflow that flows through the core portion of the engine. Fan airflow passes over the outer part of the fan blade and then out of the fan exhaust and back to the atmosphere. Core engine airflow passes over the inner part of the fan blades and is then compressed, combusted, and finally exhausted from the hot exhaust duct back into the atmosphere.

Generally speaking, the higher the bypass ratio, the higher the engine's propulsive efficiency. Currently, this general statement applies only up to a bypass ratio of approximately 11:1 on aircraft designed to cruise at normal airliner, commuter, and business jet speeds (Mach 0.8 to Mach 0.9). [Figure 3-32A] Wide diameter fans are necessary to achieve high-bypass ratios. With increased width, however, comes increased weight and drag. In addition, a decay in thrust occurs in fixed-pitch rotating airfoils at high flight speeds. Figure 3-32B shows the latest fan design with swept blades of composite material, which have the ability to produce thinner boundary layers with less flow separation, thereby improving blade efficiency by better managing thrust decay up to a current limit of approximately 11:1 bypass ratio. Typical bypass ratios are as follows:

- Business jets — 2:1 in older aircraft and up to 5:1 in newer designs
- Commuter (regional jets) — 4:1 or 5:1
- Older narrow-body airliners with full fan ducts — 1:1 or 2:1
- Wide-body airliners — 5:1 up to 11:1

New variable pitch airfoils in the ultrahigh-bypass propfan engines under development will greatly increase the bypass ratios characteristic of current engines. Bypass ratios for ducted propfans and future generations of turbofans are predicted to be in the range of 15:1 to 20:1; and bypass ratios for unducted propfans could be as high as 100:1, with target cruising speeds remaining in the Mach 0.8 to 0.9 range.

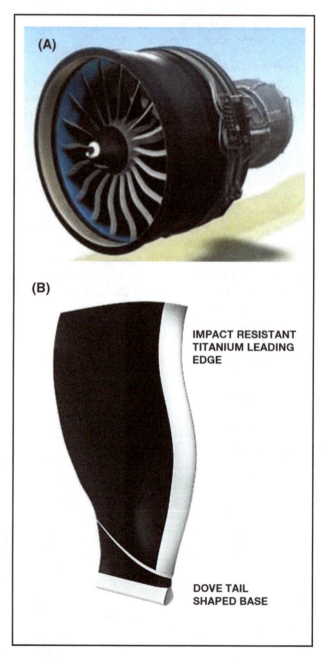

Figure 3-32A. Turbofan engine with contoured fan blades
Figure 3-32B. Contoured composite fan blade

ADVANTAGES AND DISADVANTAGES OF AXIAL FLOW COMPRESSORS

Axial flow compressors have the following advantages:

- High peak efficiencies (that is, compressor pressure ratios) that result from their straight-through design
- Higher peak efficiencies (pressure) attainable through the use of additional stages of compression
- Higher mass airflow and lower drag coefficient for a given frontal area

The disadvantages of the axial flow compressor are as follows:

- Difficulty and high cost of manufacture
- Relatively high weight
- High starting power requirements
- Low pressure rise per stage, with the best designs being in the range of 1.3:1 to 1.4:1

The relatively low rise in pressure per stage is due primarily to the fact that stage outlet pressure opposes axial flow moving rearward through the compressor stages. Newer designs are continually under development to limit the tendency to slow the airflow and thereby improve overall compression in newer engine models.

COMBINATION COMPRESSORS

To take advantage of the best attributes of both the centrifugal and the axial flow compressor and to eliminate some of their disadvantages, many small turbine engines installed in business jets and helicopters use combination axial-centrifugal compressors. An axial-centrifugal compressor produces a high mass airflow in its axial section for a small cross-sectional area, due to the high axial velocity present. The centrifugal section creates a better compressor pressure ratio over a wider operating range that would be possible with an axial compressor by itself. The combination compressor is especially well suited to engines with a reverse flow annular combustor. Engines designed to accommodate this type of combustor have a greater diameter, so there is no disadvantage in using a centrifugal compressor, which is, by nature of its design, much wider than a comparable axial flow compressor. Figure 3-33 shows a combination compressor with six axial stages and one centrifugal stage.

COMPARISON OF AXIAL AND CENTRIFUGAL COMPRESSORS AND LIFT

Both axial and centrifugal compressor sections compress air—that is, raise air pressure. The centrifugal compressor raises air pressure by accelerating the air outward into a single diffuser shaped as a divergent duct, where, in accordance with Bernoulli's principle, the air spreads out and slows, and pressure rises. Remember that when airflow slows, more air molecules must be present in the duct at any given time.

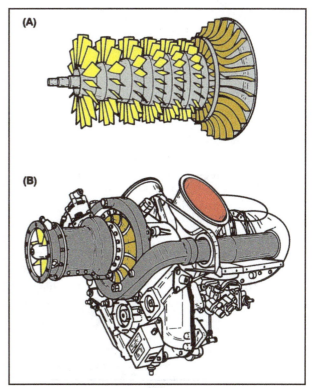

Figure 3-33A. Combination axial-centrifugal flow compressor

Figure 3-33B. Turboshaft engine with combination compressor

The axial compressor raises air pressure by accelerating air rearward into many small diffusers, or divergent ducts, formed by the shape and positions of the stator vanes. In addition, the blade pair's trailing edges also form divergent ducts, which initiate the rise in air pressure prior to its entry into the stators.

To enhance understanding of gas turbine engine compressors, examine the traditional theory of lift and airfoils. A wing exerts a downward force on the air that supports it. This force creates a downward velocity in the air equal to the lift (upward force). In much the same way, the compressor airfoil exerts a rearward force on the air. This force creates a rearward velocity in air equal to the lift (forward force). The resultant pushing force aids in propelling the engine as well as producing pressure for combustion. [Figure 3-34]

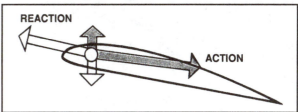

Figure 3-34. Forces acting on an airfoil

COMPRESSOR INTERSTAGE AIRFLOW

The compressor both compresses and pumps air from one stage to the next. In this process, the compressor airfoils experience an infinite variety of angles of attack (AOA) and air densities, which in turn create pressure and velocity changes. Controlling AOA is a design function of the flight inlet duct, the compressor, and the fuel controlling system. Flight inlet ducts are discussed in the first part of this chapter and fuel controls will be discussed in Chapter 7.

The principles of rotating airfoil compression can be understood by analyzing the following steps in vectoring, and the explanation of interstage airflow that follows.

A vector represents force in a particular direction. Figure 3-35 shows that if a force in the direction of arrow 1 experiences a second force in the direction of arrow 2, a new direction and force results, shown by arrow 3.

Referring to Figure 3-36, note that rotation of the compressor blades causes the initial increase in air velocity near the engine entrance in the inlet duct. Airflow is drawn through the inlet guide vanes, which impart an angular change only. No velocity or pressure change in the airflow occurs because of the straight duct flow area formed by each pair of vanes.

The straight-in angle at which the inlet guide vanes receive air and the vectored angle at which the air leaves the vanes are determined by the vane positioning and curvature. Note that the two arrows on the diagram are the same length, which indicates no change in velocity but a change in direction only. Although some designs use variable inlet guide vanes, for this discussion these vanes will remain fixed.

Two vector forces act on the airflow. One vector is inlet effect, either ram or suction, which directs air velocity into the compressor. It is depicted by the arrow labeled "guide vane discharge air velocity and direction." The other vector is created by the effect of the rotating blade. As it rotates in one direction, air flows over the airfoil in a direction opposite that of rotation. This vector is labeled "rotor speed effect on velocity and direction."

If the two combined vector forces are in the proper proportion, the resultant vector provides a suitable angle of attack of incoming air in relation to the blade chord line, and air will remain on the airfoil surfaces, producing minimal turbulence and friction. Airflow, after passing through the first stage of compression as shown on the diagram, will then proceed through each stage in this same manner. It is interesting to note that if a particular molecule of air were followed through the compressor, it would probably rotate no more than 180 degrees due to the straightening effect of the compressor stator vanes. Because the last compression stage is followed by a stationary vane set (called exit guide vanes), the airflow is turned completely back to an axial direction on its way to the combustor.

Keeping in mind the angular direction of airflow, next examine how the passage of air through the blades of the compressor creates pressure. Note that the passageway, formed by the top (cambered side) of one blade and the bottom side of the blade next to it, is diverging. This diverging shape causes a slight rise in static pressure of the air as it passes through. Concurrently, the blades are acting on the air to increase its velocity.

When the air leaves the compressor blades, it flows into a row of stator vanes. The stator vanes also form diverging ducts, which decrease the velocity of the air and increase the static pressure. The compressor blade and stator vane action continues through all the stages of the compressor. When the air leaves the compressor, its velocity will be approximately the same as when it entered, but its static pressure will be much greater.

A careful examination of the passageway formed by any of the pairs of blades or vanes reveals that the shape is actually convergent at the leading edges and divergent toward the trailing edge, forming what is called a convergent-divergent duct or passageway. This does not create a sonic shock because airflow is subsonic in this area of the engine, and the net effect is that of a divergent duct. The result is the same as what occurs in a convergent-divergent flight inlet at subsonic flight speeds, which is discussed in the first part of this chapter.

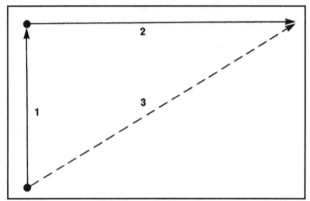

Figure 3-35. Steps in vectoring airflow

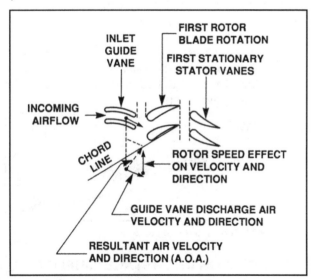

Figure 3-36. Vector diagram of interstage compressor airflow

CASCADE EFFECT

The axial compressor is described as containing sets of airfoils in cascade. This means that the airfoils are arranged in series, which influences air under low pressure in the front stages to flow into an area of higher pressure. Forcing air to flow rearward against an ever-increasing pressure is similar to forcing water to flow uphill. Pressure must be constantly applied to achieve the correct flow. The following narrative and drawings explain the concept of constantly applied pressure. Figure 3-37 shows that if a slight positive angle of attack exists, a relatively high pressure is present on the bottom of the airfoil in relation to the pressure on the top of the airfoil. These high- and low-pressure zones apply to both the rotating airfoils (rotor blades) and to the stationary airfoils (stator vanes); they permit the air in one set of airfoils to come under the influence of the next set, resulting in the cascade effect.

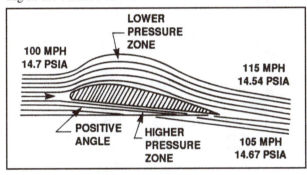

Figure 3-37. Pressure zones on an airfoil

Figure 3-38 shows high-pressure zone air of the first stage blade being pumped into the low-pressure zone of its stator. Note that the stator's leading edge faces in the opposite direction of the rotor blade's leading edge, which causes the pumping action to occur. The high-pressure zone of the first stage stator vane then pumps into the low-pressure zone of the second stage rotor blade. This cascade progress continues through to the last stage of compression.

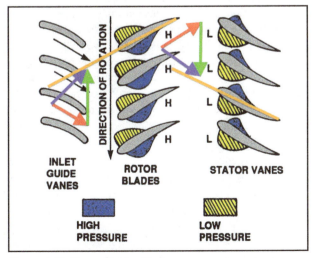

Figure 3-38. The cascade effect

Figure 3-38 also shows the effect that RPM and airflow velocity have on the angle of attack. The air entering the inlet guide vanes on the left is shown in red, with the arrow showing the direction and the length of the line representing the velocity. The effect of the rotating blades on the air is shown in green, and the resultant air direction is shown in purple. The chord line of the rotor blade is shown in orange. The angle between the purple and orange lines is the angle of attack on the rotor blade. The air leaving the rotor blades also has an angle of attack with respect to the stator vanes, and that is shown by the same color lines.

When observing Figure 3-38, the rotor blade high-and low-pressure zones might appear to cancel each other out as they blend, but the overall effect of the divergent shape of the flow path results in a net decrease in velocity and a corresponding increase in static pressure.

COMPRESSOR TAPER DESIGN

In accordance with Bernoulli's Principle, as pressure builds in the rear stages of the compressor, velocity tends to drop. This is not desirable because to create thrust, the gas turbine engine operates on a principle of velocity change in airflow. Figure 3-39 shows where velocity rises and falls through the successive stages of the compressor but maintains approximately the same inlet and outlet velocity. Even though the pressure rises dramatically, the velocity is held relatively constant. To stabilize the velocity, the shape of the compressor gas path converges, reducing to approximately 25 percent of the inlet flow area. This tapered shape provides the proper amount of space for the compressed air to occupy.

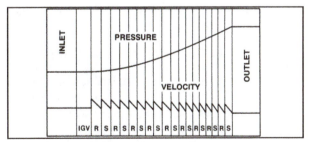

Figure 3-39. Pressure and velocity change through an axial compressor

Figure 3-40 illustrates the tapered annulus concept and reiterates the one-in, one-out idea covered in Chapter 2. That is, each unit of air passing through will have a certain physical size. If ideal compression in a particular engine is considered to be 12:1, and if airflow discontinuities in the compressor cause compression to drop to 10:1, the units will be larger and will try to accelerate in order to exit as the next unit enters. This acceleration creates a change in the angle of attack, the consequences of which are significant.

If the compressor pressure ratio is designed to be 12:1 at takeoff power, as shown in Figure 3-40B, the size of a unit of air under normal compression as it moves from the

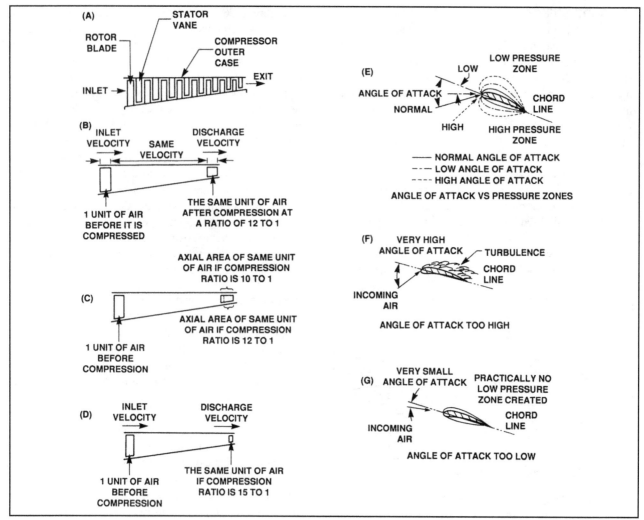

Figure 3-40. Compressor pressure ratio influence on angle of attack

compressor inlet to the compressor exit. The AOA will be normal in this case.

If the air is not properly compressed as shown in Figure 3-40C, its exit velocity will be high, its angle of attack will be low, and this will affect the pressure zone as shown in Figure 3-40E and Figure 3-40G.

Compression that is too high, as seen in Figure 3-40D, causes a low-velocity vector, a high AOA, and too large a pressure zone. The results of high AOA can be seen in Figure 3-40E and Figure 3-40F.

ANGLE OF ATTACK AND COMPRESSOR STALL

As Figure 3-41 shows, the angle of attack of the compressor blade is the result of inlet air velocity and the effect of compressor speed on airflow. The two forces combine to form a vector, which is the actual angle of attack of air approaching the airfoil. A compressor stall, a condition all gas turbine engines experience from time to time, can be described as an imbalance between the two vector quantities, inlet velocity, and compressor speed.

Compressor stalls cause air flowing through the compressor to slow down, to stagnate (stop), or to reverse direction, depending on the stall intensity. Stall conditions can usually be heard and range in audibility from an air pulsating or fluttering sound in their mildest form to a louder pulsating sound, to a sound of violent backfire or explosion. Cockpit gauges often do not indicate a mild stall condition, called a transient stall. These stalls are not usually harmful to the engine and often correct themselves after one or two pulsations. Severe stalls, called hung stalls, can significantly decay engine performance, cause loss of power, and even damage the engine or cause engine failure. Stall conditions are generally cyclic and result from a variety of causes, the most common of which are as follows:

- Turbulent or disrupted airflow to the engine inlet (which reduces the velocity vector)
- Excessive fuel flow caused by abrupt engine acceleration (which reduces the velocity vector by increasing combustor back pressure)
- Excessively lean fuel mixture caused by abrupt engine deceleration (which increases the velocity vector by reducing combustor back pressure)

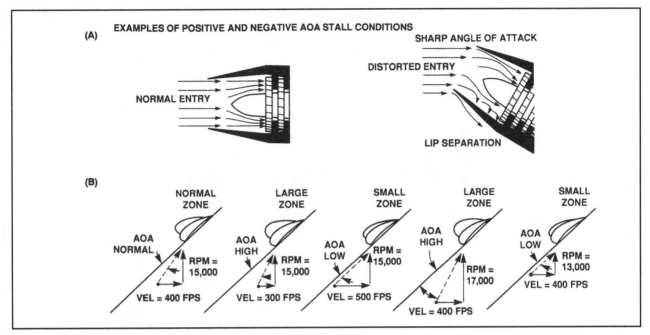

Figure 3-41A. Comparison of normal and distorted airflow into flight inlet
Figure 3-41B. Vector analysis of compressor stall

- Contaminated or damaged compressors (which increases the velocity vector by reducing compression)
- Damaged turbine components, causing loss of power to the compressor and low compression (which increases the velocity vector by reducing compression)
- Engine operation above or below designed speed (increases or decreases the speed vector).

For an example of disrupted airflow to the inlet, consider a business jet with two engines mounted at the rear of its fuselage and entering a sharp right hand turn. In this attitude, airflow to the left engine can be partially blocked by the aircraft fuselage. This sideslip could cause low inlet air velocity to result and a momentary increase in the effective angle of attack sufficient to create a compressor stall.

The indications to the pilot that an engine is experiencing compressor stall include an audible noise, fluctuation in engine speed, an increase in exhaust gas temperature, or a combination of these three. The pilot's reaction will probably be to reduce power so the inlet air velocity and engine speed will return back to their proper relationship.

In some instances of extremely severe compressor stall or surge, such as that caused by fuel system malfunction or foreign object ingestion, a reversal of airflow occurs with such force that bending stresses on the rear of compressor blades can cause them to contact the stator vanes. At that point, a series of material failures can result in total disintegration of the rotor system and complete engine failure.

RELATIONSHIP BETWEEN COMPRESSOR PRESSURE RATIO AND MASS AIRFLOW

When an engine is operating at its designed speed, the compressor blades are at a high angle of attack, which is very close to their stall angle but which generates the maximum pressure rise.

Figure 3-42 illustrates the relationship between compressor pressure ratio and mass airflow. Figure 3-42A shows that a mass airflow of 30 pounds per second, when flowing from an unrestricted nozzle, builds only a minimal amount of pressure. Entering the inlet at 15 p.s.i.a., under the influence of the compressor action and mass airflow, pressure builds to only 20 p.s.i.a., representing a compressor pressure ratio of 1.3:1.

Figure 3-42B shows that with a constricted discharge nozzle restricting the flow, pressure builds to 50 p.s.i.a. at the same mass airflow of 30 pounds per second. The result is a compressor pressure ratio of 3.3:1.

Figure 3-42C shows the final pressure rise, again under the influence of the same mass airflow of 30 pounds per second, to the designed compressor pressure ratio of 6.6 to 1. Note that combustor back pressure and the restriction to flow created by the turbine system are added to the exhaust nozzle back pressure.

For the engine to function correctly, compressor pressure ratio and mass airflow must remain within the established relationship. This can occur only if inlet compression, compressor efficiency, fuel flow, turbine efficiency, and exhaust nozzle flow all remain within the designed operating parameters. If they do not, a compressor stall or surge can result.

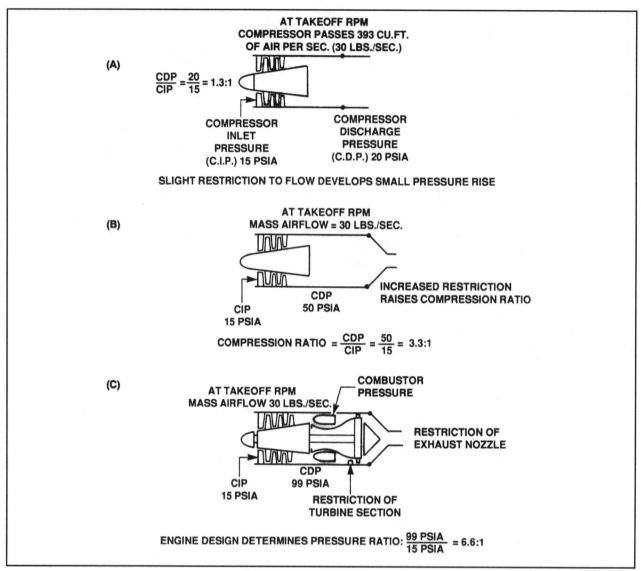

Figure 3-42. Relationship of compression ratio to mass airflow: (a) slight-restriction; (b) restricted exhaust; (c) restricted exhaust with combustor and turbine back pressures factored in

STALL OR SURGE MARGIN GRAPH

Another way to describe stall phenomena in a compressor is by way of a stall or surge margin graph. A stall is defined as a localized condition whereas a surge occurs across the whole compressor. Every compressor has an optimal operating point for a particular compressor pressure ratio (Cr), compressor speed (r.p.m.), and mass airflow (Ms), which is commonly called the design point.

The stall-surge line on the graph shown in Figure 3-43 is a series of connecting points that are plotted during the development stage of the compressor. This line represents the maximum Cr and Ms that the compressor is capable of maintaining at a particular speed. When the three factors are proportionately matched, the engine operates as expected on the normal operating line. This line is well below the surge-stall line to provide a margin for changes that occur in the atmosphere, the aircraft's flight attitude, and the engine's fuel schedule during acceleration and deceleration. If Cr increases or decreases for any reason, the design point will shift up or down and out of sync with compressor speed. If Ms increases or decreases, the design point will move to the right or left and out of sync with compressor speed.

In Figure 3-43, the normal operating line indicates that the engine will perform without surge or stall at the various compressor pressure ratios, engine speeds, and mass airflows along the length of the line, which falls well below the surge-stall zone. The design point is the point on this line at which the engine will operate during most of its service life—that is, cruise speed at altitude.

The graph reveals that at any given compressor speed, a band of compressor pressure ratios are acceptable for the engine to operate satisfactorily above the normal operating line and within the stall margin (the space between the normal operating line and the stall line).

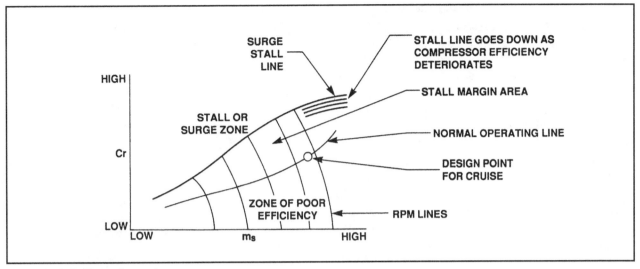

Figure 3-43. Stall margin graph

The same is true for mass airflow. At any given compressor speed, there exists a band of mass flows at which point the engine can operate satisfactorily above the normal operating line and within the stall margin.

For example, assume that the designed compressor pressure ratio is 12:1 The engine is operating at cruising airspeed with mass airflow (Ms), compressor speed, and compressor pressure ratio (Cr) plots all meeting at Point A on the stall map. [Figure 3-44]

If the aircraft were to enter turbulent weather conditions at high altitude, and at the same time the engine compressor were dirty and operating at less than peak efficiency, then a compressor pressure ratio loss down to 10:1 could occur. This loss of compression to Point B could cause mass airflow to decrease to Point C and beyond into the stall or surge zone. Note also that the normal stall line has shifted slightly downward because of the dirty compressor.

At this point, a mismatch of compressor and combustor also comes into play because the power lever has not yet been moved, fuel flow remains high, and combustor pressure is now greater than compressor discharge pressure. This causes AOA problems and adversely affects the compression process. The pilot will have to react quickly by reducing power to permit Cr and Ms to come back into symmetry with compressor speed. After recovering from the stall, the pilot must carefully accelerate the engine and try to avoid the adverse weather that caused the stall problem.

A significant factor associated with the stall map and engine performance is that a drop in compressor pressure ratio causes a drop in mass airflow. But the drop in mass airflow is more significant because it can bring the engine to the stall line. Also, with the engine operating at the right end of the normal operating line, consider the effect if the pilot were to place the aircraft nose down, making no change to the engine's compressor speed. In such a condition, a rise in compressor pressure ratio, along with increased mass airflow, could easily move the operating point above the stall line.

In flight, the fuel control senses engine parameters of Cr, Ms, and speed, and under all but the most unusual circumstances keeps all parameters in proper adjustment and in proportion at all times. If, however, the limits of the fuel control scheduling system are exceeded, the pilot must react by making a manual adjustment with the power lever.

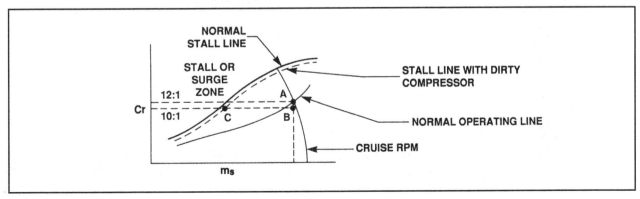

Figure 3-44. Stall map

ADVANCES IN COMPRESSOR DESIGN AND COMPRESSOR STALL AVOIDANCE

With the aid of the latest computerized 3D aerodynamic modeling, compressor designers have made significant advances in the study of flow fields of mass airflow passing through the compression process, focusing on viscosity changes, shock wave formation, flow separation, and turbulence.

Blades

Newly designed blades have radically changed the traditional airfoil shape of turbine engine compressor blades. Both the leading and trailing edges of some new blades have an irregular waviness at certain points or even all along the entire length, base to tip. This new aerodynamic design gives a distinct stall margin at each blade station along the blade's length and permits the normal operating line to shift toward the surge-stall line. The result is a compressor that can produce a high pressure ratio for a given speed, yet remain stall free.

In low-compression engines, the axial compressor allows for only subsonic axial airflow down the gas path and only subsonic airflow over all parts of its airfoil systems in order to keep flow separation low and maintain the designed compressor pressure ratio. Higher compression engines with advanced blade designs feature both high subsonic axial flow and transonic airfoil flow characteristics. Airflow over some parts of the blades, especially near the blade tips, can exceed sonic velocity.

Transonic velocity is achieved simply by increasing compressor speed, which in turn creates higher axial airflow velocity. The significance of higher velocity is that mass airflow is equal to the flow area multiplied by the axial velocity. Because of this, designers can accommodate an increase in mass airflow without having to increase the diameter of the engine.

Because the transonic blade is designed to accommodate higher air flow, another benefit of transonic fan blades is that, in many engines, they eliminate the need for inlet guide vanes.

The discussion on compressor interstage airflow earlier in this chapter was based on the traditional compressor design in which both velocity over the airfoils and axial flow velocity were subsonic. In today's more advanced compressors, supersonic blade tip flow can reach up to approximately Mach 1.3. This condition enables axial airflow down the gas path to come much closer to sonic speeds than was previously possible. [Figure 3-45]

The high pressure ratio per stage achievable in the high-performance compressor is accomplished by supersonic diffusion. Some compressors in the newest engines (and those being developed for future engines) have overall pressure ratios as high as 50:1. Some new engines today still use high aspect ratio blades, but the highest performance is being obtained from wide chord blades that incorporate "3D aerodynamic design," a concept made possible by advances in metallurgy, new manufac-

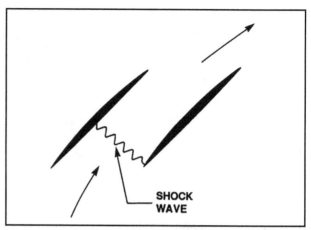

Figure 3-45. Transonic compressor blades

turing processes, and state-of-the-art compressor aerodynamics. These advances permit a supersonic airflow over airfoil sections that does not produce detrimental shock stalls and that keeps the airflow laminar to the surfaces for maximum compression. Illustrative and mathematical explanations of supersonic airfoils are beyond the scope of this book but are included in textbooks about compressor aerodynamics.

Active Clearance Control

Another compression-enhancing design used on newer engines is called active clearance control. One such system introduces cooling air into tubing external to the engine. The cooling action causes the outer compressor case to contract to the desired clearance from the compressor blade tips running within the case.

The active clearance control system schedules airflow in amounts necessary to provide the optimum compressor pressure ratio at various power settings. As a result, engine efficiency rises and fuel consumption decreases.

Another type of active clearance control is the Thermatic Compressor Rotor®. The rotor is thermally controlled (that is, heated from within), which causes it to expand. The expansion tightens running clearances between the compressor blades and the outer compressor case.

The advantage of this clearance control method over the external case shrinking method is that it can control clearances in more areas. This is because the use of external tubing is restricted due to a variety of other engine systems located on the exterior of the engine.

Mixed-Flow Compressors

Another advanced design is the mixed-flow compressor, which imparts both centrifugal and axial flow to compress air. The current mixed-flow design is an outgrowth of mixed-flow compressors that were built in the early 1950s. Production was discontinued on these early compressors because of low efficiency, but now efficiency has been improved and this compressor has been reintroduced in a small number of flight engines. [Figure 3-46A]

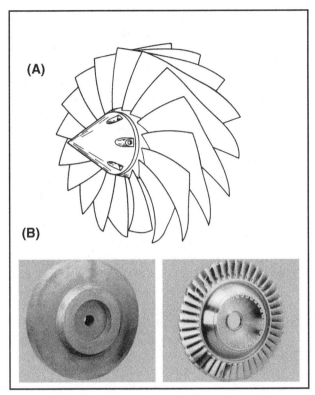

Figure 3-46A. Mixed flow compressor
Figure 3-46B. Fan blisk

Fan and Compressor Rotor Blisks

A blisk is a blade and disk unit made from a single forging rather than an assembly of many separate blades fitted to the rim of a disk. Forged blisk technology is used with many smaller fans, compressor rotors and stators, and some turbine components. Figure 3-46B shows a forging and a fan after the forging is machined to its final shape. The use of blisks can result in a weight savings of 40 to 50 percent in a given engine part because individual blades require reinforced mounting surfaces along with blade retainers, both of which add considerably to the total weight of the assembly.

COMPRESSOR-DIFFUSER SECTION

The engine section between the compressor and combustor sections is known as the compressor-diffuser because it provides additional space in which air coming from the compressor spreads out. It is a diverging duct and is usually a separate section bolted to the compressor case. The diffuser is known as the point of highest pressure in the gas turbine engine. This high wall of pressure essentially provides the combustion products something to push against. [Figure 3-47]

The concept of point of highest pressure requires additional explanation with regard to pressure total (Pt) or pressure static (Ps). At the diffuser inlet, for example, if Pt is 200 p.s.i.a., at the exit of the diffuser, Pt is also 200 p.s.i.a. The diffusing action that occurs as air moves from the inlet to the exit of the diffuser section creates an increase in Ps at the expense of velocity.

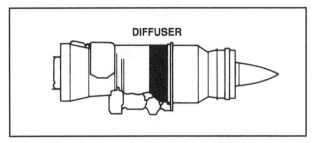

Figure 3-47. Location of compressor-diffuser section

Static pressure (measured as either absolute pressure or gauge pressure) will be higher at the diffuser exit, and this is the point of highest Ps in the engine.

If the (Pt/Ps) formula were used to calculate Ps at the diffuser inlet when velocity of airflow is Mach 0.5 (the average value for most engines), Ps would be approximately 169 p.s.i.a. The remaining 31 p.s.i.a. would be in the form of ram pressure. At the diffuser outlet, if airflow drops to Mach 0.35 (on average), Ps would be approximately 184 p.s.i.a., leaving 16 p.s.i.a. as ram pressure. Note that the total pressure (Pt) of 200 does not change if mass flow does not change; only static and ram pressure values change.

Low velocities are desirable at the combustor entrance, but if the Mach number drops too low in a divergent duct, a serious aerodynamic problem occurs as airflow starts to separate from the walls, creating turbulence. With current technology, Mach 0.35 is the approximate mean low limit.

COMBUSTION SECTION

The combustion section, or burner as it is often called, consists of an outer casing, an inner perforated liner, a fuel injection system, and a starting ignition system. The function of this section is to add heat energy to the flowing gases, thereby expanding and accelerating the gases into the turbine section. [Figure 3-48]

One way to think about combustion is that, when heat energy from fuel is added to the pressurized air from the compressor section, the volume of the gases increases. Keeping in mind that the flow area remains constant, the expansion of the gases causes them to accelerate. Furthermore, the expansion and acceleration is caused by combustion resulting from the interaction of oxygen molecules and molecules of fuel that are heated to ignition temperatures. At the high fuel flow and airflow present in large turbine engines, this combustion can generate heat energy equal to four- to eight-hundred-million BTU per hour.

The most common combustor configuration is the "through-flow," or "straight-through," combustor in which gases entering from compression are immediately ignited and then pass directly into the turbine sections. The multiple-can, annular, and can-annular combustors are generally through-flow combustors.

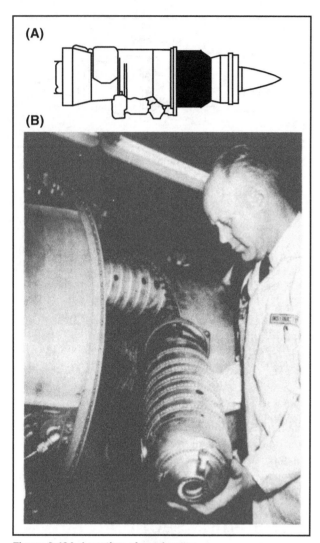

Figure 3-48A. Location of combustor
Figure 3-48B. Removal of through-flow can-annular liner from Pratt & Whitney JT8D turbofan

The other configuration is the reverse flow annular combustor in which gases make an S-turn as they enter and exit the combustor. After exiting the compressor section, the gases flow to the rear of the combustor and make a 180-degree turn to enter the flame zone. As the gases exit the combustor, they make another 180-degree turn and enter the turbine section. Illustrations of these combustor types accompany their explanations in the succeeding paragraphs.

To function efficiently, the combustion chamber must provide a means for properly mixing the air and fuel. It must also cool the hot combustion products to a temperature that the turbine section components can withstand. To accomplish this, airflow through the combustor is divided into primary and secondary air paths. Primary air is routed to the fuel nozzle area to support combustion and secondary air is used for cooling.

In early gas turbine engines, primary air was as low as 25 percent of the air leaving the compressor, the other 75 percent used for cooling. In modern engines, as much as 45 percent of the air leaving the compressor is used for combustion. Of the remaining compressor air, 35 percent is typically used to cool the combustor, and 20 percent is used to cool the turbine. With each new generation of engines, the amount of air used to support combustion versus air used to cool changes. New materials that can withstand higher heat, combined with more effective use of cooling air, enables more of the air to be used for combustion.

Approximately one half of primary air flows axially through swirl vanes located in the dome (front) portion of the combustion liner in the area of the fuel nozzle openings. The remaining primary air enters radially through small holes in the first third of the liner. Both axial and radial airflows support combustion.

A portion of secondary air (the amount varying depending on the vintage of the engine) provides a cooling air blanket over inside and outside surfaces of the liner and centers the flame, preventing it from contacting the metal surfaces. The remaining portion of secondary air enters the liner at the rear and dilutes the mixture of burned gases to a temperature that the turbine components can withstand over the long term.

Developments in recent years have led to what is called the smokeless or reduced smoke combustor. Early engines suffered from incomplete combustion, which left unburned fuel in the tailpipe to carbonize and enter the atmosphere as smoke. By shortening the flame pattern, increasing its heat intensity, and using new materials that can withstand higher operating temperatures, manufacturers have nearly eliminated smoke emissions from turbine engines.

An interesting characteristic of the traditional combustion chamber operation is the velocity of the air in the flame zone immediately in front of the fuel nozzles. Although the velocity of secondary airflow in the chamber might be several hundred feet per second, primary airflow is metered and slowed by swirl vanes. These swirl vanes create radial motion and retard axial motion of the air to an almost stagnant 5 or 6 feet per second in a vortex type flow. [Figure 3-49 and 3-51B]

By design, the combustion process is completed in the first one third of the combustion liner. In the remaining two thirds of the liner, the combusted and uncombusted gas is mixed to provide an even heat distribution at the turbine nozzle stator vanes.

The vortex created in the flame area provides the time required to mix the air and fuel. A major design problem is that in an attempt to increase mixing time by creating vortex turbulence, combustor pressure drops and combustor efficiency decreases. Because of the slow flame propagation rate of jet fuels, if primary airflow velocity is too high, it can literally blow the flame out of the engine, causing what is called a flameout.

Although flameout is uncommon in modern engines, it still occurs. Turbulent weather, high altitude, slow accel-

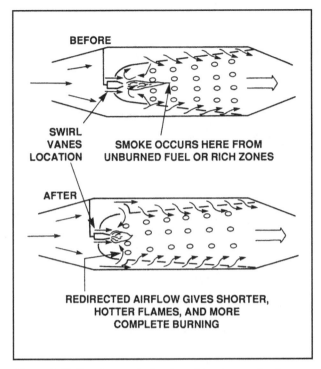

Figure 3-49. Development of reduced smoke combustors

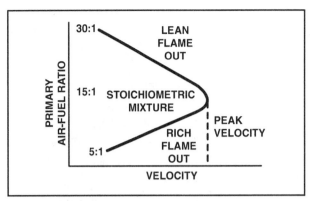

Figure 3-50. Range of burnable fuel-air ratios versus combustor gas velocity

eration during maneuvers, and high-speed maneuvers are four of the more typical conditions that set up combustor flameout.

Flameout (lean) — This condition usually occurs at low fuel pressures, at low engine speeds, or in high-altitude flight. These conditions set up a weak mixture, which can be easily blown out, even at normal airflows.

Flameout (rich) — This condition usually occurs during rapid engine acceleration in which an overrich mixture is present. This causes combustion pressure to increase until compressor airflow stagnates (slows or stops). The momentary interruption in airflow extinguishes the flame. Turbulent inlet conditions and violent flight maneuvers can also cause stalls that can result in compression stagnation and loss of combustion.

Combustor instability — Flameouts due to combustor instability can occur in a mild form from flight conditions. They are difficult to predict and sometimes allow formations of small gas pressure fluctuations in the combustor. These low-pressure cycles, if unaddressed, can generate greater and greater combustor instability until the pilot makes the necessary adjustment in flight conditions or to engine controls.

Correct velocity of airflow in the combustor depends on correctly matching compressor pressure ratio, mass airflow, and engine speed. Figure 3-50 indicates that only at the stoichiometric mixture can velocity be at its peak. If the mixture is lean or rich, the velocity will be at a corresponding lower value and the thermal efficiency will suffer.

With regard to combustor efficiency, the combustor is efficient in the range of 99 to 100 percent, meaning that the combustor extracts heat equal to 99 to 100 percent of the fuel's potential heat.

Combustor design is an inexact science and often referred to as a "black art." That is, it is not always known why one combustor design works well and gives good service life and another type does not when installed in the same engine. Just as in Whittle's time, designers today devote the bulk of the engine research and developmental time to obtaining good combustor performance.

Manufacturers tend to rely on their known technological base when developing new engines. Because of this, it is common to see familiar combustor designs from one generation of engine to the next. The various types of combustors with proven performance characteristics suitable for flight engines are of four types: multiple-can combustors, can-annular combustors, annular combustors, and annular reverse-flow combustors. All but the annular reverse-flow combustor are through-flow combustors.

MULTIPLE-CAN COMBUSTOR

The multiple-can combustor is an older type of combustion chamber no longer in common use. It consists of multiple outer housings, each with its own perforated inner liner. Each of the multiple combustors (called cans) is in effect a separate burner unit, all of which discharge into one open area at the turbine nozzle inlet. The individual combustors are interconnected with small tubes so that, as combustion occurs in the two combustors with igniter plugs, the flame can move to all of the remaining cans.

The Rolls-Royce Dart, shown in Figure 3-51, is a good example of an engine using a multiple-can combustor. The cans are mounted on a slight angle to reduce the engine's length. The cutaway view shows the various components of a can-type combustor.

CAN-ANNULAR COMBUSTOR

The can-annular combustor was once used in many commercial aircraft powered by Pratt & Whitney engines.

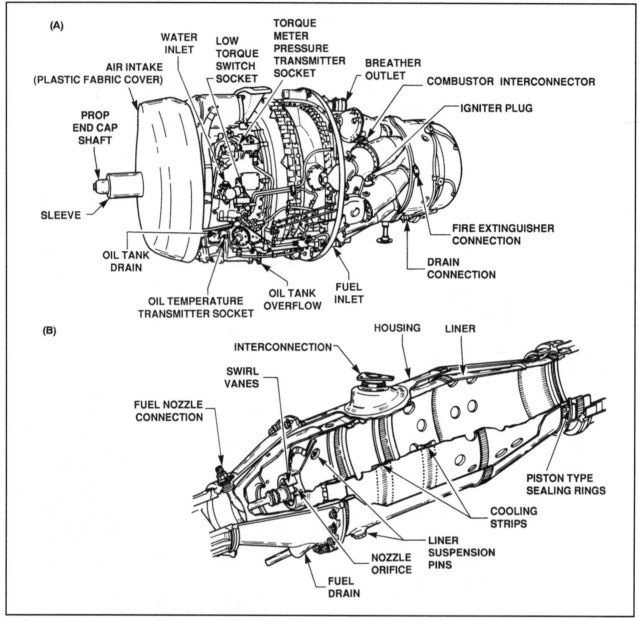

Figure 3-51A. Rolls-Royce Dart turboprop engine with multiple-can combustor
Figure 3-51B. Combustion can and its liner

This design consists of an outer case containing multiple liners located radially about the axis of the engine. The liners take air in at the front and discharge it at the rear. Flame propagation tubes interconnect the liners, with provision made for two igniter plugs in the lower cans.

The combustor shown in Figure 3-52 uses eight liners. Each liner has its own fuel nozzle cluster, which supports the liner at the front end. The outlet duct, a device with eight apertures, supports the rear of each liner. An advantage of this combustor is that it simplifies on-the-wing maintenance wherein the outer case is made to slide back to expose all of the liners within and facilitate liner inspection.

ANNULAR COMBUSTOR (THROUGH FLOW)

The annular combustor takes air in at the front dome area of the liner and discharges it at the rear. It consists of an external structural support casing that contains a single liner. The liner is often referred to as a burner, with multiple fuel spray nozzles protruding into the burner dome. Primary and secondary air provide for combustion and cooling as in other combustor designs.

As shown in Figure 3-53A, the annular combustor assembly is made up of a liner and an outer case. This forms an annulus through which the gases flow, thus the word *annular* combustor. The interior section of the liner forms an opening for the turbine rotor shaft.

Turbine Engine Design and Construction

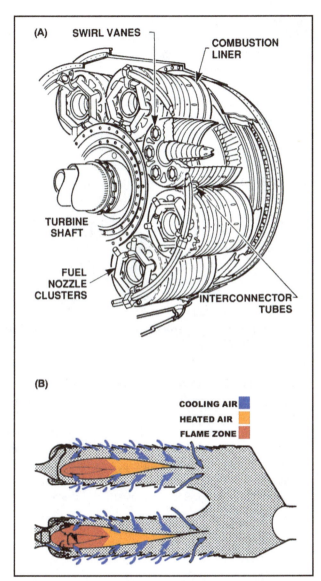

Figure 3-52A. Can-annular combustor
Figure 3-52B. Liner showing primary and secondary airflow

Figure 3-53B shows a dual annular combustor (DAC) with an inner and outer ring-shaped dome and openings for a dual ring of fuel nozzles. The pilot nozzles in the outer ring operate alone at low engine airflow conditions. At higher engine power, both main-inner and pilot-outer nozzles are in operation. The DAC was developed to help reduce gaseous oxides of nitrogen (NOx) emissions by improved mixing of fuel and air and reduction of hot zones that increase the production of NOx.

Figure 3-53C shows a Twin Annular Premixing Swirler (TAPS)® combustor, developed by General Electric. This combustor is a SAC combustor with the addition of redesigned twin annular air paths both through and around the head of the fuel nozzle and with a more sophisticated electronically controlled fuel distribution system.

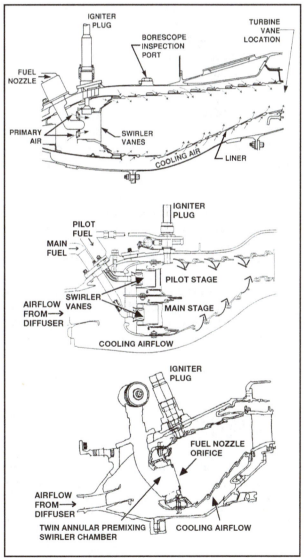

Figure 3-53A. Cross-section of a single annular combustor (SAC)
Figure 3-53B. Cross-section of a dual annular combustor (DAC)
Figure 3-53C. Cross-section of a Twin Annular Premixing Swirler (TAPS)® combustor

The annular combustor is commonly used in all sizes of engines. It is the most efficient design from the standpoint of thermal efficiency versus weight and for its shorter length than other combustor types. Its minimal surface area requires less cooling air. It makes the best use of the available space between the diffuser and turbine sections, especially on large engines where other combustor types would be much heavier for the mass airflow routed through them.

The following three combustors are of General Electric design for larger engines and are similar in many respects to Pratt & Whitney and Rolls-Royce combustors.

Figure 3-53A shows a single annular combustor (SAC), meaning that a single ring-shaped dome encircles the front portion of the combustion liner. The dome has openings for one row of fuel nozzles around which primary air flows to mix with the fuel.

In early turbine engines, the air/fuel mixture had to be slowed considerably and diluted heavily to protect the metal and center the flame. This is not the case with the TAPS® combustor, in which the air/fuel mixture at high volume is thoroughly premixed by high-velocity swirlers before it is burned. Also, stage-1 and stage-2 sets of fuel nozzles are present to flow at specified modes of engine operation. Stage-1 flows fuel for starting and low thrust settings, followed later by a combined flow of stages 1 and 2 for higher thrust operation. This results in lower gas temperatures over a wide range of engine operation. This reduces the need for radial cooling airflow through the holes, slots, and louvers found in the outer surface of traditional combustion liners. In contrast, the TAPS® liner uses only a small film of cooling air, which makes available considerably more air energy in the airflow. The desired result of this design is to further reduce NOx emissions, which increase significantly as a function of high temperatures in the burning of hydrocarbon fuels.

Other engine manufacturers have developed low-emission solutions, such as Pratt & Whitney, with its Talon-1® and Talon-2® combustors.

ANNULAR REVERSE-FLOW COMBUSTOR

The annular reverse-flow combustor is common to the Pratt & Whitney JT-15D turbofan, the PT-6 turboprop, the Honeywell (formerly Lycoming) T-53/55 turboshaft, the Honeywell TFE-731 turbofan, and several other smaller engines with smaller airflow requirements, installed in corporate aviation aircraft. The reverse-flow combustor has the same function as the through-flow combustor types. It differs only in how air flows through the combustor. Instead of air entering the combustor from the front, it flows over the liner and enters from the rear, with the combustion gas flow being opposite in direction to the normal airflow through the engine. After combustion takes place, the gases flow into a deflector, which turns them 180 degrees to exit the engine in the normal direction.

In Figure 3-54A, note that the turbine wheels are inside the combustor area rather than in tandem with it as in the other previously mentioned types. This arrangement results in shorter engine length and lower weight. It also helps to preheat the compressor discharge air with heat radiating out of the combustion liner as the air passes over the outer surface of the liner before making a turn into the combustion zone at the rear. These two factors make up for the loss of efficiency, which occurs when the gas reverses flow during combustion.

Figure 3-54B is a cutaway of the Honeywell TFE-731 turbofan engine, which uses a reverse-flow annular combustor. As air leaves the centrifugal compressor, which has thrown it to the outside, it flows around the outside of the combustor and enters from the rear (180-degree turn). After combustion takes place, the air makes another 180-degree turn and flows through the four turbine stages.

NEW COMBUSTOR DESIGNS

One new combustor design used in small engines is called the precombustor chamber. It is an annular combustor in which a portion of primary air comes first into a precombustor chamber where it mixes with fuel and ignites; the gas then enters the main chamber where it meets a second fuel nozzle and the remainder of primary airflow. Manufacturers claim that this more complex combustor promotes ease of cold weather starting, low emissions, and high resistance to flameout. [Figure 3-54D] For comparison, the traditional Allison-250 (now Rolls-Royce) combustion liner is shown in Figure 3-54C.

Another new type of liner, shown in Figure 3-54F, is the machined ring liner, constructed by welding together rings of heavy-gauge metal. This technique is said to produce a liner of much higher mechanical strength than the traditional stamped sheet metal liner as shown in Figure 3-54E. The machined ring liner is now common in the larger fan engines with annular combustors. The TAPS® combustor mentioned earlier is similar to the one shown in Figure 3-54F but with almost no radial air passages for cooling.

COMBUSTOR-GENERATED EMISSIONS

The gas turbine engine has a highly efficient combustion cycle and produces little atmospheric pollution in comparison to many industrial fuel-burning processes. Combustor efficiency is over 99 percent when the engine is operating at a high power setting, dropping to approximately 95 percent at idle. Most of the emissions from the hot exhaust are nonpollutants consisting of the following approximate values: oxygen, 15 percent; inert gas and water vapor, 82 percent; and carbon dioxide, 4 percent. Actual pollutants by weight are only about 0.04 percent at full power and 0.13 percent at idle power.

Gas turbine emissions classed as pollutants by the Environmental Protection Agency (EPA) are:

- Smoke (carbon particles).
- Unburned hydrocarbons in fuel (HC).
- Carbon monoxide (CO).
- Oxides of nitrogen (NOx).

Pollutants are formed by inefficiency in the combustion process or by high flame temperature reaction to the burning of hydrocarbon fuel in air. HC and CO result mainly from combustor inefficiencies, and NOx results from high flame temperatures, which changes atmospheric ozone to nitric acid during combustion.

HC and CO are formed primarily at low power settings near the walls of the combustor liner where cooling air inhibits complete combustion at a time when atomization of fuel by the fuel nozzle is poor and combustor temperatures are low. NOx is the natural byproduct of hydrocarbon fuel burned at the high temperature necessary for optimum power production and fuel economy.

The "reduced smoke" combustor liner mentioned in the early part of the combustor section was designed to

Turbine Engine Design and Construction

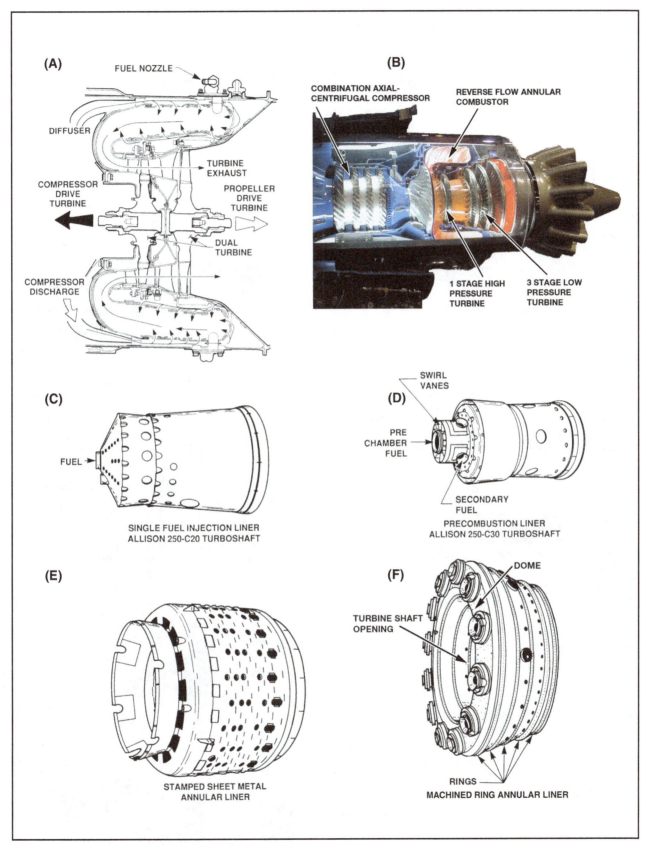

Figure 3-54A. Annular reverse flow combustor
Figure 3-54B. Honeywell TFE-731 turbofan with reverse flow combustor
Figure 3-54C and D. Comparison of single and dual fuel injection liners
Figure 3-54E and F. Comparison of early and new combustion liners

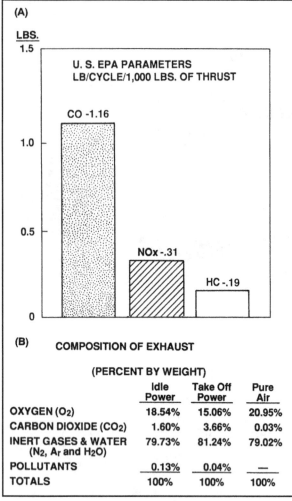

Figure 3-55A. Engine emissions limits for turbofan engines: Pound of pollutants, per takeoff and landing cycle, per 1000 pounds of rated thrust

Figure 3-55B. Typical composition of aircraft gas turbine engine emissions

reduce HC, CO, and smoke, but it slightly increased NOx emissions by producing a shorter, hotter flame pattern. These examples reveal the tradeoffs that occur between reducing various pollutants and enhancing economy of operation.

The U.S. Environmental Protection Agency tests all gas turbine engines to ensure that federal standards are met. Engine manufacturers strive to improve their products by increasing engine performance and reducing fuel consumption while meeting current EPA standards. [Figure 3-55] During one cycle of operation, which includes idle and taxi time, takeoff and climbout, and approach for landing, the current standards for pollutants are:

- Hydrocarbons — no more than 0.19 pounds per 1,000 pounds of thrust.

- Oxides of nitrogen — no more than 0.31 pounds per 1,000 pounds of thrust.

- Carbon monoxide — no more than 1.16 pounds per 1,000 pounds of thrust.

TURBINE SECTION

The purpose of the turbine section is to transform a portion of the kinetic energy and heat energy in the gases leaving the combustion section into mechanical work used to drive the compressor and accessories. The turbine section is bolted to the combustor and contains the turbine wheels and turbine stators. [Figures 3-56 and 3-57]

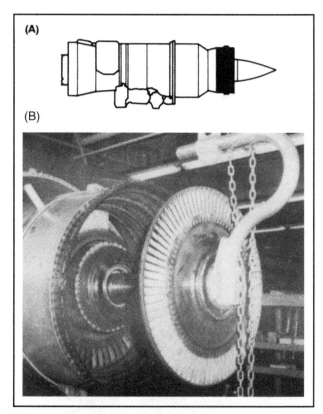

Figure 3-56A. Location of turbine section
Figure 56B. Horizontal removal of turbine wheel—Pratt & Whitney JT8D Turbofan engine

Figure 3-57. Removal of turbine stator assembly

TURBINE ROTOR AND STATOR

Recall that the compressor adds energy to air by increasing its pressure. The turbine extracts energy by reducing pressure of the flowing gases. This occurs as pressure is converted to velocity at the nozzles formed at the trailing edge of the turbine stator vanes and rotor blades. The velocity of mass flow is vectored in a tangential direction rather than axial. This slows the gas flow axially, reducing its reactive power, but adds shaft power to the rotor system.

The mass (weight) of airflow naturally does not change in the transfer of energy to the rotor system, but as the velocity of mass flow is being slowed axially, the energy of shaft power (torque) is increased. In other words, tangential velocity is essentially a loss of kinetic energy to the engine, which best explains how the turbine extracts energy from the flowing gasses.

Changes in energy extraction by the turbine are brought about to meet desired goals during the research and the development stage of the engine. These changes are usually proprietary and unpublished, and might include:

- Adding more turbine stages.
- Increasing the number of vanes and blades.
- Deflecting larger amounts of mass flow from an axial to a tangential direction.
- Narrowing the openings between vanes to increase the energy change from pressure to velocity.

The most efficient turbine performs the maximum of work from the least fuel consumption. This occurs when the turbine is operating at its design point for temperature and speed, and the compressor is operating at its design point of compressor pressure ratio and mass airflow.

The type of turbine design used in almost all flight engines is the axial flow type, in which the products of combustion pass through the turbine vanes and blades, changing angle momentarily, and then return to an axial direction.

As previously mentioned, the turbine absorbs most of the energy created in the combustion process. Consequently, this unit is one of the most highly stressed components in the engine. Stress on turbine blades can exceed 30,000 pound per square. The disk, generally a heavy forging, is subjected to many thousands of G-forces. Turbine disks and blades, sometimes referred to as buckets, are made of super alloys, usually of a nickel-base variety. The properties of these alloys are high thermal strength, resistance to corrosion, and a low coefficient of expansion.

The G-force experienced by a rotating turbine blade is a result of centrifugal force. The amount of centrifugal force, and the G-force on the blade, can be calculated as follows:

$$\text{Centrifugal Force} = \frac{\text{Weight}}{\text{gravity}} \times \frac{\text{Velocity}^2}{\text{radius}}$$

Where: $\frac{\text{Weight}}{\text{gravity}} = \text{Mass}$

Velocity = f.p.s. at blade C.G.

radius = radius (ft.) of blade C.G.

C.G. = blade center of gravity

gravity = 32.16 ft/sec^2

G - Force = Centrifugal Force ÷ Blade Weight

For example, assume that the distance between the center of gravity (CG) point of one turbine blade and its opposite blade CG is 2.0 feet (diameter), blade weight is 0.2 pounds, and the speed is 9,980 r.p.m. You can use the formula to determine the G-force on each blade.

$$\text{Velocity} = \pi \times \text{dia.} \times \text{r.p.m.} \div 60$$

$$V = 3.1416 \times 2 \times 9,980 \div 60$$

$$V = 1,045 \text{ f.p.s.}$$

$$\text{Centrifugal Force} = \frac{\text{Weight}}{\text{gravity}} \times \frac{\text{Velocity}^2}{\text{radius}}$$

$$\text{C.F.} = \frac{0.2 \text{ lb.} (1,045 \text{ ft/sec})^2}{32.16 \text{ ft/sec}^2 \times 1 \text{ ft.}}$$

$$\text{C.F.} = \frac{218,405}{32.16} \text{ lb.}$$

$$\text{C.F.} = 6,791 \text{ lb.}$$

G - Force = 6,791 ÷ 0.2

G - Force = 33,956

FUNCTION OF TURBINE STATORS

The turbine section, like the compressor section, contains many blades and vanes; but, unlike the compressor, its stator vanes are located in front of the blades. Whereas the compressor stator vanes act as diffusers that decrease velocity and increase pressure, the turbine stator vanes act as nozzles that increase velocity and decrease pressure. The turbine nozzle assembly is also known as the turbine nozzle, nozzle diaphragm, or the turbine nozzle guide vane assembly. [Figure 3-58]

Most turbine nozzles operate in a choked condition (wherein the gas flow is at Mach 1 velocity) while in the cruise to takeoff power range. Gas flow at this velocity gives a predictable energy level to the turbine wheel at any point in the normal operating range. The velocity of gases is more dependent on temperature of the gas in relation to the local speed of sound than on back-pressures within the rear sections of the engine. This is because

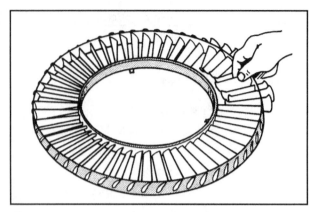

Figure 3-58. Assembly of turbine nozzle guide vanes

downstream pressure has little effect on the choked turbine nozzle, which creates its own back pressure. In addition, the downstream pressure, being much less than the head of pressure in front of the nozzle, keeps flow constant to the turbine wheel.

A secondary purpose of the turbine stator is to direct the gases at the optimum angle into the turbine blades so that the wheel turns with maximum efficiency. The greater the tangential component of the gas flow to and from the turbine wheel, the greater the torque to drive the compressor.

The turbine stator is known as the point of highest velocity in the turbine engine. The velocity, in this case, is angular velocity rather than axial velocity. The velocity is controlled by the total area of the opening between the vanes. Vane sets have flow areas of certain sizes referred to as classes. In many cases, stator assemblies are built up with varying vane classes to provide the most effective flow area according to the needs of a particular engine. For example, assume that a new compressor is installed during overhaul and that, due to back pressure at a restricted turbine nozzle, it creates more mass airflow than the engine can accommodate without stalling. In this instance, the nozzle area can be reconstructed with a larger opening to relieve the back pressure and correct the stall problem.

SHROUDS AND SEALS

The shroud ring, shown in Figure 3-59A, is used to minimize gas loss over the blade tips. Excessive air leakage over the blade tips creates turbulence, which can destroy the blade efficiency in the tip area. Air leakage also can be thought of as disrupted airflow bypassing the working portion of the engine, in effect, reducing engine efficiency.

The air seals shown in Figure 3-59B are generally a rotating knife-edge seal, sometimes called a rotating rim. This seal is made up of several thin sheet-metal rims that form seal dams and also act as metering orifices to control compressor bleed air to the inner areas of the engine. The bleed air is used to pressurize labyrinth and carbon oil seals and to cool certain hot section areas. When the bleed air has completed its cooling functions, it generally bleeds back into the gas path through other seals similar to the ones shown in the illustration.

IMPULSE-REACTION BLADES

The turbine rotor is constructed either as a disk and blade assembly with removable blading or as a single unit in which the blades are cast integral with the disk. Such a casting is called a blisk. The turbine blisk is similar to the fan blisk shown in Figure 3-46B. In either case, the turbine blades are of compound curvature, and the design is referred to as an impulse-reaction design. The twist in the blade is used to distribute the workload evenly along the blade length by keeping the exit pressure and velocity uniform from the base to the tip. This is accomplished by extracting different amounts of kinetic energy at various blade stations. In flight engines, the design usually found to be the most efficient is 50 percent impulse and 50 percent reaction.

The graph in Figure 3-60 shows that blade inlet pressure flowing from the stator vanes is lowest at the base. This occurs in relation to the high exit velocity of the turbine stator vanes at this location. The graph also shows that pressure applied is highest at the tip in relation to a lower turbine stator exit velocity. The effect of this varying inlet pressure, base to tip, results in uniform blade exit pressure and exit velocity along the length of the blade.

The following narrative and drawings explain the conditions described in the preceding paragraph. [Figure 3-61]

The reaction position is at the blade tip. This portion of the blade exerts the greatest torque arm force by rotating with greater speed than the base. The tip area is therefore designed to absorb the least kinetic energy from the flowing gases. The straight duct design of the stator at this blade position keeps pressure relatively high as the blade tips receive the gas at area A.

The converging duct formed at area B between the blade pairs accelerates the gas to counteract the tendency of high tip rotational speed to reduce the axial velocity of the gas. The turbine blade passageways (ducts) in this area are, in fact, rotating nozzles, and the turbine wheel's rotational force at the blade tips is in reaction to the axial acceleration of the gases. This is a situation of action and reaction, as described in Newton's third law. The relatively high pressure available at the tip area has a secondary purpose of counteracting the tendency of centrifugal reaction that attempts to direct air outward, thus reducing axial velocity and reducing the forward reacting force desired.

Figure 3-62 illustrates the impulse position at the blade base. The base exerts the least torque arm force by rotating slower, relative to the tip. The tendency of the base to do less work is counteracted by supplying the base with a larger share of the available kinetic energy.

Turbine Engine Design and Construction

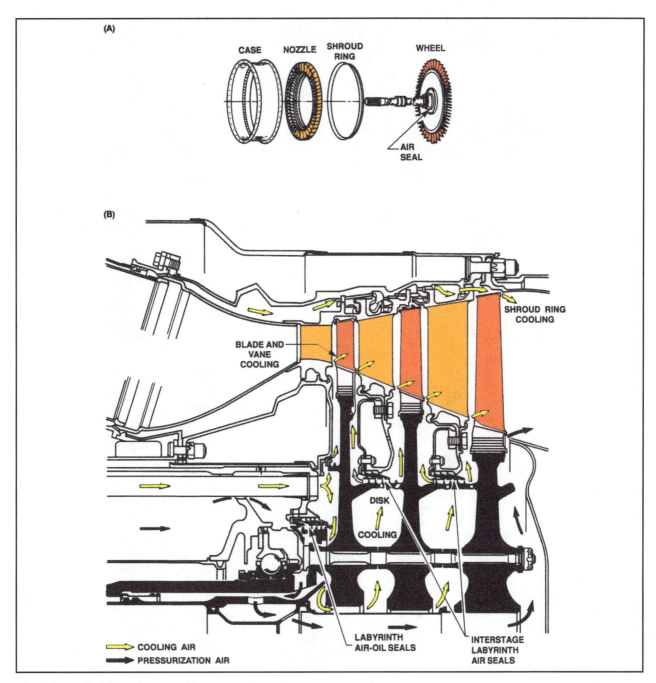

Figure 3-59A. Turbine rotor assembly
Figure 3-59B. Turbine section airflow

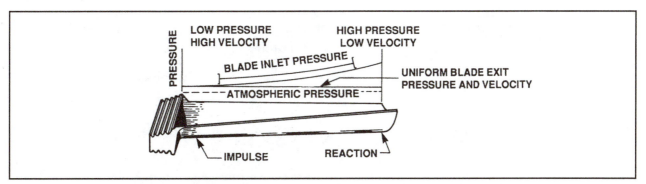

Figure 3-60. Combination impulse-reaction turbine blade

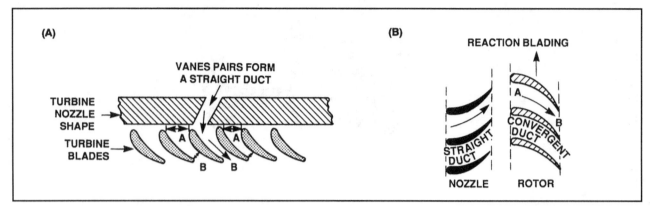

Figure 3-61A. Reaction turbine system (Newton's third law)
Figure 3-61B. Vane and blade flow areas at blade tip

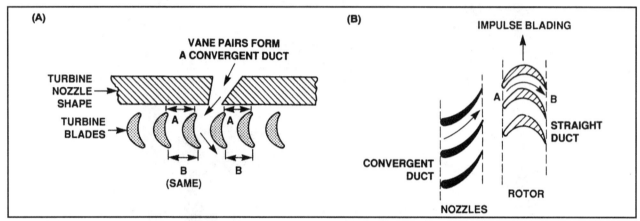

Figure 3-62A. Impulse turbine system (Newton's second law)
Figure 3-62B. Vane and blade flow area at blade base

Because work equals force times distance, more force must be applied at the base of the blade where the distance to the axis is less. The increased force enables the base to accomplish the same amount of work as the tip.

The cup-shaped base area receives the greatest amount of kinetic energy from a convergent stator vane section, and the gases force the blades around in a circular path. This is an example of unbalanced forces as described in Newton's second law.

To compare forces acting on the blade base versus forces acting on the blade tip, consider that the gases are guided onto the cup-shaped portion of each blade at a high velocity in order to apply force to the blade and thus to the wheel. At the tip area, the gases are guided into the blades at the best angle. The blades then squirt the gases out at high velocity, creating a reacting force, which turns the wheel. [Figure 3-63]

The axial velocity and pressure drop that occurs at the turbine blade base is minimized by the straight duct formed by the turbine blade pairs and the slower rotational speed. With the combination impulse-reaction design, the workload is evenly distributed along the length of the

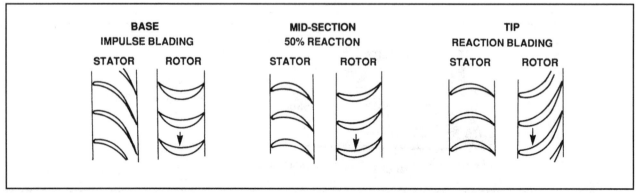

Figure 3-63. Twist changes blades from impulse to reaction

blade, and axial velocity and pressure drop across the blade, from base to tip, is uniform.

AXIAL TURBINE CONSTRUCTION

The axial turbine rotor assembly consists of drive shafts, disks with blades attached, and blade retention devices of various styles. At the front of each turbine rotor is a system of stationary vanes that direct gas flow into the turbine blading.

DRIVE SHAFTS

The engine compressors are driven by a coupling arrangement to the turbine shafts. Figure 3-64 shows the construction features of the turbine. The N_2 shaft is bolted to the turbine disk at the aft end. The turbine shaft is attached to the compressor by means of splines cut on the forward end of the shaft. The splines fit into a coupling device, which slips over the turbine shaft splines. The N_2 compressor also has a splined shaft, which fits into the coupling at the front end. The illustration shows a dual coaxial turbine shaft arrangement. The long shaft couples the rear, low-pressure (N_1) turbine to the front (N_1) compressor. The short shaft couples the front turbine to the rear (N_2) compressor.

The N_2 turbine is referred to as the high-pressure turbine because it receives the highest gas pressure from combustion. The low-pressure turbine is so named because of the pressure drop in the gas flow before it reaches the low-pressure turbine.

BLADE ATTACHMENT AND RETENTION DEVICES

Turbine blades (or buckets, as they are sometimes called) are attached to the disk in a variety of ways. One of the most common methods for positive engagement under the high heat and high centrifugal loading conditions that turbine blades experience is the fir-tree design.

An advantage of this design is that it provides more contact surface area between the blade base and the disk. Turbine blades are retained in their grooves by a variety of methods. Some of the more common methods are rivets, locktabs, lockwires, and roll pins. [Figure 3-65]

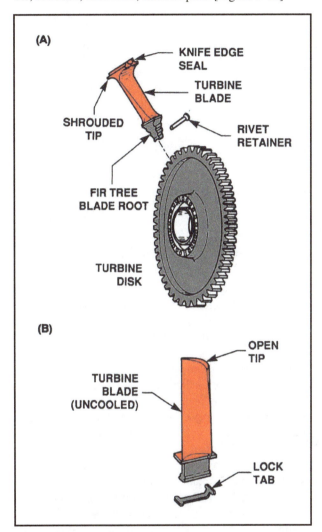

Figure 3-65A. Turbine disk and shrouded tip blade
Figure 3-65B. Open-tip blade

SHROUDED TIPS AND KNIFE-EDGE SEALS

Turbine blades are either open at the tip or fitted with interlocking shrouds, as seen in Figures 3-65 and 3-66. Both types are often used in a single engine, with the high-speed wheel using open tip blades and the low-speed wheel using shrouded tip blades. Tip loading from rotational forces often limits the use of shrouds to lower speed locations, such as low-pressure turbines in turbofan engines. This is also true of low-pressure turbines in turboshaft engines, in which all of the energy is designed to be absorbed by the turbine blades; any energy that slips over the blade tips without adding torque to the turbine rotor is sacrificed because high velocity energy leaving the exhaust duct is given up to the atmosphere. Shrouded tips reduce this energy loss.

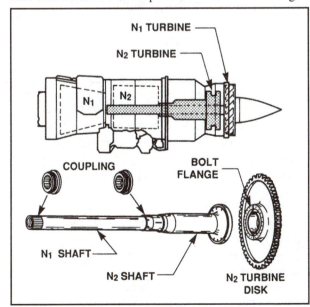

Figure 3-64. Turbine shaft locations

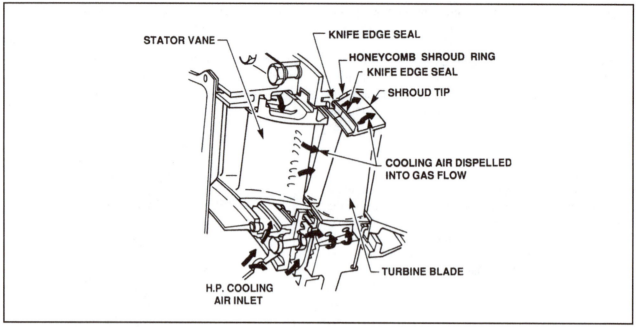

Figure 3-66. Shrouded air-cooled blade and air-cooled turbine stator vane

Tip shrouds do several things to aid turbine wheel efficiency. They enable the use of long thin blades, which results in lighter construction. They prevent air loss at the tips and blade distortion (or untwisting) under heavy gas loading. They also dampen vibration and provide a mounting base for knife-edge air seals.

The use of knife-edge seals also reduces air losses at the blade tips, and keeps the airflow in an axial direction to maximize the impact force of the flowing gases onto the turbine blades. Knife-edge seals fit in close tolerance to a shroud ring mounted in the outer turbine case. This shroud is often constructed of a honeycomb material or some other porous material. [Figure 3-66]

Occasionally, high G-forces from flight maneuvers or hard landings cause contact as cases distort and the knife-edge seals cut into the honeycomb shroud ring. This occurs with minimal wear to the seal and shroud and results in no loss of blade length.

COUNTER-ROTATING TURBINES

Some smaller turbine engines, especially turboprop and turboshaft engines, use counter-rotating free power turbines, rather than the compressor drive turbines, to drive the propeller or output shaft. In these engines, counter-rotation dampens gyroscopic effect and reduces vibration. Some larger turbofan engines also use counter-rotation in the low-pressure turbines to increase the overall efficiency of the engine. The increase in efficiency occurs because when the air flows from the high-pressure turbine into the low-pressure turbine (which causes it to turn the opposite direction) its effective velocity increases, which also increases impact force. However, designers must ensure that the effective velocity does not become so great that flow separation occurs. [Figure 3-67]

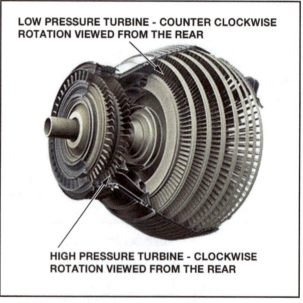

Figure 3-67. General Electric turbofan with counter-rotating low-pressure and high-pressure turbines

TURBINE VANE AND BLADE COOLING

Many modern engines, especially high-pressure turbines that experience extremely high temperatures, use air-cooled stator vanes and rotor blades. Cooling enables the components to operate in a thermal environment 600°F to 800°F above the temperature limits of the alloys used for vane and blade construction. [Figures 3-66 and 3-68]

With cooled blades and vanes, maximum turbine inlet temperature (TIT) of an engine is approximately 3,000°F. With the continual development of newer metals, inlet temperatures have risen over time and will likely continue to do so. One disadvantage of cooling blades and

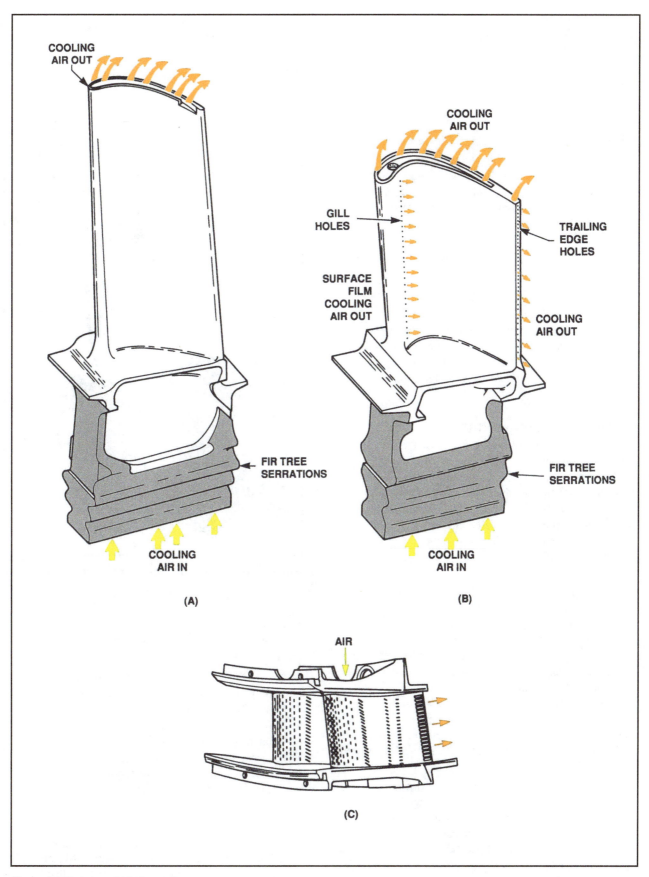

Figure 3-68A. Internal blade cooling
Figure 3-68B. Internal and surface film cooling
Figure 3-68C. Pair of surface film cooled turbine vanes

vanes is that it increases the demand on the compressor, but the consensus is that overall efficiency increases due to the higher turbine inlet temperatures that are possible. The air that is bled off the compressor to cool the blades and vanes slightly decreases engine efficiency, but the higher temperature at the turbine, which translates into higher gas velocity, more than compensates for the loss.

Three cooling methods are commonly used:

- Internal air flow cooling (convection cooling). Air flows through hollow blades and vanes and heat is carried away directly by the cooling air. This is an example of convection cooling. [Figure 3-68A]
- Surface film cooling. Air flows from small exit ports in leading edges, trailing edges, or both, of the vanes or blades to form a heat barrier on the surfaces. [Figure 3-68C]
- A combination of convection and surface cooling. [Figure 3-68B]

Cooling air is extracted from the gas path at the compressor section. After cooling is accomplished, the air is directed back into the gas path at the cooling location. At this point, some air can also cool the shroud seals and shroud rings.

ACTIVE CLEARANCE CONTROL

A method of controlling the clearance between the tips of the turbine blades and the turbine case shroud ring is called active clearance control. The term *active* means that the blade tip clearance is controlled by varying the amount of cooling air in relation to the thermal expansion rate of the turbine outer case. This in turn keeps more energy on the surface of the blade, rather than sacrificing the energy of the gas at the tip due to excessive clearance. [Figure 3-69]

The high-pressure and low-pressure turbine cases on many later model engines, when cooled for clearance control purposes, typically use a manifold that encircles the inner or outer turbine case. The manifold receives its cooling air from the fan or the compressor section. Figure 3-69 shows an air-cooling manifold around the outer portion of the low-pressure turbine case. The manifold consists of a series of tubes, each tube having many small holes drilled on the side that faces the turbine case. When air from the fan or compressor is directed to the manifold, the air blows against the turbine case, controlling its temperature and expansion.

In older engines, the amount of air extracted for cooling is a function of compressor speed and the resulting compressor discharge pressure. In new engine models that are controlled by an electronic engine control (EEC), the EEC continually schedules the cooling air with the following results:

- Compressor load during starting and transient conditions is reduced.

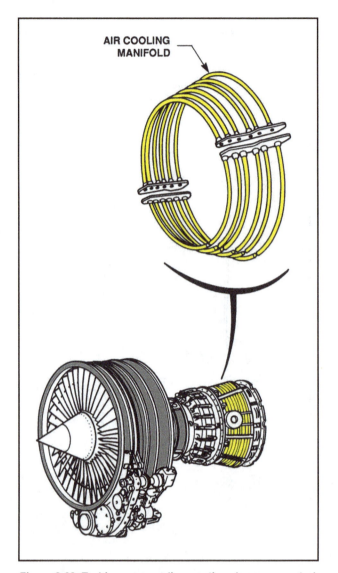

Figure 3-69. Turbine case cooling—active clearance control

- During cruise conditions, the turbine shrouds are cooled to tighter clearances, which maximizes turbine efficiency.

Typical inputs to the EEC that determine the amount of cooling air delivered to the manifolds are:
- N_1 and N_2 rotor speeds.
- Turbine case temperature.
- Total air temperature.
- Ambient air pressure.
- Compressor discharge temperature.
- Compressor inlet temperature.

A concept similar to active clearance control is used in some compressors to control the clearance between the compressor blade tips and the compressor case. This is called tip clearance control and, as with active clearance control, this system is controlled by an EEC that is often part of an engine control system known as full authority digital engine control (FADEC).

Turbine Engine Design and Construction

RADIAL INFLOW TURBINE

Another turbine design is the radial inflow turbine. Like the centrifugal compressor, its advantages are low cost and simplicity of design. Radial inflow turbines are primarily used in auxiliary gas turbine engines. The design derives its name from the fact that gases flow through a stator vane assembly located at the outer radius of the turbine. The gas then flows inward from the tip area and finally exits at the center. This design is used because it extracts up to 100 percent of the kinetic energy from the flowing gases.

The radial inflow turbine has high single-stage turbine efficiency but has poor multistage efficiency. It also has the disadvantage of low axial velocity discharge and short service life under high temperature loads due primarily to the high centrifugal loads on the disk. To date, these problems have not been resolved, making the use of these turbines unsuitable for flight engines. [Figure 3-70]

EXHAUST SECTION

The exhaust section is located directly behind the turbine section and consists in most cases of a convergent exhaust duct, an exhaust cone, and an inner tail cone. The final opening, called the jet nozzle, releases the hot gases to the atmosphere. Other terms for the exhaust duct are exhaust nozzle (including the variable exhaust nozzle and the vectoring exhaust nozzle), and the tailpipe.

EXHAUST CONE, TAIL CONE, AND TAILPIPE

The exhaust cone, sometimes referred to as the turbine exhaust collector, collects the exhaust gases discharged

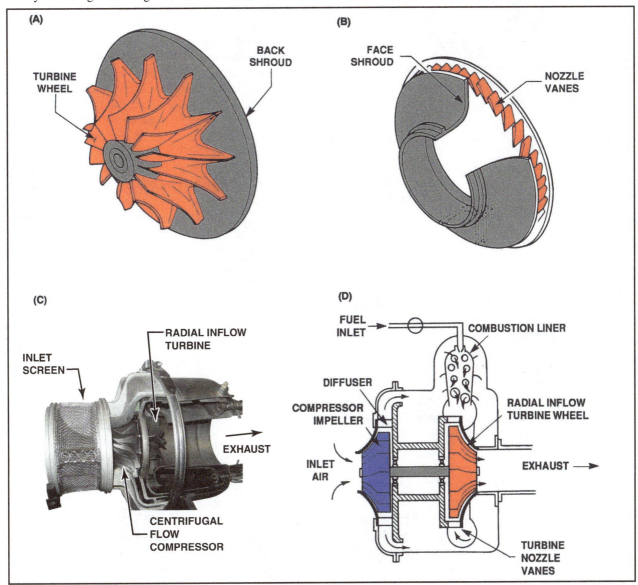

Figure 3-70A. Radial inflow turbine rotor
Figure 3-70B. Radial inflow turbine stator ring
Figure 3-70C. Gas turbine auxiliary power unit with a radial inflow turbine
Figure 3-70D. Turbine rotor location in engine

from the turbine and gradually converts them into a uniform wall of gases. This process is accomplished in conjunction with the tail cone, also called exhaust plug, and its radial support struts. The tail cone forms a diffuser-shaped duct within the exhaust cone, and the resulting pressure buildup reduces turbulence downstream of the turbine wheel. The struts redirect the swirling airflow to an axial direction. [Figure 3-71]

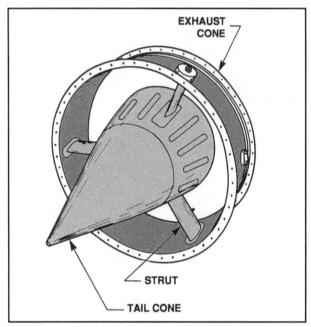

Fig. 3-71 — Exhaust cone, tail cone, and support struts

On some very early gas turbine engines, the tail cone was movable. To increase exhaust velocity and thrust, the tail cone was mechanically moved rearward, which decreased the effective size of the final opening of the exhaust duct (jet nozzle). By matching the airflow with the flow area of the jet, this mechanical arrangement provided a smooth and rapid engine and aircraft acceleration. In later engines, the problems associated with controlling airflow became a function of the fuel system.

In modern engines on subsonic airliners and business jets, the tail cone is fixed within a fixed-area exhaust duct, and smooth and rapid acceleration is accomplished by more-sophisticated fuel scheduling techniques. [Figure 3-72] Variable area exhaust systems that employ movable devices are currently in use, but only on supersonic aircraft.

The tailpipe is a component of the airframe, used to adapt an engine to a particular airplane installation. In most cases, the tailpipe is a convergent duct. It is also referred to as the jet pipe or exhaust duct. Its convergent shape causes the gases to accelerate to the design speed necessary for producing the required thrust. Convergent tailpipes are used on most subsonic aircraft. The shape is generally of fixed geometry—that is, its flow area cannot be changed during engine operation, although some tailpipes are manufactured in both standard and nonstandard sizes and can occasionally be exchanged to regain lagging engine performance.

On some older engines, small tabs (inserts) could be fitted to the tailpipe to change the effective open area of the exhaust nozzle and recover a small amount of lost performance. These tabs are rarely used today.

The convergent-shaped exhaust ducts (as described here) can accelerate the exhaust gases to Mach 1 (the speed of sound) and no faster in terms of Mach number. The exhaust nozzle opening, being an orifice, forces the gas molecules to pile up as the mass airflow throughout the engine increases with airspeed. At Mach 1, the gas flow is said to be choked at the exhaust nozzle opening to the atmosphere.

CONVERGENT "CHOKED" NOZZLE THEORY

When gas initially flows down a convergent duct, the shape accelerates the gas. As more and more airmass flows downstream, the shape of the duct starts to constrict the flow. At the point of Mach 1 airflow, the walls of the duct constrict the flow with a force equal to the air's axial flow force. The flow, therefore, stabilizes at Mach 1.

The choked nozzle condition of exhaust ducts is further explained by using the Pt/Ps formula from Appendix 8, Formula 16.

When P_t/P_s is calculated with M = 1.0, a minimum exhaust duct to ambient pressure ratio of 1.89 is required to achieve a choked condition. P_t is the exhaust duct entrance pressure, which drops to pressure ambient (equal to P_s) at the exhaust nozzle.

$$\frac{P_t}{P_s} = \left[1 + \left(\frac{\gamma-1}{2} \times M^2\right)\right]^{\frac{\gamma}{\gamma-1}}$$

Where:

γ(gamma) = 1.4 (specific heat)

M = Mach number

γ, 1, 2 = Constants

In terms of engine power during ground runup, if (P_t) represents turbine discharge pressure and (P_s) represents compressor inlet pressure, when the engine pressure ratio (EPR) gauge in the cockpit reads above 1.89, the exhaust nozzle is choked.

When the gas exits a choked orifice, it accelerates radially (spreads out) faster than it accelerates axially, the axial velocity being fixed at Mach 1. If more fuel is added after Mach 1 gas velocity is reached, engine speed, compression, and mass airflow increases, and pressure (pile-up) in the tailpipe also increases.

The additional exhaust nozzle pressure provides a small increase in thrust, as described in the Chapter 2 thrust formula for choked exhaust nozzles, but this condition would result in excess fuel consumption. Also, tem-

Turbine Engine Design and Construction

peratures within the engine would elevate significantly. When supersonic exhaust nozzle velocities are needed for supersonic flight, a convergent-divergent nozzle is required rather than a simple convergent jet nozzle.

To understand why velocity (kinetic energy) from a convergent duct cannot exceed Mach 1, bear in mind what Bernoulli's principle states about subsonic flow through a convergent duct. That is, when velocity is less than Mach 1, the potential energy (static pressure) is greater than the kinetic energy (ram pressure), and, therefore, velocity is forced to increase because of the squeezing-down action created by the shape of the duct.

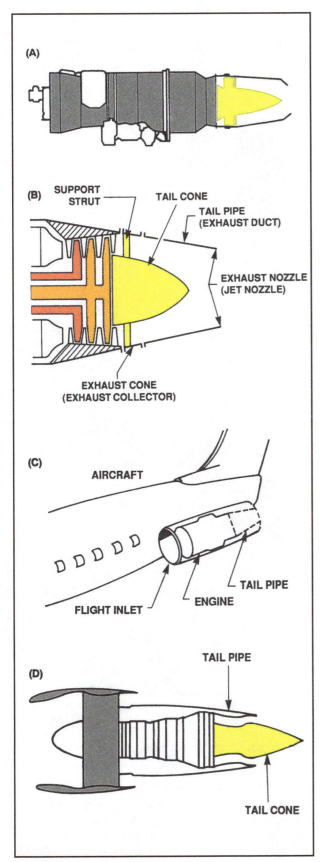

Figure 3-72A. Location of exhaust section
Figure 3-72B. Conventional convergent exhaust duct
Figure 3-72C. Tailpipe for small and medium engines
Figure 3-72D. Tailpipe for large engines

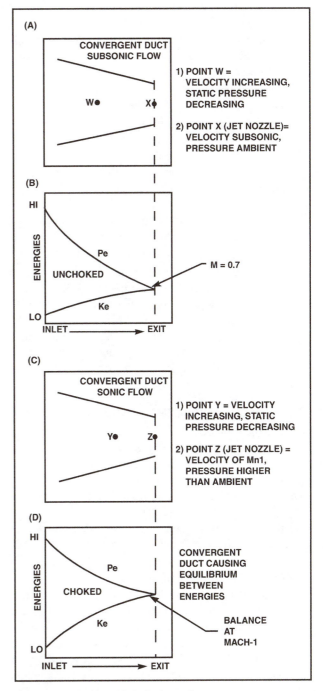

Figure 3-73. Theory of choked nozzles

As shown in Figure 3-73A, as air at subsonic speed flows through a convergent duct, the velocity at point W increases and reaches its maximum at point X. This occurs because the air molecules of potential energy, which were formally pushing outward perpendicular to the direction of flow, are now moving in the direction of flow and being converted to kinetic energy. The velocity at the jet nozzle is still subsonic, and the pressure at the nozzle is ambient.

In Figure 3-73B, gas enters the duct at high potential energy (Pe) and low kinetic energy (Ke). As the gas approaches the nozzle, kinetic energy increases as potential energy decreases. In the example, gas flow is still subsonic with a flow rate of Mach 0.7.

In Figure 3-73C, the velocity at point Y is subsonic and is increasing to its maximum at point Z. In this case, the velocity at point Z has reached Mach 1 and cannot go any faster. Any additional energy added to this duct will not increase the velocity of the air, but rather will exit the jet nozzle as a pressure higher than ambient.

Figure 3-73D shows that when the kinetic energy of the gas molecules reaches the speed of sound, Mach 1, the potential energy in the gas and the kinetic energy in the gas are in equilibrium. That is, airflow through a convergent duct, trying to move ever faster, will seek a point of balance. This occurs when the squeezing-in action on airflow caused by the shape of the duct is counterbalanced by the pushing out action of potential energy.

In practice, the nozzle will choke, in accordance with Formula 16 in Appendix 8, at an inlet to outlet pressure ratio of 1.89. An interesting note concerning choked nozzle flow is that nozzle flow Mach numbers can be less than the aircraft Mach number. This is because Mach number is influenced by the temperature of the gas. At higher temperatures, a greater velocity is required to equal Mach 1.

CONVERGENT-DIVERGENT EXHAUST DUCTS FOR SUBSONIC AIRCRAFT

Some subsonic aircraft now use convergent-divergent nozzles. These convergent-divergent nozzles are of fixed geometry with a slight increase in final opening size. They are designed to maximize cruise thrust and reduce engine noise. These convergent-divergent nozzles take the form of exhaust mixers, which are described in the noise suppression topic later in this chapter. [Figure 3-88]

DIVERGENT EXHAUST NOZZLES

The rotorcraft exhaust duct is normally divergent in shape, rather than convergent. This shape nullifies the small amount of thrust available in order to enhance the hover capabilities. [Figure 3-74A] Another design for helicopter exhaust contains a fluted or scalloped outer perimeter that is used for enhanced noise suppression. [Figure 3-74B]

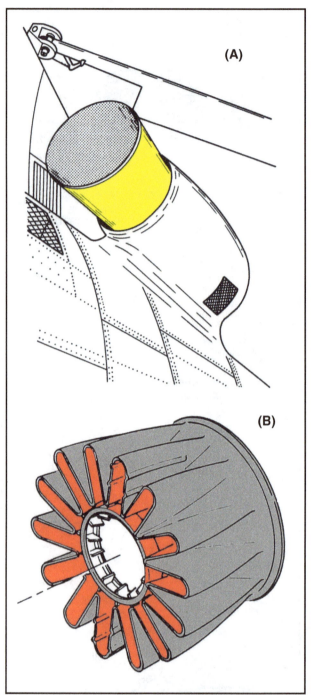

Figure 3-74A. Rotorcraft exhaust duct installation
Figure 3-74B. Noise suppressing mixer exhaust duct

CONVERGENT-DIVERGENT NOZZLE THEORY FOR SUPERSONIC AIRCRAFT

Supersonic aircraft use the variable geometry convergent-divergent exhaust duct. The advantage of the convergent-divergent duct is greatest at high Mach numbers because of the high pressure ratio available across the tailpipe. That is, high supersonic inlet ram pressure results in high exhaust duct pressure.

To ensure that a constant weight of a gas will flow past any given point after sonic velocity is reached, the rear portion of the duct is enlarged. Doing so in turn increases gas velocity after it emerges from the throat area to become supersonic.

Gas traveling at supersonic speeds expands outward faster than it accelerates rearward. This is because, as the gas is compressed axially, it releases its energy radially. [Figure 3-75A] The convergent-divergent duct uses this principle to create the thrust necessary to propel the aircraft at supersonic speeds.

The forward convergent section causes pressure to build as the throat area chokes, creating a backpressure. The aft divergent section permits velocity to increase to the desired Mach number, depending on the force being applied by combustion. If shaped properly, the convergent-divergent duct effectively controls gas expansion, captures the released energy, and produces the required thrust for limited supersonic flight. [Figure 3-75B] To achieve higher supersonic flight speeds, the exhaust duct must be enhanced by a separate fuel and ignition system referred to as an afterburner. [Figure 3-76]

In a convergent-divergent exhaust system, several events take place when the pressure ratio exceeds 1.89:1. In the converging section:

- The air stream lines converge.
- The density of the air increases at the throat.
- The velocity of the air stabilizes at Mach 1.
- The pressure at the throat is higher than ambient.

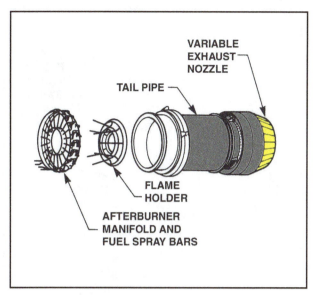

Figure 3-76. Afterburner assembly

In the diverging section:

- The density of the air decreases.
- The velocity increases to supersonic speed.
- The pressure decreases, reaching ambient at the nozzle opening.

The modern supersonic aircraft exhaust duct is shaped so that the rearmost section has a slight divergence in normal, non-afterburner mode. In this mode, many supersonic aircraft are capable of supersonic flight speeds. When afterburner mode is selected, the mechanism is designed so that the divergence of the exhaust nozzle increases to handle (properly accelerate) the new mass airflow created by afterburner fuel flow. In other words, the divergent section functions as a variable area exhaust nozzle. In non-afterburner mode, the exhaust nozzle area is smallest, but when afterburner mode is selected, the nozzle is scheduled to a more open position.

The addition of afterburner fuel—and the expansion of gases that occurs when it combusts—causes outward pressure on the walls of the afterburner rear duct, and the forces are vectored forward by the diverging shape. Research indicates that fully expanded supersonic flow results in the best thrust augmentation. That is, pressure across the exhaust duct returns to ambient value. In this case, no thrust due to pressure is available at the exhaust nozzle, but an increase in thrust still occurs because exhaust velocity increases above Mach 1 in proportion to the fuel energy supplied. [Figure 3-77]

Supersonic flow causes the familiar shock wave phenomena to occur, but a properly designed afterburner results in no shock distortion to airflow within the duct, only shock rings, which are visible in the jet exhaust stream. [Figure 3-78]

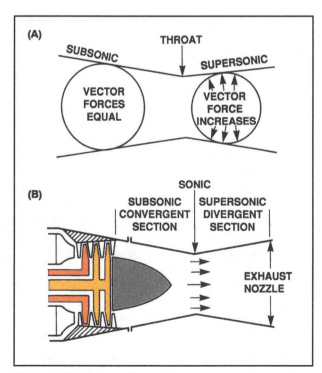

Figure 3-75A. Energy released in a convergent-divergent duct

Figure 3-75B. Gas flow in a convergent-divergent tailpipe

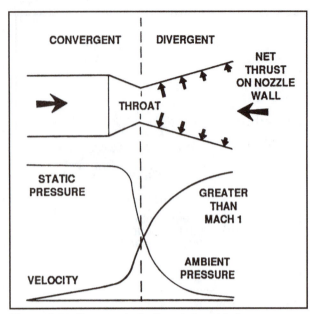

Figure 3-77. Pressure/velocity relationship in a convergent-divergent tailpipe

Figure 3-78. Afterburner operation showing shock rings in exhaust

AFTERBURNING

Afterburning is used primarily for takeoff with heavy aircraft loading, for rapid climb-out speeds, and for higher supersonic flight speeds. Afterburning provides the maximum exhaust velocity and maximum engine thrust for a given engine frontal area, but requires additional fuel. The addition of an afterburner type exhaust duct to a gas turbine engine is made possible by the fact that the products of combustion in the tailpipe contain a large quantity of unburned oxygen. The portion of compressor discharge air used for combustor cooling mixes with combusted air at the turbine and then flows downstream to the exhaust system. A set of afterburner fuel nozzles, called spray bars, along with an ignition system are fitted to the entrance of the exhaust duct. When afterburner fuel and unburned oxygen mix and ignite, additional propulsive power is created as the gases are further accelerated by the increased heat energy in the form of a large volume of burning fuel.

Along with fuel and ignition components, another device, called a flameholder, is required for good combustion. [Figure 3-76] A flameholder is a tubular grid or spoke-shaped obstruction placed downstream of the fuel nozzles. As gases impinge on the flameholder, it creates turbulence, which enhances fuel-air mixing. This promotes complete and stable combustion in a rapidly moving airstream.

In effect, the afterburner is a form of ramjet attached to the rear of a gas turbine engine. The only types of gas turbines, however, that utilize afterburning are the turbojet and the turbofans with mixed exhausts—that is, turbofans in which the fan and core engine gases premix and exit from one exhaust nozzle.

Older afterburners were two-position types. They formed a convergent nozzle in non-afterburning mode and a convergent-divergent nozzle when open in afterburning mode. In newer aircraft, the afterburner nozzle is convergent-divergent shaped in both modes, changing both the throat flow area and the final nozzle size to their largest area and flow angles in full afterburner mode. Electronic sensors match the flow area to the mass flow in afterburners of this type. Constant monitoring helps to counteract the low thermal efficiency (high fuel flow), which is typical of engines operating in afterburner mode.

Aircraft fitted with afterburners can gain as much as 100 percent additional thrust in afterburning mode, with fuel flows increasing three to five times. However, some modern aircraft with powerful engines require only limited thrust augmentation in the 15- to 20-percent range. In these aircraft, the convergent-divergent tailpipe is often referred to as a thrust augmenter rather than an afterburner.

An interesting aspect of afterburner thrust is that even a small boost to takeoff (gross) thrust can still bring about a significant boost to net thrust in flight. When an aircraft is operating in afterburner mode on the ground, gross thrust and net thrust are the same. If, at that time, the afterburner boosts gross thrust by 25 percent, in flight the same afterburner contribution to net thrust would be much greater—as much as 100 percent. This occurs because ram drag, which affects engine thrust, has no effect on afterburner thrust. In other words, ram drag is the same regardless of whether the engine is in afterburner mode. RAM drag is defined as aircraft speed times mass airflow, and net thrust is defined as gross thrust minus RAM drag.

The following are examples of thrust for an aircraft operating on the ground versus its performance in flight:

- Gross (static) thrust without afterburner = 16,000 pounds
- Gross (static) thrust with afterburner = 20,000 pounds (an increase of 4,000 pounds, or 25 percent)
- Net (in flight) thrust without afterburner = 4,000 pounds
- Net (in flight) thrust with afterburner = 8,000 pounds (an increase of 4,000 pounds, or 100 percent)

VECTORING AFTERBURNER EXHAUST NOZZLES

A variety of military aircraft use vectoring exhaust nozzles. These nozzles change the direction the flowing exhaust gases up or down at the command of the pilot to enhance takeoff performance as well as low-speed flight maneuverability of the aircraft. Vectoring nozzles can also reverse the flow of exhaust gases throughout the flight envelope, including approach, and aid in braking during landing. [Figure 3-79A]

When the nozzle is placed in the up position, it pushes the nose of the aircraft up quickly for short field takeoff or for low-speed maneuvering. When the nozzle is pointed down, the nose of the aircraft moves down in forward flight without changing altitude. This capability is not possible with conventional fighter aircraft. Only V-STOL aircraft, such as the Lockheed Martin F-35 fighter aircraft fitted with lift-fan engines, have this capability.

VARIABLE AREA EXHAUST NOZZLES FOR SUBSONIC AIRCRAFT ENGINES

Variable area exhaust nozzles are used with some subsonic airplanes. These units, such as the unit shown in Figure 3-79B, also contain a thrust reverser system. This type of exhaust nozzle operates in a manner similar to the vectoring exhaust nozzle used on the afterburners of supersonic airplanes. The unit shown can change the flow area of the exhaust throat by up to 15 percent to optimize a small turbofan engine's hot exhaust flow and performance during takeoff, climb, and cruise operation.

THRUST REVERSERS

Airliners powered by turbojets and turbofans, most commuter aircraft, and an increasing number of business jets are equipped with engine thrust reversers to:

- Aid in braking and directional control during normal landing.
- Reduce brake system maintenance.
- Provide braking and directional control during emergency landings and rejected takeoffs.
- Increase the aircraft's rate of descent by acting as speed brakes.
- Back an aircraft out of a parking spot in what is called a power back operation.

The two types of thrust reversers in common use today are the aerodynamic blockage (sometimes referred to as cascade or egg crate reversers) and the mechanical blockage (often referred to as clamshell or target reversers). Both types of reversers are commonly operated by a pneumatic actuating system powered by compressor discharge pressure. Other types are operated by hydraulic actuators. [Figures 3-80, 3-81, and 3-82]

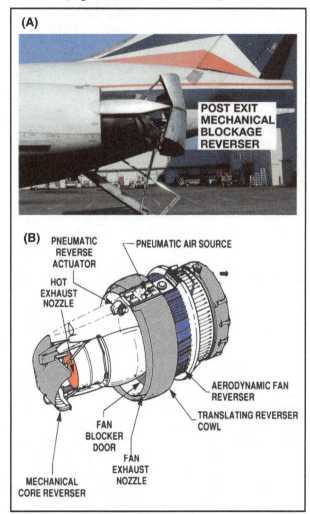

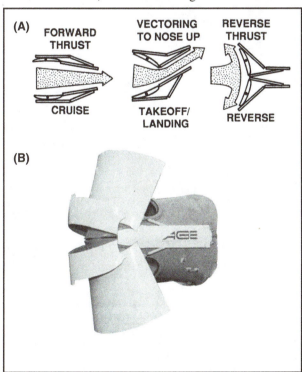

Figure 3-79A. Vectoring afterburner exhaust nozzle
Figure 3-79B. Variable area, reversing exhaust nozzle

Figure 3-80A. McDonnell Douglas MD-83 with post-exit mechanical blockage reverser deployed
Figure 3-80B. View of post-exit mechanical blockage type reverser deployed (also deployed are the fan blocker doors and aerodynamic blockage reverser)

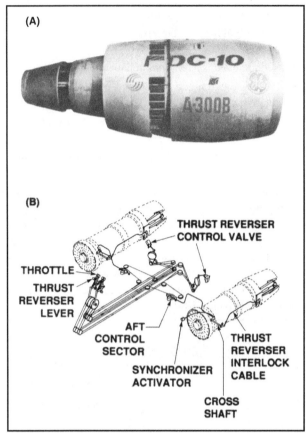

Figure 3-81A. DC-10 during landing, showing aerodynamic blockage fan and exhaust reverser in the deployed position

Figure 3-81B. Throttle and thrust reverse control system

assist in stopping the aircraft. The normal way to operate this system is to apply reverse as soon as the aircraft is firmly on the runway, and then to apply as much reverse power as necessary for existing conditions such as water, ice, and so on. When the aircraft slows to approximately 80 knots, power is reduced back to reverse-idle and then to forward thrust as soon as practical. [Figure 3-83A]

Operating in reverse thrust at low ground speeds can cause reingestion of hot gases and compressor stalls. It can also cause ingestion of fine sand and other runway debris that can abrade gas path components and even make its way through main bearing air-oil seals into oil sumps. The normal operating procedure for thrust reverse is to select reverse after touchdown at ground idle speed and reapply power to approximately 75 percent N_2 speed (100 percent in emergencies).

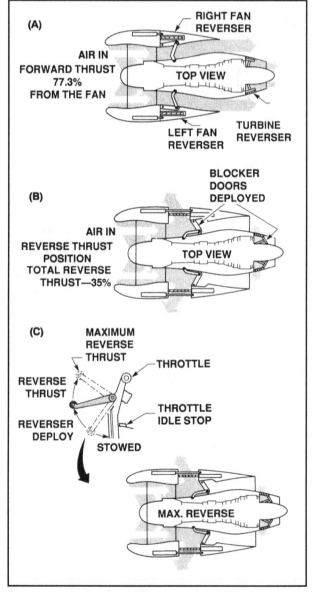

Figure 3-82A. Aerodynamic reverser stowed
Figure 3-82B. Reverser deployed
Figure 3-82C. Cockpit control lever

The aerodynamic blockage reverser consists of a set of cascade turning vanes in a pre-exit position in either the fan exhaust or hot exhaust. The vanes turn the escaping gases to a forward direction, which in turn causes a rearward thrust.

The mechanical blockage reverser can be placed in either a pre-exit or post-exit position. This type of reverser, when deployed, forms a solid blocking door in the jet exhaust path.

In reverse, exhaust gases hit the clamshell, or turning vanes, and are angled forward enough to provide reverse thrust but not enough to permit gas to be reingested into the engine inlet. Thrust reversers are controlled by a cockpit lever at the command of the pilot. After thrust reverse is selected, the pilot can move the reverse-throttle lever from idle select-position up to takeoff position, as required by landing conditions. Thrust reversers provide approximately 20 percent of the braking force under normal runway conditions. Reversers are capable of producing between 35 and 50 percent of rated thrust in the reverse direction. [Figure. 3- 82]

Reversers are especially helpful when landing on wet or icy runways and provide approximately 50 percent

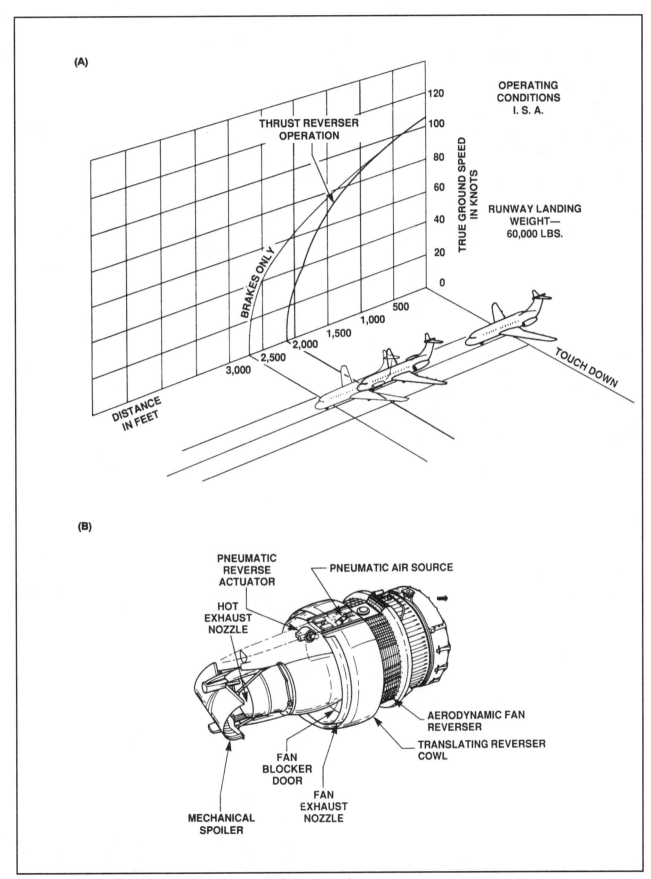

Figure 3-83A. Typical landing runs with and without thrust reversal
Figure 3-83B. High-bypass turbofan engine with unmixed exhaust, aerodynamic fan reverser and hot stream spoiler

Thrust reverse can be explained by recalling the thrust distribution example in Chapter 2, in the discussion regarding thrust distribution at the tailpipe. In that example, the jet nozzle had −681.6 pounds of thrust with a rearward velocity of 1,900 feet per second. If the velocity direction (vector) is changed to an angle in the forward direction, this velocity component changes from a positive to a negative value. Because the angle is not straight forward, for reasons already explained, the resultant velocity vector will drop to approximately 60 percent of its former value. [Figure 3-84]

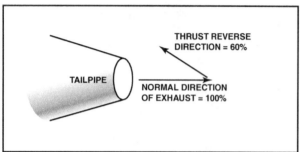

Figure 3-84. Vector example

The example engine from the thrust distribution problem in Chapter 2 had 30 pounds of mass airflow (Ms), an exhaust velocity of 1,900 feet per second (V), and a choked nozzle, which created an extra 525 pounds of thrust. The engine's total thrust was 2,295.2 pounds. The thrust distribution for the engine was as follows:

Compressor   3,673.0 pounds of thrust
Combustor   5,631.0 pounds of thrust
Exhaust Cone   542.5 pounds of thrust
                    9,846.5 pounds of thrust

Turbine   − 6,869.7 pounds of thrust
Jet Nozzle   −   681.6 pounds of thrust
                   − 7,551.3 pounds of thrust

After subtracting the negative thrust from the positive thrust, the total forward thrust equals 2,295.2 pounds.

Given that the jet nozzle of the engine is not choked when the engine is in reverse thrust, and with the exhaust velocity at 60 percent of its normal value, the jet nozzle thrust shown above would change as follows:

$$Fg = \frac{Ms \times V}{g} - i$$

$$Fg = \frac{30(-1{,}140)}{32.2} - 2{,}976.8$$

$$Fg = -1{,}062 - 2{,}976.8$$

$$Fg = -4{,}038.8 \text{ lbs.}$$

Where:

Ms = 30 lbs/sec

V = −1,140 ft/sec (60% of 1,900)

i = 2,976.8 lbs. (value at exhaust cone)

g = 32.2 ft/sec^2

By substituting the jet nozzle thrust when the engine is in reverse (−4,038.8) for the value that existed when the engine was in forward thrust (−681.3), the totals are:

Total Positive Thrust = 9,846.5 pounds

Total Negative Thrust = −10,898.5 pounds

The difference, −1,052 pounds, is the amount of thrust in reverse, which is 45.8 percent of the normal forward thrust.

OTHER ASPECTS OF THRUST BRAKING SYSTEMS

Mixed exhaust turbofans are configured with one reverser; unmixed exhaust turbofans often have both cold stream and hot stream reversers. Some high-bypass turbofans use only cold stream reversing, when most of the thrust is present in the fan discharge. In these installations, a hot end reverser would be of minimal value and add undesirable weight.

Another system similar to thrust reverse is a thrust spoiler. It looks similar to a clamshell hot stream reverser, but uses blocker panels to direct the gases out radially rather than turning them forward. The spoiler system is used when reversal of the hot jet nozzle gas would interfere with the aerodynamics of the fan section or cause hot gas reingestion into the flight inlet. [Figure 3-83B]

Some turboprop aircraft have a form of thrust reversing, namely, a full reversing propeller. This system, as well as turbofan reversers, work so well that they can be used to back aircraft into parking spots.

Backing an aircraft by way of thrust reversal is referred to as power back operation and is used with great caution due to the possibility of foreign object ingestion. Power back operation also incurs a fuel cost, which sometimes makes it more expensive than using the conventional tractor for a conventional push-back.

Another braking system, widely used by the military, is the drag chute. After the aircraft lands, a fabric canopy similar to a parachute deploys from a container in the tail section of the aircraft to produce a braking action. The chute is later released and recovered by ground personnel. Some fast-landing business jets have been configured with this system as standard or emergency braking to be used in conjunction with thrust reversers.

NOISE SUPPRESSION

The sound level of the average business jet or airliner during takeoff is in the range of 90 to 100 decibels (dB). This noise level is similar to that of a subway train as heard from the boarding platform. At close range to the aircraft, the noise level can be as high as 160 dB, which is painful to the ears without ear protection. [Figure 3-85]

Turbine Engine Design and Construction

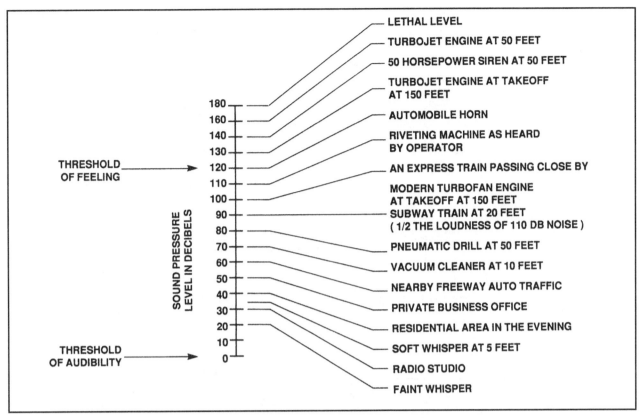

Figure 3-85. Noise levels in decibels

Even the lower level of noise (90 to 100 effective perceived noise dB) is considered by many to be excessive and harmful. The aircraft industry has continually improved noise reduction techniques on each new generation of engine and aircraft to satisfy demand for more effective noise abatement.

Effective perceived noise decibels (EPNdB) is a standard measure of the loudness (sound pressure) of sound, combined with its frequency and duration, and is used specifically to express aircraft noises in the atmosphere. EPNdB can also be an estimated value where atmospheric absorption prevents completely accurate measurement, such as an aircraft flying overhead where factors such as wind, temperature, and moisture might affect accuracy.

Part 36 of the Code of Federal Regulations (Title 14) regulates noise standards for aircraft type certification. The standards have evolved over time and are now much stricter than they used to be. Boeing 727 airplanes, for example, were certified under what was known as Stage 2 standards, as were the original Boeing 737-100 and 200 and Douglas Corporation DC-9. As time passed, and the McDonnell Douglas MD-80 series airplane was being certified, Stage 3 standards were in effect, and the MD-80 had to meet stricter standards. Aircraft certified after January 2006 must meet Stage 4 noise limits, which require aircraft to be even quieter.

When the Stage 3 limits went into effect, airplanes such as the B-727 and the DC-9 were not quiet enough, so noise suppression kits (often called hush kits) were developed for those airplanes. With Stage 4 limits now in effect, MD-80 series aircraft are no longer quiet enough and hush kits are being developed for those as well.

Figure 3-86A shows the profiles that the FAA uses to measure noise levels in reference to aircraft taking off, landing, and sideline noise. Because of the location of the microphones used to measure takeoff noise, it is evident that an aircraft that climbs out more steeply could be sensed as being quieter. Figure 3-86B shows how a few example aircraft compare in reference to the Stage 3 noise limits. The Airbus A300, for example, has a noise level of 91 EPNdB on takeoff and 101 EPNdB on approach. The measured noise and the noise limit are higher on approach because of the relatively shallow angle of the aircraft compared to the steep angle typical of climbout. Under Stage 4 noise limits, the sum of takeoff, approach, and sideline noise must be at least 10 Db lower than the limits imposed by Stage 3. Thus, if a new airplane were 3 dB below the limit at takeoff, 3 dB below the limit on approach, and 4 dB below the limit for sideline noise, the three values add up to 10 and the airplane would be Stage 4 compliant.

Noise suppression units are not generally required on new business jets or airliners today, but 14 CFR Part 36 requires their use on many older commercial jet aircraft. Newer aircraft have inlets and exhaust ducts lined with noise attenuating materials to keep sound emission within

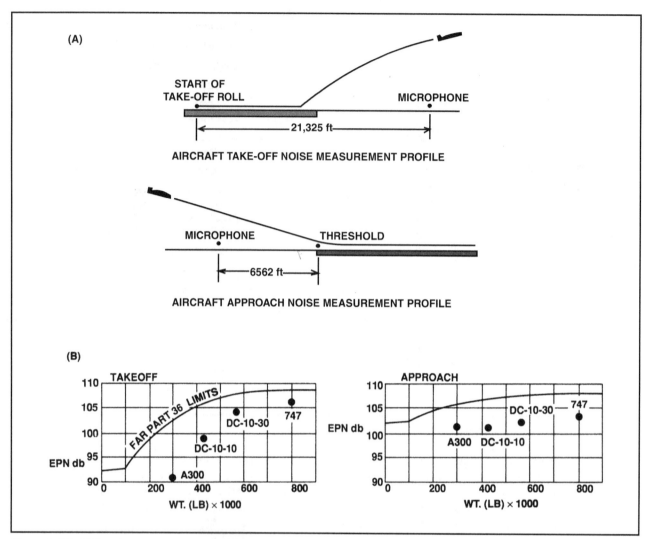

Figure 3-86A. FAA noise measurement profiles
Figure 3-86B. Typical takeoff and landing noise emission limits; approach limits are higher due to low approach altitudes

the established EPNdB. [Figure 3-87] These noise-absorbing materials function by converting acoustic energy (air pressure) into heat energy as the molecules are forced to increase in velocity by the shape of the matrix in the structure of the noise-attenuating materials.

The noise generated as the exhaust gases leave the engine is at a low-frequency level such as that from a ship's fog horn. This low-frequency noise, which carries for long distances, tends to be most bothersome to people who live close to airports.

The noise generated by a turbofan engine is much less than that generated by a turbojet. This is principally because turbofans typically employ more turbine wheels to drive the compressor and the fan. This, in turn, lowers the hot exhaust velocity and noise level.

Because low-frequency noise tends to linger at relatively high volume, one way to reduce noise is to raise its frequency. Frequency change is accomplished by increasing the perimeter of the exhaust stream, which provides more mixing space for cold and hot air. The larger space reduces the tendency of hot and cold air molecules to shear against each other; it also breaks up the large turbulence in the jet wake, which produces the low-frequency noise. [Figure 3-88A and 3-88B]

In other words, reducing large eddy turbulence to fine grain turbulence changes the frequency of noise to a higher state that is more readily absorbed by the atmosphere. The noise is then reduced for any given distance from the noise source and the effective perceived noise reading on a decibel meter is lower.

The noise suppressor shown in Figure 3-89 is an old style, hot-stream noise suppressor on a turbojet-powered aircraft, called an increased perimeter or a multi-lobed design. This suppressor, although not a current design, is still used by private owners and by unscheduled overseas cargo haulers in other parts of the world.

Most modern, fully ducted turbofan engines are designed with what is termed exhaust mixing, which blends the fan and hot airstreams more effectively and lowers the sound emission coming from a common

Turbine Engine Design and Construction

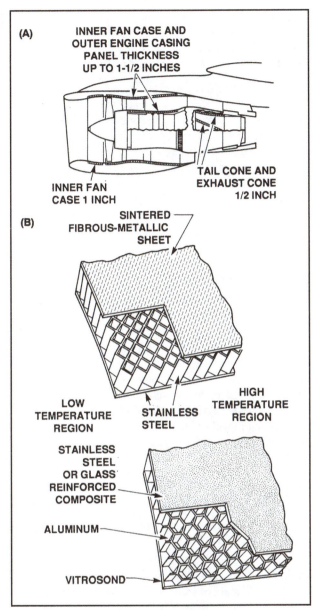

Figure 3-87A. Location of noise suppression materials
Figure 3-87B. Noise suppression materials convert acoustic energy (pressure) to friction heat energy

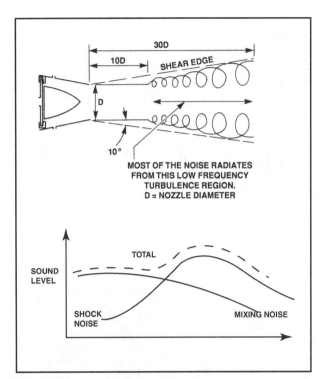

Figure 3-88A. Hot exhaust noise pattern
Figure 3-88B. Total sound versus frequencies

Figure 3-89. Older style multilobed noise suppressor

exhaust duct. [Figure 3-90] On these engines, the sound from the inlet is likely to be louder than from the tailpipe. This is also the case today with the high-bypass fan engines, which draw so much energy from the hot gases to drive the fan, compressor, and accessories that the fan emits the greatest noise.

As stated previously, some older Boeing 707 and Douglas DC-8 aircraft with turbojet powerplants had noise suppressors similar to the one shown in Figure 3-89. To meet new Stage 3 noise limits, airplanes like the Boeing 727 and 737-200 have hush kits installed similar to those shown in Figure 3-91A and 3-91B.

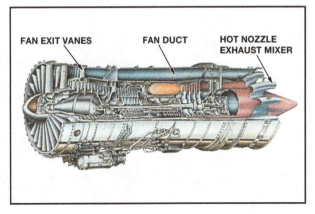

Figure 3-90. Pratt & Whitney JT8D-200-series engine with exhaust mixer

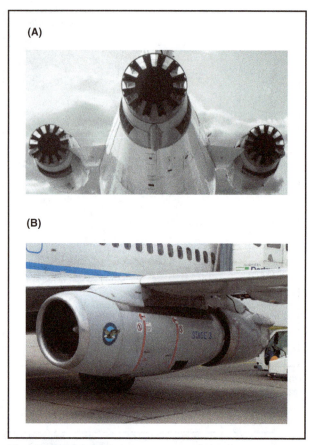

Figure 3-91A. Stage 3 noise suppressor (hush kit) for Boeing 727
Figure 3-91B. Stage 3 noise suppressor (hush kit) for Boeing 737

ENGINE COMPARTMENT VENTILATION AND COOLING

Engine nacelle ventilation and cooling is required because of the high heat radiation through engine outer cases and the presence of fuel, oil, and electrical systems located on, or adjacent to, the outer cases. Air is changed in these locations five or more times per minute. Cooling air comes either from ram air or from fan air discharge. Figure 3-92 shows the cooling arrangement for a turbojet engine nacelle that uses only ram air to ventilate and cool. Other engines, such as turbofans, instead use fan air discharge to cool the nacelle; still others use a mixture of fan air discharge and ram air for cooling.

Figure 3-93 shows typical temperature values along the length of a dual-spool engine with a peak temperature load at the turbine area. The figure also shows the two compartments to be cooled. The cold section is cooled and ventilated by ram air and is separated from the hot section by a fireproof seal. The hot section is also cooled by ram air but in higher quantity than the cold section. The fire seal prevents the high heat in the hot section from moving forward into the cold section, which contains all or most of the volatile fluid, lines, and electrical wiring.

ENGINE MOUNTS

Engine mounts for gas turbine engines are of relatively simple construction, as shown in Figure 3-94. Engine mounts attach to structures that transmit engine thrust to the airframe. Except for the turboprop, gas turbine engines produce little torque, and their mounts do not need to be of heavy construction. The mounts do, however, support the engine weight and transfer the stresses created by the engine into the aircraft structure. Because of induced propeller loads, the turboprop develops higher torque loads; therefore, the mountings are proportionately heavier.

BEARINGS

Bearings are an important construction and design feature of any gas turbine engine, and are discussed in detail in Chapter 5.

CONSTRUCTION MATERIALS

The cold and hot sections of the engine require the use of state-of-the-art materials and advanced manufacturing techniques because both cold and hot engine sections house large components and highly stressed rotating assemblies constructed of lightweight materials.

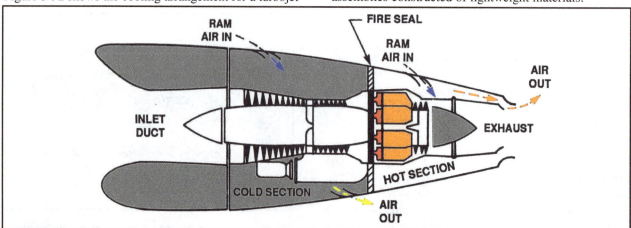

Figure 3-92. Engine compartment cooling and ventilation

Turbine Engine Design and Construction

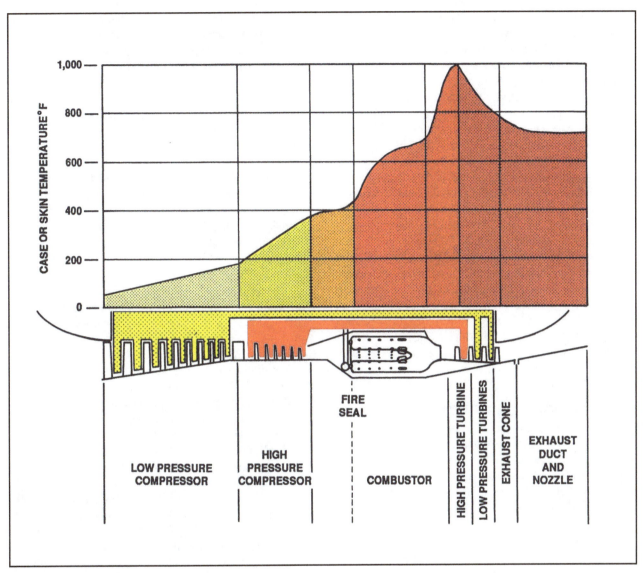

Figure 3-93. Typical outer case temperatures

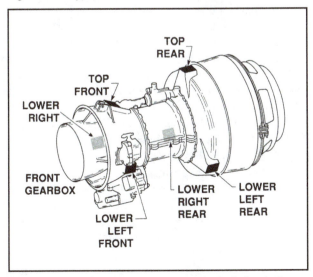

Figure 3-94. Engine mount arrangement of a turboshaft engine

COLD SECTION CONSTRUCTION

Many types of lightweight alloys and composite materials are needed in the cold section to minimize engine weight, yet they must be strong enough to provide sufficient strength to protect against distortion, wear, or failure. Aluminum and magnesium alloys are extensively used for compressor cases, inlet cases, and accessory cases where low heat and moderate strength is the primary consideration. These materials are approximately 60 to 70 percent lighter than steel.

Titanium alloys, though relatively expensive, are used for fan cases, fan blades, compressor blades, compressor disks, and centrifugal impellers where lower weight rather than high temperature steel strength is required. Although not as resistant to foreign object damage as steel, titanium has the strength of some steels of moderate to high quality but only half the weight.

Titanium is used in turbine engines because of its low density, high specific strength, and corrosion resistance. Although these are significant benefits, titanium has some unique properties that make it unsuited for some applications within turbine engines. Two properties in particular combine to make titanium vulnerable to combustion: unlike most other structural metals, titanium ignites at a lower temperature than its melting point, and it has a lower conductivity of heat. Because heat is not as readily conducted away from its source, titanium can more rapidly reach its ignition temperature. Hard rubs are the most common source of heat buildup. They can result from foreign object damage, stall damage, bearing failure, rotor imbalance, and case deflection. During a rub, the low thermal conductivity of a titanium component can rapidly rise to the ignition temperature.

In the compressor high-pressure stages, nickel-chromium alloys, referred to as stainless steels, and nickel-base alloys are often used. Nickel-base alloys are also very expensive and are primarily used in the hot section.

Epoxy-resin materials, called composite materials, have been developed for cold section construction of cases and shroud rings where lower strength is permissible and light weight is the primary consideration. This family of materials is presently undergoing major development for use in the construction of primary airfoils, such as fan blades.

HOT SECTION CONSTRUCTION

For hot sections, a variety of high strength-to-weight materials have been developed. These alloys, often referred to as super alloys, have a maximum temperature limit of 2000°F when uncooled and 2600°F when cooled internally. Super alloys were developed for use in high temperature areas where oxidation resistance is needed and where high thermal, tensile, and vibratory stresses render other materials unsuitable.

Super alloys are complex mixtures of many metals, metallic elements, and alloys such as nickel, chromium, cobalt, titanium, tungsten, and carbon. General agreement on precise mixtures by manufacturers of turbine parts is still the subject of debate. One reason for this is that the strength properties these metals ultimately have depend on the mixture. Generally speaking, the stronger the metal, the more difficult and expensive it is to form and machine into the intricate shapes necessary for turbine engine parts.

In addition to their high initial expense, components made from exotic materials and processes are expensive to replace. For example, a single replacement turbine blade for smaller engines can cost in the range of hundreds of dollars and for largest engines in the range of 10 to 20 thousand dollars. Costs depend largely on blade size, wear resistance, and the blade's ability to resist the stresses of thermal loading and centrifugal loading. [Figure 3-95]

Many manufacturing processes are utilized in the production of hot section parts. Forging, casting, plating, electrochemical machining (ECM), and electrical discharge machining (EDM) are the traditional methods.

Newer procedures include powder metallurgy, single-crystal casting, and plasma spraying.

Powder metallurgy is a forging process in which powdered super metal is hot-pressed into a solid state. This process results in a very high density material of high temperature strength. These metals have long slender crystals with axial grain boundaries, but few traverse grain boundaries, and are highly resistant to creep, the permanent elongation of parts operating under rotating loads and high thermal environments.

Another process that produces even stronger materials than those possible with the powder metallurgy process is single-crystal casting in which only one grain of material forms in the mold rather than millions of grains bound together, as is the case with traditional casting. With only one grain and no grain boundaries, corrosion due to expansion is all but eliminated.

Ceramic and aluminum alloy thermal barrier coating of super alloy parts and some titanium parts are additional processes that provide high surface strength and resistance to corrosion. These coatings are generally referred to as plasma sprays or coatings. When applied under high heat, the coatings melt into the surface of the base metal. Plasma coatings represent the best procedures for protection against the scaling corrosion or erosion that occurs at high gas temperatures. Scaling is a condition caused by the chemical reaction of sodium (salt) in the air and sulfur in the fuel with the base metals.

Each alloy, in conjunction with the process involved in forming it, usually determines its strength and workability. In some cases, the combustion liner is constructed of material as thin as 0.040 inch and must be easily weldable. For this reason, nickel-base alloys are generally used today rather than the stainless steel alloys of a few years ago. Nickel-base alloys contain little or no iron, are noncorrosive, and can be worked in thin weldable sheets.

Combustion liners sometimes experience surface erosion, which contributes to carbon buildup on the inner surfaces. To combat carbon buildup, some manufacturers apply a whitish coating called magnesium zirconate to the liners. This coating wears away during operation, taking carbon with it, and thereby maintaining surface cleanliness. During heavy repair, the coating is replaced.

Combustor cases and turbine cases are often constructed from nickel-base alloys. One such alloy is known by its trade name, Inconel®.

Turbine blades and vanes are forged either by newer powder metallurgy techniques or by traditional methods, or investment cast from nickel-base alloys. They are also cast by single-crystal methods. These materials have very high temperature strength under centrifugal loads and are highly corrosion resistant.

Temperatures in the first stage vane area of large engines can reach as high as 2500°F. To withstand such extreme temperatures, as well as the extreme mechanical and thermal loads imposed on them, turbine disks are

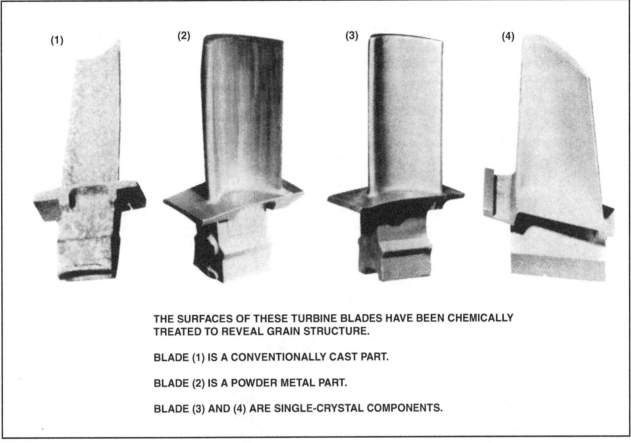

Figure 3-95. Turbine blades made of super metals

often constructed from cobalt-base alloys. Cobalt represents one of the important metallurgical developments for turbine engines.

Because of their ability to withstand higher heat than metal and their high strength to weight ratio, ceramic turbine components have been experimented with since early German development, but because of its low mechanical strength under vibrating loads, only limited use has been made of ceramic material. Some nonflight engines are currently fitted with ceramic blades and disks, but flight engines to date limit the use of ceramic coating to some stationary parts, such as combustion liners and turbine nozzle vanes. Ceramic coating can usually be recognized by its greenish glazed finish.

As mentioned previously, gas turbine engines would theoretically have unlimited power if no temperature limits were imposed by material strength. As material heat strength increases, less cooling air is necessary. Engines could then be scaled down and the power-to-weight ratio would increase significantly. But, as in Whittle's time, material strength still remains the most limiting factor in the power output of the turbine engine.

CONSTRUCTION PROCESSES

Producing compressor and turbine parts usually follows this common process:

1. The turbine disk is forged by use of powder metals.

a) A forming case is filled with powder metal and placed in a vacuum chamber to prevent air voids in the mixture.

b) The case is vibrated to tightly pack the powder.

c) The metal powder is subjected to very high mechanical pressure of approximately 25,000 pounds per square inch. High heat is applied sufficient to fuse the metal particles into a disk-shaped piece.

d) The disk is machined to its final shape.

2. The compressor blades and vanes are formed by investment casting.

a) Molten metal is poured into a ceramic mold in a furnace; then taken out to cool.

b) The mold is broken away, and the blade or vane emerges in near-final shape.

c) The part is machined to its final shape.

3. The turbine vanes and blades are formed either by the lost-wax method of casting or by the single-crystal casting method. [Figure 3-96]

For lost-wax casting:

a) A wax copy of the piece is made in a metal mold.

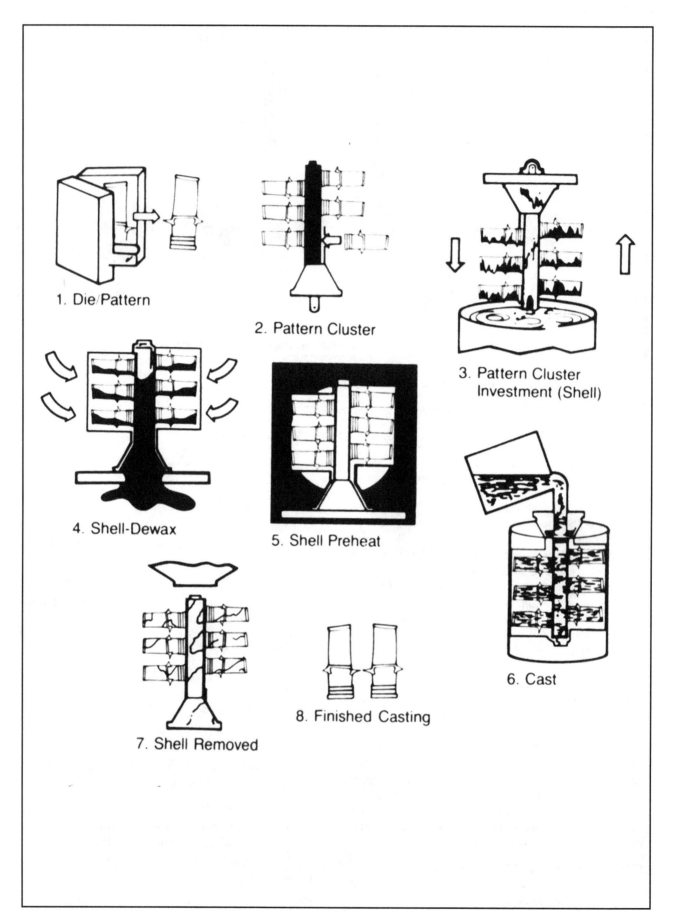

Figure 3-96. Steps in lost-wax casting method for a cluster of six blades

b) The wax piece is dipped in liquid ceramic to form a coating.

c) Molten metal is poured into the ceramic casting in a casting furnace, displacing the wax in the mold.

d) During cooling, the casting is centrifugally loaded in a spin-chamber to provide directional solidification to the piece, resulting in a long-grain structure.

For single-crystal casting:

a) Single-crystal casting is similar to the lost wax method for directional solidification, except that the molten metal is drawn into the mold through a small corkscrew channel at the base of the mold.

b) The corkscrew twist permits only one crystal through to the mold. The crystal then solidifies as perfectly aligned atoms to form a single-crystal blade or vane. With the single-crystal technology, the metal in the vane or blade has no grain structure, which makes it less prone to developing cracks.

ENGINE STATIONS

For ease of identification, engine manufacturers number locations, either along the length of the gas path or along the length of the engine. Station numbers start at either the flight cowling inlet or the engine inlet. Typical of this station numbering concept is the Pratt & Whitney turboprop, a single-spool, two-shaft engine shown in Figure 3-97A. Figure 37B and C show the numbering sequence for a Pratt & Whitney dual-spool and a single-spool engine, respectively. Although manufacturers do not always number engine stations the same way, the purpose of the numbering scheme is always the same. Figure 3-98 shows the station numbering sequence for a high-bypass turbofan, the General Electric CFM56.

Engine symbols such as Pt and Tt are often used in conjunction with subscript station numbers. For example, to describe pressure total at station 2 (the engine inlet), Pt2 is used. To describe temperature total at station 7 (the turbine outlet on a dual-spool engine), Tt7 is used. This abbreviation scheme helps eliminate cumbersome terminology in describing locations and functional data of the engine.

DIRECTIONAL REFERENCES

To identify engine construction points or component and accessory placement, directional references are used along with station numbers. These references are described as forward at the engine inlet and aft at the engine tailpipe, with a standard 12-hour clock orientation. The terms right- and left-hand, clockwise, and counterclockwise apply as viewed from the rear of the engine looking forward toward the inlet. [Figure 3-99]

QUESTIONS:

1. Is the shape of a subsonic turbofan inlet duct convergent, divergent, or both?

2. What principle is involved in inlet duct design to increase static pressure or to increase velocity of the mass airflow?

3. The centrifugal compressor is more common to which type of gas turbine engine—turboshaft or large turbofan?

4. The primary function of a stator vane in an axial flow compressor is to act as a diffuser. What is its secondary function?

5. What is the name given to the reduced thickness at the tip of some compressor blades?

6. Name another advantage of a gas turbine engine with an axial flow compressor besides a small frontal area.

7. At what location in the turbine engine is the point of highest static pressure?

8. What approximate percentage of total airflow is used for combustion?

9. What is the main purpose of the combustion section "secondary air"?

10. Why is the reverse-flow annular combustor considered an efficient design?

11. Which is the most common low-pressure turbine blade design—the open-tip blade or the shrouded blade?

12. At what location on an impulse-reaction turbine blade does the impulse concept apply?

13. From what construction materials are turbine components typically made?

14. What is the opening in the end of the tailpipe called?

15. What are the two names given to the common types of thrust reversers?

16. Why does a turbofan produce less noise than a turbojet of the same thrust rating?

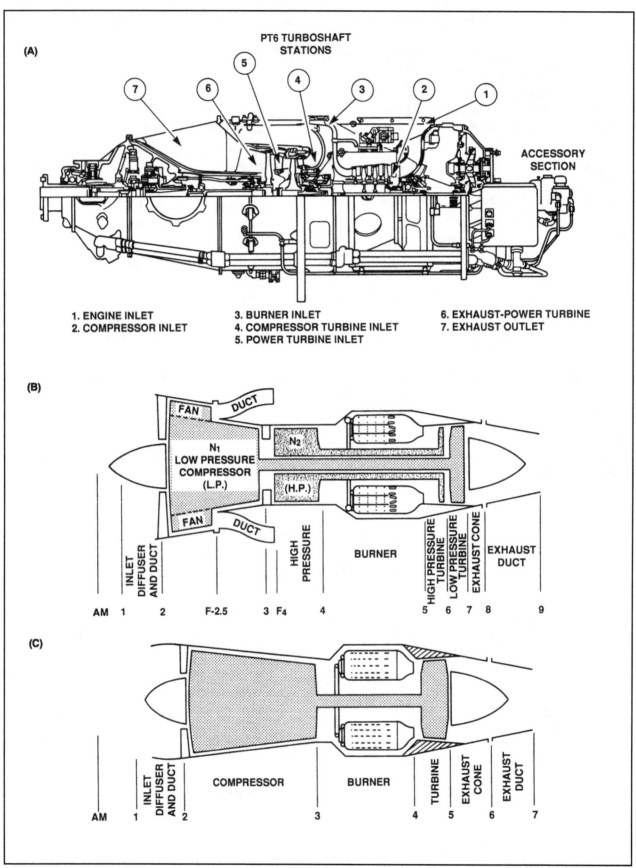

Figure 3-97A. Engine stations numbered along the gas path of the PT6 turboprop engine
Figure 3-97B. Engine stations numbered along the length of a dual-spool engine
Figure 3-97C. Engine stations numbered along the length of a single-spool engine

Turbine Engine Design and Construction

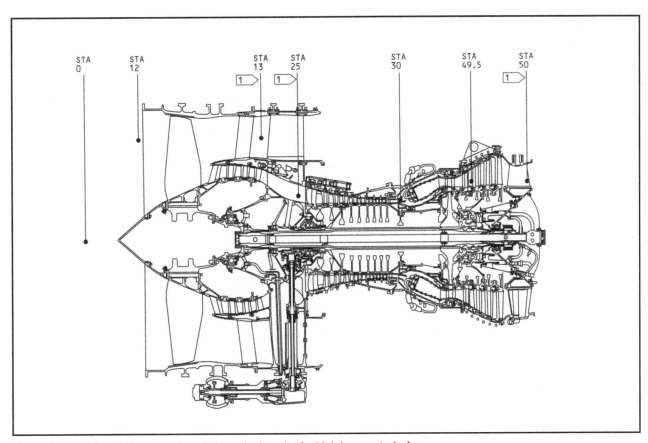

Figure 3-98. Engine stations numbered along the length of a high-bypass turbofan

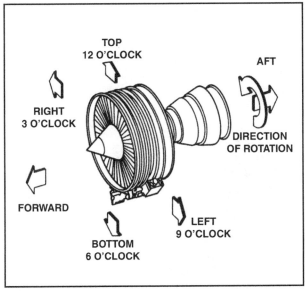

Figure 3-99. Directional references

CHAPTER 4
Engine Familiarization

This chapter covers four widely-produced gas turbine engines currently in use worldwide:

- The Pratt & Whitney JT8D turbofan, a low-bypass airliner-sized engine
- The Rolls-Royce Allison Model 250 turboshaft used in helicopters
- The Pratt & Whitney Canada PT6 turboprop, a commuter and business aircraft-sized engine
- The GE/Snecma CFM56 turbofan, a high-bypass airliner-sized engine

In addition to the overview for each of these engines, this chapter also includes data sheets for the four engines listed above and these three state-of-the-art, high-thrust engines for wide-bodied transports:

- The General Electric GE90-115B
- The Pratt & Whitney PW4090
- The Rolls-Royce Trent 895

THE PRATT & WHITNEY JT8D TURBOFAN ENGINE

The Pratt & Whitney JT8D turbofan engine is the most widely used airliner-sized engine in the history of aviation. It is the powerplant on the Boeing 727, Boeing 737, and McDonnell Douglas (now Boeing) DC-9 and MD-80. It is a low-bypass ratio, fully ducted engine, with models ranging from 12,500 to 20,000 pounds of thrust.

The JT8D is produced only as a turbofan and is an outgrowth of the J52, a Navy turbojet.

The JT8D-1 was first produced in 1963 with 14,000 pounds of thrust and, as of this writing, is being produced as the JT8D-219 model with over 20,000 pounds of thrust

This section covers the construction features and some of the operational data of the JT8D-17A.

ENGINE DESIGN FEATURES

The JT8D is a dual-spool, fully ducted, front-fan turbofan engine with a mixed exhaust. [Figures 4-1 and 4-2]

The full-bypass duct allows the cold and hot gas streams to merge before discharging to the atmosphere. The low-bypass design ensures that approximately the same amount of air is flowing through the fan duct (labeled secondary airflow in Figure 4-1) as is flowing through the core portion of the engine (labeled primary airflow in Figure 4-1).

Dual-spool refers to the split compressor design, meaning that the low-pressure compressor (LP) and the high-pressure compressor (HP) rotate independently of each other. This is possible because the LP compressor drive shaft is located coaxially within the HP compressor shaft.

The six-stage, low-pressure compressor, also called the N_1 compressor, located in front, is driven by a three-stage axial flow turbine rotor located at the rear of the high-pressure turbine.

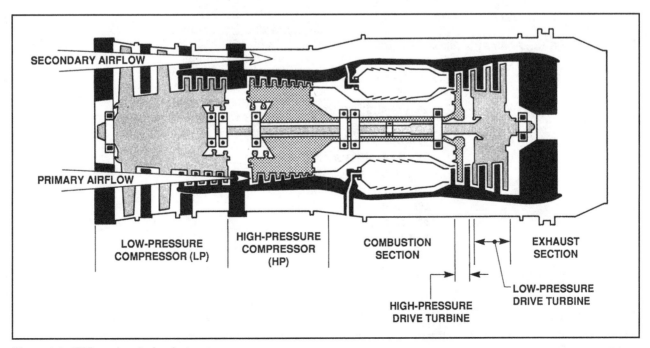

Figure 4-1. JT8D engine design features

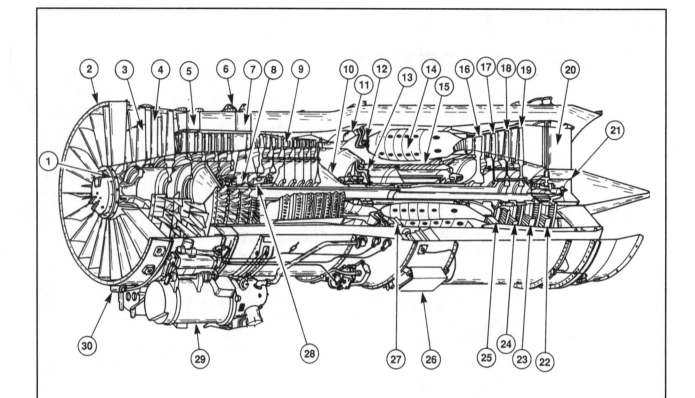

LEGEND:
1. ANTI-ICING AIR DISCHARGE PORTS
2. FAN INLET CASE
3. 1ST STAGE FAN BLADES
4. FRONT COMPRESSOR ROTOR
5. FAN DISCHARGE VANES
6. FAN DISCHARGE INTERMEDIATE CASE
7. FAN DISCHARGE INTERMEDIATE CASE STRUTS
8. NO. 2 AND 3 BEARINGS OIL NOZZLE
9. REAR COMPRESSOR ROTOR
10. REAR COMPRESSOR ROTOR REAR HUB
11. DIFFUSER CASE AIR MANIFOLD
12. FUEL NOZZLE
13. NO. 4 BEARING OIL NOZZLE
14. COMBUSTION CHAMBER
15. COMBUSTION CHAMBER INNER CASE
16. 1ST STAGE TURBINE BLADES
17. 2ND STAGE TURBINE DISK AND BLADES
18. 3RD STAGE TURBINE DISK AND BLADES
19. 4TH STAGE TURBINE DISK AND BLADES
20. EXHAUST STRUT
21. NO. 6 BEARING HEATSHIELD
22. 4TH STAGE TURBINE VANES
23. 3RD STAGE TURBINE VANES
24. 2ND STAGE TURBINE VANES
25. 1ST STAGE TURBINE VANES
26. IGNITION TRANSFORMER
27. IGNITER PLUG
28. GEAR BOX DRIVE BEVEL GEAR
29. MAIN GEARBOX
30. NO. 1 BEARING TUBE CONNECTOR

Figure 4-2. JT8D cutaway view

The first two stages of the N_1 compressor also serve as the front fan. The inner portion of the fan blades act as compressor blades and provide primary airflow, while the outer portion of the blades act as fan blades and provide secondary airflow.

The seven-stage, high-pressure compressor, also called the N_2 compressor, is driven by a single-stage axial flow turbine rotor located immediately to the rear of the combustor.

The two rotor systems, N_1 and N_2, are supported by two double and five single main bearings that are positioned within the main cases of the engine. There are chip detectors at four of the bearing locations.

The JT8D includes three borescoping ports that enable internal inspections.

MAJOR ENGINE SECTIONS

The JT8D has two major sections, as shown in Figure 4-3. The front (cold) section includes the inlet case to the diffuser case and the main accessory gearbox. The rear (hot) section includes the combustor to the fan turbine exhaust case. The engine is further divided into smaller sections shown in Figure 4-3.

Smaller sections of this engine are constructed of both unit and non-unit design similar to the current modular designs. Maintenance personnel can replace any individual components of a non-unit assembly or replace an entire unit section during overhaul, thus expediting the engine's overhaul procedure.

With unit construction, management personnel analyze the engine's total time in service and each unit section's total time in service so they can make a cost-effective match during maintenance. This ensures that a low-time unit section is not placed on a high-time engine, unless existing stock precludes the proper match. In some instances, a module will be repaired instead of being replaced to prevent mismatching.

LOW-PRESSURE COMPRESSOR — N_1

The low-pressure compressor (N_1) has six stages of compression: two fan stages and four compressor stages. At rated thrust, the N_1 has a compressor pressure ratio of 4.33:1, with a discharge pressure of 63.6 pounds per square inch—absolute at standard conditions.

The N_1 compressor has two functions. First, it accelerates secondary airflow into the fan duct at a rate of 164 pounds per second, at 8,589 r.p.m, which is 100 percent takeoff speed (pressure ratio of the fan is 2.1 to 1 with a fan discharge pressure of 31.0 pounds per square inch—absolute). Second, the N_1 compressor provides the N_2

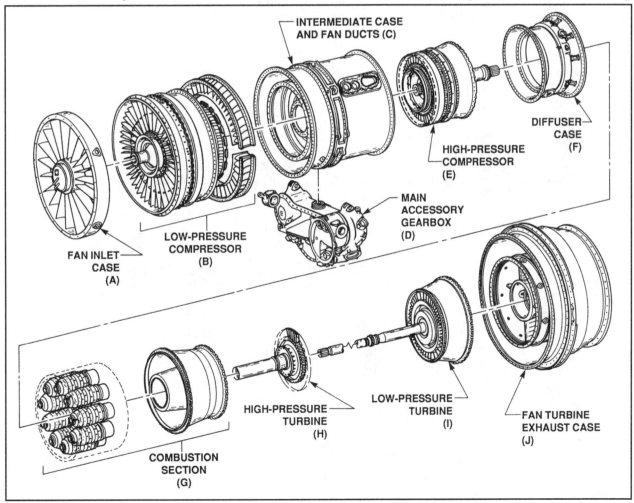

Figure 4-3. Major engine sections—JT8D

compressor with supercharged primary air of 4.33 times atmospheric, at 160 pounds of mass airflow per second.

A single-roller bearing (number 1) located in the inlet case supports the front of the compressor for radial loads, and a double ball bearing (number 2) supports the rear of the N_1 rotor for both axial and radial loads. [Figure 4-4]

The first-stage fan blades are attached to the disk by a dovetail blade root and retained by a locking ring. The second-stage fan blades are attached by a dovetail attachment and retained by tab locks.

The six stator stages are individual, continuous welded ring assemblies. To assemble the N_1 compressor, this design requires that the compressor be stacked, starting with the last stator, then the last rotor, then the next stator, and so forth through the successive stages to the number one stage. Each rotor stage has a shroud ring that acts as a spacer between stator assemblies.

The N_1 compressor is mechanically coupled to the N_1 turbine shaft at the number 2 bearing area. The turbine shaft runs co-axially through the N_2 compressor shaft.

HIGH-PRESSURE COMPRESSOR — N_2

The high-pressure compressor (N_2) has seven stages of compression. At rated thrust, the N_2 compressor has a compressor pressure ratio of approximately 4:1, with a discharge pressure (total of N_1 and N_2) of 254 pounds per square inch—absolute at standard conditions.

The N_2 compressor provides the combustor with sufficient air at all operating conditions. At rated power, the N_2 moves 160 pounds of mass airflow per second.

A single ball bearing (number 3) supports the front of the compressor and a double ball bearing (number 4) supports the rear for both axial and radial loads. An air balance chamber at the number 4 bearing assists in absorbing thrust loads. [Figure 4-4]

The seventh-stage blades (first stage of N_2) are pin-mounted and retained with rivets. Stages 8 through 13 are dovetail slotted to the disk and retained by tablocks.

The seven stator stages are continuous welded ring assemblies that are stacked from the rear, rotor on stator, during reassembly.

The N_2 compressor is mechanically coupled to the N_2 turbine shaft at the number 4 bearing area.

DIFFUSER CASE

The diffuser case is the engine's mid-supporting member. It contains the thirteenth-stage stators and the thirteenth-stage rotor shroud ring. The diffuser houses the number 4 bearing, which supports the rear of the high-pressure compressor. [Figure 4-5]

The outer case contains air extraction points for customer bleed air, engine anti-ice air, and anti-surge bleed air. It also contains external bosses to which the fuel nozzles mount.

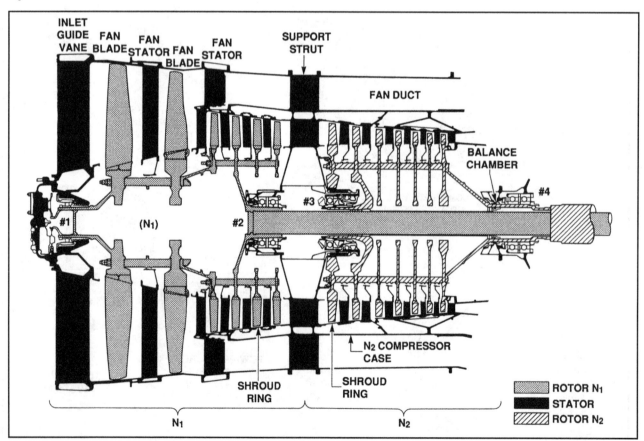

Figure 4-4. JT8D compressor section and bearings 1, 2, 3, and 4

Engine Familiarization

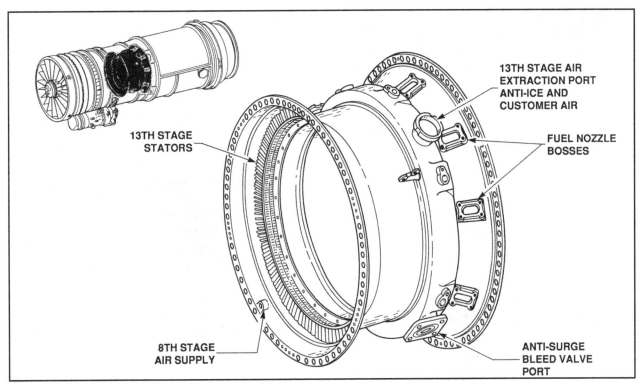

Figure 4-5. JT8D diffuser case

The diffuser straightens airflow and diffuses it to the correct pressure and velocity in preparation for combustion.

COMBUSTION CASE

The combustion section houses the combustion liners. The turbine shaft passes through the inner case, which forms the inner walls of the combustion chamber. The outer case forms the outer walls of the combustion chamber. [Figure 4-6]

The front end of each of the nine can-annular combustion liners has a locating lug that connects to a hangar pin

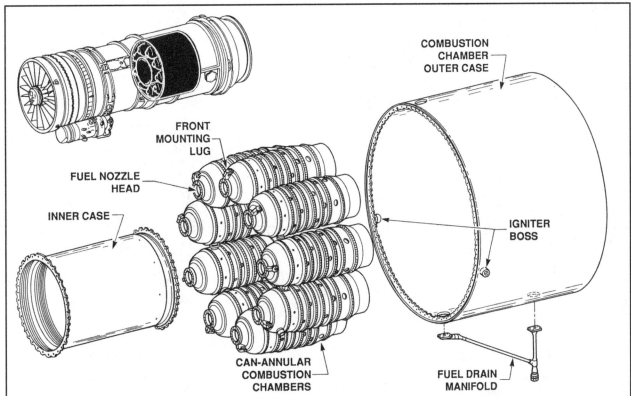

Figure 4-6. JT8D combustion section

within the diffuser case. Circular clamps hold the liners to the rear support assembly at the aft end.

The combustor rear support and outlet assembly supports the rear of the nine liners and has two configurations, louvered and non-louvered. [Figure 4-7] Both perform essentially the same task, but the louvered, which is a newer design, is cooled by thirteenth-stage air, giving the assembly a higher tolerance to thermal shock and increasing its expected service life.

The entry points for combustion air, as well as the fuel nozzle head mounting points, are located in the front portion of the liners.

The purpose of the combustion section is to add thermal energy to the air passing through it, to enclose the fuel-air mixture during combustion, and to discharge that mixture to the turbine via the outlet duct assembly.

TURBINE NOZZLE VANES

The turbine nozzle vanes are individually installed in all four stages of the turbine. The first stage contains 46 vanes, which are located in front of the first-stage N_2 turbine wheel. The N_1 turbines have, respectively, 95 vanes in the second stage, 79 vanes in the third stage, and 77 vanes in the fourth stage. [Figures 4-8 and 4-9]

The first-stage vanes can be removed individually from the front by sliding the outer combustion case back, removing the liners, and sliding the vanes forward. In the unit module low-pressure turbine, the three turbines and stators are removed as one piece. In the non-unit low-pressure turbine, the wheels and stators are unstacked one at a time starting at the number 4 turbine wheel.

The first-stage vanes are air-cooled by both convection (through-flow cooling) and film cooling from a combination of trailing edge slots and cambered-side slots. The difference can be seen in the vanes for the -9, -15, and -17 model engines.

The turbine outer air seals act as turbine blade shroud rings and reduce air leakage at the blade tips. They also act as spacers between vane stages.

The vane trailing edges act as nozzles and form an effective flow area, which helps maintain correct back-pressure of gas flow through the turbine system. Airseals also accelerate and direct the gases at the most effective angle onto the turbine blades.

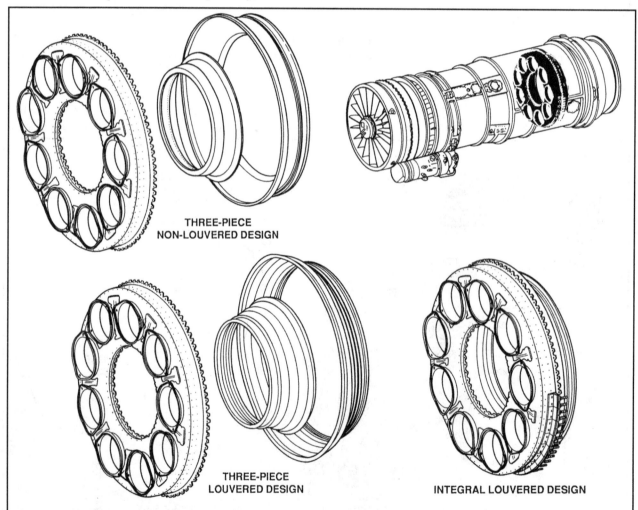

Figure 4-7. JT8D combustion chamber rear support and outlet

Engine Familiarization

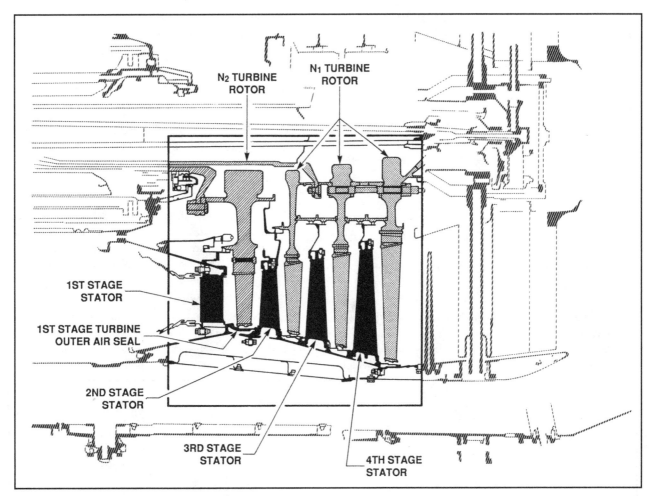

Figure 4-8. JT8D turbine nozzle vanes

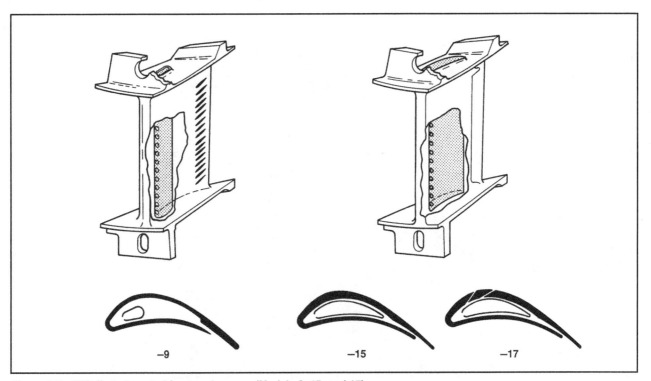

Figure 4-9. JT8D first-stage turbine nozzle vanes (Models 9, 15, and 17)

Vanes come in several sizes, called classes, by which the effective flow area can be adjusted by maintenance personnel to meet certain operational performance requirements of an engine.

HIGH-PRESSURE TURBINE ROTOR (N_2)

The high-pressure turbine rotor is a single-stage axial flow rotor with shrouded, impulse-reaction turbine blades. The blades are designed with fir tree-shaped bases that fit into turbine disk slots of the same shape. The blades are retained by rivets on models -1, -7, -9, -11, -15, and by side plates on the -17 model engines. [Figure 4-10]

On early model engines, the shrouded tips contain no knife-edge seals; the seals are located in the turbine outer air seal and shroud ring. [Figure 4-11] On the -15 and -17 engines, the knife-edge seals are located on the blade tip shrouds, which results in better sealing. The outer air seal for the -15 and -17 models are of the honeycomb design, which allows for tighter running clearances and lower air leakage.

The number 5 bearing supports the N_2 turbine. The N_2 turbine shaft houses the number 4-1/2 bearing, which centers the N_1 turbine shaft, located coaxially within the N_2 shaft. Splines on the front end of the N_2 turbine shaft connect to the N_2 compressor rear shaft.

The function of the N_2 turbine is to convert a portion of the combustor discharge energy into shaft horsepower to drive the N_2 compressor and the main accessory gearbox.

LOW-PRESSURE TURBINE (N_1)

The low-pressure turbine has two configurations, the non-unit and the unit module. The non-unit is removed and unstacked during repair and the unit module is removed and replaced as a single assembly. [Figure 4-12]

The N_1 turbine is a three-stage axial-flow turbine with shrouded, impulse-reaction blades. The blade bases are configured with fir tree serrations that fit into the turbine disk serrations. The blades are retained in the disk by rivets. The turbine blade tips are sealed by continuous ring shrouds containing knife-edge seals.

The N_1 turbine shaft houses the number 4-1/2 bearing on its outer diameter. The outer race of this bearing is located within the N_2 turbine shaft. This bearing prevents the N_1 shaft from whipping at high torque loads.

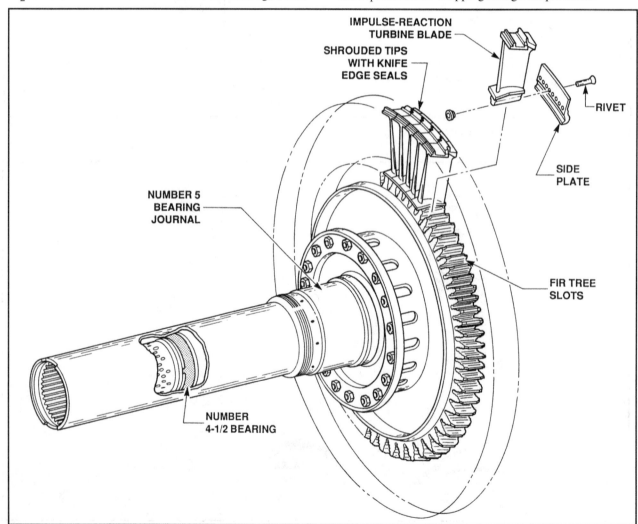

Figure 4-10. JT8D high-pressure turbine

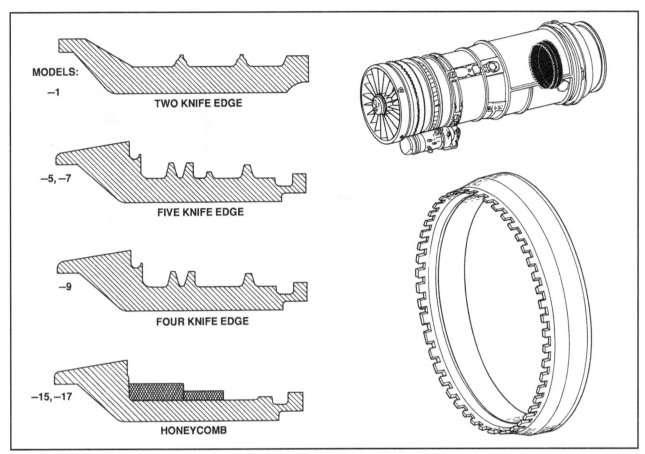

Figure 4-11. JT8D first-stage turbine outer air seal

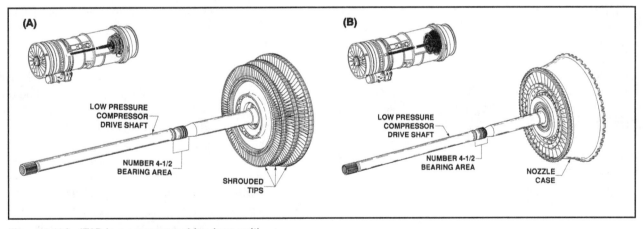

Figure 4-12A. JT8D low-pressure turbine (non-unit)
Figure 4-12B. JT8D low-pressure turbine (unit type) models (9, 15, and 17)

The function of the N_1 turbine is to convert the gas energy, which spills over from the N_2 turbine, into horsepower to drive the N_1 compressor.

MAIN ACCESSORY GEARBOX

The main accessory gearbox is located at the six o'clock position on the fan outer case below the N_2 compressor front shaft. The gearbox is driven by a radial (tower) shaft that connects to a bevel gear drive mechanism located at the front of the N_2 compressor. [Figure 4-13]

The gearbox provides reduction gearing to the drive pads on which components and accessories such as the fuel pump/fuel control unit, constant speed drive (C.S.D.), starter, hydraulic pump, and tachometer generator are mounted. The front face of the gearbox is a mounting point for the main oil tank.

The gearbox housing also contains integral mounting points for the main oil pump, scavenge oil pump, oil filter, oil pressure regulating valve, and vent system air-oil separator (de-oilers).

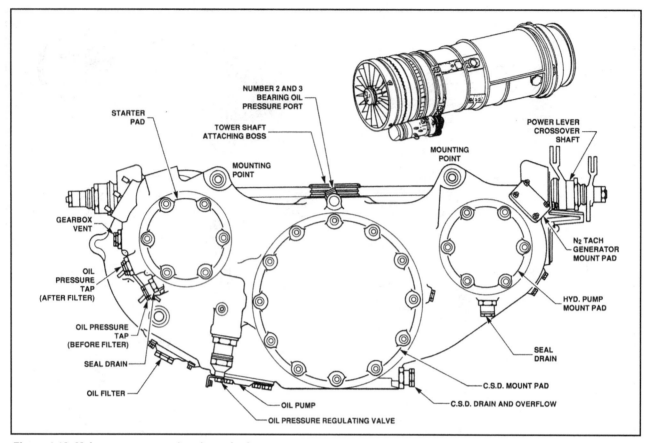

Figure 4-13. Main accessory gearbox (rear view)

TURBINE EXHAUST CASE

The turbine exhaust case forms the exhaust nozzle for primary airflow through the core of the engine. The rear part of the fan duct forms the combined primary and secondary exhaust nozzle. [Figure 4-14]

The turbine exhaust case houses the turbine exhaust duct, which is supported by four airfoil shaped struts designed to provide the final straightening of primary air flow before discharge into the mixed-flow duct. This case also contains the number 6 bearing, which supports the rear of the low-pressure turbine. The bearing housing is positioned by four support rods that pass through the struts of the turbine exhaust duct.

The outer case also provides mounting points for six turbine discharge, total-pressure (Pt_7) probes, which are part of the engine pressure ratio (EPR) cockpit indicating system. The eight turbine discharge total temperature (Tt_7) probes installed in this case are part of the exhaust gas temperature (EGT) cockpit indicating system.

MAIN BEARINGS

There are seven main bearings of the ball-and-roller type supporting the rotor systems. [Figure 4-15] Four bearings support the N_1 system, and three bearings support the N_2 system as follows:

- Number 1 bearing is a roller bearing that supports the front of the N_1 compressor for radial loads. It is mist and vapor lubricated. Oil leakage into the gas path is prevented by labyrinth air-oil sealing, which is pressurized with sixth-stage bleed air.

- Number 2 bearing is a duplex-ball bearing that supports the rear of the N_1 compressor for both radial and axial loads. It is directly lubricated by a fluid oil stream and fitted with labyrinth air-oil sealing. It is also pressurized with sixth-stage bleed air.

- Number 3 bearing is a single-ball type that supports the front of the N_2 compressor. It is directly lubricated by an oil jet, fitted with a labyrinth air-oil sealing, and pressurized by sixth and seventh-stage bleed air.

- Number 4 bearing is a duplex-ball type that supports the rear of the N_2 compressor. It is directly lubricated by an oil jet, fitted with labyrinth air-oil sealing, and pressurized by eight-stage bleed air.

- Number 4½ is a single-roller type bearing. Its outer race is located midway within the N_2 turbine shaft, and the roller and cage assemblies are located on the N_1 turbine shaft. This bearing prevents the N_1 shaft from whipping at high rotational speeds. An oil jet directly lubricates this bearing, and it uses a ring-type carbon seal to prevent loss of oil to the gas path.

- Number 5 bearing is a single-roller bearing that supports the front of the N_2 turbine shaft. It is mist-lubricated and sealed by the use of face-type carbon

Engine Familiarization

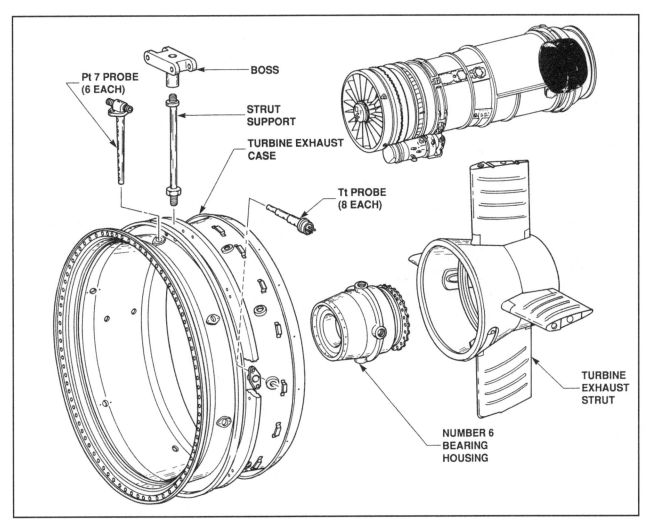

Figure 4-14. JT8D turbine exhaust case

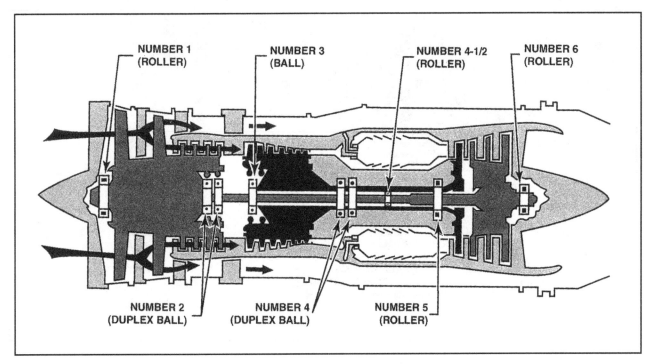

Figure 4-15. JT8D bearing locations

seals. Last (thirteenth) stage air is used to preload the carbon seal to its rub ring.
- Number 6 bearing is a single-roller type that supports the rear of the N_1 turbine. It is a direct-lubricated bearing and protected from leakage by carbon-ring type seals. The seal is pressurized by last (thirteenth) stage bleed air.

ADDITIONAL INFORMATION

Engine stations, directional references, and construction materials are given in Figures 4-16, 4-17, and 4-18.

Figures 4-19, 4-20, 4-21, and 4-22 contain performance figures.

FAMILIARIZATION WITH THE ROLLS-ROYCE ALLISON MODEL 250 TURBOSHAFT ENGINE

The Allison-250 [Figure 4-23] was originally developed as both the military T-63 and the commercial 250 model. It is produced in turboshaft and turboprop models, the turboshaft model being the most popular. Rolls-Royce acquired the manufacturing rights in 1995 from the General Motors Corporation and now markets the engine as the Rolls-Royce Allison Model 250. From this point on, this engine will be referred to as the Rolls-Royce 250.

As of this writing, this engine is one of the most widely used helicopter engines in the world. There are several different models of the Rolls-Royce 250, including some turboprop models. Only the C-20B, F, and J models will be described here.

The C-20B, F, and J models are a two-shaft turboshaft with a combination compressor, consisting of six axial stages attached to a one-stage centrifugal compressor. It has a reverse-flow annular combustor, a two-stage high-pressure turbine, also referred to as the gas producer turbine or N_1 turbine, and a two-stage low-pressure turbine called the power turbine, or N_2 turbine.

GAS PATH OF THE ROLLS-ROYCE 250

The C-20 has a compressor pressure ratio of 7.1:1 and a mass airflow of 3.6 pounds/second at 52,000 r.p.m.

Airflow along the engine's gas path, shown in Figure 4-23, is as follows: From the flight inlet, air moves straight into the compressor first stage and out of the centrifugal last stage into two external air transfer tubes and to the combustor at the very rear of the engine. The gases then turn forward and through a two-stage compressor turbine—also called a gas producer—(N_1) and a two-stage power turbine (N_2). Finally, the gases are directed out of the exhaust duct and upward through two outlets that are twenty degrees from top center at the mid-point on the engine.

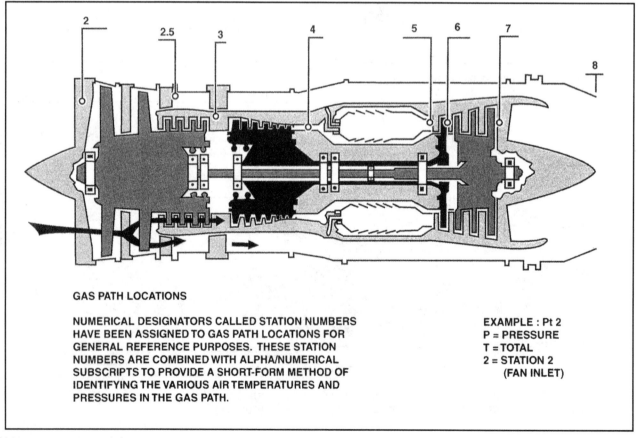

GAS PATH LOCATIONS

NUMERICAL DESIGNATORS CALLED STATION NUMBERS HAVE BEEN ASSIGNED TO GAS PATH LOCATIONS FOR GENERAL REFERENCE PURPOSES. THESE STATION NUMBERS ARE COMBINED WITH ALPHA/NUMERICAL SUBSCRIPTS TO PROVIDE A SHORT-FORM METHOD OF IDENTIFYING THE VARIOUS AIR TEMPERATURES AND PRESSURES IN THE GAS PATH.

EXAMPLE : Pt 2
P = PRESSURE
T = TOTAL
2 = STATION 2
    (FAN INLET)

Figure 4-16. JT8D engine station locations

Engine Familiarization 4-13

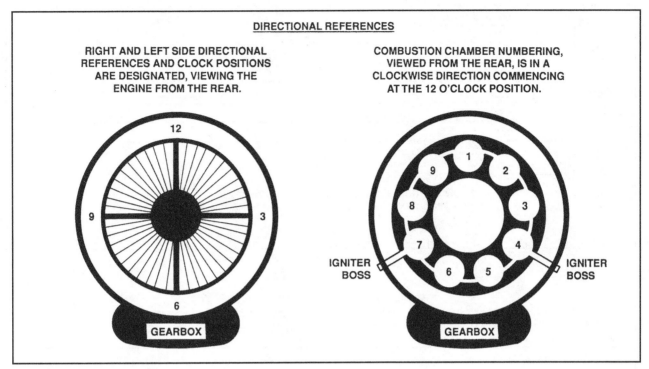

Figure 4-17. JT8D directional references

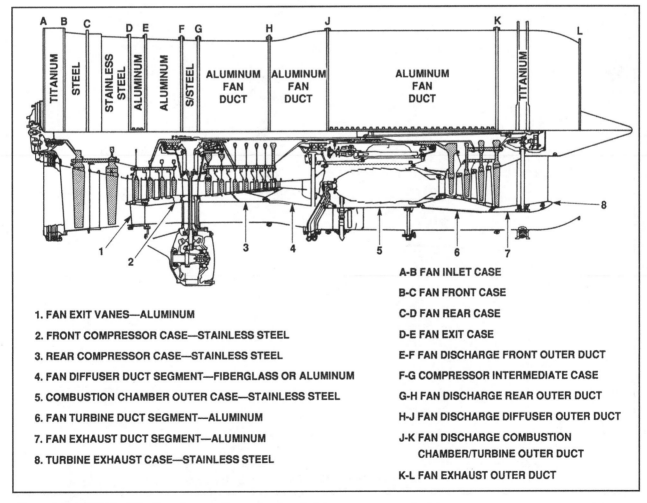

Figure 4-18. JT8D identification of cases, flanges, and materials

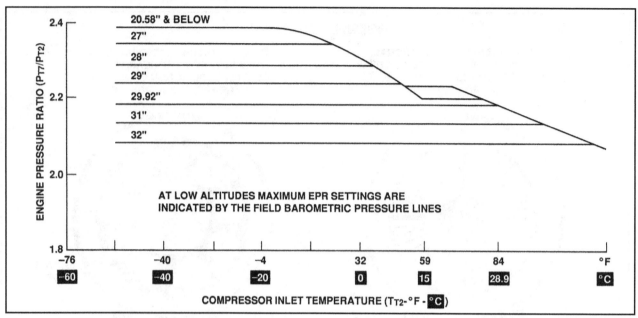

Figure 4-19. JT8D-17 takeoff EPR setting

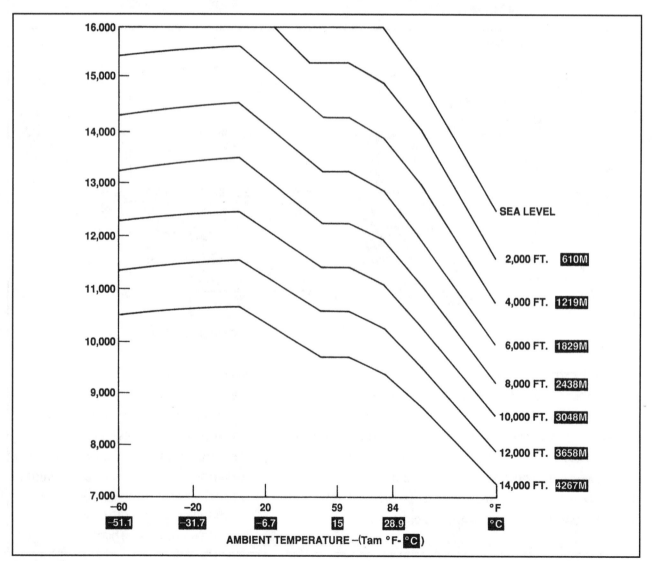

Figure 4-20. JT8D-17 thrust according to runway altitude

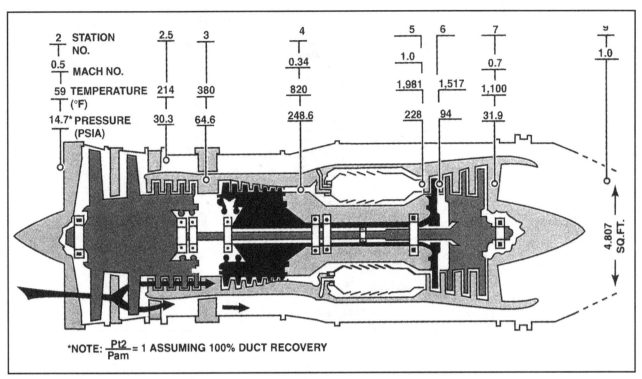

Figure 4-21. JT8D takeoff values (average performance)

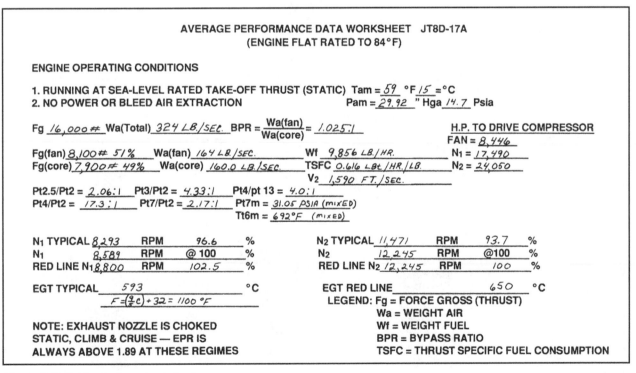

Figure 4-22. Engine test-run worksheet

FOUR MAJOR ENGINE SECTIONS (MODULES)

The four major engine sections in Figure 4-24 are:

- **Compressor section** — Consists of inlet housing, combination axial-centrifugal compressor, and diffuser at the rear.

- **Combustion section** — Consists of two external air transfer tubes that carry air from the diffuser to a single basket, reverse-flow annular combustor. The combustor contains one duplex fuel nozzle and a single igniter plug.

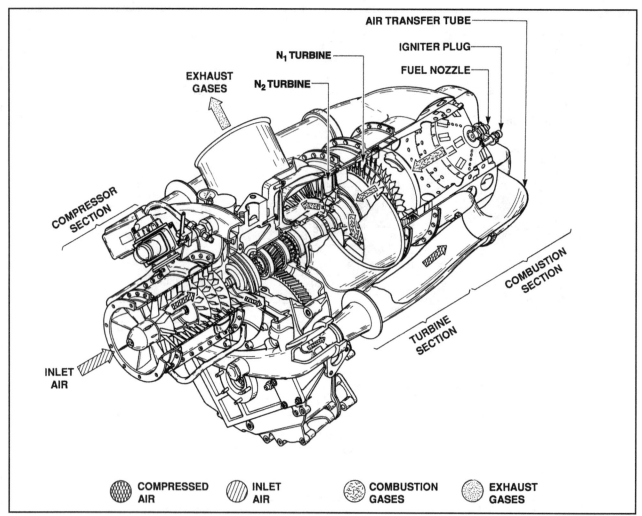

Figure 4-23. Gas path of the Rolls-Royce Allison 250-C20B, F, and J

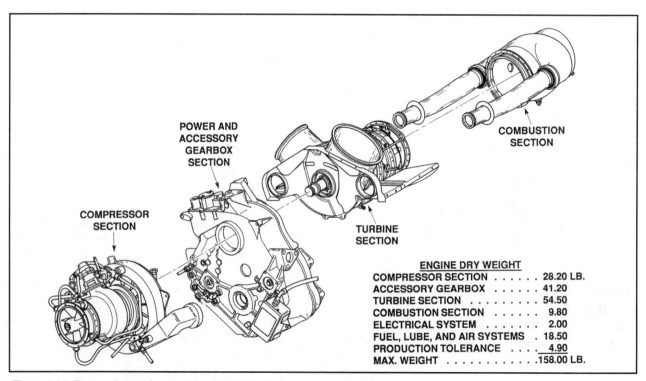

Figure 4-24. Four major engine sections 250-C20B, F, J

- **Turbine section** — Consists of a two-shaft, four-stage turbine assembly and a dual exhaust outlet duct.
- **Power and accessory gearbox section** — Consists of a power outlet reduction gear with a ratio of 5.534:1. The output drive to the helicopter transmission is 6,016 r.p.m. at 100 percent power turbine speed. For different aircraft applications, a connecting pad is located at both the front and rear of the gearbox. The gearbox also provides mounting pads for the various engine components and accessories.

Total weight of the engine is 158 pounds. At 420 rated shaft horsepower, this is equal to a power-to-weight ratio of 2.66:1, or 2.66 shaft horsepower per pound of weight.

COMPRESSOR SECTION

The compressor assembly consists of a compressor front support assembly, compressor rotor assembly, compressor case assembly, and compressor diffuser assembly. [Figure 4-25]

The compressor consists of one double and four single axial wheel segments and one centrifugal segment. The compressor blades, both axial and centrifugal, are cast as part of the wheel and cannot be removed individually. If a blade is damaged beyond blend repair limits, the entire wheel segment must be replaced. [Figure 4-26]

The compressor is a combination axial-centrifugal type with six stages of axial compression and one stage of centrifugal compression. The wheel and blade assemblies and the impeller are made of stainless steel. The compressor rotor front (number 1) ball bearing is housed in the compressor front support, and the compressor rotor rear (number 2) ball bearing is housed in the compressor rear diffuser. The number 2 bearing serves as the thrust bearing for the compressor rotor assembly.

The compressor case assembly consists of a stainless steel upper and lower case. The stator vanes are also made of stainless steel and are brazed to stainless steel bands that are welded to the compressor case halves. Thermal setting plastic is centrifugally cast to the inside surface of the case halves and vane outer bands. To obtain maximum compressor efficiency, it is necessary to maintain as tight a clearance as possible between the compressor blade tips and the inside surface of the compressor case halves. If the blade tips contact the plastic, the plastic will be scraped away to the extent that minimum blade tip clearance will be attained without damage to either the case halves or blades.

The compressor case assembly has provisions for mounting a bleed-air control valve that bleeds air from

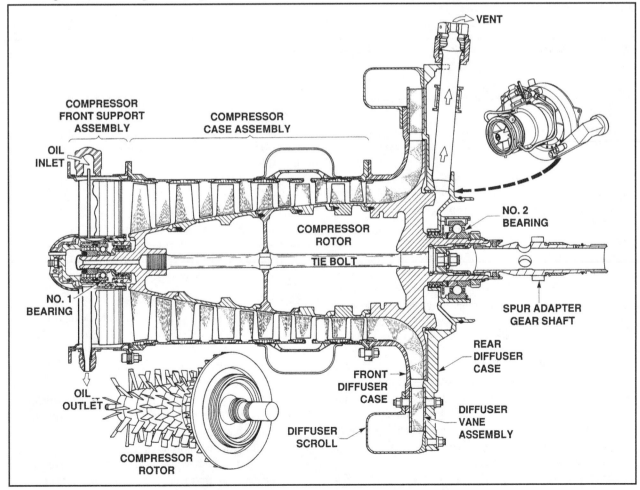

Figure 4-25. Compressor section schematic 250-C20B, F, and J

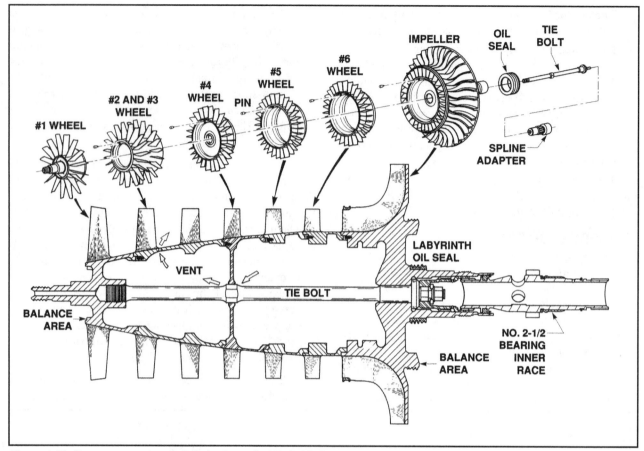

Figure 4-26. Compressor rotor exploded schematic 250-C20B, F, and J

the fifth stage of the axial compressor during starting and acceleration.

The compressor diffuser assembly consists of stainless steel front and rear diffuser cases and a magnesium alloy diffuser scroll.

The scroll collects the air and delivers it to two elbows. Each elbow contains stainless steel turning vanes that redirect the airflow from an outward to a rearward direction. Compressor discharge air tubes deliver compressed air from the outlet side of the elbows to the combustor outer case. The diffuser scroll has five ports from which air can be bled, or from which compressor discharge air pressure can be sensed. Two of these ports are customer bleeds, and the remaining ports are used by the anti-icing valve, fuel control system pressure sensing, and compressor bleed-air control valve pressure sensing.

COMBUSTION SECTION

Figure 4-27 shows the combustor assembly, which is comprised of two compressor discharge transfer air tubes, combustor outer case, and the combustor liner. The combustor outer case is a stainless steel part with tapped bosses for mounting a combustor drain valve, a fuel nozzle, and an igniter plug.

Two combustor drain valve bosses are provided. The combustor drain valve threads into the boss nearest to the 6 o'clock position with the engine installed in the aircraft, and the other boss is plugged.

The fuel nozzle positions and supports the aft end of the combustion liner, and the igniter locates the combustion liner in a circumferential position.

The combustion liner allows rapid mixing of fuel and air, and controls the flame length and position so that the flame does not contact any metallic surface. Approximately 25 percent of the total airflow passes through the liner to the combustion zone; this is referred to as primary air. The remaining 75 percent is used for cooling and is referred to as secondary air.

GAS PRODUCER TURBINE

The gas producer turbine (N_1), also called the compressor turbine, is a two-stage unit consisting of turbines number 1 and number 2, with number 1 located at the rear of the engine and nearest to the combustor. [Figure 4-28]

The function of the N_1 turbine is to drive the compressor and accessory gearbox directly from combustor discharge gases. Turbine blades are of the open-tip, integral type. (The blades are cast as part of the turbine disk and cannot be removed individually.)

The first and second turbine nozzles are located in front of the first and second turbine wheels. They increase the velocity of exhausting gases and direct the

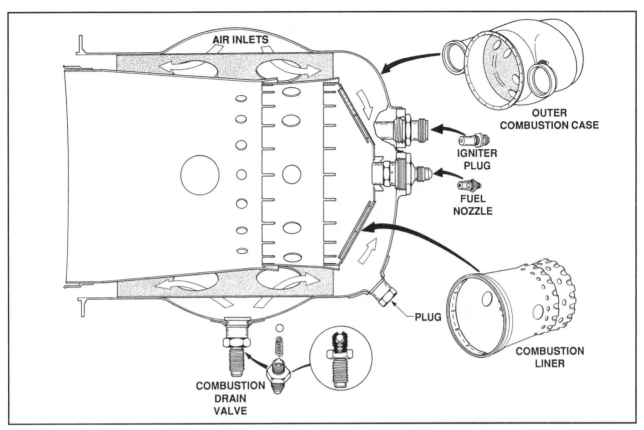

Figure 4-27. Combustion section schematic 250-C20B, F, and J

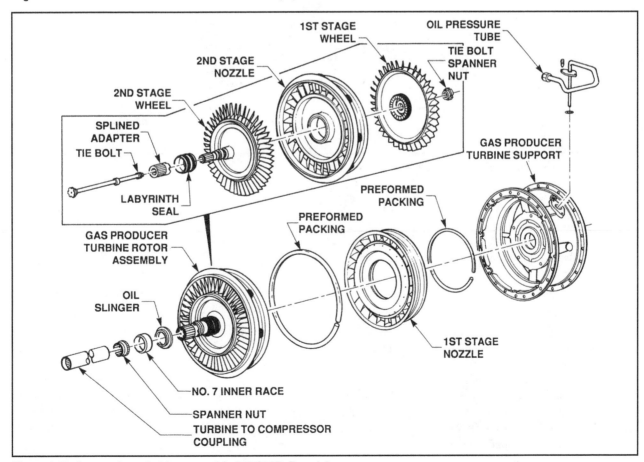

Figure 4-28. Gas producer turbine assembly 250-C20B, F, and J

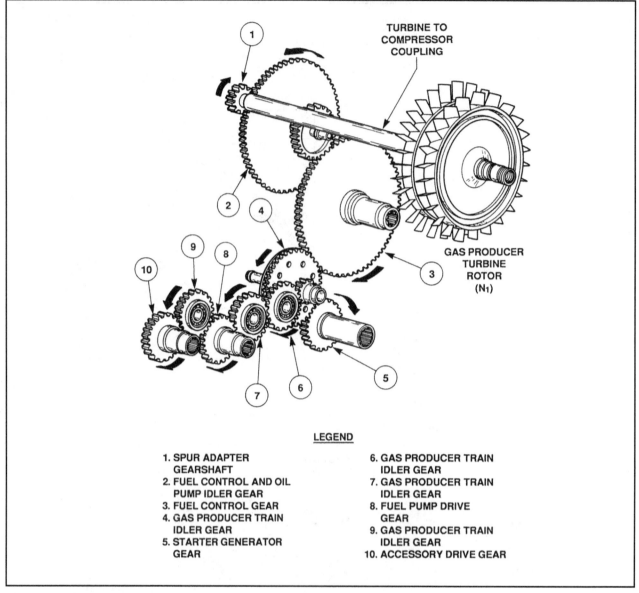

Figure 4-29. Gas producer gear train 250-C20B, F, and J

gases at the correct angle onto the turbine rotor blades of their respective stages.

The gas producer gear train in Figure 4-29 shows how the gas producer turbine rotor drives the compressor and the drive gears to the accessory drive gearbox.

POWER TURBINE

The power turbine (N_2) is a two-stage unit consisting of the number 3 turbine and the number 4 turbine, with the number 4 turbine located nearest the exhaust outlet. The function of the N_2 turbine is to drive the power output gear through a pinion gear coupling. The power turbine rotor receives the gas energy spill-over from the gas producer turbine and converts gas energy into power delivered to the output shaft. [Figure 4-30]

The power output gear can couple from either end to the power output shaft, which drives the helicopter transmission. [Figure 4-31]

The power turbine is a "free" turbine because it is free to rotate at a different speed than the gas producer turbine. The power turbine blades are of the shrouded tip, integral type. This design has several advantages:

- Added operational flexibility resulting from an independent selection of speeds between the N_1 and N_2 rotors.

- Improved overall engine performance because each turbine can be operated at a point of maximum efficiency for a given power requirement.

- Ease of starting because the starter rotates only the N_1 rotor during the start cycle.

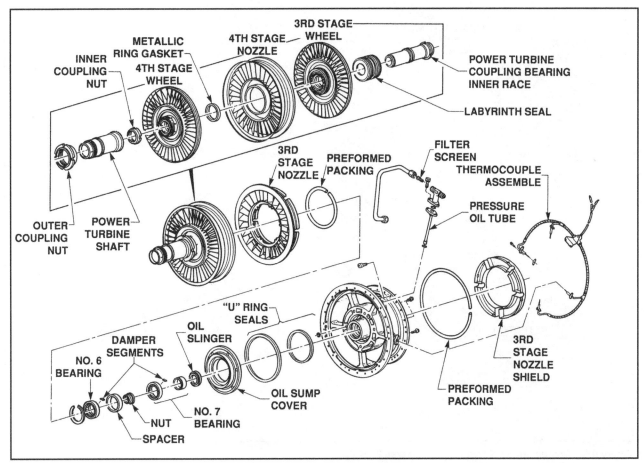

Figure 4-30. Power turbine assembly 250-C20B, F, and J

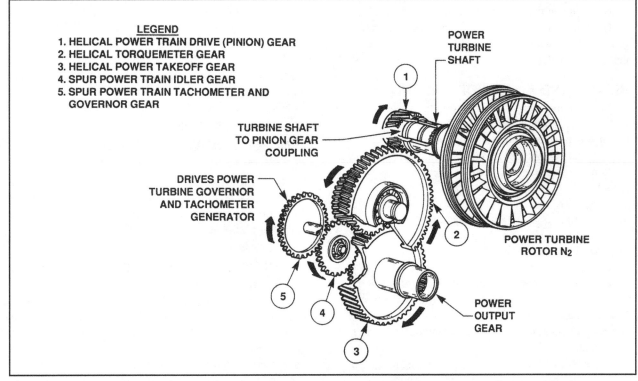

Figure 4-31. Power turbine gear train 250-C20B, F, and J

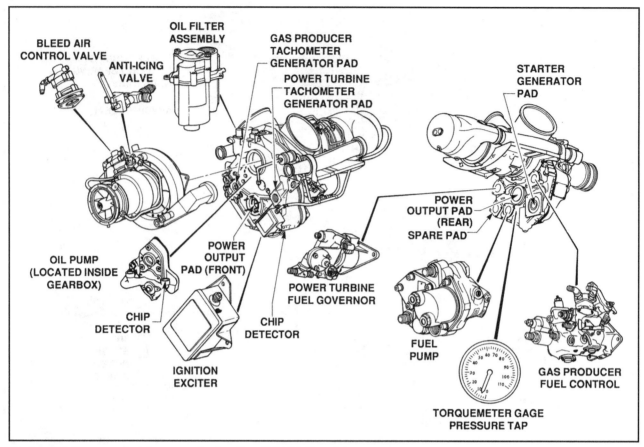

Figure 4-32. Component and accessories location, 250-20B, F, and J

The power turbine is supported for thrust loads by the number 5 main ball bearing at the front and the number 6 roller bearing at the rear, which absorbs only radial loads.

The third and fourth turbine nozzles are in front of the power turbine wheels to accelerate and direct gases onto the turbine blades.

POWER AND ACCESSORY GEARBOX

The combined power and accessory gearbox [Figure 4-32] is the primary structural member of the engine because it provides mounting and support for the compressor and turbine assemblies. The accessory gearbox contains most of the lubrication system components and incorporates two separate gear trains. The power turbine gear train reduces power turbine speed from 33,290 to 6,016 r.p.m., a gear reduction ratio of 5.53:1. The power turbine gear train also incorporates the torquemeter assembly and drives the power turbine tachometer generator and the power turbine governor. The gas producer gear train drives the oil pump, the fuel pump, the gas producer fuel control, the gas producer tachometer generator, and the starter generator. During starting, the starter-generator rotates the engine through the gas producer gear train.

The gearbox housing and cover are magnesium-alloy castings that house the bearings that support the power turbine and gas producer gear trains.

The oil pump assembly, which incorporates a single pressure element and four scavenge elements, is mounted partially within the gearbox and on the housing. An oil filter is mounted on, and extends into, the top of the accessory gearbox housing.

There are two indicating chip detectors. One is located at the bottom of the accessory gearbox and the other is at the engine oil outlet of the gearbox.

Other non-driven accessories are the anti-surge bleed-air control valve, anti-icing valve, and ignition unit.

ENGINE BEARINGS AND LUBRICATION SYSTEM

Main bearings support the compressor and turbine drive shafts. Ancillary bearings provide support at accessory drives and gear locations. The shaft bearings and gears are lubricated by engine oil from the engine lubrication system.

MAIN BEARING NUMBERING

The main bearings are numbered 1 through 8 from front to rear. The compressor rotor assembly is supported by the number 1 and number 2 main bearings. The number 3 and number 4 main bearings support the helical power train drive (pinion) gear. Bearings number 5 and number 6 support the power turbine, and the number 7 and number 8 main bearings support the gas producer turbine rotors. [Figure 4-33]

Engine Familiarization 4-23

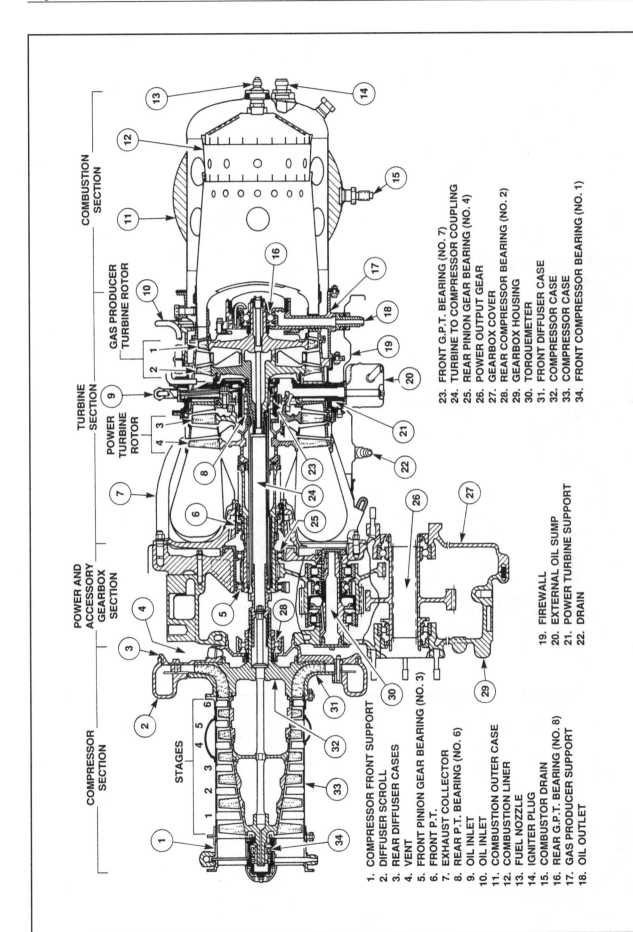

Figure 4-33. Cutaway view including bearing locations 250-C20B, F, and J

BEARING LUBRICATION

The lubrication system is a circulating dry sump with an external oil tank and oil cooler, both of which are mounted and furnished by the helicopter manufacturer.

Oil jet lubrication is provided to all compressor, gas producer turbine, and power turbine rotor bearings and to bearings and gear meshes of the power turbine gear train, with the exception of the power output shaft bearings. All other gears and bearings are lubricated by oil mist.

ADDITIONAL INFORMATION

Figure 4-34 contains performance figures for the Rolls-Royce 250 engines.

FAMILIARIZATION WITH THE PRATT & WHITNEY PT6 TURBOPROP ENGINE

The PT6 was originally developed as both a military T-76 and the commercial PT6. It is produced in turboprop and turboshaft models; the turboprop model is the most popular. [Figure 4-35A]

The PT6 Turboprop engine is produced by the Pratt & Whitney Canada, a division of United Technologies Corporation of Hartford, Connecticut.

It is the most widely used corporate/commuter sized turboprop engine in the world. There are several different models of the PT6, including some turboshaft models. All PT6 models have the same basic shape, with a circular air inlet, and dual exhaust parts located on the sides of the engine. The output drive shaft and main accessory gearbox are located at the front and back. This engine design allows it to be used in either a puller or pusher configuration. Small models of the PT6 are in the 500 shaft horsepower class and weigh approximately 300 pounds. Large models are in the 1,800 shaft horsepower class and weigh approximately 600 pounds. Only the PT6-34 engine for fixed-wing aircraft will be discussed here.

The PT6-34 is a two-shaft turboprop with a combination three-stage axial and single-stage centrifugal compressor. It has an annular reverse flow combustor, a single-stage high-pressure turbine, called the gas producer turbine (N_1), and a single-stage low-pressure turbine called the power turbine (N_2).

The PT6-34 has a compressor pressure ratio of 7.0:1, a mass airflow of 6.5 pounds/second, and 823 shaft horsepower at 38,100 r.p.m., 101.5 percent (N_1).

GAS PATH OF THE PT6 AND ENGINE STATION NUMBERING

Figure 4-35B illustrates how air flows along the engine's gas path:

Station 1 — Air enters the flight inlet (not shown) and is directed radially inward through a screened opening that encircles the entrance of the compressor. The screen is located toward the rear of the engine, just forward of the accessory gearbox, which is the rearmost section of the engine.

Station 2 — Air flows into a curved compressor inlet, which angles the air 90 degrees forward into the compressor first stage.

Station 3 — Air moves axially through the first three stages of compression and then radially out of the last (centrifugal) stage into the diffuser at station 3. From there, it continues to move forward between the combustion liner and the combustor outer case to the area of the fuel nozzle. At the forward end of the combustion liner, approximately one-fourth of the air enters the flame zone and the remainder seeps through and surrounds the liner, forming a cooling air blanket. The direction of airflow is now reversed.

Stations 4 and 5 — Air flow reverses again and passes through the single-stage gas producer turbine and the single-stage power turbine.

Stations 6 and 7 — The gases exit the turbines and flow radially outward from a dual-exhaust duct located just in front of the power reduction section.

FIVE MAJOR ENGINE SECTIONS

The five major engine sections shown in Figure 4-36 are:

- **Compressor section** — consists of an air inlet screen, a compressor inlet case, a combination axial-centrifugal compressor, and a diffuser case.

- **Combustor section** — consists of an outer casing and an annular reverse-flow, single basket-type liner. The liner contains fourteen fuel nozzle openings and two igniter plug openings.

- **Turbine and exhaust section** — consists of a two-shaft, two-stage turbine assembly, and a dual exhaust outlet.

- **Propeller reduction gearbox section** — consists of a planetary reduction gearbox of 15:1. The output flange to the propeller rotates at 2,200 r.p.m. when the power turbine is operating at 100 percent speed (33,000 r.p.m.). Mounting pads are provided for accessories on the outer case.

- **Accessory gearbox section** — consists of a reduction gear train and mounting pads for the various engine components and accessories.

COMPRESSOR SECTION

The compressor section is made up of the inlet case, the compressor rotor and stator assembly, and the diffuser. [Figure 4-37]

Engine Familiarization

PERFORMANCE RATINGS—STANDARD, STATIC SEA LEVEL CONDITIONS

MODEL 250-C20 B, F, J RATINGS	OUTPUT SHP (MIN.)	N_1 GAS PRODUCER RPM (EST.)	OUTPUT SHAFT RPM	POWER TURBINE RPM	S.F.C. LB/HR/SHP (MAX)	F.F. FUEL FLOW LBS/HR (MAX)	RAM POWER RATING AT OUTPUT SHAFT — TORQUE FT-LBS (MAX)	RAM POWER RATING AT OUTPUT SHAFT — SHP (MAX)	T.O.T. MEASURED RATED GAS TEMPERATURE °F	T.O.T. MEASURED RATED GAS TEMPERATURE °C	NET JET THRUST LBS. (MIN.)
TAKEOFF (5 MIN.) *30-MINUTE POWER	420	52,000 / 102%	6,016 / 100%	33,290 / 100%	0.630	265	367	420.4	1460	793	40
MAX. CONTINUOUS	405	51,490 / 101%	6,016 / 100%	33,290 / 100%	0.633	256	336	385	1430	777	39
MAX. CRUISE	366	50,200 / 98.5%	6,016 / 100%	33,290 / 100%	0.645	236	302	346	1358	736	36
CRUISE A (90%)	331	49,180 / 96.5%	6,016 / 100%	33,290 / 100%	0.661	218	302	346	1301	705	33
CRUISE B (75%)	280	47,900 / 94%	6,016 / 100%	33,290 / 100%	0.698	195	302	346	1245	674	30
GROUND IDLE	45 MAX.	33,000 / 64.8%	4500-75% TO 6300-105%	24,968-75% TO 34,950-105%	---	70	---	---	800 ±100	427 ±38	10
FLIGHT AUTOROTATION	0	33,000 / 64.8%	5900-98% TO 6480-106%	32,725-98% TO 35,280-106%	---	70	---	---	775 ±100	413 ±38	10

*THIS RATING IS APPLICABLE ONLY DURING ONE-ENGINE-OUT OPERATION OF MULTI-ENGINE AIRCRAFT

100% N_1 = 50,970 RPM
100% N_2 = 33,290 RPM
T.O.T. = GAS PRODUCER TURBINE OUTLET TEMPERATURE
F.F. = FUEL FLOW
S.H.P. = SHAFT HORSEPOWER
S.F.C. = SPECIFIC FUEL CONSUMPTION

$$S.F.C. = \frac{F.F.}{S.H.P.} = THUS, \text{ TAKEOFF } S.F.C. = \frac{265 \text{ LBS/HR}}{420 \text{ S.H.P.}} = 0.630 \text{ LBS./HR./S.H.P.}$$

$$S.H.P. = \frac{TORQUE \times N_2 \times 0.18071}{5252} = \frac{367 \times 6016}{5252} \quad \text{WHERE TORQUE IS IN FT. LBS. \& } N_2 \text{ IS POWER TURBINE RPM.}$$

THUS TAKEOFF RAM POWER RATING S.H.P. = $\frac{367 \times 6016}{5252}$ = 420.4

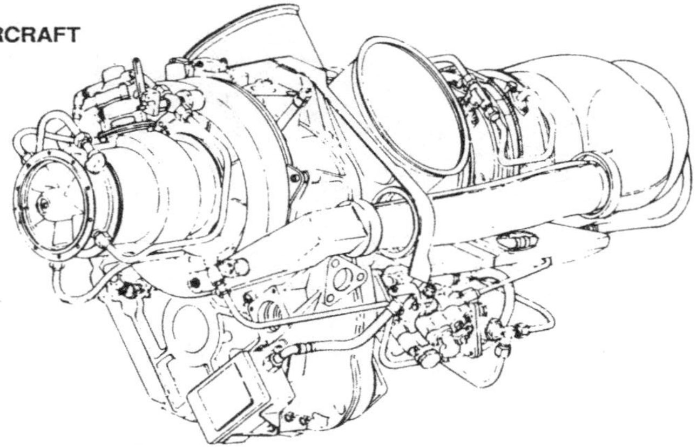

Figure 4-34. Performance Rolls-Royce Allison 250 Models 20B, F, and J

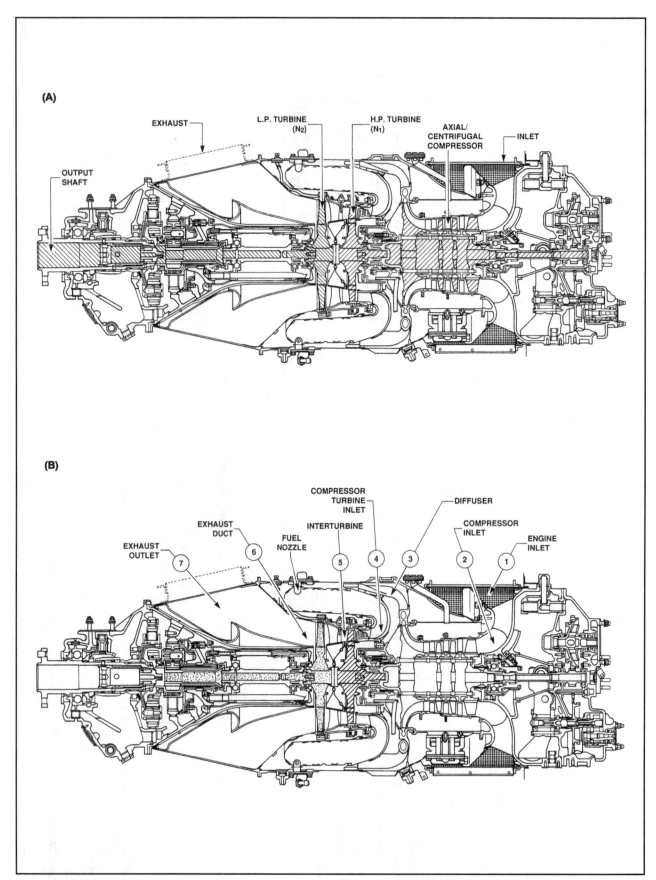

Figure 4-35A. PT6A-34 engine cross-sectional view
Figure 4-35B. Engine stations along the gas path

Engine Familiarization

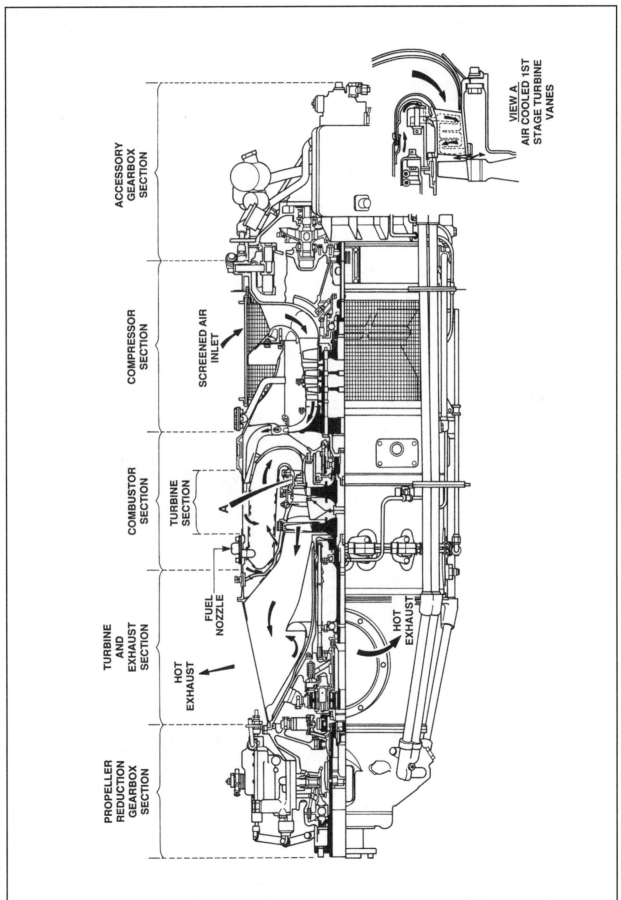

Figure 4-36. Five major sections

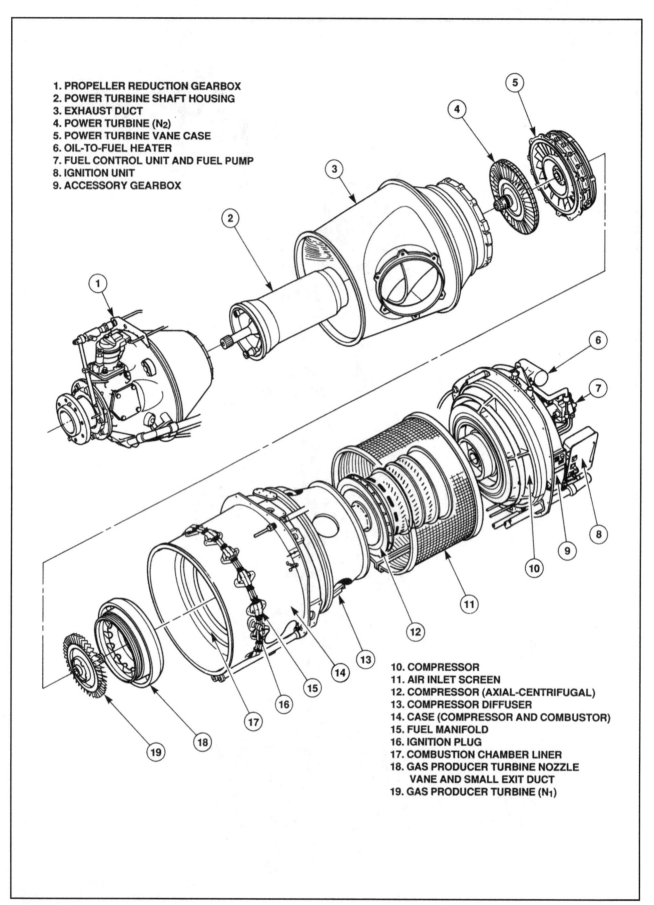

Figure 4-37. Components of major sections

The compressor inlet case consists of a circular aluminum casting, the front of which forms a plenum chamber for the passage of compressor inlet air. The rear portion forms the front of a hollow compartment that functions as an integral oil tank. A large area, circular, wire-mesh screen is located around the air inlet to prevent the compressor from ingesting foreign objects.

The compressor rotor and stator assembly [Figure 4-38] consists of three axial rotor stages, three interstage spacers, three stators, and a single-stage centrifugal impeller and diffuser. The first-stage blades are made of titanium, and the remaining blades are stainless steel. The impeller is made of aluminum alloy.

The wide cord of the first-stage blades provide increased impact tolerance. All blades are fitted to the disk by dovetail-shaped roots. The vanes are all made of stainless steel.

The number 1 main ball bearing and its labyrinth sealing are contained within the inlet case centerbore. This bearing supports the front of the compressor rotor for both axial and radial loads. It is directly lubricated by an oil jet, and this oil is prevented from leaking into the gas path by the labyrinth sealing.

The number 2 main roller bearing supports the rear of the compressor for radial loads. It is located in the centerbore of the rear gas generator case. This bearing is directly lubricated by an oil jet and is protected from leaking oil into the gas path by labyrinth sealing.

The compressor delivers pressurized air radially into the diffuser, which is located within the rear portion of

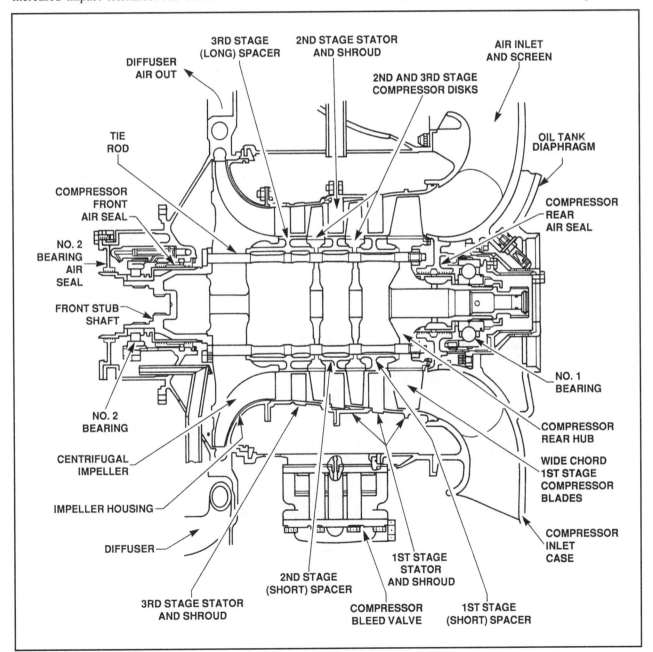

Figure 4-38. Compressor section

the gas generator case. Here the static pressure makes its final increase as air diffuses to the correct pressure and velocity for combustion. The diffuser contains straightening vanes to turn the air back to an axial direction into the combustor.

COMBUSTOR SECTION

The front of the gas generator case forms the outer housing of the combustion section. [Figure 4-39] The circular gas generator case consists of two stainless steel sections fabricated into a single structure. The case contains 14 mounting bosses (fuel nozzle support) for the fuel nozzles and 2 bosses for mounting of the igniter plugs. The PT6 uses 2 different types of igniter plugs to initiate combustion. Ignition systems are explained in detail in Chapter 11.

The combustion liner is an annular reverse-flow type and is constructed of rolled sheet stainless steel.

The combustion section receives the total airflow discharged by the diffuser. The air is channeled first to the forward (domed) end of the liner where the primary air passages are formed. Approximately 25 percent of the air is directed into the liner around the fuel nozzle openings. The remaining 75 percent of the total airflow acts as a cooling air blanket. The outside of the liner is cooled directly, and the louvers provide a film cooling airflow inside of the liner.

GAS PRODUCER TURBINE

The gas producer turbine (N_1), also called the compressor turbine, is a single-stage unit, consisting of the number 1 turbine nozzle and the number 1 turbine rotor. [Figure 4-40] The turbine nozzle is made up of 14 cast nickel alloy, air-cooled vanes. The vane assembly forms a calibrated, effective flow area for combustion gases to accelerate through and discharge into the turbine blades at the correct angle.

The N_1 turbine is fitted with individually removable blades. Each blade has a fir tree root that attaches it to the turbine disk and a rivet that retains the blade in its serrated slot. [Figure 4-41]

The open-tip blades are made of cast nickel alloy. They have a reduced thickness at the tips, called squealer tips, to provide minimum rubbing on the shroud ring if contact occurs.

The N_1 turbine is supported by the number 2 bearing, which also supports the rear of the compressor. The N_1 turbine drives the compressor and accessory gearbox directly from combustor discharge gases.

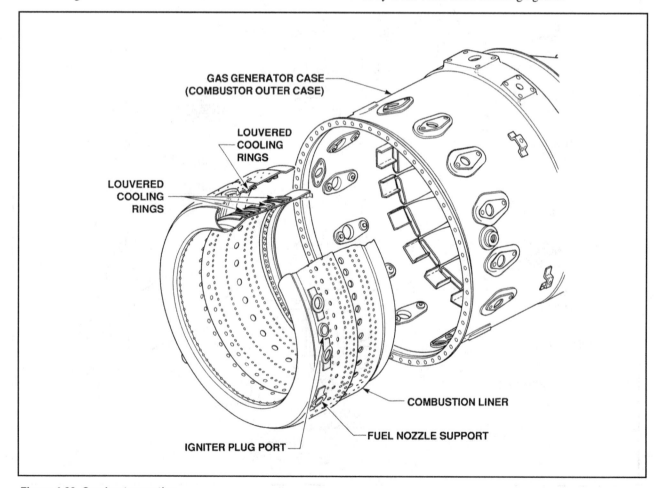

Figure 4-39. Combustor section

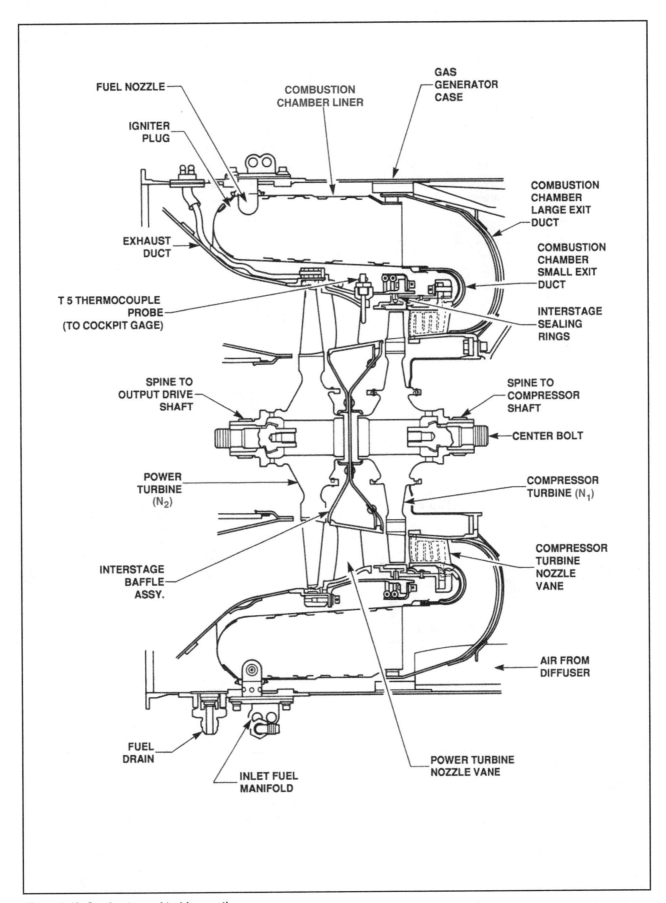

Figure 4-40. Combustor and turbine sections

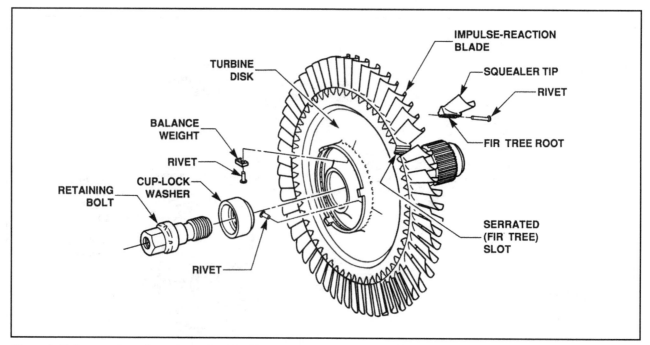

Figure 4-41. Gas producer (compressor) turbine N_1

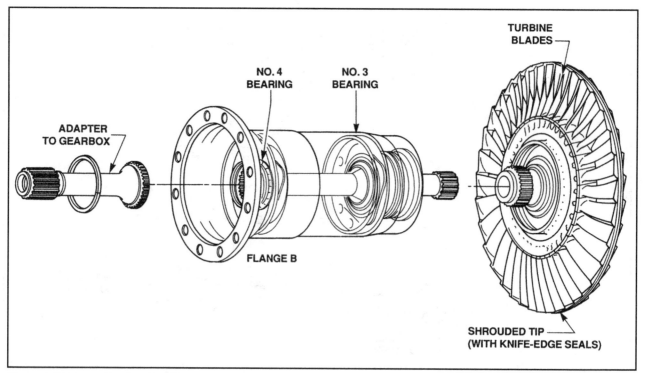

Figure 4-42. Power (free) turbine N_2

POWER TURBINE

The power turbine (N_2) is a single-stage unit, consisting of the number 2 turbine nozzle and the number 2 turbine rotor. N_2 is located toward the front of the engine, directly in front of the gas producer turbine. [Figure 4-42]

The turbine nozzle consists of 19 uncooled, cast steel vanes that direct the flow of gases from the N_1 turbine into the power turbine at the most effective angle.

The power turbine (N_2) is a free turbine, meaning that it has an independent operating speed from the compressor turbine (N_1). The advantages of the free turbine can be found in the power turbine information of the Rolls-Royce 250 turboshaft engine earlier in this chapter.

The power turbine is supported forward of the turbine disk by the number 3 main bearing. It is a roller bearing and supports radial loads. The number 4 main bearing is a ball bearing that supports the front of the N_2 turbine shaft for both radial and axial loads.

Power turbine blades are made of cast nickel alloy and have fir tree roots similar to the N_1 turbine, but the blade tips are shrouded to form a circular support ring. This support ring rides within an outer shroud ring fitted with a double knife-edge seal. This reduces tip leakage and increases turbine efficiency by extracting the required energy before the gases exit the engine via the exhaust duct.

The function of the power turbine is to receive the gas energy spill-over from the N_1 turbine and convert most of this energy into power delivered to the propeller reduction gearbox. Approximately 95 percent of the hot exhaust power is delivered to the propeller, and the remaining 5 percent creates thrust.

EXHAUST DUCT

The exhaust duct is made of heat-resistant sheet stainless steel and provides two outlet ports. [Figure 4-43] The duct is attached to the front flange of the gas generator case and consists of an inner and an outer section. The outer conical section contains the flanged outlet ports and forms the outer gas path. The aircraft tailpipe attaches to these outlet ports and carries the exhaust away from the aircraft in the aft direction, producing approximately 82 pounds of jet thrust at takeoff power.

The inner section forms a compartment for the power reduction gearbox rear case.

The insulation blanket keeps the high temperature exhaust gases from heating the power turbine shaft that runs through it to connect into the power reduction gearbox.

PROPELLER REDUCTION GEARBOX

The propeller reduction gearbox is located at the front of the engine. [Figure 4-36] It consists of magnesium alloy cases that attach to the front of the gas producer case.

Torque from the power turbine is transmitted into the first-stage planet gear to start the reduction in speed of the propeller shaft. The first-stage planet reduction system is located in the rear of the propeller reduction case. The power turbine shaft adapter splines into this reduction system.

The first-stage planet gear is connected to the second-stage planet gear by a shock absorbing coupling and the second-stage planet gear is connected to the propeller shaft. In the second stage, the final reduction takes place, converting, at takeoff power, 33,000 r.p.m. at the power turbine to 2,200 r.p.m. at the propeller shaft.

There are two bearings in the power reduction gearbox. The rear roller bearing supports loads from the planet gear system and the ball bearing supports the propeller for thrust loads. These bearings are not engine main bearings and are not numbered as such. However, engine lubricating oil supplied to the main engine bearings is also routed to the gears, bearings, and torquemeter of the power reduction gearbox.

Figure 4-44 shows the torquemeter, which is located within the power reduction gearbox. It is a hydro-mechanical device connected to the first-stage reduction gear to provide an accurate indication of engine power output. The mechanism consists of a cylinder, piston, and oil metering plunger valve. A helical spline resists the rotation of the first-stage reduction output drive ring gear that imparts an axial movement to the first-stage ring

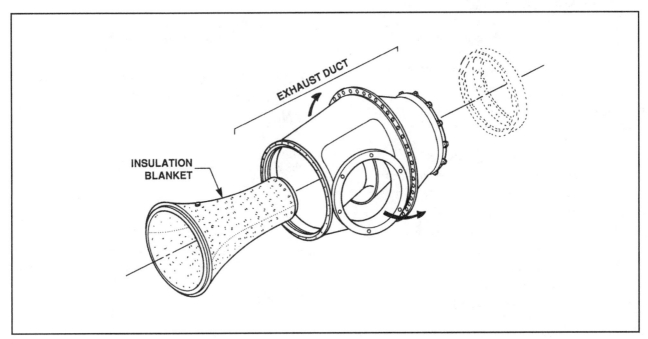

Figure 4-43. Exhaust duct

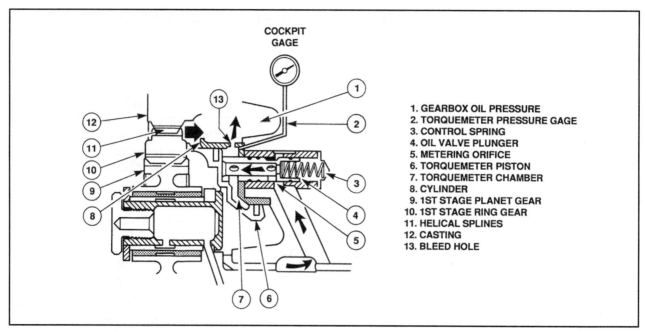

Figure 4-44. Torquemeter assembly

gear and to the torquemeter piston. In turn, this forces the piston onto the oil valve plunger, allowing engine lubricating oil to enter the cylinder. This movement continues until the oil pressure within the torquemeter is equal to torque being applied to the first-stage ring gear. A bleed hole in the torquemeter cylinder allows a continuous flow of oil and bleeds pressure when engine power is reduced.

When engine oil pressure is supplied to the plunger valve, it acts as a variable inlet metering orifice. The bleed hole acts as a fixed calibrated leak. On acceleration, more oil is supplied than is bled away, so pressure builds up in the torquemeter cylinder. This pressure is directed to an electrical transmitter that operates either a cockpit "%" torque gauge or a "psi" torque gauge. When power is reduced, more oil bleeds away through the calibrated leak than enters the system, and the cockpit gauge reading diminishes, showing the reduction in engine power.

ACCESSORY GEARBOX

Figures 4-45, 4-46, and 4-47 show the accessory gearbox, which consists of two magnesium alloy casings attached to the rear of the compressor inlet case. It provides gear reduction and drive pads for the:

- Starter/generator, fuel pump/fuel control unit.
- Tachometer generator.
- Vacuum pump.
- Propeller reduction section scavenge pump.
- Two optional mounting pads.

The gearbox housing also contains mounting points for the oil pressure relief valve and the main oil filter. The gearbox housing contains a pressure oil pump for the entire engine lubricating system, a scavenge pump for the accessory case sump, an impeller type air-oil separator and vent to the atmosphere, and an oil tray, designed to prevent oil foaming during engine operation. The tray inhibits splashing of scavenged oil that drains down to the sump.

The forward bulkhead of the accessory gearbox, called the accessory diaphragm, forms one of the walls of the integral dry sump oil tank compartment. The other oil-tight wall is formed by the compressor inlet case.

ADDITIONAL INFORMATION

Figure 4-48 shows the bearing locations.

Figures 4-49A and 4-49B show engine leading particulars.

The PT6 lubrication system is explained in Chapter 6, and the fuel system is explained in Chapter 7.

FAMILIARIZATION WITH THE GE/SNECMA, CFM56 TURBOFAN ENGINE

All Boeing 737 models from -300 to -900 use the CFM56 engine. [Figure 4-50] A number of Airbus airplanes and engine retrofits on DC-8 and KC-135 aircraft also use the CFM56.

The CFM56 turbofan engine is manufactured by a multi-national company that combines General Electric of the United States and Safran Group-Snecma of France. A number of different models have been made since the engine was introduced in 1978, but this familiarization section concentrates on the -7B model used in the newer generation Boeing 737 aircraft.

The CFM56-7B is available in several different thrust ratings, ranging from 19,500 pounds to 27,300 pounds. The engine is a two-spool, high-bypass turbofan. It has a

Engine Familiarization

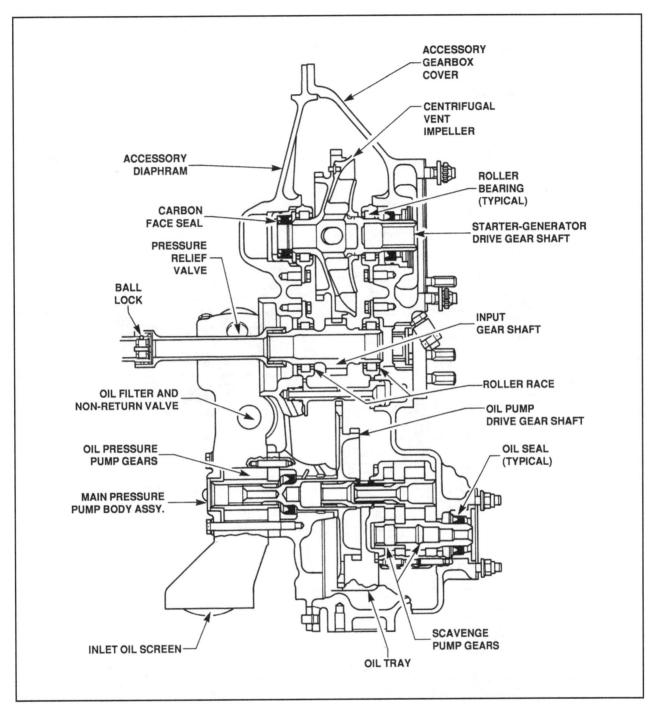

Figure 4-45. Accessory gearbox

single-stage fan plus four additional stages making up the low-pressure compressor. It has a nine-stage, high-pressure compressor. The combustion chamber is an annular type, available as either a single- or dual-annular design. The high-pressure turbine is a single-stage, and the low-pressure turbine has four stages. The engine weighs 5,300 pounds, and is 99 inches in length, 72 inches high, and 83 inches wide.

The CFM56-7B is a modular engine. Seventeen different sub-modules are enclosed in three major engine modules and an accessory drive module. The four modules, shown in Figure 4-51, are:

- The fan module.
- The core engine module.
- The low-pressure turbine module.
- The accessory drive module.

FAN MODULE

The fan module is at the front of the engine, downstream from the air inlet cowl. The fan module is made up

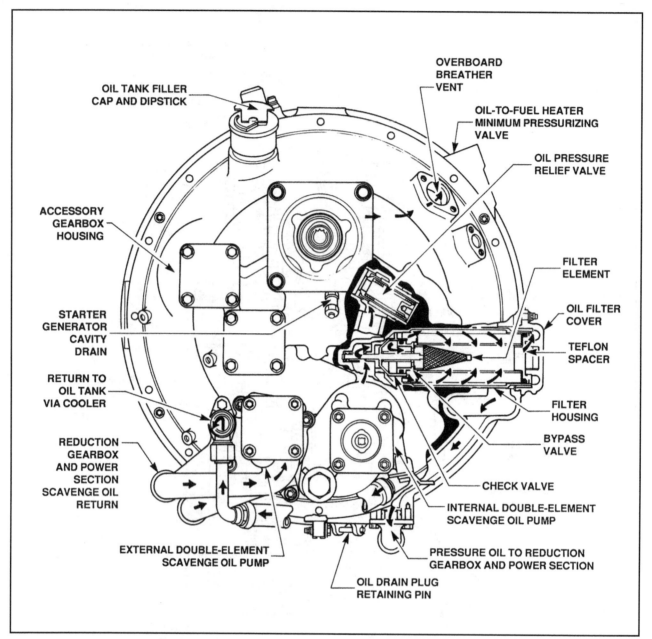

Figure 4-46. Location of components and accessories

of four sub-modules: the fan and booster sub-module, the number 1 and number 2 bearing support sub-module, the fan frame sub-module, and the inlet gearbox and number 3 bearing sub-module.

The main purposes of the fan module are to provide:

- Approximately 80 percent of the engine thrust.
- The engine/pylon front attachment.
- The fan stage and low-pressure compressor stages.
- Structural rigidity in the front section.
- Containment for major deterioration or damage of the front section.
- Noise reduction for the fan section.
- Attachment for gearboxes and nacelle equipment.
- Attachment for the core engine.

FAN AND BOOSTER

The fan and booster sub-module is at the front of the engine, downstream from the air inlet cowl. [Figure 4-52] This sub-module consists of:

- A spinner front cone.
- A spinner rear cone.
- A single-stage fan rotor.
- A three-stage axial booster.

The fan and booster rotating assembly is mounted on the fan shaft, and its fixed assembly is secured to the fan frame.

The spinner front cone is made of a black sulfuric anodized aluminum alloy to minimize ice build-up. The spinner rear cone smoothes airflow at the inlet of the

Engine Familiarization

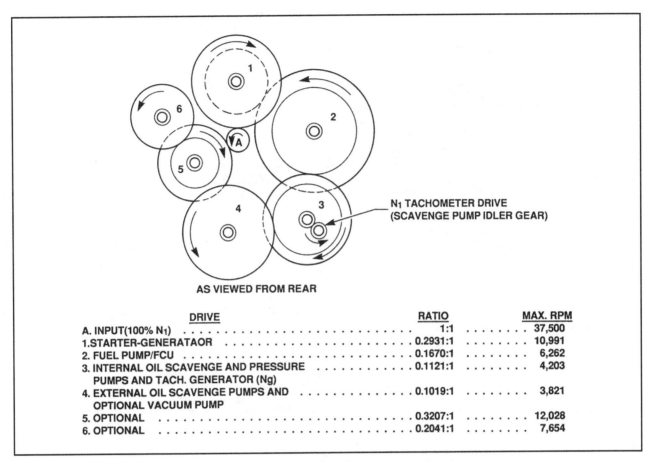

Figure 4-47. Location and gear ratios of components and accessories

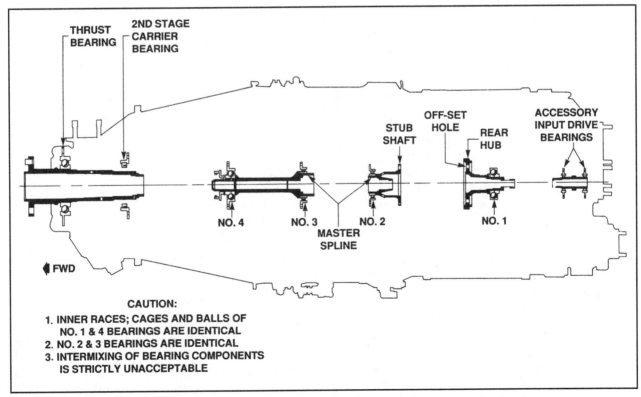

Figure 4-48. Main bearing locations, propeller reduction gearbox bearings, and accessory gearbox bearings

(A)

RATING PT6A-34/-34B/-34G	ESHP	SHP	PROP. RPM	JET THRUST LBS.	FUEL CONSUMPTION (LB./ESHP/HR) AT 15°C (59°F)
TAKEOFF	823	790*	2200	82	0.595
MAX CONTINUOUS/ ENROUTE EMERG.	823	790	2200	82	0.595
MAX CLIMB	769	736	2200	82	0.604
MAX CRUISE	700	667	2200	82	0.604

NOTE: 1. *AVAILABLE TO +30°C (+87°F) AMBIENT
2. H.P. (JET) = JET THRUST ÷ 2.5 = 33
3. CORRESPONDING ROTOR SPEEDS: GAS GENERATOR—38,100 RPM MAX.
POWER TURBINE—33,000 RPM

ENGINE TYPE	FREE TURBINE
TYPE OF COMBUSTION CHAMBER	ANNULAR REVERSE FLOW
COMPRESSOR RATIO	7.0.:1
PROPELLER SHAFT ROTATION (LOOKING FORWARD)	CLOCKWISE
PROPELLER SHAFT CONFIGURATION	FLANGED
PROPELLER SHAFT GEAR RATIO	0.0668:1
ENGINE DIAMETER, BASIC AT ROOM TEMPERATURE	19 INCHES
ENGINE LENGTH, BASIC AT ROOM TEMPERATURE	62 INCHES
OIL CONSUMPTION, MAXIMUM AVERAGE	0.2 LB/HR.
DRY WEIGHT (APPROXIMATELY)	292 LBS.

(B)

PT6A-34/-34B/-34G

OPERATING CONDITIONS			LIMITS							
POWER SETTING	TEMP. AVAILABLE TO	MAX. ESHP	N_1 (100 = 37500 RPM) %	RPM	N_2 (100 = 2200 RPM) %	RPM	MAXIMUM OBSERVED ITT(T_{t5})	MAXIMUM TORQUE FT. LB. PSI		NORMAL OIL PRESSURE (PSIG)	OIL TEMPERATURE RANGE
TAKEOFF AND MAX. CONTINUOUS, ENROUTE EMERGENCY	30.6°C (87°F)	823	101.5	38,100	100	2200	790°C	1970	64.5	85 TO 105	+10° TO +99°C (+50° TO +210°F)
MAX. CLIMB	28.3°C (83°F)	769	101.5	38,100	100	2200	765°C	1840	60.2	85 TO 105	+10° TO +99°C (+50° TO +210°F)
MAX. CRUISE	19.4°C (67°F)	700	101.5	38,100	100	2200	740°C	1840	60.2	85 TO 105	0° TO +99°C (+32° TO +210°F)
GROUND IDLE			52.5	19,750 (TYPICAL)			685°C			40 (MIN)	−40° TO −99° (−40° TO +210°F)
STARTING							1090°C				−40° (MIN.)
MOMENTARY ACCELERATION			102.6	38,500	110	2420	850°C	2100	68.4	85 TO 105	0° TO 99°C (+32° TO +210°F)
MAX. REVERSE		750	101.5	38,100	95(±1%)	2100	790°C	1970	64.5	85 TO 105	0° TO 99°C (+32° TO +210°F)

Figure 4-49A. PT6A-34 engine leading particulars
Figure 4-49B. Operating conditions and limits

engine and provides anti-rotation of the fan retaining ring. It also accommodates the fan retaining flange and balancing screws used in fan trim and static balance procedures.

The fan disk is forged from a titanium alloy. The outer front flange provides attachment for the rear cone and the retaining flange. The outer rim of the fan disk has 24 curved, dovetail slots for fan blade retention.

The fan blades form the first stage of the low-pressure compressor and accelerate the air entering the engine through the air inlet cowls. There are 24 titanium alloy, wide-chord fan blades, each with a dovetail base that slides into a recess on the outer rim of the fan disk. A retainer lug, machined at the rear end of the blade root, engages the forward flange of the booster spool and limits axial movement.

The part number, the serial number, the moment weight, and the manufacturer code are engraved on the bottom of the blade root. The fan blade root faces have an anti-friction plasma coating and a top coat of cured molybdenum-base varnish, which acts as a lubricant.

The three-stage booster rotor consists of a booster spool, forged and machined from titanium alloy, which is cantilever-mounted on the rear of the fan disk. The inner front flange acts as a stop for the fan blades. The booster rotor blades are installed in dovetail slots and supercharge the high-speed compressor.

Engine Familiarization

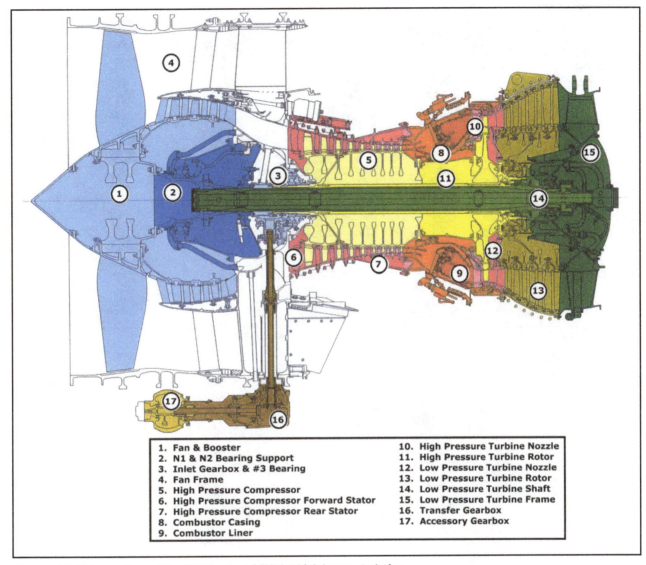

Figure 4-50. Major sections of the G.E./Snecma CFM56-7 high-bypass turbofan

NUMBER 1 AND 2 BEARING SUPPORT SUB-MODULE

The number 1 and number 2 bearing support module belongs to the fan module. [Figure 4-53] The sub-module has a number of functions:

- Supports the fan booster rotor
- Encloses the front section of the forward oil sump
- Supports one of the vibration sensors
- Vents the forward sump
- Provides the fan speed indication
- Directs bearing lubrication

The number 1 bearing support is a titanium casting. The front flange of the support holds the number 1 ball bearing, and its rear outer flange is bolted to the fan frame center hub. The support front flange provides an attachment to the number 1 bearing stationary air/oil seal and the number 1 bearing vibration sensor. The number 1 bearing is a ball bearing that takes up the axial and radial loads generated by the low-pressure rotor system.

The number 2 bearing support is a titanium casting. Its front inner flange holds the number 2 bearing outer race and also allows for the installation of the number 2 bearing oil nozzle. The support also accommodates a guide sleeve for installation of the N_1 speed sensor probe. The number 2 bearing is a roller type and takes up some of the radial loads from the fan and booster rotor.

FAN FRAME SUB-MODULE

The fan frame sub-module is the structure at the front of the engine. [Figure 4-54] It consists of four major assemblies: the containment case, the outlet guide vane assembly, the fan frame assembly, and the radial drive shaft housing. The main purposes of the fan frame sub-module are to:

- Provide ducting for both the primary and secondary airflows.
- Transmit the engine's thrust to the aircraft.
- Support the low-pressure compressor rotor, through the number 1 and 2 bearing support.

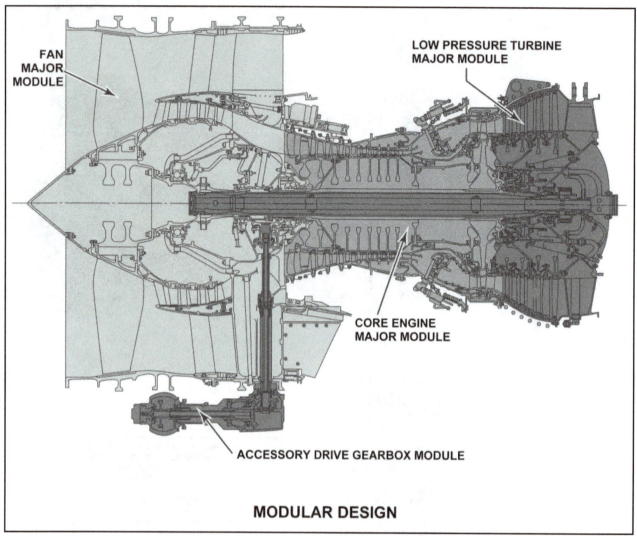

Fig. 4-51 — CFM56-7 Modular design

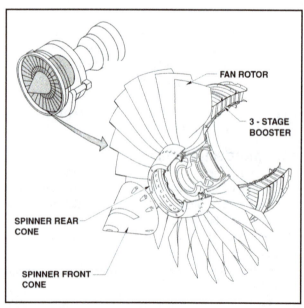

Figure 4-52. CFM56-7 fan and booster module

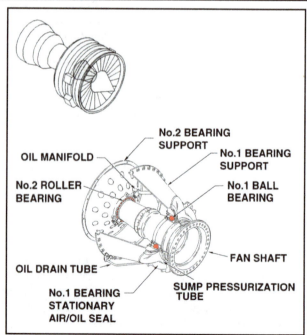

Figure 4-53. CFM56-7 number 1 and 2 bearing support module

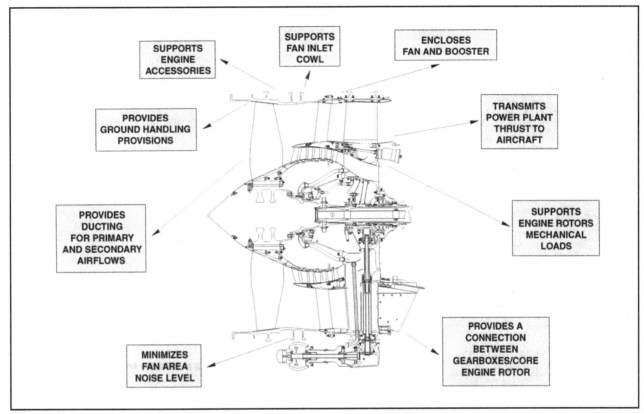

Figure 4-54. CFM56-7 fan frame module main purposes

- Support the front of the high-pressure compressor rotor through the number 3 bearing support.
- Enclose the fan and the booster.
- Support various engine accessories.
- Minimize fan area noise levels.
- Provide attachment for the forward engine mounts, front handling trunnions, and lifting points.
- Support the fan inlet cowl.
- Provide a connection between gearboxes and core engine rotor.

The containment case is a single part made of aluminum alloy. Its outer rear flange is bolted to the outer front flange of the frame shroud. The flanges and ribs on the outer surface provide more strength to the case during engine operation and also provide attachment for equipment brackets. Its inner surface houses an abradable shroud, located radially in line with the fan rotor blades.

The outlet guide vane assembly is at the rear of the containment case. Its purpose is to direct and smooth the secondary airflow to increase thrust efficiency. The assembly consists of the fan outlet guide vane inner shroud and 76 aluminum-alloy vanes.

The fan frame assembly is the major structure at the forward section of the engine. It consists of the fan frame shroud, a 12-strut hub, and a radial drive shaft housing. The fan frame shroud is made from aluminum alloy, and the strut hub is made from titanium alloy.

The strut at the 9 o'clock position contains both the forward sump oil supply tube and the radial drive shaft housing. The radial drive shaft is the mechanical rotating link between the inlet gearbox and the transfer gearbox.

CORE ENGINE MODULE

Figure 4-55 shows the core engine major module, which is made up of the high-pressure compressor rotor, the combustion case and combustion chamber, and the high-pressure turbine.

HIGH-PRESSURE COMPRESSOR

The high-pressure compressor consists of nine stages. It is housed in the compressor case, and the rotor front end is supported by the number 3 bearing (combination ball and roller).

Stages 1 and 2 are cantilever mounted on the front face of the rotor shaft flange and welded together as one unit. The disks are titanium alloy, with 38 blades fitted to stage 1 and 53 blades fitted to stage 2 by dovetail attachments. All blades are titanium alloy.

The stage 3 disk mates with the rotor shaft flange and supports the stage-four through stage-nine disks. It is made of titanium alloy and has individual axial dovetail slots for its 60 titanium alloy blades. Retainer hooks are machined on either side of the disk to provide a slot for the installation of split-ring blade retainers.

The nickel-based alloy spool, made up of stages 4 through 9, is bolted onto the stage-three disk rear face. The outer surface of each disk has a circumferential dovetail groove for the installation of the blades. Each

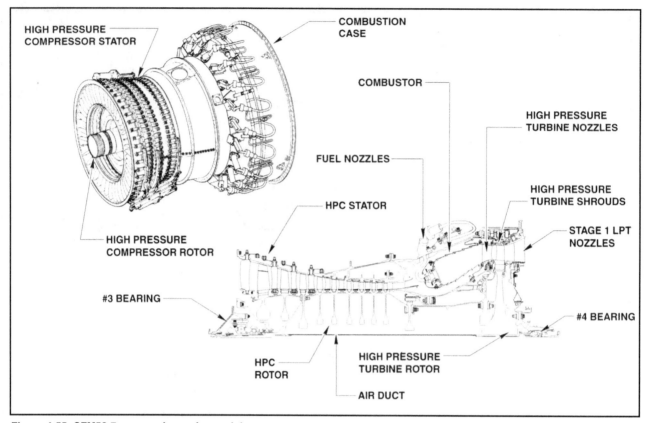

Figure 4-55. CFM56-7 core engine major module

blade tip has a reduced thickness, known as a profile tip or squealer tip. The blades are all made of nickel alloy. The blade count is as follows:

Stage	Blades
1	38
2	53
3	60
4	68
5	75
6	82
7	82
8	80
9	76

The high-pressure compressor case forms the load carrying structure between the fan frame and the combustion case. The case is made up of a front and a rear section, each with a top and a bottom half.

The front case [Figure 4-56] contains the first five stages of the high-pressure compressor, with the two halves being machined as a matched set from a steel forging. Housed within the front case are the inlet guide vanes, the variable stator vanes for stages 1, 2, and 3, and the fixed stator vanes for stages 4 and 5. The inner surface of the case is machined to provide a smooth air flow path through all five stages.

There are ports at stages 4 and 5 to accommodate pipes that supply bleed air for both engine and aircraft use. Bleed air from the stage 4 is extracted for high-pressure turbine cooling and clearance control and for low-pressure turbine cooling. Bleed air from stage 5 is for customer service air.

The rear case shown in Figure 4-57 is for stages 6 through 9 of the high-pressure compressor, with the two halves being machined as a matched set from a zinc-nickel-cobalt alloy forging. The fixed stator vanes for stages 6, 7, and 8 are in the rear case. The fixed stator vane for stage 9 is part of the combustion case.

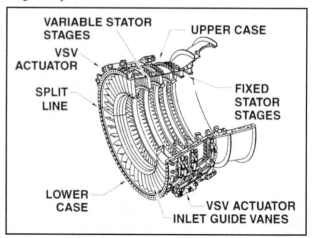

Figure 4-56. CFM56-7 high-pressure compressor front stator design

Engine Familiarization

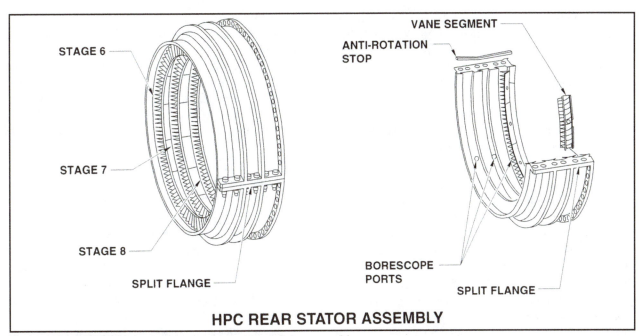

Figure 4-57. CFM56-7 high-pressure compressor rear stator assembly

COMBUSTION SECTION

The combustion section is located between the high-pressure compressor and the low-pressure turbine, and is made up of a combustion case and a combustion chamber. [Figure 4-58] There are two versions of combustion chamber, a single annular combustor (SAC) and a dual

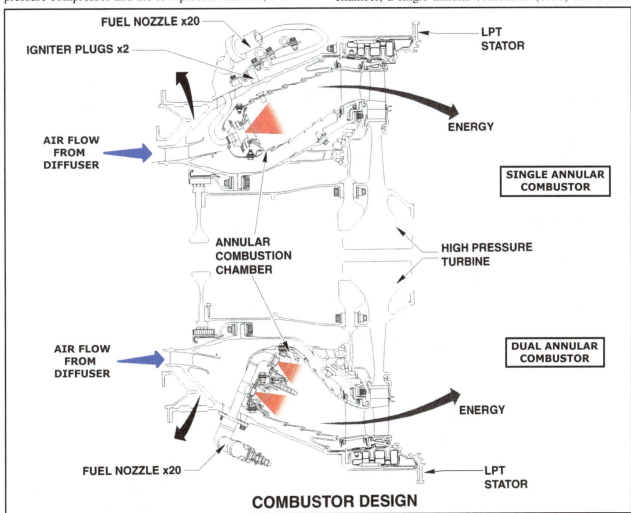

Figure 4-58. CFM56-7 combustor design (single annular, top; dual annular, bottom)

annular combustor (DAC). The SAC has 20 individual locations around its circumference for 20 single-line duplex fuel nozzles; the DAC has 10 circumferential locations for 10 pairs of fuel nozzles. In the SAC and DAC, air from the compressor, called primary airflow for combustion, mixes with fuel supplied by 20 fuel nozzles. (SAC and DAC combustors were discussed in chapter 3.) The combustion case also provides the ports for high-pressure compressor stage-nine bleed air.

The combustion case is a weldment structure that provides the structural interface between the high-pressure compressor, the combustor, and the low-pressure turbine. It also transmits the engine axial loads. It incorporates the compressor outlet guide vanes and a diffuser, which slows the air flow prior to delivering it to the combustion area. The mounting pads around the outer surface accommodate 20 fuel nozzles and 2 igniter plugs.

The combustion chamber is a short annular structure housed in the combustion case. It is installed between the high-pressure compressor stage-nine stator and the high-pressure turbine nozzle. The chamber is made from a nickel-chrome alloy and coated with a thermal barrier material

HIGH-PRESSURE TURBINE

The high-pressure turbine (HPT) is a single-stage, air cooled assembly that converts the kinetic energy in the gasses leaving the combustion chamber into torque to drive the high-pressure compressor. [Figure 4-59] It is housed in the aft portion of the combustion case. The assembly consists of the high-pressure turbine nozzle and rotor, the high-pressure turbine shroud, and the stage-one low-pressure turbine nozzle.

The high-pressure turbine nozzle consists of 21 nozzle segments, each with two vanes that are brazed to inner and outer platforms. Each vane is a cast shell divided into forward and aft cooling compartments by an inner rib.

The vanes and platforms are cooled by compressor discharge air that enters the vane compartments through inserts in the inner and outer ends of the vanes. The air exits through leading edge holes and trailing edge slots. The vanes are made of a nickel base alloy and covered with a thermal protective coating.

The high-pressure turbine rotor front shaft forms the structural connection between the high-pressure compressor and the high-pressure turbine. It is made from a nickel-chrome alloy. The front flange on the shaft is

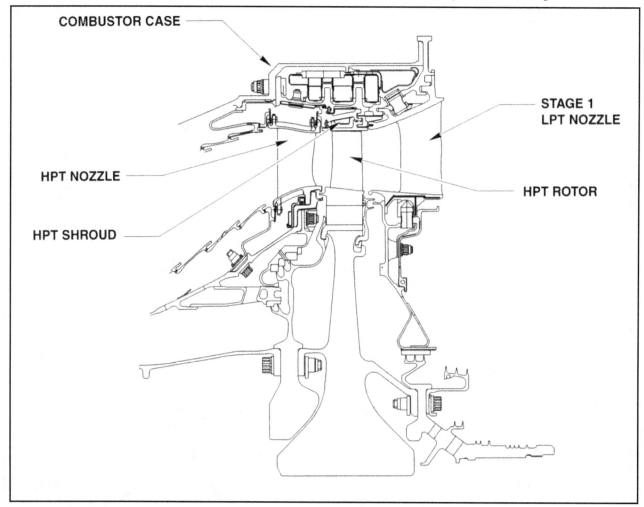

Figure 4-59. CFM56-7 high-pressure turbine

bolted to the high-pressure compressor, stages 4 to 9. It includes a damper sleeve on its inner surface to change vibration frequency.

The high-pressure turbine disk is a forged and machined part, with individual axial dovetail slots that retain the turbine blades. The blades are held in position at the front by a rotating air seal and at the rear by blade retainers and a seal ring. The inner part of the disk, as well as the front and rear faces, are cooled by compressor bleed air.

The high-pressure turbine blades are made of a high-temperature, single-crystal nickel alloy. There are 80 individually replaceable blades, with open tips, internally cooled by compressor bleed air that enters through the blade root and exits through holes in the leading edge, tip, and trailing edge.

The high-pressure turbine rear shaft provides aft support for the rotor through the number 4 bearing, which is a roller type. Thirty-six radial and axial holes allow the passage of oil in order to cool the number 4 bearing outer race. It also has holes providing passages for booster discharge bleed air to cool the low-pressure turbine, and booster air to pressurize the aft sump.

The high-pressure turbine shroud and the stage-one, low-pressure turbine nozzle assembly form the connection between the core section and the low-pressure turbine module of the engine. This assembly is located inside the aft end of the combustion case, and it performs two main functions:

- The shroud is part of the high-pressure turbine clearance control mechanism. It uses high-pressure compressor bleed air to maintain close clearances with the high-pressure turbine rotor blades throughout flight operations.
- The stage-one, low-pressure turbine nozzles direct the core engine exhaust gas onto the stage-one low-pressure turbine blades.

Between the combustion case and the high-pressure turbine case, there is an air impingement manifold that circulates stage 4 and 9 bleed air for active clearance control of the high-pressure turbine blades and for cooling of the low-pressure turbine nozzle. There are three air supply tubes on the manifold's inner surface that circulate the air to cool down the high-pressure turbine shroud.

The low-pressure turbine nozzle directs high-velocity gasses from the high-pressure turbine rotor onto the blades of the low-pressure turbine rotor stage 1. The assembly consists of 24 nozzle segments of 4 vanes each. The nozzle is air cooled by air from stage 4 of the high-pressure compressor.

LOW-PRESSURE TURBINE MODULE

The purpose of the low-pressure turbine (LPT), shown in Figure 4-60, is to transform the pressure and velocity of the gasses from the high-pressure turbine into torque

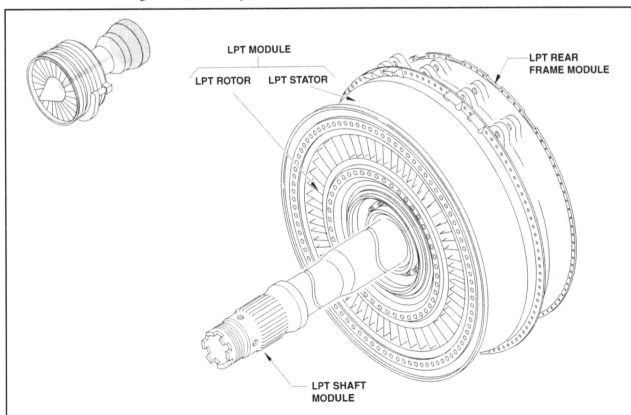

Figure 4-60. CFM56-7 low-pressure turbine major module

to drive the fan and booster module. It also provides support for the high-pressure system and a rear mount location for installation on the aircraft. It is a four-stage, axial-flow design.

TURBINE CASE

The nickel alloy turbine case incorporates eight thermocouple mounting pads and three borescope ports. The case is air cooled for active clearance control, and it uses six cooling air tubes, which surround the engine. The tubes are pressurized with fan discharge air.

TURBINE NOZZLES AND DISKS

The low-pressure turbine module incorporates the nozzles for the stage 2, 3, and 4 turbine wheels. The nozzle for the first-stage wheel is part of the high-pressure module. The nozzle assemblies are made of nickel alloy, protected against oxidation by a vapor-phase aluminization treatment. There are 108 vanes in the stage-two nozzle, 140 vanes in the stage-three nozzle, and 132 vanes in the stage-four nozzle.

The turbine disks in the low-pressure turbine are made of nickel alloy. They have dovetail slots to accept the turbine blades.

TURBINE BLADES

The four stages of the low-pressure turbine have shrouded tip blades made of nickel alloy. On stages 1 and 2 only, the blades are protected against oxidation by a vapor-phase aluminization treatment. There are 162 blades in stage 1, 150 blades in stage 2, 150 blades in stage 3, and 134 blades in stage 4. Three blades of each stage have a hard coating on their tips, to rub against the honeycomb material of the stator seal segments.

TURBINE SHAFT

The low-pressure turbine shaft is made of steel alloy. [Figure 4-61] It transmits torque from the turbine to the fan and booster module. It is installed concentrically inside the high-pressure rotor system. The shaft is supported by the number 5 main bearing, which is a roller type.

The forward end of the low-pressure turbine shaft has outer splines that engage inner splines on the fan shaft. It also has a shoulder that is secured against a mating shoulder in the fan shaft by a coupling nut. The shoulder and coupling nut provide axial retention of the low-pressure turbine shaft.

Running through the middle of the low-pressure turbine shaft is a vent tube that provides overboard venting for the engine forward and rear oil sumps. A centrifugal air/oil separator is installed at the end of the tube to separate the vaporized oil from the aft sump pressurization air. The separated oil joins the oil supply to the number

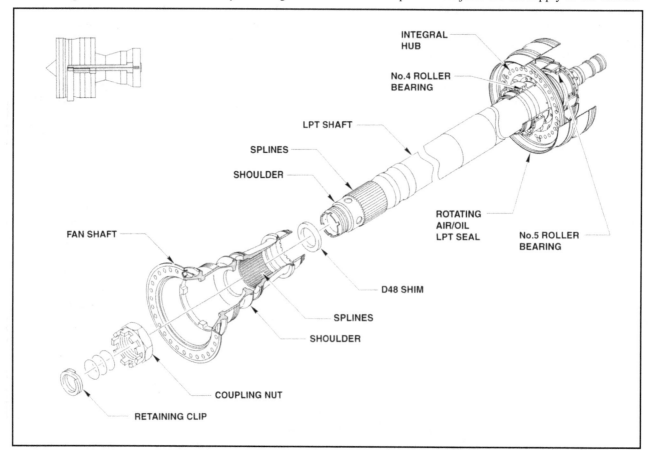

Figure 4-61. Low-pressure turbine shaft

4 and 5 main bearings. The air that vents overboard exits through a flame arrestor in the middle of the last low-pressure turbine stage.

REAR FRAME

The low-pressure turbine rear frame at the rear of the engine is one of the engine's major structural assemblies. It is made of nickel alloy. Its front section is bolted to the rear flange of the low-pressure turbine case, and its rear section provides attachment for the exhaust nozzle and exhaust plug, which are both part of the nacelle.

ACCESSORY DRIVE MODULE

At engine start, the accessory drive system transmits external power from the engine's air turbine starter to drive the core engine. [Figure 4-62] When the engine is running, the accessory drive system extracts part of the core engine power and transmits it through a series of gearboxes and shafts to drive the engine and aircraft accessories.

The accessory drive system is located at the 9 o'clock position and consists of:

- The inlet gearbox, which takes power from the high-pressure compressor front shaft.
- The radial drive shaft, which transmits the power to the transfer gearbox.
- The transfer gearbox, which redirects the torque.
- The horizontal drive shaft, which transmits power from the transfer gearbox to the accessory gearbox.
- The accessory gearbox, which supports and drives both engine and aircraft accessories.

INLET GEARBOX

The inlet gearbox transfers torque between the high-pressure compressor front shaft and the radial drive shaft. It also supports the front end of the core engine. It is located in the fan frame sump and bolted to the forward side of the fan frame aft flange. It is only accessible after many of the other engine modules have been removed.

The inlet gearbox contains:

- The horizontal bevel gear, with a coupling/locking nut.
- The radial bevel gear.
- The number 3 main bearing (ball and roller).
- The rotating air/oil seal.

RADIAL DRIVE SHAFT

The radial drive shaft transmits power from the inlet gearbox to the transfer gearbox. The assembly is installed inside the fan frame number 10 strut at the 9 o'clock position. It consists of an inner radial drive shaft and housing, a shaft mid-length bearing, and an outer radial drive shaft and housing.

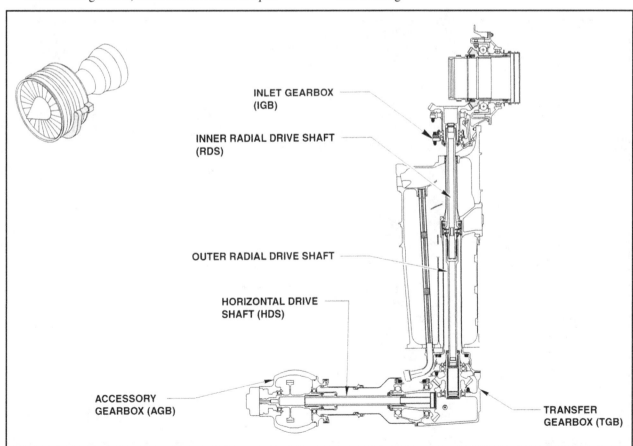

Figure 4-62. CFM56-7 accessory drive section design

TRANSFER GEARBOX

Driven by the radial drive shaft, the transfer gearbox reduces rotational speed and redirects the torque from the inlet gearbox to the accessory gearbox, through the horizontal drive shaft. It is secured under the fan frame module at the 9 o'clock position.

HORIZONTAL DRIVE SHAFT

The horizontal drive shaft provides power transmission between the transfer gearbox and the accessory gearbox. It consists of a steel and aluminum outer tube that encloses the inner drive shaft. The steel drive shaft is splined at both ends for connection to the transfer and accessory gearboxes.

ACCESSORY GEARBOX

The accessory gearbox supports and drives both aircraft and engine accessories. [Figure 4-63] It is mounted on the left hand side of the fan frame at the 9 o'clock position. The housing is an aluminum alloy casting.

The accessory gearbox consists of a gear train that reduces and increases the rotational speed to meet the specific drive requirements of each accessory. Figure 4-64 shows the gearbox arrangement and the relationship of rotational speeds. The front face of the gearbox has mount pads for the following accessories:

- The hydraulic pump, with a ratio to the N_2 of 0.257
- The integrated drive generator, with a ratio to the N_2 of 0.565
- The starter, with a ratio to the N_2 of 1.002
- The hand-cranking drive, with a ratio to the N_2 of 0.986
- The control alternator (FADEC power supply), with a ratio to the N_2 of 1.301

The rear face of the gearbox has mount pads for the following accessories:

- The lubrication unit, with a ratio to the N_2 of 0.423
- The scavenge oil filter
- The fuel pump and hydromechanical unit, with a ratio to the N_2 of 0.426

ENGINE DATA SHEETS

The Engine Data Sheets [Figures 4-65 to 4-71] show data and specifications for selected engines. A complete set of specifications for nearly every engine in world use is available in the *Encyclopedia of Jet Aircraft and Engines*.

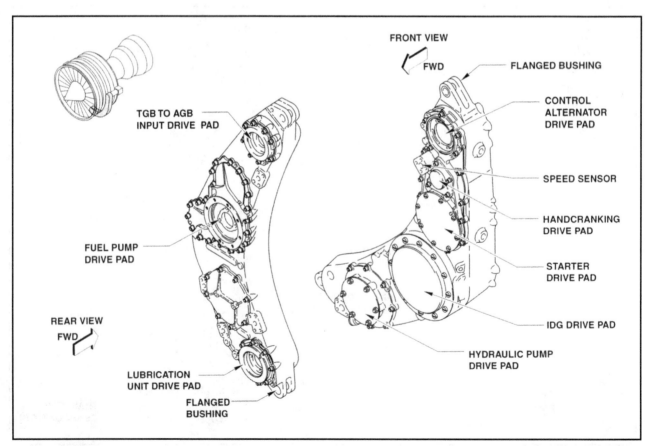

Figure 4-63. CFM56-7 accessory gearbox housing

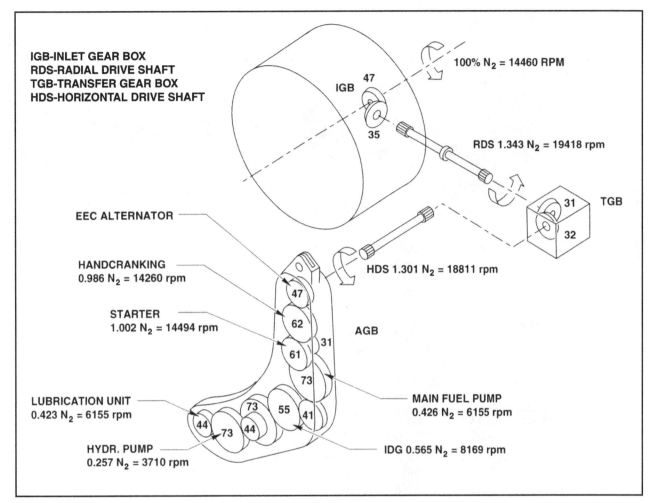

Figure 4-64. CFM56-7 accessory drive system gear train

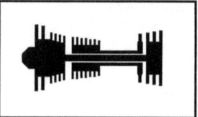

MANUFACTURER: **UNITED TECHNOLOGIES CORP.**
(Pratt & Whitney Aircraft Group)
Commercial Products Division, East Hartford, Conn.

DESIGNATION: JT8D-17A.

BACKGROUND: Derivative of the Military J52 Turbojet. Originally developed for the Boeing B727 Airliner.
Date First J52 Engine Produced: 1958.
Date First JT8D Engine Produced: 1963.

ENGINE TYPE: Turbofan
Dual-Shaft, Low-Bypass, Front Fan.

COMPRESSOR TYPE: 13-Stage Dual-Spool, Axial Flow Compressor including: 2-Stage Front Fan and 4 Axial Stages in the Low Pressure Compressor, 7-Stage High Pressure Compressor.

COMPRESSOR DATA (Take-Off): Compressor Pressure Ratio: 16.9 : 1, Fan Pressure Ratio: 2.11 : 1, Fan Bypass Ratio: 1.0 : 1, Total Mass Airflow: 331 lb/sec. Fan Diameter: 42.5 inch.

TURBINE TYPE: 4-Stage Axial Flow Turbine including: 1-Stage High Pressure Turbine, 3-Stage Low Pressure Turbine.

COMBUSTOR TYPE: Can-Annular, Through-Flow, with (9) Combustion Liners.

POWER (take-off) RATING: 16,000 lbt. Rating Approved to: 84°F (29°C).
Cruise TSFC: 0.806 lb/hr/lbt.

TAKE-OFF SPECIFIC FUEL CONSUMPTION (TSFC): 0.62 lb/hr/lbt.

ENGINE WEIGHT (less tailpipe): 3,500 lbs.

POWER/WEIGHT RATIO: 4.97 : 1 lbt/lb.

APPLICATION: Boeing B727, B737, McDonnell-Douglas DC-9-30, -50 Airliners.

OTHER ENGINES IN SERIES:
JT8D-1 in Boeing B727 Airliner and McDonnell-Douglas DC-9-5 and DC-9-10 Airliners.
JT8D-7 (14,000 lbt) in B727, DC-9, Aerospatiale Caravelle and Super Caravelle Airliners.
JT8D-9,-9A (14,500 lbt) in B727, B737, DC-9, Caravelle Airliners.
JT8D-11 (15,000 lbt) in DC-9, Dassault Mercure And Caravelle Airliners.
JT8D-15 (15,500 lbt) in B727, B737, DC-9, Dassault Mercure-2 Airliners; Boeing C-22B.
JT8D-15AR (16,400 lbt) in B727-100/200, B737, DC-9 Airliners.
JT8D-17 (16,000 lbt) also in Indonesian "Surveiller" Patrol Aircraft.
JT8D-17R in Boeing B727-100, and -200 Airliners.
JT8D-9 (14,500 lbt) In Kawasaki C-1 Transport Aircraft.
JT8D-200 in B737, MD-80, Boeing E-8

Figure 4-65. Data sheet, Pratt & Whitney, USA, JT8D-17A turbofan engine

Engine Familiarization

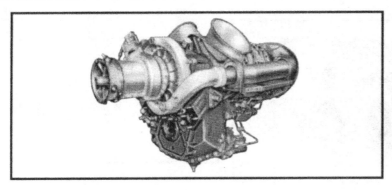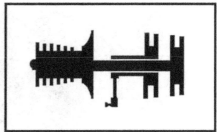

MANUFACTURER:	**ALLISON GAS TURBINE COMPANY** (DIVISION OF ROLLS-ROYCE) **Indianapolis, Indiana.**
DESIGNATION:	250-C20B.
BACKGROUND:	Civil version of the military T-63 Turboshaft. Date First 250-C20R Engine Produced: 1970.
ENGINE TYPE:	Turboshaft Dual-Shaft, Single Compressor.

COMPRESSOR TYPE: Combination Compressor: 6-Stage Axial, 1-Stage Centrifugal.

COMPRESSOR DATA (Take-Off): Compressor Pressure Ratio: 7.2 : 1, Total Mass Airflow: 3.8 lb/sec.

TURBINE TYPE: 4-Stage Axial Flow Turbine, including a 2-Stage Gas Producer (compressor drive) Turbine, 2-Stage Power (free) Turbine.

COMBUSTOR TYPE: Reverse-Flow, Can Type Combustor.

POWER (take-off) RATING: 420 shp. Rating Approved to: 59°F (15°C).

TAKE-OFF SPECIFIC FUEL CONSUMPTION (SFC): 0.65 lb/hr/shp.

ENGINE WEIGHT (less tailpipe): 161 lbs.

POWER/WEIGHT RATIO: 2.6 : 1 shp/lb.

APPLICATION:

250-C20B, F, J; in:	Bell 206B/L, Bell TH-67, and Hughes 500D/E, USA.
250-C20B in:	MBB BO.105, Germany. Brenda-Nardi 369D, India. Agusta AB 206, Italy. IPTN NBO.105, Indonesia. Kawasaki OH-6D, Japan. WSK-PZL Mi-2, Poland. Rogerson-Hiller UH-12, USA.
250-C20R in:	Agusta A.109A, Italy.MDHC MD-500/530, USA, Rhein-Flugbugbar, FT-400 "FanTrainer" Ducted Fan type Helicopter.
250-C20W in:	Enstrom TH-28 & Enstrom 480, USA. Schweizer TH-330, USA.

Figure 4-66. Data sheet, Rolls-Royce Allison, USA, 250-C20B turboshaft engine

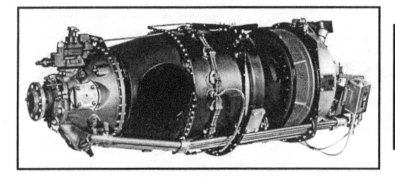
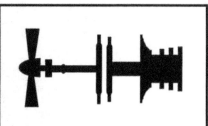

COUNTRY: CANADA

MANUFACTURER: PRATT & WHITNEY OF CANADA, INC. LONGUEUIL, QUEBEC.

DESIGNATION: PT6A-34.

BACKGROUND: Military version designated T-74-CP-701. The PT6 Series ranges in power output from 500 eshp (373 ekw) to 1,875 eshp (1,398 ekw). It is the most widely used Small Gas Turbine Engine in world service.
Date First PT6 Produced: 1963.

ENGINE TYPE: Turboprop
Rear Drive, Dual-Shaft (Compressor Drive & Power Output Drive).

COMPRESSOR TYPE: Combination, Axial-Centrifugal Flow Compressor including: 3-Stages of Axial Flow Compression, 1-Stage of Centrifugal Flow Compression.

COMPRESSOR DATA (Take-Off): Compressor Pressure Ratio: 7 : 1, Total Mass Airflow: 6.5 lb/sec.

TURBINE TYPE: 2-Stage Axial Flow Turbine including: 1-Stage Gas Producer (compressor drive) Turbine, 1-Stage Power (free) Turbine.

COMBUSTOR TYPE: Annular, Reverse Flow.

POWER (take-off) RATING: 750 eshp. Includes 80 shp from 200 lbt. thrust.
Rating Approved to: 71°F (22°C).

TAKE-OFF SPECIFIC FUEL CONSUMPTION (SFC): 0.59 lb/hr/eshp.

ENGINE WEIGHT (less tailpipe): 331 lbs.

POWER/WEIGHT RATIO: 2.27 : 1 eshp/lb.

APPLICATION: Embraer EMB-110 and EMB-111.

OTHER ENGINES IN SERIES: PT6A Series: -10, -11, -11AG, -112, -15AG, -21, -25, -25A, -25C, -27, -28, -34B, -34AG, 110, -112, 114, -135, -135A, -36, -41, -41AG, -42, -45, -45R, -50, -60, -65B, -65R, -66, -67. PT6B Series: -35F, -36. PT6T Series: -3B, -6. ST6L-73. In many models of fixed-wing aircraft including: Avtec, IAI Arava, Ayres, Basler, Beech, Cessna, Cinair, Commuter, DeHavilland, Dornier, Embraer, Gates, Harbin, IMP, LearFan, Maul, Mooney, New-Cal, Norman, Omac, Omni, Pezetel, Piaggio, Pilatus, Pox, iper, Shorts, TBM (Aerospatiale-Mooney), Valmet. Also Rotor-Wing aircraft including: Agusta-Bell, Bell, SikorskyT-74 US Army applications include: RC-12, UV-18, UV-20, RU-21, UV-21, UV-24 ,UV-27. T-74 US Navy Applications include: T-34, T-44, UC-12.

Figure 4-67. Data sheet, Pratt & Whitney, Canada, PT6A-34 turboprop engine

Engine Familiarization

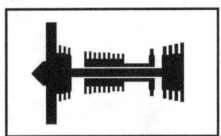

MANUFACTURER: CFM INTERNATIONAL (CMFI): GENERAL ELECTRIC AND SNECMA
Cincinnati, Ohio, USA.

COUNTRY: USA, FRANCE.

DESIGNATION: CFM56-7B27

BACKGROUND: The original CFM56 Utilized a General Electric, F101 Engine as its core. Date First CFM56 Engine Produced: 1978.

ENGINE TYPE: Turbofan
Dual-Shaft, High-Bypass, Front Fan.

COMPRESSOR TYPE: 13-Stage Dual-Spool, Axial Flow Compressor including: 1-Stage Front Fan and (3) additional Axial Stages in the Low Pressure Compressor, 9-Stage High Pressure Compressor. Fan Diameter 72.3 inch.

COMPRESSOR DATA (Take-Off): Compressor Pressure Ratio: 28.9 : 1, Fan Pressure Ratio: 1 : 1, Fan Bypass Ratio: 6.5 : 1, Total Mass Airflow: 1,045 lb/sec.

TURBINE TYPE: 5-Stage Axial Flow Turbine including: 1-Stage High Pressure Turbine, 4-Stage Low Pressure Turbine.

COMBUSTOR TYPE: Annular (ring), Through-Flow.

POWER (take-off) RATING: 27,300 lbt. Rating Approved to: 86°F (30°C).

TAKE-OFF SPECIFIC FUEL CONSUMPTION (TSFC): 0.38 lb/hr/lbt.

ENGINE WEIGHT (less tailpipe): 5,234 lbs.

POWER/WEIGHT RATIO: 5.75 : 1 lbt/lb.

APPLICATION:
Boeing and Airbus Airliners.

OTHER ENGINES IN SERIES: As of this writing: CFM56-7B18 (19,500 LBT), -7B20 (20,600 LBT), -7B22 (22,700 LBT), 7B24 (24,000 LBT), -7B26 (26,300 LBT).

Figure 4-68. Data sheet CFM Int'l, USA/France, CFM-56-7B27 turbofan engine

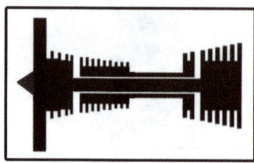

MANUFACTURER: GENERAL ELECTRIC AIRCRAFT ENGINES.
Evandale, Ohio.

DESIGNATION: GE90-115

BACKGROUND: Date First GE90 Produced: 1994.

ENGINE TYPE: Turbofan
Dual-Shaft, High-Bypass, Front Fan.

COMPRESSOR TYPE: 14-Stage Dual-Spool, Axial Flow Compressor including: 1-Stage Front Fan followed by four additional Low Pressure Stages, 9-Stage High Pressure Compressor. Fan: Shroudless, Composite Blades with Titanium Leading Edges, Diameter: 123.0 inch.

COMPRESSOR DATA (Take-Off): Compressor Pressure Ratio : 42 : 1. Fan Pressure Ratio: 1.6 : 1. Fan Bypass Ratio: 9 : 1, Total Mass Airflow: 3,150 lb/sec.

TURBINE TYPE: 8-Stage Axial Flow Turbine including: 2-Stage High Pressure Turbine, 6-Stage Low Pressure Turbine.

COMBUSTOR TYPE: Annular (ring), Through Flow.

POWER (take-off) RATING: 115,400 lbt. Rating Approved to: 86°F (30°C).

TAKE-OFF SPECIFIC FUEL CONSUMPTION (TSFC): Range of 0.30 to 0.35 lb/hr/lbt.

ENGINE WEIGHT (less tailpipe): 19,300 lbs.

POWER/WEIGHT RATIO: 5.99 : 1 lbt/lb.

APPLICATION: Boeing B777B, Twin-Engine, Wide-Bodied Airliner.

OTHER ENGINES IN SERIES:
GE90-76B (78,700 lbt), Boeing B777-200.
GE90-85B (84,930 lbt), Boeing B777-200ER, -200LR and -300.
GE90-90b (90,000 lbt), Boeing B777-200ER, -200LR and -300.
GE90-94B (94,930 lbt), Boeing B777-200ER/LR.
GE90-115B (115,000 lbt), Boeing B777-200ER, -200LR and -300.

Figure 4-69. Data sheet, General Electric, GE90-115 high-bypass turbofan engine

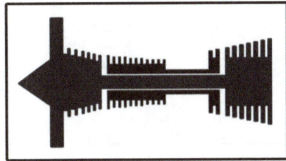

MANUFACTURER: UNITED TECHNOLOGIES CORP. (Pratt & Whitney Aircraft Group) Commercial Products Division, East Hartford, Conn.

DESIGNATION: PW 4090

BACKGROUND: Developed for commercial aircraft. Date 1st PW 4000 Engine Produced: 1986.

ENGINE TYPE: Turbofan
Dual-Shaft, High-Bypass, Front Fan.

COMPRESSOR TYPE: 18-Stage Dual-Spool, Axial Flow Compressor including: 1-Stage Front Fan followed by 6-Low Pressure Stages in the Low Pressure Compressor, 11-Stage High Pressure Compressor. Fan: 22 Hollow Titanium, Wide Chord, Shroudless blades, 119 inch Diameter.

COMPRESSOR DATA (Take-Off): Compressor Pressure Ratio: 38.6 : 1, Fan Pressure Ratio: 1.7 : 1, Fan Bypass Ratio: 6.4 : 1, Total Mass Airflow: 2,900 lb/sec.

TURBINE TYPE: 9-Stage Axial Flow Turbine including: 2-Stage High Pressure Turbine, 7-Stage Low Pressure Turbine.

COMBUSTOR TYPE: Annular, Through Flow.

POWER (take-off) RATING: 91,790 lbt. Rating Approved to: 86°F (30°C).

TAKE-OFF SPECIFIC FUEL CONSUMPTION (TSFC): Range of 0.30 to 0.35 lb/hr/lbt.

ENGINE WEIGHT (less tailpipe): 15,585 lbs.

POWER/WEIGHT RATIO: 5.89 : 1 lbt/lb.

APPLICATION:
Boeing B777A, Twin-Engine, Wide-Bodied Airliner.

OTHER ENGINES IN SERIES:
PW 4050 series, B747 (4-Engine), B767 (2-Engine); 4100 series, A310, A330
PW 4060 series, B747, B767, A330 (2-Engine); 4400 series, MD-11
PW 4080 series, B777 (2-Engine)

Figure 4-70. Data sheet, Pratt & Whitney, PW4090 high-bypass turbofan engine

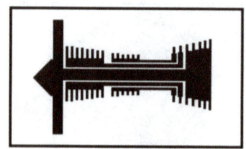

MANUFACTURER: ROLLS-ROYCE LTD., Derby, England.

DESIGNATION: TRENT 895

BACKGROUND: Follow-on turbofan of the RB211 series. Date first Trent 800 Run: 1993. Date Trent 800 in Service: 1998.

ENGINE TYPE: Turbofan
Three Shaft, High-Bypass, Front Fan.

COMPRESSOR TYPE: 15-Stage triple spool, Axial Flow: 1-Stage Front Fan acting as a Low Pressure Compressor;
8-Stage Intermediate Compressor; 6-Stage High Pressure Compressor. Fan Diameter: 110 inch.

COMPRESSOR DATA (Take-Off): Compressor Pressure Ratio: 42.7 : 1. Fan Pressure Ratio: 1.782 : 1. Fan Bypass Ratio: 5.75 : 1. Total Mass Airflow: 2,720 lb/sec take-off.

TURBINE TYPE: 7-Stage Axial Flow Turbine including: 1-Stage High Pressure Turbine, 1-Stage Intermediate Pressure Turbine, 5-Stage Low Pressure Turbine.

COMBUSTOR TYPE: Annular, Through-Flow.

POWER (take-off) RATING: 95,000 lbt. Rating approved to: 86°F (30°C).

TAKE-OFF SPECIFIC FUEL CONSUMPTION (TSFC): Range of 0.30 to 0.35 lb/hr/lbt.

ENGINE WEIGHT (less tailpipe): 13,000 lbs.

POWER/WEIGHT RATIO: 7.3 lbt./lb.

APPLICATION:
Boeing B777, Twin-Engine, Wide-Bodied Airliner.

OTHER ENGINES IN SERIES:
500 series A340, 4-Engine, (53-56,000 lbt)
700 series A330, 2-Engine, (67-71,000 lbt)
900 series A380, 4-Engine, (70-75,000 lbt)
1000 series B787, 2-Engine (53-70,000 lbt)

Figure 4-71. Data sheet, Rolls-Royce, G.B., Trent-895 high-bypass turbofan engine

CHAPTER 5
Inspection and Maintenance

The gas turbine engine has two levels of maintenance: line maintenance and shop maintenance. Maintenance includes inspection, parts replacement, repair, and overhaul. Although the tendency today is to perform more maintenance on the flight line, heavy maintenance is performed on engines removed from the aircraft in shop maintenance facilities. Shop maintenance is also referred to as heavy maintenance or overhaul maintenance.

Remember that all turbine engines are lightweight, high-speed machines that are manufactured to very close tolerances, so technicians must be very careful during any maintenance procedure. This includes rigid adherence to established technical procedures, correct use of tools, and cleanliness of parts and shop environment. [Figure 5-1]

LINE MAINTENANCE

Line maintenance encompasses all the inspections, parts replacement, and repairs that can be made to the powerplant while it is installed in the aircraft. [Figure 5-2]

Some airline repair programs include module replacement in the line maintenance category. Others have a separate maintenance category that fits between line maintenance and shop maintenance.

Some airline repair programs include module replacement in the line maintenance category. Others have a separate maintenance category for modular maintenance, discussed later in this chapter, which places modular maintenance at a higher level of line maintenance but not as high as shop maintenance.

Figure 5-2. General Electric CF6 engine undergoing flight line maintenance

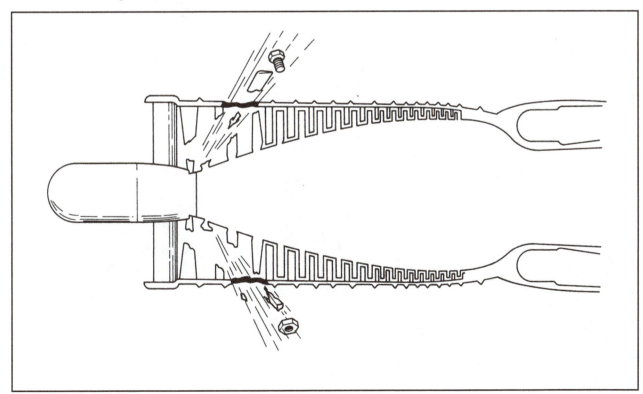

Figure 5-1. Foreign object damage requiring line or shop maintenance

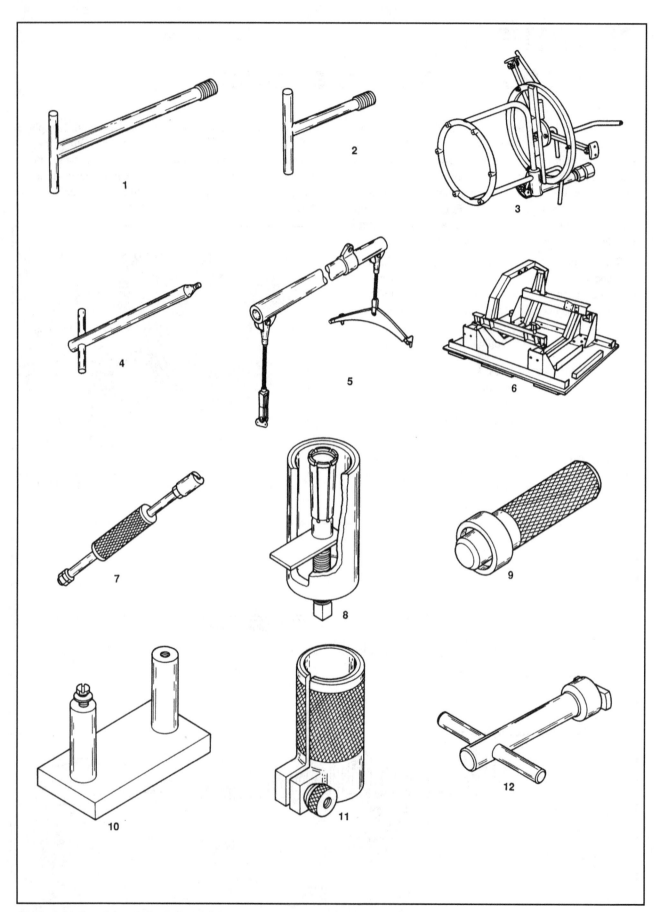

Figure 5-3A. Special tools for Pratt & Whitney JT15 Turbofan line maintenance

Inspection and Maintenance

REF. NO.	PART NUMBER	NOMENCLATURE	APPLICATION
1	CPWA30128-02	PULLER	ANTI-ICING LINE TRANSFER TUBE
2	CPWA30123-07	PULLER	OIL FILLER PLUG
3	CPWA31498	WASH RIG	LOW COMPRESSOR
4	CPWA30271	SPREADER	EXHAUST DUCT AND GAS GENERATOR CASE SHANK NUTS
5	CPWA31001	SLING	ENGINE ASSEMBLY COMPLETE
6	CPWA31002	SKID	LINE MAINTENANCE ENGINE HANDLING
7	CPWA31013-00	PULLER	ACCESSORY GEARBOX RETAINING PIN
8	CPWA31061-00	PULLER	CENTRIFUGAL BREATHER CARBON SEAL
9	CPWA31062-00	DRIFT	CENTRIFUGAL BREATHER CARBON SEAL
10	CPWA31063	SUPPORT	CENTRIFUGAL BREATHER CARBON SEAL
11	CPWA31080	PULLER	CHECK VALVE HOUSING
12	CPWA31081	ADJUSTING TOOL	OIL PRESSURE RELIEF VALVE

Figure 5-3B. Identification of special tools for Pratt & Whitney JT15 Turbofan

GAS TURBINE SPECIAL TOOLS (FOR LINE MAINTENANCE)

The special tools and fixtures necessary for line maintenance on the engine, and to prepare the Pratt & Whitney of Canada JT15D Turbofan engine for storage or service, are listed in Figure 5-3. Standard tools that normally form part of a technician's tool kit are not included. Shop maintenance tools are also too numerous to include here.

FOREIGN OBJECT DAMAGE

Much of the damage to the compressor section encountered on the flight line is the result of foreign matter being drawn into the engine inlet. [Figure 5-4] Compressor blade damage causes changes in compressor geometry that can result in malfunctions such as performance deterioration, compressor stalls, and even engine failure. Objects dropped into the engine gas path or internal parts during maintenance can also cause foreign object damage (FOD).

Figure 5-4. Fan damage from failed blades, caused by bird strike

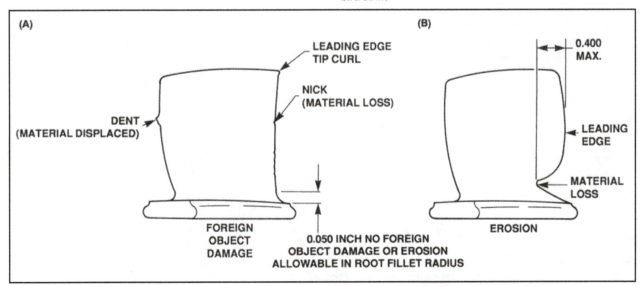

Figure 5-5. Compressor blade damage from FOD (A) and erosion (B)

FOD prevention is a concern of all flight line personnel. Sometimes the most harmless looking piece of debris can cause thousands of dollars in maintenance costs to the aircraft owner. The following is a list of suggested FOD prevention methods. Managers, technicians, and pilots must ensure that:

- Maintenance personnel keep ramp and hangar areas clean.
- Other flight line personnel are made aware of the importance of cleanliness in work areas.
- All personnel keep articles of clothing and materials in pockets secured when working on operating aircraft.
- Engine operators check inlets for foreign objects before engine run-up and avoid run-ups and taxiing into exhaust blasts of other operating aircraft.
- Everyone who maintains jet aircraft keeps the inlet and exhaust covers in place when the engine is static (not operating) to prevent contamination and windmilling.

NOTE: Damage incurred in the gas path from material failure of aircraft or engine parts is normally termed Domestic Object Damage rather than foreign object damage.

EROSION

Gas path erosion occurs from ingestion of sand, dirt, dust, and other fine airborne contaminants. Figure 5-5 shows the material loss that can occur from erosive contaminants that enter the inlet and pass through the engine. This ingestion affects both the compressor and the turbine sections. The abrasive effect of repeated ingestion can wear through the surface coating and even into the base metals of the fan, the compressor blades, and vanes. It can even cause similar damage to the turbine before leaving the engine via the exhaust.

Designers of modern aircraft understand this problem better today and try to engineer the slipstreams to carry contaminants around the aircraft rather than into the inlets. However, many older aircraft have ingestion problems. In addition, some have been reconfigured from narrow nacelles to wide, high-bypass, fan engine nacelles and have very low ground clearance. These aircraft are especially prone to performance loss and an increase in maintenance and fuel costs due to the effects of erosion on compressor and turbine parts. [Figure 5-6]

COMPRESSOR FIELD CLEANING

Accumulation of contaminants in the compressor reduces the aerodynamic efficiency of the blades, thereby reducing engine performance. Contaminants, mainly salt, airborne pollutants from smokestacks, and agricultural chemicals, all pass through the engine and build up on internal surfaces over time.

Two common methods for removing dirt, salt, and corrosion deposits are a fluid wash and an abrasive grit blast. Before field cleaning, it may be necessary to blank off certain sensing and bleed ports to prevent contamination or blockage.

FLUID CLEANING PROCEDURE

Perform the fluid cleaning procedure by first spraying an emulsion surface cleaner and then applying a rinse solution into the compressor. Figure 5-7 shows a Pratt & Whitney PT6 turboprop performance recovery wash apparatus. It is extremely important to perform the wash procedure in strict accordance with the instructions in the manufacturer's maintenance manual.

There are two methods of performing compressor washes:

- While motoring the engine with starter only
- While running the engine

Depending on the nature of the operating environment and the type of deposits in the engine gas path, you can use either of these two methods to remove accumulated salt, dirt, and other baked on deposits that cause engine performance deterioration.

A water wash performed solely to remove salt deposits is known as a desalination wash. A solution wash used solely to remove baked on deposits to improve engine performance is known as a performance recovery wash.

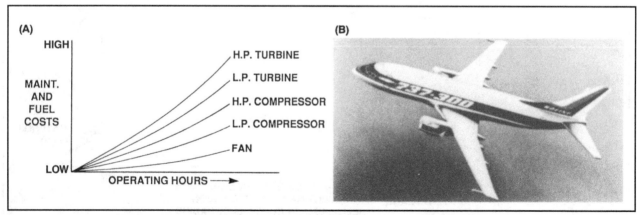

Figure 5-6A. Maintenance and fuel costs due to component efficiency losses
Figure 5-6B. High-bypass engine conversion to Boeing 737 aircraft

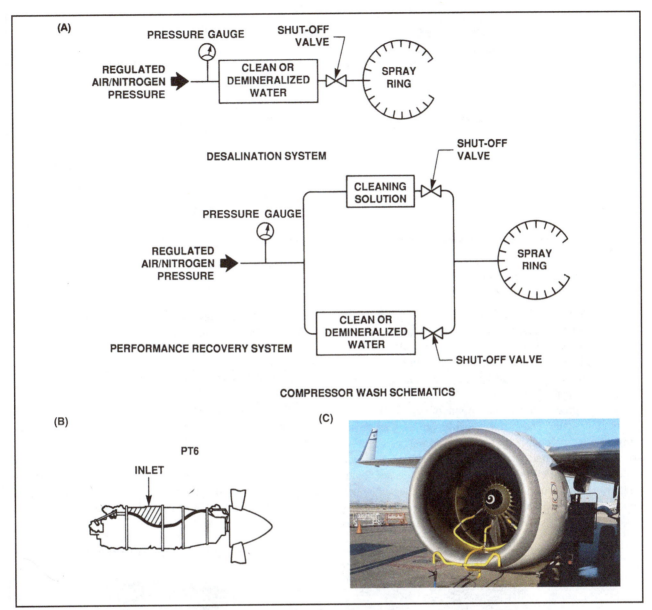

Figure 5-7A. PT6 turboprop compressor wash schematic
Figure 5-7B. Water is introduced into engine inlet
Figure 5-7C. Large engine compressor wash

In a motoring wash, engine speed is 14 to 25 percent, and the cleaning mixture is injected at a pressure of 30 to 50 pounds per square inch gauge.

In a running wash, engine speed is approximately 60 percent, and the cleaning mixture and rinsing solution is injected at a pressure of 15 to 20 pounds per square inch gauge.

Figure 5-8 represents a typical wash schedule.

NOTE: Perform multiple motoring wash procedures to the extent permitted by the starter operating limitations. Observe the starter cooling period indicated in the manufacturer's manual. After finishing the motor washing, a five-minute drying out period at idle speed is required.

The fluid wash method also cleans the turbine area. Turbine sulfidation (sulfur deposits from burning fuel that collect on turbine components) causes surface damage over time, and the frequent use of surface cleaning solvents in a motoring wash procedure extends the service life of some engines. [Figure 5-9]

Fresh water rinsing to remove salt deposits (if weather conditions permit) and the use of inlet and exhaust plugs greatly reduce the need for heavy cleaning procedures. Some manufacturers of small engines have authorized fogging of the compressor with anti-corrosive fluids such as WD-RD® after the wash procedure to slow the contamination process.

OPERATING ENVIRONMENT	NATURE OF WASH	RECOMMENDED FREQUENCY	RECOMMENDED METHOD	REMARKS
Continuously salt laden	Desalination	Daily	Motoring	Strongly recommended after last flight of day.
Occasionally salt laden	Desalination	Weekly	Motoring	Strongly recommended. Adjust washing frequency to suit condition.
All	Performance Recovery	100 to 200 hours	Motoring or Running	Strongly recommended. Performance recovery required less frequently. Adjust washing frequency to suit engine operating conditions as indicated by engine condition monitoring system. Motoring wash for light soil and multiple motoring or running wash for heavy soil is recommended.

NOTE: On some engines, a turbine wash is possible via the ignitor plug opening.

Figure 5-8. Typical compressor wash schedule

ABRASIVE GRIT PROCESS

A second more vigorous method of compressor cleaning is to inject an abrasive grit (one popular material being a mixture of ground walnut shells and apricot pits called Carboblast) into an engine operating at selected power settings. [Figure 5-10] The manufacturer prescribes the procedure and the amount of material for each particular engine. The greater capability of the Carboblast grit cleaning procedure in the engine compressor section over the solvent and water methods can extend the time interval between cleanings. However, because the cleaning grit is mostly burned up in combustion, the agent does not clean the turbine vanes and blades as effectively as the fluid wash. In many cases, maintenance technicians carry out both procedures, depending on their experience and the costs involved.

SCHEDULED LINE MAINTENANCE INSPECTIONS

Scheduled line maintenance includes inspections, such as the 100-hour, annual, continuous, and progressive, which are frequent tasks performed by the maintenance technician. FAR Parts 43, 65, and 91 describe the scope of these inspections, and the manufacturer publishes the specific inspection procedures for the particular engine. Figure 5-11 shows an engine with the cowling open and ready for inspection.

BEFORE A COMPRESSOR WASH
(A)

AFTER A COMPRESSOR WASH
(B)

Figure 5-9. PT6 turboprop engine compressor

Inspection and Maintenance

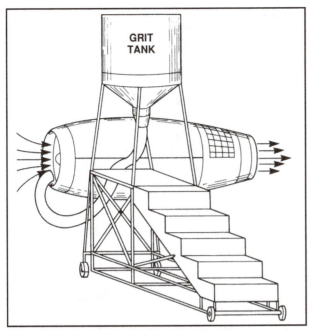

Figure 5-10. Abrasive grit compressor cleaning

Figure 5-11. Engine cowling open for inspection

SMALLER TURBINE-POWERED AIRCRAFT

A typical 100-hour inspection of a turbine engine in a small aircraft would include, but not be limited to, the following items:

- Oil changed every third inspection (300 hours)
- Oil filter cleaned or replaced
- Oil filter and chip detector debris analyzed
- Oil analyzed by means of a spectrometer check
- Igniter plugs visually inspected and operationally checked
- Fuel pump filter(s) cleaned or replaced
- Engine inlet and exhaust visually inspected for FOD and turbine distress
- Engine exterior visually inspected for leaks and the condition of the lines and electrical leads
- Engine operationally checked and a compressor wash done
- Engine vibration analysis performed

BUSINESS AND COMMUTER JET AIRCRAFT

A turbine-powered business or commuter aircraft will typically undergo a set of routine inspections to ensure the engine remains in an airworthy condition. The following is an example of a typical inspection schedule:

Check 1 — After each flight, perform the following transit checks:
- Check the engine cowling for signs of leaks, the intake and low-pressure compressor rotor blades for damage, and the engine exhaust for damage and metal deposits.
- Check the oil level and oil filter blockage indicator.

Check 2 — At 25 hours of run time, perform the transit checks plus:
- Check the last stage of the low-pressure turbine for cracking and damage by using a strong spotlight.
- Check the nose cone fairing for damage and security, the low-pressure compressor lining, and the rotor blades.
- Check the low-pressure compressor outlet guide vanes and the intermediate compressor inlet guide vanes.

Check 3 — At 150 hours or 3 months, perform checks 1 and 2, plus:
- Check the oil system master chip detectors.
- Check the fan bypass duct, exhaust cone, and fairings for damage.
- Audibly checking the igniter plugs for required spark emissions per second.
- Check the low-pressure and high-pressure air supply ducting and joints for damage and leaks.
- Check the fuel system for contamination.
- Check the freedom and security of mechanical controls, and grease those controls.

Check 4 — At 600 hours or 12 months, perform checks 1, 2, and 3, plus:
- Replace the fuel filter element.
- Perform a functional test of the temperature control system.

LARGER COMMERCIAL JET AIRCRAFT

Large commercial aircraft, like Boeing 767s or Airbus A340s, undergo a Continuous Airworthiness Inspection Program. This program involves daily inspections, known as layover inspections, and letter (alphabet) checks. Letter checks are typically divided into "A," "B," "C," and "D" checks.

Each higher letter check incorporates all the previous inspection items, plus a more detailed look at the aircraft and its engines. By the time the "D" check takes place, the aircraft is ready to be completely stripped to its shell and rebuilt. What happens to the engines depends on how long it has been since they were overhauled; they may just be removed, inspected, and reinstalled as the aircraft goes back together.

SCHEDULED LINE MAINTENANCE REPAIRS

Scheduled line maintenance concepts vary by manufacturer; however, a typical maintenance plan might include the following:

Task-Oriented Maintenance Plan — A plan in which maintenance tasks are completed at established intervals such as engine flight hours (EFH). Ground-operating time is usually not counted as part of total time, but it is accounted for in the EFH time requirements. The task-oriented maintenance plan typically includes mandatory repair or replacement of engine components referred to as line replaceable units (LRUs) at the established EFH. LRUs include such items as fuel controls, fuel pumps, oil pumps, ignition units, and numerous smaller mechanical and electronic units. The task-oriented maintenance plan also includes more-extensive maintenance, such as hot section replacement and even engine change.

On-Condition Maintenance Plan on a Time Schedule — An engine and engine component inspection, repair, and replacement plan based on calendar time or engine hours, at which time maintenance personnel evaluate the condition of the items involved. The final determination of on-condition maintenance actions is based on carefully planned trend analysis of engine operating parameters and maintenance history for selecting the most prudent procedures.

On-Condition Maintenance Plan Without a Time Schedule — An engine and engine component inspection based on an item's condition, determined by recorded electronic alerts or by flight and maintenance personnel observations. The maintenance action is based on trend analysis.

Within the two on-condition maintenance plans, many of the items referred to as LRUs mentioned in the task-oriented plan could remain in place for many engine flight hours.

UNSCHEDULED LINE MAINTENANCE

Maintenance section technicians perform unscheduled line maintenance as they correct discrepancies identified by crewmembers during flight or, in larger aircraft, that have been detected electronically. Unscheduled maintenance is also necessary to correct discrepancies found during walk-around and scheduled inspections and to comply with Service Bulletins and while performing Airworthiness Directives (ADs), etc.

Another data collection system for many aircraft is the electronic Aircraft Condition Monitoring System (ACMS), which is capable of analyzing aircraft and engine data on removable PC cards. It also produces hardcopy printouts. The ACMS can be programmed to analyze the health of the engine and to generate reports when exceedances such as high engine temperatures and high rotor speeds occur. The engine system chapters in this text include the line maintenance repairs and troubleshooting necessary to locate and correct common malfunctions observed during engine operation.

SHOP MAINTENANCE

Whenever the engine cannot be repaired in the aircraft, it is removed for shop maintenance or for test cell operation and troubleshooting. The FAA requires that this level of maintenance be accomplished only at a manufacturer's facility or at a certified repair station that has the necessary tooling, technical data, and trained personnel.

The FAA divides most engine heavy maintenance into limited and unlimited categories. These procedures are generally carried out by either the original equipment manufacturer's in-house facility or an independent, commercial maintenance repair and overhaul facility.

LIMITED HEAVY MAINTENANCE

Many privately-owned repair stations operate under a Limited Heavy Maintenance license. Factory-operated repair stations may operate in the limited category. Normally, both types of repair stations are authorized to perform any maintenance up to removal and replacement of the entire hot section. They can perform some cold end repairs, but cannot rebuild the compressor.

UNLIMITED HEAVY MAINTENANCE

Both privately-owned and factory-operated overhaul facilities fall into the Unlimited Heavy Maintenance category. They can remove and replace any part, perform limited remanufacture of parts, and zero out the engine time.

Note: Shop Maintenance in terms of engine time change, on-condition maintenance, and trend analysis is described in detail later in this chapter under "Engine Time Change and On-Condition Maintenance Concepts."

MODULAR MAINTENANCE

Modular maintenance is a maintenance concept that allows what were formerly heavy maintenance tasks to be completed during flight line maintenance procedures. In modular engine construction, the engine is assembled as a set of separate modules that can be more easily removed and replaced with a minimum expenditure of man-hours. Each module has its own data plate that maintenance personnel can use to track the operating time of cycles (engine starts) or hours by serial number. Most or all of the modules are pre-balanced and can be replaced while the engine remains in the aircraft. This eliminates engine removal and test-cell running of the engine.

Figures 5-12A, 5-12B, and 5-13 show two kinds of maintenance actions:

- **Line Maintenance Actions** — Maintenance procedures that can be completed while the engine remains on the aircraft or dropped into a maintenance stand without leaving the flight line.

Inspection and Maintenance

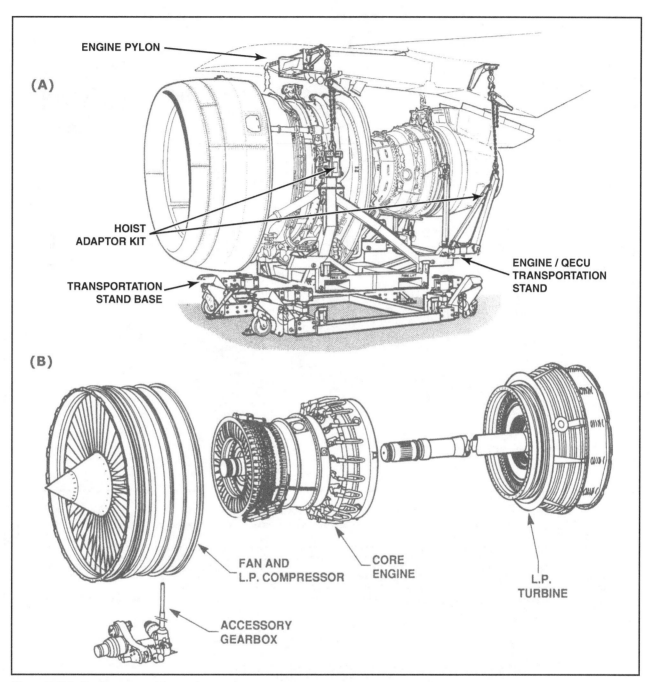

Figure 5-12A. Engine removal from wing
Figure 5-12B. G.E./Snecma CFM56 turbofan major modules

- **Shop Maintenance Actions** — Maintenance procedures that require engine removal from the aircraft and work completed at a licensed maintenance facility.

When rebuilt modules are installed in engines with high service time, achieving a good aerodynamic and thermodynamic match is extremely difficult. An engine's total time since new continues to increase, even though many of the engine's modules may have been replaced. Because of the nature of module maintenance, the FAA classifies the replacement of most modules as a minor repair, many of which can be accomplished at line maintenance level and require no FAA Form 337. Overhaul of modules is considered a major repair, and requires the submission of FAA Form 337 to the local FAA Records Office. [Figure 5-14]

Note: Further discussion of engine time change, modular maintenance, and on-condition maintenance concepts can be found later in this chapter under "Engine Time Change and On-Condition Maintenance Concepts."

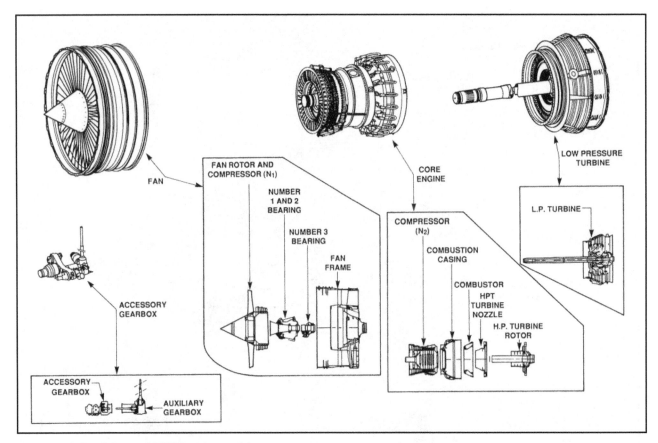

Figure 5-13. Breakdown of CFM56 major modules

AIRWORTHINESS INSPECTOR'S HANDBOOK, SECTION 15 "POWERPLANT REPAIRS" FAA ORDER 8300.9 -EXCERPT-

630. PURPOSE. THIS SECTION PROVIDES GUIDANCE TO FIELD PERSONNEL CONCERNING MAJOR/MINOR REPAIRS TO POWERPLANTS AND CLASSIFIES THE STRUCTURAL PARTS OF TURBINE ENGINES.

631. BACKGROUND. FIELD PERSONNEL ARE BEING ASKED TO PROVIDE GUIDANCE CONCERNING REPAIRS TO STRUCTURAL PARTS OF AIRCRAFT POWERPLANTS. FAR 43, APPENDIX A (B) (2), DEFINES POWERPLANT MAJOR REPAIRS AND SPEAKS TO STRUCTURAL ENGINE PARTS, HOWEVER, THE SECTION ADDRESSES ITSELF SPECIFICALLY TO RECIPROCATING ENGINES. THIS LEADS TO A PARTICULAR NEED FOR GUIDANCE CONCERNING TURBINE ENGINE REPAIRS AND THE CLASSIFICATION OF TURBINE ENGINE STRUCTURAL PARTS. THEREFORE, IN ORDER TO ARRIVE AT A UNIFORM POLICY CONCERNING REPAIRS TO TURBINE AND RECIPROCATING ENGINES, THE FOLLOWING CRITERIA ARE OFFERED AS GUIDANCE.

632. TURBINE ENGINE PARTS. EACH MANUFACTURER MAY NOT USE THE IDENTICAL TERMINOLOGY USED BELOW, HOWEVER WHAT IS USED WILL BE EQUIVALENT TO THESE TERMS.

    A. THE STRUCTURAL ENGINE PARTS:
        (1) ALL FRAMES.
        (2) ALL CASINGS OR HOUSINGS.
        (3) ENGINE MOUNTS, AND ASSOCIATED ENGINE STRUCTURE.
        (4) COMPLETE ROTOR ASSEMBLY.

    B. THE ENGINE FRAMES:
        (1) FRONT FRAMES OR FRONT BEARING SUPPORT.
        (2) COMPRESSOR REAR FRAME.
        (3) TURBINE MIDFRAME.
        (4) TURBINE REAR FRAME OR REAR BEARING SUPPORT.

    C. THE ENGINE CASINGS OR HOUSINGS:
        (1) FAN CASING.
        (2) COMPRESSOR, BOTH LOW AND HIGH PRESSURE.
        (3) COMBUSTOR CASING OR HOUSING.
        (4) TURBINE CASING OR HOUSING.
        (5) ACCESSORY GEAR CASE HOUSING.

633. TURBINE ENGINE REPAIRS. REGARDING MODULAR AND NON-MODULAR DESIGNED TURBINE ENGINES THE FOLLOWING WOULD APPLY:
A. MODULAR DESIGN TURBINE ENGINES: THE CHANGING OF MODULES SHOULD "NOT" BE CONSIDERED A MAJOR REPAIR. THE DISASSEMBLY OF A MODULE SHOULD BE CONSIDERED A MAJOR REPAIR.
B. NON-MODULAR DESIGN TURBINE ENGINES: THE DISASSEMBLY OF ANY OF THE MAIN SECTIONS OF A TURBINE ENGINE SHOULD BE CONSIDERED A MAJOR REPAIR. THE MAIN SECTIONS ARE:
    (1) FAN SECTION.
    (2) COMPRESSOR SECTION, BOTH LOW AND HIGH PRESSURE.
    (3) COMBUSTION SECTION.
    (4) TURBINE SECTION.
    (5) ACCESSORY SECTION.

Figure 5-14. Turbine engine major versus minor repair

Inspection and Maintenance

REMANUFACTURING FACILITY

Some manufacturers offer their customers a remanufacture option. Under this option, the manufacturer repairs the engine and installs updated, remanufactured parts as necessary so that the engine returns to service with additional capabilities and greater expected service life than on overhauled engines.

All line maintenance, including changing of modules, falls under the category of minor repairs and only the overhaul of modules is considered a major repair. When the repair shop facility completes a major repair, personnel complete a FAA Form 337 or an FAA-approved Manufacturer's Release Form to certify the repairs.

POWERPLANT REMOVAL AND DISASSEMBLY

There are two ways to remove powerplants from an aircraft. One method involves lowering the engine from its mounting location using a hydraulically operated installation stand, which looks similar to a large scissor jack. Generally, this method is used when working with large engines. The other method, more common to general aviation, requires a sling and hoist arrangement. Figure 5-12A shows an engine being removed from an airplane wing engine pylon, and Figure 5-15 shows an engine ready to be hoisted into a transportation dolly and delivered to a maintenance area for installation of an aircraft adapter kit.

In the shop, the engine is installed on a maintenance stand for repair. Some stands are on casters while others look similar to the one in Figure 5-16. Many stands are designed to keep the engine perfectly horizontal. The engine in Figure 5-16 is undergoing an inspection prior to being routed into the appropriate shop for maintenance.

Figure 5-17 shows a turbine wheel being removed with a special tool called a pivoting lifting adapter and an overhead shop hoist. The turbine, as well as many of the large components, will be placed in its own transport fixture, commonly called a roll-around maintenance stand.

At some point in engine disassembly, such as the removal of the compressor, the work is usually completed vertically. [Figure 5-18] On some engines, the entire reassembly is done vertically so that weight assists in component alignment. One standard maintenance practice during disassembly is to cover all openings as they become exposed, using plugs, caps, and other suitable material to prevent contamination and to maintain the utmost in shop cleanliness and safety procedures.

Another general rule that applies during any maintenance is never to reuse lockwire, lock washers, tab locks, cotter pins, gaskets, packings, or rubber O-rings, and to reuse locknuts and other fasteners only within the limits prescribed in the manufacturer's instructions.

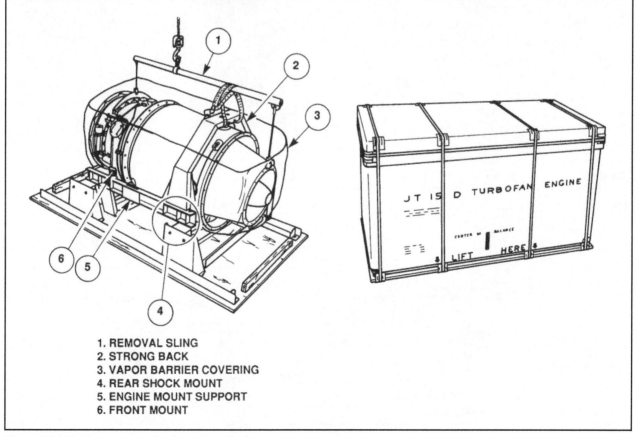

1. REMOVAL SLING
2. STRONG BACK
3. VAPOR BARRIER COVERING
4. REAR SHOCK MOUNT
5. ENGINE MOUNT SUPPORT
6. FRONT MOUNT

Figure 5-15. Replacement engine from the manufacturer

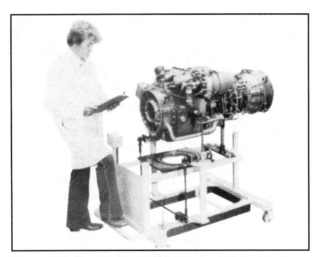

Figure 5-16. General Electric CT-7 Turboshaft engine at overhaul facility

NONDESTRUCTIVE INSPECTIONS AND REPAIRS

For purposes of inspection and maintenance, the engine is divided into two main sections: the cold section and the hot section. The cold section includes the engine inlet, compressor, and diffuser sections. The hot section includes the combustor, turbine, and exhaust sections. [Figure 5-19]

BORESCOPING

The fundamental inspection technique for engine inlets, exhausts, and other exterior areas of built-up (completely assembled) engines is to visually look for tell-tale signs of air, fuel, and oil leaks and items that are loose, chafed, broken, or otherwise damaged.

Borescoping of inner parts of the engine is another valuable inspection technique. [Figure 5-21] The lighted borescope eyepiece is capable of magnification and adaptable for photography. The borescope can be rigid or flexible, but the flexible types feature a fiber optics core that allow technicians to view areas where the probe of the rigid type cannot reach.

Figures 5-20 and 5-21 show typical access port locations for inserting the eyepiece. The entire inner portion of the engine cannot be viewed with the borescope, only selected areas that the manufacturer identifies as critical.

The photographs in Figure 5-22 show the borescope views and the actual views with the piece out of the engine. It is obvious that a trained technician must interpret the findings when performing the borescope inspection.

Figure 5-23 shows a more advanced borescope design equipped with a video viewing system, a camera, and a grinding tip. The rotary file or stone at the tip is for use in specific engine locations to blend out small areas of damage in order to remove stress points. In the illustration, the area being accessed is the first stage of the high-pressure compressor.

OTHER NONDESTRUCTIVE INSPECTIONS

Nondestructive inspection (NDI), sometimes referred to as nondestructive testing (NDT), is a means of checking the external and internal condition of aircraft and engine parts without affecting their airworthiness. If these

Figure 5-18. Vertical engines assembly

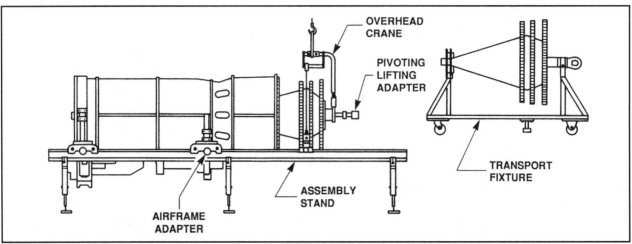

Figure 5-17. Turbine rotor removal

Inspection and Maintenance

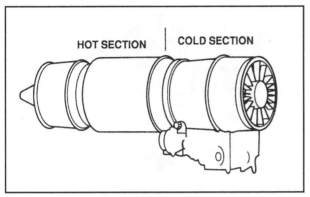

Figure 5-19. Engine cold and hot sections

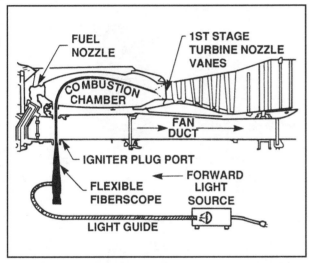

Figure 5-20. Flexible borescope

inspections are accomplished in a timely manner on a gas turbine engine, they can avert costly unscheduled maintenance resulting from part failures due to fatigue and wear.

Some inspection methods require a part to be disassembled into its basic components before testing, but other inspection methods can be accomplished on a built-up assembly or a completely assembled engine. The inspector determines the most appropriate inspection method and the degree of disassembly required for the most accurate results.

There are many nondestructive inspection methods. The five most commonly used methods in gas turbine engine overhaul are covered here.

MAGNETIC PARTICLE METHOD

The magnetic particle method requires the use of special test apparatus and is an effective method of detecting defects such as cracks, porosity, inclusions, and voids at or near the surface in ferrous materials.

In this method, the part to be inspected is first magnetized, and then a layer of fine magnetic test particles is applied to its surface. When the part is arranged in the magnetic field created by the test device, a material defect creates a magnetic field leakage that attracts the test particles. The particles align with the defect, giving a visible indication of the shape and extent of the problem area.

The test particles can be applied in dry form or wet in a kerosene-type fluid. Dry particles best detect subsurface defects in cast or forged parts that have rough surfaces. Wet fluorescent particles are best for detection of fine

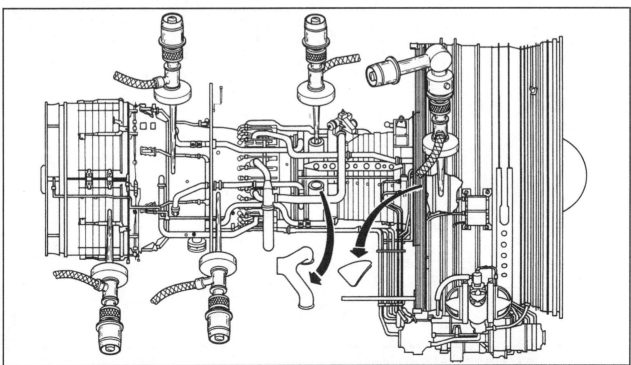

Figure 5-21. Borescope locations of a General Electric CF6 turbofan; inspection interval 150 to 500 engine cycles

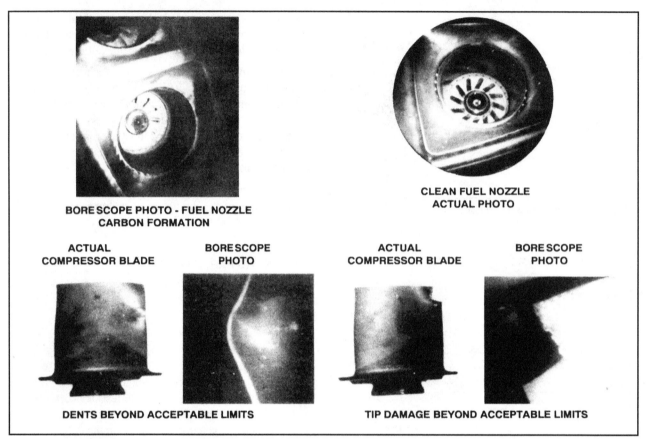

Figure 5-22. Borescope photography of a General Electric CF6 turbofan

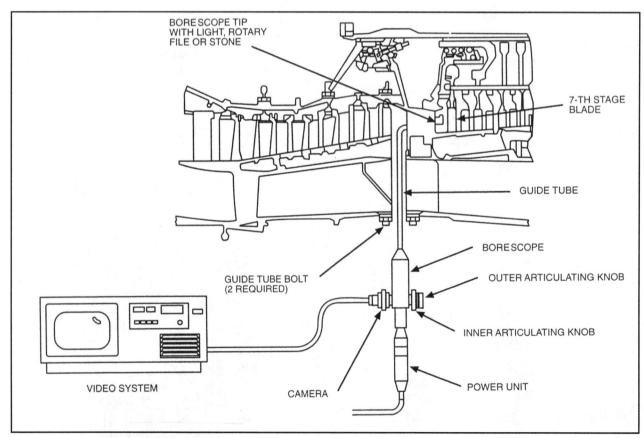

Figure 5-23. Borescope with blending tool

cracks in smooth surfaces. Wet inspection requires an ultraviolet light and a room that is sufficiently dark for the best visibility of the suspect area. [Figure 5-24A]

DYE-PENETRANT METHOD

The two common dye check methods used to detect cracks and voids open to the surface in most ferrous and nonferrous materials are the red-dye method and the fluorescent green-dye method.

The red-dye kit typically consists of three aerosol containers for the application of a penetrating red dye, a cleaning fluid, and a developer.

When the penetrating fluid is applied to a clean surface, it seeps into defects and remains even after the surface is wiped dry of the penetrant. Application of a chalk-colored spray developer will make any defect appear as a red mark or red line on the whitened surface.

The green-dye method is used for detecting the same types of defects as red dye, but it is sometimes more convenient when inspecting larger parts. Clean the test item and place it in a drip tray, and then spray it with a green fluorescent penetrating fluid. After a drying interval, usually five to thirty minutes, inspect the item visually under an ultraviolet light in a darkened room. Cracks show up as bright yellow-green lines, and voids show up as yellow-green marks defining the shape of the defect. [Figure 5-24B]

THE RADIOGRAPHIC METHOD

The radiographic method uses X-rays, gamma rays, and other penetrating radiation to reveal cracks, voids, or inclusions in the subsurface or deep interior of solid materials. Defects that will not show up in the magnetic-particle and dye-check nondestructive inspection procedures can be found with radiographic inspection. This inspection requires special test apparatus and licensed operators.

When penetrating rays are introduced into a part that contains an interior discontinuity, the rays create an image of the defect on a photographic plate that is positioned on the exterior surface opposite the point of introduction. This method detects flaws in most metallic and nonmetallic solids and even measures the thickness of plating surfaces.

Radiographic inspection provides a permanent record of the findings for comparison to past and future radio-

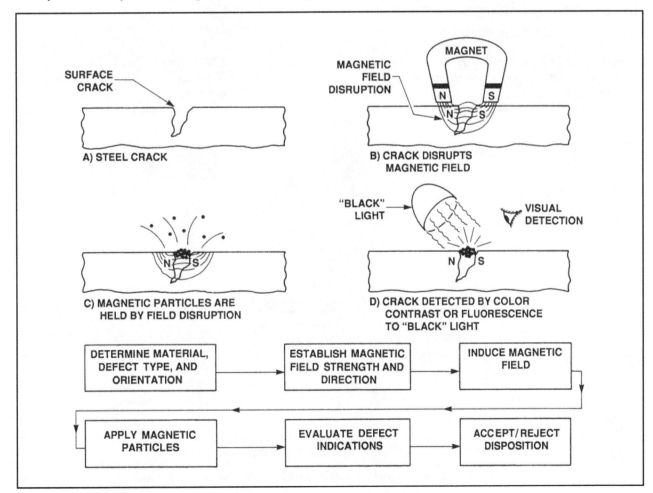

Figure 5-24A. Magnetic particle inspection method

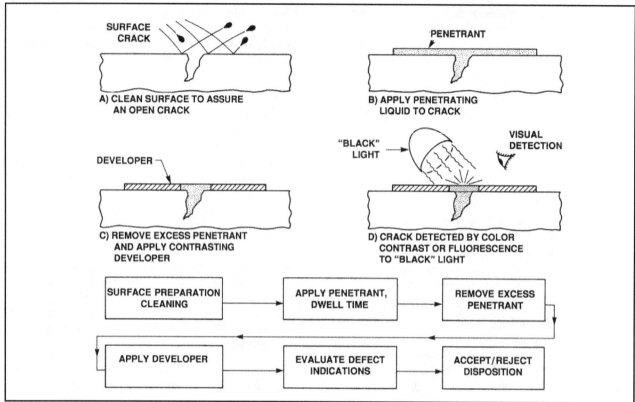

Figure 5-24B. Liquid penetrant inspection method

graphic inspections, and it can show the progression of some types of defects from one inspection to the next. [Figure 5-24C]

THE EDDY CURRENT METHOD

The eddy current method is accomplished by placing a metallic part in a test device, then passing an electrical

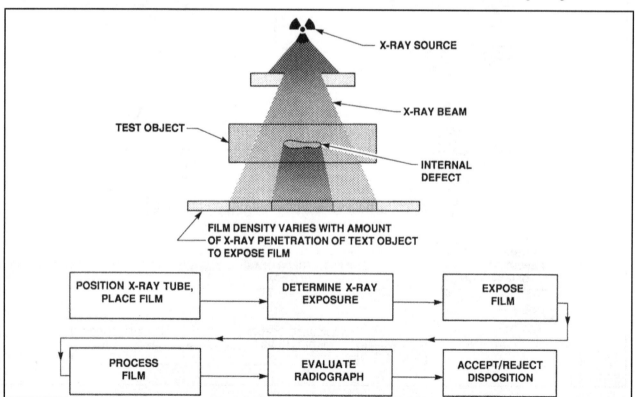

Figure 5-24C. Radiographic inspection method

Inspection and Maintenance

current through it to create a secondary magnetic field within the induced magnetic field created by the test device. The presence of a surface or subsurface flaw in the part alters the eddy current of the magnetic fields, which is measured by a special detection coil in the test unit. This test can also be used to measure thickness of platings applied to metallic surfaces. It is widely used with simple parts such as turbine and compressor blades that can be tested in place or removed from the engine and placed into a fixture on the eddy current device. [Figure 5-24D]

THE ULTRASONIC METHOD

The ultrasonic method introduces sound waves through a part and measures the time rate of pulses of energy. Discontinuities in the material are identified by comparing this time factor from the established time factors of a good part. This method is most effective in more dense metallic and nonmetallic materials of regular shape and smooth surfaces. The ultrasonic method will detect very small surface and subsurface defects in parent material, discontinuities in bonded materials, and delamination of base materials. [Figure 5-24E]

COLD SECTION INSPECTION AND REPAIR

The cold section is the front, air inlet section of the engine and includes the fan of a turbofan engine and all of the compressor section components up to the front of combustor section.

COMPRESSOR DISASSEMBLY

Figure 5-25 illustrates how the N_1 fan and LP compressor can be removed from the core (N_2) case as a single unit for further disassembly, inspection, and repair. The N_2 compressor in the forward section of the core module is also exposed for further disassembly, inspection, and repair.

TYPICAL FAN BLADE DAMAGE LIMITS

Repair to coded areas A to E, shown in Figure 5-26, is accomplished by blending. Blending is a method of re-contouring damaged blades and vanes by hand using

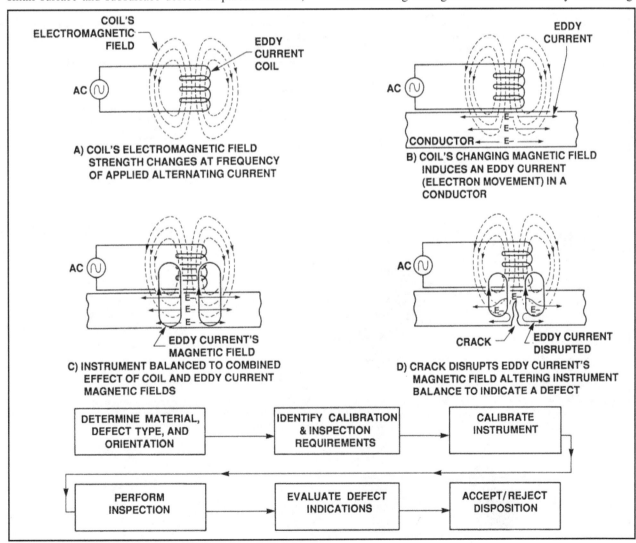

Figure 5-24D. Eddy current inspection method

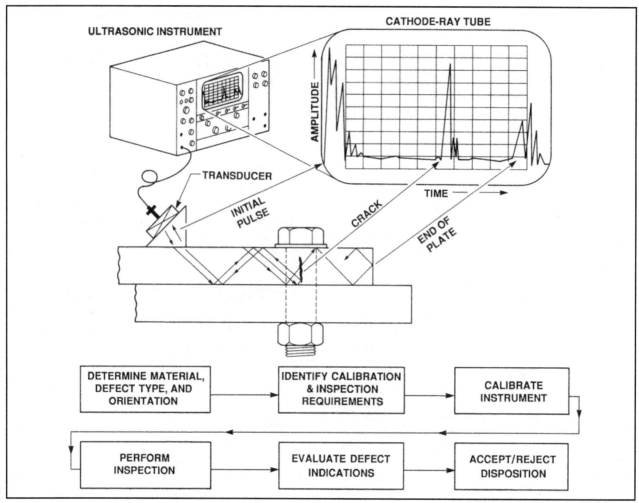

Figure 5-24E. Ultrasonic inspection method

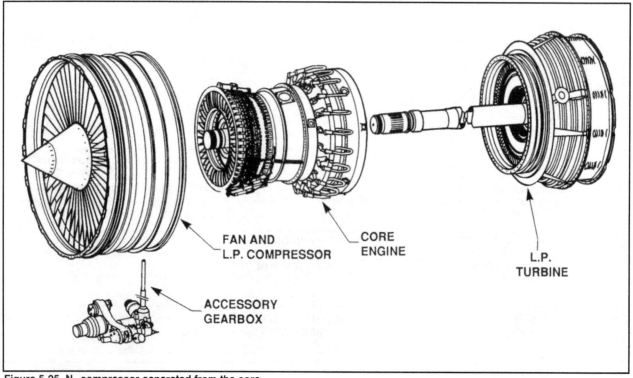

Figure 5-25. N_1 compressor separated from the core

Inspection and Maintenance

common and dye sinker type files, crocus and emery cloth, and India or Carborundum stones. Power tools are seldom used on installed blades because of the possibility of heat stress buildup and inadvertent damage to adjacent parts in restricted working areas.

Blending is performed parallel to the length of the blade to minimize stress points and to restore as smooth an aerodynamic shape as possible. You can often complete this procedure on the flight line if damage is limited to the first one or two stages. Generally, it is only necessary to blend the damaged blade. Occasionally, the manufacturer will require making an identical blend on the blade 180 degrees opposite to maintain rotor balance.

Note that also in Figure 5-26 no damage is allowed in the blade fillet area (Area E), because of the concentration of mechanical stresses that occur at these points during engine operation.

After repair, some manufacturers recommend covering the blend with a felt tip dye marking material or similar solution to identify it as a reworked area. This is helpful to those maintenance personnel who view it later while performing inlet inspections.

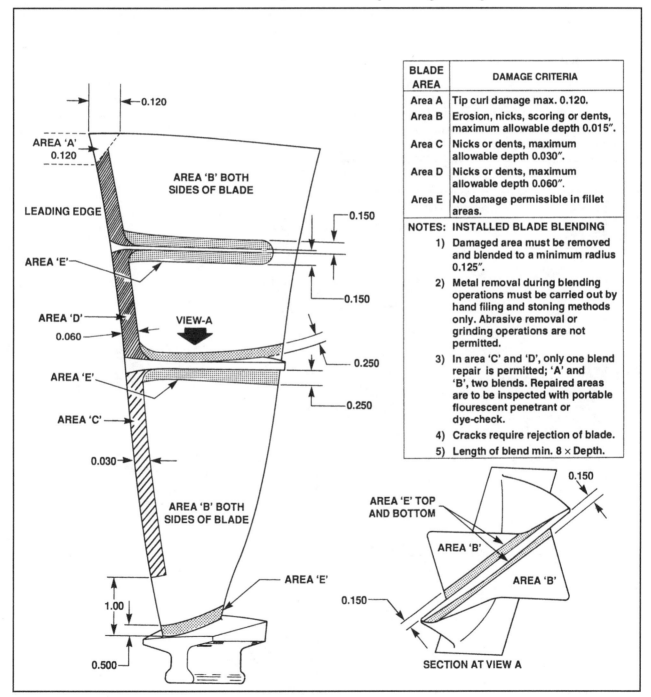

Figure 5-26. Typical fan blade damage limits

AXIAL COMPRESSOR INSPECTION AND REPAIR

You can repair minor impact damage to compressor blades either on the flight line or in the shop if you can remove the damage without exceeding allowable limits. If repairs are completed within the prescribed limits, there will be no compressor imbalance, and balancing checks are not usually required.

Figures 5-27 and 5-28 show typical gas-turbine cold section repairs. This information is general in nature, so rely only on the information in the manufacturer's manuals for making these repairs.

ELECTRON BEAM WELDING

Welding and straightening of rotating airfoils usually requires special equipment and quite often only overhaul facilities or the manufacturer are authorized to do it. One technique, called electron beam welding, permits the reworking of many formerly unserviceable compressor blades. This beam welding procedure is especially useful on titanium alloy, from which many blades are made. A beam-weld results in a strength factor equal to a new blade.

Figure 5-29 illustrates the electron beam welding apparatus. Notice that the piece is welded in a vacuum chamber. Controlling the oxygen level concentrates the heat at the weld point better than welding in atmospheric air.

Figure 5-30 illustrates the difference between conventional welding methods and the narrow bead that is produced by concentrating the heat. A lower stress is placed on the base metal with this process.

Figure 5-31 shows a compressor/fan blade with leading edge damage beyond the limits of a blend repair. The damaged area is ground off and an insert piece is beam-welded. The piece is then ground down to the blade's original shape.

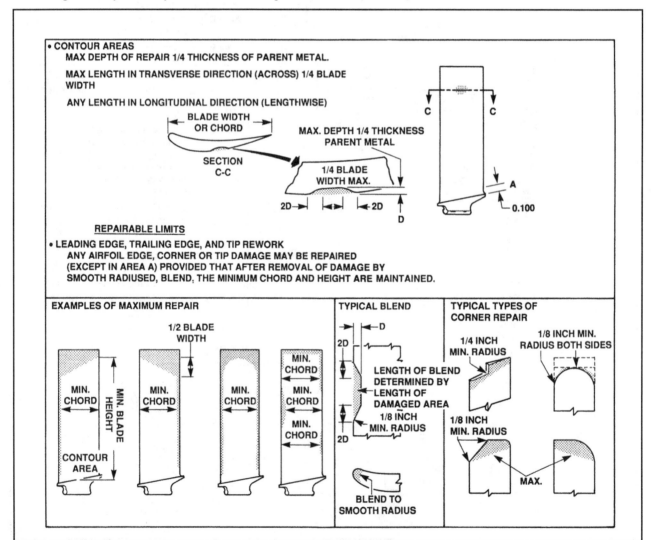

Figure 5-27. Typical compressor blade repairable limits and examples of maximum repair by blending

Inspection and Maintenance

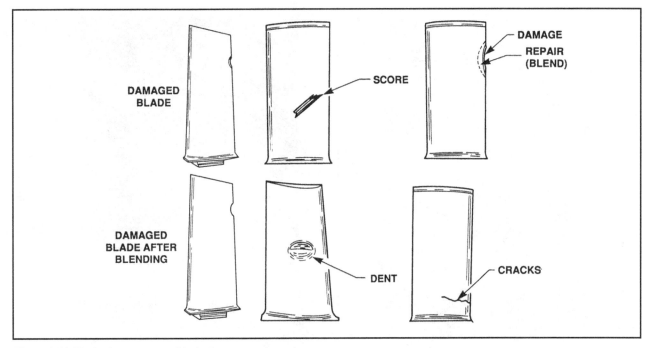

Figure 5-28. Typical compressor blade damage and repairs

PLASMA SURFACE REPAIR COATING

Another valuable overhaul process is to repair blades and vanes by applying a coating of material to its surface. For instance, a process called plasma coating can restore a worn blade to its original specifications. [Figure 5-32]

The plasma spray process has become one of the most successful techniques for reclaiming formerly unusable parts. A recoated part is typically one-half the cost of a new replacement part.

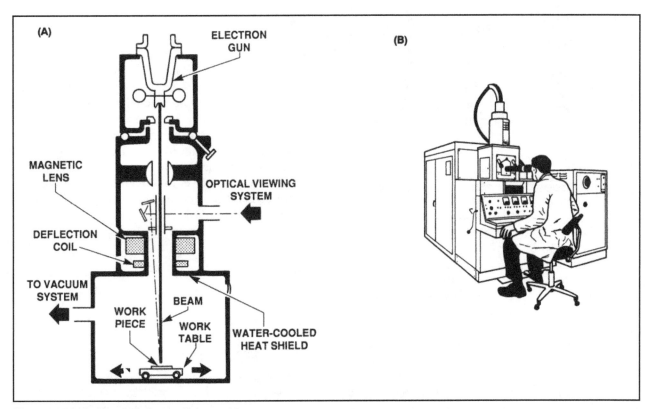

Figure 5-29A. Cutaway of electron beam welder
Figure 5-29B. Electron beam welding apparatus

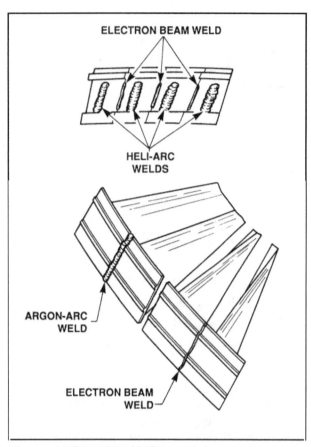

Figure 5-30. Examples of heli-arc and electron beam welds

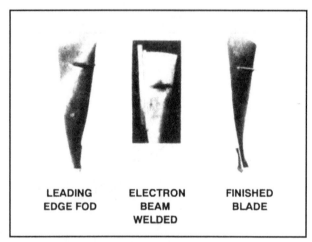

Figure 5-31. Fan blade leading edge repair

The plasma spray process consists of applying a metallic spray material, in an atomized state, to the base metal at high velocity and heat. The base metal is at room temperature, but the gas carrying the spray is super-heated to as high as 50,000°F and travels at approximately Mach 2 velocity. Coatings as thin as 0.00025 inches are possible, and multiple coats can build up to several thousandths of an inch and be completely fused to the base metal. In many instances, the new surface will be stronger than the original. After the coating is applied, the piece is ground to its final shape and dimensions.

Figure 5-32. Plasma spray process

The plasma spray is equally applicable to hot-end parts as well as cold-end parts.

Spray coatings for anti-corrosion purposes and for enhancing airflow can be used on compressor parts. One such process, called SermeTel™, is sprayed onto a prepared surface and has a ceramic-like finish when dry. This greatly reduces surface drag and air friction, thereby promoting good compression and reduced fuel consumption.

TIP CLEARANCE

Plasma and other coating techniques are especially valuable in returning compressor blade tip clearances to original specifications. Correct clearances between blades and housings are important because compressor performance depends on the controlled aerodynamic effect of its airfoils. For instance, a large engine with a 0.035-inch, cold-tip clearance might typically reduce to 0.002-inch clearance during operation. Case distortion and blade radial loading during operation can occasionally allow contact that will increase the running clearance by tip rubbing. The resulting loss of air over the blade tip, and the boundary layer distortion which will occur, can cause serious loss of compression, compressor stalls, and overtemperatures.

On small engines, in which the clearance is a greater percentage of blade height, excessive clearance can greatly affect compressor efficiency. Tip clearances are generally taken with a thickness (feeler) gauge with the upper compressor case removed. Maintaining correct tip clearances is equally applicable to hot-end blading.

BLADE REPLACEMENT

Blade replacement is allowed, but with a restriction placed on the number of blades replaced per stage and per entire rotor. The blades are moment-weighted and coded to provide a guide for exact replacement that maintains

Inspection and Maintenance

compressor balance. Moment-weight accounts for both the mass weight and the center of balance.

On compressor stages with an even number of blades, you can replace the damaged blade and its opposite blade as a pair if a blade of the appropriate moment-weight is not available.

If the compressor stage has an odd number of blades, you can replace three blades 120 degrees apart as a set under the same circumstances. [Figure 5-33] Under severe restrictions, some manufacturers allow replacement by mass weight, and other replacement criteria exist for specific installations. Some fan blades, for instance, are replaceable on the wing, while others are replaceable only during heavy maintenance.

If compressor blades can be individually removed, there is a maximum number of damaged blades that can be replaced without rebalancing the compressor. If that maximum number of blades is exceeded, the unit will require a balance check after repair. The photograph in Figure 5-34 shows a typical balancing machine for large compressors. During the check, small weights are added or removed, or small portions of metal are removed with a hand grinder to achieve the balance.

CENTRIFUGAL COMPRESSOR INSPECTION AND REPAIR

Inspect the impeller for nicks, dents, and cracks [Figure 5-35] using the following criteria:

- **Critical Area** — No cracks or nicks allowed. Smooth dents are permitted, provided they do not exceed 0.030 inch in diameter or 0.010 inch in depth.
- **Leading Edge** — No cracks allowed. Nicks or dents are permitted, provided they do not exceed 0.100 inch in depth and 0.300 inch in length after blend repair. Distance between repairs must be equal to or greater than the length of longest repair.
- **Trailing Edge** — No cracks allowed. Nicks or dents are permitted, provided they do not exceed 0.060 inch

Figure 5-34. Axial compressor rotor assembly in balancing machine

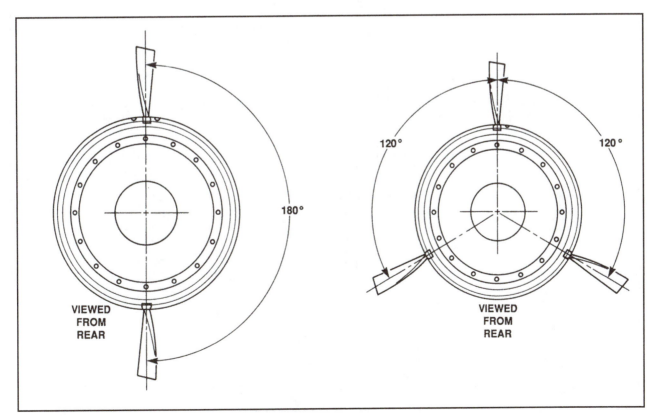

Figure 5-33A. 180° compressor blade replacement method
Figure 5-33B. 120° compressor blade replacement method

in depth or 0.300 inch in length after repair. Distance between repairs must be equal to or greater than the length of the longest repair.

- **Blade Tips** — No cracks allowed. Six nicks or dents are permitted, provided they do not exceed 0.060 inch in depth or 0.300 inch in length after repair. Distance between repaired areas must be at least 3/8 inch.

- **Airfoil (sides of blades)** — No cracks allowed. Nicks and dents are permitted, provided they do not exceed 0.030 inch in depth or 0.350 inch in length after repair. Distance between repaired areas, regardless of location, must be at least ½ inch.

STATOR VANE AND COMPRESSOR CASE INSPECTION AND REPAIR

Generally, repairs of slight impact damage to stator vanes and compressor cases are made by blending. Cracks are usually weld-repairable with traditional inert gas welding apparatus. Figures 5-36 and 5-37 show typical observable damage in the interior of the compressor cases where the stator vanes are located. After repair, if weld beads in the vanes interfere with fits or airflow, grind them back as nearly as possible to the original contour.

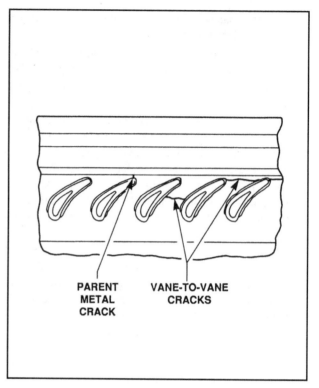

Figure 5-36. Typical weld repairable damage

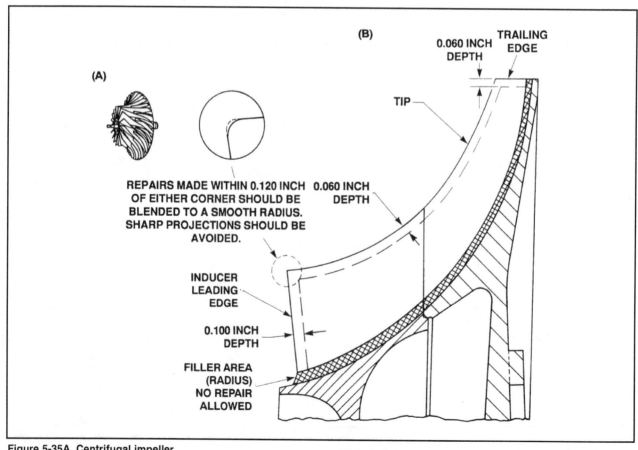

Figure 5-35A. Centrifugal impeller
Figure 5-35B. Repair limits

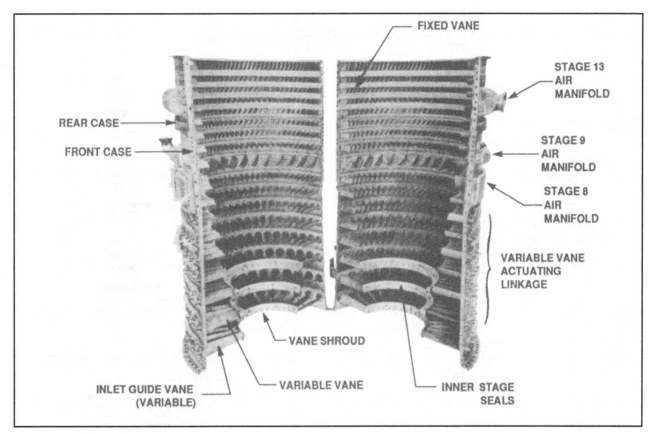

Figure 5-37. Compressor front and rear casing components

HOT SECTION INSPECTION AND REPAIR

The hot section of a gas turbine engine starts at the front of the combustor section and includes all outer and inner parts up to and including the exhaust duct.

COMBUSTION SECTION

Cracking is one of the most frequent discrepancies found in the outer cases and inner parts of a turbine engine combustor. The combustion liner within is constructed of thin stainless steel material that is subjected to high concentrations of heat.

VISUAL INSPECTION

Inspection of removed components is the first step in the determining airworthiness. Beyond that, many of the nondestructive inspections mentioned earlier in this chapter also apply.

The most common method of checking for misalignment, cracks, and other hot distress on installed engines is by using a borescope. Both rigid and flexible types are available with different illumination and magnification capabilities similar to the units discussed for compressor inspection. [Figures 5-20 and 5-21]

Maintenance personnel can easily view internal engine components and determine airworthiness of parts with the borescope. Figure 5-38 shows a combustion liner removed to illustrate the critical borescope inspection points. During a borescope inspection, the operator gains access to the interior of the engine through access ports on the exterior of the engine and inserts the device looking for distress that is out of the manufacturer's limits. Distressed areas showing cracking, warpage, burning, erosion, and sometimes obscure yet tell-tale hot spots are often enough reason for removing the parts. Hot spots, especially, are possible indicators of a serious condition, such as malfunctioning fuel nozzles or other fuel system malfunctions, and require careful interpretation in determining the necessity for further maintenance actions.

Another important aspect of borescoping is checking for misalignment of combustion liners. This so-called "burner-can shift" can seriously affect combustor efficiency and engine performance because the fuel spray pattern will be out of alignment with its airflow component.

The technician determines whether the engine is fit to remain in service or requires disassembly for repair or replacement of combustor section parts. The technician's expertise and training make this important determination possible.

TURBINE SECTION

As shown in Figure 5-39, the inner turbine section can also be inspected with a borescope either visually through

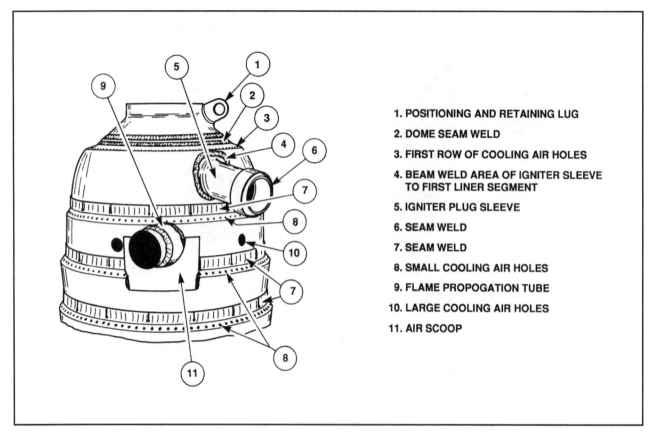

Figure 5-38. Typical combustion chamber liner inspection points

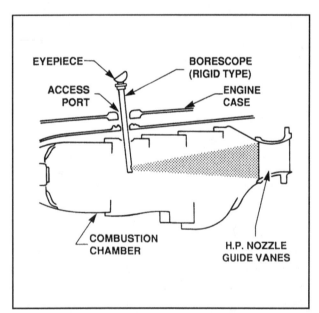

Figure 5-39. Borescoping the liner and first-stage turbine stator

the tailpipe with a strong light, mirror, and a magnifying glass, or by disassembling the engine. On the flight line, nondestructive inspection techniques such as the dye penetrant method are also useful in external inspection. As in other hot section inspections, the technician is most likely to see small cracks caused by compression and tension loading from heating and cooling. [Figure 5-40A] Other than on turbine blades [Figure 5-40B], much of this type of distress is acceptable and requires no maintenance action because, after initial cracks relieve the stress, the cracks do not expand. Erosion is another common inspection finding. Erosion is the wearing away of metal either from the gas flow across its surfaces or surface impingement by impurities in the gas flow. Hot spots are generally the first indication of a malfunction in fuel distribution. A mixture that is too rich can lengthen the flame until it reaches the turbine nozzle vanes. A condition called hot streaking can cause a flame to penetrate through the entire turbine system to the tailpipe. Hot streaking is caused by partially clogged fuel nozzles, which do not atomize the fuel but allow a small fuel stream to flow with sufficient force to cut through the cooling air blanket and impinge directly on the turbine surfaces.

TURBINE WHEEL

Figure 5-41 shows typical turbine blade serviceable and repairable limits and corrective actions, which include repairing, replacing smaller parts, or returning whole assemblies to repair facilities. Blending is a common repair for filing out small areas of distress. The illustration shows blend repairs that are common to both flight line and shop maintenance. Note that cracks are

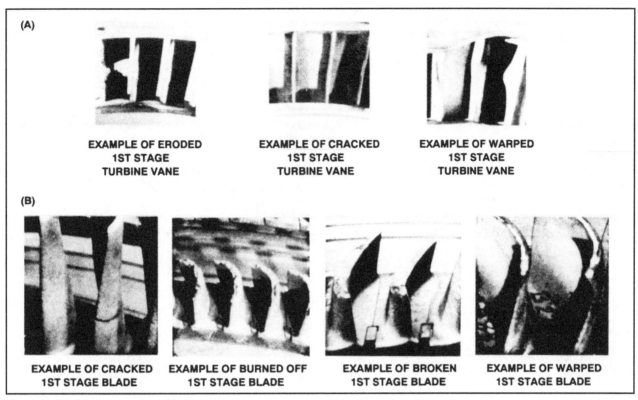

Figure 5-40A. Borescope view of turbine vanes
Figure 5-40B. Borescope view of turbine blades

not acceptable in this example. This is typical of most rotating parts of any hot section of the gas turbine engine.

Stress rupture cracks on turbine blade leading or trailing edges are of particular concern during visual inspections. Stress rupture cracks are perceptible as minute hairline cracks at right angles to the blade length. This condition, and rippling of the trailing edge, is an indication of a serious overtemperature, and a special in-shop manufacturer's inspection will probably be required. [Figure 5-42]

Generally, single turbine blades are replaced with a new blade of equal moment-weight to maintain turbine wheel balance. [Figure 5-43] If you cannot match the blade's moment-weight, replace the damaged blade and one 180 degrees opposite with blades of equal weight, or replace the damaged blade and the blades 120 degrees from it with three blades of equal moment-weight in the same manner as was mentioned for compressor blades.

Today, turbine blades are rarely replaced on the wing; however, shop procedures usually allow for entire turbine reblading, after which the rotor is checked on a special balancing device.

Code letters indicating the moment-weight in inch-ounces or inch-grams are marked on the fir tree section of the blade, as shown in Figure 5-44.

CREEP AND UNTWIST

Creep is the permanent elongation that occurs to rotating parts. Creep is most pronounced in turbine blades because of the heat loads and centrifugal loads imposed during operation. Each time a turbine blade is heated, rotated, and stopped (referred to as an engine cycle), it remains slightly longer than it was before. Under normal circumstances, the additional length may be only millionths of an inch, but after experiencing an engine overtemperature or overspeed condition, the part might be close to its failure point. Measurements for creep are accomplished using micrometer-type instruments and electronic scanning devices.

If the blade remains in service long enough, chances are that it will eventually make contact with its shroud ring and begin to wear away. When this occurs, an audible rubbing can be heard on engine coast-down. Clearance checks are then taken and appropriate maintenance action is determined. [Figure 5-45]

Creep occurs in primary, secondary, and tertiary stages. The primary and tertiary stages occur relatively quickly. Primary creep occurs during the engine's first run, tertiary during operating overloads, but secondary creep occurs quite slowly, as illustrated by the flat portion on the strain/time graph in Figure 5-45A. The engine manufacturer bases turbine service life on the secondary creep region.

Accelerated (tertiary) creep during the engine's service life can be attributed to any of the following:

- Hot starts and overtemperatures
- Extended operation at high power (high EGT and centrifugal loading)
- Erosion of the blades from ingestion of sand or other foreign objects

INSPECTION	MAXIMUM SERVICEABLE	MAXIMUM REPAIRABLE	CORRECTION ACTION
BLADE SHIFT	Protrusion of any blade root must be equal within 0.015" either side of disk.	Not repairable	Return bladed disk assembly to an overhaul facility.
AREA A			
Nicks (3 max.)	0.015" long by 0.005" deep	.015 long by 0.010" deep	Blend out damaged area / Replace blade
Dents and pits (3 max.)	0.010" deep	.015 long by 0.010" deep	Blend out damaged area / Replace blade
Cracks	Not acceptable	Not repairable	Replace blade
AREA B			
Nicks, dents, and pits (No cracks allowed)	One 0.020" deep	Not repairable	Replace blade
LEADING AND TRAILING EDGES			
Nicks, dents, and pits	One 0.020" deep	Two 1/8" deep	Blend out damaged area/ Replace blade
Cracks	Not acceptable	Not repairable	Replace blade

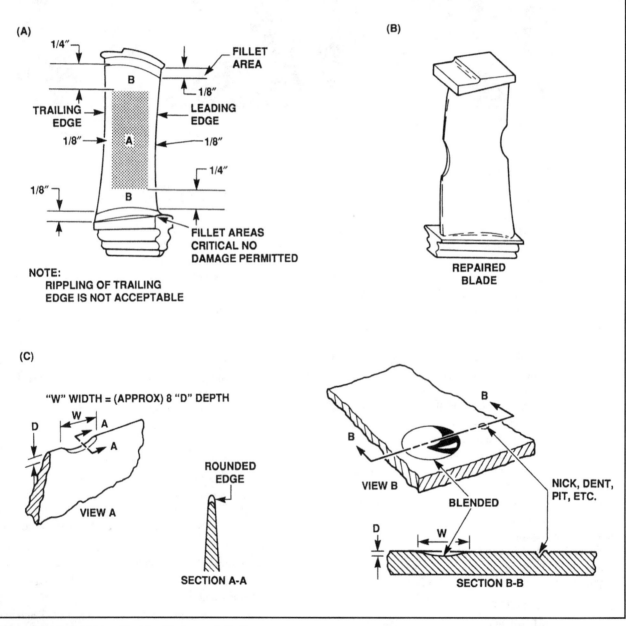

Figure 5-41A. Example of turbine blade repair limits
Figure 5-41B. Repaired blade
Figure 5-41C. Typical blending guides for turbine blade defects other than cracks

Inspection and Maintenance

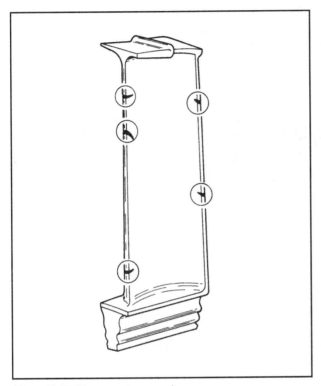

Figure 5-42. Stress rupture cracks

Untwist occurs in both turbine blades and turbine vanes because of gas loads on their surfaces. Loss of correct pitch affects efficiency of the turbine system, and engine performance deteriorates. The check for untwist is generally only possible after engine tear down when parts can be measured in special shop fixtures.

TURBINE CASE, TURBINE VANES, EXHAUST SECTION

Turbine section parts record all operational abuses as well as the deterioration that results from the normal aging process in the form of cracking, warping, bowing, and eroding.

Certain types of small visible cracks commonly found after periods of normal operation are the result of thermal stresses. The progress of many such discrepancies with further operation is often negligible because the cracks relieve the original stress condition. The manufacturer's limits, based on this consideration, incorporate certain distress conditions as acceptable. It is the job of the technician performing the inspection to determine whether the part will remain airworthy until the next inspection or whether the cracks will converge and permit a portion of the material to break away. This condition can cause impact damage to downstream components and result in serious burn-through damage by misdirection of the hot gases. [Figure 5-46]

You can repair worn or burned turbine cases by a process called plasma coating. Often, the slots or channels that vanes fit into become worn and allow the vane to shift. Vane cases that form turbine blade shrouds erode after time. The plasma coating restores the case to an "as-new" condition and is much less costly than replacement. Plasma coating was previously discussed in "Axial Compressor Inspection and Repair."

Technicians can use conventional shielded gas welding, generically called heli-arc methods, to weld cracked or burned turbine cases, but the electron beam and laser

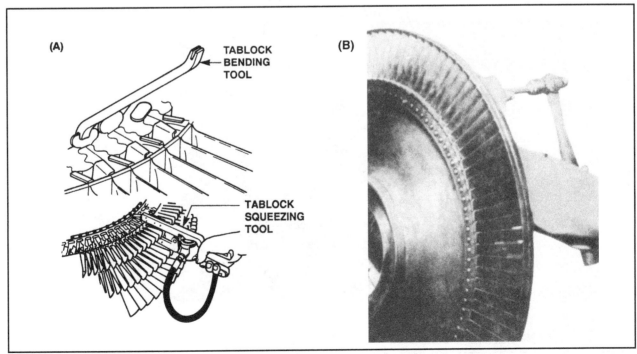

Figure 5-43A. Replacing turbine blade and tab lock retainer
Figure 5-43B. Removing rivet retainer and turbine blade from disk

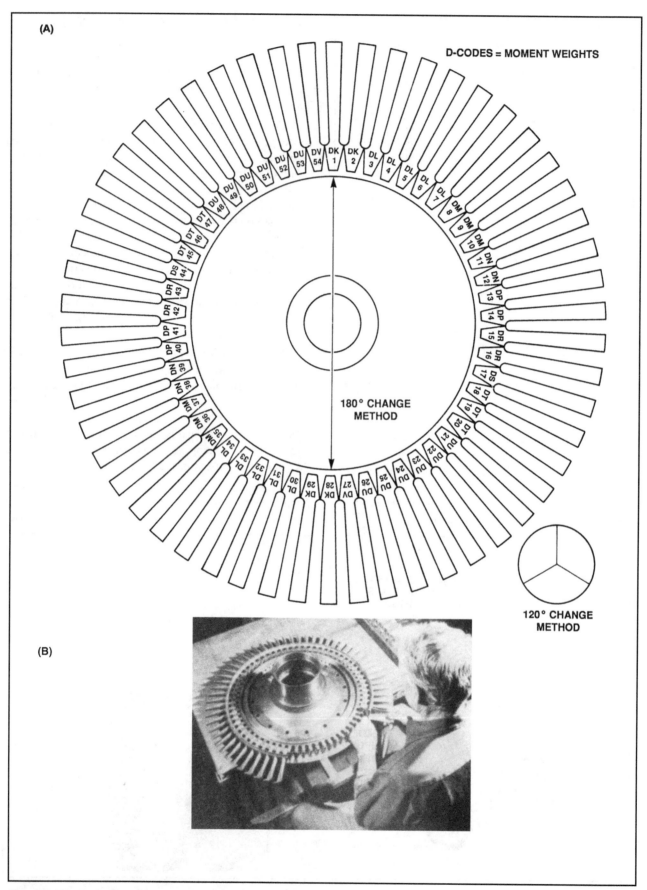

Figure 5-44A. Typical turbine blade moment weight coding
Figure 5-44B. Blade replacement in Pratt & Whitney PW2037 high-pressure turbine

Inspection and Maintenance 5-31

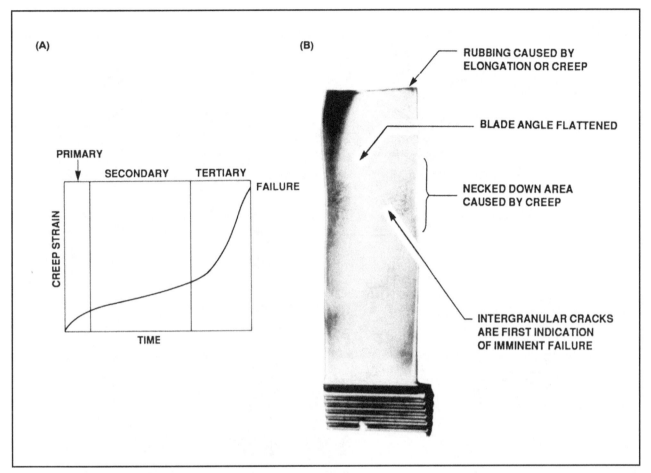

Figure 5-45A. Creep over time
Figure 5-45B. Turbine blade damage caused by excessive temperatures

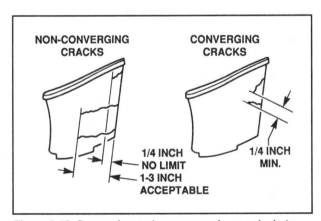

Figure 5-46. Converging and nonconverging cracks in turbine vanes

beam welding techniques are quickly becoming the standard practice because they localize the heat and cause less stress to areas surrounding the welds.

Turbine vanes with burned or eroded outer surfaces can often be repaired by applying the same types of plasma coatings as those used for turbine cases.

Technicians can beam weld cracked or bowed vanes or even restore them by cutting away the damaged area and welding in a segment of new material. Most manufacturers authorize this procedure and claim that the process will produce a strength factor that exceeds the original because the replacement material carries higher heat loading, has higher tensile strength, and is processed after welding by advanced heat treating and plating methods.

Figure 5-47A shows a vane that is ready for a bowing check on a flat plate. This check is accomplished by inserting a thickness gauge under the leading and trailing edge. If the piece is out of limits, you can straighten it if the material will permit such a process. If it cannot be straightened, you can remove a section and weld in a new section.

Figure 5-47B shows a vane that was bowed, cracked, eroded, or burned through so completely that replacement of a section of material is the only possible repair solution. The damaged area will be ground out and a new section beam-welded in its place. The vane will be ground to its original shape and then placed in an oven to relieve stress and unify its strength. More than likely, the vane will be recoated by a plasma spray before being placed back in the engine.

Figure 5-47C shows vane cracks that are acceptable without repair, provided they fall within the limits. When

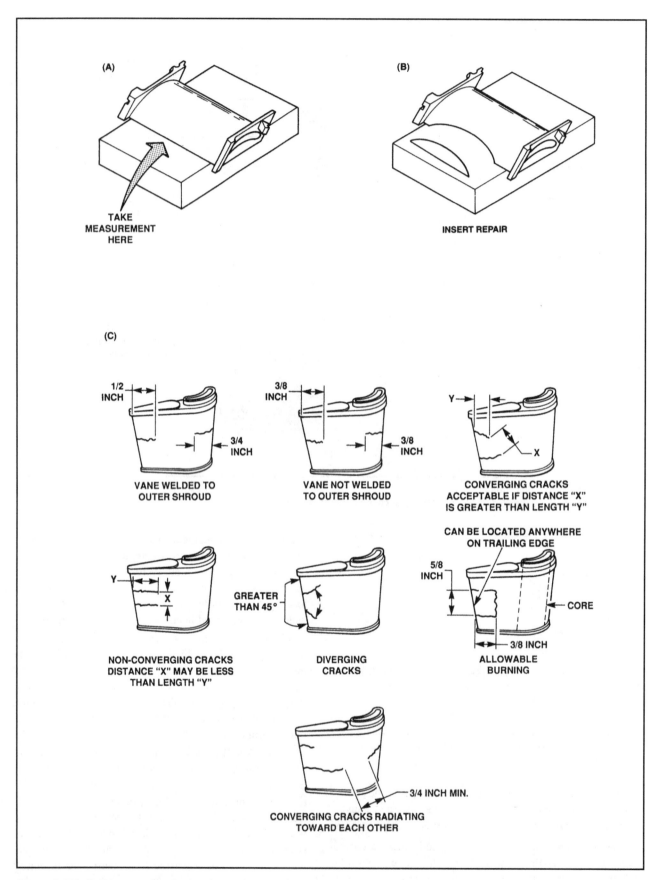

Figure 5-47A. Turbine nozzle vane bowing check
Figure 5-47B. Vane insert repair
Figure 5-47C. Vanes acceptable if they do not exceed these limits

beyond these limits, welding of cracks or replacement of small sections will be required.

Exhaust cases are also susceptible to all of the previously mentioned hot gas path problems. Most of the material in this part of the engine is a type of rolled stainless steel and can be weld repaired by conventional or beam welding for cracking or patched at burned-through areas. Figure 5-48 shows typical damage and repairs.

MARKING PARTS

The general marking procedure for identifying areas to be repaired in both hot and cold section parts is to apply chalk, special layout dye, or to mark with a commercial felt-tip applicator or special marking pencil. Do not use a substance that leaves carbon, copper, zinc, or lead deposits because these deposits are drawn into heated metal and can cause intergranular stress. Marking with a common graphite lead pencil is strictly prohibited. Specific marking procedures will always take precedence over general procedures.

This caution note excerpted from a gas turbine engine maintenance manual highlights the importance of never using these substances:

CAUTION: Deposits left on stainless and high temperature alloy parts where marked with carbonaceous materials such as graphite, wax, or grease pencils, may lead to failure of the parts in service. Even dychem (layout dye) is potentially hazardous if not completely removed. This type of failure occurs when parts are heat treated, welded, or exposed in any manner to elevated temperatures of 700°F or more. The exposure causes localized carbon enrichment and intergranular embrittlement, which can lead to crack initiation and propagation.

MAIN BEARINGS AND SEALS

Main engine bearings support the rotating shafts of the compressor and turbine sections. The bearings are lubricated by the engine lubrication system. Seals keep the oil in the bearing sumps and prevent oil from entering the gas path of the engine.

BEARINGS

The main bearings of a gas turbine engine are either ball or roller anti-friction bearings. Ball bearings ride in a grooved inner race and support the main engine rotor for both axial (thrust) and radial (centrifugal) loads. Roller bearings ride on a flat inner race. Because of their greater surface contact area, roller bearings absorb the bulk of the radial loading and allow for axial growth of the engine during operation. For this reason, tapered roller bearings are seldom used. [Figure 5-49]

Plain bearings are not used as main bearings in turbine engines, as they are in reciprocating engines, because turbines operate at much higher speeds and friction heat buildup would be prohibitive. However, plain bearings (bushings) are used in some minor load locations such as in accessories.

The primary loads acting on main bearings are from the following sources:

- Weight of the rotating mass (compressor and turbine) magnified many thousands of times by radial G-forces
- Axial forces from power changes and thrust loading
- Gyroscopic effect of heavy rotating masses trying to remain in place as the aircraft changes direction
- Compression and tension loads between the stationary casings and the rotor system caused by thermal expansion
- Vibrations induced by the airstream, the aircraft, and the engine itself

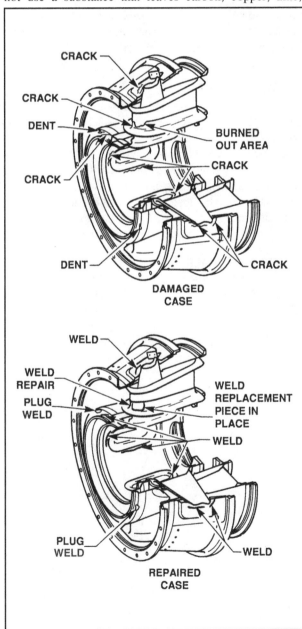

Figure 5-48. Turboshaft engine exhaust collector showing typical damage and repairs

The main bearings support the rotor assemblies and then transfer the various loads through the bearing housings and support struts to the outer engine cases and ultimately into the aircraft mountings.

The number of main bearings varies by engine model. One manufacturer might install three heavy bearings while another might use five or six lighter bearings to accommodate the same load factors.

Figures 5-49 and 5-50 show construction features of ball and roller bearings. Note that only one of the roller bearing races is grooved, allowing the roller freedom to move axially when the engine expands and contracts during operation. The split inner race is a design feature of the ball bearing that allows for ease of bearing disassembly, maintenance, and inspection, after the bearing is removed from the engine.

The inner races of bearings are normally interference-fitted to the rotor shafts to prevent movement on the shaft and must be removed with special puller tools. Also shown in Figure 5-50 is the oil damped bearing, which is provided with an oil film between the outer race and the bearing housing to reduce vibration tendencies in the rotor system and to allow for a slight misalignment of up to five thousandths of an inch.

Turbine components have serial numbers to prevent intermixing. Gas turbine anti-friction bearings are matched sets of races, cages, etc. that conform to extremely close production tolerances. Remember that the gas turbine is a high speed, lightweight device that requires absolute minimum vibration, even under great G-forces and gyroscopic loads.

This list is an example of the typically close tolerances that make up a gas turbine engine's main bearing:

- Sheet metal casings: ± 0.02"
- Machined casings: ± 0.002"
- Bearing races: ± 0.0002"
- Bearing rollers: ± 0.00005"
- Bearing balls: ± 0.00001"

Because of these extremely tight mechanical tolerances, many bearings are installed with their serial numbers, alignment marks, and other manufacturing tolerance marks placed in a very specific manner, as prescribed by the manufacturer. [Figure 5-51]

The air balance chamber, shown in Figure 5-52, aids the compressor thrust bearing (number 2) in combating high gas-path pressures that try to push the compressor forward. The balance chamber and the thrust bearings help restrain the compressor against the axial pushing force. Some engines do not need an air balance chamber because the opposite (rearward) thrust load at the turbine adequately cancels the forward pushing loads on the compressor.

BEARING SEALS

Most bearing housings contain seals to prevent loss of oil into the gas path. Oil seals are usually either labyrinth or carbon rubbing seals, and it is common to see one or the other, or a combination of the two, in the same engine because of the temperature gradient differences in the hot and cold sections of the engine. That is, if a labyrinth seal is used in some hot locations it might expand and contact its seal land, causing wear. The seal land is the name generally given to the rotating portion of the labyrinth seal.

LABYRINTH SEALS

The two labyrinth seals shown in Figures 5-52 (in context) and 5-53 (in isolation) form a compartment in which the bearing is housed. Air from the gas path outside of

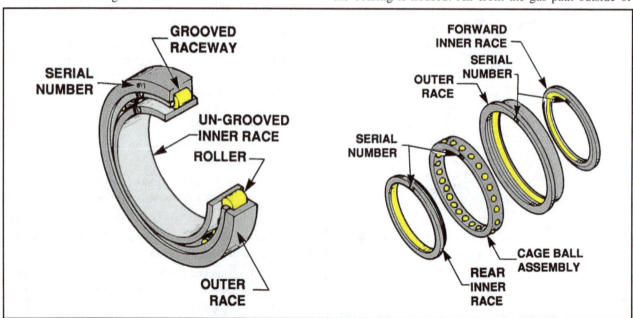

Figure 5-49A. Main bearing, roller type
Figure 5-49B. Main bearing, ball type

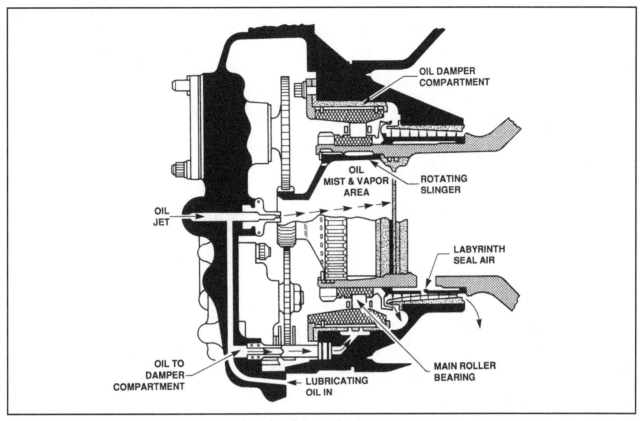

Figure 5-50. Front compressor main roller bearing with oil damped outer race

the bearing compartment bleeds inward across grooves cut in the labyrinth seal. These grooves form sealing rings in either a concentric path similar to a screw thread or a nonconcentric path with each ring in its own plane. In any case, the seal dams formed by the rings allow for a metered amount of air from the engine gas path to flow inward. Pressure within the bearing compartment is maintained slightly above atmospheric level in most engines. This is discussed in detail in Chapter 6.

The air entering across the labyrinth seal prevents the oil mist created by the oil jet spraying on the rotating bearing from exiting the bearing compartment. The seal pressurizing air then leaves the bearing area [Figure 5-52] by way of the scavenge oil system. Dead headed air pressure in the balance chamber pushes against the compressor and prevents sudden thrust loads from being absorbed totally by the bearing when the engine power changes. Most high-compression engines are designed with a separate vent subsystem. [Figure 5-53]

CARBON SEALS

Carbon seals are a blend of carbon and graphite. They are similar in function and location to labyrinth seals, but the main design difference is that the carbon seal rides on a highly polished chrome carbide surface, while the labyrinth seal maintains an air gap clearance.

The carbon seal is usually spring-loaded and sometimes pressurized with air to create a uniform pressure drop across the seal. The pressurized air also preloads the carbon segment against its mating surface and provides a more positive oil sealing capability.

The carbon seal shown in Figure 5-54A is a carbon-ring seal. Its stationary sealing rings ride circumferentially against a finely ground metallic seal race that is attached to a rotating shaft. Another common design is the carbon-face seal that is in contact horizontally with its seal race. [Figure 5-54B] Although generally larger, this seal is identical to those used as drive shaft seals in many fluid carrying accessories. The carbon surface in this illustration is stationary with its highly polished mating surface, called a seal or seal race, attached to and turning with the main rotor shaft.

Carbon seals, with their tighter clearances, are found where more positive control over airflow into the bearing sumps is required or where a full contact seal is needed to hold back oil that might puddle before being scavenged away from the sumps. Conversely, labyrinth sealing will usually be associated with oil system locations that are designed for higher vent subsystem pressures.

BRUSH SEALS

The newest generation of oil seal is the brush seal, in which a metal bristled element rides on a smooth rub

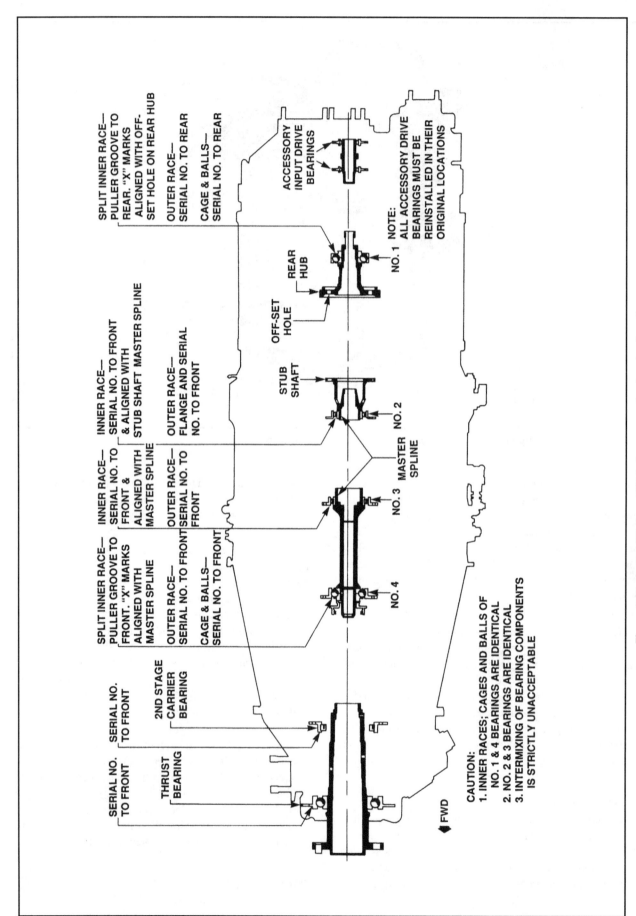

Figure 5-51. Pratt & Whitney PT6 turboprop engine bearing locations

Inspection and Maintenance

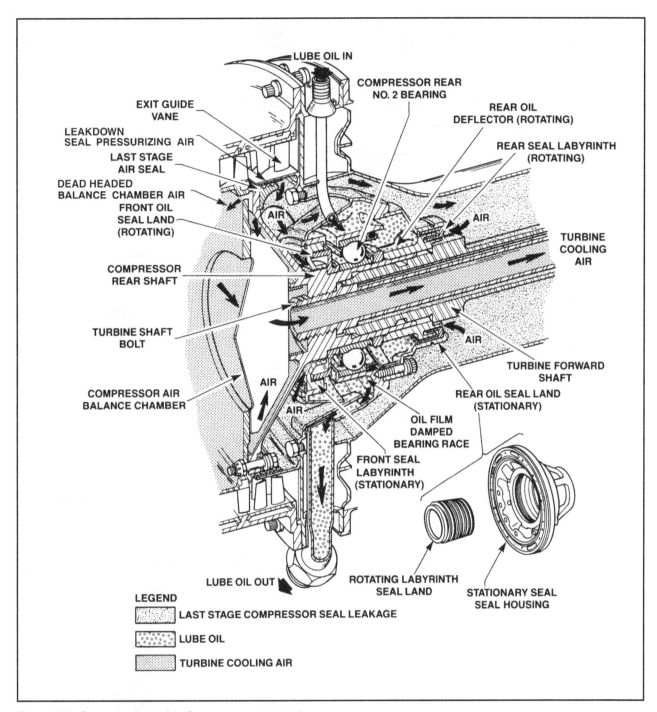

Figure 5-52. Compressor rear bearing sump arrangement

ring. This type of seal loses less air than the labyrinth seal and has a longer service life than the carbon seal.

The brush seal is becoming more widely used in the turbine engine. [Figure 5-54C] It functions much like a labyrinth seal by taking a pressure drop across the interface of the stationary bristle section and its rotating rub-ring. Because the bristles maintain contact with the runner, brush seals do not leak as much as labyrinth seals.

As the engine experiences thermal and mechanical transient loading during power changes, gyroscopic deflections of the engine rotor system promote wear on both labyrinth and carbon seals. The brush seal has an advantage in this case because it is able to accommodate rotor excursions, both radial and axial, without permanently opening up the seal's clearance. Because this type of seal does not need as much gas path air bleeding across it, less hot air enters the oil system sumps, so the heat load on the oil system is reduced.

BEARING HANDLING AND MAINTENANCE

Most manufacturers require that bearings be cleaned and inspected in an environmentally controlled bearing

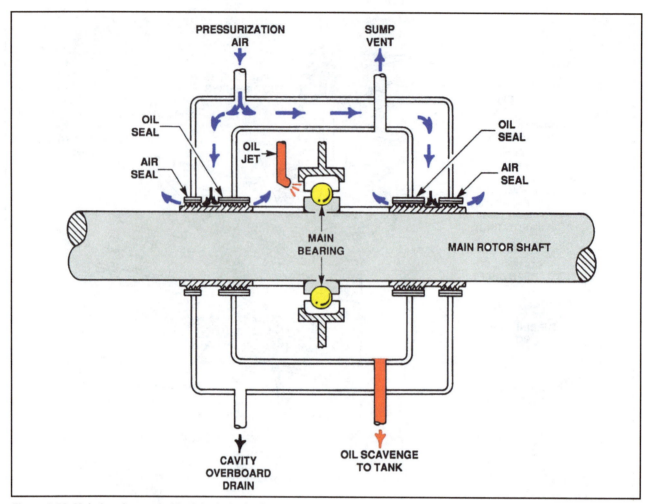

Figure 5-53. Main bearing sealed by labyrinth air-oil seals

handling room to prevent surface corrosion when bearings are out of the engine. To prevent even the slightest damage from occurring to their very close tolerance surfaces, never leave bearings unprotected. [Figure 5-55]

When inspecting bearings, wear lint-free cotton or synthetic rubber gloves to prevent acid or moisture on your hands from contacting the bearing surfaces. Bearing inspection is usually conducted under strong light and magnification to determine their serviceability. Only very minor surface defects are allowable.

Bearings tend to gain work-hardness over time. They are often checked for excessive hardness with special equipment procedures because this condition makes bearings susceptible to chipping.

During inspection, bearings also receive a feel test by an experienced technician who compares the rotational feel of one bearing against the feel of a new one. After inspection, many measurement checks are performed on the bearings with special measurement devices provided by the manufacturer.

PRECAUTIONARY MEASURES

Managers and technicians should take the following precautions during bearing inspection:

- Do not spin dry bearings because dust particles can scratch surfaces.
- Do not blow bearings dry with shop air because moisture content in the air can cause corrosion.
- Do not vapor degrease bearings because vapors support contaminants.
- Do not use petroleum oils on bearings intended for use in engines that use synthetic oil. A chemical reaction can result.
- Do not use the shop cleaning vat. Instead immerse bearings in clean fluid or wipe clean, using a lint-free cloth or suitable paper wiper and an approved cleaning solvent.

MAGNETISM CHECK

After inspection, check bearings for the presence of magnetism with a device called a magnetic-field detector. If magnetism is present, demagnetize the bearing with a suitable degausser to prevent ferrous particles from accumulating on the bearing during engine operation.

Inspection and Maintenance

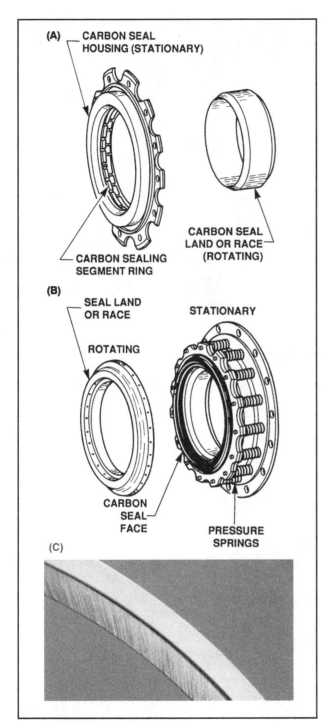

Figure 5-54A. Carbon ring seal
Figure 5-54B. Carbon face seal
Figure 5-54C. Brush seal

Magnetism occurs mainly from the effects of bearing rotation at high speeds and from lightning strikes absorbed by the aircraft.

Another possible cause of bearing magnetism is using improperly grounded equipment for electric arc welding of the assembled engine. The ground lead of the welding equipment must not be secured to an outer casing, but rather to the part being welded in a manner that prevents high electrical current flow through the entire engine. The result is that ferrous particles generated by normal engine wear in bearings and other ferrous materials will adhere to the bearing surfaces rather than be flushed away to the oil system filters.

BEARING INSTALLATION

Bearings are stored in vapor-proof paper before installation. As appropriate, the inner and outer races are either heated in a clean bath of engine oil or chilled in a refrigerator before being fitted into their installation positions. Figure 5-56 shows a bearing installation with a special tool, torque device, and sling. Figure 5-57 shows the bearing arrangement in a turbofan engine fan support shaft assembly.

BEARING DISTRESS TERMS [Figure 5-58]

Abrasion — A roughened area caused by the presence of fine foreign material between moving surfaces.

Brinelling (true) — A shallow indentation sometimes found at one location on the surface of ball or roller bearing races, caused by shock loads to the bearing when not rotating.

Brinelling (false) — A satin finish or a series of shallow depressions in the surface of ball or roller bearing races.

Burning — An injury to the surface caused by excessive heat and evidenced by discoloration or, in severe cases, by loss of material.

Burnishing — A mechanical smoothing of a metal surface by rubbing. It is not accompanied by removal of material but sometimes by discoloration around the outer edges of the area.

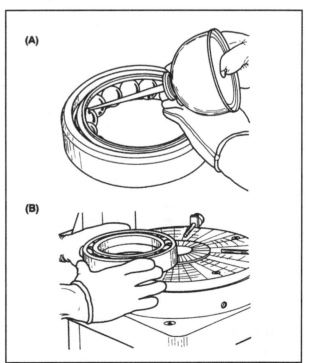

Figure 5-55A. Wear lint-free gloves when lubricating bearings
Figure 5-55B. Positioning bearing on flat plate for measurement check

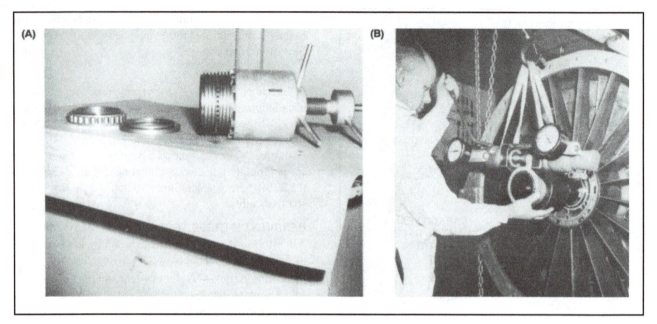

Figure 5-56A. Bearing and labyrinth seal ready for installation
Figure 5-56B. Installing bearing retaining nut on Pratt & Whitney JT8D Turbofan

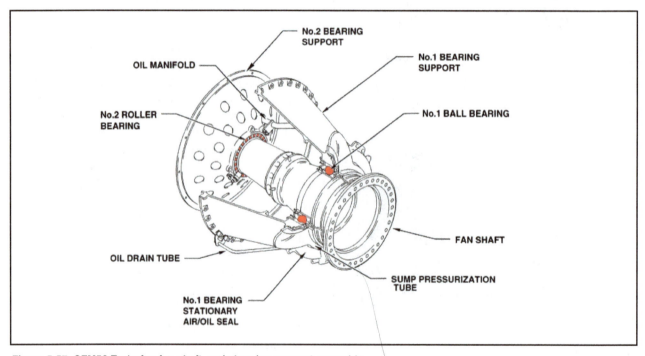

Figure 5-57. CFM56 Turbofan fan shaft, main bearing support assembly

Burr — A sharp projection or rough edge.

Chafing — A rubbing action between two parts that have limited relative motion.

Chipping — Breaking out of small pieces of material.

Corrosion — Breakdown of the surface by chemical action.

Fretting — Discoloration on surfaces that are pressed or bolted together under high pressure. On steel parts the color is reddish brown. On aluminum, the oxide is white.

Galling — The transfer of metal from one surface to another, caused by chafing.

Gouging — The displacement of materials from a surface by a cutting or tearing effect.

Grooving — Smooth rounded furrows, such as score marks, where the sharp edges have been polished off.

Guttering — A deep concentrated erosion caused by overheat or burning.

Inspection and Maintenance

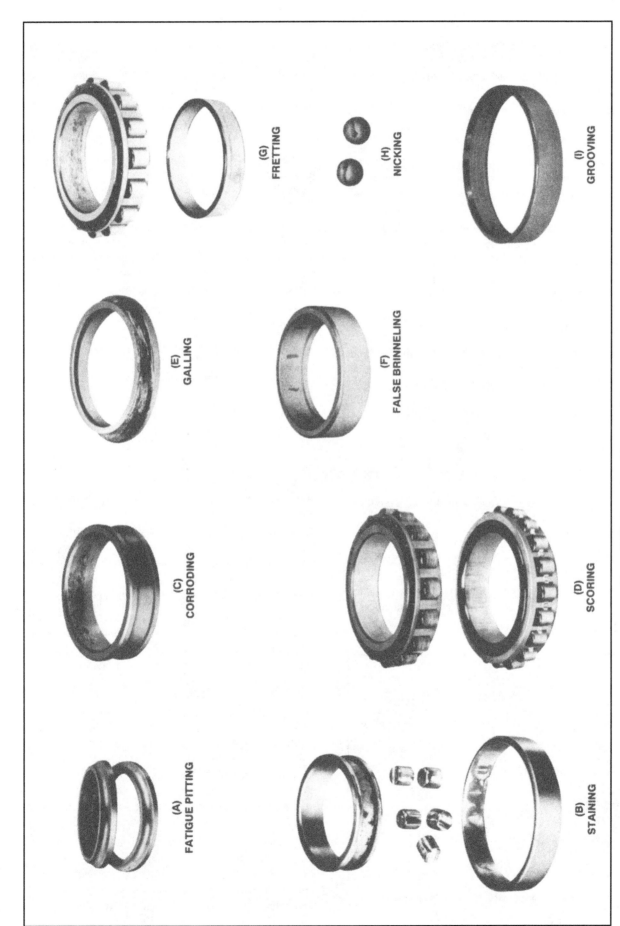

Figure 5-58. Examples of bearing distress

Inclusion — Foreign material enclosed in the metal. Surface inclusions are indicated by dark spots or lines, an inherent discontinuity in the material.

Nick — A sharp indentation caused by striking one part against another metal object.

Peening — Deformation of the surface caused by impact.

Pitting — Small irregularly shaped cavities in a surface from which material has been removed by corrosion or chipping. Corrosive pitting is usually accompanied by a deposit formed by the action of a corrosive agent on the base material.

Scoring — Deep scratches made by sharp edges or foreign particles during engine operation; elongated gouges.

Spalling — Sharply roughened area characteristic of the progressive chipping or peeling of surface material, caused by overloading.

TORQUE WRENCH USE

The torque wrench is required for both line and shop maintenance. [Figure 5-59] Before using a torque wrench, calibrate it with a weight and lever arm tester. All gas turbine engine manufacturers require careful torquing (application of twisting force), and most recommend the following calibration schedule for torque wrenches used in engine maintenance:

- Micrometer-type torque wrenches. Check once a week.
- Non-set-type torque wrenches. Check once a month.

Larger shops often have a torque wrench calibration tester in all workstations where torque wrenches are frequently used, so technicians can calibrate the wrench daily or even before each use.

The micrometer torque wrench is the most widely used in the industry because almost every fastener on a gas turbine engine requires a specific torque. This type of wrench can be used quickly and accurately in positions and places difficult to work in with other types. Torque with this wrench is applied by feel. The correct torque has been applied when the wrench breaks, so you do not have to see the scale. To prevent a micrometer torque wrench from losing calibration, return it to its lowest setting after use.

The beam and dial torque wrenches apply a more accurate initial torque if you hold the torque for a few seconds after reaching the desired amount to allow a set to occur between mating parts. You must always have an unobstructed, straight-on view of the scale or an inaccurate torque will result.

With the micrometer wrench, if the engine manufacturer feels a time interval is needed for mating surfaces to close a gap when assembling close fitting parts, then the appropriate maintenance manuals will stipulate the accurate torque application procedure as follows:

- Torque the series of fasteners to required value, then loosen and re-torque.
- Torque the series of fasteners to minimum value, and then apply a second torque to the required value.
- Stipulate an arrangement that will bring about the desired alignment of mating parts, such as using a stagger procedure.
- Stipulate an arrangement that uses a combination of the above procedures.

Another method of applying torque is to measure the stretch of a bolt rather than measuring the amount of twist applied. This is more the case with large bolts found in larger engines.

Figure 5-60A shows the technician setting initial torque with a beam torque wrench on nuts that attach to long hollow tie bolts (tie rods). The tie rods hold the fan to the front of the compressor.

In Figure 5-60B, the technician has installed an adapter plate containing a number of dial type depth micrometers that fit into the hollow tie rods. The technician would then apply final torque on the nut by measuring the stretch of the tie bolt using the dial micrometers.

TORQUE WRENCH EXTENSIONS

Occasionally, a torque wrench with an extension attached is needed to gain access to a particular fastener. In this situation, the reading on the torque wrench will not be the actual torque applied because the torque arm (length) of the wrench has changed. The following information describes the procedure for calculating the necessary indicated torque value on the wrench that will provide the true torque applied to the fastener. [Figure 5-61]

Suppose you need a torque of 1,440 pound-inches (lb-in.) on a part, and you use an extension that has a length of 4 inches from the center of its wrench slot to its square drive. The torque wrench measures 16 inches from the center of its handle to the center of its square adapter.

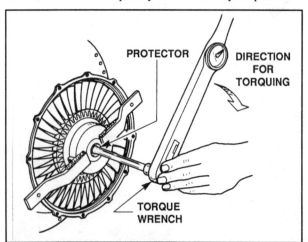

Figure 5-59. Using a torque wrench to install a turbine wheel

Inspection and Maintenance

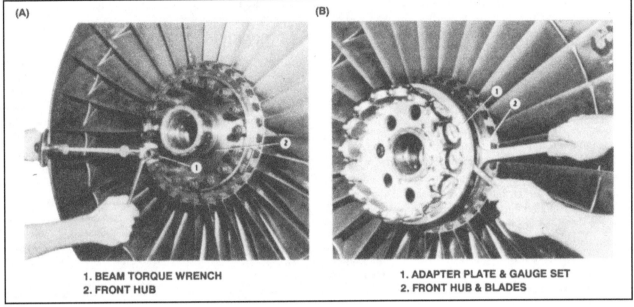

Figure 5-60A. Tightening front compressor tie rod nuts
Figure 5-60B. Stretching front compressor tie rods

What torque must the wrench indicate in order to apply the required torque to the fastener?

$$R = \frac{L}{L + E} \times T$$

$$R = \frac{16}{16 + 4} \times 1{,}440$$

$$R = 1{,}152 \text{ lb-in}$$

With the axis of the extension and torque wrench in a straight line, tightening to a wrench reading of 1,152 pound-inches will provide a desired torque of 1,440 pound-inches.

TORQUE PROCEDURE

The manufacturer usually specifies the torque to apply and the torquing procedure to use. This procedure must be followed conscientiously to avoid stress between the mating flanges.

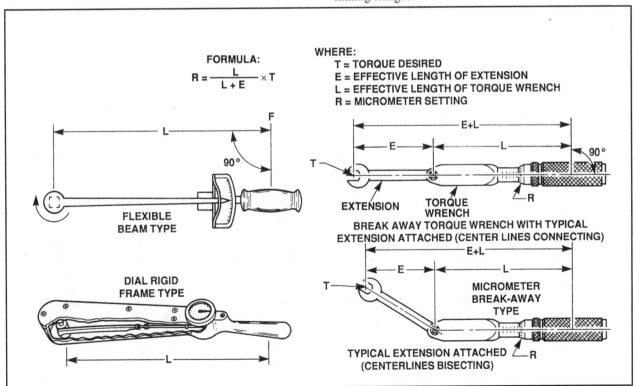

Figure 5-61. Using a torque wrench extension

The cylindrical turbine engine has many circular bolt-ring sets. Often the manufacturer will stipulate stagger torquing the entire ring to the low limit and then loosening and retorquing to the median value. [Figure 5-62] This procedure allows an even set to take place between the two surfaces, and it allows for a small torque wrench calibration error. For example, if the manual torque chart indicates a torque of 90 to 100 inch-pounds, you would torque all bolts initially to 90 inch-pounds and then loosen and retorque to 95 inch pounds.

If there is no special procedure, the standard maintenance practice is to torque tighten gradually at staggered locations until you reach the required torque value. When torquing castellated nuts or nuts and bolts with tab-washers, apply the low torque and then apply additional torque up to the maximum value, if necessary, for alignment of the cotter key slot or the tab lock slot. If you cannot make alignment, install a new nut or bolt until you can acquire the right combination of torque and alignment.

Another widely used procedure is to initially torque one bolt at each 90-degree location and then stagger torque the remaining bolts in the ring at 180-degree locations.

If you are torquing the bolt head rather than the nut (because the nut is not accessible or the bolt is being installed into a nut-plate), calculate the running torque and add this value to the median torque value. The same is true when torquing steel locking and fiber locking nuts.

If the manufacturer has not indicated a special torque value, use an appropriate standard torque table similar to the example in Figure 5-63.

LOCKING METHODS FOR ENGINE FASTENERS

Fasteners in critical locations are fitted with drilled heads or drilled shanks to accommodate a locking method that prevents rotation and loosening of the fastener and provides safety for the part that the fastener secures. Fasteners include the traditional bolts, nuts, screws, and locking tabs of various types.

LOCKWIRING

Lockwiring, sometimes called safety wiring, is a common line and shop maintenance procedure that prevents threaded parts from loosening after they have been torqued. This is a significant airworthiness consideration on turbine engines because dangerous air, oil, and fuel leaks can occur at loose lines and flanges and present serious flight hazards. Figure 5-64 shows the conventional tools required to accomplish the lock wiring task.

Be careful to select only the correct type and diameter lockwire recommended by the manufacturer. If the wire is over-twisted, it work-hardens and could break during service. For example, the twisting for 0.032-inch lockwire is usually recommended at 8 to 10 twists per inch and for 0.041-inch diameter lockwire, 6 to 8 twists per inch.

The common practice in the industry is to use stainless steel, aircraft-grade lockwire of a sufficient heat range for the intended location and of approximately ¾ the diameter of the hole in the fastener. The maximum span between tension points, if possible, should be no longer than 6 inches. Nicks, kinks, or other mutilation of the wire is unacceptable. Cut off the lockwire ends, commonly called pigtails, at least three complete twists from the last tension point, then turn it in to prevent snagging.

The commonly accepted lockwiring techniques are indicated in Figure 5-65A.

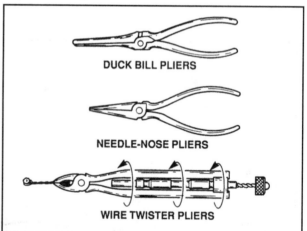

Figure 5-64. Common lockwiring tools

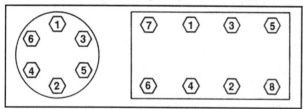

Figure 5-62. Stagger torque patterns

DIAMETER AND THREADS PER INCH	(NATIONAL COARSE) SIZE	TORQUE VALUES	DIAMETER AND THREADS PER INCH	(NATIONAL FINE) SIZE	TORQUE VALUES
NC-8-32	.164	13-16 LB-IN.	NF-8-36	.164	16-19 LB-IN.
10-24	.190	20-23 LB-IN.	10-32	.190	24-27 LB-IN.
1/4-20	.250	40-60 LB-IN.	1/4-28	.250	55-70 LB-IN.
5/16-18	.3125	70-110 LB-IN.	5/16-24	.3125	100-130 LB-IN.
3/8-16	.375	160-210 LB-IN.	3/8-24	.375	190-230 LB-IN.
7/16-14	.4375	250-320 LB-IN.	7/16-20	.4375	300-360 LB-IN.
1/2-13	.500	420-510 LB-IN.	1/2-20	.500	480-570 LB-IN.

Figure 5-63. Standard torque table for steel bolts and self-locking nuts

Inspection and Maintenance

(A) NOTE: LOCKWIRING AROUND THE HEAD RESULTS IN BETTER LOAD DISTRIBUTION THAN ACROSS THE HEAD.

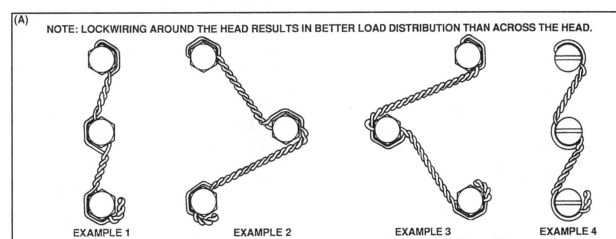

EXAMPLE 1   EXAMPLE 2   EXAMPLE 3   EXAMPLE 4

EXAMPLES 1, 2, 3, AND 4 APPLY TO ALL TYPES OF BOLTS, FILLSTER HEAD SCREWS, SQUARE HEAD PLUGS, AND OTHER SIMILAR PARTS THAT ARE WIRED SO THAT THE LOOSENING TENDENCY OF EITHER PART IS COUNTERACTED BY TIGHTENING OF THE OTHER PART. THE DIRECTION OF TWIST FROM THE SECOND TO THE THIRD UNIT IS COUNTERCLOCKWISE TO KEEP THE LOOP IN POSITION AGAINST THE HEAD OF THE BOLT. THE WIRE ENTERING THE HOLE IN THE THIRD UNIT WILL BE THE LOWER WIRE AND BY MAKING A COUNTERCLOCKWISE TWIST AFTER IT LEAVES THE HOLE, THE LOOP WILL BE SECURED IN PLACE AROUND THE HEAD OF THAT BOLT.

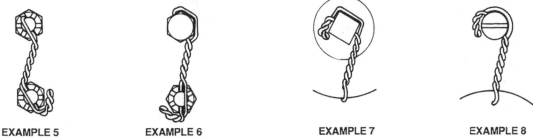

EXAMPLE 5   EXAMPLE 6   EXAMPLE 7   EXAMPLE 8

EXAMPLES 5, 6, 7, AND 8 SHOW METHODS FOR WIRING VARIOUS STANDARD ITEMS. NOTE: WIRE MAY BE WRAPPED OVER THE UNIT RATHER THAN AROUND IT WHEN WIRING CASTELLATED NUTS OR ON OTHER ITEMS WHEN THERE IS A CLEARANCE PROBLEM.

(B)

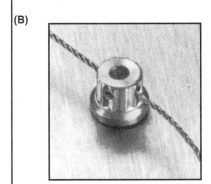

1. INSTALL CABLE THROUGH FASTENERS IN A NEUTRAL-TO-POSITIVE POSITION. INSERT LOOSE FERRULE ONTO CABLE WITH MAGAZINE LOADER.

3. CRIMP FERRULE AND CUT CABLE FLUSH IN ONE MOTION.

2. STRING END OF CABLE THROUGH TOOL AND TENSION ASSEMBLY TO THE PRESET LOAD.

4. TOTAL INSTALLED TIME AVERAGES LESS THAN HALF THAT OF LOCKWIRE.

Figure 5-65A. Twist lockwiring examples
Figure 5-65B. Cable lockwiring method

Another lockwiring technique requires pre-twisted wire, referred to as a cable and crimp-ferrule method. [Figure 5-65B] The special installation tool called a magazine loader tool tensions the cable, crimps the ferrule, and cuts off the excess cable flush with the ferrule.

LOCK WASHERS AND TABS

Lock washers found in gas turbine engines are more often the lock tab and cup-washer varieties than the traditional split ring or the internal/external tooth types seen in other industries. [Figure 5-66A]

These locking devices are placed under the nuts or bolt heads with the locating tabs in a recess in the parent material. Then, after the nut or bolt is torqued, the locking tabs or crimp flanges are bent to prevent or interfere with rotation and loosening.

O-RING SEALS

An o-ring seal is a type of elastomer that is used at two mating surfaces to prevent the loss of a fluid (liquid or gas). [Figure 5-66B] The o-ring is compressed between the two surfaces, typically fitting into a groove that holds it securely in place. The types of o-ring seals most common to aviation are:

- Nitrile — Wide temperature range; good resistance to natural petroleum products.
- Flurocarbon — A type of neoprene with a wide temperature range; good resistance to natural and synthetic lubricating products and jet fuels.
- Silicones — Wide temperature range; when combined as flurosilicone, good resistance to fuel products.
- Polyacrylate — Excellent resistance to fuel and petroleum oil products and to oxidation.
- Ethylene propylene and butyl rubber — Used mainly with ester-type hydraulic fluids.

All o-ring seals are manufactured with a specific purpose in mind, and using the wrong one can result in a serious engine malfunction. An o-ring seal must be the part number specified by the manufacturer, not just a seal of the proper size.

TEST CELL MAINTENANCE

After manufacture, heavy repair, and even some minor repairs, the engine may require an integrity check in a specific test facility similar to the one illustrated in Figure 5-67. This facility has instruments that can provide operational data beyond the capability of the aircraft cockpit. For instance, the test bed instruments for thrust-producing engines are configured to electronically measure engine thrust in pounds, which can be compared to other aircraft type performance gauges that read out in engine speed (percent of r.p.m.) or engine pressure ratio. In this manner, you can accurately measure the thrust parameters of turbojet and turbofan engines. In addition, in the case of torque producing engines, output can be indicated as brake horsepower that can then be compared to the torque output gauge reading of a turboprop or turboshaft engine.

Another very important primary engine inspection deals with vibration analysis during test cell operation. It checks for component imbalance, a hazardous condition in the low-weight, high-speed gas turbine engine, where rapid wear can occur quickly from even very slight induced vibration. Many larger aircraft cockpits are also fitted with vibration monitoring equipment.

While reciprocating engine vibration is visible to the naked eye, gas turbine engines have minute, visually undetectable vibration characteristics with their limits in the order of only 2 to 4 thousandths of an inch. It is not unusual for an engine to have vibration of less than

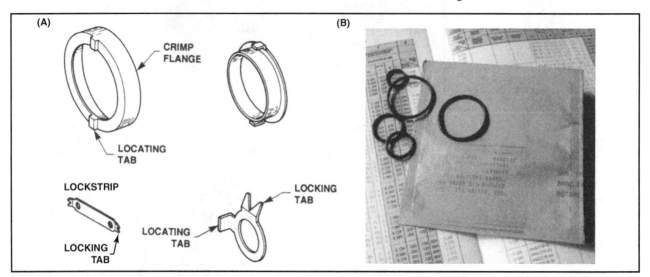

Figure 5-66A. Types of lock tabs and lock cups
Figure 5-66B. O-ring seals and packaging specifications

Inspection and Maintenance

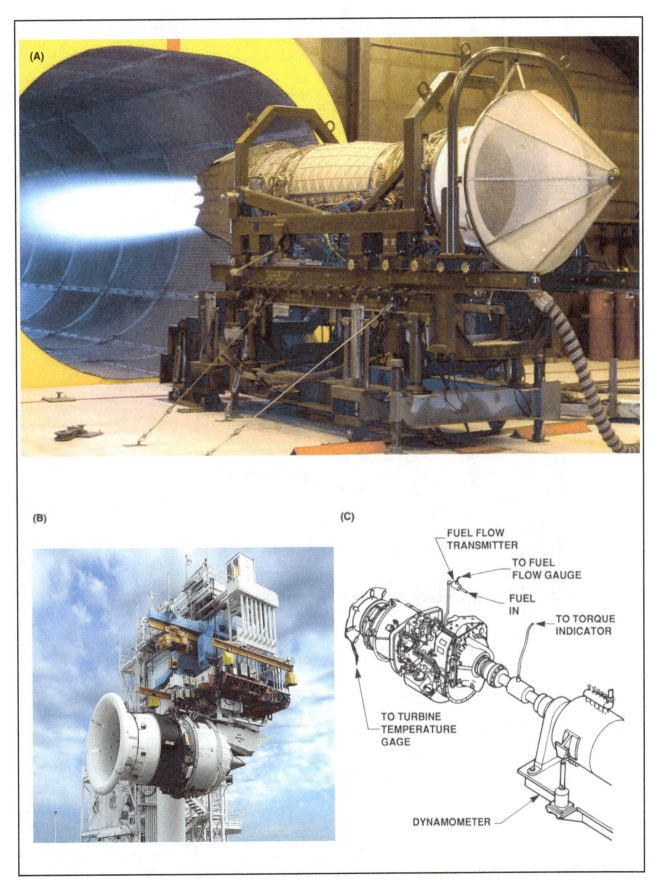

Figure 5-67A. Engine in test facility (floor type), thrust measuring bed
Figure 5-67B. General Electric Gen-X, turbofan test facility (overhead type), thrust measuring bed
Figure 5-67C. Turboprop and turboshaft test facility, dynamometer providing a substitute load

one-thousandth of an inch. Vibration is measured with a meter and special engine-mounted detectors called vibration transducers (also referred to as accelerometers) that respond to oscillatory motion and send the amplified data via a signal conditioner to the test cell instrumentation, or in the case of an aircraft installed engine, to the flight deck display.

Figure 5-68A shows one of several engine vibration transducers that might be installed on an engine. These externally mounted transducers send a signal that indicates the vibration levels of the various parts of the engine on the test cell vibration display. Typical locations include low- and high-pressure compressors and low- and high-pressure turbines. [Figure 5-68B]

Figure 5-68C shows a test cell instrument with a four-position selector switch, one position for each of four transducer locations on the engine.

- Selecting LP/FWD displays the LP compressor rotor vibration level, and selecting LP/AFT displays the vibration of the LP turbine rotor.
- Selecting HP/FWD displays the HP compressor rotor vibration level, and selecting HP/AFT displays the vibration of the HP turbine rotor.

The vibration gauge is operating correctly if the pointers move to full scale when the test button is pressed and return when the button is released.

If an engine vibrates beyond the allowable limit during operation, the rotating component causing the imbalance is identified and the engine is sent back to the repair facility for rework.

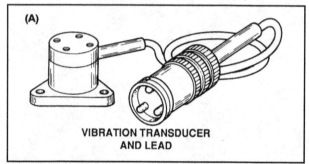

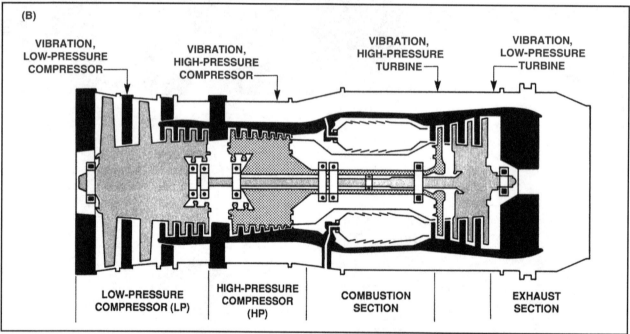

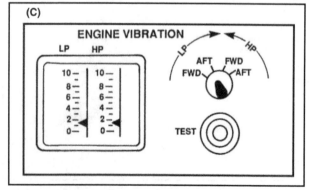

Figure 5-68A. Vibration transducer and lead
Figure 5-68B. Transducer locations on dual-spool turbofan
Figure 5-68C. Vibration instrument

ENGINE VIBRATIONS CHARACTERISTICS

The repairs described in this chapter ensure that all rotating airfoils maintain their strength, aerodynamics, and balance. The original design specifies engineering techniques that eliminate vibration, resonance, and harmonics to ensure that there is little or no inherent imbalance in the engine.

Inspection and Maintenance

These terms are defined as follows:

Natural frequency of vibration — the speed at which rotating objects vibrate. Engine parts are designed to rotate so that natural frequency speeds are never reached. Improper repairs, however, can lower the natural frequency into the operating r.p.m. range to a point where part failure occurs from vibratory stresses.

Resonance — Occurs when two mechanical systems, closely mounted, have the same natural frequency of vibration. If one malfunctions and reaches its natural frequency, the other will also vibrate along with the first, failing both systems.

Harmonics — Severe vibrations that occur at one-times the magnitude of vibration at the natural frequency and, if unattended, two-times the natural frequency, and so on until the part fails.

ANALYSIS OF TEST CELL DATA

Test cells are also used by repair facilities to troubleshoot engine malfunctions, leak-test engines after minor repairs, perform research and development, and test after modifications and for various other maintenance support reasons. [Figure 5-69]

When all parameters are recorded, test cell personnel plot observed readings against standard data to give a permanent record of the test run.

STANDARD DAY CONDITIONS

To produce meaningful data from an engine test run and check its thrust performance on any given day, correct the gauge readings to Standard Day conditions. Do this by recording the observed engine data along with the present day conditions of ambient temperature and pressure. Then compare this data to Standard Day values of 29.92 inches Hg and 519°R (59°F). To use the same

Figure 5-69. Test console

type data for in-flight recording and monitoring of engine performance, correction factors are programmed into the aircraft instrument systems, which bias the ambient conditions at altitude to Standard Day atmospheric conditions (see Appendix 7). The data then becomes a tool for both maintenance and management to use in determining such factors as engine economy of operation, maintenance planning, and flight safety.

Consider the following run data taken on a test cell run-up of an engine when ambient temperature is 545°R (85°F) and ambient pressure is 30.1 inches Hg.

Engine run data is:
- R.p.m. = 15,000
- EGT = 1,560°R (1,100°F)
- Fuel flow = 1,500 lbs./hr
- Mass air flow = 65 lbs./sec

To find out how these values relate to a standard day, you need two correction factors, referred to as Delta (δ), the pressure correction factor, and Theta (θ), the temperature correction factor.

Pressure correction factor ($\delta t2$) calculations:

$$\delta t2 = \frac{\text{observed ambient pressure}}{29.92 \text{ in. Hg}} = \frac{30.1}{29.92} = 1.006$$

Temperature correction factor ($\theta t2$) calculations:

$$\theta t2 = \frac{\text{observed ambient temperaure}}{519°R} = \frac{545}{519} = 1.050$$

For ease of computations, test cell personnel use Delta and Theta tables, such as provided in Appendix 9.

The following formulas can now be used in conjunction with the two correction factors:

$$\text{Corrected r.p.m.} = \frac{\text{observed r.p.m.}}{\sqrt{\theta t2}} = \frac{15,000}{\sqrt{1.051}} = 14,634$$

$$\text{Corrected EGT} = \frac{\text{observed EGT (°R)}}{\theta t2} = \frac{1,560}{1.051} = 1,484°R$$

$$\text{Corrected W}_f = \frac{\text{observed Wf (pph)}}{\delta t2 \times \sqrt{\theta t2}}$$

$$= \frac{1,500}{1.006 \times \sqrt{1.051}} = 1,455 \text{ pph}$$

$$\text{Corrected M}_s = \frac{\text{observed Ms} \times \sqrt{\theta t2}}{\delta t2}$$

$$= \frac{65 \times \sqrt{1.051}}{1.006} = 66 \text{ lbs/sec}$$

Gas turbine engine performance is sensitive to ambient conditions. When conditions are different from International Standard Day (ISD) values, the observed readings are not the same as they would be on a Standard Day. The values in the calculations above reflect ISD conditions. Compare these values with the manufacturer's specifications to determine engine condition.

Corrected revolutions per minute (r.p.m.) — At higher than Standard Day ambient temperatures, r.p.m. (observed compressor speed) is higher than Standard Day r.p.m. because 85°F air requires more work than 59°F air to provide the necessary compressor pressure ratio and rated thrust.

Corrected exhaust gas temperature — In order to increase the r.p.m., as mentioned above, more fuel is required. This, of course, is what elevates the observed exhaust gas temperature.

Corrected fuel flow (W_f) — The increase in observed fuel flow over standard day fuel flow occurs because the operator adds fuel energy to increase r.p.m. to obtain rated thrust.

Corrected Mass Airflow (M_s) — When ambient temperature is 85°F, mass airflow is 65 pounds/second relative to a standard of 66.21 pound/second. See Appendix 10 for typical flight correction data.

Consider that 14,634 r.p.m. represents 100 percent r.p.m. It then follows that 15,000 r.p.m. represents 102.5 percent r.p.m. Percent of revolutions per minute is the traditional frame of reference for r.p.m.

Note also that three parameters, r.p.m., exhaust gas temperature, and fuel flow, are all set by the operator at higher than International Standard Day values in order to maintain rated thrust, but the observed M_s value is lower than ISD value. This indicates that r.p.m. is at its limit of 102.5 percent and creating only 65 pound/second mass airflow. The reason that rated thrust can be maintained in the presence of low M_s value is that mass airflow energy losses within the engine are being replaced by a fuel energy increase. This is always the case with the gas turbine engine. Whenever mass airflow decreases, fuel flow must increase if the engine is to produce the same thrust.

ENGINE TIME CHANGE AND ON-CONDITION MAINTENANCE CONCEPTS

Time between overhaul on gas turbine engines has changed greatly in recent years. Small gas turbine engines may have a manufacturer's recommended time between overhaul of 3,000 to 5,000 hours on average, with a half-life hot section inspection in between. If a small engine is of modular construction, only its component parts have time-between-overhaul requirements. In fact, the phrase "engine overhaul" is fast losing its meaning in terms of the gas turbine engine.

Large commercial turbine engines do not generally have hard time-between-overhaul limits, in either hours or cycles. In conjunction with the FAA, operators base major component or module removal for overhaul on an inspection schedule and trend analysis of engine performance. Using this method, some large engines remain on the wing for many thousands of hours until one of its components or modules requires removal.

Most aircraft users follow one of three primary maintenance programs:

- **Hard Time (HT)** — A preventive, primary maintenance program, analogous to the older time between overhaul (TBO) program, which requires that engines, engine modules, or engine accessories are overhauled at specific intervals well within the safe limits of expected service life. Time can be defined as hours, calendar time, or operating cycles.
- **On-Condition (OC)** — A preventive, primary maintenance program that requires that engines, modules, or engine accessories are periodically inspected against an established, documented standard to determine whether they can safely continue in service.
- **Condition Monitoring (CM)** — A primary maintenance program for engines and accessories that have neither HT nor OC replacement time requirements. CM is accomplished by adhering to current FAA standards, manufacturer's standards, and Civil Aviation Safety Authority (CASA) recommendations and to the sound technical judgment of the operator to detect potential failures.

The electronic trend monitoring procedures for engine and accessory inspection during service are shown in Figure 5-70. Data that is collected and evaluated includes in-flight electronic data collection, vibration monitoring, spectrometric oil analysis, X-ray analysis, engine borescope results, and hardcopy operational data. In addition, many sensing devices are installed on engines for gathering trend analysis data.

Hard time, also called life limited cycle time, means a mandatory replacement of the unit. This system tracks total time since new (TTSN) but not the familiar time between overhaul (TBO) or time since overhaul (TSO).

Operators base inspection intervals on hours, calendar time, and cycles. A cycle is generally considered one engine start, run, and stop. Total time since new runs through various component or module changes, so an engine can have a very high TTSN and still be airworthy and remain in service. The actual change interval for many newer engines is based strictly on cycles rather than hours of operation.

Certain smaller engine parts also have life limited cycle time, meaning they have a scheduled hard-time cycle life between the time they are new or zero-timed and the time at which they must be replaced. Zero-timed means an overhauled part brought back to an as-new condition.

For all other non-life-limited parts, the concept of on-condition maintenance prevails, meaning that the part will remain in place through successive inspections as long as it is airworthy.

Many aircraft have cycle counters, and they usually function by electronically recording engine starts. If counters are not available, flight crew and ground crew must ensure accurate recording of hours or cycles so that all inspections and part changes are accomplished on time.

Turbine engines are expensive. The new list price of one of the smallest flight engines, the Rolls-Royce 250 turboshaft engine, is approximately $300,000; the Pratt & Whitney Canada JT15D, a small turbofan engine, costs approximately $700,000; and a single jumbo aircraft fan engine, such as the Rolls-Royce Trent in the Boeing B777, costs upwards of $20 million. From this standpoint alone, it is evident that good record keeping and proper recording of operating time becomes essential.

COMPONENT EXPECTED SERVICE LIFE

The service life design of modern gas turbine engines is much improved over engines of the past. This is true for business jet powerplants and for airliner powerplants alike.

For example, the design life for the main engine structure of a General Electric CF-6 high-bypass fan engine is 50,000 hours or 35,000 flight cycles. The expected service period is 15 years.

A partial list of component design life objectives of the CF-6 engine can be seen in Figure 5-71.

TROUBLESHOOTING – AIRCRAFT GROUND OPERATION

Troubleshooting is a major part of both line and heavy maintenance. Internal engine malfunction is likely to be a troubleshooting task for line or shop technicians and in many cases managers, engineers, and factory representatives. The troubleshooter must follow an intelligent sequence of procedures to ensure efficient correction of the problem. Too often a remove-and-replace philosophy prevails because the engine problem at hand looks similar to one that has happened in the past, and the troubleshooter makes a snap judgment that is incomplete or incorrect. Here are a few guidelines to follow:

- Interview the flight crew, read the logbook, and review the work order file to find all the facts surrounding the current problem.
- Review the same documents for previous related discrepancies.
- Research the maintenance manual thoroughly for system operation and troubleshooting clues.

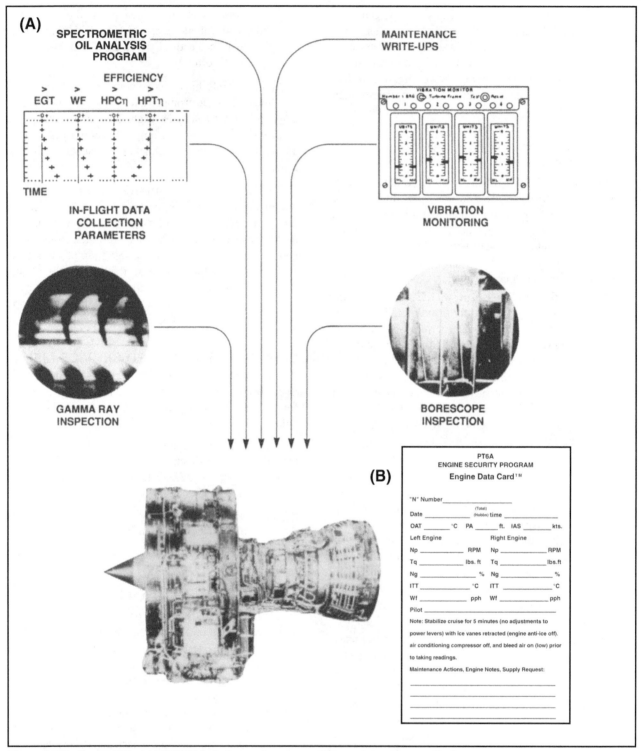

Figure 5-70A. General Electric CFM-56 turbofan engine on-condition maintenance monitoring
Figure 5-70B. PT-6A Turboprop manual trend monitoring data card

- Make a written list in order of priority of possible causes.
- Troubleshoot by inspecting, testing, and, if possible, duplicating the malfunction until you determine the cause of the problem.
- Make the necessary repairs to resolve the problem or remove the engine for shop repair.

Where possible flight line troubleshooting can give recommendations to shop maintenance for possible repairs.

CF6-6 AND CF6-50
COMPONENT DESIGN LIFE OBJECTIVES

	NORMAL MAINTENANCE AND REPAIR ASSUMED SERVICE LIFE PER INSTALLATION (INSPECTION SCHEDULE)		TOTAL SERVICE LIFE (REPLACEMENT SCHEDULE)	
	HOURS	**FLIGHT CYCLES**	**HOURS**	**FLIGHT CYCLES**
STATIONARY COMPONENTS (UNLESS NOTED)	12,000	12,000	50,000	35,000
CASINGS	12,000	12,000	50,000	35,000
FRAMES	12,000	12,000	50,000	35,000
COMBUSTOR	6,000	6,000	18,000	15,000
HP TURBINE VANES	6,000	6,000	15,000	12,000
LP TURBINE VANES	6,000	6,000	18,000	15,000
TURBINE FRAME LINERS	6,000	6,000	18,000	15,000
NOISE SUPPRESSION PANELS	12,000	12,000	12,000	12,000
ROTATING COMPONENTS (UNLESS NOTED)	15,000	15,000	30,000	30,000
FAN BLADES	12,000	12,000	30,000	25,000
HP COMPRESSOR BLADES	12,000	12,000	30,000	25,000
HP COMPRESSOR DISCS	15,000	15,000	30,000	30,000
FAN DISCS	15,000	15,000	30,000	30,000
HP COMPRESSOR HUBS AND SHAFTS	15,000	15,000	30,000	30,000
HP TURBINE BLADES	6,000	6,000	15,000	12,000
LP TURBINE BLADES	6,000	6,000	18,000	15,000
HP TURBINE HUBS, SHAFTS, AND SPACERS	15,000	15,000	30,000	25,000
LP TURBINE DISCS	15,000	15,000	30,000	25,000
HP TURBINE DISCS	15,000	15,000	30,000	25,000
LP TURBINE HUBS, SHAFTS	15,000	15,000	30,000	25,000
GEARBOXES	12,000	12,000	50,000	35,000
GEARBOX BEARINGS	10,000	10,000	16,000	9,000
MAIN ENGINE BEARINGS	7,500	4,500	16,000	9,000
SEALS (MAIN ENGINE)	12,000	12,000	50,000	35,000
FAN THRUST REVERSER	6,000	4,000	30,000	20,000
TURBINE REVERSER	6,000	4,000	30,000	20,000

Figure 5-71. Table of component expected service life

FADEC INTERFACE WITH TRADITIONAL ENGINE SYSTEMS

The original method of controlling the engine consisted of levers, cables, and linkages that connected the cockpit throttle lever to a hydro-mechanical fuel-metering device for manual modulation of engine power.

The standard for controlling the gas turbine engine in modern aircraft is a highly sophisticated, computerized system called the Full Authority Digital Engine Control (FADEC). Now in wide use in practically every new generation of gas turbine-powered aircraft, FADEC provides a commonality among engines that optimizes reliability and reduces operation, maintenance, and training costs. The General Electric CFM56, for instance, has six thrust ratings that can easily be changed by electronic plug-in devices. In this way, the same dash-model engine can be used in several dash-model aircraft and even in other aircraft types, with no further maintenance required.

FADEC also contains a built-in-test-equipment (BITE) system that is capable of fault diagnosis and fault correction in the event of overspeed, overtemperature, or other out-of-range parameters. The ability of the BITE system to diagnose and display cockpit readouts leads to faster and more precise troubleshooting that was not possible with older hydro-mechanical fuel scheduling systems.

A sequence of troubleshooting procedures is included at the end of Chapters 6 through 12. FADEC interface with these systems will be mentioned, but troubleshooting is beyond the scope of this text due to the highly electronic nature of that material, which requires specialized equipment and training.

If a formal troubleshooting document is not available, compose a sample troubleshooting and information priority listing as shown in Figure 5-72 for the type or aircraft and engine being maintained.

TROUBLESHOOTING AIRCRAFT IN-FLIGHT DATA

Another important troubleshooting technique is to analyze in-flight data gathered either manually or electronically. The flight crew or the personnel at a maintenance management facility then plot the data into a trend analysis that can assist in making timely maintenance decisions or pinpointing impending or actual parts failures.

The fundamental idea in gathering in-flight data is that it is obtained while the problem is ongoing in the engine rather than later during maintenance check runs. It then allows maintenance personnel to address the problem quickly with little or no troubleshooting other than to study the data collected.

The data can be in either observed readings or corrected readings, as was discussed for test cell readings of engine parameters.

MONITORING ENGINE OPERATIONAL TRENDS AND ANALYSIS

Two categories of trend parameters are available during engine operation:

- **Mechanical Monitoring** — The traditional cockpit instrument readings of oil pressure, oil temperature, oil quantity, vibration, and low oil-pressure warning lights and filter bypass lights.
- **Performance Monitoring** — The instrument readings that indicate how hard the engine is working to produce power, such as engine pressure ratio, N_1 speed, N_2 speed, exhaust gas temperature, and fuel flow.

The success of instrument analysis depends on the operator's ability to observe small shifts in operating parameters on one or more gauges and to compare these data accurately against standard or baseline data supplied by the manufacturer. For instance, a small shift in only one gauge reading may likely be a problem in the gauge itself, whereas multiple small shifts may indicate engine performance change and possible contamination, wear, or damage within the engine.

The following hypothetical trend analysis sheets show typical data plotted by calendar time and engine time since overhaul.

NORMAL ENGINE

Case 1 shows parameter plots and oil consumption data for a normal engine. [Figure 5-73] All parameters are relatively flat and consistent. This is a good engine that shows no performance loss or mechanical problems.

COMPRESSOR SECTION MALFUNCTION

Case 2 shows compressor contamination from inlet water injection on a JT8D engine. [Figure 5-74]

This is a plot of corrected flight log data for an engine water injection system that was probably serviced with water containing more solids than the 10 parts per million typically allowed. Exhaust gas temperature, fuel flow, and N_2 are up significantly while N_1 is up slightly. Abrasive grit cleaning this engine brought all parameters back down almost to their original level, as shown by the squares at 1,175 hours TSO.

Troubleshooting Information and Priority Listing (To be filled out by personnel performing troubleshooting)
Aircraft No. __542__   Engine No. __#2__   Date: __05/13/87__

1. Problem:
NO ENGINE OIL PRESSURE INDICATION ON COCKPIT GAUGE ON START

2. Cockpit Indications:
   a. EPR: OK
   b. EGT: OK
   c. RPM N1: OK
      N2: OK
   d. W_f : OK
   e. Fuel Temp.: HIGH (21°C)
   f. Oil Temp.: SLIGHTLY HIGH (215°C)
   g. Oil Pressure: ZERO
   h. Oil Quantity: OK
   i. Warning Lights: NONE

3. Other Factors to Consider:
From flight log: SAME PROBLEM 4 FLIGHTS PREVIOUS — CHANGED INDICATOR
Normal oil consumption: LAST SERVICE 1 PINT
Other information:
FLIGHT CREW INTERCHANGED INDICATORS #1 TO #2 STILL NO INDICATION

4. Suspect Causes: (in priority order)
   a. LOW OIL QUANTITY (COCKPIT QUANTITY INDICATOR MAY BE INACCURATE)
   b. CIRCUIT BREAKER TRIPPED
   c. DEFECTIVE INDICATOR INPUT SIGNAL
   d. DEFECTIVE TRANSMITTER OR INPUT SIGNAL
   e. OBSTRUCTION IN LINE TO OIL PUMP
   f. DEFECTIVE OIL PUMP

Figure 5-72. Sample of a troubleshooting information and priority listing

Inspection and Maintenance

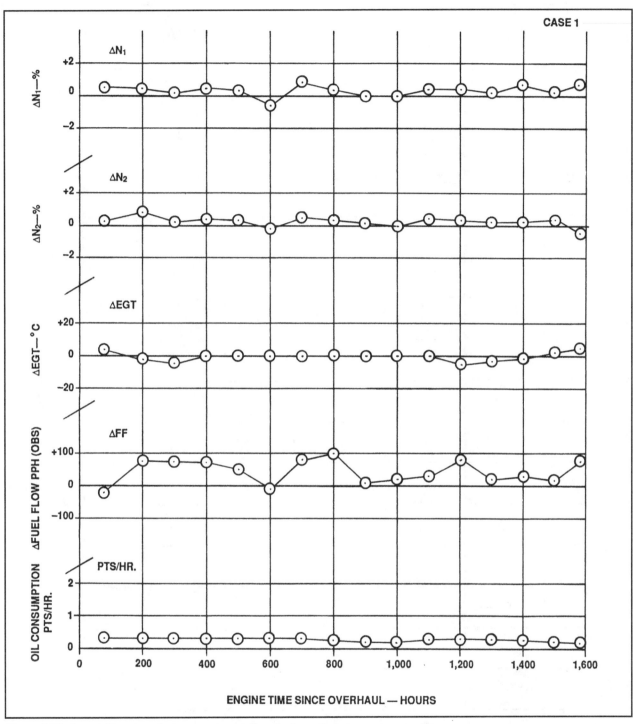

Figure 5-73. Case 1: Trend analysis normal operation dual-spool engine

Compressor contamination occurs mainly when the dissolved solids in the water adhere to blades and vanes, changing their aerodynamic shape, roughening their surfaces, and reducing the airflow area. This reduces compressor efficiency and airflow capacity. Consequently, the engine must work harder to produce a given thrust. When water contamination occurs as the result of inlet water injection for thrust augmentation, the low-pressure compressor (N_1) parts get little or none of these deposits. They normally settle out in the high-pressure compressor (N_2). This is due to the combination of temperature and pressure existing in the N_2 compressor and the time element involved in vaporizing the water.

COMBUSTOR SECTION MALFUNCTION

Case 3 shows a detached combustion chamber inner liner. [Figure 5-75]

The engine was shut down in flight when it stalled during operation at cruise. Subsequent disassembly and inspection revealed that a section of one of the combus-

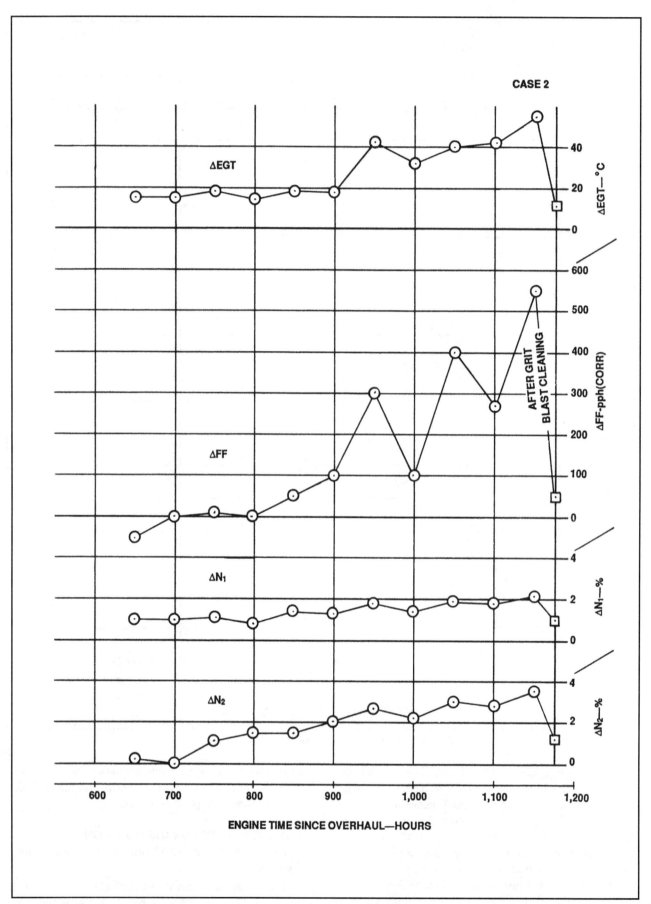

Figure 5-74. Case 2: Compressor contamination from water injection dual-spool engine

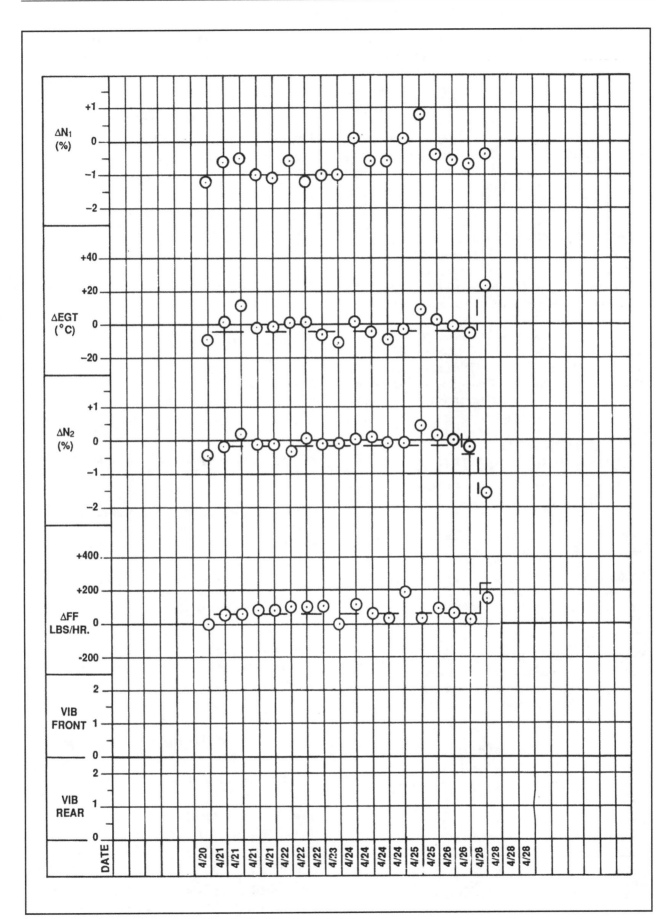

Figure 5-75. Case 3: Combustor section malfunction

tion chamber liners had become detached and passed through, lodging against the turbine nozzle vanes.

The flight engineer's log shows that on 4/28, the liner section became dislodged in the combustion chamber. The piece lodged in the nozzle vane area and the engine began to stall. The sudden depression in N_2 and increase in exhaust gas temperature and Wf resemble a classic high turbine efficiency loss. Nozzle blockage blanks off a number of turbine vanes, decreasing turbine efficiency. The decrease in turbine efficiency is the overriding effect in this case, causing N_2 to decrease.

TURBINE SECTION MALFUNCTION

Case 4 shows first-stage turbine seal erosion. [Figure 5-76]

Investigation revealed the knife-edges of the first-stage turbine outer seal to be eroded, allowing an excess of exhaust gases to bypass the first turbine, resulting in a rise in N_1 speed and a rise in exhaust gas temperature and fuel flow to obtain a given N_2 speed and thrust. The seal erosion began to be appreciable after about 1,800 hours after overhaul. This malfunction can be tracked accurately enough to plan maintenance action in time to prevent major engine problems.

INSPECTION AND TROUBLESHOOTING TERMS

The following is a list of terms commonly used to describe inspection findings during gas turbine engine maintenance:

Abrasion — Wearing away of small amounts of metal because of friction between parts.

Blister — The raised portion of a surface, caused by separation of layers of material.

Bowing — Bends or curves in a normally straight or nearly straight line.

Buckling — Large-scale deformation from the original shape of a part, usually caused by pressure or impact of a foreign object, unusual structural stresses, excessive localized heating, or any combination of these.

Burn — Discoloration from excessive heat.

Burr — A sharp projection or rough edge.

Converging — Two or more lines (cracks) that approach one another and which, if allowed to continue, will meet at a single point.

Corrosion — A surface chemical action resulting in surface discoloration, a layer of oxide, or, in advanced stages, the removal of surface metal.

Crack — Fissure or break in material.

Crazing — Minute cracking that tends to run in all directions, often noticed on glazed or ceramic-coated surfaces; occasionally referred to as "china cracking."

Deformation — Alteration of form or shape.

Dent — A smooth, round-bottomed depression.

Distress — An umbrella term to mean any of the problems included in this listing.

Distortion — A twisted or misshapen condition.

Erosion — Wearing away of metal or surface coating.

Flaking — Loose particles of metal on a surface or evidence of removal of surface covering.

Frosting — An initial stage of scoring caused by irregularities or high points of metal welding together with minute particles of metal transferring to the mating surface, giving a frosted appearance.

Galling — Chafing caused by friction.

Gouging — A removal of surface metal, typified by rough and deep depressions.

Grooving — Smooth, rounded indentation caused by concentrated wear.

Inclusion — Foreign matter enclosed in metal.

Metallization — Coating by failed molten metal particles sprayed through the engine.

Nick — A sharp-bottomed depression with rough outer edges.

Peening — Flattening or displacing of metal by repeated blows. A surface may be peened by continuous impact of foreign objects or loose parts.

Pitting — A surface condition recognized by minute holes or cavities that occur on overstressed areas. The pits may occur in such profusion as to resemble spalling.

Scoring — A form of wear characterized by a scratched, scuffed, or dragged appearance with markings in the direction of sliding. It generally occurs at or near the top of a gear tooth.

Scratches — Narrow, shallows marks or lines resulting from the movement of a metallic particle of sharp-pointed object across a surface.

Scuffing — A dulling or moderate wear of a surface resulting from a slight amount of rubbing.

Seizure — A welding or binding of two adjacent surfaces, preventing further movement.

Spalling — A separation of metal by flaking or chipping.

Stress — Metal failure due to compression, tension, shear, torsion, or shock.

Tear — Parent metal torn by excessive vibration or other stresses.

Unbalanced — A condition created in a rotating body by an unequal distribution of weight about its axis. Usually results in vibration.

Inspection and Maintenance

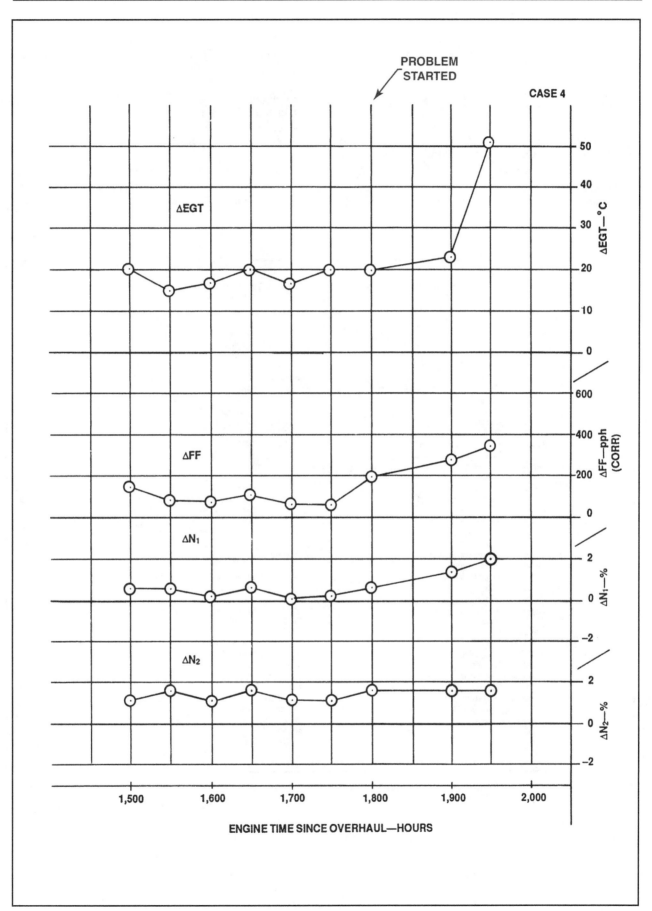

Figure 5-76. Case 4: Turbine malfunction

Wear — A condition resulting from the relatively slow removal of parent material, frequently invisible to the naked eye.

TECHNICAL DATA STANDARDS

The Air Transport Association of America (ATA), an organization of air carriers, has established many standards and procedures that make airline operation more effective and efficient. One of the specifications of value to the maintenance field is the technical data identification system. Specification 100, which is a standard for the presentation of technical information, standardizes how manufacturers of transport aircraft present maintenance information.

For example, regardless of the aircraft manufacturer, Chapter 72 of an aircraft maintenance manual deals with the turbine engine powerplant. More specifically, section 30 of Chapter 72 deals with the engine's compressor.

The ATA Specification 100 system has now found its way into all facets of aviation, including general aviation aircraft. Figure 5-77 shows the breakdown of the system.

First Element	Second Element	Third Element
Chapter (System)	Section (Subsystem)	Subject (Unit)

Example

71 - 50 - 00
Powerplant, general — Electrical harness — Unit of harness

Aircraft, General
- 05-00-00 Time Limits/Maintenance Checks
- 06-00-00 Dimensions and Areas
- 07-00-00 Lifting and Shoring
- 08-00-00 Leveling and Weighing
- 09-00-00 Towing and Taxiing
- 10-00-00 Parking and Mooring
- 11-00-00 Placards and Markings
- 12-00-00 Servicing

Airframe Systems
- 20-00-00 Standard Practices, Airframe
- 21-00-00 Air Conditioning
- 22-00-00 Automatic Flight
- 23-00-00 Communications
- 24-00-00 Electrical Power
- 25-00-00 Equipment/Furnishings
- 26-00-00 Fire Protection
- 27-00-00 Flight Controls
- 28-00-00 Fuel
- 29-00-00 Hydraulic Power
- 30-00-00 Ice and Rain Protection
- 31-00-00 Indicating and Recording Systems
- 32-00-00 Landing Gear
- 33-00-00 Lights
- 34-00-00 Navigation
- 35-00-00 Oxygen
- 36-00-00 Pneumatic
- 37-00-00 Vacuum
- 38-00-00 Water/Waste
- 39-00-00 Electrical/Electronic Panels and Multipurpose Parts
- 49-00-00 Airborne Auxiliary Power

Structure
- 51-00-00 Structures
- 52-00-00 Doors
- 53-00-00 Fuselage
- 54-00-00 Nacelles/Pylons
- 55-00-00 Stabilizers
- 56-00-00 Windows
- 57-00-00 Wings

Propeller/Rotor
- 60-00-00 Standard Practice - Propellers/Rotors
- 61-00-00 Propellers
- 65-00-00 Rotors

Powerplant
- 70-00-00 Standard Practices - Engine
- 71-00-00 Powerplant, General
- 72-00-00 Engine
- 73-00-00 Engine Fuel and Control
- 74-00-00 Ignition
- 75-00-00 Air
- 76-00-00 Engine Controls
- 77-00-00 Engine Indicating
- 78-00-00 Exhaust
- 79-00-00 Oil
- 80-00-00 Starting
- 81-00-00 Turbines
- 82-00-00 Water Injection
- 83-00-00 Accessory Gearboxes
- 91-00-00 Charts

Figure 5-77. ATA Standard for presentation of technical data

Inspection and Maintenance

QUESTIONS:

1. What is the name of the grit blast and wash procedure for removing the accumulation of dirt deposits on compressor blades?
2. Is the straightening of compressor blades typical of flight line maintenance?
3. What is one of the most frequent discrepancies detected when inspecting the combustor?
4. On which hot section component will stress rupture cracking most commonly occur?
5. Why must turbine blade replacement procedures be strictly adhered to?
6. Why is rippling and stress cracking more critical on the turbine blade trailing edge than on the leading edge?
7. What component malfunction do hot spots possibly indicate?
8. Which types of loads are ball bearings positioned on the compressor or turbine shaft to absorb?
9. Why are main bearings of ball and roller types used in preference to plain types?
10. What does the abbreviation NDI mean?
11. What is the plasma spray process used for?
12. What is the purpose of a borescope device?
13. In what units does the vibration meter measure engine vibration?
14. What is the purpose of using the dynamometer during turboshaft engine testing?
15. What is the purpose of a torque wrench?

CHAPTER 6
Lubrication Systems

Two basic types of self-contained lubrication systems are used in today's gas turbine engines: the pressure-regulated system and the variable pressure system. The pressure-regulated system controls oil flow by limiting the pressure from the oil pump to a given value. In the variable pressure system, pressure changes with change in engine and pump speed. This is the preferred system when the bearing vent cavities contain high air pressures. This chapter discusses both systems in detail.

The primary function of the lubrication system is to supply oil to the various engine parts that are subjected to friction loads from engine rotation and heat loads from the gas path. Engine heat rejection radiates outward and is addressed by the nacelle ventilation system. Engine heat rejection that radiates inward is addressed by the lubrication system. Oil is supplied under pressure along the main rotor shaft and to the gearboxes to reduce friction, to cool, and to clean. It then returns, by means of a scavenging system, to the oil storage tank to be filtered, cooled, and recirculated.

Oil consumption is low in gas turbine engines as compared to piston engines, which accounts for the relatively small bulk oil storage tanks used. Tank capacity can be as small as three to five quarts in smaller business jet engines and 20 to 30 quarts on large commercial aircraft engines. The oil is not exposed to substantial quantities of combustion products and stays clean by filtration. Heat, however, can cause rapid oil decomposition, which is why temperature is carefully controlled by automatic cooling devices and closely monitored by the flight crew.

PRINCIPLES OF ENGINE LUBRICATION

A lubricant's primary purpose is to reduce friction between moving parts. In theory, lubricating fluids provide an oil film that fills all surface irregularities. The oil films slide against each other and prevent metal-to-metal contact. As long as this oil film remains unbroken, metallic friction is replaced by internal fluid friction. The heated oil is then carried away to be cooled and reused.

Secondary purposes of an engine lubricant are to act as a cushion between metal parts, to cool, and to clean. As oil circulates through the engine, it collects foreign matter, deposits it into the filtration system, and absorbs engine heat.

REQUIREMENTS OF TURBINE ENGINE LUBRICANTS

Gas turbine engine oil must have a high enough viscosity for good load-carrying ability, but it must also be of sufficiently low viscosity to flow well. Because of these requirements, synthetic lubricants, rather than petroleum-base lubricants, are used in turbine engines.

CHARACTERISTICS OF SYNTHETIC LUBRICANTS

Synthetic lubricants have a number of desirable characteristics:

- Low volatility, which minimizes evaporation at high altitudes

- Antifoaming quality, which ensures more positive lubrication

- Low lacquer and coke (carbon) deposits, which minimizes solid particle formation

- High flash point (flash point refers to the temperature at which oil, when heated, emits flammable vapors that will ignite if exposed to an ignition source)

- Low pour point (the lowest temperature at which oil will flow by gravity)

- High film strength, which refers to the cohesion and adhesion, characteristics of oil molecules that enable them to stick together under compression loads and stick to surfaces under centrifugal loads

- Wide temperature range, from -60°F to +400°F, with preheating not required to approximately 40°F

- High viscosity index, which refers to how well the oil retains its viscosity when heated to its operating temperature

FAA REQUIREMENTS OF LUBRICATION SYSTEMS

The following is a list of minimum oil system requirements from Title 14 of the Code of Federal Regulations, Parts 23, 25 and 33:

- The word oil must be stenciled in the area of the oil tank filler opening.

- An oil tank expansion space of 10 percent must be provided.

- A means must be provided to prevent the ability to inadvertently fill the oil tank expansion space.

- An oil tank scupper must be provided to carry spilled oil to a drain point on the engine.

- The oil filter must be of a type through which all of the system oil flows.

VISCOSITY

Viscosity refers to the magnitude of friction as measured by special flow devices that show a liquid's resistance to flow. Petroleum oils are assigned a Society of Automotive Engineers (SAE) viscosity rating by measuring the time necessary for oil to pass through a fixed orifice in a device called a viscosimeter. Synthetic lubricants are assigned a numerical rating in a metric system called centistokes. A centistoke rating can be derived by conversion from SAE ratings or determined with laboratory equipment.

PETROLEUM OILS

Many petroleum-based lubricants are assigned a viscosity rating by the SAE. These ratings are determined by heating 60 milliliters (cubic centimeters) of oil to one specific temperature, and measuring the flow time as the oil is poured through a calibrated orifice. One device for this calculation is the Saybolt-Universal Seconds (SUS) viscosimeter. Using the table in Figure 6-1, you can extrapolate that if the flow time of an oil at 0°F is 24,000 seconds, it will be assigned an SAE 20W classification. If the flow time of an oil at 210°F is 65 seconds, it will be assigned an SAE 30 classification. The "W" indicates that the oil is designed for use in winter conditions in low-viscosity oils.

Many automotive and some aviation oils are now classified as multigrade—for example, SAE 5W-20. This means that when cold the oil has a viscosity of SAE 5W, and that, at its normal operating temperature, it will thin out no more than SAE 20. Viscosity, then, is a measure of an oil's pourability, and multiviscosity oils are designed to have low temperature fluidity for effective lubrication at low temperatures but remain thick enough for good lubrication at higher temperatures.

Although the SAE scale eliminates some confusion in the designation of engine lubrication oils, it does not describe all viscosity requirements. The SAE number merely indicates the viscosity grade; it does not indicate the quality of an oil.

SYNTHETIC OILS

Synthetic oils do not have SAE ratings to indicate viscosity. Instead, synthetics are assigned a kinematic viscosity rating in centistokes. The term "kinematics" derives from the study of the motion of fluids, and centistoke is an international system (metric) measurement of viscosity. Centistoke numbers are to synthetic oils what SAE numbers are to petroleum-based oils.

VISCOSITY INDEX

Viscosity index is determined by measuring the viscosity change when a liquid lubricant is heated to two different temperatures. An important quality of synthetic lubricants is determined in this way.

The American Society of Testing Materials (ASTM) nomograph, shown in Figure 6-2, is used to determine viscosity index (VI) when the Saybolt Universal Viscosity is known. Note that the oil in the sample plot has a viscosity of 280 SUS at 100°F, and 60 SUS at 210°F on the appropriate scales. Plots extended to the viscosity index chart indicate a viscosity index rating of approximately 170. What the nomograph reveals is a basic quality of the oil. The higher the viscosity index of the oil, the less tendency it has to thin out when heated and under friction loads.

If the viscosity of an oil is given as kinematic viscosity in centistokes (cSt) from a kinematic viscosimeter rather than in SUS units from a Saybolt viscosimeter, you can use a conversion chart such as the one in Figure 6-3 in conjunction with the chart in Figure 6-2 to determine the viscosity index. The centistoke value must, however, be known at both 100°F and 210°F.

VISCOSITY RANGE SAYBOLT UNIVERSAL SECONDS (SUS)				
SAE VIS- COSITY NO.	SECONDS POUR TIME AT 0°F.		SECONDS POUR TIME AT 210°F.	
	MIN	MAX	MIN	MAX
5W	—	LESS THAN 6,000	—	—
10W	6,000	LESS THAN 12,000	—	—
20W	12,000	LESS THAN 48,500	—	—
20	—	—	45	LESS THAN 58
30	—	—	58	LESS THAN 70
40	—	—	70	LESS THAN 85

Figure 6-1. Viscosity rating by SAE number

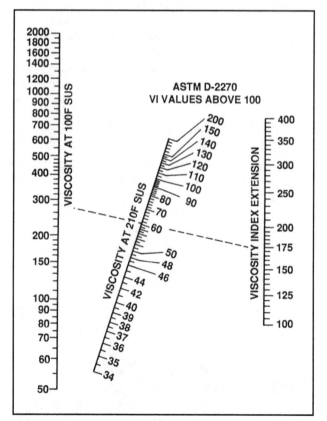

Figure 6-2. Viscosity index nomograph

Lubrication Systems

The centistoke value (metric viscosity measurement) appears on some container labels of synthetic lubricants. A rough equivalent to SAE values is as follows:

- Three-centistoke oils are approximately equal to SAE 5W oils.
- Five-centistoke oils are approximately equal to SAE 5W-10 multiviscosity oils.
- Seven-centistoke oils are approximately equal to SAE 5W-20 multiviscosity oils.

The heavier seven-centistoke oil is commonly used in turboprop engines where high gear loading is present whereas five-centistoke oils are most widely used in turbojet and turbofan engines.

OIL SAMPLING

After shutdown, and just prior to servicing, many air carriers require ground personnel to take an oil sample from a sediment-free location in the main oil tank. From this sample, the contaminants that are suspended in the oil are analyzed. Contaminants provide reliable indications of engine wear when counted in a device known as a spectrometer. The procedure, which expresses contaminants in parts per million, is referred to as spectrometric or spectrographic oil analysis. A spectrometer registers contaminant levels of silicon (dirt) and "wear-metals," as they are called, by analyzing the color and measuring the intensity of brightness that occurs when the particles are burned in a certain light spectrum.

Many private companies offer this service to customers who, in turn, use the information to plot trend analyses of internal engine wear. Knowing the trends enables operators to take timely action and avert costly repair or loss of equipment. Figure 6-6 shows a typical spectrometric oil analysis report.

SAMPLING INTERVALS

Sampling intervals are not standardized between one engine and another, or even between identical engines used by different operators. Intervals can be as low as 25 engine operating hours for smaller engines and up to 250 hours for large engines. Whatever the interval, when oil analysis trends start to rise, the interval is shortened to maintain a closer surveillance on the oil-wetted portions of the engine. Sometimes the interval is shortened to sampling after each flight.

When the first indication of excessive wear is encountered, maintenance managers typically make one of the following decisions based on the engine's history and the manager's fleet experience of oil analysis:

- Shorten the sampling interval.
- Back-flush the main oil filter to collect wear-metal particles for analysis.
- Change the oil and perhaps shorten the sampling interval.
- Flush the oil system, reservice, and perhaps shorten the interval.
- Remove the engine from service and investigate the areas of the engine that contain the types of wear-metal found.

Notice in the example shown in Figure 6-4A that the parts per million (PPM) trend is staying well below the guideline limit. In Figure 6-4B, on the sixth sample taken, the contaminant level rose significantly and management or maintenance action was determined to be necessary. The wear-metal and silicon guideline in oil trend analysis is not a firm limit, but a point at which a management decision is required concerning the engine.

The contaminant levels typically plotted include the following:

- Iron
- Tin

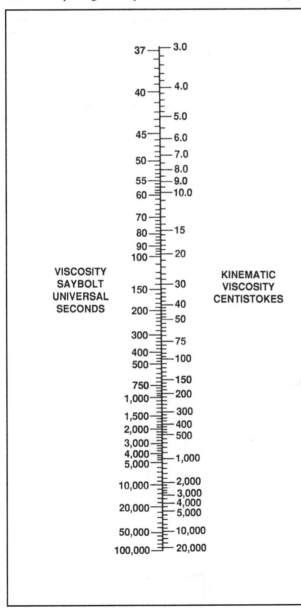

Figure 6-3. Conversion chart centistokes to SUS seconds

- Bronze
- Silver
- Aluminum
- Magnesium
- Chromium
- Copper
- Silicon
- Lead
- Nickel

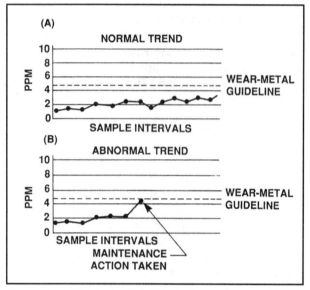

Figure 6-4A. Spectrometric oil analysis—normal trend
Figure 6-4B. Spectrometric oil analysis—abnormal trend

Maintenance personnel are aware of the points within the engine containing these types of metals and also the locations that are more suspect than others. For example, high silicon levels are not generated by the engine; they come from the airstream when the aircraft is operated in dusty environments.

TRADITIONAL SPECTROMETRY

Wear-metal particles suspended in oil can be of such microscopic size that they cannot be seen by the naked eye nor can they be felt with the fingers, yet they can flow freely through the system filters. However, wear-metals one-tenth the size of a grain of talcum powder are easily measured by a spectrometer. The spectrometer measures the particles that move in suspension in the oil and are too small to appear either in the oil filters or on chip detectors.

The spectrometer measures the contaminants present in the used oil samples as follows:

1. A film of the used oil sample is picked up on the rim of a rotating, high-purity graphite disk electrode (See Detail A of Figure 6-5).

2. A precisely controlled, high-voltage AC spark discharge is initiated between the vertical electrode and the rotating disk electrode, which burns the small film of oil.

3. Light from the burning oil passes through a slit that is positioned precisely to the wavelength for the particular contaminants being monitored.

4. The spectrometer identifies the type of contaminant by the color of the oil burn and also quantifies the amount in parts per million.

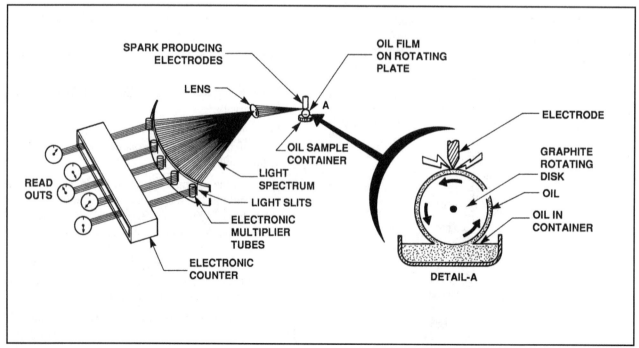

Figure 6-5. Oil spectrometer

RATHODE FILTER SPECTROSCOPY

Rathode Filter Spectroscopy (RFT) is a more recent technique for providing wear-metal analysis of particles typically larger than 10 micrometers caused from spalling, sliding, and cutting wear that can go undetected by traditional spectrographic methods. RFT samples a much larger volume of oil with a filtering and heating process in which light emitted during vaporization identifies the type of contaminants and amounts. The higher volume of oil used in this process reveals the presence of larger particles and leaves the particles in the filter for further analysis and evaluation.

ORIGIN OF THE METAL CONTAMINANTS

The moving contact between the metallic surfaces of engine mechanical systems is always accompanied by friction. Even though this friction is reduced by a thin film of oil, some microscopic particles of metal do wear away and are suspended in the oil. Thus, a potential source of information exists that relates directly to the condition of the system.

Under most conditions, the rate of wear remains constant and quite slow. The wear-metal particles are microscopic in size and remain in suspension in the lubricating system.

Any condition that alters or increases the normal friction between the moving parts also accelerates the rate of wear and increases the quantity of wear particles that result. If the condition is not discovered and corrected, the wear process will continue to accelerate, usually with secondary damage to other parts of the system and eventual failure of the entire system.

The important wear-metals produced in an oil lubrication mechanical system can be separately measured in extremely low concentrations.

Regarding the size of contaminant particles, silver is accurately measured in concentrations down to one-half part by weight of silver in 1,000,000 parts of oil. Most other metals are measured accurately in concentrations down to two or three parts per million. The maximum amount of wear-metal particles considered normal wear is determined for each metal by the engine manufacturer. This amount, called the "threshold limit" of contamination, when exceeded, requires maintenance personnel to determine the appropriate action necessary.

SYNTHETIC LUBRICANTS

Synthetic lubricants have multiviscosity properties by virtue of their structural makeup.

They are a blend of certain diesters, which are themselves man-made (synthesized) extracts of mineral, vegetable, and animal oils. In other words, synthetic oils are made by synthesizing raw materials to form a base stock rather than refining base stock from crude oil.

The blending of these diesters with suitable chemicals in different amounts produces a lubricant that meets a prescribed specification of both the petroleum and the aviation industries. Synthetic oils are not compatible and cannot be mixed with petroleum-based (mineral) oils. In addition, most manufacturers recommend either against mixing different brands or types of synthetic oils or mixing only within strict guidelines of same-type and certain compatible brands. Inadvertent or improper mixing can cause chemical shock and oil foaming and result in improper lubrication of the engine.

Three types of synthetic lubricants are used in turbine engines today: Type-1 (MIL-PRF-7808), Type-2 (MIL-PRF-23699), and Type-3 (which currently does not have a military specification, or MILSPEC). In the past, the military specification number for Type-1 and Type-2 oils had an "L" designation instead of the PRF. The "L" stood for lubricant, and the new designation PRF stands for Performance Specification. Type-3 is the most recent synthetic lubricant to be developed and is used in many of the more modern engines. It is designed to meet current engine requirements and does not necessarily have the same chemical composition as Type-1 or Type-2 lubricants. Engines originally designed to use Type-1 or Type-2 oil are still using those oils. Continuous modifications to the chemical structure of Type-1 has kept it essentially at the same quality as Type-2 or Type-3 regarding the heat range for which it is intended. Type-2 and Type-3 oils were developed to withstand higher operating temperatures and to have improved anticoking characteristics (coking refers to the accumulation of carbon deposits). Types 1 and 2 synthetic oils were originally developed to meet military specifications primarily because the military was the first to use gas turbine engines in aircraft. Type-3, also known as 3rd generation synthetic oil, was not designed to conform to a military specification but rather by industry to meet commercial aircraft specifications.

Changing over from Type-1 to the newer Type-2 or Type-3 is not generally recommended because the later generation oils have higher detergent qualities. These can be detrimental to older engines, the deposits of which have formed over long periods and are better left in place.

DISCOLORATION OF SYNTHETIC LUBRICANTS

Type-1 and Type-2 synthetic oils are straw-colored when new but darken over time. Type-3 synthetic oil is slightly darker when new. The color change comes from an oxidation inhibitor added to the oil that darkens after coming in contact with oxygen. The gradual darkening effect is not an indication of oil degradation but rather that the inhibitor performing its function of absorbing oxygen contained in air that is normally present in main bearing compartments and gearboxes.

S.O.A.P./EARLY WARNING ENGINE ANALYSIS

COMPANY: Embry-Riddle Aeronautical Univ.
ADDRESS: REGIONAL AIRPORT
CITY: DAYTONA Beach   STATE: FL   ZIP: 32015
CONTACT: Pete VOSBLAY
PHONE: (904) 252-5561
ENGINE TYPE AND MODEL: PRATT-WHITNEY PT6-21
ENGINE SERIAL NUMBER: PBE-80002
END ITEM NAME AND NUMBER: BEECHCRAFT KING AIR 302
TYPE AND BRAND OF OIL: EXXON 2389

WEAR METAL ANALYSIS OF OIL IN PARTS PER MILLION

#	SAMPLE NUMBER	DATE	OIL USED SINCE LAST SAMPLE (QT.)	HOURS SINCE: NEW OR OVERHAUL	HOURS SINCE: OIL CHANGE	HOURS SINCE: FILTER CHANGE	IRON Fe	COPPER Cu	NICKEL Ni	CHROMIUM Cr	SILVER Ag	MAGNESIUM Mg	ALUMINUM Al	LEAD Pb	SILICON Si
1	S250	12/5/80	1	435	360	360	2	<1	<1	2	<1	4	2	<1	7
2	S289	12/27/80	1	483	408	408	2	1	<1	<1	<1	3	3	<1	8
3	S1190	3/1/81	9	549	54	54	3	2	<1	<1	<1	4	3	<1	9
4	S1293	3/29/81	1	601	106	106	2	2	<1	2	<1	3	3	2	7
5	S1465	4/17/81	1	658	163	163	3	3	<1	<1	<1	10	2	<1	10
6	S1633	4/27/81	1	680	185	185	3	3	<1	<1	<1	13	3	<1	10
7	S1893	5/18/81	9	711	29	29	3	3	<1	<1	<1	4	3	<1	8
8	S2081	6/2/81	1	769	87	87	7	5	<1	<1	<1	6	4	<1	10
9	S2211	6/21/81	1	815	133	193	4	11	<1	1	1	13	4	<1	9
10															

(SAMPLE COMMENTS)

1 NORMAL SAMPLE
2 NORMAL SAMPLE
3 NORMAL SAMPLE
4 NORMAL SAMPLE
5 RECOMMEND SUBMIT RESAMPLE AFTER 15-25 FLT. HRS. - INCREASED Fe & Mg
6 RECOMMEND CHANGE OIL AND SUBMIT RESAMPLE AFTER 50 FLT. HRS. - POSSIBLE WATER CONTAMINATION CAUSING HIGH Mg IN GEARBOX
7 NORMAL SAMPLE
8 NORMAL SAMPLE
9 RECOMMEND CHECK ENGINE FOR SOURCE OF HIGH Fe, Cu, Mg. SUSPECT PROBLEM FROM ITEM 6 OR MAIN BEARING PROBLEM.

Figure 6-6. Spectrometric oil analysis report

However, abnormally rapid or heavy discoloration of oil can indicate engine problems, mainly excessive air leakage into oil-wetted areas. In this situation, the inhibitor breaks down and oxidation of oil occurs as oxygen molecules interact with molecules within the oil. Excessive oxidation results in viscosity increase and the formation of sludge.

TYPICAL PROPERTIES OF TURBINE OILS

The following table lists a variety of specifications, properties, and characteristics of Type-1 and Type-2 turbine oils, showing the differences between the two types:

SPECIFICATIONS	TYPE I	TYPE II
United States	MIL-PRF-7808	MIL-PRF-23699
Great Britain	MIL-L-7808	MIL-L-23699
France	AIR 3513	PWA 521
Pratt & Whitney	PWA 521	50TF1
General Electric	D50TFI	EMS-53
NATO Symbol	O-148	O-156

PROPERTIES		
Specific gravity at 60°F (15.6°C)	0.95	0.975
Kinematic viscosity centistokes at		
210°F (99°C)	3.26	5.09
at 100°F (38°C)	13.46	26.38
Flash point (open cup), °F (°C)	450 (232)	480 (249)
Pour point, °F (°C)	below 75 (60)	75 (60)
Evaporation loss in 6 1/2 hr. at 400°F (204°C), wt. %	17.0	4.2
Ryder gear test load, lb/in^2	2,575	2,796
Total acid number, mg KOH/gm	0.21	0.3

When working with synthetic lubricants, keep in mind the following safety and operational information:

- Synthetic turbine lubricants contain additives that are readily absorbed through the skin and are considered highly toxic. Avoid excessive and prolonged exposure to the skin.

- Silicone-based grease, such as that sometimes used to hold O-rings in place during assembly, can cause silicone contamination to the lubrication system. Silicone contamination can cause engine oil to foam and result in oil loss through oil tank vents. The foaming can also lead to engine damage from oil pump cavitation and insufficient lubrication.

- Cadmium and zinc-plated parts and fasteners are not compatible with synthetic lubricants and should not be used in oil-wetted areas. The lubricant can penetrate under the plating through small cracks or pin holes, which causes the plating to flake off and contaminate the lubricating system.

SERVICING

Before servicing an engine's oil system, the technician should refer to the engine or aircraft-type certificate data sheets or operations manual for the correct oil to use. (Appendixes 1 and 2 show a typical engine type certificate data sheet.)

COMMON SYNTHETIC LUBRICANTS FOR GAS TURBINE ENGINES

A list of typical synthetic lubricants being widely used in the aviation industry is as follows:

Type 1	Type 2	Type 3
(MIL-PRF-7808)	(MIL-PRF-23699)	No MILSPEC
3 cSt	5 cSt	5 cSt
Exxon 2389	Mobil Jet-2	Mobil 254
Aeroshell 308	Aeroshell 500	Aeroshell 560
Castrol 399	Exxon 2380	Aeroshell 750
	Castrol 5000	
	Stauffer Jet-2	

No standard identification system is currently in use. In fact, only a few oil companies include the type number or military specification on the lubricant container. Technicians often have to refer to oil company literature for specifications.

Synthetic oil for turbine engines is usually supplied in quart containers to minimize the chance of contaminants entering the lubrication system. Ground personnel must ensure cleanliness during servicing to maintain the integrity of the lubricant. In addition, use of a clean, service-station-type oil spout is recommended instead of can openers, which can deposit metal slivers in the oil.

If using bulk oil rather than quart containers, filtering with a 10-micron or finer filter is generally required.

INADVERTENT MIXING OF OILS

If incompatible lubricants are inadvertently mixed, many manufacturers require that the oil system be drained and flushed before refilling. In addition, when changing to another approved oil, a system drain and flush is typically required if the oils are not compatible.

Draining usually occurs at the oil tank, the accessory gearbox sump, the main oil filter, and other low points in the lubrication system. Flushing generally means reservicing and draining a second time after motoring the engine with the starter and no ignition.

After final servicing, the engine is generally run for a short period of time to resupply the lines, sumps, and so on with the residual oil normally held within the system.

If the oil has been replaced with a new type of oil, the placard stencil near the filler opening or metal oil identification tag, whichever is used, should be changed accordingly.

SERVICING INTERVALS

Oil servicing is generally required after the final flight of the day and whenever requested by the flight crew. When servicing the oil system, ensure that servicing occurs within the prescribed time after engine shutdown. Manufacturers normally require this in order to prevent overservicing. Overservicing can occur on some engines that have the tendency for oil in the storage tank to seep into lower portions of the engine after periods of inactivity.

When the oil level is checked later than the prescribed time after shutdown, the following actions are typical:

- If the oil level is within one quart of full, servicing is generally optional.
- If the oil level is low but still visible on the dipstick or sight gauge, motor the engine over with the starter for 20 to 30 seconds; then recheck the oil level.
- If the oil level is not visible on the dipstick or sight gauge, add oil until an indication appears; then motor the engine for 20 to 30 seconds and recheck the oil level.

After oil servicing, it is important to record the amount of oil serviced. A steady oil consumption compared against allowable limits provides valuable trend analysis data to indicate whether wear at main bearing oil-seal locations is normal.

The following are important considerations to keep in mind when servicing the lubrication system:

- To avoid serious injury and to allow time for air pressure bleed down in the oil tank, do not open the oil filler cap until a prescribed interval after shutdown.
- Always use the oil specified for the aircraft being serviced.
- Keep tools, oil containers, hands, and so on scrupulously clean when handling aircraft oils.
- To prevent contamination from moisture, use only factory-sealed cans of oil, and open only one can at a time.
- To prevent the possibility of contaminating the oil with foreign particles, do not use screwdrivers or other inappropriate tools for opening oil cans.
- With a clean, lint-free cloth or towel, wipe off the opener and the top of the oil can prior to opening.
- Protect the oil filler port during inclement weather conditions.
- Avoid overfilling the oil tank.
- Secure the oil filler cap and perform a security check after installation by pulling upward.
- Record how much oil was added to each engine as well as the time in service when the oil was added. Doing so facilitates the oil usage trend analysis, which indicates whether an engine is consuming too much oil.

TURBINE OIL STORAGE

Most companies that produce turbine engine oil state that it must be used immediately after opening the container. Unlike most other oils, turbine engine synthetic oil is hygroscopic, meaning that it readily absorbs moisture from the atmosphere. If a container is opened and not used in a short period of time, the oil will tend to absorb moisture from the air. Moisture can cause foaming, which is detrimental to the lubricating properties of oil.

OIL CONSUMPTION AND OIL CHANGE

Oil consumption in turbine engines is very low. For example, many business-jet-sized engines require only one quart of oil replenishment every 200 to 300 flight hours. A typical oil change interval is 300 to 400 operating hours, or six months on a calendar interval.

Larger engines might consume no more than 0.2 to 0.5 quarts per operating hour. By comparison, an 18-cylinder radial engine could consume as much as 20 quarts per operating hour and still be considered airworthy.

Many airlines do not establish oil change intervals because, in the average 20 to 30 quart capacity oil tank, normal replenishment automatically changes the oil.

WET SUMP LUBRICATION SYSTEMS

The wet sump system is the oldest design, and though rarely used in modern flight engines, it is still used in auxiliary power units and ground power units. Components of a wet sump system are similar to a dry sump system, except for the location of the oil supply. The dry sump carries its oil in a separate tank, whereas the wet sump oil is contained integrally in an engine sump.

Figure 6-7 shows an older engine with a wet sump lubrication system, in which all of the oil is contained in its accessory gearbox. The bearings and drive gears within the sump are lubricated by a splash system. The remaining points of lubrication receive oil from a gear-type pressure pump, which directs oil to oil jets at various locations in the engine.

Most wet sump engines do not incorporate a pressure relief valve and are known as variable pressure systems. With this system the pump output pressure depends directly on engine and pump rotational speed.

Scavenged oil is returned to the sump by a combination of gravity flow from the bearings and suction created by a gear-type scavenge pump located within the pump housing.

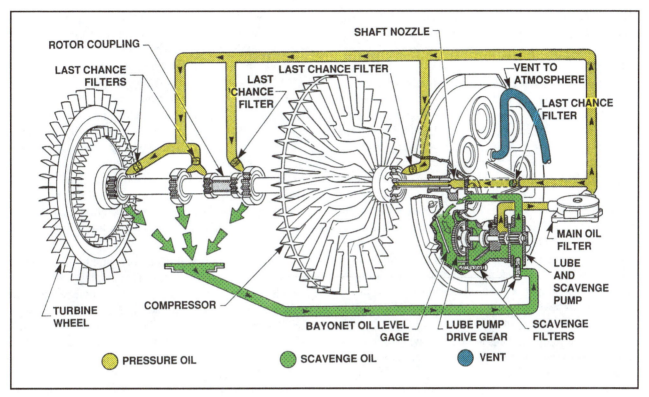

Figure 6-7. Older wet sump, variable-pressure lubrication system with no relief valve

The vent line prevents over-pressurization of the gearbox. Gas path air seeping past main bearing seals finds its way to the gearbox via the scavenge system and the vent line returns this air to the atmosphere.

DRY SUMP SYSTEMS

Most gas turbine engines use a dry sump lubrication system consisting of pressure, scavenge, and breather vent subsystems.

In the dry sump system, the main oil supply is carried in a tank mounted either within the engine or externally on the engine or in the aircraft. A smaller supply is contained in the main accessory drive gearbox and in its accessories such as the oil pressure pump, oil scavenge pump, oil filter, and other lube systems components. A small amount of residual oil is contained within the oil system internal and external lines.

The dry sump lubrication system includes:

- The oil tank (storage), which, on an airliner, typically contains 20 to 30 quarts of oil.
- The oil pressure (delivery) subsystem, which provides lubrication to parts of the engine where metal-to-metal contact could occur, such as meshing gears and rotating bearings that support all of the main and secondary shafts in the engine.
- The air pressurizing and vent subsystem, which handles the pressurized air that bleeds past oil seals, between the seal and the rotating shaft, and collects in the main bearing sumps.
- The scavenge (return) subsystem, which returns to the oil tank the oil that drains into the bottom of the sumps after it has lubricated the engine components.

Figure 6-8 illustrates the dry sump design in which the oil pressure subsystem delivers oil to various oil jets in gearboxes and bearing sumps. To prevent oil loss along the rotor shaft, pressurized air from the compressor is ported into the cavity surrounding the sump, and then directed through rotating air seals and air-oil seals. This air then leaves the sump by venting through the hollow rotor shaft. The hollow shaft, known as a "center vent" in this design, routes air out of the engine and into the tailpipe area. Any small amount of oil that leaks past the oil seal is forced out of an overboard drain. The tight clearance provided by the air seals helps maintain the vent system air pressure and the inward flow of sealing air into the oil sump, permitting only a small amount of air to flow back into the gas path.

SYSTEM COMPONENTS

The dry sump lubrication system is composed of an oil storage tank, pressure (supply) pump, scavenge (return) pumps, oil coolers, oil filters, oil jets, and the necessary indicating and warning sensors. This instrumentation provides the cockpit with an accurate method of determining the health of the oil-wetted parts of the engine.

The oil-wetted parts include internal main bearings, rotating shafts, and gearboxes.

OIL TANK

The oil supply reservoir (tank) is usually constructed of sheet aluminum or stainless steel and is designed to furnish a constant supply of oil to the engine during all authorized flight attitudes. Most tanks are pressurized to ensure a positive flow of oil to the oil pump inlet and to suppress foaming in the tank, which in turn prevents pump cavitation. Pressurization is often accomplished by running the tank overboard vent line through a relief valve to maintain a positive pressure, typically from three to six pounds per square inch—gauge (p.s.i.g.). That is, the relief valve releases excess air at a pressure differential of three to six pounds per square inch—differential (p.s.i.d.) between the tank and ambient, shown in Figure 6-9. After shutdown, a small bleed-down orifice in the relief valve relieves the pressure in the tank, allowing the filler cap to be safely removed for servicing.

Some dry sump oil tanks are integral with the engine. While the external sheet metal type is a separate assembly located outside the engine, the integral oil tank is formed by space provided within the engine. For example, a propeller reduction gearbox can house the oil supply and act as a tank; a cavity between major engine cases can also hold oil, such as in the PT6 turboprop. [Figure 6-33]

The wet sump is located in the main gearbox at the lowest point within the engine, which facilitates splash lubrication. The dry sump is seldom located at the low point on the engine. It might or might not supply oil by gravity to the main oil pump inlet. [Figures 6-9 and 6-10]

Figure 6-9 shows an oil tank with a dwell chamber, often referred to as an oil tank de-aerator, which provides a means of separating entrained air from the scavenge oil. The tank shown is of typical oil capacity for a business jet, approximately five quarts of oil, three of which are usable, plus a two-quart expansion space. The location of the outlet keeps one quart as residual oil and provides a low point for sediment and condensation to collect until drained. Other tanks take oil from a bottom location using a standpipe.

Today, some oil tanks are configured with a remote pressure fill capability. An oil pumping cart can be attached to the tank and the oil hand-pumped into the tank until it is at the proper level, at which time oil starts to flow from the overflow. The oil filler cap is usually removed during this operation to prevent overservicing in case the oil overflow is not properly connected. [Figure 6-11C] The hand gravity method of filling the oil tank is, however, still more common. The scupper shown on the illustration catches oil that is spilled during servicing or during cap blow-off and routes this spillage through a drain point location at the bottom of the engine. Due to

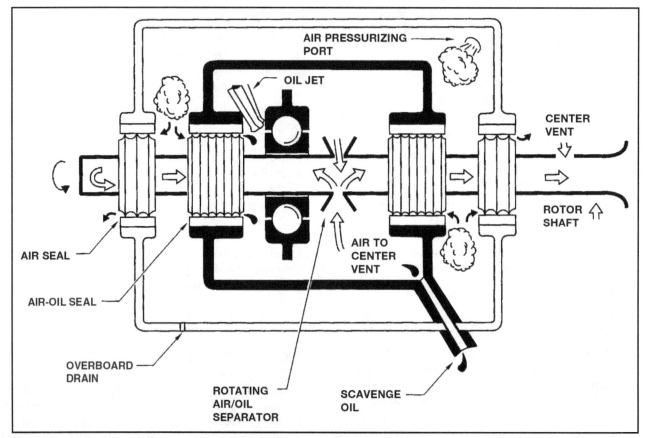

Figure 6-8. General Electric/Snecma CFM56 turbofan oil sump design

Lubrication Systems

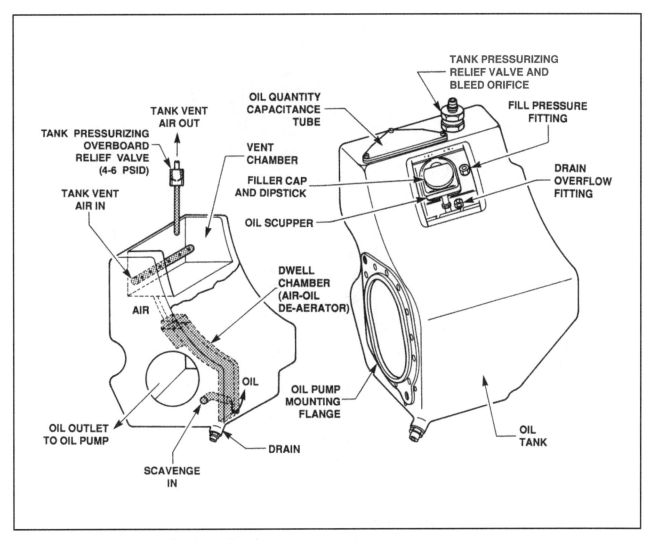

Figure 6-9. External dry sump oil tank, small engine

the position of the filler cap, it is impossible to overservice by the hand gravity method. Many filler openings are fitted with a flapper seal in the event that the oil filler cap is inadvertently left off.

In place of a dipstick, some oil tanks incorporate a sight gauge for checking oil level. [Figure 6-11A and 6-11B]. Figure 6-11D shows the oil tank on a Boeing 757 with the sight glass and oil cap identified. Note the height of the oil tank above the oil filler cap, which is used as expansion space.

OIL PUMPS

The purpose of the oil pressure pump is to supply oil under pressure to the parts of the engine that require lubrication. Many oil pumps consist of not only a pressure lubrication element but also one or more scavenge elements, all-in-one housing. Oil pumps are designed to provide a volume of flow to the engine. How much oil pressure they create is a function of the resistance to flow: the more restriction, the higher the oil pressure. For example, as an oil filter starts to clog, the resistance to flow increases in front of the filter, and the pressure increases.

The three most common oil pumps are the vane, gerotor, and gear pumps. All are classed as positive displacement pumps because they place a fixed quantity of oil in the pump outlet per revolution. They are also referred to as constant displacement types because they displace a constant volume per revolution. All three types are also self-lubricating.

Vane Pump

In a vane pump, such as the one in Figure 6-12, pumping action takes place as a rotor drive shaft and eccentric rotor, which act as one rotating piece, drive the sliding vanes around. The space between each vane pair floods with oil as it passes the oil inlet opening and carries this oil to the oil outlet. As the spaces diminish to a zero clearance, the oil is forced to leave the pump. The downstream resistance to flow determines the pump output pressure unless a relief valve is included to regulate pressure.

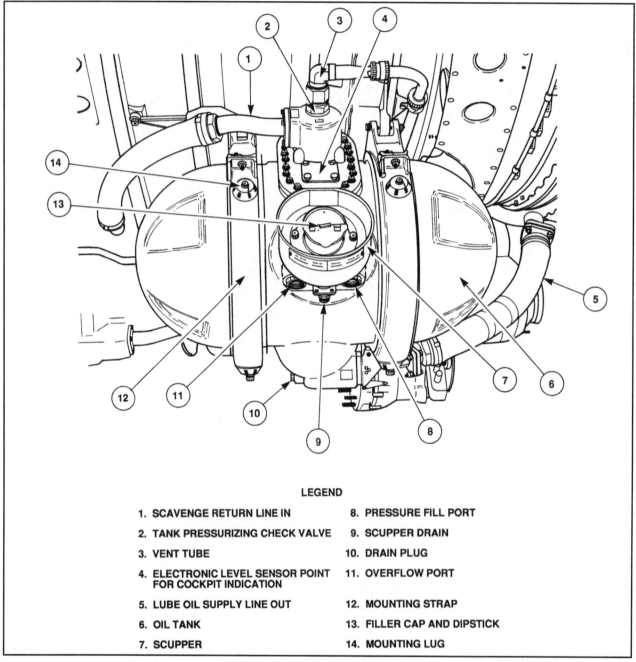

Figure 6-10. External dry sump oil tank, large engine

LEGEND

1. SCAVENGE RETURN LINE IN
2. TANK PRESSURIZING CHECK VALVE
3. VENT TUBE
4. ELECTRONIC LEVEL SENSOR POINT FOR COCKPIT INDICATION
5. LUBE OIL SUPPLY LINE OUT
6. OIL TANK
7. SCUPPER
8. PRESSURE FILL PORT
9. SCUPPER DRAIN
10. DRAIN PLUG
11. OVERFLOW PORT
12. MOUNTING STRAP
13. FILLER CAP AND DIPSTICK
14. MOUNTING LUG

The pump shown in Figure 6-12 could be a single-element pump or one element of a multiple-element pump. Multiple pumps of this type typically contain one pressure element and one or more scavenge elements, all of which are mounted on a common shaft. The drive shaft mounts to an accessory gearbox drive pad and all pumping elements rotate together.

Vane pumps are more tolerant of debris and are used more often in scavenge oil systems. They are also lighter than gerotor or gear pumps and offer a slimmer profile. Therefore, vane pumps are found in oil systems that do not require the strength of some other pumps.

Gerotor Pump

The gerotor pump, sometimes referred to as gear-rotor pump or a rotor-gear pump, uses a principle similar to the vane pump. The gerotor uses a lobe-shaped drive gear within an elliptically-shaped idler gear to displace oil from an inlet to an outlet port. Figure 6-13A shows one pumping element mounted on a multiple-element pump main shaft.

Note that the inner driving gear in Figure 6-13 has six lobes and that the outer idling gear has seven openings. This arrangement permits oil to fill the one open pocket and move inlet oil through the pump as it rotates until a zero clearance forces the oil from the discharge port. The

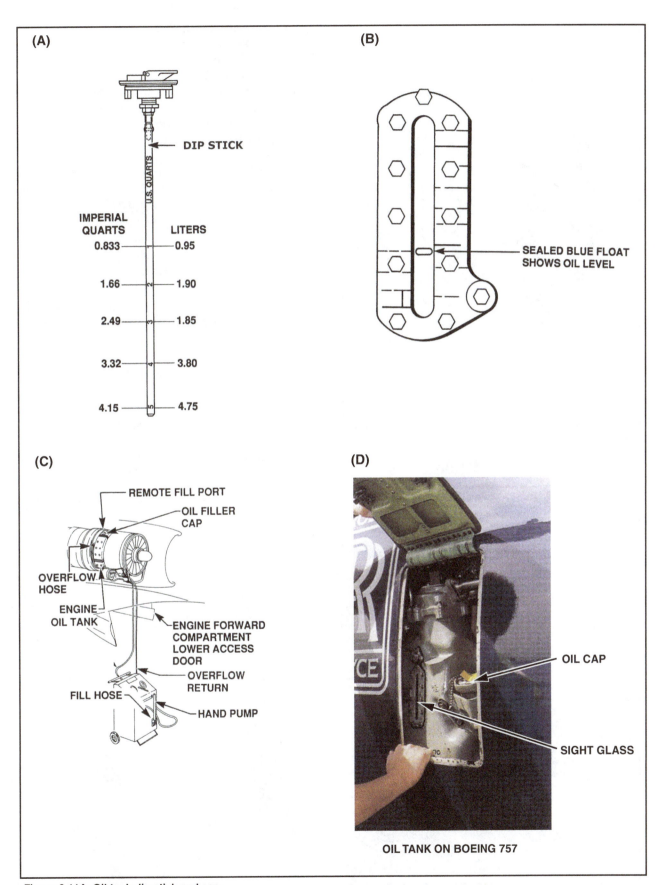

Figure 6-11A. Oil tank dip stick and cap
Figure 6-11B. Oil tank sight gauge
Figure 6-11C. Pressure oil service cart
Figure 6-11D. Boeing 757 engine oil tank

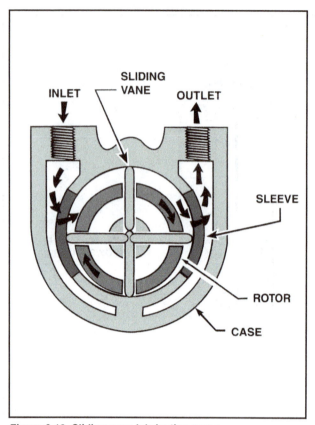

Figure 6-12. Sliding vane lubrication pump

principle of operation is that the volume of the missing tooth multiplied by the number of lobes in the outer gear determines the volume of oil pumped per revolution of the outer gear. In this example pump, in each revolution of the driven gear, six pockets of oil are pumped, because there are six lobes on the driven gear. For each revolution of the idler gear, seven pockets of oil are pumped. Keep in mind that the idler gear rotates only 6/7 as fast as the driven gear.

Figure 6-13A shows a complete pumping element, one of several that could be mounted on a single shaft within the same pump housing. As illustrated in Figure 6-13B, the operating cycle of the gerotor pump is as follows:

1. From 0 degrees to 180 degrees, interlobe space increases from a minimum to a maximum volume. For most of the 180-degree path, the space is open to the intake port, permitting it to fill with oil.

2. As the space reaches maximum volume, it is closed to the intake port and is poised to open to the discharge port.

3. At 270 degrees, the space decreases in volume, forcing the oil out the discharge port.

4. As the space reaches minimum volume at 360 degrees, it is closed to the discharge port and begins to open to the intake port, repeating the cycle.

This action takes place in each of the seven inter-lobal spaces between the inner six-lobe gerotor and the outer seven-lobe gerotor, essentially providing a continuous oil flow.

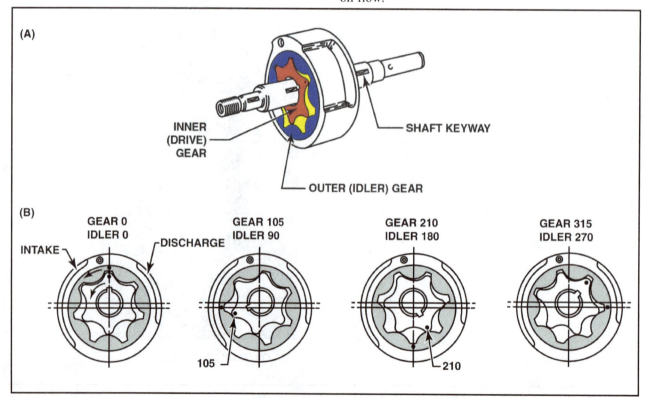

Figure 6-13A. Gerotor lubrication pumping element
Figure 6-13B. Gerotor lubrication pump cycle of operation, similar to CFM56 rotor-gear pump

Gear Pump

The single element gear type pump shown in Figure 6-14 takes in inlet oil and rotates in a direction that permits oil to move between the gear teeth and the pump inner case until the oil is deposited in the outlet. The idler gear seals the inlet from the outlet, which prevents fluid backup and doubles the capacity per revolution. This pump also incorporates a system relief valve in its housing, which returns unwanted oil to the pump inlet.

Figure 6-15 shows a dual pump with both a pressure and a scavenge element driven by a single shaft. Larger engines typically use a multi-element oil pump with one pressurizing pump delivering oil to the engine parts and two or more scavenging pumps that move oil from the various bearing sumps and gearboxes, back to the oil tank. In the CFM-56 engine (shown in Figure 6-35), the pump assembly is referred to as a lubrication unit and contains four pumps—one pressure pump and three scavenge pumps—driven by a single shaft.

OIL FILTERS

Oil filters are an important part of the lubrication system because they remove contaminant particles that collect in the oil.

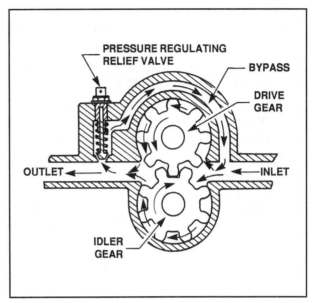

Figure 6-14. Side view of gear lubricating pump

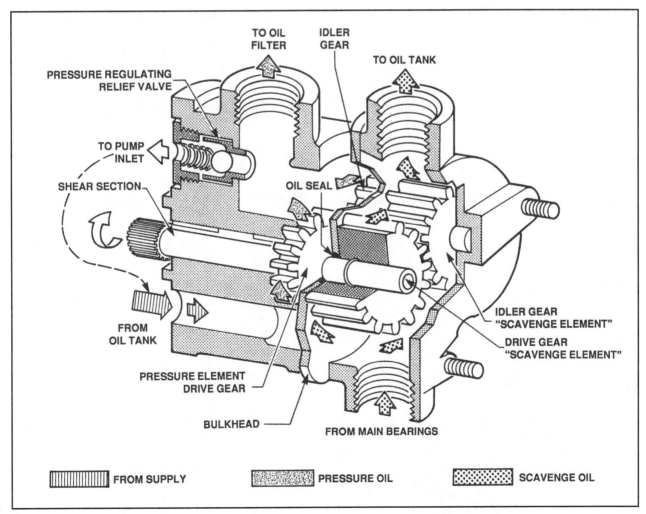

Figure 6-15. Cutaway view of combination pressure and scavenge pump

Contaminants in Oil

Contaminants found in the oil system filters come primarily from the following sources:

- Products of decomposition of the oil itself, usually seen as small black specks of carbon
- Metallic particles from engine wear and corrosion in oil-wetted areas of the engine
- Airborne contaminants entering through main bearing seals
- Dirt and other foreign matter introduced into the oil supply during servicing

The contaminants found in filter bowls or on filter screens are always a matter of concern. Usually, experienced technicians familiar with normal and abnormal levels of contamination determine an engine's airworthiness and whether it requires maintenance. If a spectrometric oil analysis is available, as is the case in many larger aviation companies, a readout of the various metal particles suspended in the oil helps to determine whether sufficient cause exists to require maintenance on the engine.

Engine oil often becomes dark brown over time, but with little or no contaminants. As mentioned earlier, this discoloration is a chemical reaction to oil oxidation and is considered normal.

Gas turbine engine oil filters, which are assigned micronic ratings, are designed to prevent passage of micron-sized contaminant particles into the system. The filters are assigned an efficiency rating based on their ability to trap and hold contaminants in accordance with their nominal or absolute rating.

The nominal rating of 10 microns, for instance, is defined as the ability of a filter to trap 98 percent of contaminant particles at the stated micron size and larger. Nominal means that the filter media has no actual micron-sized pore dimension due to the filter media (such as fiber or paper-pleated material) used; therefore it is said to have an equivalent micronic filtering capability.

The absolute rating defines the stated micron-sized pore opening, which is often referred to as the mesh or weave diameter. The capture rate is based on the ideal condition of spherically shaped particles. A filter with a 10-micron rating will capture all particles 10 microns and larger. [Figure 6-16]

Microns

A micron is a unit of the international system of measurement (SI) and represents one millionth of a meter or approximately 0.000039 inch. The unaided human eye cannot readily distinguish objects smaller than about 40 microns. The air carries many invisible particles, one to five microns in size. The airborne moisture in fog is composed of 5- to 50-micron particles.

Because of the extreme fineness of micronic particle size, preventing contamination to the oil system by these minute objects is a closely controlled process.

The following table compares microns to inches and millimeters:

1 Inch	25.4 Millimeters	25,400 Microns
1 Millimeter	0.0394 Inches	1,000 Microns
1 Micron	1/25,400 Inch	0.001 Millimeters

The following table compares the size of common objects expressed in microns:

White blood cell	25 Microns
Red blood cell	8 Microns
Bacterium (Coccum)	2 Microns

Forces Acting on Filters

The forces acting on filters are as follows:

- Pressure forces, which occur when the oil is cold. Cold-flowing oil results in high viscosity, which can build pressure up to 300 p.s.i.g. in a system normally controlled to 50 p.s.i.g. This can take place even though the pressure regulating valve and filter bypass valve are open and trying to relieve pressure.

- Pressure forces from the volume of flow. In the high flow rate, low volume type of system used in gas turbine engines, the entire oil supply can pass through the oil filter four to eight times per minute, which in large engines can be as much as 60 gallons per minute.

Figure 6-16. Filter surfaces enlarged 250 times

Lubrication Systems

- Fatigue forces from high frequency. The pressure pulsations emanating from the oil pump gear teeth occur at high frequency.
- Fatigue forces from thermal cycling. Filters located on the scavenge side of the oil system are subjected to temperatures up to 400°F.

All types of filters are constructed to withstand high fatigue forces, but they must be in perfect condition to do so. Any damage to a filter is generally cause to reject it.

Filter Types

The most common types of main system filters are the disposable fiber and the cleanable stainless steel screen. Cleanable screen filters are further classified as pleated screen, wafer screen, and screen and spacer types. All three metal types are typically cleaned at intervals based on engine cycles.

Regarding the difference between cleanable metal screens and disposable fiber filters, woven wire filters are more common in aircraft with high engine cycles in which frequent filter inspections are required. The ability to clean this type of filter saves costs. However, woven wire filters are not typically rated below 40 microns. They are also larger than disposable filters of the same rating because only about 30 percent of the surface area of the mesh remains as flow area. On the other hand, disposable filters in oil systems can filter down to 15 microns. However, it is not always possible to use a 15-micron filter with oils of high centistoke values. An advantage of disposable filters is that they are much smaller than comparable wire mesh filters. Because they have no weave, they have an effective flow area of up to 70 percent.

Filters with low micronic ratings remove all but the smallest particles, even the small carbon particles, and keep the oil in a near new condition. As the use of labyrinth main bearing oil seals has become more common, finer filtration has become necessary. This is because labyrinth air-oil seals pass more airborne contaminants into the oil than do carbon seals.

On older aircraft, designed when the harmful effect of small particles such as carbon, dust, and dirt were not as fully understood as they are today, metal mesh filters rated at 175 microns or more are common. Many of the high micronic-rated filters have since been changed because filter manufacturers now provide deeper pleated filters with low micronic ratings, which, for a given physical size, permit equal amounts of oil to flow and provide better filtration.

The current trend is to change to a lower micron filter if one is available. The difference in pressure drop across a clean filter is only about three p.s.i.d. more when changing from a 40-micron filter to a 15-micron filter. The micron rating selected is a compromise between fine filtration, overall cost, and an acceptable pressure drop that the engine can tolerate when the oil is cold. An important point to bear in mind with a lower-numbered micron filter is that the engine might be poorly lubricated during a cold weather start.

Filter Assembly Operation

To provide a maximum surface area for filtration, most paper disposable and screen mesh filters are heavily pleated or, in the case of stacked filters (wafer or screen and spacer), consist of many twin screens. The screen types have an actual micronic size, measurable in microns. The fiber type filters have an equivalent micronic rating. [Figures 6-18 and 6-19]

Figure 6-17 shows an in-line bowl-type filter, which can be either disposable or cleanable. This type of filter is typically rated at 40 microns.

Oil fills the filter bowl, and then forces its way through the filtering element to the core, exiting at the port near the spring side of the bypass relief valve. In cold conditions when oil is highly viscous or if an obstructed filter restricts oil flow through the element, the differential bypass valve opens to permit unfiltered oil to flow to the engine.

During a bypass condition, the amount of oil is reduced from that which would flow normally through the filter screen, but the reduced flow still provides initial lubrication during starting or sufficient lubrication for at least reduced power operation in flight. Note that the bypass relief valve in Figure 6-17 has a rating of 25 pounds per square inch—differential, often referred to as a differential pressure or delta-p ($\triangle P$) rating.

Assume that system pressure in which this filter is located is regulated to 45 p.s.i.g. (oil-in pressure), and

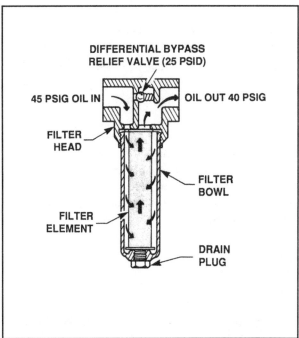

Figure 6-17. Bowl-type cleanable stainless steel mesh, pleated oil filter

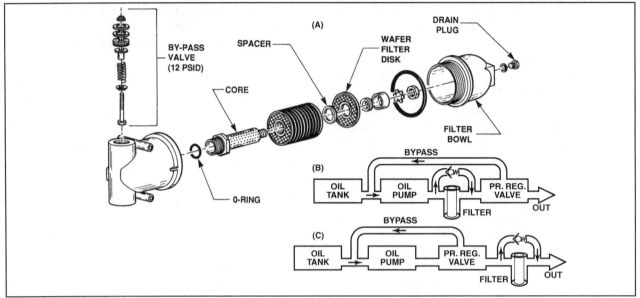

Figure 6-18A. Cleanable wafer screen-type filter
Figure 6-18B. Pressure regulating relief valve located downstream from the main oil filter
Figure 6-18C. Pressure regulating relief valve located upstream of the main oil filter

the normal pressure drop across a clean filter is 5 p.s.i.g. In this case, 40 p.s.i.g. oil-out pressure is assisting the 25 p.s.i. spring force in holding the bypass valve closed. As the filter becomes blocked by debris or, if oil is congealed during a cold-weather start, the pressure drop across the filtering element increases. When the pressure drop exceeds the rating of the bypass valve spring, the bypass valve opens and permits unfiltered oil to flow directly from the inlet to the outlet. When the bypass valve opens, the pressure downstream of the filter does not return to normal. The downstream pressure remains the same, lower than the upstream pressure by the p.s.i.d rating of the bypass valve. If the pressure were to return to normal, the pressure drop would no longer be sufficient to hold the bypass valve open.

Figure 6-19 shows filters of the cleanable pleated-screen type and the screen and spacer type, both of which fit into a gearbox annulus and provide the same service as the bowl type.

The screen and spacer type filter, also known as an edge-type filter, seen in Figures 6-18 and 6-20, can be disassembled for inspection and cleaning. This filter usually fits into an annulus in the main accessory gearbox. The filter configuration, which allows oil to flow in the inward direction, is a series of thin screens between spacers.

The filters in Figure 6-19 are more common in the pressure (oil supply) subsystem to the engine. Some engines also provide filtration for the scavenge subsystems, which route oil from the engine back to the supply tank. The three different micron ratings shown represent the range of filtration that might be used. The 140 micron filter might be used in an engine that is subject to coking problems, while the 40 and 15 micron filters would be used when coking is not a problem.

Filter Cleaning

Traditional methods of cleaning filters in solvent by hand are still commonly used and acceptable. However, several cleaning devices are also available, such as ultrasonic cleaners (which induce high frequency sound waves) and high frequency "vibrator cleaners." These cleaners do a more complete job of removing all the contaminants from the filtering elements. [Figure 6-21]

Most facilities maintain a written record of findings during filter inspections to provide a trend analysis of contamination build-up during subsequent filter inspections. Smaller particles of metal on filter surfaces are normal, but if the contamination level is in excess of the manufacturer's limits or if any large metal chips are found, the source of the contamination must be located and the problem corrected. Then the engine should be drained of all oil, reserviced, and run for a prescribed period of time. Sometimes, several cycles of this procedure are necessary to clear the system to the point where the filters remain clean.

INTERACTION OF OIL FILTERS WITH OIL PRESSURE RELIEF VALVES

Oil systems contain either a pressure regulating relief valve to maintain the oil pressure at a prescribed value or a pressure limiting relief valve to keep the pressure from going beyond a predetermined limit. The pressure regulating relief valve typically unseats by the time the engine reaches idle speed, maintaining a specified pressure even as the engine accelerates to takeoff thrust. The pressure limiting relief valve typically remains seated and only opens to limit the pressure in circumstances when it would be unsafe to let the pressure rise any higher.

On engines with pressure regulating relief valve, the valve can be located either upstream or downstream of

Lubrication Systems

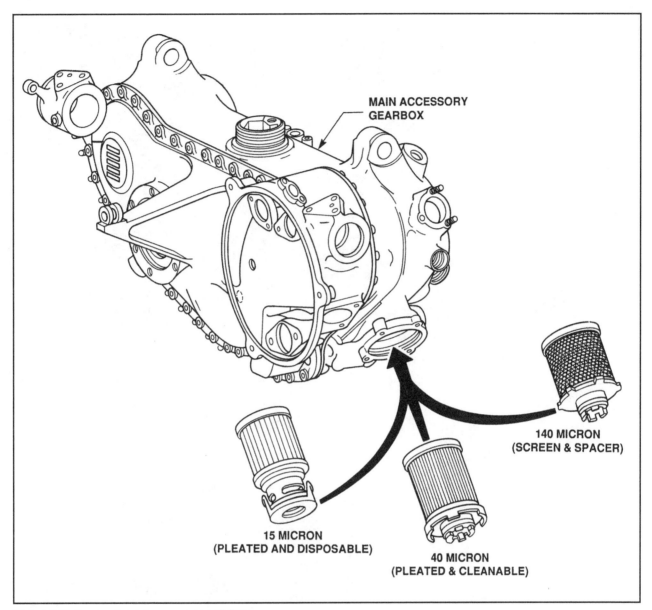

Figure 6-19. Types of gearbox-mounted oil filters

the main oil filter. The valve location plays a significant role when checking system pressures during an oil filter bypass condition. For example, if the valve is downstream of the filter (as shown in Figure 6-18B) and the filter clogs, the pressure will rise upstream of the filter, which creates the differential pressure that causes the oil to open the bypass valve at the filter. An example of an engine corresponding to this design is the Pratt & Whitney JT-8D turbofan engine shown in Figure 6-34.

If the pressure regulating relief valve is upstream of the filter (as shown in Figure 6-18C), the upstream pressure remains constant during a bypass condition as the downstream pressure drops. The drop in downstream pressure then permits the filter bypass valve to open. An example of an engine corresponding to this design is the Pratt & Whitney PT6 turboprop shown in Figure 6-33.

On engines in which the oil system contains a pressure limiting relief valve rather than a pressure regulating relief valve, if the filter becomes clogged, the oil pressure will rise up to the cracking pressure of the valve. [Figure 6-27]

LOW-PRESSURE WARNING LIGHT

All aircraft cockpits have at least one oil pressure gauge. The cockpit pressure gauge typically taps into the oil system downstream (output side) of the main oil filter to indicate actual oil pressure delivered to the engine. Many aircraft are also configured with a low-pressure warning light. When power is turned on in the aircraft, this light will illuminate. Then as oil pressure builds in the system during starting, the light will go out at a preset value equal to the low or "red line" limit for the cockpit oil pressure gauge. [Figures 6-22 & 6-23A]

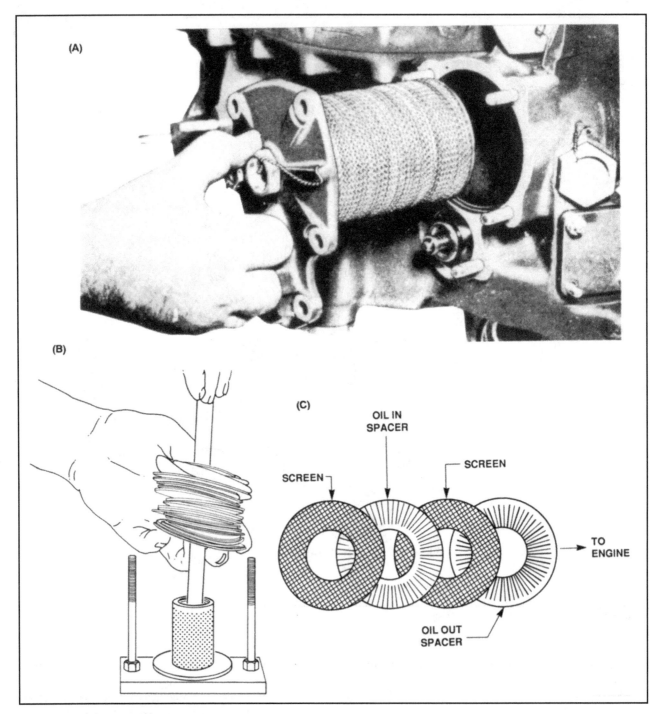

Figure 6-20A. Screen and spacer oil filter
Figure 6-20B. Disassembling a screen and spacer oil filter for cleaning
Figure 6-20C. Arrangement of screens and spacers

If the warning light fails to extinguish after start-up or if it comes back on during operation, the operator monitors the pressure gauge to confirm the extent of the low oil pressure condition and then takes the appropriate action by reducing power or by shutting the engine down. Figure 6-23A also shows the low-pressure warning light arrangement. If the filter clogs during engine operation, the low-pressure warning light acts as a bypass warning light. Its microswitch is set so that the cockpit light will illuminate at the pressure at which the filter starts to bypass oil. This situation is further explained in the following paragraphs, including a more detailed illustration of the low oil pressure warning systems.

FILTER BYPASS WARNING LIGHTS AND COCKPIT GAUGES

Filter warning lights indicate when a filter clogging (blocking) condition exists and that the filter bypass

Lubrication Systems

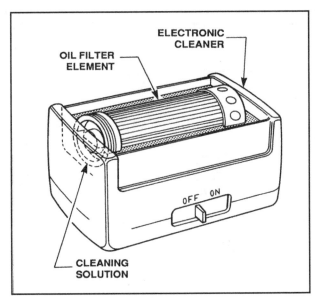

Figure 6-21. Fluid vibrator oil filter cleaner

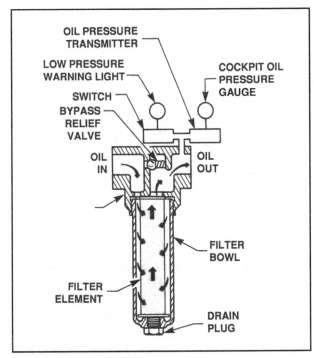

Figure 6-22. Oil filter with low oil pressure switch and oil pressure transmitter

valve is approaching the point at which it routes unfiltered oil to the engine. Pressure gauges can also be used to interpret the degree of flow blockage that has occurred and caused the filter bypass valve to open. When the flight crew or ground operating personnel observe a partial or complete bypass oil condition, they can refer to the manufacturer's instructions for the appropriate action.

Bypass Condition

After a filter is obstructed to the point that it is bypassed, unfiltered oil flows to the engine and can clog internal engine oil screens and jets. This can result in a loss of lubrication to the related bearings and seals.

Should this occur, the conditions at the bearing and seal locations throughout the engine would be similar to conditions following loss of main oil pressure.

Instrumentation to warn of an impending bypass of the oil filter is installed in many engines to provide flight and maintenance personnel with an indication that the main oil filter is approaching a blocked condition or is completely blocked. Such instrumentation is considered a maintenance aid because early action will prolong the life of the engine components in most cases. [Figure 6-23B]

In a pressure-regulated system, a change in the oil pressure indication might warn the operator because the system relief valve would simply return more oil to the pump inlet. In this case a warning device called an impending bypass light is useful. It is set to actuate at a differential pressure sufficiently lower than the differential pressure ($\triangle P$) at which the system would begin to bypass the filter, which permits the flight crew to act in time to prevent unfiltered oil from circulating.

Differential Pressure ($\triangle P$) Light

The differential oil pressure (pressure versus vent) indicating system provides a reading of the true oil pressure drop across the oil jets, because this is a measure of the quantity of oil flowing to the bearings. When a filter is configured with a $\triangle P$ light, the light remains off after power is supplied to the instrument panel because no differential pressure exists at this time. The light normally illuminates only at an impending filter bypass condition; however, it might illuminate if filter inlet pressure builds rapidly during engine starting. The reason for the rapid pressure rise is typically due to highly viscous oil brought about by cold conditions. The light typically extinguishes as oil temperature increases to normal value. Should the light stay on, continued operation above idle is not usually permitted except during in-flight emergencies because of the high probability that the filter is obstructed with solid contaminants. In such circumstances, the operator must closely monitor other engine gauge readings such as oil temperature and engine vibration for indications of major engine malfunction. [Figure 6-23B]

Dual Cockpit Gauges

Instead of a $\triangle P$ light, some aircraft are configured with a dual-pressure indicating system, which incorporates two pressure gauges—one upstream and one downstream from the filter. The gauges will be red-lined at the same value as the micro contactor in the warning switch to the light. The difference in the two gauge readings indicates whether the bypassing point is imminent or has been reached. For example, if normal pressure drop across a clean filter is 5 p.s.i.g. and the bypass valve is set to open at 28 p.s.i.d., when the two gauges have a spread of 28 p.s.i.d., bypass is occurring. This condition is explained in greater detail in the section about the General Electric CJ610 lubrication system later in this chapter.

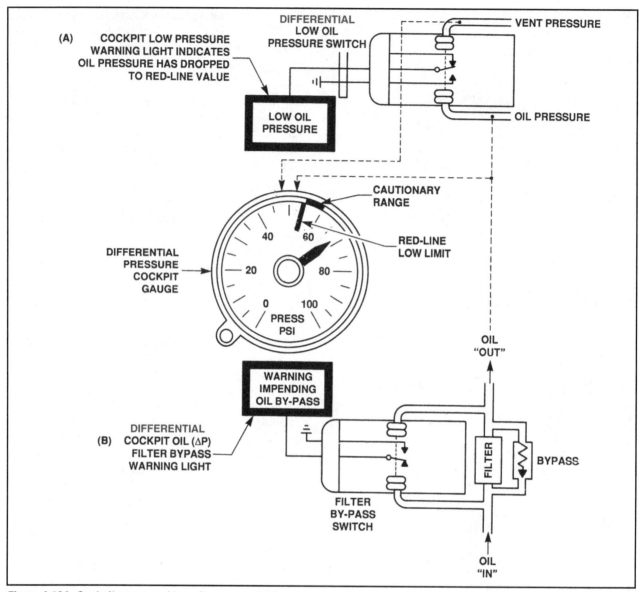

Figure 6-23A. Cockpit gauge and low oil pressure light
Figure 6-23B. Oil filter bypass light

Procedures During Low Oil Pressure Conditions

The following guidelines are recommended for engines that incorporate oil-filter pressure-drop instrumentation:

- Reduce power whenever the cockpit pressure indicator reaches the red-line limit or its back-up system, the low-pressure warning light, illuminates, or both.

- At the discretion of the flight crew, operate the engine at reduced throttle if the warning light goes out after being on for a short time and all other engine instrument indications remain at acceptable values. If high vent pressure is causing a low oil pressure indication, reducing power will often lower the vent pressure and bring the oil pressure back to a more normal value. A high oil temperature indication often accompanies high vent pressure, because more hot gas path air is in contact with the oil.

- If the oil pressure indicator reading remains at the red-line or if the low oil warning light remains on, shut the engine down or set the throttle at the minimum thrust required to sustain flight until a landing can be made.

- Whenever the oil pressure indicator reading reaches the red-line limit or the warning light illuminates, or both, report the incident as an engine discrepancy and disassemble and inspect the main oil filter.

Filter Pop-Out Warning

Some filter assemblies that do not have pressure drop indicators or warning lights are configured with a warning pop-out button on the filter bowl. Figure 6-24 shows a filter bowl with an impending bypass button. The button, which pops out when filter inlet pressure reaches a preset value, provides a visual warning that the filter is about to be bypassed or that it has already been bypassed.

Maintenance technicians inspect this warning button during routine inspections or during troubleshooting of the oil system and react by examining the filtering element for contamination. After the problem is resolved, the button is reset by hand.

During cold-weather starting, high oil pressure might cause the oil filter differential pressure bypass valve to open. This condition does not cause the impending bypass button to pop out because the pop-out assembly contains a thermal low-temperature lockout (not shown) to prevent it from tripping. As the oil warms up to approximately 100°F, the thermal lockout is disengaged and the indicator is ready to warn of filter contamination.

OTHER COMPONENTS OF DRY SUMP SYSTEMS

Several other components make up the dry sump lubricating system, including:

- System pressure relief valve
- Antistatic leak check valve
- Oil cooler, also known as an oil-fuel heat exchanger
- Oil jets
- Last chance filters
- Chip detectors
- Rotary air-oil separator
- Pressurizing and vent valve

These components are covered in the following engine-specific discussions on lubrication systems: the General Electric CJ-610 Turbojet; the Pratt & Whitney PT6 Turboprop; the JT8D turbofan; and the G.E./Snecma CFM56 turbofan.

SMALL ENGINE LUBRICATION SYSTEM — GENERAL ELECTRIC CJ610 TURBOJET

The General Electric CJ610 turbojet's lubrication system is a variable-pressure, dry sump, hot tank system in which the oil is cooled in the pressure subsystem and returns hot to the tank from the scavenge subsystem. This oil system has three subsystems:

- Pressure (supply) subsystem
- Scavenge (return) subsystem
- Vent (atmospheric) subsystem

PRESSURE SUBSYSTEM OIL FLOW

In the schematic diagram in Figure 6-27, oil flows from a 0.75 gallon tank to the pressure subsystem pumping element. The pump moves oil at the rate of 2.5 gallons per minute to a nonadjustable relief valve, set in this case to relieve at 125 p.s.i.g. It relieves the system by routing oil back to the oil tank whenever fluid pressure reaches a preset value, typically called the cracking pressure. In this system, the relief valve is referred to as

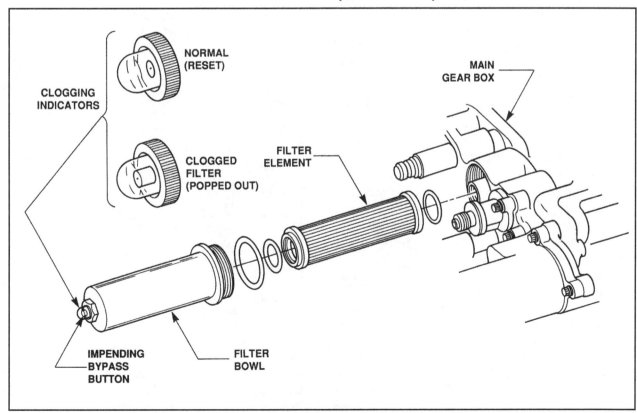

Figure 6-24. Main oil filter with bypass warning button

a pressure-limiting relief valve (also called a cold-start relief valve) because it only cracks when back-pressure caused by low ambient temperature and high oil viscosity forces it open. This full flow pressure subsystem operates with varying oil pressure from idle power (5 p.s.i.g. minimum) to takeoff power (60 p.s.i.g. maximum) at normal oil operating temperature.

As shown in Figure 6-27, after passing the system relief valve, oil flows to the fuel-oil cooler. If congealed oil or other restrictions to flow occur, the pressure downstream of the differential pressure bypass valve that backs up the tensioning spring will diminish. When a differential pressure ($\triangle P$) of 26 to 34 p.s.i.d. exists, the bypass valve opens to protect the cooler from overpressurization.

Note the antistatic-leak check valve, which is normally installed at the filter inlet to prevent oil leak-down from the tank to the sump during periods of engine inactivity. This check valve is set to open at minimal pumping pressure, in the range of 2 to 3 p.s.i.g.. In addition, this valve helps to keep the oil pump primed for immediate lubrication to the engine on start-up. A similar view of the antistatic leak valve is shown on Figure 6-26.

After the oil is cooled, it is filtered. A similar cold starting and filter clogging bypass valve is installed at the filter. It is set to open at 33 p.s.i.d.

To better understand the way in which this bypass valve operates, assume that the engine is operating at normal oil temperature with a normal differential pressure of 5 p.s.i.d. across a clean filter, oil pressure upstream of the filter at 60 p.s.i.g., and oil pressure downstream of the filter at 55 p.s.i.g. Holding the bypass valve closed is 55 p.s.i.g. downstream oil pressure plus a 33 p.s.i. spring pressure. This value is significantly higher than the pressure on the upstream side (60 p.s.i.g.). If the filter begins to clog, the pressure upstream starts to rise and the pressure downstream starts to drop. When the differential pressure reaches 33 p.s.i.d. or slightly greater, the bypass valve opens to maintain sufficient lubrication for operation at low to moderate flight requirements.

Figure 6-27 shows that after oil passes through the oil filter, the oil (under pump pressure) flows downstream to the low oil pressure switch and light and to the oil jets. Oil under pressure also flows to the oil pressure transducer (transmitter). The transducer also receives a vent pressure input.

The transducer is designed to send a corrected oil pressure (fluid pressure minus vent air pressure) to the cockpit gauge. This design is used because vent pressure opposes oil flow at the oil jets, and the operator needs to know the flow condition expressed as corrected oil pressure. The vent system is explained in detail later in this chapter. The oil pressure indicating system is explained in detail in Chapter 12, Engine Instrument Systems.

In this system, as in most gas turbine engines, the entire oil supply circulates approximately three times per minute to control oil temperatures and to ensure that desired filtration occurs. The CJ610 lubrication system is considered a hot tank system because the oil cooler is located in the pressure subsystem, downstream from the pump, and the hot oil is scavenged back to the oil tank.

If the engine does not incorporate a cold-start relief valve as shown in Figure 6-27, it provides system pressure relief by way of a pressure-regulating relief valve. [Figures 6-25 and 6-26]. With this type of regulating relief valve, the oil pressure is held in a much narrower operating range than in the cold start relief valve system. In the regulating relief valve system, for example, a typical operating range is 40 ($\pm$5) p.s.i.g. to 80 ($\pm$5) p.s.i.g. In this case, the relief valve would be cracked open constantly—slightly open at idle speed and open wider at takeoff power to maintain the preset pressure value. The oil systems shown in Figures 6-33 and 6-34 have this type of relief valve.

OIL COOLER FUNCTIONS

The oil cooler's main function is to maintain a specific oil temperature at varying engine speeds. [Figure 6-27] A similar oil cooler shown in Figure 6-28 is also known as an oil-to-fuel heat exchanger. It contains numerous thin tubular passageways in which cooler fuel flows on its way to the combustor and around which the oil circulates. This arrangement enables an exchange of heat between the fuel and the oil.

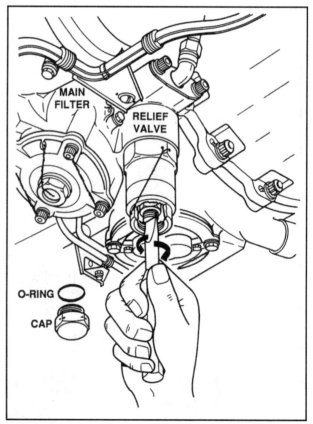

Figure 6-25. Engine oil pressure relief valve adjustment

Lubrication Systems

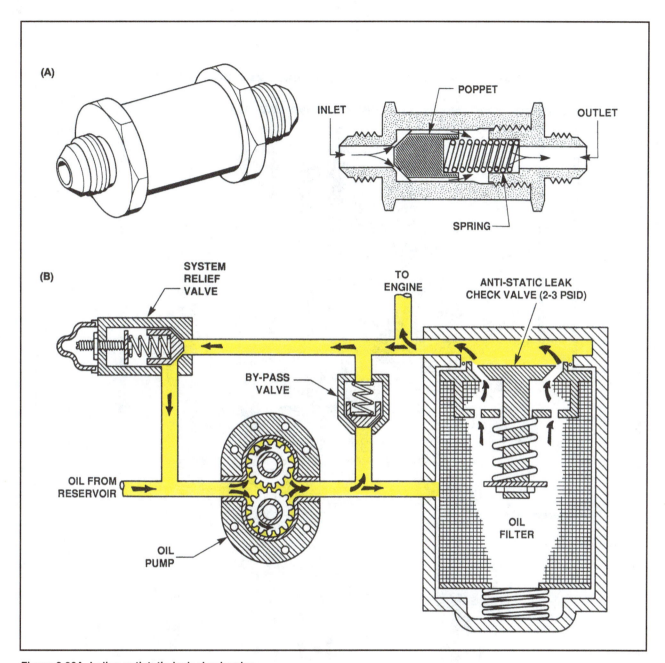

Figure 6-26A. In-line antistatic-leak check valve
Figure 6-26B. In-oil-filter antistatic-leak check valve

A combination differential pressure bypass valve and thermostatic bypass valve is positioned at the cooler inlet. [Figure 6-27 and 6-28] When the oil is cold, the valve is open, which permits oil to take the path of least resistance, bypassing the cooling chamber and flowing directly to the rest of the system. When the oil heats up, the thermostatic valve expands to close, forcing the oil to flow through the cooler. If a restriction occurs from cooler obstruction, pressure buildup unseats the bypass valve, permitting uncooled oil to flow, at a slightly reduced pressure, to the system. The thermostatic valve contains a bimetallic spring, typically constructed of an iron/nickel alloy and brass, which, because of the differing coefficients of expansion, produces movement with either loss or gain of heat.

A typical oil cooler operational schedule might be as follows: The oil cooler thermostatic valve starts to close at 165°F, becoming fully closed at 185°F, with normal engine oil temperature stabilizing at 210°F. From this point, the cooler capacity for fuel flow and oil flow regulate the operational oil temperature rather than the thermostatic valve. As the throttle is advanced for the engine to generate more power, and consequently more heat for the oil to absorb, the fuel flow through the cooler increases and absorbs this heat. The maximum continuous oil temperature in this system would be 210°F. If the

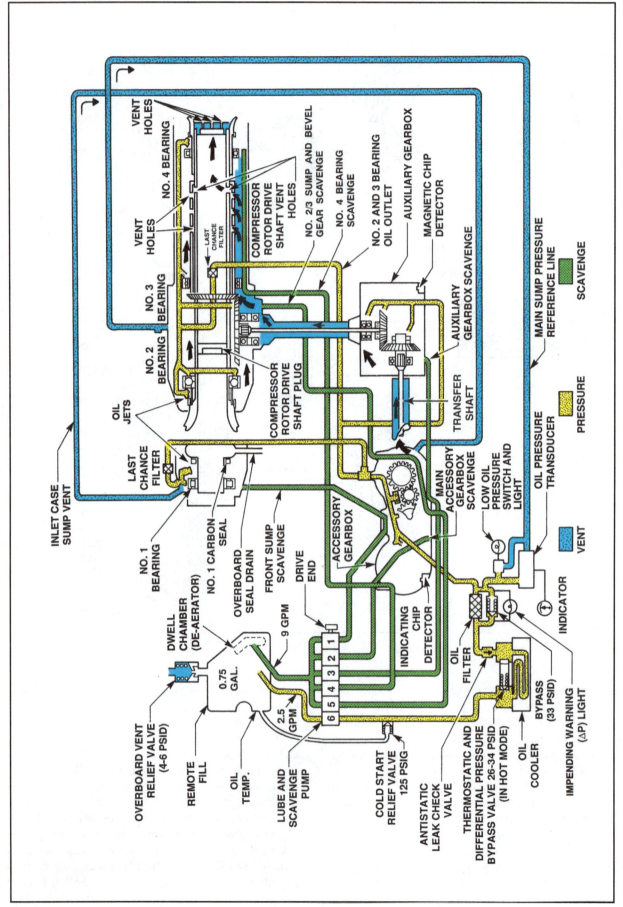

Figure 6-27. Variable pressure lubrication system with hot oil tank (General Electric CJ610 turbojet engine)

Lubrication Systems

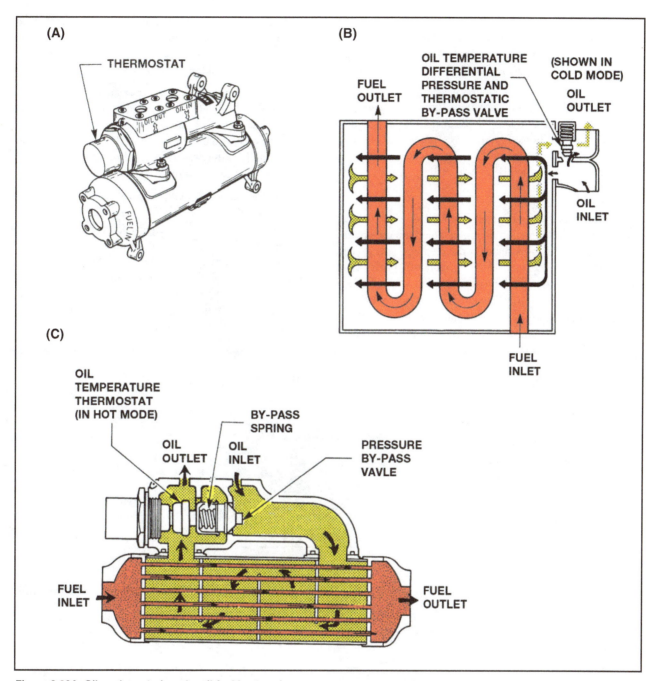

Figure 6-28A. Oil cooler exterior, aka oil-fuel heat exchanger
Figure 6-28B. Thermostatic bypass valve in transit with oil both cooling and bypassing
Figure 6-28C. Thermostatic bypass valve closed when oil is hot

temperature reached a value over 210°F but under the red-line value of 230°F, the engine would have to be operated at reduced power at the discretion of the pilot. If the oil temperature were to reach 230°F, the engine would have to be shut down.

The purpose of the thermostatic valve is to permit oil to quickly bypass the cooler and provide lubrication to the lube points on a cold start. On some engines, however, an oil cooler without a thermostatic device is used if oil can be distributed to the lube points rapidly enough when the oil is cold.

One of the checks that operators can perform on an oil cooler is to observe a momentary oil temperature rise on engine deceleration, and drop in oil temperature on acceleration as a function of fuel flow. A successful test indicates that the thermostatic valve is not stuck in a transient position and is not permitting the oil to bypass the cooler.

Oil Jets — CJ610

Oil jets (sometimes referred to as nozzles) are located at the various places within the engine that require lubrication. [Figure 6-27] Oil jets are the terminating point of the pressure subsystem. They deliver either an atomized spray or a fluid stream of oil to bearings, oil seals, gears, and other parts. Figure 6-29A shows an additional, detailed view of the oil jet locations in a main bearing sump.

The CJ610 uses a fluid stream method of oil delivery. This is the most common oil delivery method, especially in high load conditions. In most cases, the stream of oil is directed onto the bearing surfaces from what is termed a direct lubrication oil jet. [Figure 6-29B]

General Comments — Oil Jets

Another less common method of oil delivery is the mist and vapor lubrication oil jet, in which the oil stream (sometimes an air-oil stream) is directed at a splash pan and slinger ring device. This configuration provides a wider area of lubrication than possible with a single oil jet and is used in some larger engines. [Figure 6-29C]

Another type of oil jet coming into wider use is called under-race lubrication. In this configuration, oil is routed through rotor shafts and bearing journals, and then fed through slots that act as oil jets in the bearing inner races. One advantage of under-race lubrication over other oil jet configurations is superior cooling.

Over time, oil flow can be restricted at the calibrated orifice of the oil jet due to an accumulation of carbon (called coking). Coking occurs when residual engine heat acts on oil-coated metal parts. This condition occurs more rapidly if the prescribed cooling down period prior to engine shutdown is ignored.

Oil jets can be checked for size and cleanliness with a drill pin or the shank of a new numbered drill bit. Drill shanks must be free from any nicks or burrs to prevent damage to the jet. Another method of checking for restrictions to flow is the smoke check. Smoke or shop air is directed into the oil nozzle inlet port, and the discharge rate is observed as it passes through the orifice. A comparison is usually made to a known good or new oil jet.

A flow tester is often available in larger repair facili-

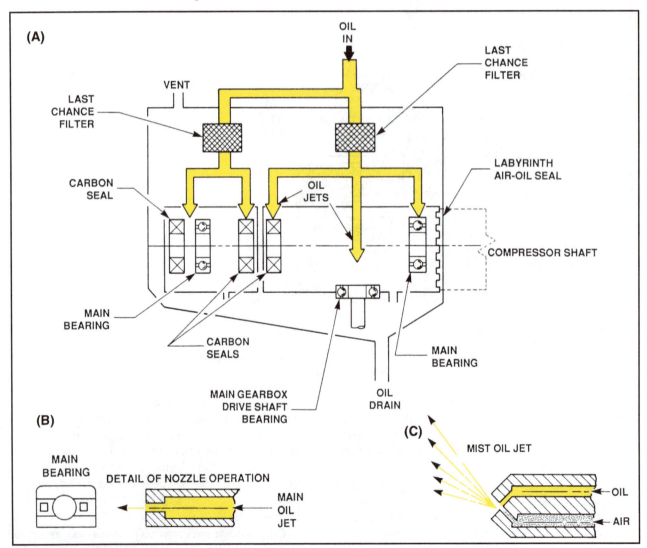

Figure 6-29A. Location of main bearing oil jets and filters
Figure 6-29B. Direct lubrication oil jet
Figure 6-29C. Mist and vapor oil jet

ties. Flow testers can accurately measure rate of flow in gallons per minute, with the oil jet installed in the engine. On some engines, bearing flow checks are part of a 100-hour inspection or a similar inspection requirement.

Last Chance Filters

Filters known as last chance filters are often installed in oil lines to prevent plugging of the oil jets. [Figure 6-27] Because of their remote location within the engine, last chance filters are accessible for cleaning only during engine overhaul. To prevent engine damage from obstructed last chance screens or oil jets, ground personnel frequently inspect the main filters. They also periodically perform flow tests to detect early signs of last chance filter blockage. [Figure 6-29A]

SCAVENGE SUBSYSTEM

The scavenge subsystem removes oil from the bearing compartments and gearboxes by suction from each of five lubrication pump scavenge return elements. [Figure 6-27] All of the scavenge return elements route oil to a single return line, which enters the dwell chamber in the oil tank. The dwell chamber acts as an air-oil separator. The total flow rate of return oil is nine gallons per minute. The entrained air that accumulates in the oil increases oil volume and requires the use of a scavenge subsystem with a capacity much higher than that of the pressure subsystem.

CHIP DETECTORS

Many scavenge systems contain permanent magnet chip detectors [Figure 6-27] that attract and hold ferrous metal particles, which would otherwise circulate back to the oil tank and the engine pressure subsystem, possibly causing wear or damage. Chip detectors are frequently inspected to detect early signs of main bearing failure.

General Comments — Chip Detectors

The presence of small fuzzy particles or gray metallic paste indicates normal wear. Metallic chips or flakes are an indication of serious internal wear or malfunction. [Figure 6-30C]

The inset in Figure 6-33 also shows an indicating magnetic chip detector. When debris bridges the gap between the magnetic positive electrode in the center and the ground electrode (shell), a warning light illuminates in the cockpit. The flight crew then takes whatever action is warranted, such as in-flight shutdown, continued operation at flight idle, or continued operation at normal cruise, depending on the other engine instruments readings. The chip detector shown in Figure 6-27 is also of this type.

Another type of chip detector, known as the electric pulsed chip detector, can discriminate between small ferrous and nonferrous wear-metal particles that are considered non-failure-related, and larger particles that can indicate bearing failure, gearbox failure, or other potentially serious engine malfunction. [Figure 6-30C]

The pulsed chip detector resembles the indicating chip detector at the gap end, but its electrical circuit contains a pulsing mechanism powered by the aircraft's 28 VDC bus.

The pulsed detectors have two operating modes: manual only or manual and automatic. In the manual mode, each time the gap is sufficiently bridged, regardless of the particle size, a warning light illuminates in the cockpit. The operator will then send an electrical pulse of energy across the gap end in an attempt to separate the debris from the hot center electrode. In this procedure, called burn-off, if the light goes out and stays out, the operator considers the bridging a result of a non-failure-related cause. If the light stays on or repeatedly comes on after multiple burn-off attempts, the operator will take appropriate action, such as reducing engine power or shutting down the engine.

In the automatic mode, if the gap is bridged by small debris, the system automatically discharges a pulse of electrical energy across the gap. The resulting burn-off prevents a cockpit warning light from illuminating by opening the circuit before a time-delay relay in the circuit activates to complete the current path to ground. If the debris is a large particle, it will remain in place after the burn-off cycle is completed and a warning light will illuminate in the cockpit when the time delay relay closes.

Another development in chip detectors is known as the quantitative debris monitor (QDM). The QDM provides an online system to compute the extent of captured ferrous particles in the oil. It can differentiate between small non-failure-related and larger failure-related particles and provide a computer readout and analysis of the results. To accomplish this, the QDM uses a dual magnet system in an indicating chip detector that can read the level of resistance between two magnets at the tip of the chip detector. When installed as part of a FADEC system, QDM provides alerts, warnings, and fault messages to the flight deck.

VENT SUBSYSTEM

Vent air (sometimes called breather air) originates in the gaspath of the CJ610 engine and then leaks into the oil wetted parts of the engine. In the CJ610 turbine engine, vent air is deposited in the main accessory gearbox along with scavenged oil from the main bearings. [Figure 6-27] This air is then routed to the mid-frame. From there, it is channeled internally along the compressor shaft and out of the turbine shaft vent holes into the gas path. A system of seals controls the rate of leakage and prevents turbine section air from backing up into the vent system. The oil tank is also fitted with an overboard relief valve, its purpose is to maintain a head pressure above the oil level that will ensure positive oil flow to the pressure subsystem pump.

GENERAL COMMENTS — VENT SUBSYSTEMS

The presence of pressurized air in the bearing cavities is a result of gas path air leaking across carbon and laby-

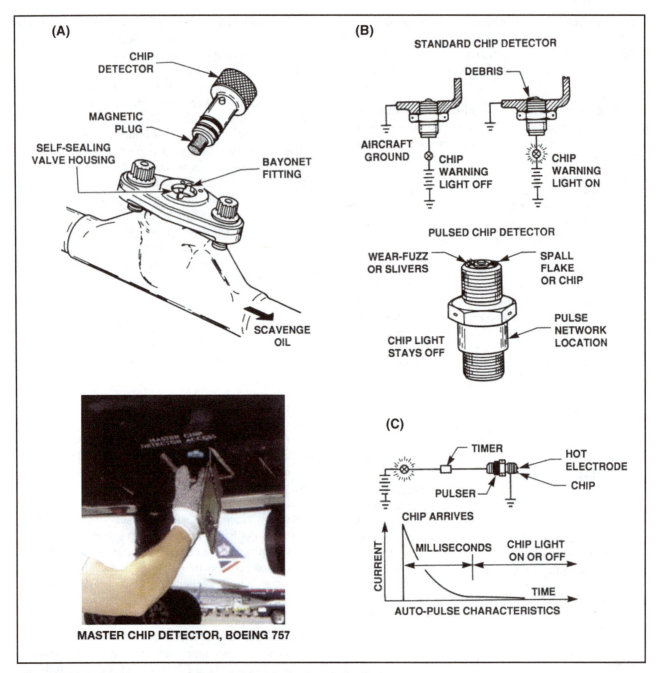

Figure 6-30A. In-line, scavenge magnetic oil chip detector (non-indicating)
Figure 6-30B. Chip detector access panel on engine cowling
Figure 6-30C. Comparison between standard, pulsed, and auto-pulse detectors

rinth oil seals. This air pressure assists in oil return to the tank by exerting a head of pressure on the scavenge oil at the bearing sumps. The air is also vented overboard by various methods before an undesirable buildup occurs. A separate subsystem is installed on some engines to vent this seal leakage air overboard.

Pressurized air in the bearing cavities also ensures a proper oil spray from the oil jet. By regulating the amount of back-pressure at the oil jet, the quantity of oil flow from the oil jet is also regulated.

A common problem associated with the vent subsystem is coking. Vent air is oil-laden and over time the heat to which this mixture is subjected causes some of the oil particles to decompose and solidify into coke. Coke buildup can slow or even block air flow through some of the smaller passageways, subjecting portions of the vent subsystem to excessive pressure.

When normal venting is restricted, it results in problems such as low oil flow to bearings and high oil temperature. To troubleshoot for this malfunction, technicians typically isolate the vent system at various points on the engine, measure the pressure, and compare it against the standards in the maintenance manual.

A rotary air-oil separator is needed in some large engines that have greater vent system airflow. This is the result of higher compression and higher gas path pressure. These engines use a centrifuge-type rotary air-oil separator to assist the vent system in releasing vent air with minimal loss of the oil supply.

The rotary separator shown in Figure 6-31 and 6-34 is an impeller or centrifuge-like device located in the main gearbox near the vent outlet. As the oil-laden vent air enters the rotating slinger chamber, centrifugal action throws the oil outward to drain back into the sump, while clean vent air is routed out of the engine or to a pressurizing and vent valve and then overboard.

A pressurizing and vent valve is also needed in some large engines to prevent releasing high volumes of air overboard at altitude. The valve shown in Figure 6-32 consists of an aneroid bellows, which is open at sea level but closed at altitude to maintain engine vent pressure. It also includes a relief valve to ensure a specified vent system back pressure at the oil nozzle and a flow similar to that which occurs at sea level.

The vent system operating pressure at sea level is approximately 5 to 7 p.s.i.g. This means that even though the pressurizing and vent valve is fully open in the ground operating condition, volume of flow creates a pressure build-up inside the vent portion of the lubrication system of 5 to 7 p.s.i.g.

The aneroid shutoff valve typically starts to close at an altitude of 8,000 to 10,000 feet and closes completely at 20,000 feet. The vent system relief valve then acts as a pressurizing check valve, maintaining 5 to 7 p.s.i.g within the vent subsystem.

The oil jets in the pressure subsystem, having the same back-pressure across their flow orifices as at sea level, provide the same lubrication in gallons per minute to the engine. Figures 6-33 and 6-34 both show the location of this valve.

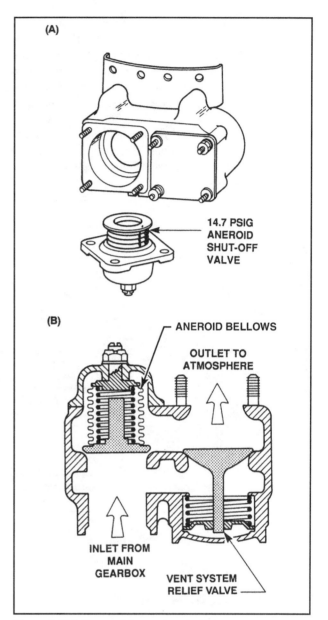

Figure 6-32A. Pressurizing and vent valve
Figure 6-32B. Cutaway view

SMALL ENGINE LUBRICATION SYSTEM — PRATT & WHITNEY PT6 TURBOPROP

The Pratt & Whitney PT6 turboprop engine is a pressure-regulated, dry sump lubricating system described as a "cold tank" oil system. Its oil is cooled in the scavenge subsystem. Although it appears to have a wet sump lubrication system, the PT6 uses an integral dry sump oil tank. Tank capacity is two gallons, with 1.5 gallons of usable oil and a 0.5-gallon expansion space. [Figure 6-33]

PRESSURE SUBSYSTEM FLOW PATH

In the schematic diagram in Figure 6-33, the oil flows from a 2.0-gallon tank to the pressure subsystem pumping element. It is a gear pump with a capacity of four

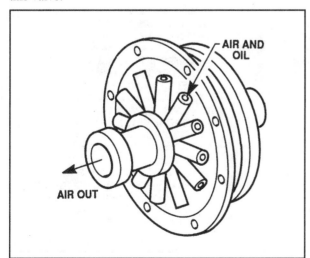

Figure 6-31. Rotary air-oil separator

gallons per minute. Oil then flows to an adjustable relief valve, which is set in this case to 80 (±5) p.s.i.g. The valve controls the system oil pressure by routing oil back to the supply tank whenever the fluid pressure reaches its preset value, typically called the cracking pressure. In this system, the relief valve is referred to as a pressure regulating relief valve because it is open and continually bypassing a portion of the oil during engine operation to maintain the system pressure. This subsystem operates at a constant pressure after the engine reaches it normal operation oil temperature.

After passing the relief valve, oil flows to the oil filter and the antistatic check valve assembly. If the oil is congealed or if other restrictions to flow occur, the build-up of oil pressure forces the filter bypass valve to open, permitting bypass oil to flow into the main bearing supply line. The oil filter bypass setting is 25 to 30 p.si.d.

Oil under system pressure also flows to the oil pressure transmitter and oil temperature bulb, and then on to the last chance filters at the four main bearing locations. Oil also flows to the propeller reduction gearbox and to the torquemeter system.

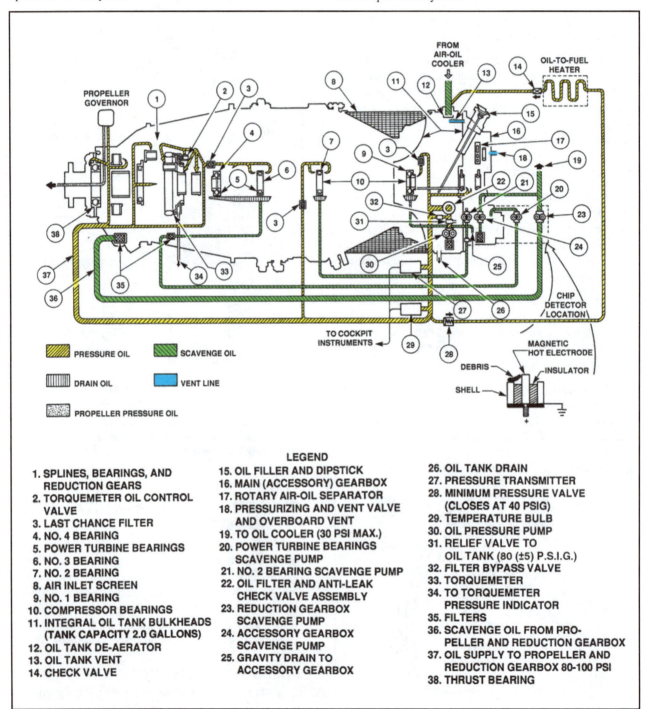

Figure 6-33. Pressure regulated lubrication system with cold oil tank (Pratt & Whitney PT6 turboprop)

As oil flows to the bearings, it also passes through the oil-to-fuel heater. The fuel heater minimum pressure valve is in place in the line to the heater to close at 40 p.s.i.g. This valve blocks the flow if the engine is shut down in flight, thus ensuring sufficient lubrication to the main bearings during windmilling.

SCAVENGE SUBSYSTEM FLOW PATH

The scavenge subsystem in the PT6 removes oil from the bearing sumps and gearboxes by suction from each of four scavenge pumps and returns the oil to the oil tank. The scavenge pumps also pump a certain amount of air along with the oil. This air creates a pressure above the tank oil level to ensure a positive pressure head. The remainder of the air is vented to the atmosphere by way of the pressurizing and vent valve and the overboard vent.

Note that the number 1 bearing sump drains directly into the accessory gearbox without the aid of a scavenge pump. Also note that a chip detector is located in the bottom of the accessory gearbox to collect ferrous particles that accumulate in the scavenged oil.

VENT SUBSYSTEM FLOW PATH

Air that leaks into the PT6 propeller gearbox and bearing sumps 2, 3, and 4 from the engine's gas path is carried away by the scavenge pumps to the accessory reduction gearbox. The number 1 bearing sump vents directly into the accessory reduction gearbox.

The oil tank also vents to the accessory reduction gearbox, and vent air leaves the engine by way of the pressurizing and vent valve and the overboard vent. This valve regulates the pressure within the main accessory gearbox. This valve also controls the pressure within the oil tank because the gearbox is connected to the tank by an internal oil tank vent tube. [Figure 6-33]

LARGE ENGINE LUBRICATION SYSTEM — PRATT & WHITNEY JT8D TURBOFAN

The lubricating system in the JT8D engine is a pressure-regulated, dry sump, hot tank system with an oil tank capacity of 6.3 gallons. Its oil is returned to the oil tank uncooled by the scavenge subsystem. The system contains one gear-type pressure pump, one dual-gear scavenge pump, and three single-gear scavenge pumps. [Figure 6-34]

Although the lubricating system does not use a thermostatic bypass valve in its fuel-oil cooler, it does use a pressure bypass valve, which permits oil to bypass the cooler when oil viscosity is high during cold weather starting or if the cooler core becomes obstructed.

The JT8D engine does not need a thermostatic bypass to supply increased oil to the bearings during starting as some engines do. Oil pressure is regulated to 40 to 55 p.s.i.g. at the fuel-oil cooler outlet by a special pressure-regulating relief valve design which assures sufficient lubrication during start and warm-up. The regulating valve mechanism is shown on Figure 6-34 at "B." The sensing oil line runs from the cooler outlet back to the regulating valve.

Because this regulating valve senses pressure downstream of the oil cooler, system pressure is maintained at the cooler outlet regardless of whether the main oil filter or oil cooler are bypassed. If oil pressure drops at this point due to high oil viscosity or blockage of some type, the sense line signals the regulating valve to bypass less oil back to the supply side of the oil pump and thus deliver more oil to the system.

The oil pressure in this system is much higher at times in the upstream side of the oil cooler than it is at the downstream side. If the inlet pressure of the main filter is 70 p.s.i.g. higher than the outlet pressure, a bypass condition exists. Similarly, if the fuel-oil cooler inlet pressure is 75 p.s.i.g. higher than the cooler outlet pressure, a bypass condition exists.

PRESSURE SUBSYSTEM FLOW PATH

In the schematic diagram in Figure 6-34, oil flows from a five-gallon tank to the pressure subsystem pumping element. The main oil pump "A" has a capacity of 35 gallons per minute at takeoff engine power. Oil then flows to the main oil filter "C," which is fitted with a differential pressure bypass valve "D." This valve has a bypass setting of 70 p.s.i.d., meaning that if the filter starts to clog and the filter inlet pressure rises to its bypass value above the outlet pressure, the bypass valve opens to provide an adequate oil supply to the engine. The flight crew uses two gauges to monitor the situation, one showing the pressure gauge reading upstream of the filter and another showing the pressure gauge reading downstream from the filter.

After passing the oil filter, the oil then flows to two locations—first to the pressure regulating valve "B" that is set at 40 to 55 p.s.i.g. downstream of the fuel-oil cooler, and second to the fuel-oil cooler inlet. The cooler is fitted with a differential pressure bypass valve "F," which is set to a bypass setting of 75 p.s.i.d. If the cooler starts to clog and the inlet pressure rises to that value above the outlet pressure, the bypass valve opens.

Oil is now directed to the sensing line that connects to the pressure-regulating valve and also downstream to the last chance filters that protect main bearings one through six.

The following system components also connect into the oil pressure subsystem at this location:

- The cockpit oil pressure transmitter and gauge, which shows a regulated oil pressure of 40 to 55 pounds per square inch-gauge
- The oil temperature gauge with a 130°C maximum allowable limit
- The low oil pressure light, which during engine start is set to extinguish at 35 p.s.i.g., approximately 28 percent N_2 speed

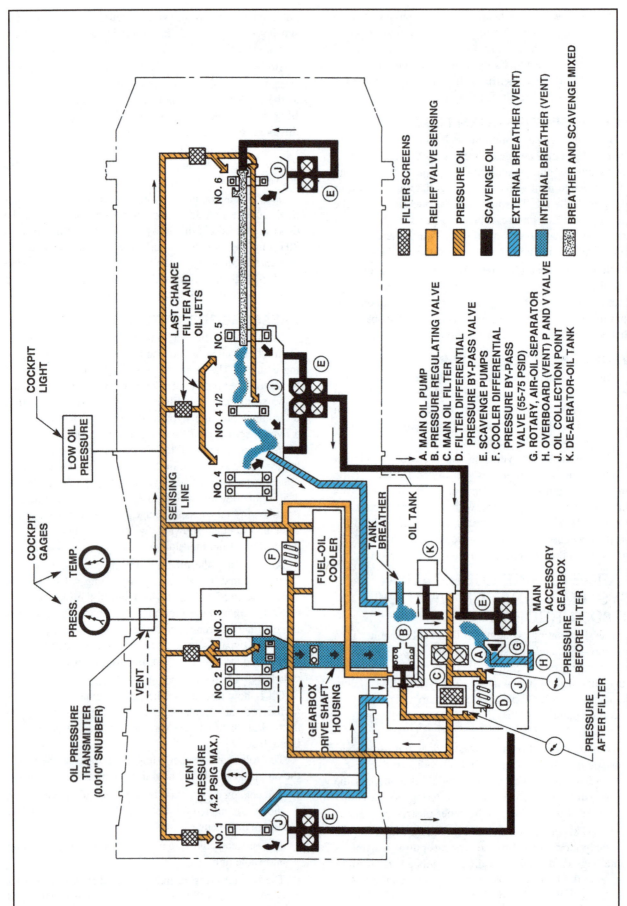

Figure 6-34. Pressure-regulated lubrication system with hot oil tank (Pratt & Whitney JT-8D turbofan)

SCAVENGE SUBSYSTEM FLOW PATH

As represented in Figure 6-34, the scavenge subsystem returns oil to the oil tank from bearing sumps and gearboxes by suction or drainage from the various sumps using five scavenge pumps as follows:

- The number 1 bearing sump "J," is scavenged by a gear pump "E," located in the bearing sump. This pump routes oil through an external line directly into the main accessory gearbox sump.
- The number 2 and 3 bearing sumps are scavenged by draining down through the gearbox drive shaft housing into the accessory gearbox sump.
- The number 4 and 4 ½ bearing sumps "J" are scavenged by one element of a dual-gear pump "E," located within the sump, which routes oil through an external line that interconnects the accessory gearbox scavenge pump return line to the oil tank.
- The number 5 bearing sump "J" is scavenged by the second element of the dual-gear pump "E," within the sump that routes oil through an external line to the accessory gearbox. This line also routes number 4 and number 4 ½ bearing oil to the accessory gearbox.
- The number 6 sump "J" is scavenged by a gear pump "E," and directed out through a combination vent and scavenge tube located within the low-pressure turbine shaft. Number 6 scavenge oil then combines with number 5 scavenge oil and returns to the accessory gearbox by way of an external line.
- The accessory gearbox is scavenged by a pump located within the sump "J." Oil is returned to the oil tank via the oil tank de-aerator "K."

VENT SUBSYSTEM SEQUENCE OF FLOW

As represented in Figure 6-34, air leaks into the following JT8D sumps from the engine gas path and is returned to the main accessory gearbox, and from there, some of the air is returned to the oil tank with the scavenged oil. The oil tank breather relieves the air pressure buildup back to the gearbox. The scavenge oil flow is as follows:

- Number 1 bearing sump "J" vents through an external line into the accessory gearbox.
- Number 2 and number 3 sumps vent down through the gearbox drive shaft housing into the accessory gearbox.
- Numbers 4, 4 ½, and 5 sumps "J" vent through an external line into the accessory gearbox.
- The number 6 sump "J" vents through a mixed vent/scavenge tube provided within the low-pressure turbine shaft, to the vent for bearings 4, 4 ½, and 5.
- The oil tank vents through a tank breather passageway, which connects the oil tank to the accessory gearbox.
- The accessory gearbox vents through the rotary air-oil separator "G" and the pressurizing and vent valve "H" to the atmosphere. This valve acts both as a vent valve and as a pressurizing valve to maintain a set vent and oil tank pressure. [Figure 6-32]

LARGE ENGINE LUBRICATION SYSTEM — CFM56-7B TURBOFAN

The CFM56 turbofan engine contains a pressure-regulated, cold-tank lubrication system. Its oil is returned to the tank cooled by oil-to-fuel heat exchangers located in the scavenge subsystem. This lubricating system includes the following major components:

- An oil tank, located on the right hand side (aft looking forward) of the fan case.
- An antileakage valve in the supply circuit located at the bottom of the fan case.
- A lubrication unit assembly installed on the accessory gearbox (AGB), which contains the pressure and scavenge pumps, the pressure relief valve, the supply oil filter, the bypass valve, and a warning indicator.
- A main oil-to-fuel heat exchanger and servo fuel heater through which scavenged oil returns to the oil tank.
- An oil scavenge filter assembly.

The lubrication system for this engine consists of three sections: the oil supply circuit, the oil scavenge circuit, and the oil venting circuit. On some engines, these are referred to as the three subsystems or circuits as shown on Figures 6-35, 6-36, and 6-37.

OIL SUPPLY CIRCUIT

General Electric refers to the CFM56's oil pressure subsystem as an oil supply circuit. The oil is drawn from the engine's oil tank through an anti-leakage valve, by a gerotor-type pressure pump within the lubrication unit. The oil then passes by the pressure limiting relief valve on its way to the oil supply filter, then flows to the engine forward sump, the aft sump, and the accessory and transfer gearboxes. [Figure 6-35 and 6-36]

OIL TANK

The oil tank is mounted on the fan case and has a maximum capacity of 22 quarts. The tank is made from a machined light alloy and covered with flame-resistant paint. Six inner bulkheads add strength and reduce oil sloshing. The tank has an oil inlet tube coming from the servo fuel heater and the main oil/fuel heat exchanger, an oil outlet to the lubrication unit, and a vent tube. [Figure 6-35 and 6-36]

A gravity filling port is provided to replenish the tank. Also provided is a remote filling port with an overflow port to indicate whether the tank is filled to the correct level. A scupper at the gravity fill point ducts any oil spillage to a drain line. A plug is provided at the bottom of the tank for draining purposes. A sight glass on the side of the tank enables service personnel to check oil quantity, and an electrical transmitter sends an oil quantity signal to a gauge on the flight deck.

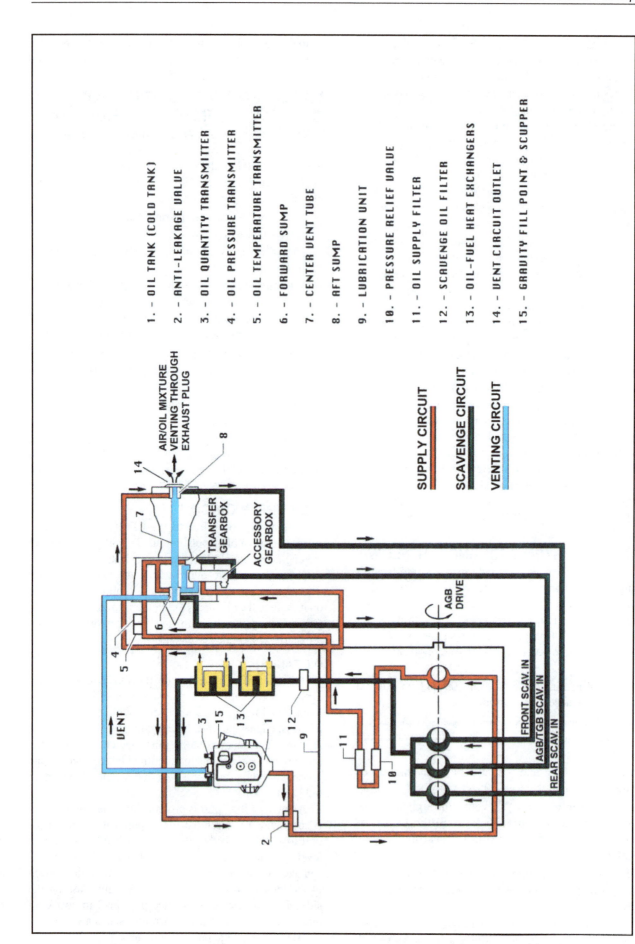

Figure 6-35. Pressure-regulated lubrication system with cold oil tank (G.E./Snecma CFM56 turbofan)

Lubrication Systems

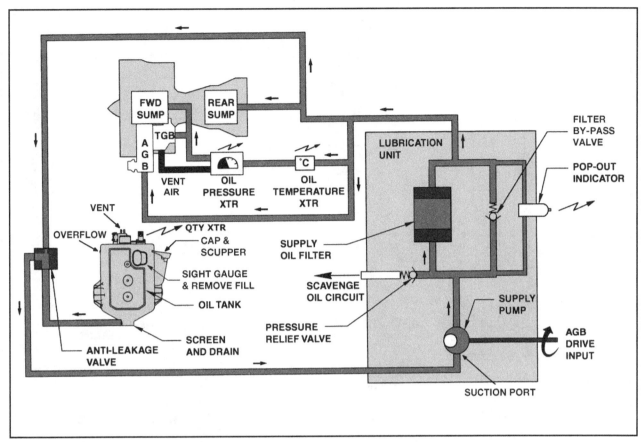

Figure 6-36. G.E./Snecma CFM56 oil supply circuit

ANTILEAKAGE VALVE

The antileakage valve [Figure 6-35 and 6-36] closes to prevent oil loss when the oil tube from the oil tank is removed during maintenance procedures for seal replacement or to replace a damaged tube. It also blocks the flow upon engine shutdown to counter a siphon effect on the oil tank. It is a pressure-actuated, spring-loaded, normally closed valve. During engine operation, oil pressure from the rear sump supply line holds the anti-leakage valve open against spring force; when the engine is shut down, spring force closes the valve.

LUBRICATION UNIT

The lubrication unit contains a pressure (supply) pump, three scavenge pumps, a pressure regulating relief valve, and an oil supply filter. It is driven by the accessory gearbox and has two purposes—it pressurizes and filters the supply oil to lubricate the engine bearings and gears, and it pumps scavenge oil back to the oil tank. The unit is mounted to the rear face of the accessory gearbox. [Figure 6-35, 6-36, and 6-37]

The unit has a suction port from the oil tank to the pressure pump, three scavenge ports, three scavenge screens, an oil-out port to the accessory gearbox and the main bearings in the forward and rear oil sumps, a supply oil filter, and an indicator that warns of an obstructed oil filter. The filter is a 44-micron-rated cleanable element. Internally, the unit has four pumps driven by a single shaft from the accessory drive gearbox. One of these pumps is dedicated to the supply circuit and the other three are scavenge pumps.

During operation, oil from the oil tank is pressurized through the supply pump and directed first to the supply oil filter. If the supply oil filter is obstructed, a bypass valve (installed in parallel) opens when the differential pressure across the valve is greater than the spring load, which is set from 17.4 to 20.3 p.s.i.d. A pop-out indicator provides visual indication of filter clogging. The button pops out at a differential pressure of 11.6 to 14.5 p.s.i.d. to warn that a filter bypass condition is approaching. A bimetallic spring prevents the button from popping out at extremely low oil temperatures. A pressure relief valve, installed downstream from the supply pump, redirects the oil to the scavenge circuit when oil pressure reaches a maximum limit of 305 p.s.i.g.

OIL SCAVENGE CIRCUIT

The scavenge oil circuit routes the oil to be scavenged from the forward sump, from the aft sump, and from the accessory drive gearbox by three scavenge pumps installed within the lubrication unit. The oil passes through hollow scavenge screens, which have threaded inserts to accommodate magnetic chip detectors. The oil then passes through a scavenge filter, the servo fuel heater, and finally the main oil/fuel heat exchanger, commonly called an oil cooler, before returning to the

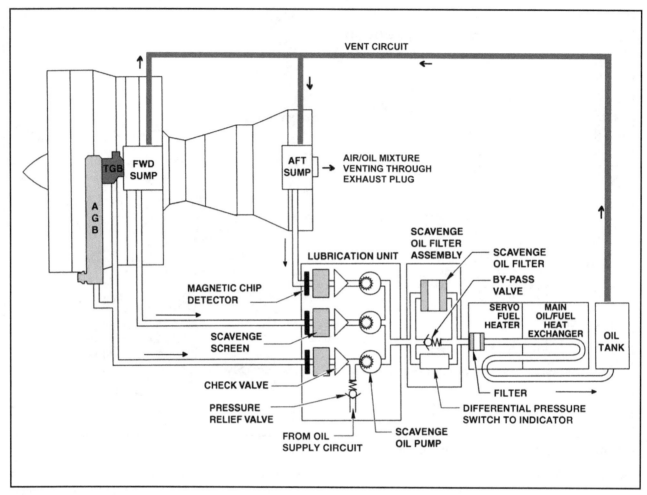

Figure 6-37. G.E./Snecma CFM56 oil scavenge circuit

oil tank. The scavenge filter has a replaceable cartridge. Oil from the transfer gearbox drains into the accessory gearbox, from where it is then scavenged. [Figure 6-35, 6-36, and 6-37]

If the scavenge oil filter begins to clog, a light on the flight deck illuminates at a pressure differential of 25 to 27 p.s.i.d. A pressure drop across the filter that reaches 28 to 34 p.s.i.d. triggers the pop-out indicator on the filter bowl to provide a visual warning that a bypass condition is approaching. As with the indicator for the supply oil filter, a bimetallic spring prevents the button from popping out at extremely low oil temperatures. If no action is taken and the pressure drop across the filter reaches 36.3 to 39.2 p.s.i.d., the filter bypass opens.

OIL VENTING CIRCUIT

As shown in Figure 6-35 and 6-37, a venting system, the purpose of which is to vent the air from the scavenge system, links the oil tank, the engine sumps, and the engine gearboxes. A center vent tube connects the forward and aft sumps to collect oil vapor and to equalize the pressure between the sumps. The forward sump and the rear sump vent through the turbine exhaust plug at the rear of the engine.

HOT TANK VERSUS COLD TANK SYSTEMS

Whether an engine has a hot or a cold oil tank system is either a matter of necessity or one of convenience of location for the manufacturer. In hot tank systems, the oil cooler is located in the pressure subsystem. An advantage of this configuration is that a maximum heat exchange occurs because oil has less entrained air in the pressure side of the lubrication system. This factor permits the use of a smaller oil cooler, which saves weight.

In cold tank systems, the oil cooler, also called the oil-to-fuel heat exchanger, is located in the scavenge subsystem, which permits the oil to return to the supply tank in a cooled condition. The oil is still aerated from the action of the rotating parts within the engine, which results in reduced heat exchange. A higher volume oil cooler is required to overcome the reduced heat exchange.

Bear in mind that some engines have normally higher oil temperatures than others. This high oil temperature in the oil tank can affect oil service life because the bulk oil storage is at a higher temperature for a longer time. Engines with high operating oil temperatures often use a cold tank system to alleviate this problem.

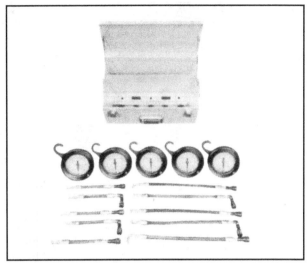

Figure 6-38. Gauge set for troubleshooting the lubrication system

TROUBLESHOOTING LUBRICATION SYSTEMS

PROBLEM/POSSIBLE CAUSE	CHECK PROCEDURE	REMEDY
1. No engine oil pressure (no oil leaks)		
a. Low oil level	Check oil level.	Add oil.
b. Circuit breaker	Locate breaker panel and check for tripped circuit breaker.	Reset if tripped. Check circuit wiring.
c. Defective indicator	1. Check power input. 2. Exchange with gauge from another engine. 3. Slave in another gauge or perform a bench check.	Repair circuit or replace indicator.
d. Defective transmitter	1. Check power input. 2. Slave in another transmitter or perform a bench check.	Repair circuit or replace transmitter.
e. Obstruction in oil tank	Remove line at pump inlet and check flow rate.	Remove obstruction or replace tank.
f. Defective oil pump	1. Motor engine with outlet line removed and check flow rate. 2. Check for leaks between elements or check for sheared drive shaft.	Replace pump.
2. Low engine oil pressure (no oil leaks)		
a. Same as 1a, 1c, 1d, 1e, 1f	Check as necessary.	
b. Improper regulating relief valve setting	1. Check security of valve and install gauges. 2. Check for high vent pressure affecting cockpit gauge reading.	Reset or replace as necessary.
c. High vent pressure from the pressurizing and vent valve outlet	Measure the vent system pressure.	Tear down engine as necessary to replace bearing seal.
d. Obstructed last chance filter (variable-pressure subsystem)	Check flow.	Clean or replace.

PROBLEM/POSSIBLE CAUSE	CHECK PROCEDURE	REMEDY
3. High oil pressure		
a. Same as item 1c, 1d, 2b	Check as necessary.	
b. Oil bypass line obstructed	Check line from the relief valve to the oil supply.	Repair or replace.
c. Low vent pressure	Check security of vent line to indicating system.	Tighten lines, replace gaskets, and so on.
4. Fluctuating oil pressure		
a. Low oil level	Check oil level in tank.	Service as necessary.
b. Loose electrical connection	Check circuit.	Tighten as necessary.
c. Defective indicator	Same as 1c	
d. Defective relief valve	Check for sticking components.	Clean or replace.
e. Defective transmitter	Bench check or slave in new transmitter.	Repair or replace transmitter.
5. Excessive oil consumption		
a. External oil leaks	Visually check entire engine.	Tighten lines, replace gaskets, and so on.
b. Gas path oil leaks	1. Check for inoperative scavenge pump. 2. Check for restricted scavenge lines or filters. 3. Check for high vent pressure forcing oil past seals.	Replace or repair pump. Clear restrictions. Tear down engine as necessary to repair or replace damaged components.
c. Overboard vent discharging oil	1. Check for damage to rotary breather. 2. Check for high vent subsystem pressure from damaged carbon or labyrinth oil seal.	Tear down accessory gearbox as necessary to repair or replace damaged components. Tear down engine as necessary to repair or replace damaged components.
d. Damaged main bearing oil seal	Check overboard vent for oil discharge. Check vent pressure.	Tear down engine as necessary to repair or replace damaged components.
e. Overboard accessory seal drains discharging excessive oil	Check drainage quantity against allowable limits.	Isolate the leaking accessory drive and replace gearbox seal.
f. Pressurizing and vent valve sticking open at altitude	Check for evidence of oil at cowling vent opening to atmosphere.	Bench-check pressurizing and vent valve.
6. Increasing oil quantity		
a. Oil cooler core leak (fuel intrusion)	Perform a bench check.	Replace as necessary.
7. Excessive oil in gas path		
a. Overservicing	Check servicing procedure; service only during prescribed period after engine shutdown.	Remove excess oil and run engine to dry out.
b. Inoperative scavenge pump(s)	Check output with direct pressure gauge.	Replace if accessible or tear down engine to gain access.

PROBLEM/POSSIBLE CAUSE	CHECK PROCEDURE	REMEDY
c. High vent pressure	1. Check for inoperative scavenge pumps.	Replace or repair pumps.
	2. Check for restricted scavenge lines or filters, raising sump pressure.	Clear restrictions.
	3. Check for high vent pressure.	Tear down engine as required to repair or replace damaged components.
8. Oil in tailpipe overnight or dripping from gearbox vent		
a. Pressure subsystem antistatic leak valve	Check for oil migration from contamination or worn check valve seals.	Clean or replace seals; then run engine and check for leaks.
9. Oil tank rupture		
a. Oil tank pressurization check	Check for valve sticking closed.	Clean or replace valve.
10. Oil pressure indication follows power lever movement		
a. Regulating relief valve	Check for sticking valve mechanism.	Clean or replace valve.
b. Cold start relief valve	Normal condition	None
11. Oil temperature high		
a. Vent subsystem coking (carbon build-up)	Check for high vent pressure caused by high scavenge-oil temperature.	Clean vent subsystem; tear down engine as required to repair or replace damaged components.
b. Oil cooler thermostat	Perform a pressure drop check to determine if thermostat is sticking in the open position.	Replace thermostat.
c. Main bearing overheating	Check flow for clogged last chance oil filter or oil jet.	
d. High ambient temperature	Low taxi engine speed.	Raise speed to correct.
12. Oil filter screen collapsed yet clean		
Filter bypass valve	Check for valve remaining closed during cold weather starts.	Clean or replace valve.
13. Oil smoke from exhaust		
Clogged vent or scavenge line	Check flow for carbon blockage.	Tear down engine as required to clean or replace damaged components.
14. Low oil level (normal consumption)		
	Check for oil migration at antistatic leak check valve.	Clean or replace valve.

QUESTIONS:

1. When heated, will oil of high viscosity index show little viscosity change or great change?

2. Do synthetic lubricants have a higher or lower flash point than petroleum-based oils?

3. What markings do federal regulations require near the oil filler opening?

4. Why is fuel-to-oil dilution not used on turbine engines as it is on reciprocating engines?

5. What device regulates oil tank pressure?

6. Where is the relief valve located in relation to the main oil pressure pump?

7. Why is the scavenge subsystem capacity greater than that of the pressure subsystem?

8. What are the two basic types of oil coolers?

9. In which of the three lubrication subsystems is the oil cooler located with a hot tank oil system?

10. Does a sliding-vane positive displacement oil pump provide a specific pressure or specific volume per revolution?

CHAPTER 7
Fuel Systems

The aircraft boost pumps pressurize the fuel sent from the fuel tanks to the gas turbine engine. The engine boost pump and the main fuel pump then further increase fuel pressure to the various components of the engine fuel system. Finally, the fuel enters the engine combustor and provides the heat expansion that produces engine thrust.

PRINCIPLES OF FUEL SYSTEMS

The primary function of a fuel system in a gas turbine engine is to supply a precise amount of fuel to the engine in all conditions of ground and air operations. The system must be free of dangerous operational characteristics, such as a vapor lock, a condition that restricts fuel flow through units designed to handle liquids rather than gases, and it must be able to increase and decrease power on command to obtain the thrust required for any operating condition. In a gas turbine engine, a device called a fuel control accomplishes this by metering fuel to the combustion chamber. The pilot selects a fuel flow condition that causes the fuel control systems to provide fuel automatically according to prevailing ambient conditions and engine mass airflow conditions. These automatic features prevent rich or lean flameout and over-temperature or over-speed conditions.

Lean die-out occurs when there is so little fuel in the air-fuel mixture that it no longer supports combustion. A rich blowout occurs when the force of fuel flow during low airflow conditions interrupts the normal burning process in close proximity to the fuel distribution nozzle. This momentary instability can cause the flame to blow away from the nozzle. Combustion ceases in both conditions, and the engine requires a relight procedure (restart). The maximum flame speed for supporting combustion using hydrocarbon fuel must be less than 0.4 Mach.

The secondary functions of the fuel system are to cool the engine oil and to provide hydraulic control for other engine systems, such as variable stator vanes and compressor bleed systems.

GAS TURBINE FUELS

Jet fuels are liquid hydrocarbons similar to kerosene; some are blended with gasoline. Hydrocarbon fuel is a compound of hydrogen and carbon found in coal, natural gas, and crude oil. This mixture freely combines with oxygen at combustion flow rates and temperatures. The blending of gasoline reduces the fuel's tendency to become too viscous at high altitudes. This problem affects performance of some high altitude aircraft.

The oxides that are formed by combustion in a gas turbine engine are mostly gases, a quality of jet fuel that minimizes solid particles that would impinge on turbine nozzle vanes and erode turbine blades.

Jet fuels are not color-coded like reciprocating engine fuels; they have a natural straw color.

The following jet fuels are most common in commercial and general aviation:

Turbo Fuel A — Commonly called Jet-A or "civil aviation kerosene," it essentially contains no gasoline blend and is the primary fuel for commercial and general aviation in the United States. Military fuel JP-8 is similar to Jet-A.

Turbo Fuel A-1 — Commonly called Jet A-1, it is a low-temperature fuel with a lower freezing point than Jet-A. International airlines are the primary users.

Specifications	Turbo Fuel A-1	Turbo Fuel A
United States	MIL-T-83133*	-------
Great Britain	DERD 2494/2453*	-------
Canada	CAN 2-3.23-M80	-------
France	AIR 3405*	-------
Pratt & Whitney Aircraft	522	522
Allison Div. of GM	EMS-64	EMS-64
ASTM D 1655	Jet A-1	Jet A
IATA Guidance Material	Kerosene*	-------
NATO Symbol	F-34*/F35	JP-8
Properties		
Aromatics, % volume	18	18
Mercaptan sulfur, % weight	0.0003	0.0003
Sulfur, % total weight	0.05	0.05
Initial boiling point, °F(°C)	325(163)	325(163)
10% evaporated, °F(°C)	355(179)	364(184)
20% evaporated, °F(°C)	364(184)	372(189)
50% evaporated, °F(°C)	379(203)	411(210)
90% evaporated, °F(°C)	450(232)	474(246)
Final boiling point, °F(°C)	498(259)	520(271)
Flash point, °F(°C)	108(42)	115(46)
Gravity, °API	44.0	42.0
Specific gravity @ 60°F(15.6°C)	0.806	0.816
Freezing point, °F(°C)	- 60(51)	- 48(44)
Viscosity @ 30°F(34.4°C)	7.9	7.9

(Continued on next page)

Specifications	Turbo Fuel A-1	Turbo Fuel A
Heat of combustion, Btu/lb(MJ/Kg)	18,600(43.1)	18,600(43.1)
Existent gum, mg/100 ml	0.2	0.2
Particulate matter, mg/liter	1.0	1.0
Free water, parts per million	30	30

Turbo Fuel B — Commonly called Jet-B, it is a blend of approximately 30 percent kerosene and 70 percent gasoline and described as a wide-cut fuel because of the high gasoline content. It has a very low freezing point and low flash point. The military uses this fuel primarily; it is similar to military fuel JP-4.

Specifications	Turbo Fuel B	Turbo Fuel 5
United States	MIL-T-5624*	MIL-T-5624*
Great Britain	DERD 2486/2454	DERD 2498/2452*
Canada	CAN 2-3.22-M80	3-GP-24M
France	AIR 3407*	AIR 3404*
Pratt & Whitney Aircraft	522	-------
ASTM	D 1655	Jet B
NATO Symbol	F-40*	43/F-44*
Properties		
Aromatics, % volume	11.0	18.0
Olefins, % volume	1.0	0.6
Mercaptan sulfur, % weight	0.0005	0.0004
Sulfur, % total weight	0.04	0.02
Initial boiling point, °F(°C)	162(72)	338(170)
10% evaporated, °F(°C)	255(125)	381(194)
20% evaporated, °F(°C)	275(135)	395(202)
50% evaporated, °F(°C)	318(159)	422(217)
90% evaporated, °F(°C)	380(193)	476(247)
Final boiling point, °F(°C)	455(235)	516(269)
Gravity, °API	53.8	41.0
Specific gravity 60°F (15.6°C)	0.764	0.820
Flash point, °F(°C)	0(18)	148(64)
Freezing point, °F(°C)	-76(60)	-58(50)
Heat of combustion, Btu/lb(MJ/Kg)	18,700(43.5)	18,500(43.1)
Existent gum, mg/100 ml	0.5	0.8
Particulate matter, mg/liter (max)	1	1
Free water, ppm (max)	30	30

Turbo Fuel 5 — A high flash point military fuel used aboard naval aircraft carriers. The military designation is JP-5.

*These specifications require special additives that normal commercial fuels may not contain. If required to meet this specification, the correct additives must be blended into the fuel.

Most gas turbine engines can use Jet-A, Jet-A1, and Jet-B commercial fuels interchangeably. Military fuels JP-4, JP-5, and JP-8 are generally suitable alternate fuels. Aviation grades 80-145 octane reciprocating engine fuels are often emergency alternate fuels for turbine engines.

Check the aircraft operator's manual or the type certificate data sheet file for the approved fuel and fuel additives when servicing a turbine engine.

When comparing the BTU value of fuels such as Jet-A and aviation gasoline, it is interesting to note that Jet-A has more BTUs per gallon, but aviation gasoline has more BTUs per pound.

	lb/gal	BTU/lb	BTU/gal
Jet-A	6.74	18,600	125,364
Av Gas	5.87	18,900	110,943

ALTERNATE FUELS, NONPETROLEUM

Nonpetroleum jet fuels under development are classed as renewable and nonrenewable fuels.

- Renewable biomass products, sometimes referred to as Biojet fuel, are manufactured from a base such as corn, soybean, algae, or similar natural products.
- Nonrenewable fuels are classed as synthetic kerosene and are produced from coal.
- A 50/50 blend of renewable (biomass) and nonrenewable (coal) materials is approved under Mil Spec 8133 as a U.S Air Force, JP-8 aircraft fuel.

FUEL HANDLING AND SAFETY

Jet fuels require the normal handling precautions observed for any flammable or explosive liquid. It is especially important that the grounding jack is in place before the refueling nozzle contacts the filler opening during refueling to avoid static sparks. [Figure 7-1]

Jet fuel in tanks is often more dangerous than gasoline. Gasoline usually maintains a vapor-to-air mixture so rich that ignition is less likely; fuel is often at its best mixture to ignite.

Personnel handling aviation fuels should observe a number of practical and precautionary measures that reduce undesirable contact with fuel products, including:

- Avoid all unnecessary contact and use protective equipment to prevent contact.
- Remove promptly any fuel product that gets on the skin.
- Do not use fuels or similar solvents to remove oil or grease from the skin.
- Never wear fuel-soaked clothing. Remove immediately and clean before re-use.

- Avoid breathing fuel vapors. Maintain well-ventilated work areas.
- Clean up spilled products immediately. Keep spills out of sewers, streams, and waterways.
- Be familiar with proper first-aid techniques for handling unexpected/gross contacts and contact proper medical authorities immediately for assistance.

FUEL ADDITIVES

Some of the more common fuel additives are the anti-icing and anti-microbiocidal agents. Anti-icing additives keep entrained water from freezing without the use of fuel heat, except at very low temperatures. The manufacturer's manual states the temperature at which fuel heat must be applied. Microbiocidal agents kill microbes, fungi, and bacteria that form a slime, and in some cases, a matted waste in fuel systems.

The fuel distribution company often premixes the additives in the fuel. If the fuel and additives are not premixed, the service person must add the agents when fueling the aircraft. A popular brand of hand-servicing anti-icing and anti-biocidal mixture is PRIST®. This mixture can reduce the freezing temperature of the fuel by 25°F. However, you must determine the type and amount to add to maintain the airworthiness of the fuel system in the existing climatic conditions. Most manufacturers of these products recommend their use year round. [Figure 7-1]

WATER DETECTION IN TURBINE FUEL

All aviation fuels contain some dissolved water and free water. Dissolved water, like atmospheric humidity, cannot be seen. It is not a problem as long as it remains dissolved. Free water, also called entrained water, is visible as tiny droplets. Large quantities of free water (over 30 parts per million) can cause engine performance loss or even flame out.

One of the principal concerns during aircraft fueling is to deliver fuel that is free of entrained water. It is desirable to test the fuel as it enters the aircraft to ensure that the clean-up system has removed any entrained water.

HYDROKIT® is a quick, go/no-go test that detects the presence of minute quantities of undissolved water in turbine fuel. The HYDROKIT indicator powder, packaged in a ten milliliter evacuated test tube, changes to a distinct pink/red color in the presence of 30 parts per million or more of undissolved water in fuel.

THRUST SPECIFIC FUEL CONSUMPTION

Thrust Specific Fuel Consumption (TSFC) is the ratio of fuel consumption to engine thrust, specifically, the amount of fuel in pounds that an engine must consume to produce one pound of thrust during one hour of operation. This ratio is usually included in any set of engine specifications and affords a means of comparing the fuel consumption or economy of operation of one engine to another, regardless of thrust rating. The formula for computing TSFC is:

$$TSFC = \frac{\text{Total weight of fuel consumed (Wf)}}{\text{Pounds of thrust (net or gross)}}$$

EXAMPLE: An engine with a TSFC of .49 lb/hr/lbt has a thrust rating of 3,500 pounds. How many pounds of fuel will it consume per hour?

$$TSFC = \frac{(Wf)}{Fn \text{ or } Fg}$$

$$0.49 = \frac{(Wf)}{3,500}$$

$$Wf = 0.49 \times 3,500$$

$$Wf = 1,715 \text{ lbs/hr}$$

The comparison of an early model turbojet, the Westinghouse J-34, with a newer small turbofan, the Honeywell TFE-731, gives a good indication of how engine efficiency (fuel economy) has improved over the years.

Engine	Gross Thrust (in pounds)	TSFC lb/hr/lbt	Wf(pph) lb/hr
J-34	3,250	1.06	3,445
TFE-731	3,500	0.49	1,715

It is clear to see that the TFE-731 turbofan engine is more than twice as efficient as the J-34 turbojet engine in terms of fuel consumption.

TURBOFANS AND TSFC

One of the reasons the turbofan is more efficient than the turbojet has to do with the loss of kinetic energy in the hot exhaust.

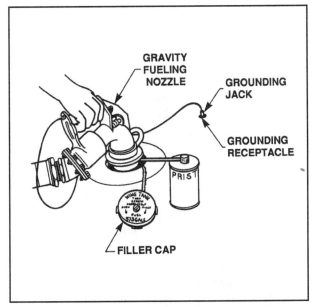

Figure 7-1. Servicing an aircraft with fuel and PRIST®

The TSFC of an engine is linked to its thermal efficiency, and thermal efficiency is a comparison of an engine's actual horsepower to the potential horsepower in the fuel. If the fuel has the potential to create 3,000 horsepower, but the engine only creates 1,000 horsepower, then the engine's horsepower is 1/3 of the potential, or 33 percent thermally efficient.

Many factors cause an engine to run at less than 100 percent efficiency, including the inefficiency of the component parts (compressor, combustor, etc.), friction losses from the rotating pieces, heat loss to the atmosphere through the exhaust and from the engine cases, and many other incidentals, such as aircraft speed and ambient conditions. One of the most significant losses is the heat in the exhaust air. Any air going out the exhaust at a higher temperature than it entered the engine represents wasted energy.

One significant factor that makes a turbofan engine more efficient than a turbojet engine is the fact that it wastes less heat energy. The turbojet engine moves its entire mass airflow through the engine combustor and turbines, and therefore adds heat energy to all of it. A turbofan engine may send 80 percent of its mass airflow out the fan duct and only 20 percent through the core and out the hot exhaust. The fan accelerates cold ambient air, so there is less wasted heat energy in the hot exhaust, which results in improved thermal efficiency. Additional turbine stages added to the engine to drive the fan extract additional heat energy that would otherwise flow out the exhaust as waste.

Because the cost of jet fuel is such a large business expense, everyone from the airlines to the corporate operators is calling for an improvement in turbine engine efficiency. Manufacturers are striving to attain an improvement of 15 to 20 percent in the next generation of engines. To generate these improvements, manufacturers are:

- Increasing fan bypass ratios.
- Improving the shape of fan and compressor blades by incorporating radical twists and curvature to make them move more air.
- Developing higher strength metals that will allow higher internal engine temperatures.
- Developing fans driven through a gearbox so the fan and turbine can achieve a more ideal r.p.m.
- Investigating variable pitch fans to improve fan efficiency.
- Refining electronic engine controls so they manage the flow of fuel more efficiently.

The following data shows the TSFC for a General Electric CF-6 high-bypass turbofan engine, used in the McDonnell Douglas MD-11, the Boeing 767 aircraft, and quite a few others. The data is for the engine operating static on the ground, under standard day conditions, at various thrust settings.

Thrust Setting	Gross Thrust (in pounds)	TSFC (lb/hr/lbt)	Fuel Flow (lbs/hr)
Takeoff (S.L.)	50,200	0.394	19,779
Max. Continuous	46,200	0.385	17,787
75% Takeoff	37,600	0.371	13,579
Flight Idle	5,190	0.450	2,320
Ground Idle	1,740	0.850	1,490

The following data shows the TSFC for a General Electric CF-6 high-bypass turbofan engine, operating in a McDonnell Douglas MD-11 at altitude, in both a climb configuration and at cruise (Mach 0.85).

Thrust Setting	Gross Thrust (in pounds)	TSFC (lb/hr/lbt)	Fuel Flow (lbs/hr)
Max. Climb	11,500	0.664	7,636
Max. Cruise	10,800	0.654	7,063

EXAMPLE 1: Using the ground performance specifications for the CF-6 engine, it is possible to verify the maximum continuous fuel consumption in pounds per hour, as follows:

$$TSFC = \frac{(Wf)}{Fg}$$

$$0.385 = \frac{(Wf)}{46,200}$$

$$Wf = 0.385 \times 46,200$$

$$Wf = 17,787 \text{ lbs/hr}$$

EXAMPLE 2: Using the altitude performance specifications shown for the CF-6 engine, it is possible to verify the maximum cruise fuel consumption in pounds per hour, as follows:

$$TSFC = \frac{(Wf)}{Fn}$$

$$0.654 = \frac{(Wf)}{10,800}$$

$$Wf = 0.654 \times 10,800$$

$$Wf = 7,063 \text{ lbs/hr}$$

Even though the TSFC for the CF-6 engine is not as good in cruise flight as it is static on the ground (0.654 versus 0.385), the engine burns significantly less fuel (7,063 lbs/hr versus 17,787 lbs/hr) because it produces so much less thrust in cruise flight. So in terms of thrust produced versus fuel consumed, the turbofan engine does best operating static on the ground, at sea level, but the airplane (airframe and engines) is most efficient when operating at altitude in cruise flight. [Figure 7-2]

TSFC IN FLIGHT

From the takeoff roll through rotation and the climb to altitude, the turbine engine experiences a sequentially different set of operating conditions.

Fuel Systems

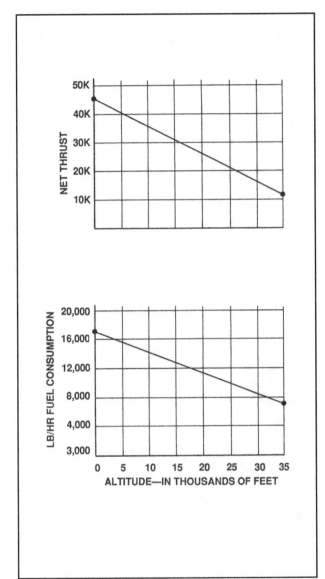

Figure 7-2. The effect of altitude on engine performance

1. When the airplane begins to accelerate, two things affect engine thrust. Acceleration forces more air into the engine, causing an increase in mass airflow and a subsequent tendency for thrust to increase. At the same time, the change in velocity experienced by the air (V_2-V_1) decreases, and thrust tries to decrease. The V_2-V_1 effect has the greatest influence, and net thrust decreases.

2. As the airplane continues to accelerate, rotates, and starts climbing to altitude, both the air ramming into the engine and the V_2-V_1 effect (described in Chapter 2) continue to influence the thrust being produced by the engine. At the same time, an increase in altitude causes the outside air temperature and the ambient pressure to drop.

The changes in temperature and pressure have the following effects:

- The drop in temperature with increasing altitude tries to make the air denser.

- The drop in atmospheric pressure tries to make the air less dense.

- The drop in atmospheric pressure has the greatest impact, and the density of the air ultimately decreases with altitude, decreasing engine thrust.

- As the density of the air decreases with altitude, the compressor must work harder to increase the pressure (p.s.i.) of the air.

The turbofan is essentially a multi-bladed fixed pitch propeller. Like the propeller on a piston engine airplane, the fan becomes less efficient with increased airspeed and altitude. Whereas at takeoff the fan might produce 80 percent of the total engine thrust, in cruise flight the percentage decreases and the core must make up the difference. Because the core is the source of so much wasted heat energy, this decreases the thermal efficiency of the engine in cruise flight.

Even though the engine is optimized for efficiency in cruise flight, its best TSFC occurs when operating static at sea level.

When considering a flight speed increase and an altitude increase, TSFC also increases when compared to a similar sea level throttle setting. When viewing Figure 7-3, consider the following points:

- Fuel flow (Wf) decreases to about 40 percent of its sea level value when the airplane reaches its cruise altitude and airspeed (Curve A).

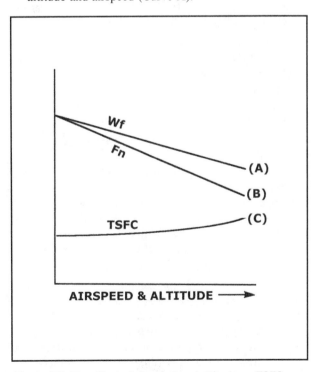

Figure 7-3. The effect of airspeed and altitude on TSFC

- Flight thrust (Fn) drops to about 20 percent of its sea level value when the airplane reaches its cruise altitude and airspeed (Curve B).
- TSFC increases because fuel flow remains higher than thrust when applied to the TSFC formula (Curve C).

A TSFC OBSERVATION

An interesting observation about TSFC can be made between large sized fan engines and small sized fan engines. The TFE-731 is a business jet engine, and it has a sea level TSFC of 0.51 lb/hr/lbt. The CF-6 is a commercial engine with a much higher bypass ratio, and its sea level TSFC is 0.38 lb/hr/lbt. It appears that the smaller engine is inferior in terms of fuel consumption per pound of thrust produced, but it actually has a TSFC advantage over the larger engine during climb to altitude. Both engines experience degradation in their TSFC, but the small engine will degrade to a lesser extent.

The larger engine is more efficient at sea level because it has a large diameter fan, but the fan loses some of its efficiency at altitude cruise, in the manner of a fixed pitch propeller. The favorable efficiency of the fan blades at sea level, where the air is more dense, is diminished at altitude, so the core portion of the engine has to make up for it with an increase in fuel flow. In this way, TSFC increases more on a high-bypass ratio engine going to altitude than it does on a smaller engine with a lower bypass ratio, as follows:

- CF-6, TSFC increases from 0.380 at sea level maximum continuous to 0.654 at altitude maximum cruise. Change in TSFC = 72 percent increase.
- TFE-731, TSFC increases from 0.51 at sea level maximum continuous to 0.80 at altitude maximum cruise. Change in TSFC = 56 percent increase.

The high-bypass fan engine is still more efficient at 0.654 TSFC than a low-bypass engine operating at 0.800 TSFC, but not by the same degree as seen by the sea level figures alone.

THRUST SPECIFIC FUEL CONSUMPTION VS. THRUST-HORSEPOWER SPECIFIC FUEL CONSUMPTION

Another interesting comparison can be made between engines designed for subsonic flight and engines designed for supersonic flight, comparing the amount of fuel they burn per thrust horsepower (THP), instead of fuel burned per pound of thrust. While fuel burned per pound of thrust is known as TSFC, fuel burned per horsepower is often referred to as just SFC, or SFC (Hp).

The Concorde SST, for example, had a cruise TSFC of 1.200. This looks rather high when compared to the MD-11 or B-767 engine, which have a cruise TSFC of 0.654, but the fuel consumed by the Concorde per thrust horsepower is lower. Instead of comparing thrust and fuel flow to form the ratio SFC(Fn) = Wf ÷ Fn, thrust horsepower can be compared with fuel flow to form the ratio SFC(THP) = Wf ÷ THP.

EXAMPLE: What would the SFC be for the engine in the MD-11 while operating in cruise if the thrust is 10,800 pounds, the fuel consumption is 7,063 pounds per hour, and the speed is 600 m.p.h.?

The thrust horsepower would be 17,280, and the SFC(Hp) would be 0.41, as shown by the calculations below.

$$THP = \frac{\text{Net Thrust} \times \text{Aircraft Speed}}{375}$$

$$THP = \frac{10,800 \times 600}{375}$$

THP = 17,280

SFC = Wf ÷ THP

SFC = 7,063 ÷ 17,280

SFC = 0.41

The Concorde engine at cruise produces 10,500 pounds of thrust and consumes 12,600 pounds of fuel per hour. If the airplane is flying at 1,250 m.p.h., what is the SFC(Hp)?

The thrust horsepower would be 35,000, and the SFC(Hp) would be 0.36, as shown by the calculation below.

The cruise TSFC for the Concorde engine (1.2), when compared to the cruise TSFC of the MD-11 engine (0.654), is considerably worse.

NOTE: Notice the improvement in fuel consumption for the Concorde, 0.36 vs. 0.41 for the MD-11, when the comparison is based on thrust horsepower in flight.

$$THP = \frac{\text{Net Thrust} \times \text{Aircraft Speed}}{375}$$

$$THP = \frac{10,500 \times 1,250}{375}$$

THP = 35,000

SFC = Wf ÷ THP

SFC = 12,600 ÷ 35,000

SFC = 0.36

BEST TSFC VS. BEST SFC(HP)

As noted earlier, the best TSFC for an engine occurs at a high power setting under static sea level conditions. However, the best SFC(Hp) for a turbine engine occurs at an ideal cruise altitude and airspeed.

Even though the turbofan engine will not create as much thrust for each pound of fuel burned at cruise altitude and airspeed, the amount of thrust it does create will propel the airplane to a much greater true airspeed. Because the formula for thrust horsepower includes the speed of the airplane, higher airspeeds at higher altitudes means each pound of thrust equals a higher thrust horsepower.

For example, consider the following two options for a large, twin-engine transport airplane. The first option is to take off and climb to an altitude of 1,000 feet and cruise at a relative ground speed of 400 m.p.h. With this option, the two engines would need a combined thrust of 90,000 pounds, and the engine TSFC would be 0.512. The second option is to take off and climb to an altitude of 35,000 feet and cruise at a relative ground speed of 550 m.p.h. With this option, the two engines would need a combined thrust of 22,000 pounds, and the engine TSFC would be 0.654.

The following table compares the relative values of these two options.

	Option 1:	Option 2:
Airspeed	400 m.p.h.	550 m.p.h.
Thrust	90,000 pounds total	22,000 pounds total
TSFC	0.512	0.654
Fuel Consumption	46,080 lb/hr	14,388 lb/hr
Thrust Horsepower	96,000 total	32, 267 total
SFC(Hp)	0.480	0.446

Even though the TSFC in the first option is 21.7 percent better, the SFC(Hp) is 7 percent better in the second option. In addition, the fuel consumed per hour is 31,692 pounds less in the second option, and the distance traveled per hour is 150 miles farther. It is impossible not to conclude that an airplane should fly at the designed cruise airspeed and altitude where the entire package (airframe and engines) is most efficient.

NOTE: Specific airplane data of this sort is unavailable because of its proprietary nature. These numbers are hypothetical.

FUEL CONTROLLING SYSTEMS

The fuel control is an engine-driven accessory that operates by various combinations of mechanical, hydraulic, electrical, or pneumatic forces. The purpose of the fuel control is to maintain a correct combustion zone primary air-to-fuel mixture ratio of 15:1 by weight. Sometimes this is expressed as a fuel-air ratio of 0.067:1. All fuels require a certain proportion of air for complete burning, but the fuel will burn but not completely at rich or lean mixtures. The ideal proportion for air and jet fuels is 15:1, and it is called the stoichiometric (chemically correct) mixture.

Quite often, the air-fuel ratio is expressed as 60:1, which refers to the total airflow rather than the primary combustor airflow. If primary airflow is approximately 25 percent of total airflow, then 15:1 is 25 percent of 60:1. A gas turbine engine will experience a rich to lean mixture of about 10:1 during acceleration and 22:1 during deceleration. If the engine is using 25 percent of its total airflow in the combustion zone, the mixture, when expressed in terms of total airflow, will be 48:1 on acceleration and 80:1 on deceleration.

When the pilot moves the cockpit power lever forward, fuel flow increases, which creates increased gas expansion in the combustor and raises the level of power in the engine. For the turbojet and turbofan engines, that means a thrust increase. For turboprop and turboshaft engines, it means an increase in power to the output drive shaft. This could mean a speed increase at a given propeller load or a stabilized speed at an increasing blade angle and load.

Figure 7-4A shows the air-fuel mixture range of a typical gas turbine engine. Air-fuel represents the mixture range being plotted and percent N_2 speed, the speed range of the engine being plotted, as the fuel control sees it at its governor flyweight drive shaft. Note that % N_2 is actually the speed of the high-pressure compressor, and this compressor drives the accessory gearbox that drives the fuel control, therefore the fuel control recognizes percent N_2 speed as speed of the engine.

Note that at idle the mixture on the steady state (S.S.) line contains a little more than 20 parts of air to 1 part of fuel and that 15 parts of air to 1 part of fuel occurs in the 90 to 100 percent N_2 range.

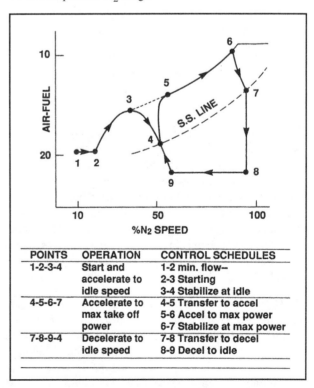

Figure 7-4A. Air-fuel operational diagram

As an engine ages, the air-fuel ratio of 15:1 changes because compression tends to deteriorate with increasing engine service time, but the engine must maintain its rated compressor pressure ratio (Cr) to remain efficient and stall free. When Cr starts to decrease due to engine aging, contamination, or damage, more power lever, fuel flow, and compressor speed will be required to bring Cr back to normal, which results in a richer mixture for a given Cr. Later, maintenance personnel may have to clean, repair, or replace the compressor or turbine as the engine nears its internal temperature limits. All engines are temperature limited, and how these limits come into play will be discussed later.

FUEL CONTROL SIGNALS

Many signals are sent to the fuel control for the automatic control of the air-fuel ratio. How many signals come into play will depend on the engine, and whether electronics are involved. Newer engines with electronic engine controls (EEC) sense many more engine and aircraft parameters than a hydro-mechanical unit on an older aircraft. Some of the more common signals sent to a hydro-mechanical fuel control are:

Engine speed signal (Nc) — A direct drive to the engine accessory gearbox sends this signal to the fuel control through a flyweight governor in the control for both steady state and acceleration/deceleration fuel scheduling. (Acceleration of many gas turbine engines is in the range of 5 to 10 seconds from idle to full power.).

Inlet pressure (Pt_2) — A total pressure signal transmitted to a fuel control bellows from a probe in the engine inlet gives the control a sense of aircraft speed and altitude as ram conditions in the inlet change.

Compressor discharge pressure (Ps_4) — A static air pressure signal sent to a bellows within the control to give the fuel control an indication of mass airflow at that point in the engine.

Burner can pressure (Pb) — A static pressure signal sent to the fuel control from within the combustion liner. There is a linear relationship between burner pressure and weight of airflow at this point in the engine. If burner pressure increases 10 percent, the mass airflow has increased by 10 percent and the burner bellows will schedule 10 percent more fuel to maintain the correct air-fuel ratio. The quick response this signal gives makes it valuable in preventing stalls, flameouts, and over-temperature conditions.

Inlet temperature (Tt_2) — A total temperature signal sent from the engine inlet to a temperature sensor connected by a capillary tube to the fuel control. It is filled with a heat sensitive fluid or gas that expands and contracts as a function of inlet temperature. This signal provides the fuel control mechanisms with a baseline airflow density value for establishing the fuel schedule.

SIMPLIFIED FUEL CONTROL SCHEMATIC (HYDRO-MECHANICAL UNIT)

Figure 7-4B is a simplified schematic of a gas turbine fuel control, which uses two sections to meter fuel.

FUEL METERING SECTION

Moving the shut-off lever (1) during the engine start cycle allows fuel to flow out to the engine. [Figure 7-4B] A manual shut-off lever (1) is necessary because the minimum flow stop (2) prevents the main metering valve (3) from closing completely. This design is necessary in case the speeder spring breaks or if the idle stop is improperly adjusted. The full rearward position of the power lever is the idle position against the idle stop. This prevents the power lever from becoming a shut-off lever. The shut-off lever in this illustration also ensures the correct working pressure buildup within the control during the starting cycle. This prevents roughly metered fuel from entering the engine before its correct time.

Fuel from the supply system is pumped through the main fuel pump (4) to the main metering valve (3). As fuel flows through the orifice created by the taper of the valve, pressure drops. Fuel from the metering valve to the fuel nozzles is referred to as metered fuel. In this instance, fuel is metered by weight rather than volume, because BTU per pound is constant regardless of fuel temperature, while BTU per unit volume is not. Fuel now flows in a correctly metered condition to the combustor.

Metering fuel by weight is mathematically expressed as:

$$Wf = KA\sqrt{\Delta P}$$

Where:

Wf = weight of fuel flow in lbs/hr
K = constant for a particular fuel control
A = area of orifice of main metering valve
ΔP = pressure drop across the orifice

If engines only operated in one set of conditions, only one fuel metering orifice size would be necessary, and there would be no variables in this formula because the pressure drop would always be the same value; but aircraft engines change power settings when the pilot moves the power lever. When the power lever is advanced, the orifice area at (3) subsequently increases. This action creates a mathematical variable. If it were not for the presence of the differential pressure regulating valve (5), the pressure differential across the metering orifice would create a second variable. This arrangement is referred to as a linear relationship between orifice size and weight of fuel flow. With only one variable, orifice size, such a relationship exists. That is, if the opening changes, the weight of fuel flow changes proportionally.

Fuel Systems

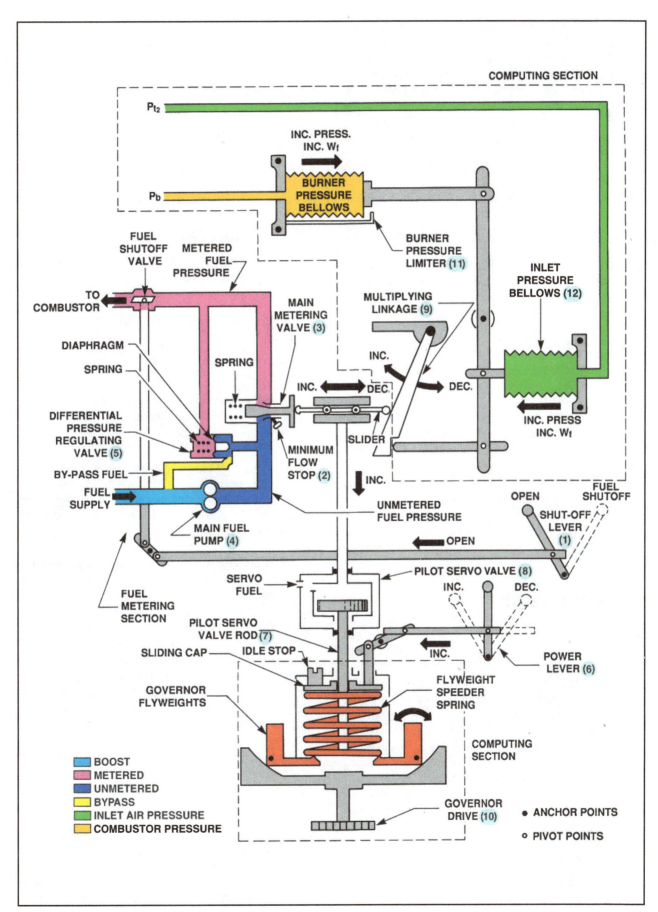

Figure 7-4B. Simplified diagram of hydro-mechanical fuel control

A constantly changing fuel bypass maintains the pressure differential at a constant value regardless of orifice size. By directing metered fuel to the spring side of the hydraulically operated differential pressure regulator diaphragm, the pressure differential will always return to the value of the spring force. Because this spring force is a constant value, the pressure differential across the orifice ($\triangle P$) will also become a constant.

The fuel pump always delivers more fuel than the fuel control needs, and the differential pressure regulator valve continually returns excess fuel back to the pump inlet.

EXAMPLE: The un-metered fuel pressure is 500 pounds per square inch-gauge (p.s.i.g.); metered fuel pressure is 420 p.s.i.g., and spring force is 80 pounds per square inch. At this point, there is 500 p.s.i.g. on both sides of the differential pressure regulator diaphragm. The bypass valve will be in a state of equilibrium and will be bypassing fuel that is surplus to engine needs.

If the pilot moves the power lever forward, the orifice size at the metering valve increases, and the metered pressure downstream also increases. For this example, assume the metered pressure increases to 440 p.s.i.g. This action will create a total pressure of 520 p.s.i.g. on the spring side of the regulator diaphragm, pushing the bypass valve toward closed. The reduced amount of fuel bypass will cause un-metered pressure to rise until 80 p.s.i.g. is re-established for the new orifice size. This happens because increased revolutions per minute cause the positive displacement fuel pump to produce more fuel flow. The $\triangle P$ will always come to the setting of the differential pressure regulator valve spring as equilibrium occurs.

COMPUTING SECTION

Referring again to Figure 7-4B, movement of the power lever (6) during engine operation causes the spring cap to slide down the pilot servo valve rod (7) and compress the flyweight speeder spring. The spring base depresses the flyweights, causing an under-speed condition. The pilot servo valve (8) prevents sudden movement as its fluid is displaced bottom to top. The multiplying linkage (9) remains stationary, and the slider moves down the inclined plane and to the left, forcing the main metering valve (3) to the left against its spring force, increasing fuel flow to the engine. With increased fuel flow, the engine speeds up and drives the governor shaft (10) faster. The new flyweight force comes to equilibrium with the speeder spring force as the flyweights return to an upright position. They are now in position to act at the next speed change.

The flyweights always return to the upright position so they can be ready for use at the next load change as follows:

- Over-speed condition

  1. Load on the engine decreases and the engine tends to speed up.

  2. The flyweights fly out, closing off some of the fuel.

  3. The engine returns to an on-speed condition. As the flyweights come upright, flyweight force comes into equilibrium with the speeder spring force.

- Under-speed condition

  1. Load on the engine increases, and the engine tends to slow down.

  2. The flyweights move in at the top, adding fuel.

  3. The engine returns to an on-speed condition as the flyweights move outward to the upright position into equilibrium with the speeder spring force.

- Power lever movement (forward)

  1. The speeder spring is compressed and the flyweights move in at the top in a false under-speed condition.

  2. Fuel is increased and the flyweights start to fly out again to come into equilibrium with the new speeder spring force.

NOTE: The flyweights will not return completely to their former position unless the power lever is adjusted because the speeder spring now has a greater force value. This is called droop—the slight loss of speed due to governing system mechanisms.

On many engines, static pressure in the cumbustor (burner) is a useful measure of mass airflow. The air-fuel ratio can be controlled more carefully for a known mass airflow. As burner pressure (Pb) increases, the burner pressure bellows expands to the right. The burner pressure limiter (11) restricts excessive movement. If (7) remains stationary, the multiplying linkage forces the slider to the left, opening the metering valve to match fuel flow to the increased mass airflow. This condition could occur in an aircraft nose-down condition, which would increase airspeed, inlet ram air, and engine mass airflow.

An increase in inlet pressure would also cause the inlet pressure bellows (12) to expand, forcing the multiplying linkage to the left, and the metering valve to open wider.

When the engine is shut down, the flyweight speeder spring expands in both directions, moving the sliding cap up against the idle stop and pushing the main metering valve off the minimum flow stop. When the engine is started the next time and goes to idle speed, the governor flyweights keep the sliding cap on the idle stop and move the main metering valve toward the minimum flow stop.

Fuel Systems

HYDRO-PNEUMATIC FUEL CONTROL SYSTEM, PT6 TURBOPROP (BENDIX FUEL CONTROL)

The basic fuel system, as depicted in Figure 7-5, consists of a single, engine-driven pump; a fuel control unit; a starting control; and a dual fuel manifold with 14 simplex (single orifice) fuel nozzles. Two drain valves on the gas generator case ensure drainage from the fuel manifold after engine shutdown.

FUEL PUMP

The fuel pump (1) is a positive displacement gear pump driven off the accessory gearbox. Fuel from a booster pump enters the fuel pump through a 74-micron (200-mesh) inlet screen (2) and then flows into the pump gear chamber. From there, the fuel moves at high pressure to the fuel control unit through a 10-micron pump outlet filter (3). The inlet screen is spring-loaded, and if it becomes blocked, an increase in fuel pressure differential will overcome the spring, lift the screen from its seat, and allow unfiltered fuel to flow into the system. A bypass valve (4) and cored passages in the pump casing enable unfiltered high-pressure fuel to flow from the pump gears to the fuel control unit when the outlet filter is blocked. An internal passage (5), originating at the fuel control unit, returns bypass fuel from the fuel control unit to the pump inlet downstream of the inlet screen.

FUEL CONTROL SYSTEM

The fuel control system consists of three separate units with interdependent functions:

- The fuel control unit (FCU) (6) determines the proper fuel schedule for engine steady-state operation and acceleration.
- The starting flow control (7) acts as a flow divider, directing fuel control unit metered fuel output to the primary fuel manifold or to both primary and secondary manifolds as required.
- A governor package that contains a typical propeller governor section (not shown) and an N_2 power turbine governor (8) provides full propeller control during forward and reverse thrust operation.
- The N_2 governor section provides power turbine overspeed protection during normal operation.

The propeller governor is inoperative during reverse thrust operation, and the N_2 governor section controls power turbine speed.

FUEL CONTROL UNIT

The fuel control unit (FCU) is mounted on the engine-driven fuel pump and is driven at a speed proportional to compressor turbine speed (N_1). The FCU determines the fuel schedule necessary for the engine to provide the required engine output and for controlling the speed of the compressor turbine (N_1). Engine power output is directly dependent on compressor turbine speed. The FCU governs N_1, thereby governing the power output of the engine. Regulating the amount of fuel supplied to the combustion section of the engine controls N_1.

Fuel Metering Section

The FCU is supplied with fuel at pump pressure (P_1). A main metering valve (9) and a differential bypass valve (10) establish fuel flow. Unmetered fuel at P_1 pressure is applied to the entrance of the metering valve. The fuel pressure immediately after the metering valve is metered fuel pressure (P_2). The differential bypass valve maintains an essentially constant fuel pressure differential (P_1–P_2) across the metering valve. The orifice area of the metering valve changes to meet specific engine requirements. Fuel pump output in excess of these requirements returns to the pump inlet downstream of the inlet filter (5) via internal passages in the fuel control unit and fuel pump. This returned fuel is referred to as P_0. The differential bypass valve consists of a sliding valve in a ported sleeve, actuated by a diaphragm and spring. In operation, the P_1–P_2 differential working on the diaphragm balances the spring force. The bypass valve will always be in a position to maintain the P_1–P_2 differential and to bypass fuel in excess of engine requirements.

A relief valve (11) is incorporated parallel to the bypass valve to prevent an excessive P_1 buildup in the FCU. The valve is spring-loaded closed and remains closed unless the inlet fuel pressure (P_1) overcomes the spring force and opens the valve. As soon as the inlet pressure diminishes, the valve closes.

The metering valve (9) consists of a contoured needle working in a sleeve. The metering valve regulates the flow of fuel by changing the orifice area. Fuel flow is a function of metering valve position only, because the differential bypass valve maintains an essentially constant differential fuel pressure across the orifice regardless of variations in inlet or discharge fuel pressures.

The bimetallic disks under the differential bypass valve spring compensate for variations in specific gravity resulting from changes in fuel temperature.

Pneumatic Computing Section

The power lever (12) incorporates a speed-scheduling cam that depresses an internal rod when the power is increased. [Figure 7-5] The governor lever pivots against an orifice to form the governor valve (13). The enrichment lever (14) pivots at the same point as the governor lever and has two extensions that straddle a portion of the governor lever so that after a slight movement, a gap will close and then both levers must move together. The enrichment lever actuates a fluted pin that operates against the enrichment "hat" valve. Another smaller spring connects the enrichment lever to the governor lever.

The speed-scheduling cam applies tension to the governor spring (15) through the intermediate lever, which applies a force to close the governor valve. The enrich-

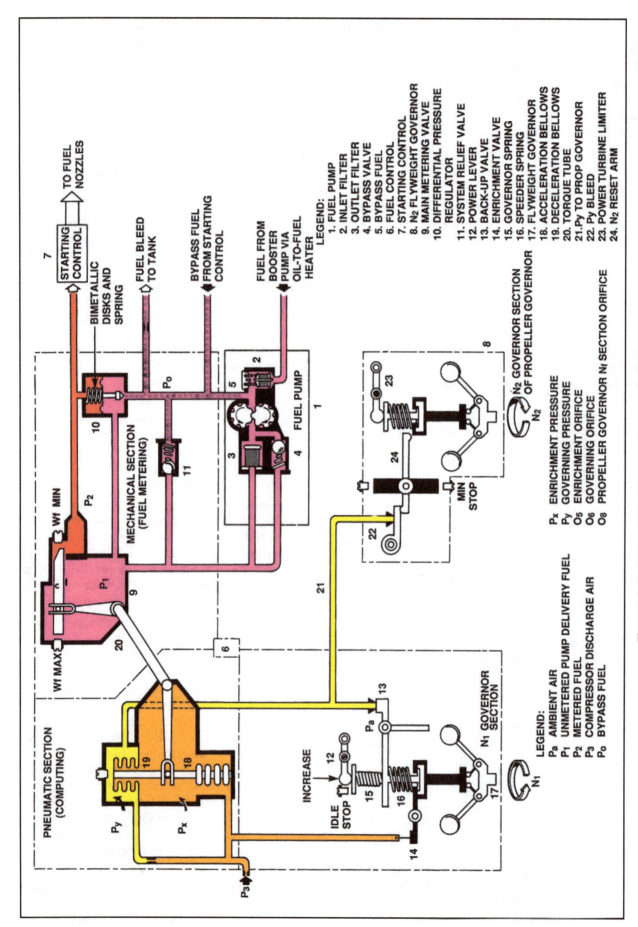

Figure 7-5. Hydropneumatic fuel controlling system (PT6 turboprop)

ment spring (16), between the enrichment and governor levers, provides a force to open the enrichment valve.

As the drive shaft rotates, it in turn rotates a table (17) on which the governor flyweights are mounted. Small levers on the inside of the flyweights contact the governor spool. As N_1 increases, centrifugal loading causes the flyweights to apply increasing force against the spool. This tends to move the spool outward on the shaft against the enrichment lever. As governor flyweight force overcomes opposing spring force, the governor valve opens and the enrichment valve closes.

The enrichment valve begins to close whenever N_1 increases enough to cause the flyweight force to overcome the smaller spring. If N_1 continues to increase, the enrichment lever continues to move until it contacts the governor lever, at which time the enrichment valve closes fully. The governor valve opens if N_1 increases sufficiently to cause the weight force to overcome the force of the larger spring. At this point, the enrichment valve closes as speed increases to keep working air pressure constant.

Bellows Assembly

The bellows assembly [Figures 7-5 and 7-6] consists of an evacuated (acceleration) bellows (18) and a governor bellows (19) connected by a common rod. The acceleration bellows provides an absolute pressure reference. The governor bellows is secured in the body cavity, and its function is similar to that of a diaphragm. The cross shaft and associated levers (20) move within a torque tube attached near the bellows lever to transmit bellows movement to the metering valve (9). An adjustment bushing secures the tube in the body casting at the opposite end, so any rotational movement of the cross shaft increases or decreases the force of the torque tube. The torque tube forms the seal between the air and fuel sections of the control. The torque tube is positioned during assembly to provide a force in a direction tending to close the metering valve. The bellows acts against this force to open the metering valve. Py pressure is applied to the outside of the governor bellows; Px pressure is applied to the inside of the governor bellows and to the outside of the acceleration bellows.

For purposes of illustration, the governor bellows is shown as a diaphragm in Figure 7-6. Py pressure is applied to one side of the diaphragm and Px is applied to the opposite side. Px is also applied to the evacuated acceleration bellows attached to the diaphragm. The force of Px applied against the evacuated bellows is cancelled by application of the same pressure on an equal area of the diaphragm as the forces act in opposite directions.

All pressure forces applied to the bellows section can be resolved into forces acting on the diaphragm only. These forces are Py pressure acting on the entire surface of the top side, the internal pressure of the evacuated bellows acting on a portion of the under side (within the area of pressure cancellation), and Px acting on the remainder of that side. Any change in Py will have more effect on the diaphragm than an equal change in Px, due to the difference in effective surface areas.

Px and Py vary with changing engine operating conditions. When both pressures increase simultaneously, such as during acceleration, downward bellows movement moves the metering valve (9) to the left in the opening direction. When Py dumps away at the governor valve as the desired N_1 approaches (for governing after acceleration), the bellows moves up to reduce the opening of the metering valve.

When both pressures decrease simultaneously, the bellows travels up to reduce the metering valve opening because the acceleration bellows is now acting as a spring. This occurs during deceleration as Py dumps away at the governor valve and Px dumps away at the enrichment valve, moving the metering valve to its minimum flow stop.

Power Turbine (N_2) Governor

The N_2 governor section of the propeller governor senses Py pressure through an external pneumatic line (21) from the body of the flow control unit to the governor. In the event of a power turbine over-speed condition, flyweight action opens an air bleed orifice (22) in the N_2 governor section to bleed off Py pressure through the governor. When this occurs, Py pressure acting on the flow control unit bellows decreases to partially close the flow control unit metering valve and reduce fuel flow. Reduction in fuel flow decreases N_1 speed and consequently N_2 speed. The speed at which the air bleed orifice opens depends on the propeller governor control lever (23) setting and the N_2 reset arm (24) setting. Power turbine (N_2) speed, and hence propeller speed, is thus limited by the N_2 governor.

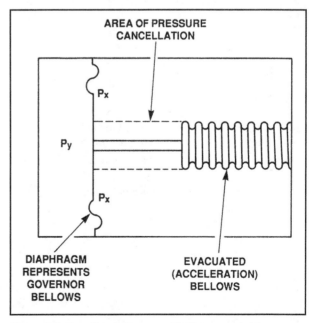

Figure 7-6. Functional diagram of bellows assembly

Starting Flow Control

The starting flow control [Figure 7-7] consists of a body assembly incorporating a ported plunger (25) sliding in a ported housing. Rotational movement of the input lever (26) is converted to linear movement of the plunger through a rack and pinion. Rigging slots are provided at the 45 degree and 72 degree RUN positions. One of these positions, depending on the installation, rigs the system to the cockpit lever.

A minimum pressure valve (27), located at the inlet to the starting flow control, maintains a minimum pressure in the flow control unit to ensure correct fuel metering. Two connections are provided to the dual manifolds, which are interconnected via the transfer valve (28). This valve permits the number 1 primary manifold to fill initially for light-up, and, as pressure increases in the control, the transfer valve opens, allowing fuel into the number 2 secondary manifold.

When the lever is in the CUT-OFF AND DUMP (zero degree) position [Figure 7-7A], the fuel supply to both manifolds is blocked. At the same time, drain ports align (via porting in the plunger) with the dump port, allowing the residual fuel in the manifolds to drain overboard. This prevents the fuel from boiling and forming carbon in the system due to heat absorption. Fuel entering the starting flow control during engine rundown is diverted through the bypass port to the fuel pump inlet.

When the lever is in the RUN position [Figure 7-7B], the outlet port to number 1 manifold is uncovered, and the bypass port is completely blocked off. As the engine accelerates, both the fuel flow and manifold pressure increase until the transfer valve opens, and the number 2 manifold fills. When the number 2 manifold is filled, the total flow is increased by that amount now being delivered through the number 2 system, and the engine further accelerates to idle. When the lever is moved beyond the RUN (45-degree or 72-degree) position towards the maximum stop (90 degrees), the starting flow control has no further effect on fuel metered to the engine.

STARTING AND OPERATION — FOR A TYPICAL INSTALLATION

The engine starting cycle begins with the power control lever in the cockpit placed in the IDLE position and the starting control lever in CUT-OFF. The ignition and starter are switched on and, when required N_1 is attained, the starting flow control lever is advanced to the RUN position. Successful ignition normally occurs in approximately ten seconds, and the engine accelerates to idle.

During the starting sequence, the fuel control unit metering valve is in a low flow position. As the engine accelerates, the compressor discharge pressure (P_3) increases. Px and Py increase simultaneously (Px = Py) during engine acceleration. The increase in pressure sensed by the bellows (18) causes the metering valve to open partially. [Figure 7-5] As N_1 approaches idle, the centrifugal effect of the flyweight begins to overcome the governor spring force and opens the governor backup valve (13). This creates a (Px - Py) differential that causes the metering valve to begin to close until the required-to-run idle fuel flow is obtained.

The governor flyweights sense any variation in engine speed from the selected (idle) speed and increases or decreases flyweight force. This change in flyweight force moves the governor valve, which changes the fuel flow to re-establish the proper speed.

Acceleration

As the power control lever (12) advances above idle, it increases the governor spring force. The governor spring then overcomes the flyweight force and moves the lever, closing the governor valve and opening the enrichment valve. Px and Py immediately increase and cause the metering valve to begin to open. Acceleration is then a function of increasing Px and Py.

When fuel flow increases, the compressor turbine N_1 accelerates. When N_1 reaches a predetermined point (approximately 70 to 75 percent), flyweight force overcomes the enrichment spring force and starts to close the enrichment valve. When the enrichment valve starts to close, Py and Px pressures increase, causing an increase in the movement rate of the governor bellows and metering valve, thus providing speed enrichment to the acceleration fuel schedule.

Meanwhile as N_1, and hence N_2, increase, the propeller governor increases the pitch of the propeller to control N_2 at the selected speed and to apply the increased power as additional thrust. Acceleration occurs when the centrifugal effect of the flyweights again overcomes the governor spring and opens the governor valve.

Governing

When the acceleration cycle is complete, the governor flyweights sense any variation in engine speed from the selected speed and increase or decrease flyweight force. This change in flyweight force either opens or closes the governor valve, which changes the fuel flow necessary to re-establish the proper speed.

Altitude Compensation

Altitude compensation is automatic with this fuel control system because the evacuated acceleration bellows assembly [Figure 7-5, #18] provides an absolute pressure reference. Compressor discharge pressure P_3 is a measurement of engine speed and air density. Px is proportional to compressor discharge pressure, so it will decrease with a decrease in air density. The acceleration bellows, also shown in Figure 7-6, senses this and reduces fuel flow.

Deceleration

Retarding the power control lever reduces the governor spring force, allowing the governor valve (13) to move in an opening direction. The resulting drop in Py moves the metering valve in a closing direction until it

Fuel Systems

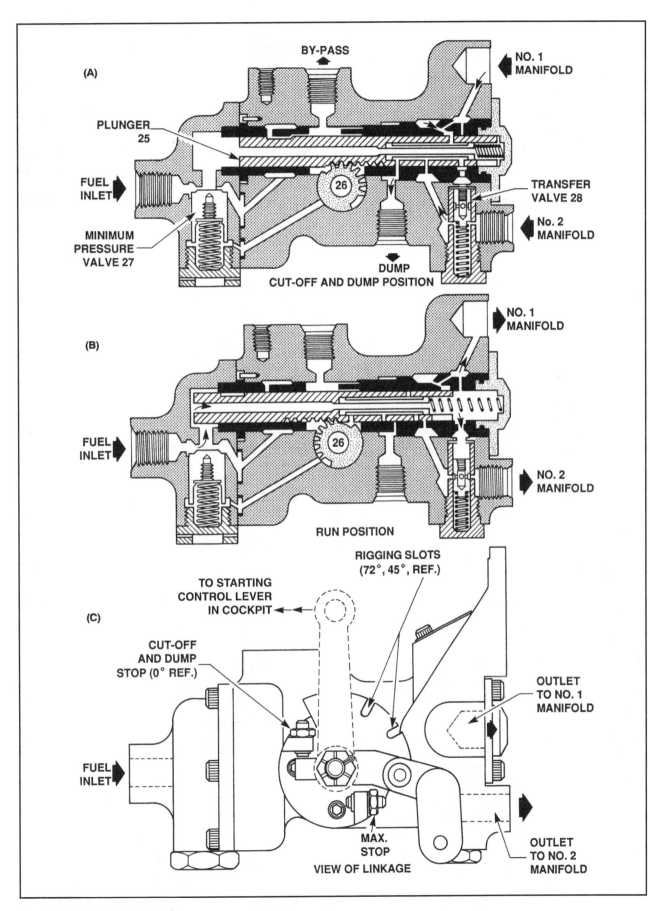

Figure 7-7. Starting control unit

contacts the minimum flow stop. This stop ensures sufficient fuel to the engine to prevent flameout. The engine will continue to decelerate until the governor flyweight force decreases to balance the governor spring force at the new governing position.

Power Turbine Limiting

The N_2 governor section of the propeller control senses Py pressure through a line from the fuel control. If a power turbine over-speed occurs, the N_2 air bleed orifice opens to bleed off Py pressure through the propeller governor. This decrease in Py moves the metering valve in the fuel control unit in a closing direction, reducing fuel flow, and consequently, gas generator speed.

Engine Shutdown

Placing the starting flow control lever in CUT-OFF position shuts down the engine. [Figure 7-7C] This action moves the manually-operated plunger to the CUT-OFF AND DUMP position, stopping all fuel flow to the engine and dumping the residual fuel contained in the dual manifold overboard.

BENDIX DP-L2® FUEL CONTROL (HYDRO-PNEUMATIC UNIT)

This hydro-pneumatic fuel control is installed on the JT15D turbofan. [Figure 7-8]

Fuel is delivered to the fuel control main metering valve at P_1 pump pressure. The main metering valve, in conjunction with the differential metering head regulator, establishes fuel flow. The fuel pressure immediately downstream of the differential metering valve is P_2 pressure. The fuel that bypasses as P_0 fuel maintains an essentially constant fuel pressure differential (P_1-P_2) across the metering valve, assuring that fuel flow is a function of orifice area only.

COMPONENTS/FUNCTIONS

There are several components in the DP-L2 fuel control and supporting system:

Fuel inlet — From fuel storage tank.

Filter — Coarse screen, self-relieving type.

Gear pump — Discharge referred to as P_1 fuel.

Filter — Fine mesh.

Relief valve — Prevents excessive P_1 fuel-pump discharge-pressure buildup and assists the differential metering head regulator during rapid deceleration.

Differential metering head regulator — Hydraulic mechanism that bypasses unwanted (P_0) fuel and establishes a constant fuel pressure differential (P_1-P_2) across the metering valve.

Fuel temperature bi-metallic disks — Automatically compensates for changes in specific gravity with fuel temperature changes. It can be manually adjusted for the differing specific gravity values of various jet fuels.

Metering valve — Meters P_2 fuel to the fuel nozzles; positioned by the torque tube connecting the bellows unit to the metering valve.

Minimum flow adjustment — Prevents metering valve from completely closing on deceleration.

Maximum flow stop adjustment — Sets maximum rotor speed for limit of engine.

Dual bellows units — Governor bellows receives Px and Py air pressure to position the torque tube and change fuel schedule and engine speed. Deceleration bellows expands to its stop when Py air pressure decreases to cause a reduction in engine speed.

Temperature sensor — Bi-metallic disks sensing engine inlet temperature T_2 to control Px air pressure to the bellows unit.

Enrichment valve — Receives Pc compressor air pressure and controls Px and Py pressure to the dual bellows unit. It closes down as speed increases to keep approximately the same working pressure.

High rotor governor — Flyweights throw outward under centrifugal loading of increased engine speed. This action modifies Py air pressure.

Power lever — Exerts a direct force to position the governor.

OPERATION OF CONTROL

When fuel is delivered to the engine-driven fuel pump by the aircraft fuel system, the following sequence of fuel flow occurs in conjunction with proper operation of the various system components within the engine fuel system:

1. The fuel pump supplies unmetered fuel P_1 to the fuel control.

2. P_2 pressure drops across the metering valve orifice. P_1 then becomes P_2 pressure, which flows out to the engine and influences the operation of the differential pressure-regulating valve, referred to as the differential metering head regulator.

3. The fuel that bypasses to the fuel pump is labeled P_0. Its pressure is maintained at a higher value than fuel pump inlet pressure via the P_0 line restrictor.

4. Compressor discharge air Pc operates the pneumatic section. When modified, this air becomes Px and Py air, which position the main metering valve.

5. When the power lever is advanced:

   a. The flyweights droop because the force on the speeder spring is greater than the flyweight force.

   b. The governor valve closes off the Py bleed.

   c. The enrichment valve moves toward closed, reducing Pc airflow. (Not as much air pressure is required when Py bleeds are closed.)

   d. Px and Py air pressures equalize on the surfaces of the governor.

Fuel Systems

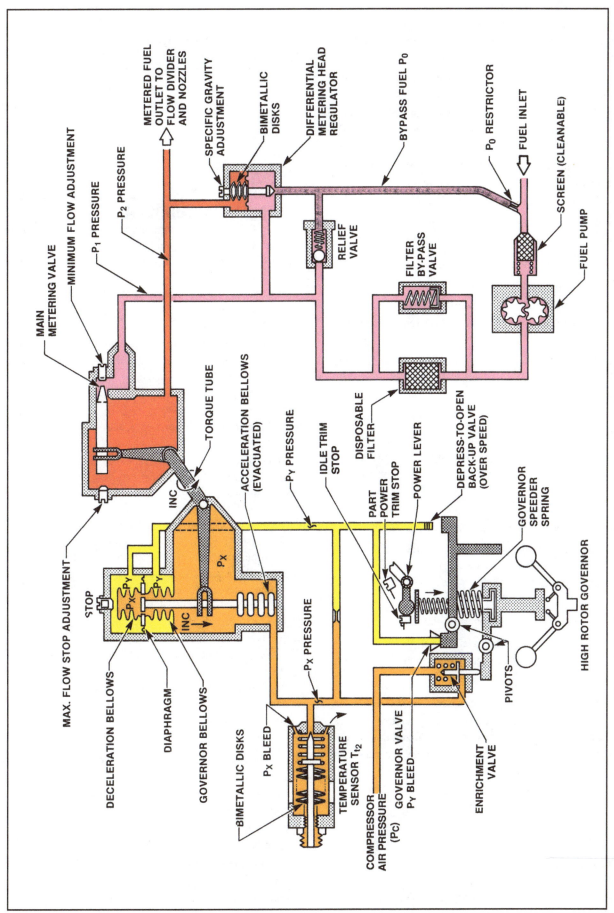

Figure 7-8. Bendix DP-L® hydro-pneumatic fuel control (Pratt & Whitney JT-15 turbofan engine)

e. Py air becomes the predominant force and the acceleration bellows and the governor bellows rod are both forced downward. The diaphragm allows this movement.

f. The torque tube rotates counterclockwise, and the main metering valve moves open.

g. The flyweights move outward as engine speed increases, and the governor valve opens to bleed Py air.

h. The enrichment valve reopens, and Px air increases over Py air value.

i. Reduced Py value allows the governor bellows and rod to move back up.

j. The torque tube rotates clockwise to decrease fuel flow and engine speed stabilizes.

6. When the power lever is retarded to the idle stop:

a. The flyweights move outward because speeder spring force is now less than flyweight force under high engine speed.

b. The governor valve opens, dumping Py air, and the backup valve is also depressed, dumping additional Py air.

c. The enrichment valve opens, allowing increased Px airflow.

d. Px air expands the governor and deceleration bellows to its stop, the governor rod also moves up, and the main metering valve moves toward closed.

e. Px air decreases with engine speed decrease, but the acceleration bellows holds the governor rod up.

f. As engine speed slows, the flyweights come back in, closing the Py bleed at the governor valve and the backup valve.

g. The enrichment valve also moves toward closed as Py air increases in relation to Px value.

h. The deceleration bellows moves downward, the metering valve moves slightly open, and engine speed stabilizes.

7. When ambient temperature goes up for any fixed power lever position, the Tt_2 sensor expands to reduce Px bleed to keep Px air pressure stabilized during low Pc pressure conditions. This maintains the acceleration bellows position and the acceleration schedule. The spool up time from idle to takeoff power is the same on hot days as on cold days.

ELECTRONIC FUEL SCHEDULING SYSTEMS

In the past, fuel electronic metering systems have not been as widely used as the hydro-mechanical or hydro-pneumatic controls. In recent years, however, the electronic engine control (EEC) has been incorporated into newer engines designed for both commercial and business size aircraft. The EEC is actually a basic hydro-mechanical control with the addition of an electronic sensor circuit. The electronic circuitry is powered by the aircraft bus or by its own dedicated alternator, and it analyzes engine operating parameters such as exhaust temperatures, gas path pressures, and engine r.p.m. As a result of these sensed parameters, the electronics portion of the system ensures delivery of the correct fuel flow.

EXAMPLE SYSTEM (ROLLS-ROYCE RB-211, HIGH-BYPASS TURBOFAN)

The RB-211 is a large, three-spool, front turbofan engine with a part-time (supervisory) EEC incorporated into its hydro-mechanical fuel scheduling. The electronic control amplifier protects the engine from over-temperature conditions when operating at takeoff power. In any other operating condition, the fuel control operates only on its hydro-mechanical system.

Figure 7-9 illustrates how the control amplifier receives signals from turbine gas temperature (TGT) and two compressor speed signals (N_1 and N_2).

This control operates on a hydro-mechanical schedule until near full engine power, then the electronic control amplifier circuit functions as a part-time fuel limiting device.

The differential pressure regulator in this installation is similar to the differential pressure regulating valve in the simplified hydro-mechanical fuel control diagram in Figure 7-4B, except that in this system fuel bypass occurs at the fuel pump outlet rather than within the fuel control. Near full power, at predetermined turbine gas temperature and compressor speed values, the pressure regulator reduces fuel flow to the spray nozzles by returning increased amounts of fuel to the fuel pump inlet. The fuel-flow regulator in this control acts as a hydro-mechanical control, receiving signals from the high-pressure compressor (N_3), gas path air pressure (P_1, P_2, P_3), and power lever position.

Figure 7-9 shows that the fuel control receives the following signals from the engine upon which the fuel schedule is established:

PLA — Power lever angle.

P_1 — Compressor inlet total pressure (fan).

P_3 — Second compressor discharge total pressure (intermediate-pressure compressor).

P_4 — Third compressor discharge total pressure (high-pressure compressor).

N_3 — Third compressor rotational speed (high-pressure compressor).

N_1 — First compressor rotation speed (fan).

N_2 — Second compressor rotation speed (intermediate-pressure compressor).

Fuel Systems

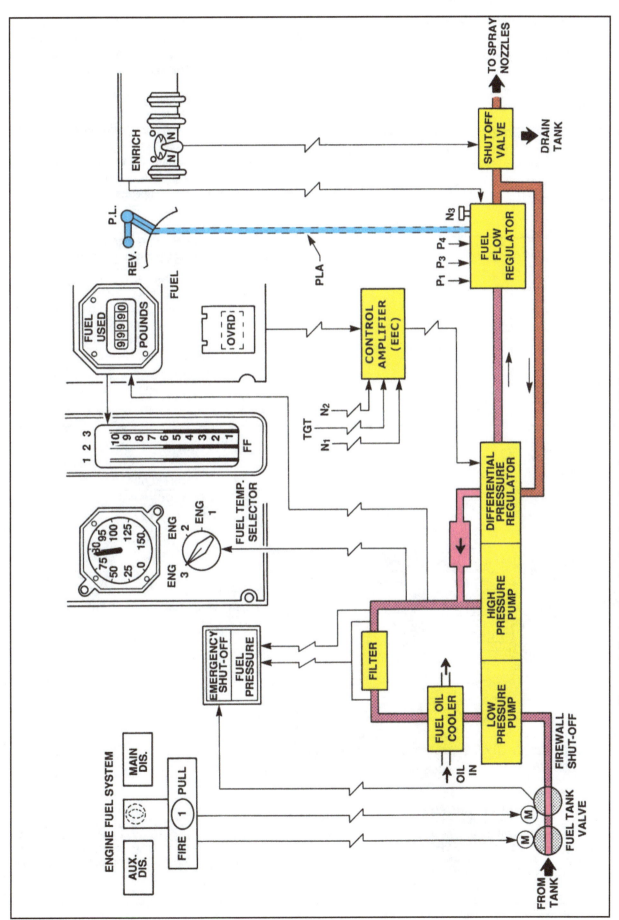

Figure 7-9. Fuel system showing electronic engine control (EEC) with supervisory schedule

TGT — Turbine gas temperature (low-pressure turbine outlet).

OVRD — Override command to block control amplifier functions.

Enrichment — Fuel enricher used to start engine below 0°F ambient.

EXAMPLE SYSTEM (HONEYWELL TFE-731)

The TFE-731 fuel system is representative of business jets fitted with a turbofan engine. It incorporates a full schedule EEC system. Figure 7-10 shows the following electronic computer inputs:

N_1 — Fan speed.

N_2 — Intermediate pressure compressor speed.

N_3 — High-pressure compressor speed.

T_{t2} — Inlet total temperature.

T_{t8} — High-pressure turbine inlet temperature.

P_{t2} — Inlet total pressure.

Input power — 28 volt DC.

PMG — Permanent magnet A.C. generator.

PLA — Power lever angle.

IGV — Inlet guide vane position.

P_{s6} — High-pressure discharge static pressure.

The electronic portion of the fuel control analyzes the input data and sends a command to position the inlet guide vanes and to schedule fuel flow at the hydro-mechanical portion of the fuel control unit.

Manufacturer's information states that this is a full-schedule (full-time) system that schedules fuel flow more accurately than a comparable hydro-mechanical unit. From engine start to takeoff thrust, the EEC protects the engine from over-temperature and over-speed conditions and provides stall-free rapid acceleration by continually monitoring turbine inlet temperature and several other important engine parameters.

EXAMPLE SYSTEM (G.E./SNECMA CFM56-7B, HIGH-BYPASS TURBOFAN)

The CFM56-7B operates through a system known as Full Authority Digital Engine Control (FADEC). It takes complete control of engine systems in response to command inputs from the aircraft and various engine systems. [Figure 7-11A] The FADEC also provides information to the aircraft for flight deck indications, engine condition monitoring, maintenance reporting, and troubleshooting. The FADEC system accomplishes the following functions:

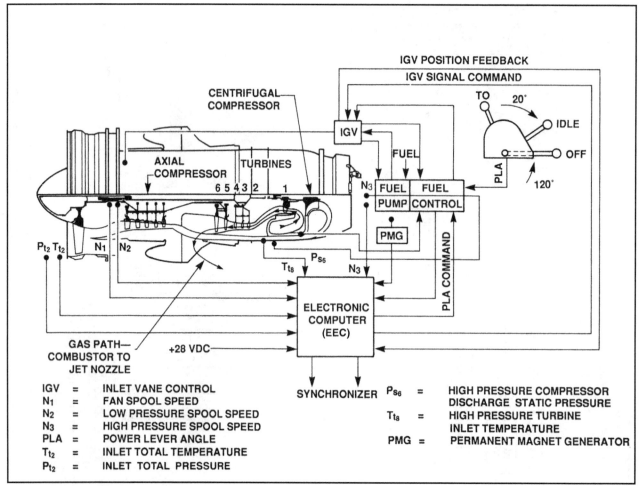

Figure 7-10. Honeywell-Garrett fuel system with EEC

Fuel Systems

- Performs fuel scheduling and limits N_1 and N_2 speed.
- Controls the engine parameters during the starting sequence and prevents the engine from exceeding starting EGT limits.
- Manages the thrust according to manual and auto-thrust modes.
- Provides optimal engine operation by controlling compressor airflow and turbine clearances.
- Controls the two thrust lever interlock solenoids located in the electronic throttle system.

Because the FADEC is a full authority system, the flight crew has few or no opportunities to interrupt its operation. For example, in the event of a loss of oil pressure, EGT over-limit, or various other critical faults, the FADEC shuts down the engine after sufficient warning.

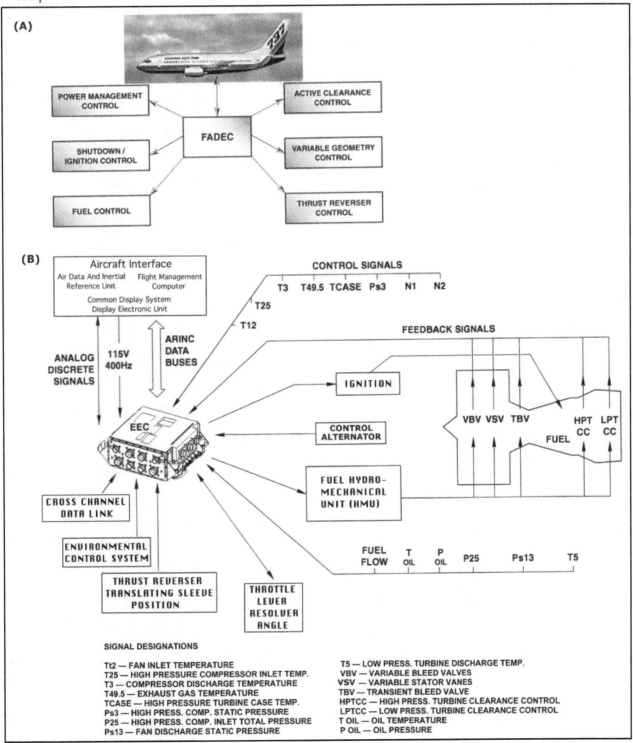

Figure 7-11A. Purpose of FADEC system
Figure 7-11B. Fuel system schematic, G.E./Snecma CFM56-7

The General Electric CFM56-7B material that follows uses these abbreviations:

ADIRU — Air data and inertial reference unit
ARINC-429 — Aeronautical Radio, Inc.; data bus standard for avionics
ASM — Auto throttle servo mechanisms
ATC — Auto throttle computer
BITE — Built-in-test-equipment
CCDL — Cross channel data link
CDS — Common display system
CDU — Control display unit
DEU — Display electronics unit
DFCS — Digital flight control system
EEC — Electronic engine control
EHSV — Electro-hydraulic servo valve
FADEC — Full authority digital engine control, or full authority digital electronic control
FMC — Flight management computer
HMU — Hydro-mechanical unit (fuel)
PDL — Portable data loader
TRA — Throttle resolver angle

FADEC COMPONENTS

The FADEC system consists of:

- An EEC containing two identical computers, designated channel A and channel B. The EEC electronically performs engine control calculations and monitors the engine condition.
- A hydro-mechanical unit (HMU), which converts electrical signals from the EEC into hydraulic pressures to drive the engine valves and actuators.
- Peripheral components such as valves, actuators, and sensors used for control and monitoring.

AIRPLANE/EEC INTERFACE

As shown in Figure 7-11B, the airplane provides engine thrust and control commands as well as airplane flight and status information to the EEC as follows:

- Thrust lever position is provided to the EEC by an electro-mechanical device called a throttle lever resolver. This device is mechanically linked to the thrust levers on the flight deck to measure the throttle lever angle.
- The airplane display electronic units (DEU) transmit air data information and engine-specific commands and data to each engine via an ARINC-429 serial databus.
- Selected airplane discrete command and data signals are hardwired to the EEC.
- Thrust reverser (T/R) position signals from each translating sleeve are wired to the EEC.
- The EEC uses bleed-discrete information and flight-configuration data (flight/ground and flap position) from the airplane for thrust setting compensation and for biasing the acceleration fuel topping schedule.

FADEC INTERFACES

The FADEC system is a built-in test equipment (BITE) system. This means it is able to detect internal and external faults. To perform all its tasks, the FADEC system communicates with the aircraft computers through the EEC.

The EEC receives operational commands from the common display system (CDS) display electronic unit (DEU), which is an interface between the EEC and aircraft systems. Both CDS-DEU 1 and 2 provide the following data from the two air data and inertial reference units (ADIRU) and the flight management computer (FMC):

- Air data parameters (altitude, total air temperature, total pressure, and Mach number) for thrust calculation.
- The position of the throttle resolver angle (TRA).

FADEC DESIGN

The FADEC system is fully redundant and built around the two-channel EEC. The valves and actuators are fitted with dual sensors to provide the EEC with feedback signals. All control inputs are dual, but some parameters used for monitoring and indicating are single.

To enhance system reliability, all inputs to one channel are made available to the other, through a cross channel data link (CCDL) that allows both channels to remain operational even if important inputs to one of them fail.

The two channels, A and B, are identical and permanently operational, but independent from each other. Both channels always receive inputs and process them, but only the channel in control, called the active channel, delivers output commands. The other is called the standby channel.

Active and standby channel selection is performed at EEC power-up and during operation. The BITE system detects and isolates failures to determine the health status of the channels and to transmit maintenance data to the aircraft. Active and standby selection is based upon the health of the channels and each channel determines its own health status. The healthiest is selected as the active channel.

When both channels have equal health status, active/standby channel selection alternates with every engine start, as soon as N_2 is greater than 10,990 r.p.m. If a channel is faulty and the active channel cannot ensure an engine control function, this function is moved to a failsafe position that protects the engine.

CLOSED-LOOP CONTROL OPERATION

To control the various engine systems, the EEC uses an operation known as closed-loop control. The EEC calculates a position for a system component, known as the command. The EEC then compares the command with the actual position of the component, known as the feedback, and calculates a position difference, which is known as the demand.

The EEC, through the electro-hydraulic servo valve (EHSV) of the hydro-mechanical unit (HMU), sends a signal to a component (valve, actuator) which causes it to move. The movement of the system valve or actuator provides feedback about the component's position to the EEC. The process is repeated until there is no longer a position difference.

INPUT PARAMETERS

All sensors are dual, except $T_{49.5}$ (exhaust gas temperature), T_5 (low-pressure turbine discharge temperature), Ps_{13} (fan outlet static air pressure), P_{25} (high-pressure compressor inlet total air temperature), and Wf (fuel flow). T_5, Ps_{13}, and P_{25} are optional sensors that are not installed in every system.

Each EEC channel receives a local value and a cross channel value through the cross channel data link to perform its calculations. Both values pass through a validation test program in each EEC channel. The EEC selects a value based on the assessed validity of each reading, or an average of both values.

In case of a dual sensor failure, the EEC selects a model value, computed from other available parameters such as the following:

- Fan speed (N_1).
- High-pressure compressor speed (N_2).
- Compressor discharge static air pressure (Ps_3).
- High-pressure compressor inlet air temperature (T_{25}).
- Position of the fuel metering valve (FMV).
- Position of the variable bleed valves (VBV).
- Position of the variable stator vanes (VSV).

For all other parameters, if the EEC cannot select a valid value, it uses failsafe values.

EEC LOCATION

The EEC is a dual-channel computer housed in an aluminum chassis secured to the right side of the fan case at the 2 o'clock position. [Figure 7-12] Four mounting bolts, with shock absorbers, provide isolation from shocks and vibrations.

To maintain an acceptable internal ECC temperature, ambient air enters an air scoop on the fan inlet cowling, flows into the ECC internal chamber and around channel A and B compartments, and exits through the cooling air outlet.

In addition to processing data and controlling many engine systems, the EEC also outputs information to the BITE system, the display electronics unit, and ultimately to the control display unit (CDU) located on the flight deck. By accessing the proper engine pages on the CDU, a technician can check and troubleshoot the operation of the EEC-controlled fuel metering system.

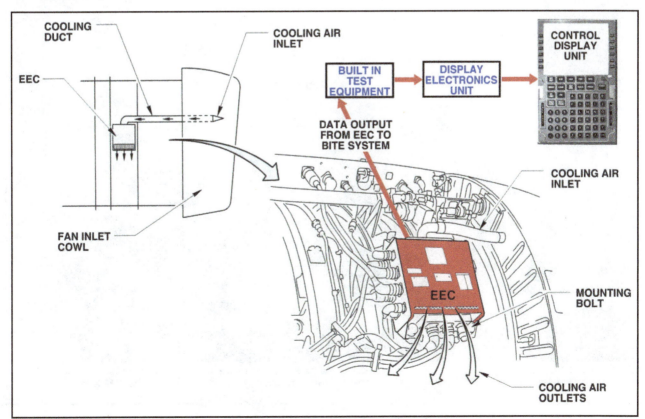

Figure 7-12. G.E./Snecma CFM56-7B electronic engine control and BITE display

EEC REPROGRAMMING (BY GROUND CREW)

Each EEC can be reprogrammed with a portable data loader (PDL). The PDL connects to the EEC at three of the cannon plug locations, and then both are powered up to allow the latest software to be downloaded. After the download, a PDL display shows either "Load Complete" or "Transfer Fail."

ENGINE RATING IDENTIFICATION PLUG

The engine rating/identification plug (#5), also called the EEC identification plug, provides the EEC with engine configuration information for proper engine operation. [Figure 7-13] It is plugged into one of the connectors on the EEC and attached to the fan case by a metal strap. It remains with the engine even after EEC replacement. The plug includes a coding circuit, soldered to the plug, which the EEC interprets and uses to determine how much thrust the engine will be able to produce.

The EEC stores schedules in its non-volatile memory for all available engine configurations. During initialization, it reads the voltages present on certain pins in the plug and selects a particular schedule from ROM based on those readings. In case of a missing or invalid ID plug, the EEC uses the value stored in the non-volatile memory for the previous plug configuration.

The ID plug has fuse and push-pull links. The fuse links provide the EEC with thrust information at power up. They are made by metallization of an area between two contacts on the plug. These links can only be opened by burning them out, thus their reconfiguration is not possible.

By design, all 7B engines can produce a takeoff thrust of 27,300 pounds. Depending on the application, the ID plug changes the takeoff thrust to 19,500; 20,600; 22,700; 24,200; or 26,300 pounds.

Bump is an option provided to achieve power levels greater than the normal take-off levels within specific limitations. Specific bump rating capabilities may be set by the engine ID plug. The bump rating does not influence power levels that are at or below Max Continuous Thrust. For any available bump, the redline values for N_1, N_2, and EGT remain identical to the baseline rating.

When new engines are built, a small variation may exist in the thrust they create at a certain N_1 speed. To account for this, the ID plug may include a modifier to

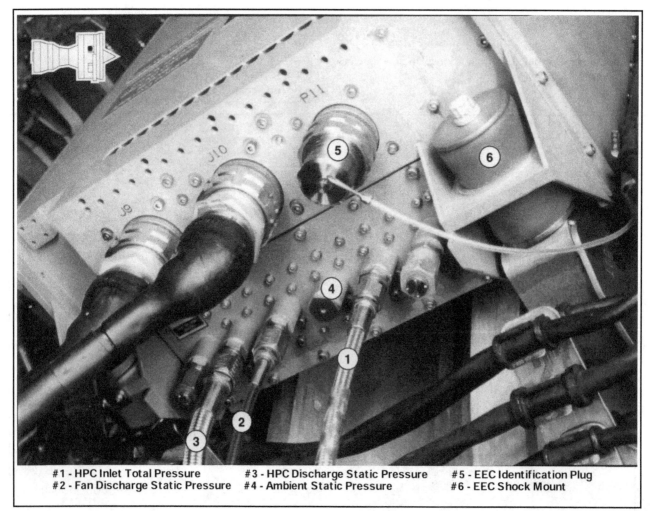

#1 - HPC Inlet Total Pressure
#2 - Fan Discharge Static Pressure
#3 - HPC Discharge Static Pressure
#4 - Ambient Static Pressure
#5 - EEC Identification Plug
#6 - EEC Shock Mount

Figure 7-13. G.E./Snecma CFM56-7B engine rating identification plug

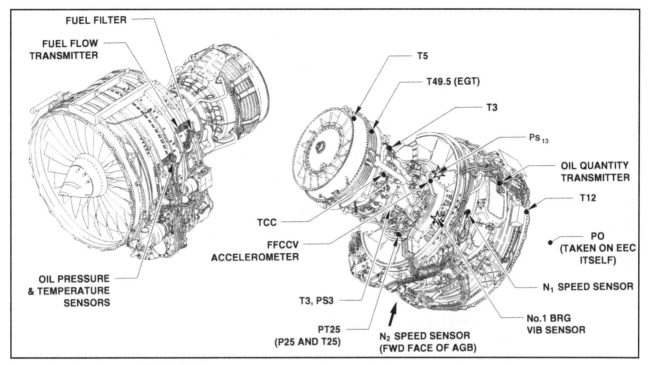

Figure 7-14. G.E./Snecma CFM56-7B engine sensors

slightly alter the N_1 speed and make an engine identical to what is considered the norm. Even though the modifier may cause an engine to have a lower N_1 speed, the signal sent to the flight deck gage will not show this reduction. In a twin engine airplane, both N_1 tachometers will show the same r.p.m.

EEC POWER SUPPLY

The EEC is provided with redundant power sources to ensure an uninterrupted and failsafe power supply. A logic circuit within the EEC automatically selects the correct power source in the event of a failure. The power sources are:

- The aircraft 115 VAC, 400 Hz normal bus.
- The aircraft 115 VAC, 400 Hz emergency bus.
- The control alternator can provide power from two separate windings, above an engine speed of approximately 12 percent N_2.

The control alternator is the primary source of electrical power for the EEC. If this unit malfunctions, the EEC automatically switches to aircraft electrical power.

ENGINE SENSORS

The EEC requires information on the engine gas path and operational parameters in order to control the engine during all phases of flight. [Figure 7-14] Sensors at aerodynamic stations and various engine locations measure engine parameters and provide them to the EEC subsystems. Sensors located at aerodynamic stations have the same number as the station, for example T_{25}. Sensors placed at other engine locations have a particular name, for example T case sensor.

The EEC uses the following engine sensors:

Speed Sensors

- Low-pressure rotating system speed, N_1.
- High-pressure rotating system speed, N_2.

Resistive Thermal Devices (RTD sensors)

- Fan inlet temperature, T_{12}.
- High-pressure compressor inlet temperature, T_{25}.

Thermocouples

- Compressor discharge temperature, T_3.
- Exhaust gas temperature, EGT or $T_{49.5}$.
- Low-pressure turbine discharge temperature, T_5.
- High-pressure turbine shroud support temperature, TCC.

Pressures

- Ambient static pressure, Po.
- High-pressure compressor discharge static pressure, Ps_3 or CDP.
- Fan discharge static pressure, Ps_{13}.
- High-pressure compressor inlet total pressure, P_{25}.

Vibration Sensors

- Number 1 bearing vibration accelerometer.
- Fan frame compressor case vertical (FFCCV) accelerometer.

POWER MANAGEMENT AND FUEL SCHEDULING (CFM56-7B)

Power management controls the engine thrust levels by means of throttle lever inputs. [Figure 7-15] It uses

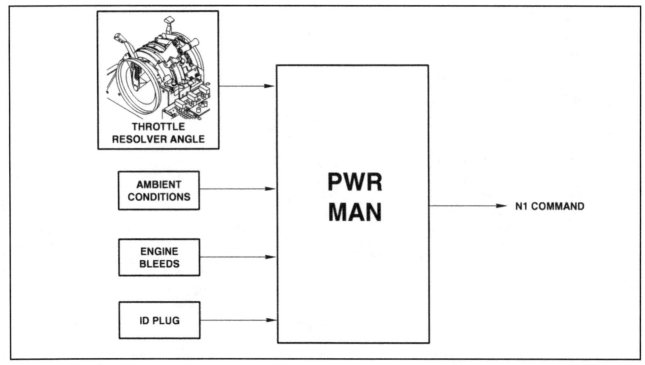

Figure 7-15. G.E./Snecma CFM56-7B power management.

fan speed (N_1) as the thrust setting parameter. The EEC calculates five reference fan speeds (idle, max climb, max continuous, max takeoff/go-around, and max reverse thrust) for the appropriate engine rating (ID plug).

THROTTLE LEVER (THRUST LEVER)

The throttle lever assembly is mechanically connected to an electronic device called a resolver The resolver transforms the mechanical movement into an electrical signal representing the angular position. The electrical signal is transmitted through hardwire connections directly to the EEC for use in thrust calculations.

Either the flight crew or the auto-throttle system positions the throttle lever. The N_1 command is calculated from the angular position of the throttle lever and other parameters.

AMBIENT CONDITIONS

The power management uses ambient condition parameters, which are static pressure (Ps/Po), total pressure (Pt), and total air temperature (TAT/T_{12}). Each EEC channel has independent sources of data available for selection. These sources are:
- Static pressure, as the Po input from the engine or as the Ps input from the Air Data and Inertial Reference Unit (ADIRU).
- Total pressure, as an input from the ADIRU.
- Total air temperature (TAT), as the T_{12} input from the engine or as the TAT input from the ADIRU.

BLEEDS

Engine compressor bleed is used to deice the engine nacelles and wings and to provide high-pressure air to the aircraft environmental control system (ECS). Each engine provides its own cowl thermal anti-icing (CTAI) bleed. The EEC controls the compressor bleeds, integrating the needs of the engine and aircraft with the thrust requirements and the appropriate engine limits.

THRUST CONTROL OPERATING MODES

The CFM56-7B engine has three thrust control operating modes, the normal thrust control mode and two alternate thrust control modes that provide fault accommodation for the loss of total pressure data from the ADIRU.

The EEC switches into the soft alternate mode if it loses ADIRU communication, pressure total data, or pressure total probe heat, or if there is a disagreement between the data coming from ADIRU 1 and 2. In soft alternate mode, the EEC does not calculate a Mach number from PT coming from a single valid input, it calculates the Mach number with the last valid delta temperature standard day and the current ambient static pressure. Because both engines usually receive the same set of data, the two engines switch into soft mode at the same time. The only time a single engine can be in soft mode is if the engine encounters a data bus failure.

The EEC switches automatically from soft alternate mode into hard alternate mode if the throttle lever is placed below the max climb position. Hard alternate mode can be manually selected by the EEC switch on the flight compartment overhead panel. In this control mode, the EEC calculates Mach number with a fixed total air temperature value (30°C) and ambient static pressure.

In the hard alternate mode, the maximum N_1 data provided by the EEC is greater than, or equal to, the maximum N_1 thrust rating in normal mode. During hot day operation, it is possible to exceed engine limits by a significant amount.

AUTO-THROTTLE FOR THE CFM-56-7B

The full range auto-throttle system provides automatic positioning of the throttle lever during all flight operations. [Figure 7-16] The system consists of:

- A flight management computer (FMC), with a second FMC being optional.
- A digital flight control system (DFCS).
- An auto-throttle computer (ATC).
- Two auto-throttle servo mechanisms (ASM).

The flight management computer provides a target N_1 power setting or target airspeed to the auto-throttle computer. Alternatively, the digital flight control system may provide the auto-throttle computer with a target airspeed. When automatic thrust control is engaged, the auto-throttle computer positions the throttle lever of both engines using the two auto-throttle servo mechanisms to obtain the target N_1 power setting or target airspeed.

The FMC and the EEC both calculate thrust using information from the ADIRU. Unlike the EEC, however, the FMC can use parameters from just one ADIRU. This means that when the EEC is missing an ADIRU parameter, it switches to the alternate mode, but the FMC is still able to calculate the correct thrust.

GENERIC INFORMATION ON AUTO-THROTTLE SYSTEMS

Many corporate to commercial size aircraft have an auto-throttle (A/T) system installed as an adjunct to the FADEC system because it provides more efficient fuel consumption by assisting the flight crew in more precisely metering fuel to the engine in various flight regimes. The A/T operates in one of the following two modes:

True airspeed mode — Ensures that the aircraft will remain within the safe stall speed and maximum speed limits.

N_1 or EPR mode — Ensures that the engines will remain within the selected thrust limits for takeoff, climb, descent, approach, landing, go-around, etc.

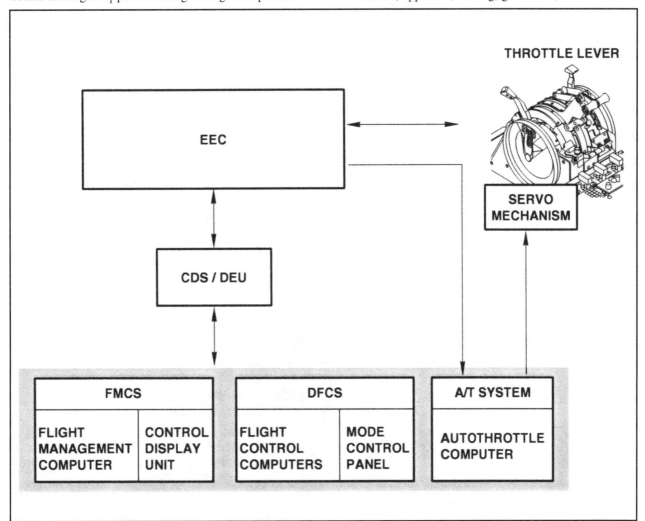

Figure 7-16. G.E./Snecma CFM56-7B autothrottle system

A/T systems in all aircraft receive signals from a flight data computer in order to maintain a set engine thrust level or true aircraft airspeed. In some aircraft, the throttles automatically move during power changes, in others the throttles remain in a selected position, called a detent, as engine power increases or decreases.

When the A/T system is disengaged, the pilot moves the throttle in a standard manner, with the throttle position providing a signal to the EEC, which then controls the amount of fuel sent by the fuel control. When the A/T system is engaged, the flight data that the pilot has entered into the flight management computer interfaces with the A/T system, and the thrust levels change automatically based on aircraft requirements.

If the aircraft throttles have detent positions, the detents correspond to various engine operational modes such as takeoff, climb, cruise, go-around, and others, depending on the aircraft type. Unlike the FADEC system, which the pilot cannot generally override, the pilot can turn the A/T system on and off at any time.

AUXILIARY POWER UNIT FUEL CONTROLLING SYSTEM

Auxiliary gas turbine engines are widely used to supply electrical power and pressurized air to the aircraft systems when the main engines are not operating. Ground power units (GPU) use similar types of gas turbine engines.

EXAMPLE SYSTEM (HONEYWELL COMPANY GTP-30), BUSINESS AND COMMUTER AIRCRAFT APU (30 TO 100 HP)

Auxiliary gas turbine fuel systems are fully automatic and do not require a power lever. After actuation of a start switch, the fuel system provides the correct amount of fuel for smooth acceleration to the rated speed. Thereafter, the fuel system schedules fuel to maintain a constant engine speed under varying pneumatic bleed and electrical loads. [Figure 7-17]

The controlled-leak acceleration and overload thermostat located in the exhaust stream is normally a closed unit, but at certain times it opens to dump a portion of the diffuser pressure signal, which goes to the top side of the bellows in the acceleration limiter. The thermostat expands, acting as a safety device in the presence of excessive exhaust heat, and relieves some of the diffuser signal pressure into the exhaust stream. This action prompts the acceleration limiter to function. The acceleration limiter diaphragm controls a bypass valve that returns excess fuel to the pump inlet and protects against engine over-temperature during acceleration from 0 to 95 percent engine speed.

A flyweight governor also controls fuel bypass to maintain a steady state speed condition by returning unwanted fuel to the pump inlet. This governor protects

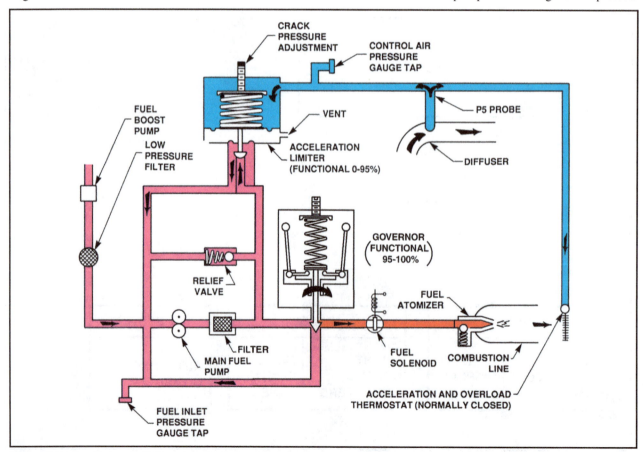

Figure 7-17. Small aircraft APU system (hydromechanical control with pneumatic temperature limiting)

Fuel Systems

against over-speed from 95 to 100 percent engine speed. As long as the governor flyweight remains loaded or turned by engine rotation, the engine will remain at rated speed.

This is the sequence of fuel flow in the APU fuel system:

1. Fuel flows from the aircraft boost pump through the low-pressure filter to the main fuel pump under low pressure.
2. Fuel flows from the main fuel pump to the governor under higher pressure and to the fuel (atomizer) nozzle.
3. Fuel bypasses back to the main pump inlet via the acceleration limiter if an over-temperature occurs when the acceleration overload thermostat expands to leak control air overboard into the engine exhaust.
4. Fuel bypasses above 95 percent r.p.m. to control engine speed as per the preset value of the speeder flyweight governor spring.
5. The relief valve limits pump pressure in the event of a malfunction in the bypass portions of the system.
6. The fuel solenoid opens and closes for starting and stopping the engine.

COMMERCIAL AIRCRAFT APU STARTING AND OPERATION (200 TO 1000 HP)

Figure 7-18 shows the location of the APU in a typical aircraft installation; it also shows the cockpit switch panel and the remote control panel from which ground personnel can operate the APU. The operator must be thoroughly familiar with the following procedures and APU operation in order to ensure the safety of personnel and of the aircraft.

1. The operator places the door switch to Auto, which opens the air inlet door on the side of the fuselage.
2. The operator places the APU master switch to Start, which energizes the starter and ignition circuits.
3. The operator moves the start switch to Run after r.p.m. and exhaust gas temperature start to read. Termination of starter and ignition occurs automatically at approximately 30 percent engine speed.
4. At approximately 10 percent engine speed, the fuel solenoid automatically opens fuel flow to the combustor, and combustion occurs.
5. The acceleration limiter starts to receive compressor discharge air, and fuel bypass decreases to allow a rapid acceleration.

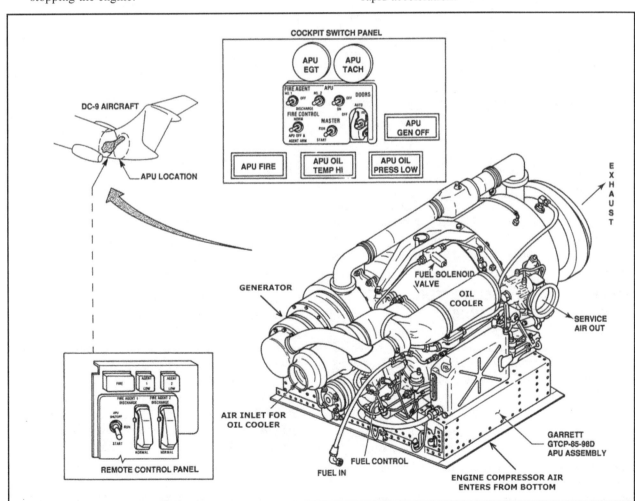

Figure 7-18. Commercial aircraft APU installation

6. The acceleration thermostat protects against overtemperature by dumping compressor discharge air into the exhaust if exhaust gas temperature becomes excessive during engine acceleration from start to 95 percent r.p.m.

7. At 95 percent r.p.m., the governor overrides the acceleration limiter and bypasses fuel to cause a steady state operation at 100 percent r.p.m.

8. When the generator is turned on, or when air is drawn away from the unit, the governor flyweights droop at the top and deliver more fuel to keep the engine on-speed.

9. During climb-out, the auxiliary power unit is generally shut down. However, the APU can be restarted during flight in many aircraft to provide air for starter-assisted engine relights or to provide electrical power to the airplane if one of the main generators has failed.

FUEL CONTROL ADJUSTMENTS, MAIN ENGINES

Fuel control maintenance on the flight line is usually limited to removal and replacement of the fuel control unit, and readjusting the specific gravity, idle r.p.m., and maximum power on hydro-mechanical or hydro-pneumatic controls. On engines with full schedule electronic engine controls, or with FADECs, few if any adjustments are necessary because the system adjusts and compensates from within its own logic systems.

SPECIFIC GRAVITY ADJUSTMENT

When running-up a gas turbine engine for performance checks, use the normal fuel prescribed by the manufacturer because the BTU value and specific gravity may be different in an alternate fuel, which could compromise the validity of the check.

Otherwise, you can adjust specific gravity. [Figure 7-19A] It is a means of resetting force on the differential pressure regulating valve spring within the fuel control when an alternate fuel is used and the engine is undergoing performance testing. [Figure 7-8]

PERFORMANCE CHECKS (TURBOJET AND TURBOFAN ENGINES)

During engine troubleshooting for performance loss or after undergoing maintenance procedures that could affect engine performance, several checks such as trimming, acceleration, or throttle adjustment may be required before certifying the engine as airworthy.

TRIMMING

Trimming refers to adjusting idle speed and maximum thrust during performance testing. [Figure 7-19B] You can trim the engine while it is in the airplane or in a test cell. Idle speed adjustment sets engine idling speed to the manufacturer's best economy and performance range. Idle speed is used during periods of operation when thrust

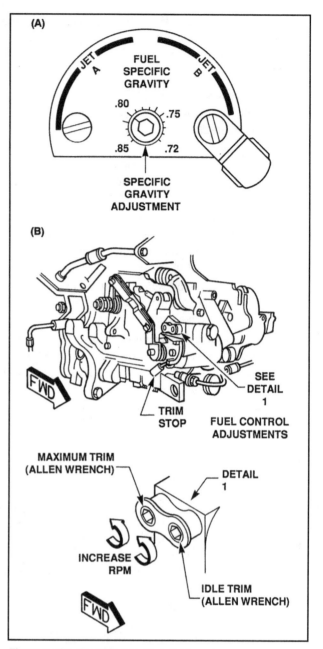

Figure 7-19A. Specific gravity adjustment
Figure 7-19B. Trim adjustment

is not required. Depending on the particular engine, a maximum percent r.p.m. adjustment, or maximum engine pressure ratio (EPR) adjustment ensures that the engine produces correct thrust. This thrust value is referred to as manufacturer's guaranteed rated thrust, sometimes shortened to rated thrust.

Many manufacturers recommend that all final trim adjustments be made in the increase direction in order to stabilize cams, springs, and linkages within the fuel control. If over-adjustment occurs, repeat the procedure by decreasing trim to below target values, and then increasing trim to the desired values.

Check trim whenever engine thrust is suspect and after maintenance tasks prescribed by the manufacturer. A few

Fuel Systems

of these might include trimming after engine change, module change, or fuel control change. Trimming is otherwise required from time to time due to deteriorating engine performance as engine service time takes its toll. Aircraft linkage systems stretch with age, causing misalignment in the cockpit to engine control systems or loss of cushion in the power lever. This condition may require a trim check.

ACCELERATION CHECK

In conjunction with the trim procedure, an acceleration check is usually accomplished as an additional test of engine performance. After the trim check, mark the cockpit power lever quadrant at the takeoff position. Advance the power lever from idle to takeoff position and measure the time against a published tolerance. Even for a large gas turbine engine, the time is quite low, in the range of five to ten seconds. [Figure 7-20A]

THROTTLE SPRING-BACK AND CUSHION CHECKS (NON-ELECTRONIC THROTTLES)

Another important part of the trim procedure is to check for throttle spring-back and cushion. [Figure 7-20B] The operator, before and after the trim run, moves the power lever full forward and releases it. The distance the lever springs back is measured against prescribed tolerances. On an airliner, this distance might measure ¼ inch or more. When spring-back is correct, the fuel control reaches its internal stops before the cockpit quadrant reaches its forward stop. If out of limits, the technician must adjust the aircraft control system.

Cushion is the distance in inches from the power lever at takeoff setting to full power lever travel.

The cushion check ensures that the pilot will not only be able to obtain takeoff power but also additional power lever travel in case of emergencies.

PART POWER TRIM

In order to save wear on the engine and to save fuel, trim both engine pressure ratio-rated engines and speed-rated engines at less than takeoff power. This procedure involves closing all service bleeds to avoid compression loss and placing a physical obstruction, called a part power trim stop, in the path of the fuel control lever linkage. The power lever is advanced to hit the trim stop during trimming, and the trimming adjustment is made at this position with the engine operating at approximately the maximum continuous thrust rating. To stabilize internal fuel control linkages, make trim adjustments in the increase direction. After trimming, remove the stop to perform a takeoff power check.

ENGINE PRESSURE RATIO TRIM AND SPEED TRIM

Thrust-producing turbine engines use either the engine pressure ratio trim or the fan speed trim procedure. If the engine is configured with an engine pressure ratio sys-

tem, the pilot uses a cockpit engine pressure ratio gauge to set engine power. In terms of trimming, the engine is referred to as an engine pressure ratio rated engine. If the engine does not have an engine pressure ratio system, it is trimmed in accordance with fan speed, and the pilot uses a tachometer indicator to set engine power. In terms of trimming, this engine is referred to as a fan speed rated engine.

ENGINE PRESSURE RATIO

The aircraft uses an engine pressure ratio (EPR) gauge for thrust indication. This gauge reads the ratio of turbine discharge pressure divided by compressor inlet pressure and automatically corrects for changing ambient conditions.

EXAMPLE: If turbine discharge pressure is 58.2 inches of mercury when the engine is correctly trimmed, and engine inlet pressure reads 30.0 inches of mercury, the engine pressure ratio is calculated as follows:

$$EPR = \frac{\text{Turbine Discharge Pressure}}{\text{Compressor Inlet Pressure}}$$

$$EPR = \frac{58.2}{30.0}$$

$$EPR = 1.94$$

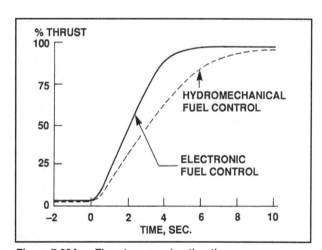

Figure 7-20A — Thrust vs. acceleration time.

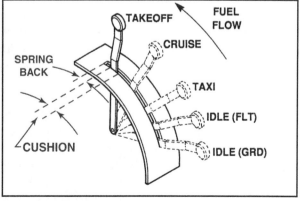

Figure 7-20B. Spring back and cushion checks

If the cockpit indicator reads within the accepted tolerance of 1.94, the engine pressure ratio indicating system and the engine are performing satisfactorily.

TRIMMING PROCEDURE FOR EPR-RATED ENGINES

On many axial flow engines, there exists a better relationship between internal engine pressures and thrust than engine speed and thrust. In fact, on some dual-spool engines the last ten percent of the r.p.m. range can increase thrust by as much as 30 percent. On these engines, EPR is a quicker measure of thrust than r.p.m./thrust charts.

Turning the maximum trim adjustment, as shown in Figure 7-19B, will increase or decrease fuel flow and thrust. This affects the relationship between compressor inlet pressure and turbine discharge pressure. As compressor inlet pressure increases with fuel flow increase, engine pressure ratio also increases for a given compressor inlet condition.

The trim procedure is as follows:

With finely calibrated gauges, maintenance personnel measure inlet conditions of barometric pressure and ambient temperature before running the engine. They insert the part power trim stop and install the necessary fittings to measure turbine discharge pressure. Finally, with the engine running on the part power trim stop, they trim the engine to a value prescribed by a manufacturer's graph. [Figure 7-21]

When performing a trim procedure, do not use the temperature given at the control tower because there could be a measurable difference between that reading and the onsite reading. Do not use the aircraft outside air temperature gauge because it could be heat-soaked from exposure to the sun, and the reading might be significantly different from a thermometer reading taken at the engine. An industry-wide procedure is to hang the thermometer in the shade of the nose wheel-well until the temperature stabilizes.

Manufacturers also commonly recommend that you accelerate the engine to a high power setting two or more times to pre-load the internal mechanisms within the fuel control and ensure a higher degree of repeatability before making the actual acceleration to trim power setting.

Figure 7-21 shows a typical trim curve for an EPR-rated business jet's part power engine. After calculating the necessary turbine discharge pressure for an outside air temperature of 75°F and inlet pressure of 30 inches of mercury, if the engine is not producing 58.20 inches of mercury turbine discharge pressure, up-trim the engine to this value.

At that time, divide 58.2 inches of mercury turbine discharge pressure by 30.0 inches of mercury compressor inlet pressure, to find the engine pressure ratio of 1.94. The cockpit gauge must read 1.94, plus or minus a typical tolerance value. If it does not, check the engine pressure ratio indicating system.

Note that Figure 7-21 uses barometric pressure (Pam) rather than compressor inlet pressure (Pt_2). This is common practice because there is no convenient way to measure Pt_2 on many aircraft, and total pressure is only slightly different from ambient pressure. The graph is corrected for this, and the engine is trimmed to an engine pressure ratio of Pt_5 divided by Pt_2.

FULL POWER CHECK AFTER TRIMMING

After completing the part power trim, remove the part power stop and advance the power lever toward the full power turbine discharge pressure value of 67.0 inches of mercury. [Figure 7-21] If you can achieve this value without exceeding the limits of engine condition instruments, such as engine speed, exhaust gas temperature, and fuel-flow, the engine full power check is satisfactory.

TRIMMING PROCEDURE FOR SPEED-RATED ENGINE

A fan speed trim is generally performed on turbofans of the dual-spool configuration where there exists a direct relationship between fan speed (N_1) and thrust. Counterclockwise rotation of the maximum adjustment [Figure 7-19B] will increase fuel flow to the engine, increase fan speed, and, consequently, increase engine thrust output. Adjusting the idle setscrew resets idle speed to the manufacturer's recommended percent r.p.m. value. The amount of adjustment depends on the parameters of an engine performance curve, such as the one in Figure 7-22.

In this case, the fan speed trim determination depends on ambient temperatures. The example engine is speed rated. That is, its thrust is determined by a comparison to fan speed. High-pressure compressor speed, turbine temperature, and other engine operational parameters must fall within an allowable range when rated fan speed is obtained. If they do not, one of two conditions probably exists, a turbo-machinery malfunction or a fuel scheduling malfunction due to:

- Dirty compressors and damaged compressors.
- Damaged hot sections (thermodynamic problems).
- Poor fuel scheduling (compressor stalls, over temperatures, and flameout).

To obtain required thrust, some part of the engine is being over-taxed, and this shows up on one of the condition-monitoring instruments in the cockpit, i.e., r.p.m., exhaust gas temperature, fuel flow, etc. Determine the cause of the high indicator reading and correct the problem before releasing the engine for service.

To ensure accuracy of readings, many operators slave a portable precision tachometer into the aircraft percent r.p.m. indicating system. This gives the trim crew personnel an immediate indication of the condition of the cockpit instrument and more information with which to assess the condition of the engine.

Fuel Systems

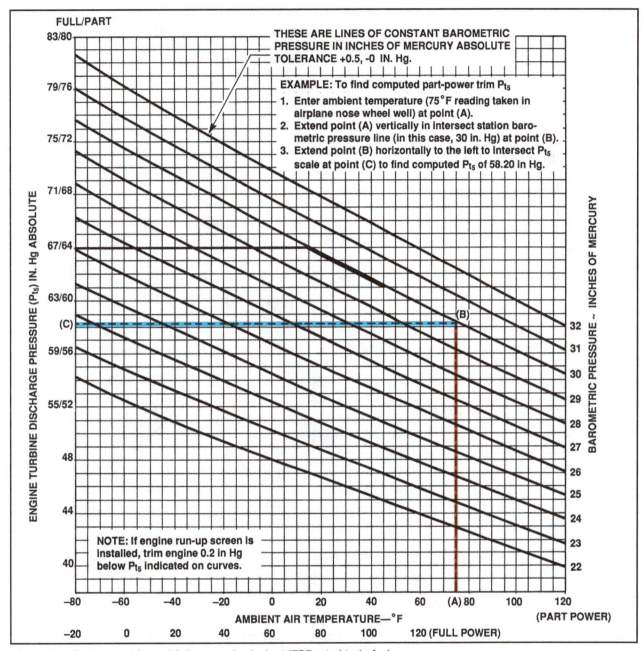

Figure 7-21. Part power trim and full power check chart (EPR-rated turbofan)

The trim procedure is as follows:

1. With a precision thermometer reading taken at the aircraft, plot the fan (N_1) speed for the ambient temperature on Figure 7-22.

2. Deploy trim part power stop.

3. Run aircraft, advancing power lever until linkage hits trim stop.

4. Adjust maximum setting and record gauge readings, and then check against manufacturer's limits.

5. Retract trim stop and advance power lever to N_1 value on Figure 7-23. Check N_2 speed and T_5 to be within limits.

EXAMPLE:

1. With an ambient temperature at the aircraft of 65°F, operate the engine with the power lever advanced to the part power stop. [Figure 7-24A] The engine should be operating at 83 percent fan (N1) speed in accordance with Figure 7-22.

2. If the N_1 speed is not 83 percent, make a max-trim adjustment.

3. Reduce power and check idle speed to be 50, ±1 percent.

4. Remove part power stop and advance power lever toward 99 percent, N_1 speed, in accordance with Figure 7-23. Exhaust gas temperature (T_5) must remain under 700°C and the high-pressure compressor

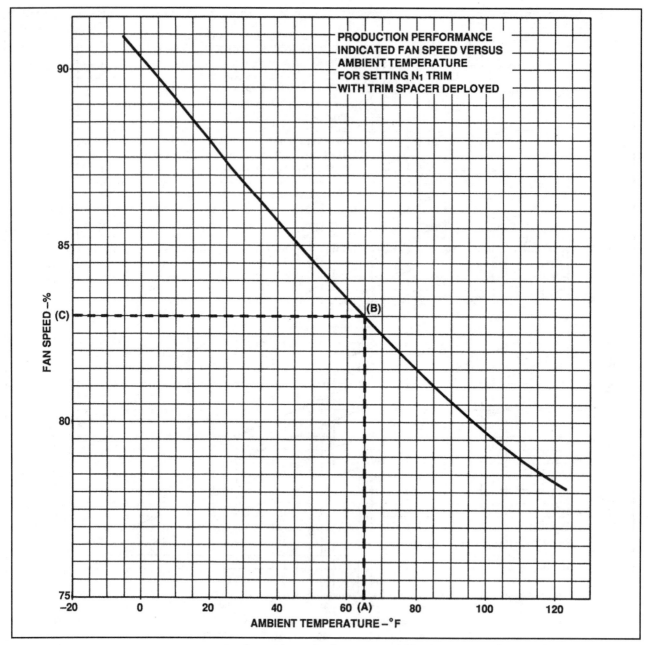

Figure 7-22. Part power trim chart (fan speed-rated turbofan)

(N_2) speed must remain under 96 percent; otherwise, do not advance the power lever further. Shut the engine down and perform troubleshooting procedures. Note that Figure 7-21 is biased for both ambient pressure and ambient temperature, compared to Figure 7-22, which is biased for only ambient temperature. The reason is that the fuel control used on the engine in question has an acceleration bellows that compensates for changes in ambient pressure. [Figure 7-8]

TRIM PROCEDURES FOR FADEC CONTROLLED ENGINES

Engines under the full authority of a FADEC do not employ the traditional trim methods of physical adjustments for the previously mentioned EPR-rated engines or speed-rated engines. The word "trim," however, still refers to a leveling out of thrust that may vary between engines of the same type. The difference in thrust is primarily due to the clearances achieved between stationary and rotating components during engine assembly. Wider clearances relate to air losses or leakages that affect compressor and turbine efficiencies and to thrust output of the engine at its top rotor speed. On engines in which thrust levels are read as N_1 speed on a flight deck display, it is possible that at the same N_1 speed, thrust levels may differ between engines on the same aircraft installation and the engine with the higher thrust must be trimmed down. The trim procedure logic within the EEC is designed to detect any thrust mismatch and to make the necessary corrections without affecting the flight deck N_1 readout.

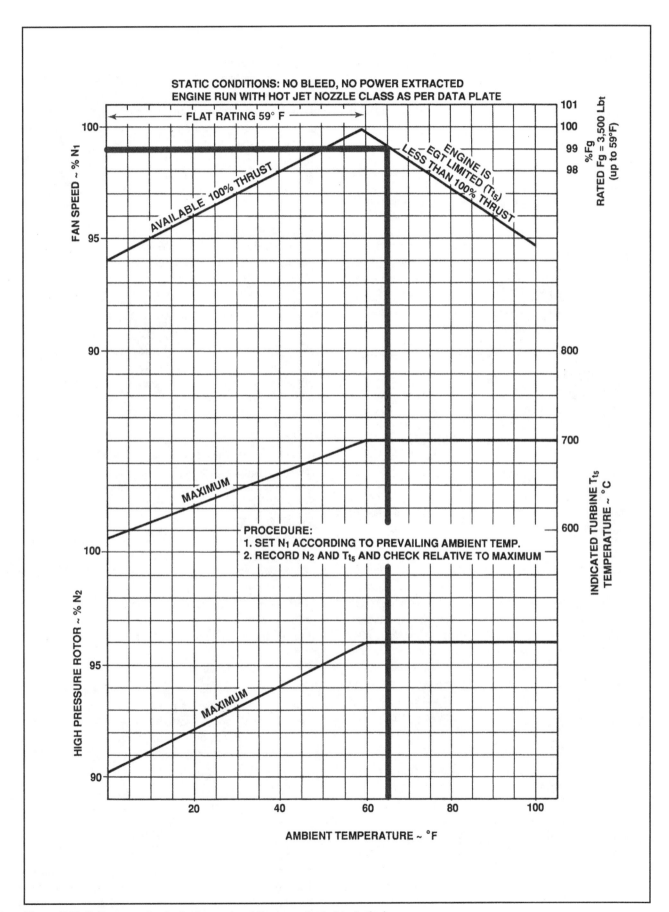

Figure 7-23. Full power check chart—sea level (fan speed-rated turbofan)

The following example describes how an automatic engine trim matching might occur when the number 2 engine is out of match with the number 1 engine. Consider that the readout for the number 1 engine is accurate and 96% (N_1) represents a takeoff thrust of 26,300 pounds, but the EEC senses that the number 2 engine is capable of producing 26,450 pounds of thrust at the same 96% N_1 speed.

The EEC would then react as follows:

1. The EEC logic creates a demand signal to cut back on fuel to the number 2 engine, causing a decrease in N_1 speed to 95.6 percent and the necessary down trim to 26,300 pounds of thrust.

Here is an example of an engine down trim:

Engine #1	Engine #2	→ Engine #2
EEC Senses 96% N_1 26,300 lbt	EEC Senses 96% N_1 26,450 lbt	EEC Down Trims 95.6% N_1 26,300 lbt

2. The EEC modifies the signal, creating the N_1 reading on the flight deck for the number 2 engine, causing it to show an r.p.m. of 96%, like the other engine's N_1 reading. Even though the number 2 engine has an actual r.p.m. of 95.6 percent, it is better for the flight crew to see matching N_1 readings when the thrust of both engines is the same.

3. The EEC retains trim authority throughout the life of the engines as changes occur in their performance or when one of the engines is replaced.

DATA PLATE SPEED CHECK

The data plate speed check is a performance check that is completed with the part power trim check. On many gas turbine engines, a small metal plate is attached at the time of manufacture during final performance testing. The plate is stamped with the engine speed at which required thrust value at part power trim was obtained. No two engines would necessarily be stamped with the same speed because production tolerances of engine parts vary the speed-to-thrust relationship on nearly every engine. However, all engines will probably be within several percent r.p.m. of each other.

The purpose of this check is to compare future engine performance against new performance data. For example, consider a hypothetical data plate stamped 87.25 percent N_2 speed at 1.61 engine pressure ratio, 59°F. At this time the engine would have been operating with the part power trim pin in place. In the future service life of the engine, with the pin removed, you can check the data plate speed as part of a ground performance check on engine condition when the engine accumulates service time (cycles and hours).

The data plate speed check is performed along with the part power trim check. First, install the trim pin as shown in Figure 7-24A and complete the engine trim run. Then remove the trim pin and perform the full power check mentioned earlier in this chapter. Next, throttle back and operate the engine at 1.61 EPR and observe the N_2 tachometer indication, and compare that indication to the "as new" speed on the data plate. If the tolerance is +2.0 percent and the engine goes to 89.5 percent N_2 speed, the engine is out of limits for the data plate speed check because the limit is 89.25 percent. [Figure 7-24B]

This check is an assessment of engine performance, not a pass/fail check. If the engine is otherwise performing satisfactorily, the operator might decide to keep the engine in service, even though it is no doubt consuming more fuel to give the required 1.61 EPR than when new.

The check might also tell the operator that the compressor needs field cleaning or that the hot section is deteriorating and should be scheduled for repair at the next inspection interval. The test run will seldom be accomplished on a Standard Day 59°F, so correct the observed speed on the tachometer indicator as per the manufacturer's charts before comparing it to the data plate speed.

This discussion applies to EPR-rated engines, but the data plate speed check is equally applicable to the turbofan speed rated engine or the turboprop engine, which is rated in torque units or horsepower units.

TRIM RESTRICTIONS

When you trim an engine, you must be aware of ambient conditions. Figure 7-25 shows typical wind direction and velocity restrictions. Excessive wind in the direction of the tailpipe will cause a false high turbine discharge pressure and subsequent low trim. Excessive wind in the inlet will cause a false high compression and turbine discharge pressure and a subsequent low trim.

These situations occur as follows:

- Wind up the tailpipe causes a backpressure and a false high turbine discharge pressure for which the technician would compensate by down trimming. Then, later, in calm air, turbine discharge pressure would be low and, consequently, engine pressure ratio would be low.

- Wind into the inlet causes a false high compressor inlet pressure that generally affects compression to a greater degree than it affects the cockpit EPR reading.

The compressor magnifies the false high inlet pressure by increased compression, which creates a rise in turbine discharge pressure. This in turn causes what appears to be a higher EPR reading or over-trimmed engine. The trim crew will compensate for this by down trimming, and

Fuel Systems

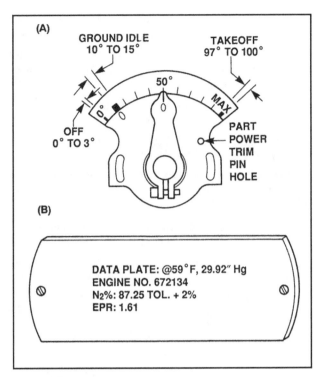

Figure 7-24A. Power lever protractor, part power approximately 90° power lever angle

Figure 7-24B. Example of data plate check results at new or overhaul

then later in calm air, the engine will be under-trimmed. Wind is seldom steady, and when gusting, causes erratic gauge readings that make trimming calculations difficult to obtain.

There are other trim restrictions in the aircraft operations manual, such as moisture content (rain) and moisture (icing). Follow them carefully or risk making a false trim.

The same restrictions apply to the speed-rated engines. Even though the trim instrumentation is not as directly affected, the engine performance will be affected, and an incorrect trim could result.

TRIM DANGER ZONES

An inherent danger to personnel and equipment exists in the vicinity of operating gas turbine engines. [Figures 7-26A and B] All flight line personnel must be constantly alert to keep out of the danger areas when approaching or leaving an operating engine. Items such as loose clothing, microphone chords, mechanic wipe rags, and tools must be carefully secured so the engine will not ingest them. For maximum safety, use an intercom system or hand signals (Appendix 5) for communication between the cockpit and the ground crew.

EAR PROTECTION FROM NOISE

A large turbojet or turbofan engine operating at full power can generate sound levels up to 160 decibels at the aircraft. [Figure 7-27] Smaller engines of all types can generate sound levels up to approximately 130 decibels. This noise intensity is sufficient to cause either temporary or permanent hearing loss if ground personnel do not use adequate ear protection.

The muff is the most effective ear protection. It fits over the entire ear and protects against noise to the ear opening and to the bone structure behind the ear. Earplugs provide minimal hearing loss protection and are generally only recommended for use in lower noise areas or for brief exposure in higher noise areas.

The Federal Standard for noise protection is outlined in the Occupational Safety and Health Administration Standard, 36th Federal Register, 105, Section 19-10.95.

FLAT RATING

Today, most gas turbine engines are flat-rated. This refers to the flat shape of the full power curve and the point on the ambient temperature scale at which the power starts to drop below 100 percent. Figure 7-28 illustrates this concept for a fan speed-rated engine. A fan speed of 96 percent r.p.m. corresponds to 100 percent thrust on this engine, and this value can be obtained at any ambient temperature up to 90°F. That is, by moving the power lever more and more forward,

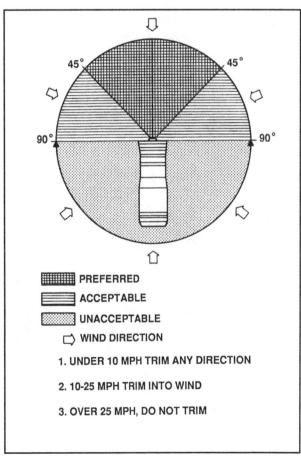

Figure 7-25. Wind direction and velocity limits (Pratt & Whitney JT12)

the pilot can obtain rated thrust at any temperature up to 90°F. After 90°F, forward movement of the power lever is not permitted because it most likely will result in an engine over temperature.

When ambient temperature exceeds the flat rating of the engine, 100 percent thrust can no longer be obtained. This being the case, the aircraft's gross weight might need to be adjusted, or, at the very least, runway takeoff roll will increase and the flight crew will need to account for this in their takeoff procedures.

Some engines are flat rated to only 59°F, others over 100°F. This consideration depends largely on the needs of the aircraft manufacturer. Generally, flat rating enables the engine to produce a constant rated thrust over a wide range of ambient temperatures without working the engine harder than necessary, which prolongs engine service life.

For example, an engine rated at 3,500 pounds thrust at 59°F might be re-rated to 3,350 pounds thrust at 90°F. The aircraft user might not need 3,500 pounds of thrust or the maximum gross weight of the aircraft, and he would like to benefit from increased engine service life and lower fuel consumption by operating at 3,350 pounds thrust maximum. Flat rating is an engine manufacturer's way of re-rating an engine to a lower rated thrust than it would have at Standard Day temperature. The engine will be able to use that lower rated thrust over a wider ambient temperature range. Flat rating is equally applicable to all types of gas turbine engines, both thrust-producing engines and torque-producing engines. The aircraft manufacturer will probably use the following process, or one very similar, when selecting the best flat rating:

1. The user decides the takeoff power needed for his aircraft configuration, route requirements, runway lengths, runway altitudes, etc.
2. The user calculates the highest ambient temperature at which required takeoff power can be obtained.
3. The engine and aircraft manufacturer print all of the flight manuals, operational instructions, etc., to reflect the selected takeoff power as the maximum usable for normal operation.

If an engine is re-rated to a lower power level than it is capable of producing, the engine retains its full power capability as an emergency reserve. No mechanical changes are needed to the engine or fuel scheduling system, merely changes in the printed operational data.

TURBOPROP AND TURBOSHAFT ENGINE PERFORMANCE CHECKS

Turboprop and turboshaft engines are torque producers rather than thrust producers. Performance calculations of torque-producing engines are very different from those of turbofan and turbojet engines, which use engine pressure ratio or fan speed as power indicators in the cockpit.

The turboprop and turboshaft aircraft cockpit contains a torque indicator calibrated in either torque (psi) oil pressure, torque (ft.lbs.), or torque (%). The gauge reading is produced most often by either a "phased shift" electronic torquemeter system or a "balanced piston" torquemeter oil system (discussed in Chapter 12).

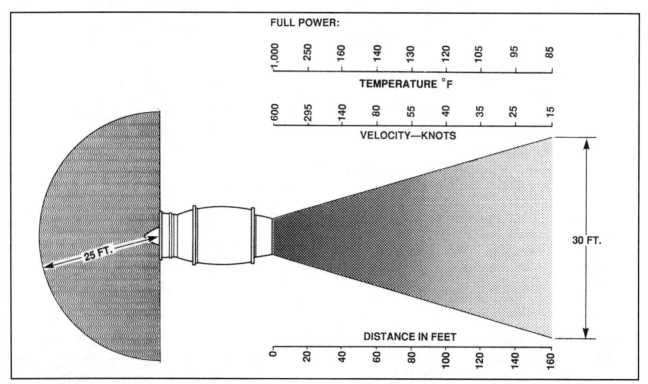

Figure 7-26A. Inlet and exhaust jet wake danger areas (Pratt & Whitney JT15D turbofan)

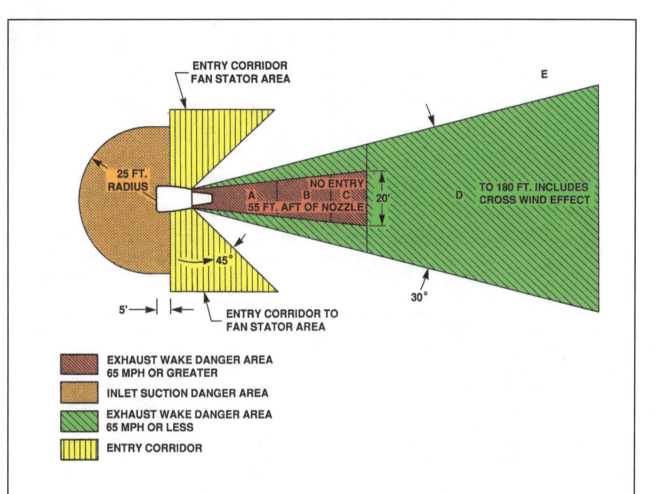

Figure 7-26B. Inlet and exhaust wake areas (General Electric CF6 high-bypass turbofan)

TYPE EAR PROTECTIVE DEVICES	ALLOWABLE NOISE EXPOSURE SOUND LEVEL IN dB						
	EXPOSURE TIME, HOURS*						
	1/4	1/2	1	2	4	6	8
NO PROTECTION	115	110	105	100	95	92	90
EAR PLUGS WITH AVERAGE SEAL	127	122	117	112	107	104	102
EAR PLUGS AND EARMUFFS	135	130	125	120	115	112	110

*DURATION OF EXPOSURE PER DAY

EAR PROTECTIVE DEVICES

UNIVERSAL FIT EARPLUG	EAR PLUG V-51-R TYPE OR SIMILAR	TYPICAL EARMUFF

Figure 7-27. Ear protection guidelines

EXAMPLE 1: The PT-6 is a turboprop engine, and a torque gauge calibrated in foot-pounds indicates its power output in the cockpit. To the pilot, this is representative of a certain shaft horsepower value. The process by which the foot-pound reading of the cockpit gauge is produced and by which the actual shaft horsepower within the engine is being produced is as follows:

$$\text{Shaft Hp} = \text{Torque (lb. ft.)} \times \text{r.p.m.} \times K$$

Where:

Torque = Flight deck gauge reading

r.p.m. = Turbine speed going to prop

K = A derived constant

Recall from Chapter 2 that:

$$\text{Power} = \frac{\text{Force} \times \text{Distance}}{\text{Time}}$$

$$\text{Hp} = \frac{\text{Power (ft. lbs./min.)}}{33,000}$$

Where:

Force = pounds

Distance = feet

Time = minutes

In the previous formula, when horsepower is applied to a turboprop or turboshaft engine, time and distance become a function of the r.p.m. of the free power turbine, and force is the turning force called torque. Torque is measured in pound-feet, and is created because of a force of one pound acting through a moment arm, or radius, of one foot. Torque is often expressed in units of foot-pounds, but in formula calculation the units are expressed as pound-feet.

The power turbine generates power to drive the propeller through a reduction gearbox. For example, the PT6-34 power turbine speed is 33,000 r.p.m. at rated power, and its propeller reduction gearbox has a 15:1 ratio. This results in a 2,200-r.p.m. drive shaft speed at the propeller. The torque produced when the propeller is under load is therefore an indication of the engine shaft horsepower being produced.

The torque (T) produced by the power turbine in Figure 7-29 is the force developed in the plane of the turbine rotor times the moment arm (radius). As a formula, it would be expressed as follows:

Torque = Force × Moment Arm

To calculate horsepower, the torque, r.p.m., and distance around the mean circumference of the rotor blades are used. The force acts during each revolution of the turbine wheel through this distance.

The force value "F" can be arrived at by direct measurement during factory testing or by calculations involving British thermal units of fuel energy available at the power turbine. One British thermal unit equals 778 foot-pounds of work. For this discussion, F equals force and will not actually work out its value because that will be done automatically within the engine by the torque meter and the cockpit gauge that reads out in pound-feet (or foot-pounds).

EXAMPLE 2: To calculate shaft horsepower, change Time and Distance in the horsepower formula to r.p.m. multiplied by circumference, as follows:

$$\text{Hp} = \frac{F \times N_p \times 2\pi r}{33,000}$$

Where:

F = Force in lbs.

N_p = Propeller r.p.m.

r = Mean radius in feet

33,000 = Conversion to Hp

The horsepower formula shown above can be rearranged as follows:

Fuel Systems

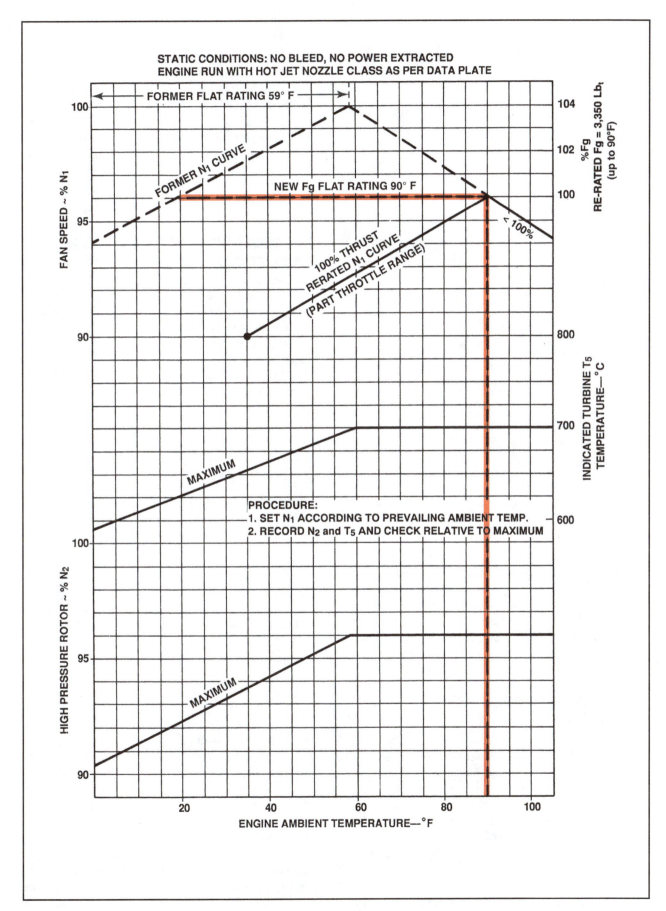

Figure 7-28. Example of flat rating (typical engine at sea level)

$$Hp = \frac{(F \times r) \times Np \times 2\pi}{33,000}$$

$$Hp = \frac{Torque \times Np \times 2\pi}{33,000}$$

$$Hp = \frac{Torque \times r.p.m.}{5252}$$

Where:

F = Force in lbs.

Np = Propeller r.p.m.

r = Mean radius in feet

33,000 = Conversion to Hp

Torque = F × r

$\frac{1}{5252} = 2\pi \div 33,000$

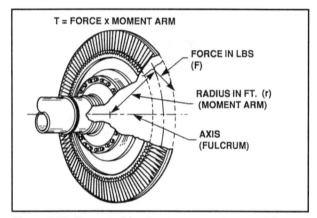

Figure 7-29. Power turbine torque, moment arm and force

The formula shows that the actual shaft horsepower produced by the engine can be obtained by the use of the cockpit torque gauge reading in pound-feet and the prop r.p.m. gauge. The torque reading may be in p.s.i. and must be converted to pound-feet. The prop r.p.m. reading may be in percent r.p.m. and must be converted to actual r.p.m.

CONVERTING TORQUE (PSI) TO TORQUE IN POUND-FEET

If the gauge on the flight deck shows the engine torque as a p.s.i. value, this can be converted to a pound-feet value by using a conversion factor. Each engine and model will use a different conversion factor. The Pratt & Whitney PT6-34 turboprop, for example, uses a conversion of 30.57 when the engine is at 100 percent r.p.m. The formula would be as follows:

Torque (pound-feet) = Torque p.s.i. × 30.57

EXAMPLE: If the torque gauge on the flight deck of a PT6-34 powered airplane shows a value of 42.05 p.s.i., what would be the engine's torque in pound-feet?

Torque (lb.ft.) = 42.05 × 30.57

Torque (lb.ft.) = 1,285

CONVERTING PERCENT RPM TO ACTUAL REVOLUTIONS PER MINUTE

With regard to actual revolutions per minute and percent r.p.m., if 100 percent equals 2,200 revolutions of the propeller per minute, then a gauge reading of 98% represents 98 percent of 2,200. As a formula, the relationship would be expressed as follows:

Actual r.p.m. = % r.p.m. (100% value)

CALCULATING TORQUE (POUND-FEET) FROM TAKEOFF GRAPH

Using a typical takeoff power setting curve like the one shown in Figure 7-30, when the ambient temperature is 77°F and the field barometric pressure is 29.92 inches of mercury, the takeoff torque value is 1,285 pound-feet.

The operator will start the engine and accelerate to this value for takeoff or during a maintenance power check. The operator will also ensure that, when obtaining the correct takeoff power, all other cockpit gauges pertaining to engine conditions are reading satisfactorily. This indicates that the engine is performing as designed and is airworthy in terms of this check.

COMPUTING SHAFT HORSEPOWER FROM COCKPIT READING

Shaft horsepower can now be computed if the r.p.m. of the propeller (Np) is known. In this instance, all of the PT6 turboprop engines that drive propellers through reduction gearing use 2,200 r.p.m. as 100 percent Np speed.

EXAMPLE:

$$Shp = \frac{Torque \times Np}{5252}$$

$$Shp = \frac{1,285 \times 2,200}{5252}$$

Shp = 537

After cruise r.p.m. is set, the propeller governor and fuel control will keep the power turbine (N_2) on speed even though ambient conditions and load conditions change at the propeller and engine. Fuel flow will be varied and N_1 speed will vary by action of sensors within the prop and fuel scheduling systems, but the power turbine, and thus propeller speed, will be held constant.

The torque and the resulting shaft horsepower will vary with the load applied, in accordance with Newton's first law, which states: "Objects at rest tend to remain at rest (resisting increase in motion). Objects in motion tend to remain in motion (resisting decrease in motion)." If, for instance, flight conditions cause an increase in fuel

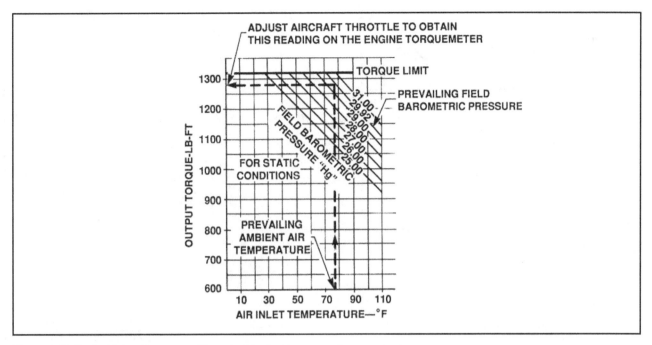

Figure 7-30. Typical takeoff power setting chart for turboprop engine

flow and N_1 speed, the N_2 speed will try to increase; but, the propeller governor will select a higher blade angle, and the propeller will stay on-speed. The increase in blade angle will create more resistance to movement, and torque and shaft horsepower will increase.

WATER INJECTION THRUST AUGMENTATION

Some gas turbine engines require the use of a water injection, power augmentation system to increase flat rated thrust or to regain thrust when operating under high ambient temperatures or high altitude runway conditions. Water, in a fine spray, is introduced into the compressor inlet, the combustion inlet, or both, in an attempt to increase thrust or to regain lagging thrust created by these poor ambient conditions. Recall that flat rating was discussed earlier in this chapter.

- Observe that flat-rated dry thrust can be extended to a higher ambient temperature by water injection. [Figure 7-31A]
- Observe that when an aircraft is taking off from a runway higher than sea level some of its lost thrust can be recovered by water injection. [Figure 7-31B]
- Observe that the flat-rated dry thrust can be increased by water injection. [Figure 7-31C]

PRINCIPLES OF OPERATION

The principle of latent heat of vaporization applies to the water injection process in the gas turbine engine; that is, injection of fluid into the gas path causes a heat transfer. When the fluid evaporates, heat in the air will be transferred into the fluid droplets, cooling the air and increasing gas flow density. When water is vaporized in the engine, it absorbs heat from the air at the rate of approximately 1,000 BTUs per pound of water.

Water injection in a gas turbine engine is a means of augmenting engine thrust in two ways. First, addition of water to air in the compressor increases compression and mass flow. Second, water cools the combustion gases, which allows additional fuel to be used without exceeding maximum temperature limits during takeoff. Increases in these three engine parameters result in a thrust increase in the range of 10 to 15 percent. This means that when the engine is operating at 100 percent thrust without water injection and water is injected, the thrust level will be raised to 115 percent. [Figure 7-31C]

Inlet water injection is designed for use at ambient temperature above 40°F. Below this temperature, icing is likely to occur in the water injection system and in the engine inlet. There is no temperature restriction concerning combustor inlet water injection.

The principle of latent heat of evaporation lowers the compressor inlet temperatures during water injection. Water injection is only used at takeoff power settings because the combination of cooling effect of high velocity airflow and absorption of heat by water molecules sets up conditions for icing well above 32°F ambient temperature.

When the temperature approaches 40°F and water injection is required, heated water is serviced into the aircraft tanks. The tanks are also configured with heating elements to keep the water at the required temperature until use.

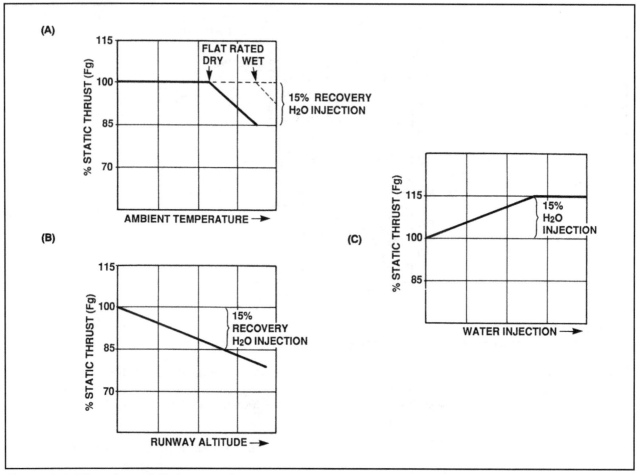

Figure 7-31A. Effect of water injection on thrust versus ambient temperature
Figure 7-31B. Effect of water injection on thrust versus runway altitude
Figure 7-31C. Added thrust with water injection

WATER INJECTION FLUIDS

Pure demineralized or distilled water is the most common water injection fluid. Ordinary tap water is not used because its high mineral solid content can cause severe turbine distress when the minerals impinge on the turbine blades. Pure water is also widely used because it produces a greater cooling effect than a mixture of water and methyl or ethyl alcohol. Airliners can take advantage of this and not worry about altitude freeze up by using the complete supply of water at takeoff. Aircraft such as helicopters and turboprops, which make frequent takeoffs and landings, are forced to use a water-alcohol mixture to protect against freeze up.

Typical fluid properties are as follows:

- Demineralized water or distilled water must have less than 10 parts per million (ppm) of solids.
- Methyl/ethyl mixtures will generally be a blend of 35 to 50 percent alcohol in either demineralized or distilled water.

The following table shows the heat absorption or vaporization effect of the most common injection fluids.

Fluid Type	BTU/lb. Absorbed	Temp.	Heating Value BTU/lb.
Water	970	212°F	0
Methyl alcohol	481	148°F	9,000 approx.
Ethyl alcohol	396	173°F	12,000 approx.

Even though water does not contain the heating value of alcohol, because of its heat absorption capability more thrust can be obtained by injecting a given volume of water into the engine than an equal mixture of water and alcohol. Although alcohol can be used as fuel after it is used as a coolant, the thrust augmentation factor per unit volume in a water/alcohol mixture is less than that of pure water.

WATER INJECTION SYSTEMS

Not many large aircraft today use water injection because the modern turbofan engine generally has enough thrust capability to offset the negative effect that high ambient temperatures and high runway altitudes have on thrust. However, military transports converted to commercial freighter operations and other smaller aircraft like turboshaft helicopters, may need water injection to meet performance requirements. An advantage is that, when the water is all used, the aircraft is lighter. If a larger engine were to be used, the added engine and subsequent aircraft weight would still be present.

WATER INJECTION SYSTEM (LARGE ENGINE)

Since available thrust quite often determines allowable aircraft takeoff weight, water injection is used almost exclusively at takeoff power settings. For instance, Boeing 707 and DC-8 airplanes carried approximately 300 gallons of water injection fluid per engine, using up the entire supply in a three-minute takeoff and climb. This would equal an air-water ratio of approximately 12 to 1, based on a mass airflow of 160 pounds per second and a water injection rate of 100 gallons per minute (13.6 lb/sec).

In terms of fuel flow, this engine has a takeoff fuel flow of 9,000 pounds per hour (22 gallons per minute). Therefore, with a 100 gallons per minute water flow, a 4.5:1 water to fuel ratio exists.

A typical water injection system is shown in Figure 7-32. Notice that it contains two independent injection nozzles, one to spray water into the compressor inlet and the other to spray into the diffuser/combustor area. Compressor injection increases mass air flow and also cools the combustion air-fuel mixture, allowing increased fuel flow. The addition of fuel increases acceleration of gases exiting the tailpipe. Both of these factors increase the thrust output of the engine.

In the system shown, full thrust augmentation, when required, will necessitate the use of both compressor and diffuser injection. In other installations, it is common to see injection at only one location, either the compressor or diffuser. Although diffuser injection alone will be less effective for a given water flow rate.

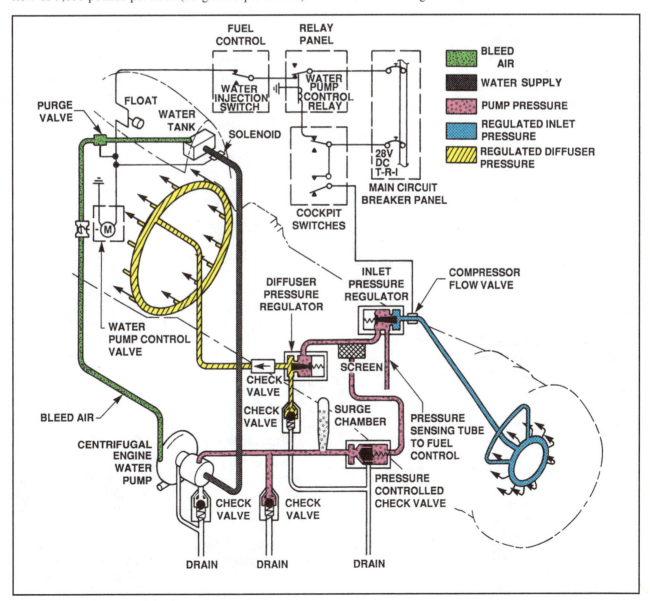

Figure 7-32. Typical water injection system

When the ambient temperature is low, only the diffuser injection system can be used. Below 40°F, at takeoff revolutions per minute, there is a danger of ice formation. At low ambient temperatures, thrust is usually high enough without water injection for almost any aircraft gross takeoff weight.

This water-injection system is controlled by a cockpit switch that arms the circuit and makes flow into both manifolds possible. When closed, the cockpit switch allows electrical current to flow to the fuel control microswitch. As the power lever reaches takeoff power, the microswitch is depressed and the water pump valve will be powered to open. This allows compressor bleed air to flow through the air-driven water pump, which supplies water under a pressure of 200 to 300 pounds p.s.i.g. to the dual manifold.

If compressor flow is not needed, a cockpit switch deactivates the flow valve. The pressure sensing tube to the fuel control alerts the control to increase fuel flow when water is flowing. This system is not generally needed if water/alcohol is used because combustion of the alcohol keeps turbine inlet temperature at its required value.

A tank float level circuit cuts off power to the pump when the tank is empty and prevents the system from operating if the circuit is activated when the water supply is low or unserviced. When the water injection system is not in use, the check valve at the diffuser prevents high temperature air from backing up into the water system.

Drains are present to drain the lines when the system is not in use, preventing freeze-up. The surge chambers alleviate water pressure peaks by providing an air cushioning effect to the system. In some installations, a bleed air system allows the pilot to purge the system of water after terminating water injection. In this system, it will occur automatically when the water supply is depleted, and the water pump control valve redirects bleed air through the purge valve.

WATER INJECTION SYSTEM (SMALL ENGINE)

The system shown in Figure 7-33 uses only compressor inlet injection; compressor discharge air pressure is the motive force for pumping the fluid to the engine. The water line restrictor creates a predictable pressure drop and establishes the correct water schedule at the takeoff power setting. System water flow is between 1.2 and 1.3 gallons per minute at a discharge pressure of approximately 40 p.s.i.g. The duration time for this system is three minutes.

In the example schematic, the following sequence occurs when selecting water injection:

1. Push in the Warning Light circuit breaker. The Water/Alcohol Low Level light will not illuminate because the circuit is open at the System Switch.
2. Push in the System circuit breaker. The Circuit is open at the System Switch.
3. Turn on the System Switch.

   a. The Low Fluid Warning Relay coil circuit is completed to Low Level Float switch.

   b. The Low Fluid Warning Relay coil is energized and contactors move down if the water/alcohol tank is serviced to cause the float switch to be closed.

   c. The circuit is now open to the Water/Alcohol Low Level Light. This light will only illuminate if fluid level is low in the tank, keeping the warning relay contractor closed.

   d. The Injection Switch is powered but the circuit is open.

   e. The Water/Alcohol Injection Light is powered but the circuit is open at the Pressure Switch.

4. Turn on the Injection Switch.

   a. The Solenoid Valve opens and water flows to the engine.

   b. The Pressure switch expands to complete the Water/Alcohol Injection light circuit through the differential pressure switch. Equal pressure on both sides of the diaphragm results in contactor closing.

   c. The Water/Alcohol Injection light illuminates to show normal water flow condition exists. The light will not illuminate if the water tank is not pressurized correctly due to system air leak, loose filler cap, etc., because weak air pressure on the contactor side of the diaphragm will allow contactor to open. This is a safety feature because low air pressure could result in a low water/alcohol flow and could cause low engine power to result.

   d. A low water level in the fluid tank will cause the Water/Alcohol Low Level light to illuminate. When the tank has 30 seconds of water remaining, the float contactor will open, de-energizing the low fluid warning relay.

   e. The Water/Alcohol Injection light will go out when the tank is empty and the contactor side of the differential pressure switch diaphragm experiences a pressure drop in excess of 4.5 to 7.0 pressure per square inch-differential.

   f. Loss of water pressure will also cause the pressure switch to open the circuit to the Water/Alcohol Injection light.

5. Turn off the Injection Switch.

For normal termination of water injection with some water remaining in the tank, turning off the Injection switch will cause the solenoid valve to close and the pressure switch to open the Water/Alcohol Injection light circuit.

At standard conditions, an engine of this type will produce 310 shaft horsepower dry and 335 shaft horsepower wet. [Figure 7-34] This engine would also be capable of attaining its dry-rated power of 310 shaft horsepower, in water injection, up to 95° F.

Fuel Systems

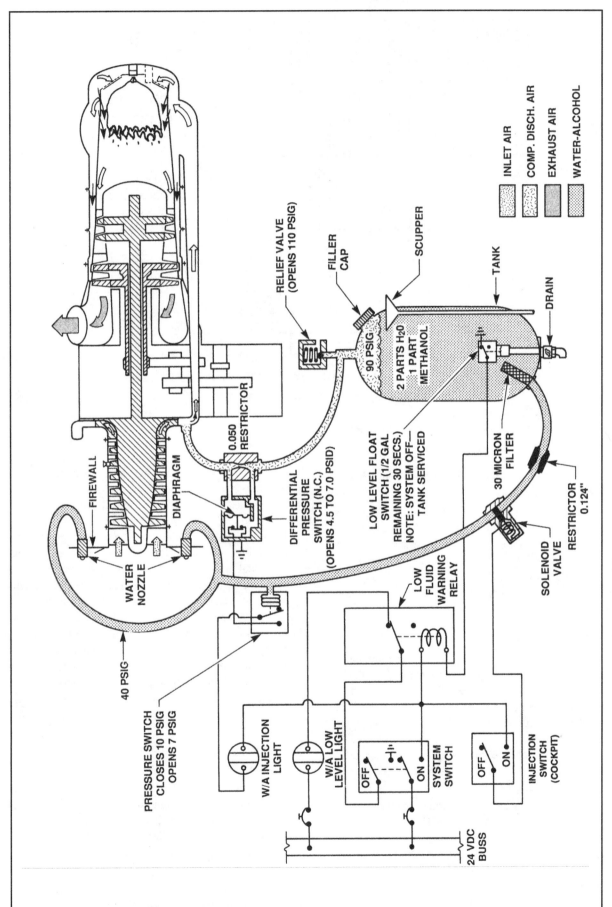

Figure 7-33. Small engine water-alcohol injection system (Allison 250 Turboshaft)

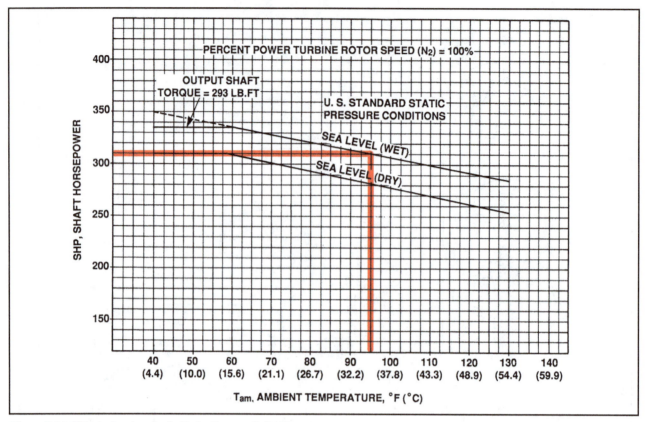

Figure 7-34. Effect of water-alcohol injection on shaft horsepower

FUEL SYSTEM COMPONENTS AND ACCESSORIES

The engine fuel system receives the fuel supply under pressure from electrical aircraft low-pressure booster pumps. This system then increases the pressure using its own pressure booster pump and a high-pressure pump that can produce more than 2000 p.s.i.g. This pump and other fuel system accessories are generally driven by the engine.

MAIN FUEL PUMP

The main fuel pump is an engine-driven component; as a result, when the engine speeds up, the pump also speeds up and delivers more fuel. [Figure 7-35A] The pump delivers a continuous supply of fuel to the fuel control at a quantity in excess of engine needs. After metering the required amount of fuel to the combustor, the fuel control returns the surplus fuel to the pump inlet via the differential pressure-regulating valve previously discussed in the fuel control section.

Main fuel pumps are self-lubricating, and are mainly spur-gear types as shown in Figure 7-35A with single or dual elements. Main fuel pumps often include a centrifugal boost element. The gear pump is classed as a positive displacement pump because it delivers a fixed quantity of fluid per revolution. In this respect, it is very similar to a gear-type oil pump.

In some cases, the main fuel pump is a sliding vane pump and is also classed as a positive displacement pump. Figure 7-35A shows a typical positive displacement pump with an impeller type boost pump installed at its inlet. The boost element is geared to produce the required inlet pressure to the dual high-pressure gear elements. Dual primary and secondary elements, with shear sections on the drive shaft, ensure that if one section fails, the other will continue to function and provide sufficient fuel for cruise and landing operation. Both elements have the same flow capacity. Should either of the gear elements stop rotating because of a malfunction and a subsequent broken shear section, the inner portion of the shaft will continue to drive the boost impeller.

Check valves are present in the outlet to prevent fuel re-circulation into an inoperative element, and a further loss of fuel to the fuel control. A relief valve is incorporated to provide protection to the fuel system if over-speeding or restrictions cause high pressures.

Pumps of this type produce the high pressure necessary for atomization of fuel in the combustor. Many large gear pumps can produce up to 2,000 pounds per square inch and a volume up to 40,000 pounds per hour.

On some engines, the fuel pump provides a mounting base for the fuel control [Figure 7-35B], on others, the fuel pump is not a separate unit; rather the pump housing is integral in the base of the fuel control. [Figure 7-36]

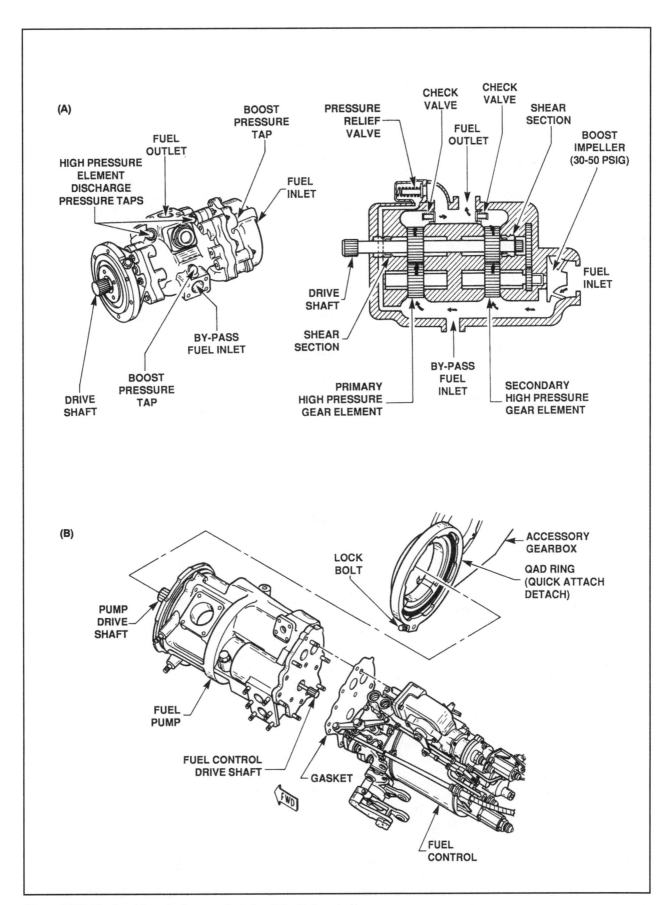

Figure 7-35A. Engine-driven fuel pump, dual element with boost stage
Figure 7-35B. Engine-driven fuel pump with fuel control in tandem

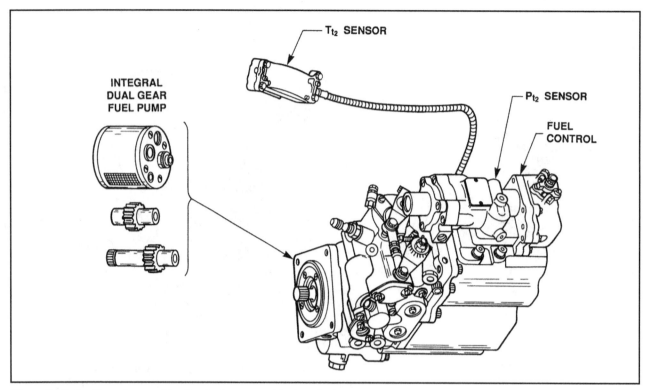

Figure 7-36. Small engine combination fuel pump and fuel control

In the pump illustration shown in Figure 7-37, a coarse screen, low-pressure fuel filter is added to the head end of the pump. In this pump, fuel enters the boost impeller stage and is directed to the outer portion of the low-pressure filter bowl. From there it flows into the core of the filtering element, through an external line, and into the gear element inlet of the main gear pump (A). The bypass referred to in the figure is the fuel control differential bypass regulator valve return line discussed earlier. (See Figure 7-4B) After the fuel leaves the pump outlet, it passes through a fine mesh filter and to the fuel control.

FUEL HEATER (DEICER)

Some engines use only the lubrication system oil cooler for heat transfer to the fuel, while others incorporate a separate fuel heater. [Figure 7-38] The fuel heater is often positioned between the engine fuel boost pump and the engine main fuel pump filter inlet to prevent icing of the filter screen. The fuel-system schematic [Figures 7-54] shows the placement of the fuel heater in relation to other components of the fuel system.

Fuel heat prevents ice crystal formation in entrained water in the fuel supply. When ice forms, it clogs the fuel filter, which can cause the filter to bypass. This condition allows unfiltered fuel to flow to downstream components. In severe cases, icing can cause flow interruption and engine flameout as ice re-forms in components downstream of the filter.

Fuel heat is used when the fuel temperature approaches 32°F. Fuel heat is either automatically activated 3 to 5°F above the freezing point of water or it is selected by a toggle switch in the cockpit. [Figure 7-38] In this system, fuel on its way to the engine low-pressure filter passes through the cores of the heater assembly. When the solenoid switch is open, it allows bleed air to pass through the air shutoff valve and over the cores to warm the fuel.

Typical operational restrictions of fuel heat are as follows:

- Operate for one minute prior to takeoff. Keep in mind that excessive heating can cause vapor lock or heat damage to fuel control.
- Operate as needed should fuel filter bypass light illuminate.
- Do not operate during takeoff, approach, or go-around because of the flameout possibilities from vaporization during these critical flight regimes.

On some installations, an electric timer and gate valve arrangement automatically controls the cycle. To check on the operation, as the system cycles on, the operator can observe cockpit indications such as engine pressure ratio, oil temperature, and the fuel filter light as follows:

- Engine pressure ratio will usually drop a slight but noticeable amount, due to compression loss as bleed air flows.
- Oil temperature will usually rise slightly as fuel temperature rises within the oil cooler.
- If a filter bypass light is illuminated due to filter icing, the light should extinguish as the fuel heat system cycles on and ice dissipates.

Fuel Systems

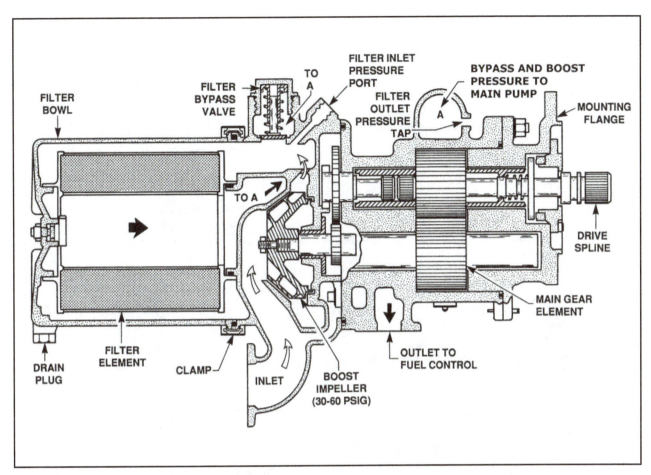

Figure 7-37. Engine-driven fuel pump, single element with low pressure filter

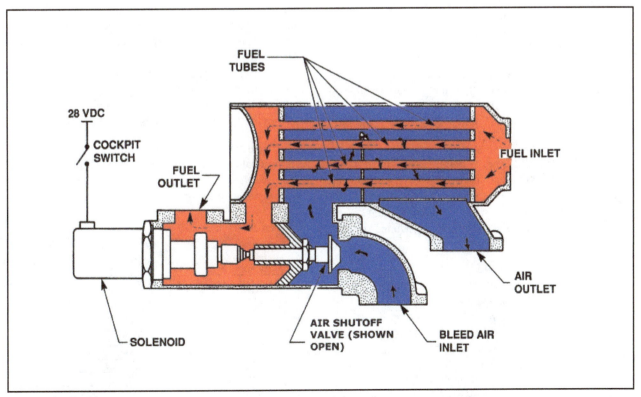

Figure 7-38. Fuel heater

NOTE: If the fuel bypass light remains on, the operator would suspect a solid contamination at the fuel filter rather than icing.

In some aircraft, a separate fuel heat system is not installed because the fuel-oil cooler and additives in the fuel give sufficient protection against fuel icing. If an air-oil cooler is used in place of a fuel-oil cooler, a fuel heat system is generally used.

FUEL FILTERS

Turbine engine fuel systems generally require two levels of filtration: a low-pressure, coarse-mesh filter between the supply tank and the engine and a fine-mesh filter between the fuel pump and the fuel control. The fine filter is necessary because the fuel control has minute passageways and fine tolerances.

Filters for this application have a rating of 10 to 500 microns, depending on the amount of contamination protection needed. A micron is a metric linear measurement of one millionth of a meter, equal to 39.4/1,000,000 of an inch (39.4 millionths of an inch).

Fuel systems use several varieties of filtering elements. The most common are the wafer screen, the steel mesh pleated screen, the steel mesh cylindrical screen, and the cellulose fiber elements. The cellulose fiber filter has an equivalent micron rating. A 35-micron filter of the wafer screen type will have square openings with a size of 35 microns (side to side) and will prevent particles larger than 35 microns in diameter from passing through to the system. The cellulose element with its overlapping fiber design will filter out particles of relatively the same size.

Fuel filter checks are frequent inspection card items for maintenance personnel. If water or metal contaminants are present in the filter element or in the filter bowl, the source of the problem must be determined before returning the aircraft to service.

Figure 7-39A illustrates a wafer screen bowl filter containing a bypass valve. This bypass valve will open at 12 p.s.i.d. In other words, it will open if the downstream pressure is less than the upstream pressure by 12 p.s.i., as would occur if the filter started to accumulate ice crystals or solid contaminants.

In Figure 7-39B, one filter contains two elements. The pleated mesh element filters main system fuel on its way to the combustor and has a filtration rating of 40 microns. A bypass valve relieves at 32 p.s.i.d. if this element clogs. The cylindrical mesh element is rated at 10 microns and filters fuel being routed to the fuel control. The minimal flow in this part of the fuel system permits the use of a very fine filter. This fine filter is needed to protect the highly machined parts of the fuel control, and protect against clogging of the numerous small fluid passageways.

FUEL FILTER WARNING SWITCHES (BYPASS AND LOW PRESSURE)

Fuel filters have warning systems similar to those found in oil systems. A differential pressure switch detects a partial blockage of the filter screen and indicates that an impending bypass condition exists by illuminating an Impending Bypass warning light in the cockpit. [Figures 7-40 and 7-41]

If the filter continues to clog and fuel boost pressure becomes low enough to actuate the low-pressure switch at the outlet of the filter, a Low Fuel Pressure warning light will illuminate in the cockpit, indicating a filter bypass condition. The operator will try to clear the blockage with fuel heat, and, if unsuccessful, most likely reduce power to a safe level, or the operator might elect to shut down the engine.

The fuel temperature transmitter in the filter outlet sends an impulse to a cockpit temperature gauge. If the gauge reading drops close to 32°F, the pilot will turn on fuel heat to prevent ice formation on the surface of the filtering element in the event that there is a high level of water entrained in the fuel.

MICRON RATING VERSUS MESH SIZE

Some fuel filters, rather than having a micron rating, are described in technical literature as having a U.S. sieve number, also called a mesh number. An analysis of the screen size chart of common filter sizes reveals a relationship between a micron rating and the mesh openings per linear inch. The mesh size is very close to, or in some cases the same as, the U.S. sieve number. For example, a 44-μ (micron) filter indicates that the opening size or the square mesh is 44 microns in diameter, or in English measurement equivalents, 0.0017 inches. There are 323 square meshes per linear inch.

The difference in the two ratings is that the micron rating deals with the diameter of the filter screen openings and the U.S. sieve number deals with the number of openings per linear inch.

Screen Size Chart

Opening in Microns	U.S. Sieve #	Opening in Inches	Meshes per Linear Inch
10	---	.00039	1407.94
20	---	.00078	768.07
44	323	.0017	323.00
53	270	.0021	270.26
74	200	.0029	200.00
105	140	.0041	140.86
149	100	.0059	101.01
210	70	.0083	72.45
297	50	.017	52.36

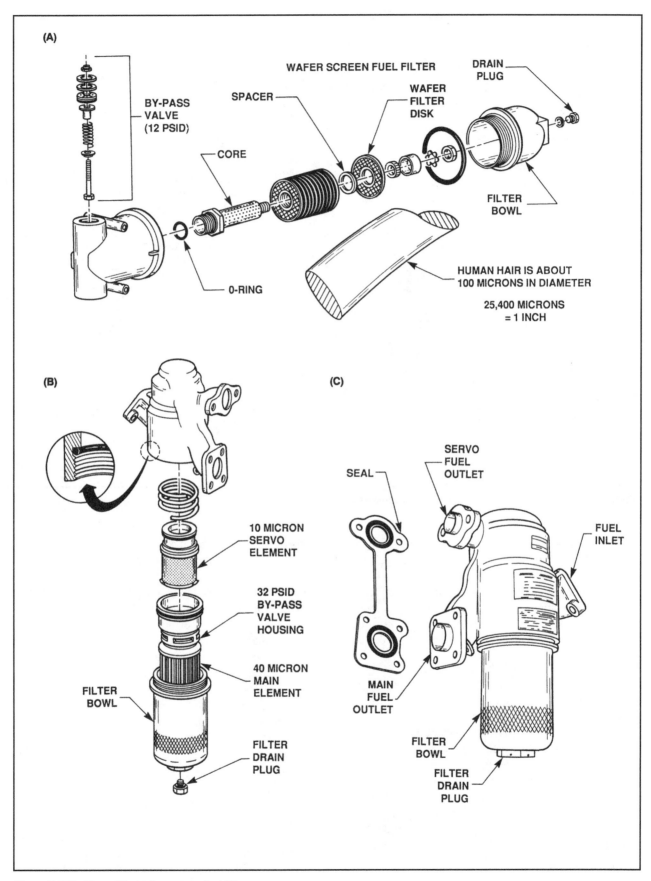

Figure 7-39A. Cleanable wafer screen fuel filter
Figure 7-39B. Dual cleanable steel mesh and pleated filter (exploded view)
Figure 7-39C. Dual cleanable steel mesh filter (assembled)

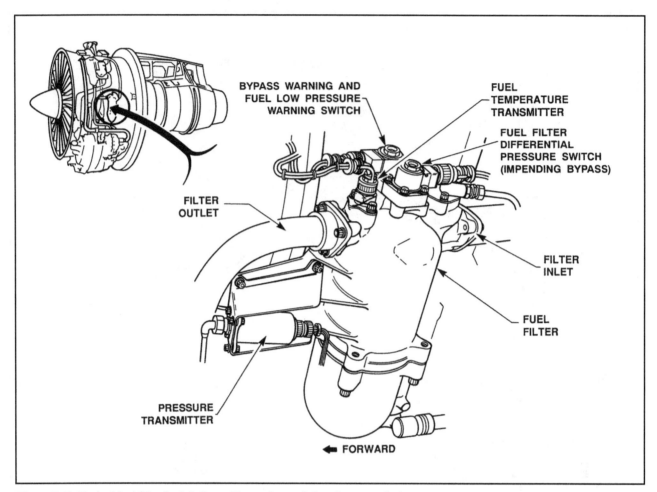

Figure 7-40. Typical fuel filter installation with warning switches (large engine)

FUEL NOZZLES

Fuel nozzles, also called fuel distributors, are the terminating point of the fuel system. They are located in the inlet of the combustion liner to deliver fuel in a defined quantity. Fuel cannot be burned in a liquid state. It must first be mixed with air in correct proportions by atomization or vaporization. The two types of fuel nozzles used in engines today are atomizing and vaporizing nozzles.

PRESSURE-ATOMIZING FUEL NOZZLES

The pressure-atomizing nozzle receives fuel under high pressure from a manifold and delivers it to the combustor in a highly atomized, precisely patterned spray. The cone shaped, atomized spray pattern provides a large fuel surface area of very fine fuel droplets to optimize air-to-fuel mixing and ensure the highest heat release from the fuel. The most desirable flame pattern occurs at higher compressor pressure ratios. Consequently, during starting and other off-design speeds, leading up to cruise power settings the lack of compression allows the flame length to increase with less heat release to the combustor.

If the spray pattern is slightly distorted, as shown in Figure 7-42A, the flame can touch the liner surface and cause a hot spot, or even burn through, rather than being held centered in the liner. Contaminant particles within the nozzle or carbon buildup outside the nozzle orifice also distort the spray pattern. [Figure 7-42B] This can cause hot streaking, which is an un-atomized stream of fuel that forms and tends to cut through the cooling air blanket and impinge on the liner or on downstream components such as the turbine nozzle.

Fuel pressures sufficient for good atomization are very high. Small- to medium-sized engines have a fuel pressure at the nozzle of 800 to 900 p.s.i.g. and large engines up to 2,000 p.s.i.g.

Some fuel nozzles are mounted on pads external to the engine to facilitate removal for inspection. Others are mounted internally and are only accessible when the combustion outer case is removed. Once removed, the nozzles can be flow tested on shop equipment as shown in Figure 7-42C.

Simplex Fuel Nozzles

The simplex design is a small round orifice that provides a single spray pattern. It also incorporates an internally fluted spin chamber to impart a swirling motion and to reduce the axial velocity of the fuel to provide atomization as it exits the orifice. The internal check valve, present in the simplex nozzle shown in Figure 7-43, is there to prevent dribbling of fuel from the fuel manifold into the combustor after shutdown.

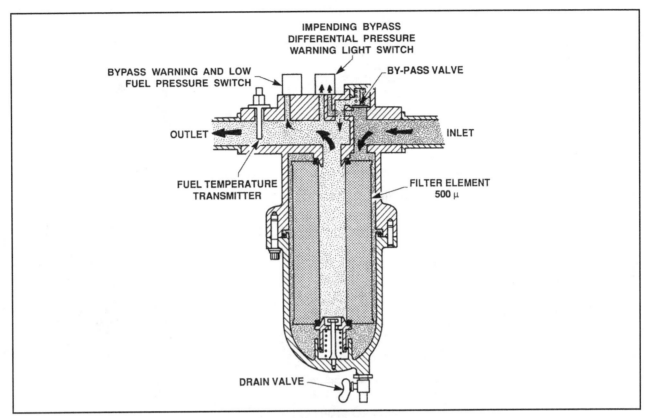

Figure 7-41. Low-pressure filter with bypass warning switches

Some fuel systems with simplex nozzles as their main fuel distributors incorporate a second smaller simplex nozzle, called a primer or starting nozzle, which sprays a very fine atomized mist for improved light-off. After light-off, start/primer systems are generally turned off.

Another configuration with simplex nozzles is called stage or sector burning. The engine is started on one-half or more of the fuel nozzles and operated in that manner up to ground idle speed or slightly above. Then, at approximately flight idle speed, fuel pressure is sufficiently high to overcome check valves, which allows the remaining fuel nozzles to flow.

Single-Line Duplex Fuel Nozzles

The duplex nozzle shown in Figure 7-44A, referred to as a single-line duplex nozzle, receives fuel at one inlet port and becomes two separate flow paths directed to two separate spray orifices by a flow divider valve. Often, the center orifice sprays at a wide angle during engine start and acceleration to idle. The fuel coming from the center orifice is referred to as pilot fuel. The annular outer orifice does not start to receive fuel until the flow divider valve opens at a preset, higher fuel pressure. Fuel, referred to as main fuel, flows from this outer orifice at a narrower angle and much higher volume and pressure, forcing the still flowing pilot fuel to conform to a narrower angle. The narrow angle of the combined pilot and main fuel helps keep the flame front from impinging on the combustion liner at higher power settings. [Figure 7-44B]

There are, however, engines with single-line (or dual-line) duplex nozzles that have flow angles that are different from what is identified in the preceding paragraph. The CFM56 turbofan has single-line duplex nozzles that have the widest flow angle coming from the main orifice, and the narrower angle from the pilot fuel orifice. With advancements that have taken place in combustor design and materials and better control of airflow in the flame zone within the combustor, engines today are able to flow main fuel flow at a wider angle and still protect the metal. This in turn facilitates a more complete mixing of fuel and air.

The duplex nozzles also utilize a spin chamber for each orifice. This arrangement provides an efficient fuel atomization and fuel-air mixture residence time, as it is called, over a wide range of fuel pressures. The high pressure supplied to create the spray pattern, generally 800 to 2,000 p.s.i.g., also gives good resistance to fouling of the orifices from entrained contaminants.

The head of the fuel nozzle is sometimes configured with a series of small air passageways that cool and clean the nozzle head, especially in the area of the spray orifices.

A distortion of the orifice flow area by carbon buildup around the orifice opening can alter the spray pattern. This buildup can be seen on a borescope check on some engines and, if severe enough, could require removal of the nozzles for cleaning. In some installations, the carbon

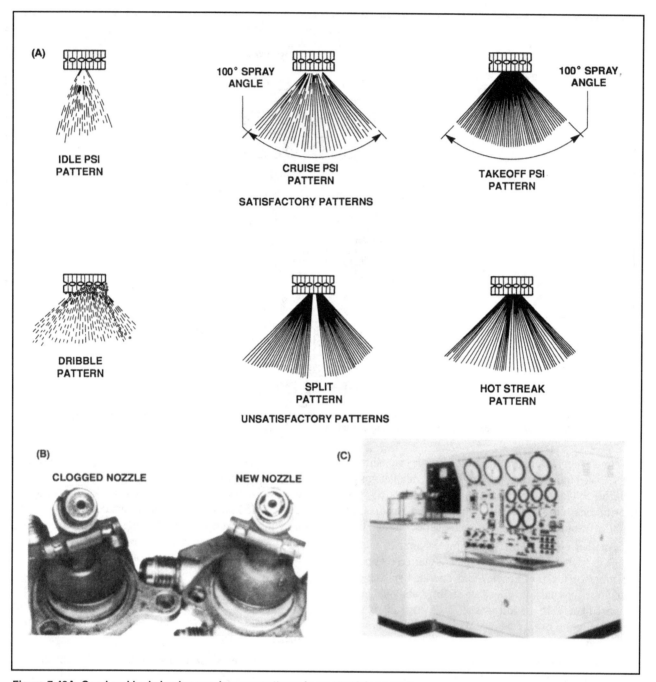

Figure 7-42A. Good and bad simplex nozzle spray patterns in an atomizing nozzle
Figure 7-42B. Carbon build-up on fuel nozzles
Figure 7-42C. Fuel nozzle test stand

buildup could require a flushing procedure or even an engine tear-down to remove the carbon.

Staged Fuel Nozzles

Staged nozzles are an advanced type of single line duplex nozzle. Staging indicates that fuel can be signaled to flow individually at the pilot stage and the main stage or to flow at different rates at the command of an electronic engine controlling (EEC) system. Staged nozzles that schedule fuel flow by computerized signals are not classed as simplex or duplex nozzles previously mentioned. The simplex and duplex nozzles divide the flow using only a simple pressure operated check valve.

The purpose of staging is to achieve leaner, cooler burning; to burn less fuel per pound of thrust; and to meet stricter EPA and FAA emission standards, especially for oxides of nitrogen (NOx) emissions. The idea of trying to reduce NOx is not new, but achieving reliable engine power output at the same time has taken many years of research and development.

Fuel Systems

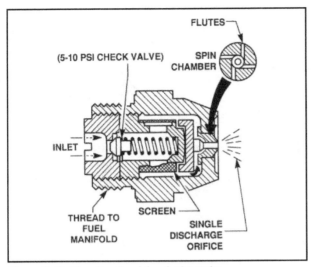

Figure 7-43. Simplex atomizing fuel nozzle

Figure 7-44C shows the dual dome method of staging, using two rings of nozzles with differing flow regimes. The pilot fuel flows from the outer ring initially and the main fuel flows later from the inner ring.

The fuel nozzle used in the newer twin annular premixing swirler (TAPS®) combustor shown in Figure 7-44D is also a staged nozzle system. The term "twin annular" means that two annular air paths, for primary air flowing in a single nozzle head enter into a premixing swirler where air is mixed with fuel. The TAPS® nozzle has the following features:

- Allowable high-volume primary airflow moves from the compressor to the combustor, and then goes through a cyclonic premixing swirler that imparts a high velocity swirl to the fuel-air mixture. The air then ejects through a set of circular openings in the fuel nozzle head. The result is a high-volume, highly atomized fuel flow delivered to the flame zone.

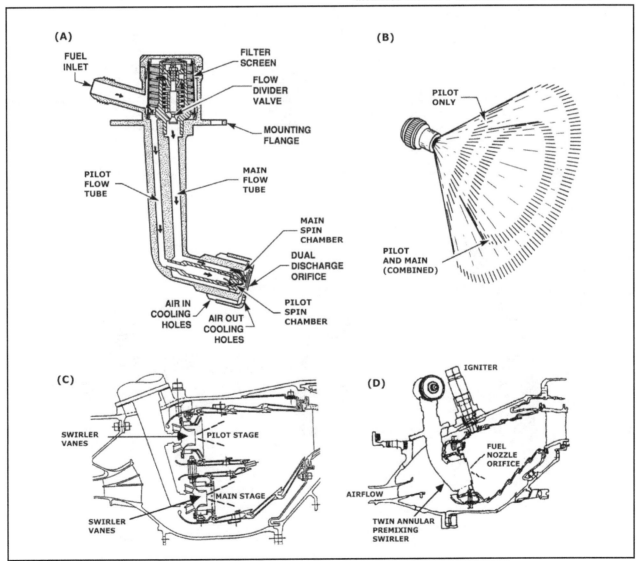

Figure 7-44A. Single-line duplex atomizing fuel nozzle
Figure 7-44B. Duplex nozzle spray pattern
Figure 7-44C. Dual dome staged combustor fuel flow
Figure 7-44D. Twin annular premixing swirler (TAPS)® combustor fuel flow

- Discrete modes with a fixed split of pilot and main fuel flow are present. Pilot fuel is used at start, idle, and taxi operations, then main fuel during power up for takeoff. During the remainder of the engine's operational envelope fuel is constantly modulated across an infinite range of pilot to main flow ratios.
- Accurate flow is determined by an electronic controlling system that provides reliable thrust throughout the entire engine operational range while maintaining a lean fuel mixture, low-combustion temperatures, and low oxides of nitrogen emissions.

Dual-Line Duplex Fuel Nozzles

A dual-line duplex nozzle, like those used in older Pratt & Whitney engines, is quite similar to the single-line duplex nozzles previously mentioned except that it contains no flow divider check valve to separate pilot and main fuel. [Figure 7-45A and 7-45B] The check valve in this system is discussed later at the pressurizing and dump valve [Figure 7-49]; it is labeled "Pressurizing Valve." The pressurizing valve acts as a single, main flow divider for all of the fuel nozzles, whereas in the single-line duplex nozzle, each has its own flow divider in the form of its check valve.

Air Blast Simplex and Duplex Fuel Nozzles

The air blast fuel nozzle is another design used in various sized engines because it enhances the atomization process and produces finer fuel droplets. [Figures 7-46A and B] This nozzle is more effective during starting when

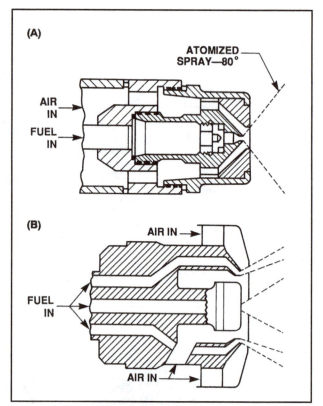

Figure 7-46A. Air-blast fuel nozzle (simplex)
Figure 7-46B. Air-blast fuel nozzle (duplex)

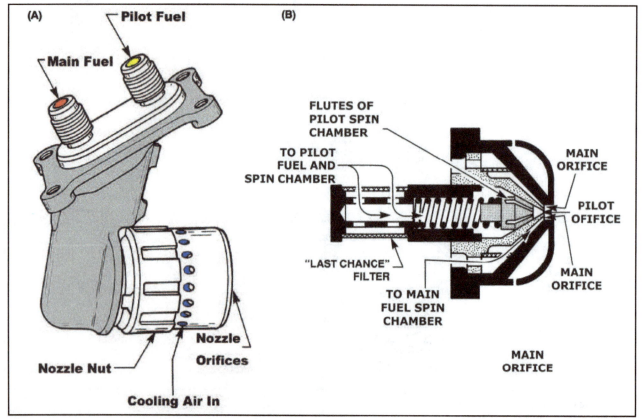

Figure 7-45A. Dual-line duplex atomizing fuel nozzle assembly
Figure 7-45B. Duplex fuel nozzle (cutaway view)

Fuel Systems

low fuel pressure causes atomization problems. By using high-velocity airflow, air blast nozzles more completely atomize the fuel than pressure alone can. This nozzle also has an advantage in that it uses a lower system working pressure than the basic atomizing nozzles.

FUEL NOZZLES (VAPORIZING TYPE)

The vaporizing fuel nozzle shown in Figure 7-47 connects to a fuel manifold in an arrangement similar to the atomizing nozzle, but instead of delivering the fuel directly into the primary air of the combustor, the vaporizing tube premixes the primary air and fuel. Combustor heat surrounding the nozzle causes the mixture to vaporize before exiting into the combustor flame zone. [Figure 7-48A and 7-48B] This type of nozzle uses high heat to get the fuel into a combustible state, whereas atomizing nozzles use high pressure. This very old design is still in use today in a small number of engines.

Whereas the atomizer nozzle discharges in the downstream direction, the vaporizer discharges in the upstream direction and the mixture then makes a 180-degree turn to move downstream. This arrangement provides a slow moving, fine spray over a wide range of fuel flows and produces more stable combustion than atomizing nozzles in some engines, especially at low engine speed. Some vaporizers have only one outlet and are referred to as cane-shaped vaporizers.

Figure 7-47 shows a tee-shaped vaporizer, one of a set of eleven used in some models of the Lycoming T-53 turboshaft engine. Because vaporizing nozzles do not provide an effective spray pattern for starting, the T-53 incorporates an additional set of small atomizing spray nozzles that spray into the combustor during starting. After light off, start fuel is terminated on spool-up to idle. This system is generally referred to as a primer or starting fuel system.

FUEL PRESSURIZING AND DUMP VALVE

A pressurizing and dump valve (P & D valve) is used along with a duplex fuel nozzle of the dual inlet line type. [Figures 7-49A, 7-49B, and 7-49C] Rather than providing a flow divider in each nozzle, as with the single-line duplex fuel nozzle, this arrangement has one central flow divider, called a pressurizing and dump (P & D) valve. The term "pressurizing" refers to the fact that at a pre-set pressure, a pressurizing valve within the P & D valve opens and fuel flows into the main manifold as well as through the pilot manifold.

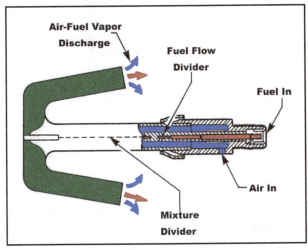

Figure 7-47. Heat-vaporizing fuel nozzle

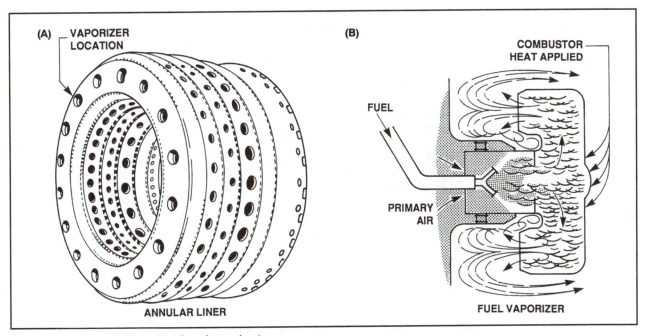

Figure 7-48A. Vaporizer tube locations in combustor
Figure 7-48B. Vaporizer tube in operation

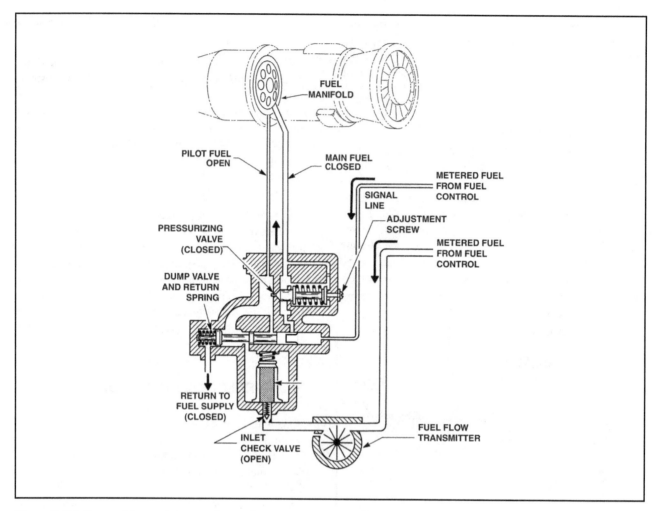

Figure 7-49A. Pressurizing and dump valve, engine operating at ground idle

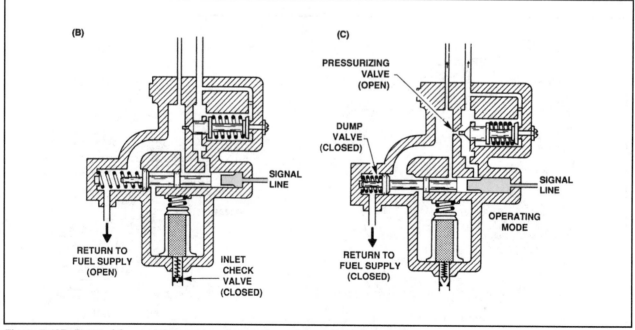

Figure 7-49B. Pressurizing and dump valve, dump valve open, engine not operating
Figure 7-49C. Pressurizing valve open, engine operating above flight idle speed

Fuel Systems

The term "dump" refers to a second internal valve that has the capability of dumping the entire fuel manifold after shutdown. Manifold dumping is a procedure that sharply cuts off combustion and prevents fuel boiling because of residual engine heat. This boiling leaves solid deposits in the manifold that could clog the fuel nozzles.

In Figures 7-49A, a pressure signal from the fuel control arrives at the P & D valve when the power lever is opened for engine start. This pressure signal shifts the dump valve to the left, closing the dump port and opening the passageway to the manifolds. Metered fuel pressure builds at the inlet check valve until it overcomes the spring force and fuel flows through the filter to the pilot manifold. At a speed slightly above ground idle, fuel pressure will be sufficient to overcome the pressurizing valve spring force, and fuel will also flow to the main manifold. [Figures 7-49C]

Adjusting the tension on the pressurizing valve spring is a line maintenance task. A valve opening too early can give an improper fuel spray pattern and create hot starts or off-idle stalls. A late-opening valve can cause slow-acceleration problems. To delay the opening of the main manifold and eliminate hot start or off-idle stalls, turn the adjusting screw in to increase tension on the pressurizing valve spring. Conversely, turn the adjuster out to cause early fuel flow to the main manifold and enhance acceleration.

To shut off the engine, the fuel lever in the cockpit is moved to off. The fuel control pressure signal is lost, and spring pressure shifts the dump valve back to the right, opening the dump valve port. At the same time, the inlet check valve closes, keeping the metered line flooded and ready for use on the next engine start. [Figure 7-49B]

DUMP VALVE

The dump valve, sometimes called a drip valve, is incorporated in the low point of fuel manifolds with simplex and single-line duplex fuel nozzles. [Figure 7-50] Its sole purpose is to drain the fuel manifold after engine shutdown. The dump valve in this illustration works identically to the dump valve in the P & D valve.

COMBUSTOR DRAIN VALVE

The combustor drain valve shown in Figure 7-52 is a mechanical device in the low point of the combustor case. Gas pressure within the combustor closes this valve during engine operation and spring pressure opens it when the engine is not in operation. This valve prevents fuel accumulation in the combustor after a false start or whenever fuel might puddle at the low point. This fuel is then directed to a drain tank.

A false start is defined as a no-start or hung-start condition that results in a fuel soaked combustor and tailpipe.

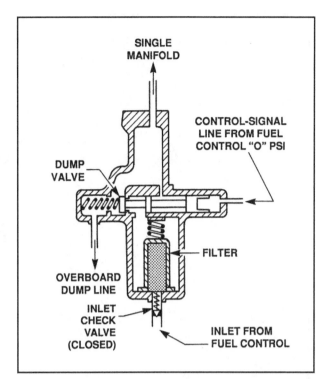

Figure 7-50. Dump valve, shown with dump valve open—engine not operating

Draining fuel in this manner prevents such safety hazards as after-fires and hot starts. This drain also removes unatomized fuel that could ignite near the lower turbine stator vanes and cause serious local overheating during starting, when cooling airflow is at the lowest flow rate.

DRAIN TANKS

Dump fuel, in years past, had been allowed to spill onto the ground or siphon from a drain tank in flight. However, FAA regulations now prohibit this form of environmental pollution, and the drain tank fuel must be captured and later manually or automatically drained. Figure 7-51 shows this drain tank. To prevent hand-draining, several types of recycling systems have also evolved; one returns fuel to the aircraft fuel supply while

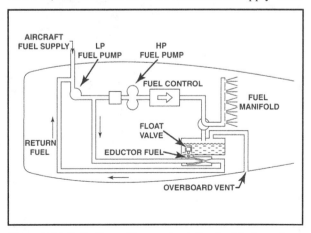

Figure 7-51. Rolls-Royce Tay—recirculating fuel drain system

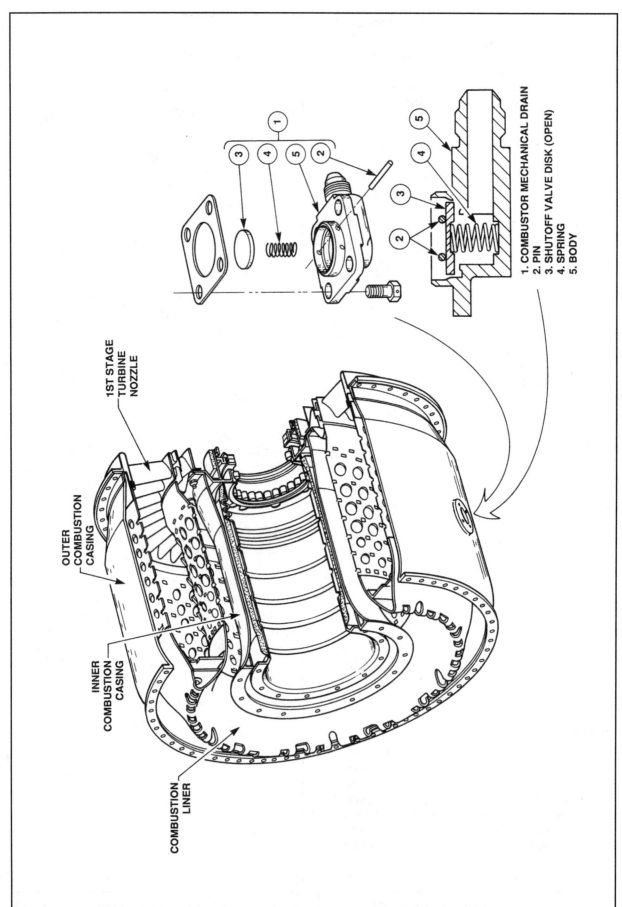

Figure 7-52. Combustor fuel drain valve

Fuel Systems

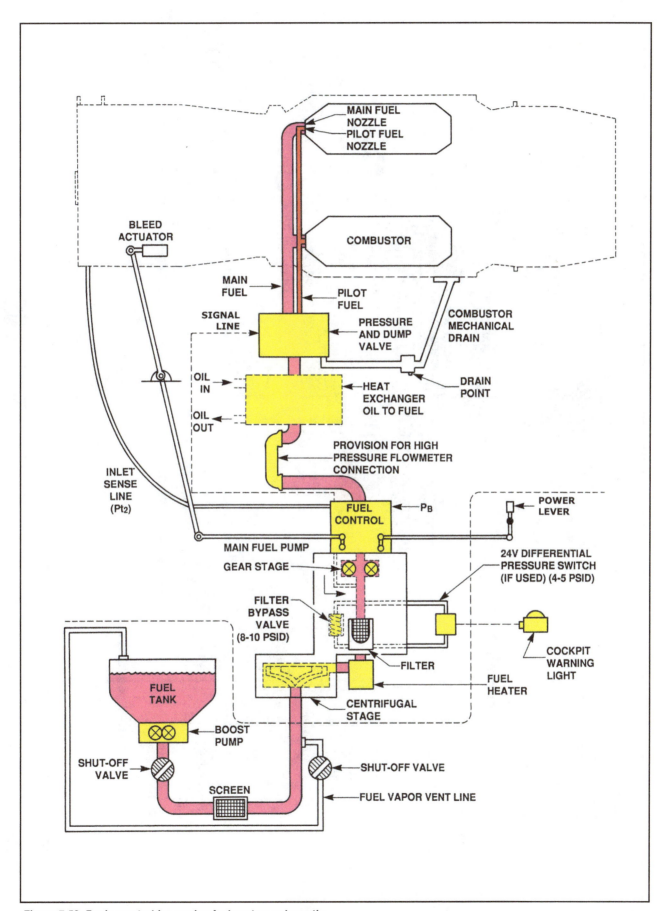

Figure 7-53. Basic gas turbine engine fuel system schematic

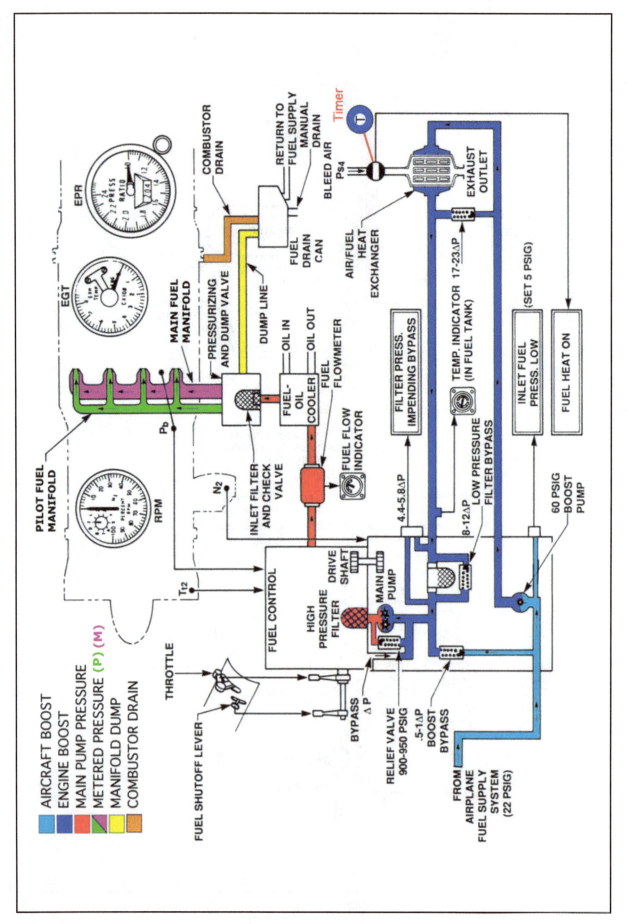

Figure 7-54. Fuel system schematic (Pratt & Whitney JT8D turbofan)

another uses bleed air to push fuel out of the fuel nozzles. This prolongs combustion slightly until fuel starvation occurs. In the system shown in Figure 7-51, a full tank causes a float valve to actuate and drain the tank. In this instance, this is accomplished by an eductor siphoning system. Fuel manifold drain tanks are also shown on Figures 7-53 and 7-54.

EXAMPLE OF A CORPORATE ENGINE FUEL SYSTEM

The following is a complete fuel system schematic that shows the relationship of component parts. This configuration is typical of a basic gas turbine engine fuel system. [Figure 7-53]

1. Fuel storage tank
2. Boost pump — present to help eliminate vapor lock
3. Shutoff valve — FAA regulation requires its presence
4. Fuel screen — coarse mesh (200 micron)
5. Vapor vent — present to help eliminate vapor lock
6. Centrifugal stage — incorporated in the main fuel pump
7. Fuel heater
8. Fine filter — (20 micron)
9. Gear stage main fuel pump — operating range 100 to 800 p.s.i.g.
10. Fuel control — hydro-mechanical unit
11. Fuel flow meter
12. Heat exchanger — (fuel cooled oil cooler)
13. P & D valve
14. Pilot fuel manifold and fuel nozzles
15. Main fuel manifold and fuel nozzles

The 24V differential pressure switch illuminates a cockpit warning light if the fuel pump filter is clogged and approaching a bypass condition.

EXAMPLE OF A COMMERCIAL ENGINE FUEL SYSTEM (PRATT & WHITNEY JT8D)

The following is a complete fuel system schematic showing the relationship of the components on a typical commercial-sized engine. This fuel system is in a Boeing 727 aircraft. [Figure 7-54]

1. Aircraft fuel tank and boost pump
2. Engine centrifugal boost pump — bypass set 0.5 to 1.0 p.s.i.g.
3. Air-fuel heater — bypass set to 20, ± 3 pounds per square inch–differential (p.s.i.g.)
4. Low pressure fuel filter — (40 micron disposable) bypass set to 8 to 12 p.s.i.g.
5. Main gear-type fuel pump — operating range 150 to 900 p.s.i.g.
6. Fuel control — fuel flows via high pressure filter (20 micron cleanable) bypass set to 27 to 30 p.s.i.g.
7. Fuel flowmeter transmitter
8. Fuel-oil cooler
9. Pressurizing and dump valve
10. Pilot fuel manifold and pilot fuel nozzles
11. Main fuel manifold and main fuel nozzles

EXAMPLE OF A COMMERCIAL ENGINE FUEL SYSTEM (G.E./ SNECMA CFM56)

The schematic shown in Figure 7-55 is for the fuel system in the CFM56 engine, as used on the Boeing 737-800 aircraft.

1. Aircraft boost pumps provide fuel to the engine driven centrifugal boost pump.
2. The engine driven low-pressure boost pump provides fuel to the integrated drive generator (IDG) fuel/oil cooler. The cooler incorporates a bypass valve equipped with an IDG bypass switch that alerts the cockpit if the cooler clogs and a pressure differential occurs between the cooler inlet and outlet.
3. From the IDG cooler, fuel flows to the engine fuel/oil heat exchanger. The heat exchanger incorporates a bypass valve equipped with a heat exchanger bypass switch that alerts the cockpit if the heat exchanger clogs and a pressure differential occurs between the cooler inlet and outlet.
4. From the fuel/oil heat exchanger, fuel flows to the low-pressure fuel filter. The filter incorporates a bypass valve equipped with a bypass switch that illuminates a cockpit warning light, alerting the flight crew if the filter clogs and a pressure differential occurs between the filter inlet and outlet.
5. Low-pressure filter fuel discharge goes to the gear type high-pressure pump.
6. From the high-pressure pump, fuel flows in two directions:

   a. Fuel flows to the servo wash filter, which cleans it for use in the hydro mechanical unit (HMU) as servo fuel. If this filter clogs, the filter bypass valve will route a sufficient amount of high-pressure fuel to operate the servo system. The servo fuel also powers the actuators for the variable vane system and the compressor bleed system.

   b. Fuel also flows from the high-pressure pump directly into the HMU fuel metering valve (FMV). If the pressure of this fuel is too high, the pressure relief valve will route fuel back to the low-pressure side of the system.

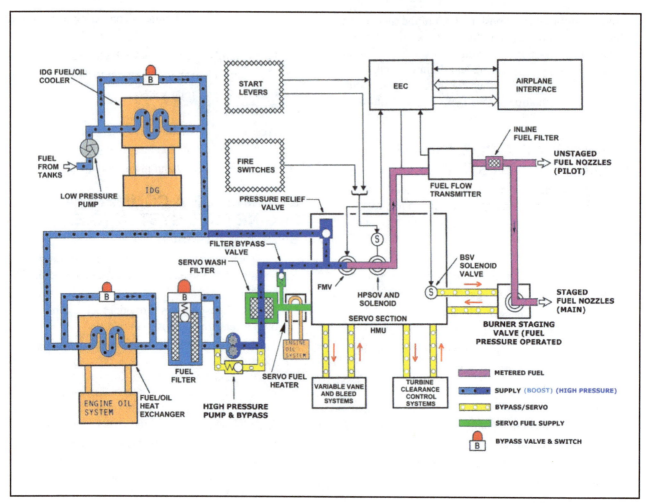

Figure 7-55. Fuel system schematic (G.E./Snecma CFM56-7)

7. Servo fuel on its way to the HMU also flows through the servo fuel heater, using the engine oil supply as a heat source to prevent fuel icing. Heat transfer into the fuel also tends to cool the oil supply.

8. Within the metering portion of the HMU, the fuel flows to the metering valve (FMV) and the high-pressure shutoff valve (HPSOV), and then exits the HMU. The position of the FMV is controlled by the EEC. The high-pressure shutoff valve and its solenoid, shown as a circled "S" in the illustration, is controlled by the start levers and fire switches on the flight deck. In the event of a fire, the fire switches close the HPSOV.

9. After exiting the HMU, the fuel goes through a fuel flow transmitter and an inline fuel filter (last chance filter).

10. From the inline fuel filter, fuel goes out to the un-staged fuel nozzles (10 single-line duplex nozzles), and to the burner staging valve (BSV).

11. The burner staging valve (BSV), which is controlled by the EEC and operated by fuel pressure, prevents fuel from flowing to the 10-staged fuel nozzles at low engine speeds and airflow to the combustor. As engine speed and airflow increase, the burner staging valve opens and allows fuel to flow to the staged nozzles.

For the CFM56 engine, the terms un-staged fuel and staged fuel have the same application as the concept of pilot and main fuel. Fuel flows to the un-staged nozzles (pilot fuel) during engine start and at low-power operation. As the engine accelerates beyond idle r.p.m., the EEC controls the opening of the burner staging valve and the flow of staged fuel (main fuel).

Figure 7-56A shows the fuel system overhead panel display located on the flight deck. This display provides information about the airframe and the engine fuel system and gives the flight crew control over the fuel tank boost pumps and cross feed. The electronic engine control and the FADEC system provide engine-related information, such as "Filter Bypass" and "Eng Valve Closed," to this display.

If the "Filter Bypass" indication illuminates, the flight crew knows the EEC has detected an unacceptable pressure drop across the low-pressure fuel filter. Because this problem is often caused by ice clogging the filter, which

Fuel Systems

is related to fuel temperature, the fuel temperature gauge is located right above the bypass lights.

The "Eng Valve Closed" indication on Figure 7-56A shows the status of the high-pressure shutoff valve located in the hydro-mechanical unit (HMU) [Figure 7-55]:

- The light is off when the valve is open.
- The light is dim when the valve is closed.
- The light is bright when a fault is detected.

Figure 7-56B shows an example of a message being generated by the BITE system for an airplane powered by the CFM56-7 engine. The message appears on the CDU, which is located on the flight deck forward of the throttles. [Figure 7-56C] If an engine malfunctions during flight, the aircraft's computers store information about the malfunction. After the airplane lands, maintenance personnel can access information about the malfunction by bringing up the engine page on the CDU. The BITE system, and the information it transmits to the CDU, is invaluable in helping the technician troubleshoot an engine malfunction and correct a problem. The information can be so detailed that it identifies the cause of the problem and what will fix it.

NOTE: Chapter 5 details general troubleshooting procedures, Chapter 7 touches on FADEC interface.

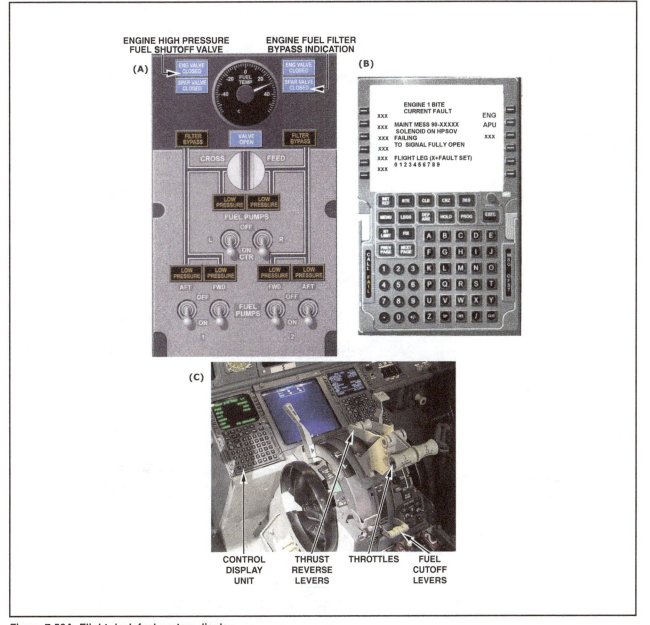

Figure 7-56A. Flight deck fuel system display
Figure 7-56B. Control display unit showing a BITE message
Figure 7-56C. Boeing 737 throttle quadrant and control display unit

TROUBLESHOOTING FUEL SYSTEMS

PROBLEM/POSSIBLE CAUSE	CHECK FOR	REMEDY
1. Engine motors over but does not start—No fuel or low fuel when fuel control shutoff valve is opened.		
a. No fuel to engine	Correct fuel tank level	Service
b. Improper rigging of shutoff valve (aircraft and engine)	Full travel	Re-rig linkage
c. Engine filters	Clogging or icing, degrading spray pattern	Clean
d. Malfunctioning fuel pump	Correct output pressure	Adjust relief valve or replace pump
e. Malfunctioning fuel control	Correct output pressure	Replace control
2. Engine motors over but does not start—Good fuel flow indication but no exhaust gas temperature.		
a. Ignition system	Weak or no spark	See ignition troubleshooting
b. P and D valve	1. Dump valve stuck open	Replace valve
	2. Pressurizing valve stuck open (also affects working pressure and atomization at fuel nozzles)	Adjust or replace
3. Engine starts but hangs up and will not self-accelerate to idle.		
a. Starter	Cut-out speed—too early	See starter troubleshooting
b. Fuel control	Entrapped air preventing proper operation	Bleed unit as per manual
c. Fuel control sensing lines	Looseness causing loss of signal	Tighten
d. P & D valve	Pressurization valve stuck open, degrading spray pattern	Adjust or replace valve
4. Engine hot start.		
a. Fuel control	High fuel flow indication	Replace control
b. P & D valve	1. Partially open dump valve affecting fuel schedule and atomization at fuel nozzles causing late hot start	Replace P & D valve
	2. Partially open pressurizing valve, which causes late hot start	
5. Engine unable to attain takeoff power.		
a. Improper fuel control setting	Partially open pressurizing valve, which causes trim adjustment or linkage problem	Re-trim or re-rig
b. Fuel filters	Partial clogging, degrading spray pattern	Clean
c. Fuel pump	1. Correct output pressure	Adjust relief valve
	2. One pumping element sheared	Replace pump
d. Fuel control	Correct output pressure and fuel flow	Replace fuel control

Fuel Systems 7-69

PROBLEM/POSSIBLE CAUSE	CHECK FOR	REMEDY
6. Engine unable to attain full power without exceeding limits of EGT or r.p.m.		
a. Compressor or turbine	Contamination or damage	Possible teardown
b. Bleed air	Engine or customer service bleed air flowing when it should not be	Replace air valve or correct electrical fault
7. Flame-out—When applying takeoff power.		
a. Fuel pump — one element sheared shaft or relief valve open	Low pressure at high r.p.m.	Replace pump
b. Fuel control	Correct fuel flow indication	Replace control
8. Engine is slow to accelerate/engine off idle stalls.		
a. Same as 5 and 6		
b. P & D valve	Correct pressurizing valve adjustment	Adjust spring force or replace P & D valve
9. Transitory combustor rumble on acceleration.		
a. P & D valve	Correct cracking point of pressurizing valve	Reset to decrease cracking point
b. Fuel control	Proper output pressure	Replace fuel control

QUESTIONS:

1. *What is the name of the fuel scheduling device most widely used on gas turbine engines?*
2. *What is the name of the control lever on the fuel control?*
3. *Is there a mixture control lever on a turbine engine fuel control?*
4. *What fuel control input signal is a measure of mass airflow through a gas turbine engine?*
5. *What type of fluid is used in water injection systems?*
6. *At what power setting is water injection used?*
7. *What term refers to making fuel control idle speed and maximum power adjustments during performance running?*
8. *What is the purpose of the engine trim check?*
9. *What does the EPR gauge indicate?*
10. *What are the two best ambient conditions for trimming?*
11. *Of the two types of fuel pumps (spur gear and centrifugal), which is a positive displacement pump?*
12. *Where is fuel system icing most prevalent?*
13. *During which engine operational mode is pilot fuel used by itself?*
14. *What are the two purposes of a pressurizing and dump valve?*
15. *What force closes the combustion case drain?*
16. *What is the function of the FADEC system?*
17. *What is the function of the EEC unit?*
18. *What is the function of the BITE system in a FADEC system?*
19. *What is the function of the Auto-throttle system?*
20. *Where in the FADEC system is the control display unit (CDU) located?*

CHAPTER 8
Compressor Anti-Stall Systems

Anti-stall systems are incorporated on many gas turbine engines, both large and small. They are needed where compressor stall frequently presents problems during acceleration or deceleration at either low compressor speeds or intermediate compressor speeds. Stalling can be controlled by varying the angle of the inlet guide vanes or the compressor stator vanes, or both, to partially block excess airflow. Another way to provide an anti-stall capability is by bleeding unwanted air overboard using a compressor anti-stall bleed system.

VARIABLE ANGLE COMPRESSOR STATOR VANE SYSTEM (LARGE ENGINE)

The variable angle compressor stator vane system is required on most high-compression engines. Stalling occurs because the low-pressure compressor supplies more air than the high-pressure compressor can accept. The variable stator vanes automatically vary the geometry (both area and shape) of the compressor gas path to exclude unwanted air and maintain the correct relationship between compressor speed and airflow, especially in the front compressor stages.

At low compressor speeds, the variable stator vanes are partially closed off to decrease airflow. As compressor rotor speed increases, the stator vanes open to permit more air to flow through the high-pressure compressor. In effect, varying the stator vane angle schedules the correct angle-of-attack relationship between the angle of airflow approaching the rotor blades and the rotor blade leading edges. A correct angle-of-attack facilitates smooth and rapid engine acceleration at the highest degree of compressor efficiency. Another way to consider the situation is that the deflection of airflow imposed on the airstream by varying the stator vane angles slows the airstream's axial velocity before it reaches the rotor blades, thus matching the low speed of the rotor blade and the low axial velocity of the airstream.

For example, keeping in mind the angle of attack of the compressor blades as discussed in Chapter 3, the vector diagram would look like Figures 8-1A and 8-1B. Figure 8-1A represents a normal condition of approximately 15 degrees effective angle of attack with the variable vanes at their normal 30-degree closed position. The upper portion of Figure 8-1C shows this relationship viewed from the blade and vane tips. Figure 8-1B shows that if the variable vane system malfunctioned in the 40-degree closed position (as shown in the lower portion of Figure 8-1C), the velocity in the axial direction would decrease, even though idle speed remains the same. For example, assume that inlet velocity in this case decreased from 200 feet per second to 100 feet per second, and the effective angle-of-attack increased from 15 degrees to 25 degrees. The result of this change would be a loss of compression and the increased possibility of a stall upon acceleration off idle due to the mismatch in airflow between the front stage and the rear stages.

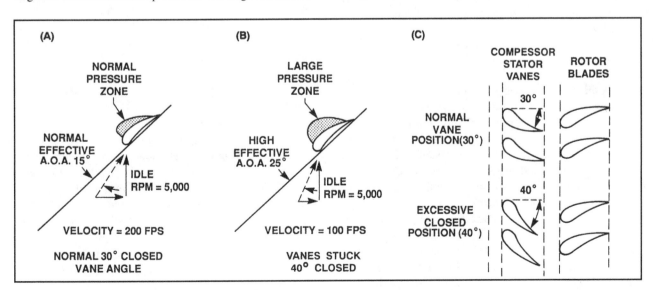

Figure 8-1A. Compressor blade with normal A. O. A.
Figure 8-1B. Compressor blade with high A. O. A.
Figure 8-1C. Stator vane positions

SYSTEM OPERATION — GENERAL ELECTRIC CF-6 TURBOFAN

The system illustrated in Figure 8-2 shows the inlet guide vanes and the six stator stages of the N_2 compressor as being variable. To permit movement, the vanes are fitted with Teflon® sockets at both ends. The remaining vane stages are conventionally installed stationary vanes.

This system uses fuel-control-discharge pressure to position hydraulic actuators, which are located on the compressor case. The actuators move the vanes open by a beam arrangement. The beam attaches to vane actuating rings that connect to the variable stator vanes.

As the power lever is moved forward, fuel pressure increases at the head end of the actuator to open the vanes. The mechanical feedback cable signals the fuel control to cut off fuel pressure and permits the position of the vanes to stabilize at the correct angle.

The compressor inlet temperature (CIT) sensor (also referred to as the Tt_2 sensor) shown in Figure 8-2 is a heat-sensitive, gas-filled bulb that receives a fuel signal at constant pressure. The sensor also manages return pressure of a regulated value based on the temperature in the engine inlet. The CIT sensor contains a fuel-metering orifice to accomplish this. The fuel control uses the return signal to schedule vane position through the rod end and head end fuel-actuating lines. Even when the power lever is in a fixed position, the CIT sensor continues to control compressor vane angles.

Because changes to ambient temperature also affect mass airflow, the CIT sensor is configured to reset the vane-open schedule to match those changes. At low Tt_2 values, the air is more dense, and the vane system will start to open at a lower compressor speed to increase airflow. This is necessary because cool, dense air has a tendency to move more slowly than warm air. In this way, the air velocity and compressor speed stay in the proper relationship to maintain a correct angle of attack.

Another way to consider the situation is that if compressor inlet temperature decreases, compression increases in the rear stages, which do not have variable vanes. Added compression in the rear stages starts to slow airflow. When the CIT sensor schedules the vanes to open earlier, increased airflow (mass and velocity) occurs in the front stages to accelerate air in the rear stages to its former velocity. This keeps the proper relationship between compressor speed and compressor air velocity to maintain the angle-of-attack. If a temperature shift downward occurs when the variable vanes are fully open, they obviously cannot open wider. In this case, other sensors in the fuel control bring about a reduction in fuel flow and compressor speed, which in turn brings compressor speed back down to match air velocity.

VARIABLE ANGLE COMPRESSOR VANE SCHEDULE

The operational aspects of the variable system are best illustrated in its operating schedule. In Figure 8-3, note that when on normal schedule (indicated by "Standard Day"), the vanes remain closed up to 65 percent N_2 speed, at which time they begin to open; by 95 percent N_2 speed, they are fully open.

When inlet temperature increases or decreases from Standard Day conditions, the vane schedule also changes. For example, if ambient temperature drops to 30°F, the vanes start to open at approximately 60 percent N_2 speed instead of 65 percent, and they would be fully opened at 92 percent instead of 95 percent. This accomplishes the same change in relationship between compressor and air velocity as in the previous discussion about temperature shifts and angle of attack. If the CIT sensor fails or the linkages to the variable vanes are incorrectly adjusted, the correct vane schedule will not be met and a compressor stall is likely to occur.

The engine-mounted protractor shown in Figure 8-2 provides the technician with a means of checking the vane position while the engine is operating, which enables the technician to plot the vane schedule of operation against a standard curve.

NECESSITY OF VARIABLE ANGLE COMPRESSOR VANES

A comparison of compressor stall-line curves for engines with and without variable vanes reveals the necessity of a variable-vane system for high-compression engines.

Compressors are designed such that for any given mass airflow and compressor speed, a certain compressor pressure ratio (Cr) exists. In Figure 8-4, which corresponds to an engine with no means of varying the angle of the compressor stator vanes, the line A-B represents the results of factory testing to establish the maximum mass airflow to compressor pressure ratio relationship that can exist without a compressor stall. This curve is similar to the stall margin curve discussed in Chapter 3, except that it is simplified to include only two plots, compressor pressure ratio and mass airflow; the compressor speed lines are not included.

Any compressor pressure ratio above the stall line A-B indicates a compressor ratio that is too high for existing mass airflow and that will result in a stall. Operating line C-D indicates a normal relationship of compressor ratio to mass airflow. However, if too much fuel flow is applied during acceleration, excessive combustor pressure can result, which causes a blockage of mass airflow and a rise in compressor pressure ratio. This condition results in line A-B being exceeded with a resulting compressor stall.

Engines equipped with variable vanes use them to establish the correct relationship of compressor pressure

Compressor Anti-Stall Systems

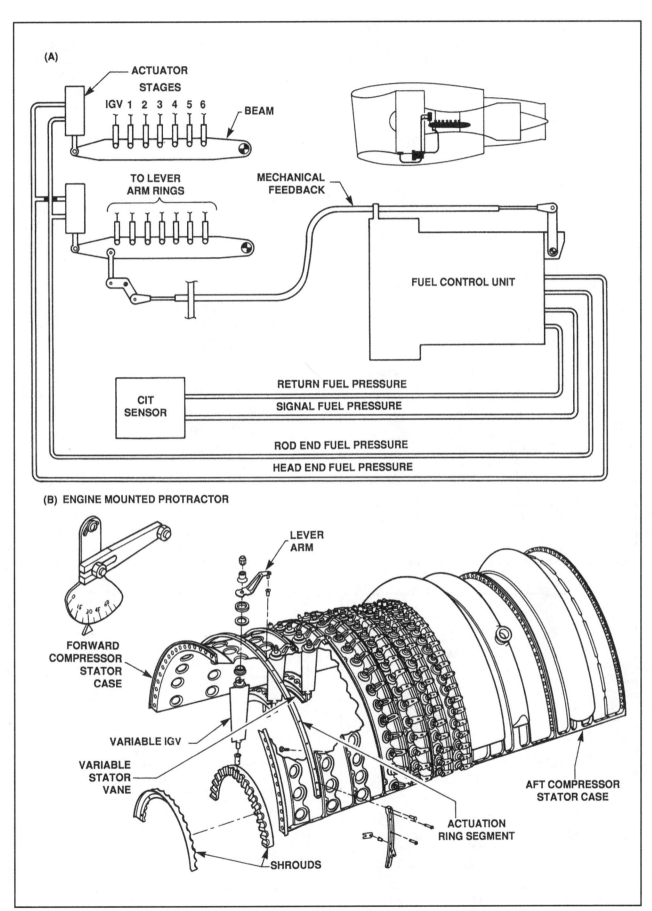

Figure 8-2. Typical variable IGV and stator vane system

ratio (Cr) and mass airflow (ms) during acceleration and deceleration. The variable vanes (whose operating schedule is depicted in Figure 8-3) operate on an r.p.m. schedule biased to compressor inlet temperature (T_{t_2}). Figure 8-5 (which corresponds to an engine with variable compressor stator vanes) shows the relationship between compressor pressure ratio and mass airflow (Ms) over r.p.m. This chart shows that by incorporating variable vanes, the operating line (C-D) can be raised, enabling the engine to operate at a higher compressor pressure ratio for a given speed without the tendency to stall.

Line C-D represents a normal compressor pressure ratio to r.p.m. relationship of an engine with fixed stator vanes, similar to that in Figure 8-5. At this safe, low-line position, the maximum compression of the engine is also low. With variable vanes installed, the compression can be raised in the engine and the operating line can be safely raised to position E-F. The higher operating line is possible because for any given speed where the variable vane system regulates airflow, it automatically schedules the correct compressor pressure ratio and mass airflow.

Variable vane systems keep the engine from stalling during normal acceleration and deceleration. Designing a high-compression engine is not possible without incorporating some form of air regulating system because the compressor will stall if its airflow is not managed. The variable angles of the compressor stator airfoils accomplish this airflow management.

VARIABLE ANGLE COMPRESSOR VANE SYSTEM WITH FADEC INTERFACE (GENERAL ELECTRIC CFM56 TURBOFAN)

Figure 8-6 illustrates the Variable Stator Vane (VSV) system, with a FADEC/EEC control as described in Chapter 7. The electronic engine control (EEC) receives several signal inputs, such as:

- Engine N_1 and N_2 speeds.
- Thrust lever angle (TLA).
- Ambient temperature.
- Ambient altitude pressure.

Taking into account the various inputs, the EEC calculates the command signals that best keep the variable stator vane system on track for a selected and stall-free thrust schedule. The vanes are positioned anywhere from

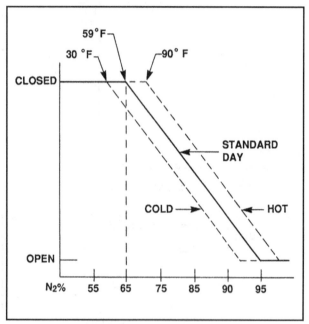

Figure 8-3. Example of vane operating schedule

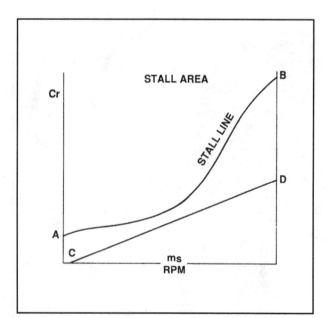

Figure 8-4. Typical stall line chart, engine with fixed compressor stator vanes

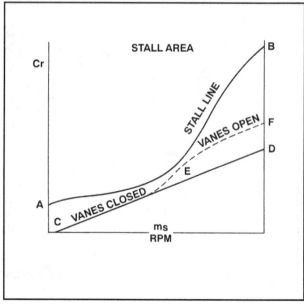

Figure 8-5. Typical stall line chart, engine with variable angle compressor stator vanes

partially closed at low engine speeds to fully open at high speeds. To check the operation of the system or to troubleshoot a problem, a technician can access the engine screens on the Control Display Unit (CDU) located on the flight deck. The CDU is located just forward of the throttles. As shown in Figure 8-6, information about the position of the variable stator vanes is transmitted to the EEC, which sends the data (by way of the ARINC-429 data bus) to the Display Electronics Unit (DEU) and ultimately to the CDU. The CDU displays the position of the vanes as follows:

- **Start** — vanes partially closed
- **Idle** — vanes partially closed
- **From idle to 82.5 (±2.5) percent N_2** — vanes modulating
- **Above 82.5 (±2.5) percent N_2** — vanes fully open

VARIABLE ANGLE INLET GUIDE VANE SYSTEM (SMALL ENGINE)

The anti-stall system shown in the Figure 8-7 and 8-8 vane position illustrations are typical of many smaller gas turbine engines in that the compressor stator vane angles are fixed and only the inlet guide vanes are variable. The inlet guide vanes have a 45-degree range of movement, from 51.5 degrees closed at low compressor speed (idle speed), gradually opening during engine acceleration to the to 6.5-degree closed position at high compressor speed. This action maintains the correct angle-of-attack relationship between inlet airflow and compressor speed and enables the engine to accelerate rapidly without experiencing a compressor stall. [Figure 8-7]

This system is operated by fuel pressure under command of the power lever. Similar to its large-engine counterpart, the system interprets fuel signals from the fuel control to determine its operating schedule.

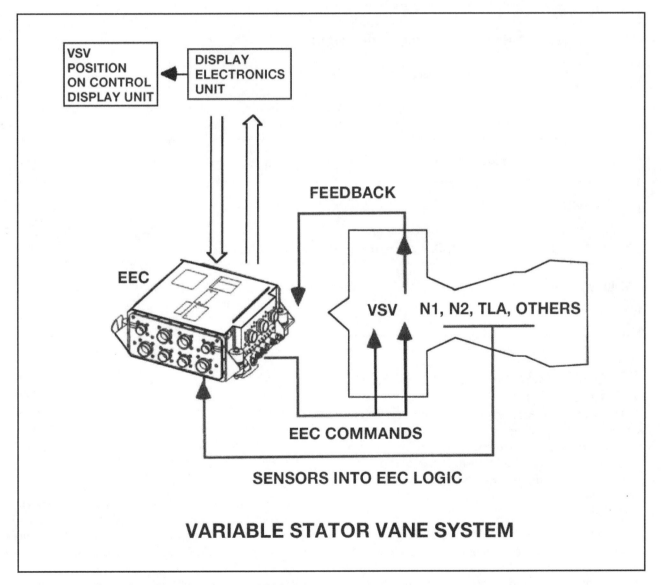

Figure 8-6. Variable stator vane system with FADEC interface

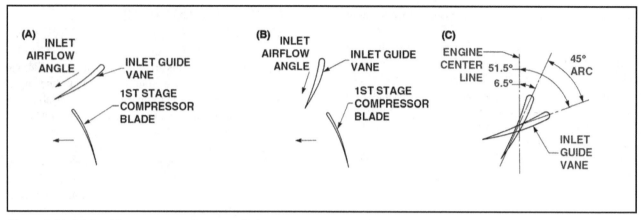

Figure 8-7A. Inlet guide vanes at maximum angle, low compressor speed, 51.5 degrees closed
Figure 8-7B. Inlet guide vanes at minimum angle, high compressor speed, 6.5 degrees closed
Figure 8-7C. Inlet guide vane full angular range = 45 degrees

TROUBLESHOOTING THE VARIABLE VANE SYSTEM

PROBLEM/POSSIBLE CAUSE	CHECK PROCEDURE	REMEDY
1. Compressor stall on acceleration or deceleration		
a. Malfunctioning variable vane system	1. Check for out-of-track or for binding mechanism. 2. Check for binding or out-of-adjustment feedback cable.	Rerig the system. Adjust or clean the feedback cable.
b. Malfunctioning compressor inlet sensor (Tt_2)	Slave in a known-good sensor.	Replace sensor.
c. Faulty fuel control	Check for correct fuel pressure to the vane system.	Replace the fuel control.
2. Engine unable to attain full power (without exceeding EGT limit)		
Malfunctioning variable vane system	Verify whether vanes are fully opening (observe vanes and protractor).	Rerig the system.

COMPRESSOR ANTI-STALL BLEED SYSTEMS

To minimize compressor acceleration and deceleration stall problems at low and intermediate speeds, some gas turbine engines use a compressor anti-stall bleed system rather than a variable vane system. Rather than exclude unwanted air, as in the case with the variable vane system, the compressor bleed system automatically bleeds away unwanted air.

Except at cruise speed and higher, some compressors cannot handle the amount of air passing through the engine without an air bleed system. For example, in a compressor with a 30 to 1 overall compressor pressure ratio, during starting, a compressor pressure ratio of only approximately 2 to 1 exists. In this condition, the flow outlet area of the compressor would have to be about 80 percent of its inlet area to be able to move the air without a substantial decrease in velocity. The average outlet area being only about 25 percent of the inlet area necessitates the use of a compressor bleed air system.

Another way to describe the situation is that in some engines at low and intermediate speeds, a relationship between compressor rotor speed and airflow cannot be maintained to provide the rotating airfoils the correct effective angle of attack to the oncoming airstream unless some of the compressor air is being bled away.

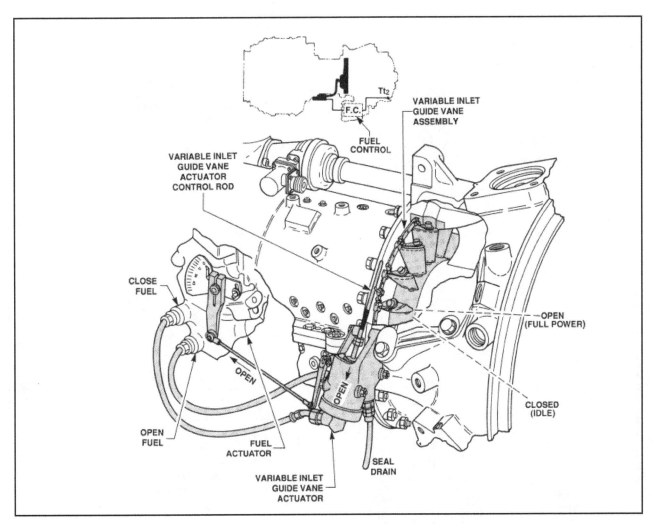

Figure 8-8. Variable inlet guide vane system

Conversely, at high rotational speeds in which the compressor is designed to handle maximum airflow without aerodynamic disturbance, the bleed system is scheduled in the closed position.

COMPRESSOR BLEED SYSTEM OPERATION

In engines equipped with variable vane systems, at the low end of the compressor speed range, the variable vane system permits less air to enter, which keeps compression low and prevents air molecules from piling up in the rear stages and blocking airflow. Conversely, in engines equipped with compressor bleed systems, at low compressor speeds, the system bleeds away the excess of air molecules in the rear stages, effectively accomplishing the same result as that of the variable vane system.

On larger engines, one or more bleed valves fitted to the compressor's outer case are used to bleed unwanted air either into the fan duct or directly overboard. On some large engines, a combination of bleed valves *and* variable vanes might be used. The higher the compressor pressure ratio, the greater the need for more complex systems that can control a wider stall margin.

On smaller engines, a single sliding band, which uncovers bleed ports to bleed away the unnecessary air, is more practical. [Figures 8-9 and 8-10]

COMPRESSOR BLEED BAND SYSTEM

The bleed band system is incorporated on many small engines to control the stall margin of the engine. The band is positioned to dump air from a rearward stage of compression selected to achieve the best operating condition of that engine. This system is needed on

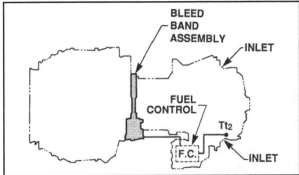

Figure 8-9. Location of bleed band assembly, Lycoming T53 turboshaft

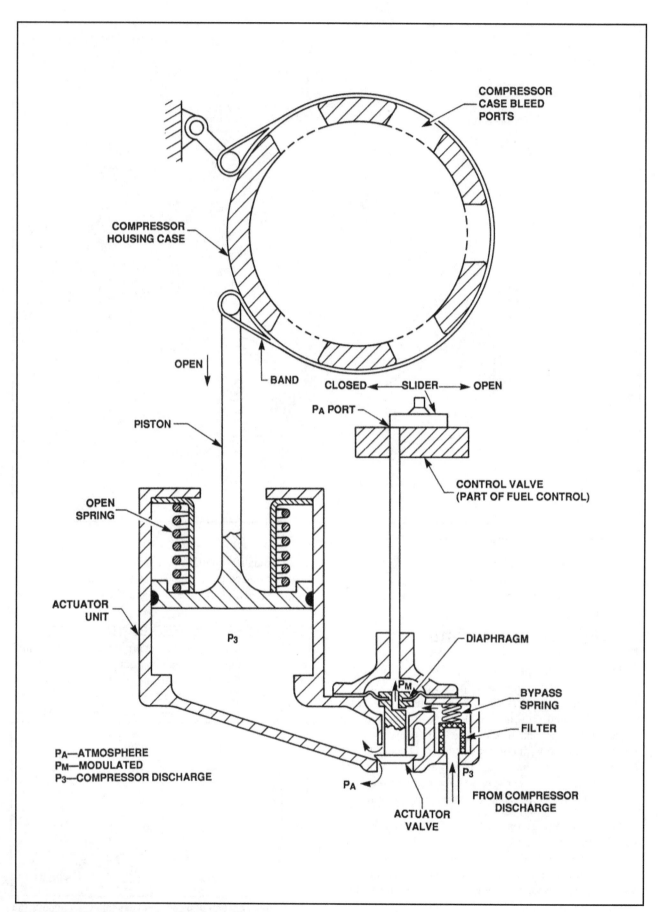

Figure 8-10. Bleed band system (band closed)

many engines because at lower compressor speeds the relatively high pressure ratio in the rear stages tends to slow airflow in the front stages. In the system depicted in Figure 8-9, the band bleeds air from the last axial stage of compression in an engine with a combination axial-centrifugal compressor. At low and intermediate speeds, the band is fully open. In the cruise to takeoff power range, the band is fully closed.

In the schematic view shown in Figure 8-10, note that P_3 air, which is tapped from the last stage of compression, pressurizes the actuator cavity, holding the piston up against the force of the open spring. In this position, Pm air is trapped by the slider; as long as pressure on both sides of the Pm diaphragm is equal, the actuator valve remains in the closed position. This operational mode occurs when the fuel control is set at a predetermined high power setting and after the engine has had a stall-free acceleration from a lower power setting.

When the power lever is moved rearward, the fuel control schedules the control valve slider to move to the right, which uncovers the Pa port. In this position, Pm control air bleeds to the atmosphere, which causes a pressure drop on the Pm side of the diaphragm. An upward movement of the diaphragm (brought about by an oil-canning-type action) occurs, which opens the actuator valve, permitting P_3 air to dump from the actuator cavity. With no pressure in the actuator cavity to overcome, the force of the open-spring pushes the piston downward, which slackens the band to uncover the bleed ports. In this operational mode, the bleed ports release a portion of the pressurized air in the compressor to the atmosphere, which increases the axial compressor velocity of flow in the front stages to match compressor speed for optimal angle of attack.

Operationally, when the bleed band opens and closes, cockpit instruments that indicate parameters such as engine pressure ratio and engine speed shift noticeably to alert the pilot.

To bias system operation to ambient temperature, the slider opens and closes in response to a Tt_2 sensor in the fuel control. [Figure 8-9] At cooler ambient temperatures, the slider closes earlier upon engine acceleration so that the heavier, slower moving airflow will be accelerated during the compression process to maintain the correct angle-of-attack relationships within the compressor.

BLEED BAND SCHEDULE

Figure 8-11 shows a typical anti-stall bleed band schedule. In this example, at 60°F, if the engine is accelerated from idle to a high power setting, the bleed band must close no earlier than 66 percent N_1 speed and no later than 72 percent N_1 speed. In deceleration, the bleed band must open below 72 percent and no lower than 66 percent N_1 speed. Additionally, if the bleed band closes, for example, at 69 percent on acceleration, it must open at 67 percent minimum and within the limits of the band schedule.

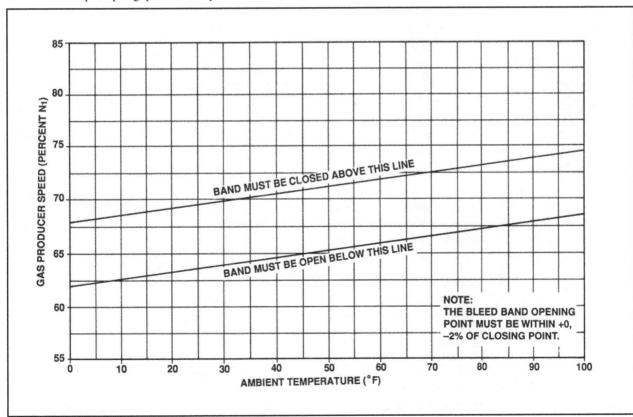

Figure 8-11. Anti-stall bleed band operational schedule

Note that as ambient temperature on the operational schedule increases, the bleed band is scheduled open longer on acceleration, meaning to a higher N_1 speed. As ambient temperature increases, airflow velocity tends to increase. The bleed stays open longer to prevent a pile up of molecules in the rear stages. After accelerating to a sufficient speed to close the bleed, the compressor can then handle the additional airflow and maintain the correct angle-of-attack relationships without stalling.

Bear in mind that compressor bleed air refers to several air bleed systems related both to engine operation requirements and non-engine-related applications. The bleed band does not provide a compressor air bleed source for applications such as aircraft air conditioning or fuel tank pressurization; the bleed air for those applications is properly referred to as *customer* bleed air.

COMPRESSOR BLEED VALVE SYSTEM

Due to their increased complexity, larger engines require additional bleed capabilities to prevent compressor stall at various stages of compression. Simple bleed band systems are unable to fulfill these requirements. This discussion of compressor bleed valve systems uses the Pratt & Whitney JT8D turbofan engine as a representative example. The JT8D engine employs a system known as the Pressure Ratio Bleed Control System to provide compressor anti-stall protection. [Figure 8-12]

The system consists of three bleed valves—two to bleed 13th-stage air (the last stage of compression), and one to bleed 8th-stage air. This system does not proportionally meter bleed air. Each valve is either in the fully open or fully closed position.

This system uses three sources of air pressure from the engine to operate the valves: low-pressure compressor discharge static pressure (Ps_3), compressor inlet total pressure (Pt_2), and high-pressure discharge pressure (Ps_4). Ps_3 and Pt_2 are sensing pressures and Ps_4 is used to operate the mechanisms.

The system schedules the bleed valve operation as a function of the pressure ratio across the low-pressure compressor. The three bleed valves are scheduled to be open when the engine is operating at low power and to be closed at slightly below cruise power.

When the engine is not operating, the Pt_2 diaphragm is in the upward position in response to Pt_2 pressure and spring pressure. This correctly positions the linkage to the two transfer valves. [Figure 8-12]

During engine starting, Ps_3 pressure enters the cavity above the diaphragm through a filter and a pressure control restrictor. It is also vented overboard through a venturi fitting. The venturi lowers the pressure of Ps_3 to a value less than actual Ps_3 value. As the engine comes up to idle speed, the venturi "chokes" and provides a steady back-pressure on the diaphragm to act against Pt_2 pressure and spring pressure. At this time, Pt_2 pressure, aided by spring pressure, is greater than Ps_3 pressure.

When the engine is between idle speed and valve-closing speed, pressure at the top of the servo piston is vented overboard by way of the top transfer valve and the Ps_4 vent. Control pressure, Ps_4, is blocked at the servo piston center section but routed to the bottom side through the lower transfer valve. This pressure, plus the spring pressure, holds the servo piston in the upward position. The bleed valve close-line is vented overboard at this time; simultaneously, pressure within the compressor forces the bleed valves open.

As engine speed increases, modified Ps_3 pressure overcomes Pt_2 pressure plus the spring pressure and forces the diaphragm downward to reverse the position of the transfer valves. [Figure 8-13]

When the transfer valves change position, Ps_4 is routed to the top surface of the servo piston on which it applies downward pressure. Ps_4 is also routed to the center surface of the servo piston, which has a larger area than the top surface. The pressure differential causes a downward movement of the servo piston.

With the servo piston down, Ps_4 is directed to the bleed valve close-line, and all three bleed valves close simultaneously because the area under the floating pistons is greater than the cone-shaped area at the close-off point at the compressor case.

If this engine had no bleed air system, the fuel schedule would have to be reduced to enable the heavier low-pressure compressor time to speed up and stay in step with the high-pressure compressor; such a reduction would adversely affect the acceleration schedule of the engine. In the same way, if the bleed valves close too early, acceleration time increases.

Deceleration is also aided by the compressor bleed valves. Opening the valves at a point just below cruise speed relieves some of the airflow, which slows the compressor more quickly.

In this pressure ratio system, no inlet temperature sensor is necessary to change the opening and closing schedule according to temperature. This is because at lower inlet air temperatures, the air is more dense and Ps_3 will overpower Pt_2 sooner, which causes the bleed valves to close earlier.

Some systems of this type have been modified so that the bleed valves can be scheduled closed electronically during the start cycle, to initially provide better starting air flow. As the engine accelerates toward idle, the valves open to aid in acceleration.

Compressor Anti-Stall Systems

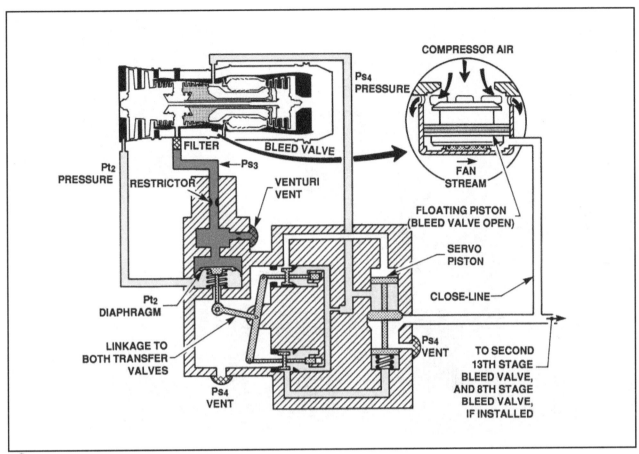

Figure 8-12. JT8D anti-stall bleed valve system (bleeds open)

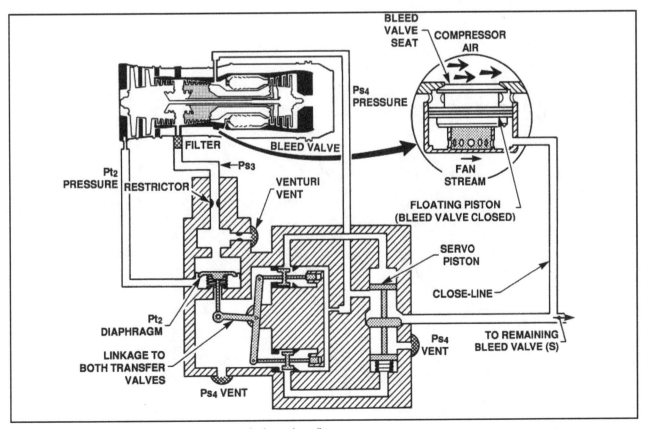

Figure 8-13. JT8D anti-stall bleed valve system (valves closed)

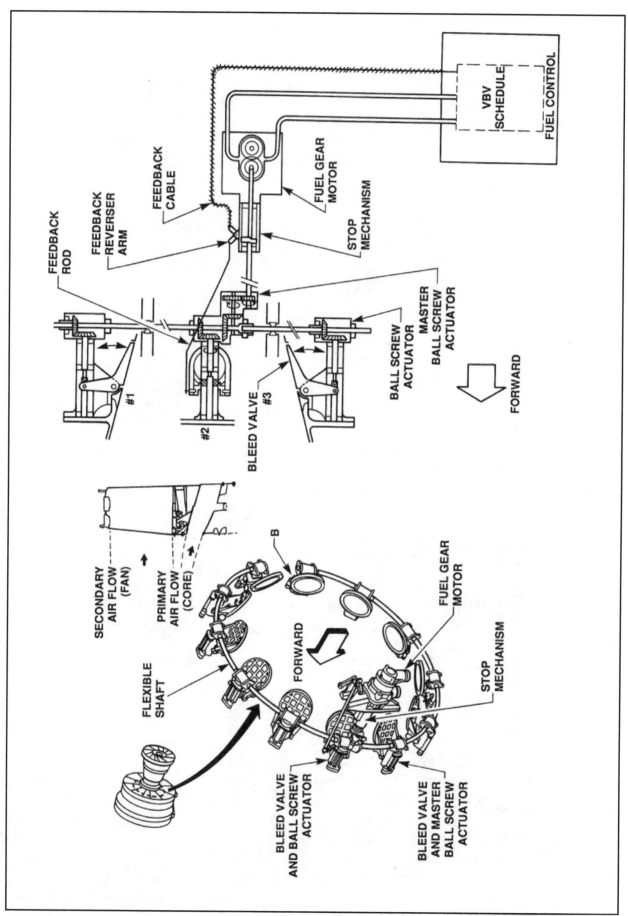

Figure 8-14. Variable bleed valve system

VARIABLE BLEED VALVE AND TRANSIENT BLEED VALVE SYSTEMS WITH FADEC INTERFACE

The variable bleed valve system in the General Electric CFM56 turbofan engine functions similarly to the JT8D turbofan bleed valve system to optimize the performance of the high-pressure compressor. However, in the CFM56 bleed system, the bleed valve position can be varied to bleed the proper amount of air according to specific engine requirements. [Figure 8-14]

The CFM56 uses an EEC as part of a FADEC system to regulate its low-compressor discharge bleed air system. The system contains 12 variable-position bleed valves, or doors, which are operated by a hydromechanical mechanism that receives commands from the EEC.

The bleed valves are located around the circumference of the low-pressure N_1 compressor outer case and release some of the N_1 discharge air pressure into the fan duct. The valves are fully open at idle speed and slowly close on a schedule controlled by the EEC and by mechanisms within the fuel control. Full closing occurs at approximately 85 to 88 percent N_2 speed, which is slightly below cruise speed. Figure 8-15 shows the interface between the engine's variable bleed valve system, the EEC, and the control display unit on the flight deck. As with the variable vane system that is controlled by a FADEC, a technician can check the operation of the variable bleed system by bringing up the engine pages on the CDU located on the flight deck.

The valves are operated by a mechanical actuator and a flexible shaft mechanism, which is powered by a fuel-driven motor. The bleed valves respond to two principle controls. The first control is the movement of the power lever (throttle) on the flight deck. Advancing the power lever causes the valves to move toward closed; retarding the power lever moves them toward open. The valves also move in response to changes in operational parameters of N_2 speed and fan discharge temperature that are received by the fuel control. The feedback cable in the illustration provides the fuel control with a continual mechanical signal of bleed valve position against which the automatic signals of speed and temperature can be compared.

The CFM56 engine also uses a second air bleed system (not shown) called a Transient Bleed Valve (TBV), which is located at the exit of the high-pressure compres-

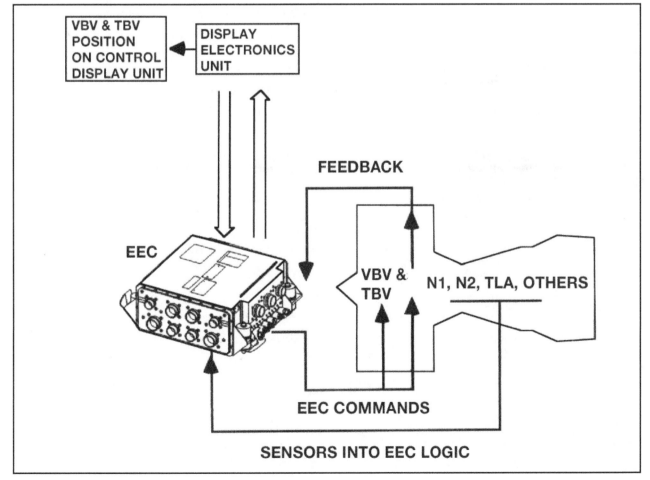

Figure 8-15. Compressor bleed valve systems with FADEC interface

sor (N_2). This system bleeds unwanted air from the last stage of the high-pressure compressor and delivers it back into the engine at the first stage turbine vanes.

The TBV is a two-position valve for which the EEC calculates when to open and when to close. The operating schedule is as follows:

- **Engine start** — valves are open
- **Engine idle** — valves are closed
- **Engine acceleration** — valves are open
- **N_2 above 80 percent** — valves are closed

The TBV, with its second bleed valve, provides better control over the compressor blade angle of attack and stall margin during acceleration and deceleration of the N_2 compressor. The TBV operates under the authority of the EEC and FADEC system. The EEC receives several signals from the aircraft and engine, as well as ambient conditions, and determines when to open and close the valves.

TROUBLESHOOTING COMPRESSOR BLEED SYSTEMS

PROBLEM/POSSIBLE CAUSE	CHECK PROCEDURE	REMEDY
1. Compressor stall on acceleration from low or intermediate speeds		
Bleed system opening or closing off schedule	1. Determine if the air bleed ports are closing early. 2. Check for binding mechanism.	Reset schedule or replace control device. Adjust mechanism.
2. Compressor stall on deceleration from high speeds		
Bleed system opening or closing off schedule	Check for late opening of bleed ports.	Adjust mechanism.
3. Engine unable to attain full power (without exceeding EGT limit)		
Bleed system opening or closing off schedule	1. Determine if the air bleed ports are not fully closing. 2. Check for binding mechanism.	Rerig system. Adjust mechanism.
4. Fluctuating RPM and EGT		
Bleed system opening or closing off schedule	Check for a modulating bleed mechanism.	Adjust mechanism or replace system parts as necessary.

QUESTIONS:

1. What is the purpose of the variable stator vane system installed on some gas turbine engines?

2. How many vanes in a single stage have controllable angles?

3. An angle-of-attack relationship occurs at the compressor blade leading edge from inlet airflow and what other factor within the engine?

4. Is the compressor bleed system closed at takeoff power?

5. Where is the compressor bleed system air directed?

6. If an engine with a compressor bleed system experiences compressor stalls, what is the probable cause?

7. What FADEC system manages the operation of the electronic stator vane system?

8. In a dual-spool engine, for which of the compressors (N_1 or the N_2) does the variable stator vane system control airflow?

CHAPTER 9
Anti-Icing Systems

On many turbine-engine-powered aircraft, the flight cowling, fan, fan spinner, compressor inlet case, inlet guide vanes, nose dome, and nose cowling are configured with internal passages that permit hot air to circulate for anti-icing purposes. On some aircraft, icing is not a problem for the core of the engine because ice does not form in sufficient quantity; for these aircraft, no engine anti-icing provisions are necessary. On some turboprops, the oil reservoir is located within the propeller reduction gearbox, which provides some anti-icing capability, and only a minimum of hot air flow is required to keep the flight inlet area free of ice.

When an anti-icing system is required to provide protection against ice formation in the flight inlet, engine service bleed air is extracted from the compressor or diffuser of the engine being anti-iced. The air is extracted from the point in the engine that provides the correct pressure and temperature to satisfy the needs of the engine during both ground and flight operations. If only the flight cowl requires anti-icing, electrical heat strips are often used.

Anti-icing air is directed radially in a high-pressure spray pattern at the flight inlet to heat all the surfaces upon which ice might form. Unlike certain deice systems on leading edges of wings and propellers, this system does not permit ice to form. If the anti-icing system is used inadvertently to deice the inlet area after ice formation caused a compressor stall, the impact forces of ice on compressor blades and vanes would severely damage the engine or possibly cause the engine to fail completely.

Conditions are most conducive to icing when the engine is operated at high speeds on the ground. Ice can form in the inlet up to 40°F ambient temperature in relatively dry air and up to 45°F in visibly moist air, such as fog or rain, due to the cooling effect of high inlet airflow velocities. [Figure 9-1] The inlet super cooling effect, concerning the use of water injection in the inlet below 40°F (discussed in Chapter 7), can also result in inlet icing. This icing is similar to the icing that can occur in the carburetor throat in a reciprocating engine due to airflow through the venturi. The combination of high velocity and the high volume of atomized fuel create conditions in which ice can form in temperatures as high as 70°F.

In the flight inlet of a gas turbine engine, the large flow area would not support a 70°F freeze-up condition, but the same processes by which ice can form are present:

Increased velocity of air causes a pressure drop and increases the cooling effect on the air.

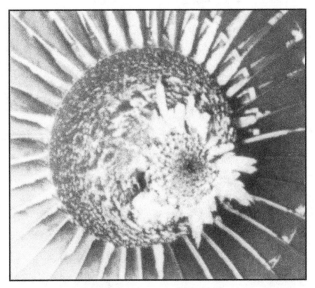

Figure 9-1. Fan icing tests showing ice formation on the fan spinner and fan blades

Evaporation of water at low pressure increases the cooling effect.

Freezing of condensed water vapor occurs in air because of the effect of low pressure has on air temperature.

Water suspended in air comes into contact with metal surfaces of 32°F or below.

Consider the following example using Formula 7, Appendix 8, by which you can calculate the temperature drop in the inlet when inlet velocity is Mach 0.5 and ambient temperature is 40°F.

$$\frac{Tt}{Ts} = 1 + \left(\frac{\gamma-1}{2}\right) \times M^2$$

$$\frac{500}{Ts} = 1 + \left(\frac{1.4-1}{2}\right) \times 0.5^2$$

$$\frac{500}{Ts} = 1 + (0.2 \times 0.25)$$

$$\frac{500}{Ts} = 1.05$$

$$Ts = 476°R \; (16°F)$$

Where:

γ (gamma) = 1.4 (specific heat of air)

40°F = 500°R

M = Mach number

This indicates that the temperature is between 16°F and 40°F in different parts of the inlet. Molecular motion is a function of temperature. When velocity is high, pressure is low. When pressure is low, molecular motion decreases, as does temperature.

It might seem that to prevent freeze up, anti-icing should be used at much higher temperatures than 40 to 45°F, but industry testing has proven that it is a safe limit. It takes time for water suspended in air passing through the inlet to turn to ice, and if the temperature in the inlet is no lower than 45°F, ice will not form.

During flight, the anti-icing system is turned on before entering the icing condition. Anti-icing heat is required when visible moisture is present in the form of clouds or precipitation and the true air temperature (ambient plus ram effect) in the inlet is typically between 5°F and 40°F. Below 5°F, ambient air is dry and ice is not likely to form; in these conditions anti-icing is used at the discretion of the pilot.

At all cruise altitudes for a gas turbine-powered aircraft, the ambient temperature is well below 5°F, and ram pressure will not raise inlet temperature sufficiently above freezing. However, most of the flight time is above cloud level and anti-icing is not required. When anti-icing is required, the usual method of initiating anti-icing is to select one engine and watch the engine parameters stabilize, after which the remaining engines are selected and monitored.

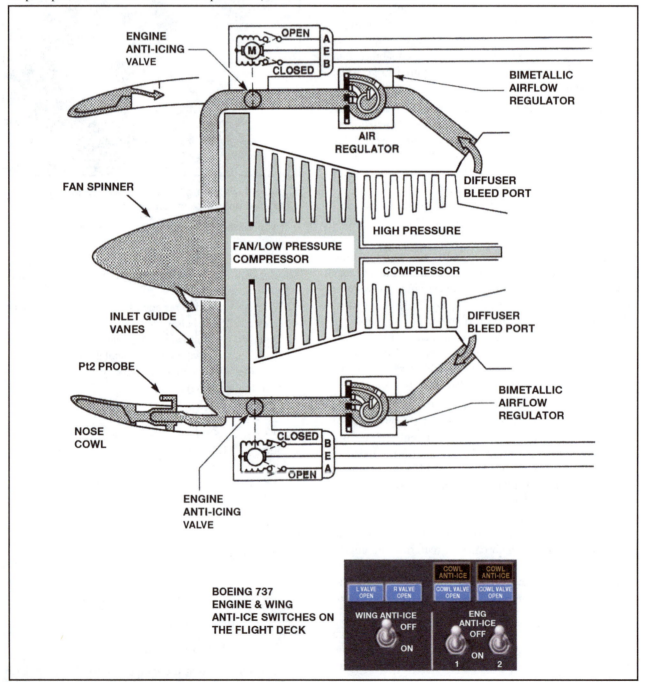

Figure 9-2. Typical engine inlet anti-icing system

On takeoff, climb-out, descent, and landing, the pilot must carefully assess the need for anti-icing according to the prevailing weather conditions. To prevent engine malfunction or damage, the pilot will have to make the same assessment when running the engine on the ground.

SYSTEM OPERATION

Figure 9-2 shows a basic anti-icing system that contains two electric-motor-driven air shutoff valves that are opened simultaneously when a cockpit switch is actuated. After the valves are opened, bimetallic coils inside the air regulator valves react to air temperature to control the amount of airflow. Air that is too hot can affect the material strength of inlet components and can also affect engine performance as the anti-icing air is ingested into the compressor.

In some engines, the increase in temperature of compressor bleed air at high power settings can adversely affect engine performance, so the anti-icing airflow is typically regulated. Some aircraft, however, have no need for regulator valves because the effect of the change in temperature on performance and material strength is negligible. In these cases, the systems contain only the electric shutoff valves. On some large fan engines, only the flight inlet receives anti-ice protection because the absence of inlet guide vanes and the slinging action of the fan eliminates ice formation in the engine inlet.

The Pt_2 probe shown in Figure 9-2 is part of an engine indicating system known as engine pressure ratio (EPR). On some turbojet- and turbofan-powered airplanes, the EPR gauge on the flight deck is the primary indication of engine thrust. It compares the total pressure leaving the engine (Pt_7) to the total pressure entering the engine (Pt_2). If the Pt_2 probe in the inlet duct ices over, the influence of ram pressure is unavailable to the EPR system and the probe acts as a Ps_2 probe. This false indication will result in a rise in the engine pressure ratio indication on the flight deck. A dangerous false high engine pressure ratio for takeoff will result because Ps_2 is always less than Pt_2 when the engine is moving forward.

When anti-icing protection is selected, an indicator light illuminates in the cockpit and a slight rise in exhaust gas temperature (approximately 20°F) occurs to indicate proper operation of the anti-icing system. Other engine parameters such as EPR and tachometer indicators might also shift noticeably due to the momentary change in compression delivered to the combustor.

REGULATOR VALVE

The regulator valve shown in Figure 9-3 is set to automatically provide 500°F air at its maximum flow position at idle engine power settings and 650°F air at its minimum flow position near takeoff power. When cool, a bimetallic spring holds the valve disk open. Then, corresponding with increased engine power, as air delivered to the system increases in flow and temperature, the disk moves toward closed until it reaches the limit of motion governed by the minimum flow stop. This restriction to flow prevents the inlet from overheating, which could result in loss of engine power, compressor stalls, or heat damage to the inlet structure.

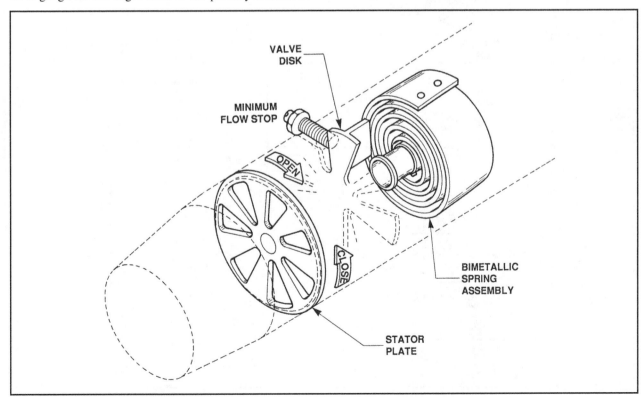

Figure 9-3. Anti-ice bimetallic regulator valve

COCKPIT CONTROLS AND ANTI-ICE VALVE OPERATION

The following is the sequence of operation of the anti-ice valves and the cockpit indicator lights when the cockpit on/off switch is actuated as seen in Figure 9-4.

ANTI-ICE SWITCH "ON"

The following sequence of events occurs when the anti-ice switch is turned on:

1. When the anti-ice switch is first turned on, the four limit switches are in a position opposite to that shown in the diagram, and AC power will actuate the two motors and valves open through limit switches 2 and 4. As the valves reach their open limit, the limit switches are forced to move into their present position. They are now in the correct position in anticipation of a later command to close the valves.

2. Before the limit switches change position, the amber light is illuminated in the cockpit through limit switches 1 and 3. When the limit switches reach their present position (as shown in the diagram) the amber light extinguishes and the blue light illuminates.

3. If the blue light does not illuminate, it is a warning to the operator that neither motor has fully actuated its airflow valve to the fully opened position.

4. If one of the motors does not actuate fully, the amber light remains illuminated (along with the blue light) to warn the operator of the malfunction.

ANTI-ICE SWITCH "OFF"

The following sequence of events occurs when the anti-ice switch is turned off:

1. When the cockpit switch is turned off, the blue light remains illuminated and the amber light again illuminates.

2. At that time, the 115 VAC circuit powers the two motors to close the valves, and the four limit switches cycle back to the position opposite the diagram to await the next command for anti-icing protection.

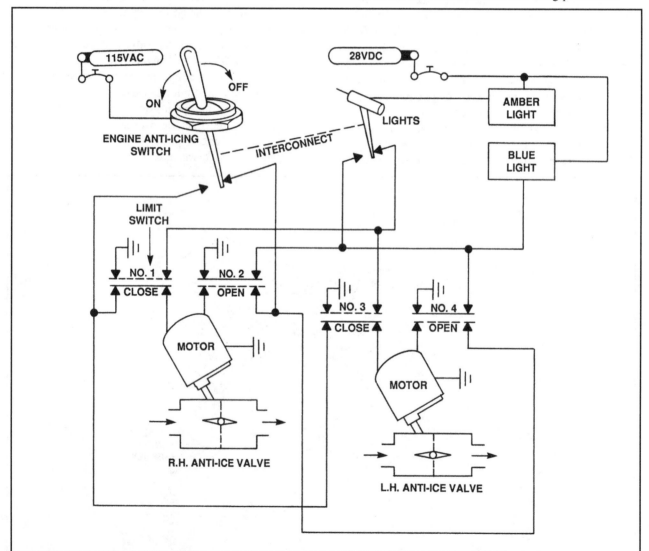

Figure 9-4. Cockpit switch, cockpit indicator lights, and anti-ice valves shown in system "on"

3. As the motor limit switches move off of their open contactors, both lights extinguish.

ANTI-ICING INTERFACE WITH AN ELECTRONIC ENGINE CONTROL AND FADEC

When a turbine engine is controlled by an Electronic Engine Control (EEC) as part of a FADEC system (Full Authority Digital Engine Control), the anti-icing system will be linked to the EEC. After the flight crew makes the choice to turn on anti-icing, the EEC controls the flow of hot air to the engine inlet based on input from ambient, aircraft, and engine sensors. Controlling the flow of anti-icing air, in an infinitely variable manner based on multiple inputs, increases the efficiency of the engine.

ELECTRO-THERMAL ANTI-ICING SYSTEM

Some smaller turboprop and turboshaft engines use electric heat strip systems, which are classed as electro-thermal anti-icing systems. They are constructed of electrical resistance wire embedded in layers of reinforced neoprene materials and located primarily at the lip of the nacelle flight inlet. Other possible locations are the engine inlet case and the engine inlet struts.

Similar to hot air anti-icing systems, electro-thermal systems are cycled on and off as required by ambient conditions. They are designed to operate only when the engine is running, because without air passing over it, operating the strip can overheat both the strip and the part of the engine to which it is attached.

TROUBLESHOOTING THE ANTI-ICING SYSTEM

PROBLEM/POSSIBLE CAUSE	CHECK PROCEDURE	REMEDY
1. Ice forms in the inlet with the anti-icing system turned on		
Anti-ice valves fail to open	1. Verify correct power source at valve. 2. Check for proper operation of valves.	Correct as necessary. Replace valves.
2. Compressor stalls at high power setting with anti-icing system off		
Inlet icing (during ground runup)	Ensure that ambient conditions are within operational guidelines.	Shut down and remove ice; then continue run with anti-icing system on.
3. Engine unable to attain full power (at EGT limit)		
a. Anti-ice shutoff valves (system off but valve stuck open)	Check for leak-through by carefully feeling forward side of valve with hand or suitable heat detector for heat from air leak.	Replace valve.
b. Air regulator stuck fully open	Bench check for correct operation of bimetallic coil.	Replace regulator.
4. Fluctuating EGT and engine speed		
a. Anti-icing valves intermittently open (system off)	Check for modulating valve motor.	Adjust micro-switch or replace motor.
5. EPR Rise (flight)		
a. Inlet probe icing or otherwise obstructed	Check for ice buildup causing decrease in inlet pressure in flight. Inspect for probe obstruction or damage after landing.	Turn on anti-ice to remove ice in flight. Clear probe obstruction or replace damaged probe.

QUESTIONS:

1. Is the anti-icing system designed to remove ice from the engine inlet?

2. Is the anti-icing regulator electrically controlled?

3. How does inlet ice cause a compressor stall?

4. Does the heated air used in the anti-icing system come from the compressor or the combustor?

5. Is the inlet electro-thermal anti-icing system selected whenever ice conditions are present or only when the engine is running?

CHAPTER 10
Starter Systems

Gas turbine engines are typically started by applying starter power to the main accessory gearbox, which in turn rotates the compressor. [Figure 10-1]

- On dual-compressor gas turbine engines, the starter rotates only the high-pressure compressor system.

- On free turbine, turboprop, and turboshaft engines with single compressors, and on turbojets with single compressors, only the compressor and its turbine are rotated by the starter through the accessory gearbox. The free turbine may rotate slowly under the influence of air passing through the engine but not at compressor speed because it is not coupled to the main accessory gearbox and the starter.

- The compressor of a fixed turbine type turboprop and turboshaft is directly coupled to the starter drive system through the main accessory gearbox. Therefore, they are started in low pitch to reduce drag on the starter.

The starter rotates the compressor fast enough to provide the engine with sufficient air for combustion. After combustion occurs, the starter remains engaged to help the engine accelerate to idle speed. Neither the starter nor the turbine wheel has sufficient power on its own to bring the engine from rest to idle speed, but when both components work in tandem, the starting process occurs in approximately 30 seconds for the typical engine. Although the starter is normally initiated by a cockpit toggle switch, a speed sensor device typically disengages the starter at 5 to 10 percent r.p.m. after self-accelerating speed is reached. For example, if the speed at which an engine can self-accelerate is 35 percent N_2 speed, the speed sensor disengages the starter when the engine reaches 40 to 45 percent N_2 speed. At this point, turbine power alone is sufficient to power the engine to idle speed.

If the engine is not assisted to the correct speed, a hung (stagnated) start can occur. That is, the engine remains at

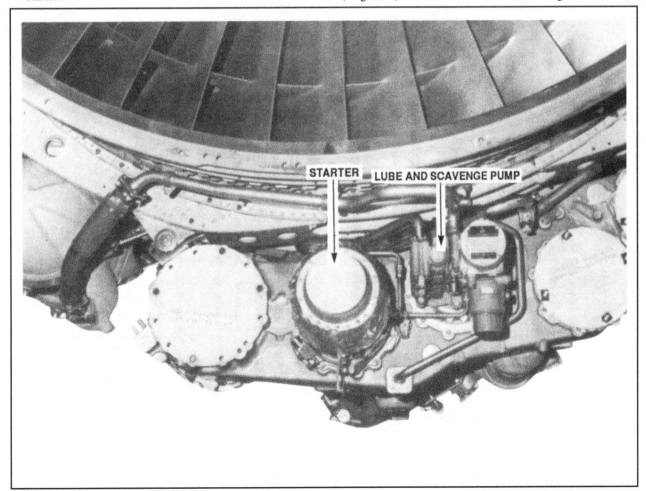

Figure 10-1. CF6 starter installation on forward face of main accessory gearbox

or near the point of starter cutoff. To remedy this situation, the engine must be shut down and the source of the problem identified. Attempts to accelerate the engine by adding fuel often result in a hot start as well as a hung start.

The usual starting sequence is to energize the starter, then at 5 to 10 percent r.p.m. compressor speed to energize ignition and open the fuel lever. A normal light-off will occur in 20 seconds or less. If light-off does not occur within the prescribed time limit, the start should be aborted to investigate the malfunction. Problems such as low starting power, weak ignition, or air in the fuel lines can degrade the starting process and cause a slow or no light-off condition.

The charts in Figure 10-2 show the typical starting events of starter-on, ignition-on, and fuel-on in relationship to time, compressor speed, and exhaust gas temperature. Bear in mind that a rich fuel mixture is scheduled for

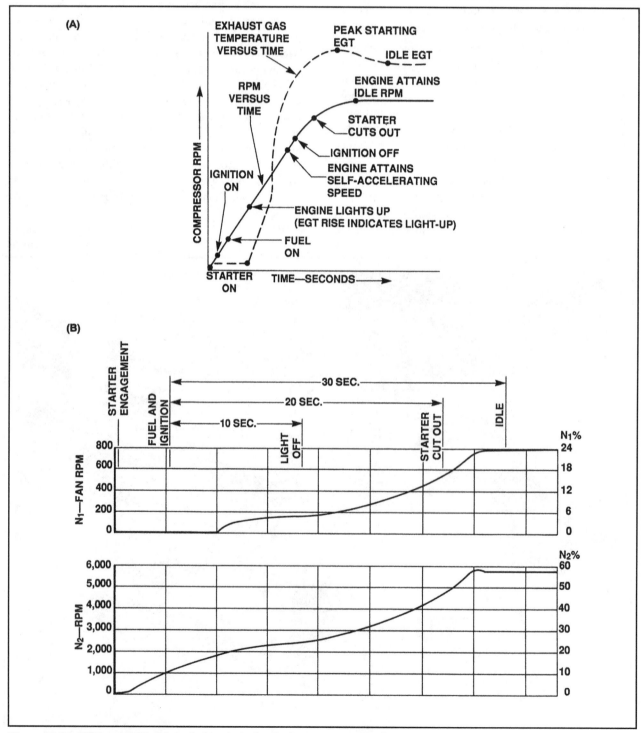

Figure 10-2A. RPM and EGT curves during start of a single-compressor engine
Figure 10-2B. RPM and percent RPM curves during start of a dual-compressor engine

the starting cycle to reduce time from start to idle. When idle speed is reached, the flyweights in the fuel control governor move outward to cause the main metering valve to move slightly toward closed. This sequence of events is represented in Figure 10-2A at the top of the exhaust gas temperature curve and the top of the compressor RPM curve. At these points, the curves peak and start to turn horizontally to a stabilized compressor speed and exhaust gas temperature.

Figure 10-2B shows a typical dual-compressor relationship of N_1 and N_2 speeds during the start cycle. Because the N_2 compressor is powered directly by the starter, it starts to rotate immediately after starter engagement, and the N_1 fan starts to rotate only after air pressure within the engine builds sufficiently to cause it to rotate. This curve is typical of a high-bypass fan engine. The starter cuts out at approximately 4,800 r.p.m., which represents 48 percent N_2 speed. The engine then stabilizes at idle N_2 speed of 58 percent (5,800 r.p.m.) after a slight overshoot at the point when the flyweights in the fuel control governor begin to control the fuel schedule. At idle, the N_1 compressor and fan are at 24 percent N_1 speed, and its speed curve stabilizes when N_2 speed stabilizes.

Engines that use an electronic engine control (EEC) might be capable of starting in an automatic mode. When the start sequence is initiated in this mode, ignition and fuel come on automatically, the starter and ignition turn off at the appropriate time, and the engine is protected from hung starts, hot starts, and from exceeding the idle speed limit.

ELECTRIC STARTERS

Standalone electric starters, similar to those used on piston engines, are often used on auxiliary and ground power units but are not typically used on flight engines because they are heavy and serve no other purpose than to start the engine. In contrast, dual-purpose starter-generators provide an overall weight savings that makes them more suitable for small engines. Standalone electric starters have not been in common use on flight engines since the 1950s.

Many electric starters contain an automatic release clutch mechanism to disengage the starter drive from the engine drive. Figure 10-3 shows a clutch assembly that performs this function as well as two additional functions.

The clutch assembly's next function is to prevent the starter from applying excessive torque to the engine drive. For this small auxiliary power unit (APU) starter, at approximately 100 to 200 inch-pounds of torque, clutch plates within the clutch housing slip and act as a friction clutch. The torque setting is adjustable by means of the slip torque adjustment nut. [Figure 10-3B] Larger starters with higher torque outputs would have appropriately higher slip torque settings.

During starting, the friction clutch is designed to slip until engine speed more closely matches starter speed, at which point the torque differential is negligible and the full torque from the starter is applied to the engine drive.

The third function of the clutch assembly is to act as an overrunning clutch, which prevents the engine as it approaches idle speed from running the starter. For this purpose, a pawl and ratchet mechanism is included, which contains three spring-loaded pawls that rest in the disengaged position. When the starter shaft starts to turn, inertia causes the pawls to move inward to engage a ratchet-type engine drive gear. This occurs because the pawl cage assembly, which floats within the overrunning clutch housing, tries to remain stationary when the armature starts to drive the clutch housing around. The overrunning clutch housing, however, quickly forces the pawls inward by a bumping action, which overcomes the force of the disengage spring. When engine speed approaches idle, its speed exceeds that of the starter and the pawls slip out of the tapered slots of the engine drive gear and are driven outward from the force of the retract spring. [Figure 10-3C]

STARTER-GENERATOR, SMALL ENGINES

The starter-generator, shown in Figure 10-4, is the most widely used starting unit on small gas turbine engines, including turbojets, turbofans, turboprops, and turboshafts. Turboprop aircraft such as the Beechcraft King Air and the Cessna Caravan, or business jets such as the Cessna Citation and the Learjet 60, do not have a source of bleed air from an onboard auxiliary power unit. The absence of auxiliary bleed air means that these aircraft cannot use pneumatic (air turbine) starters. The same is true for most turboshaft-powered helicopters. The starter-generator is particularly suitable for these aircraft because it can be powered by the aircraft battery, and it eliminates an accessory by combining the starter with the generator.

By analyzing the schematic in Figure 10-4, you can trace the circuitry and better understand how starter-generators operate. The following step-by-step sequence aids in understanding the process:

1. External power supplies current to the DC bus via wire no. 6.

2. With the engine master switch in the ON position, current flows to the:

- Fuel valve via the DC bus and wire number 2.
- Power lever relay coil via the DC bus, wires number 2 and number 12, and the power lever switch.
- Fuel pumps via the DC bus, wire number 3, and the power lever relay.
- Ignition solenoid coil via the DC bus, wire number 2, the start switch, and wire number 10.

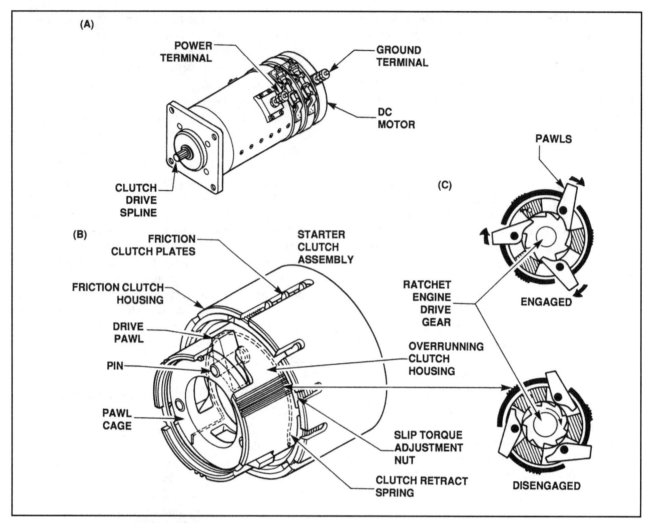

Figure 10-3A. 28VDC electrical starter
Figure 10-3B. Starter clutch assembly
Figure 10-3C. Overrunning clutch

- Ignition exciters via the DC bus, wire number 3, the power lever relay, wires number 11, number 14, and the ignition solenoid contacts.

  Note: The test switch also activates the ignition exciters via wire number 15 when the ignition solenoid contacts are in the open position. You can verify proper operation of the ignition exciters and igniter plugs by listening for a sharp snapping sound.

- Start solenoid coil via the DC bus, wire number 2, the master switch contacts, the start switch, and wire number 8. Wire number 8 also supplies power to the contact of the under current solenoid.

- Starter circuit via the DC bus, wire number 4, the starter solenoid contacts, the coil of the under current solenoid, and wire number 9.

3. As long as contacts of the under current solenoid are closed, the starter remains energized— even when the spring-loaded start switch is released. This is possible because the starter solenoid coil is now powered via the DC bus, wire number 5, and the under current solenoid.

4. The under current solenoid reopens as engine speed increases or when current flow drops below 200 amperes.

5. The stop relay enables the operator to terminate the start cycle by moving the start switch to the stop position; this action opens the circuit to the starter solenoid coil via wire number 5.

6. A microswitch on the external power door prevents both external power and battery power from powering the bus simultaneously.

7. The generator circuit activates via terminals B and ground after the engine approaches idle speed. Voltage is regulated via terminal A.

LARGE ENGINE STARTER-GENERATORS

Prior to the development of Boeing's 787 Dreamliner, most large aircraft (from the size of larger corporate jets

Starter Systems

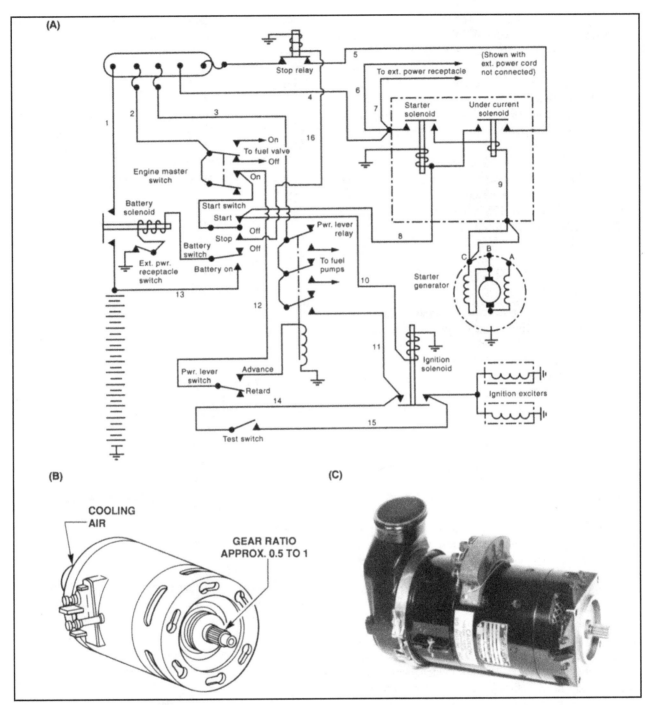

Figure 10-4A. Starter-generator electrical circuit
Figure 10-4B. Starter-generator gear ratio
Figure 10-4C. Starter-generator unit

such as the Gulfstream V and larger) did not use starter-generators. Large turbine engines require a starter with substantial power, and the size and weight of a starter-generator with this power potential has been prohibitive. Based on the electrical requirements of the aircraft, for the unit to be powerful enough to operate as a starter, it would have to be significantly oversized when operating as a generator. Because the component operates as a generator 99.9 percent of the time, the extra weight of the starter section would present a severe weight penalty.

However, the Boeing 787 aircraft, with its "no-bleed-air" technology, has begun to change the way starter-generators are considered with respect to their use on large engines.

The B-787 uses electrical systems to perform functions that were commonly carried out by engine bleed air and hydraulics. For instance, the airplane is pressurized by driving standalone compressors with electric motors instead of bleeding air off of the engine's compressor, and the wing leading edges use electric heating instead of engine bleed air for anti-icing. The brakes are electrically energized rather than hydraulic. With so many systems now relying on electricity, the generator output must be significantly greater than that for other large airplanes. For example, the engine on a Boeing 777 drives a single, 120,000-watt generator while the Boeing 787 engine drives two starter-generators of 250,000 watts each for a total of 500,000 watts. When used as a starter, just one of the units produces more than 300 horsepower, which is more than enough power to rotate the airplane's large turbofan engine. In start mode, the starter-generator on the 787 draws its power from the auxiliary power unit, which drives two generators of 125,000 watts each for a total of 250,000 watts. The APU receives its starting power from the aircraft battery bus or from a ground power unit.

PNEUMATIC (AIR TURBINE) STARTER

In contrast to the large starter-generator system used on the Boeing 787, most large commercial and regional aircraft, including an increasing number of corporate jets, use some type of pneumatic (air turbine) starter. This type of starter is a type of low-pressure, axial-flow air motor, and was developed to have a high power-to-weight ratio. It has approximately one-fifth the weight of a comparable electric starter. [Figure 10-5A and B]

A low-pressure, high-volume air source of approximately 45 p.s.i.g., at 50-100 pounds per minute, is supplied to the starter from an onboard auxiliary power unit (APU), a ground power unit, or from the cross-bleed air source of another operating main engine. As shown in Figure 10-6A, air enters the starter inlet and passes through a set of turbine nozzle vanes, changing pressure to velocity and impinging at high kinetic energy levels on the turbine blades. The exhaust air exits overboard through a cowl fairing. In some installations, starting is terminated by manually shutting off the air supply with a cockpit toggle switch connected to the starter pressure-regulating and shutoff valve. [Figure 10-8] As shown in Figure 10-6A, the air supply is terminated automatically by a centrifugal flyweight cutout switch, which causes the inlet air supply shutoff valve to close. The cutout switch in the starter provides the path to ground for the solenoid valve in the air supply shutoff valve. At the proper speed, the path to ground is interrupted and the shutoff valve closes.

On engines equipped with an EEC or with a full authority digital engine control (FADEC), starter operation is often controlled through these electronic systems. The activation of the starter circuit takes place through the EEC, and when the speed-sensing devices on the engine indicate that the proper speed has been reached, the start signal is removed. The system on the Boeing 737-800 is sophisticated enough to sense a possible hot start and shut off fuel, yet leave the starter engaged to rotate the engine and provide sufficient gas path cooling within the engine. It can also sense a wet start—a situation in which fuel is introduced but no ignition takes place—and keep the engine rotating to purge the fuel out of the combustor.

The turbine in this starter rotates at 60,000 to 80,000 r.p.m. and is geared down 20 to 30 times to achieve its high torque rating. At approximately 30 pounds, a large unit for the Boeing 747 aircraft develops 200 horsepower. Smaller units, down to approximately 20 horsepower, are available.

Most starters contain an integral oil supply of the same type of oil used by the engine. Depending on the size of the unit, anywhere from 4 to 12 ounces of oil provide lubrication for the gear train. The oil level and magnetic drain plug must be frequently inspected. On some engines, the lubricating oil for the starter comes from the engine's accessory gearbox, rather than having its own self-contained oil supply. The CFM56-7 engine starter utilizes this type of lubrication system.

During engine shutdown, at approximately 20 percent engine speed, the pawls of the overrunning clutch on this starter re-engage sufficiently for restarting, if it should be required. [Figure 10-6B] This procedure can damage some starters and must only be performed within the manufacturer's recommended limits. The only conditions under which starter engagement on a rotating engine is likely to be necessary are to purge the engine gas path of fuel vapors if a tail pipe fire occurs during ground shutdown, and during starter-assisted air-starts if windmilling speed is too low to obtain a relight.

Safety features usually incorporated in this starter include a drive shaft shear point, which will break at a predetermined gear-train-induced torque force to prevent damage to the engine. Another safety feature to prevent the starter from reaching burst speed if inlet air does not terminate on schedule is that airflow at the turbine nozzle vanes becomes choked and the turbine wheel speed will stabilize in a controlled over-speed condition. After either of these malfunctions occur, a special inspection of the magnetic drain chip detector is generally required. [Figure 10-6C]

Figure 10-6B shows the overrunning clutch, called a sprag (or sprague) clutch assembly, which is configured differently than those used for electric starters. The clutch in this installation is in a drive shaft housing that stays permanently engaged to the engine gearbox drive. The pawls are forced inward by small leaf springs to engage the sprag clutch ratchet. At a preset engine speed, the pawls experience sufficient G-force to be thrown outward, disengaging the drive shaft assembly from the sprag clutch ratchet.

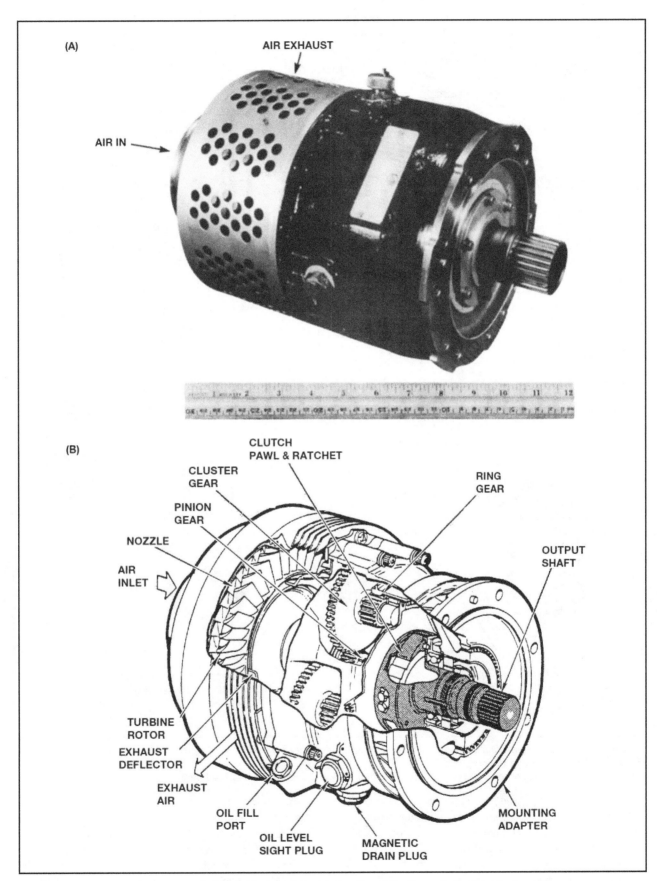

Figure 10-5A. Large engine pneumatic (air turbine) starter, showing its relatively small size (physical weight approximately 30 lbs.)
Figure 10-5B. Cutaway view of large engine pneumatic starter

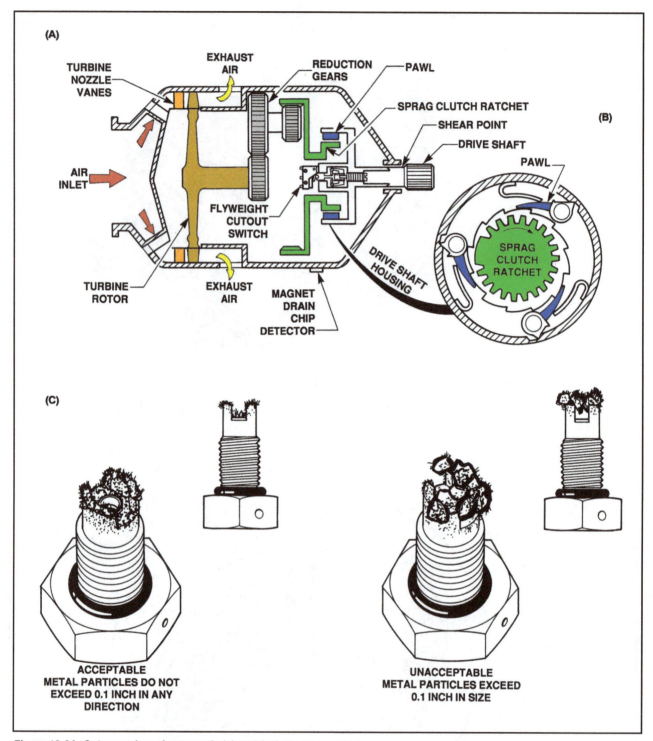

Figure 10-6A. Cutaway view of pneumatic (air turbine) starter assembly
Figure 10-6B. Overrunning or sprag clutch
Figure 10-6C. Examples of magnetic chip detector contamination found during a special inspection

The sprag clutch ratchet and starter gear train coast to a halt and the drive shaft housing that contains the pawls will continue to rotate at engine gearbox speed. A clicking sound heard during coast down on this type starter is not a malfunction, but rather the result of the pawls re-engaging and riding on the ratchet.

Pneumatic starters fitted with pawl and ratchet drives can undergo what is called a crash engagement, a dangerous situation that can occur if the air supply to the starter is turned on after the engine is running. In a crash engagement, the ratchet gear in the starter will be turning at an extremely high speed. If the engine speed is reduced to the speed at which the pawls try to engage the ratchet gear, a violent clash occurs between these two pieces. This can seriously damage the starter and possibly the accessory gearbox.

STARTER PRESSURE-REGULATING AND SHUTOFF VALVE

The starter pressure-regulating and shutoff valve, as seen in Figure 10-7 and commonly referred to as the starter air valve, is installed in the inlet air line to the starter. It consists of a control head and a butterfly valve that is powered open electrically by means of a cockpit switch. [Figure 10-10]

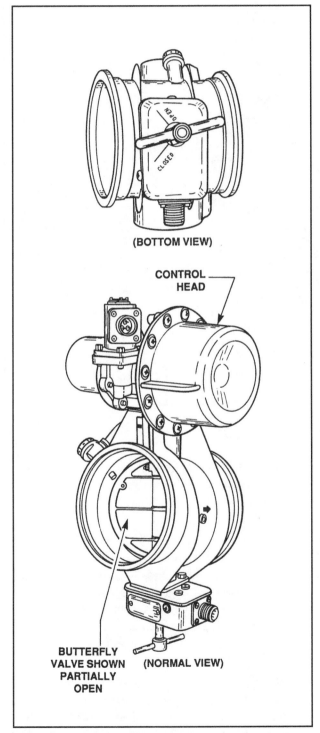

Figure 10-7. Starter pressure-regulating and shutoff valve with manual override handle in partially open position

As shown in Figure 10-8, when the operator engages the cockpit start switch, the solenoid is energized upward and the following events occur:

1. The control crank rotates counterclockwise, pushing the control rod to the right and extending the bellows fully. The butterfly regulating valve, currently in the closed position, permits this movement because no pressure is present in the sensing line.

2. The control crank also forces the pilot valve rod and cap to the right against spring tension.

3. Air that had been blocked in the filtered inlet line flows past the cap to the servo piston and opens the butterfly valve.

4. As pressure builds in the downstream supply line, the sensing line directs air to partially compress the bellows. As this occurs, the pilot valve rod unseats, which permits some of the servo piston air to vent to the atmosphere. This action causes the butterfly valve to reset in a slightly closed position.

5. When downstream air pressure reaches a preset value, the amount of air flowing to the servo piston through the restrictor equals the amount of air being bled to the atmosphere, and the system is in a state of equilibrium. This feature protects the starter if inlet air pressure is set too high.

6. When the starter drive reaches a predetermined speed, the centrifugal cutout flyweight switch in the starter de-energizes the solenoid, which causes the butterfly to return to a closed position.

MANUAL OPERATION WITH THE T-HANDLE

A manual override handle, available through a cowl access panel, enables the operator to manually rotate the butterfly open and closed if an electrical failure has occurred or if corrosion or icing causes excessive friction within the system during attempted ground starts. If the valve does not operate normally after the restriction to movement has been freed, the valve must be replaced.

The procedure for using the T-handle to override the electrical operation of the air valve has three steps:

1. Using a hook or lightly gripping it by hand, pull out on the T-handle to vent the servo piston chamber. If gripping by hand, wear gloves to prevent burns. Note also that the handle might turn quickly, which could cause hand injury.

2. Turn the T-handle to the open position and hold it so throughout the starting period. This overcomes the close spring in the servo piston.

3. At the specified speed, typically 35 percent N_2 speed, turn the T-handle to the close position and push the handle in until it seats. (Caution: This is very important because at 40 percent N_2, the starter will overspeed and require a bench check.)

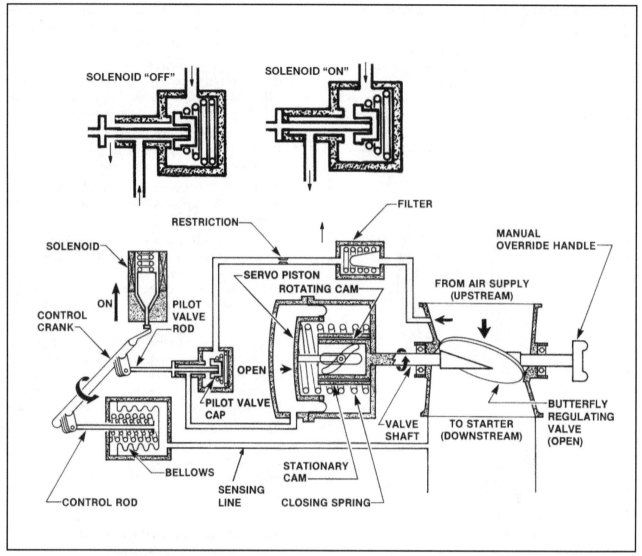

Figure 10-8. Pressure-regulating and shutoff valve in the ON position

PNEUMATIC (AIR TURBINE) STARTING SYSTEM

The auxiliary power unit is typically mounted in the rear of the airplane or in a lower fuselage compartment. An air manifold, which runs through the entire aircraft, interconnects the auxiliary power unit, the ground service connection, the engine bleed air ports, and the starter inlets. [Figure 10-9] It is possible with this system to start one engine from a ground or onboard starting unit and then to start the remaining engines from the cross-bleed air source of an operating main engine.

STARTING PROCEDURE

Air supplies for pneumatic starting systems are subject to low pressure but very high volume; creating heavy forces if air is released improperly. Before starting, be sure that procedures are in place to ensure personnel and equipment safety. For example, be sure to:

- Lay out the ground power unit (GPU) air hose free of kinks to prevent sudden movement when pressurized.
- Momentarily blow out the hose to clear it of foreign objects that could enter the starter.
- Completely engage the hose adapter to the aircraft start air connection. [Figure 10-11]

Although each aircraft likely has a specific starting procedure and checklist, the following starting procedure is typical of a dual-spool engine as depicted in Figure 10-10:

1. Start the auxiliary power unit or ground power unit and monitor the Start Air Manifold gauge in the cockpit until it indicates 45 p.s.i.g.

2. Open Cross-Bleed valve number 2.

3. Move the Start Switch to the number 2 engine position (this energizes the solenoid, as shown in Figure 10-8) and ensure that the cockpit light shown on Figure 10-10 is illuminated, which indicates that the valve is open.

4. Watch for a slight drop in starter air manifold pressure.

5. Note the increase in N_2 speed as indicated on the cockpit tachometer indicator.

6. Note the increase in N_1 speed, which should occur within five to ten seconds of N_2 indication.

7. Place the Fuel/Ignition lever to the ON position.

8. Watch for a rise in exhaust gas temperature and oil pressure.

9. Watch for the cockpit light to go out and watch for a slight rise in air manifold pressure as the number 2 start air valve and ignition de-energizes. This should occur at approximately ten percent below idle speed.

10. Monitor all engine instruments as the engine spools up to idle speed; then close cross-bleed valve number 2 after idle speed is reached.

11. Start the remaining engines from the auxiliary power unit or ground power unit.

12. Follow the prescribed checklist for the remainder of the run.

CROSS-BLEED STARTING

After one engine is started, the remaining engines can be started with cross-bleed air, but this is not desirable under normal circumstances. It requires approximately 80 percent N_2 speed to obtain the necessary air pressure, which results in excessive noise and jet blast on the ramp as well as wasted fuel.

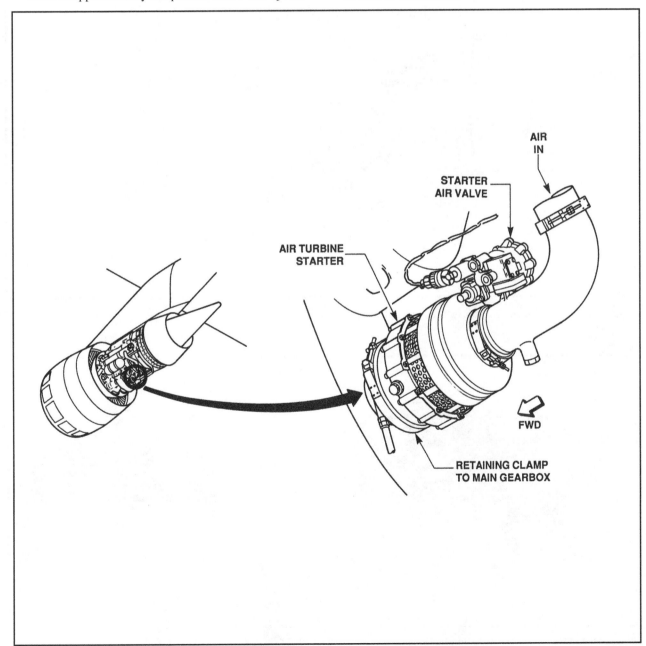

Figure 10-9. Relationship of starter air valve to starter

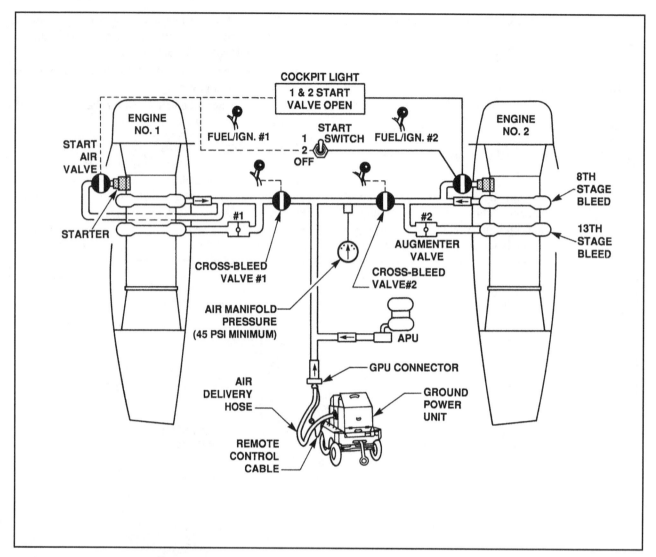

Figure 10-10. Air sources available to pneumatic starters

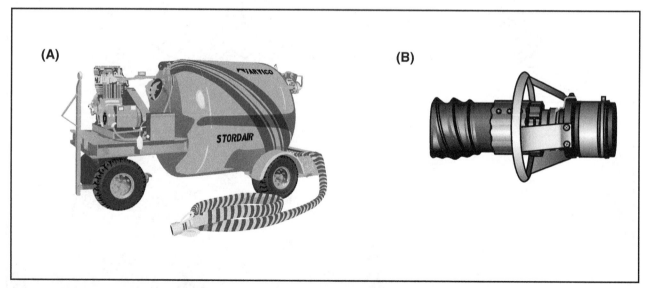

Figure 10-11A. Ground power starting unit
Figure 10-11B. Hose-to-aircraft adapter

1. To start number 1 engine from cross-bleed air, open cross-bleed valves number 1 and number 2.

2. Open the number 2 augmenter valve if air manifold pressure is low on a hot day or if customer bleed air is being used.

3. Place the start switch to number 1 and follow the same procedure as for the number 2 engine.

AIR STARTER DUTY CYCLE

Air starters have a restricted operating cycle time (or duty cycle) due to their ring gear reduction system, which rapidly builds up friction heat due to the low-volume splash-type wet sump oil system contained in the gear section. The typical prescribed duty cycle for engine starting is five minutes on; then two minutes off for cooling. During motor over checks, when the engine is rotated with the starter and no ignition, the typical duty cycle is five minutes on; then five minutes off to cool the starter due to the additional loading. Motor over checks are frequently used to inspect for various engine problems such as leaks, to listen for rubbing sounds on coastdown, and to measure the coastdown time.

STARTER-FADEC INTERFACE

Many modern aircraft are configured with a Full Authority Digital Engine Control (FADEC) system that incorporates an EEC. [Figure 10-12] These computerized systems automatically monitor and govern many engine operating parameters, giving the EEC complete control of the starting process. The FADEC system assists the flight crew during engine ground starting as well as during in-flight relights.

- FADEC monitors engine parameters such as N_1 and N_2 speeds, engine temperatures, oil pressure, and several others provided by engine- and aircraft-mounted sensors and prevents parameters from exceeding their limits.

- The EEC meters fuel and controls ignition and starter air valve functions for ground starts and in-flight relights.

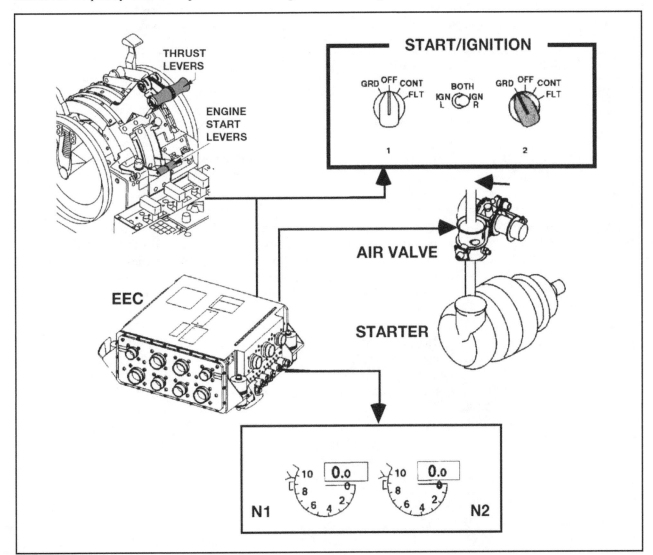

Figure 10-12. Pneumatic starter in FADEC system

If the exhaust gas temperature (EGT) exceeds the starting limit, causing a hot start, the EEC will cut off the fuel supply. Similarly, when EGT does not rise in the prescribed time, which indicates that combustion has not occurred, the EEC terminates the fuel supply to prevent a wet start. Wet starts are a safety hazard because they leave the exhaust section dangerously overloaded with fuel that can ignite when subsequent start attempts are initiated.

TYPICAL START PROCEDURE

The start levers on the throttle quadrant, shown in Figure 10-12, are used to initiate the flow of fuel during engine starting and to turn the fuel off at engine shutdown. The thrust levers modulate engine power throughout the operational range.

The following steps outline a typical start procedure:

1. Select the ignition position (IGN-L or IGN-R).
2. Move the engine start switch to the GRD (ground) position.
3. Observe the start valve open indication.
4. Observe N_2 rotation, and then N_1 rotation.
5. Monitor oil pressure and ensure that it starts to rise.
6. Move the engine start lever from the cut-off position to the idle position at designated N_2 percent.
7. Ensure that the fuel flow is within limits.
8. Monitor the EGT as it start to rise, and ensure that it stays within limits.
9. Note when the starter cuts out, typically between 50 and 55 percent N_2.

As the flight crew carries out the steps above, the FADEC system simultaneously checks and records and provides advisory information by way of flight deck lights and message displays. If, during the start cycle, the engines do not reach idle speed successfully, the EEC automatically cuts off fuel flow.

OTHER STARTING SYSTEMS

Many other starting systems have been developed in the past for military and commercial engines. They are not in common use in either business or commercial aviation today, but are still used in older special aircraft and military conversions. The following table describes several alternative starting systems.

Starter Type	Description
High-Low Pressure Pneumatic Starter	This system consists of a type of air turbine starter mounted on the accessory gearbox that can use either conventional low-pressure air starting or a high-pressure (3,000 p.s.i.) air source from an onboard storage bottle. [Figure 10-13] High-pressure air starting (usually used on only one engine) gives the aircraft a self-starting capability without the necessity of an auxiliary power unit or ground power unit.
Cartridge-Pneumatic Starter	This system consists of a starter mounted on the accessory gearbox that can use either a low-pressure, high-volume air source similar to the pneumatic (air turbine) starter or an explosive solid propellant charge The charge is ignited electrically from the aircraft battery, giving the aircraft a self-starting capability without the necessity of an auxiliary power unit or ground power unit. [Figure 10-14]
Fuel-Air Combustion Starter	This system consists of an accessory gearbox-mounted starter that uses a high-pressure (3,000 p.s.i.) air source and a combustion process. It is similar to a small gas turbine engine. Combustion is initiated electrically from the aircraft battery, giving the aircraft a self-starting capability. [Figure 10-15]
Turbine Impingement Starting	This system consists of a low-pressure, high-volume air source of 45 p.s.i.g. at 200 to 300 pounds per minute that is directed onto the engine turbine wheel. The air source terminates after the engine reaches self-accelerating speed. Although this system requires an inlet air port, no other accessory is required. [Figure 10-16]
Hydraulic Starter	This system consists of a hydraulic starter motor mounted on the accessory gearbox. It is driven by fluid from a hydraulic pump mounted on the APU or by a hand pump and accumulator arrangement.

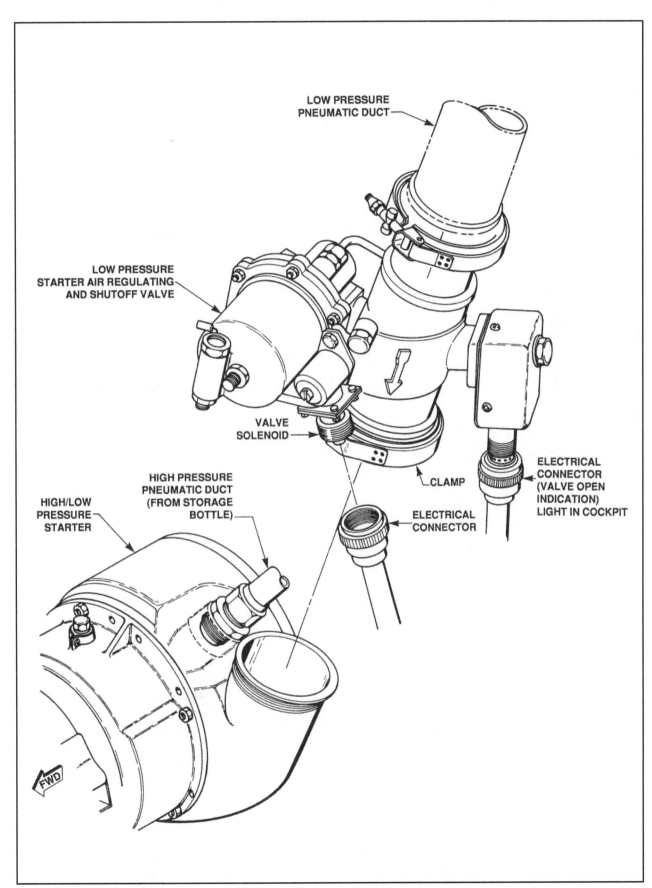

Figure 10-13. High-low pressure pneumatic starter

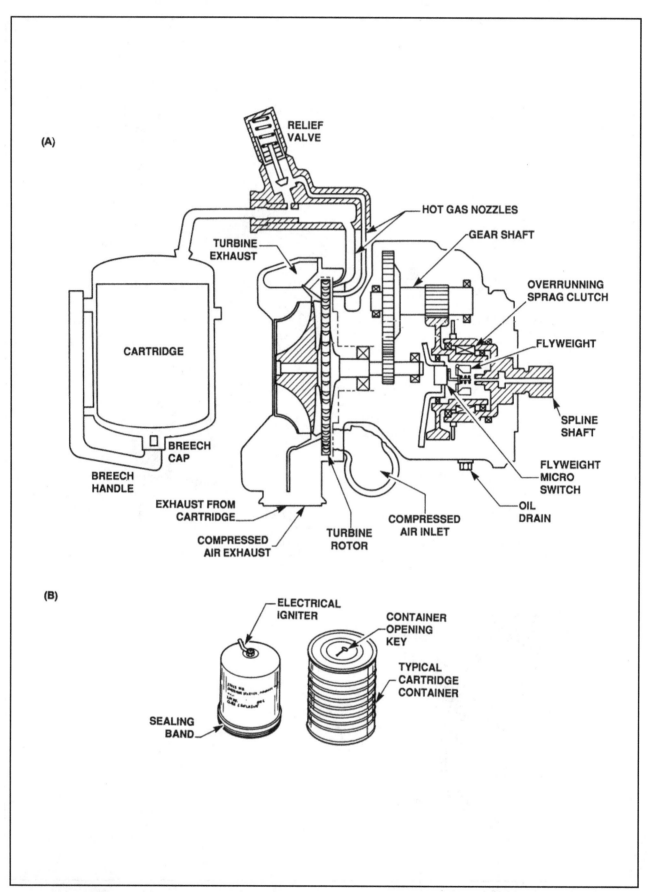

Figure 10-14A. Cutaway view of a cartridge/pneumatic starter
Figure 10-14B. Solid propellant cartridge

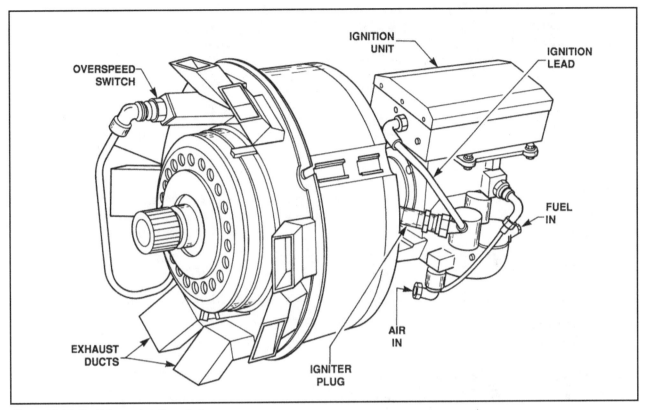

Figure 10-15. Fuel/air combustion starter

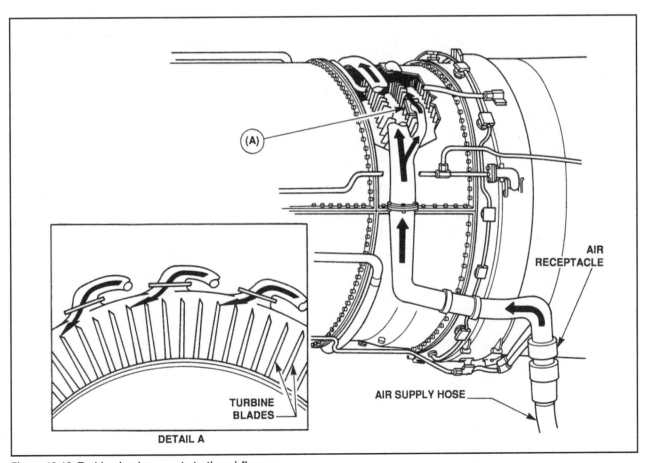

Figure 10-16. Turbine impingement starting airflow

TROUBLESHOOTING THE STARTER SYSTEM

PROBLEM/POSSIBLE CAUSE	CHECK PROCEDURE	REMEDY
Problems associated with starter-generators		
1. Engine does not rotate when the starter switch is closed during a battery start		
a. External power receptacle door left open or faulty microswitch	Check for open door or determine whether a faulty microswitch indicates a false door-open condition.	Close door or repair switch.
b. Defective battery relay	Check for power at DC start bus.	Repair as necessary.
c. Defective motor relay	Determine whether the motor relay closes properly.	Repair or replace as necessary.
d. Defective starter-generator	a) Check for correct input voltage. b) Inspect shaft to determine if it is sheared.	Change battery. Replace starter.
2. Engine does not rotate when the start switch is closed during external power start		
a. External power source failing to power the aircraft	Check for correct connection to aircraft.	Make connection.
b. See 1a through 1d above.		
3. Starting terminates when start switch is released		
Undercurrent relay fails to close properly	Check for proper relay operation.	Replace as necessary.
4. Engine starts but will not self-accelerate (hung start)		
a. Inadequate power supply	Check for low voltage condition.	Charge or change battery.
b. Faulty starter-generator	Check for signs of overheating or sounds associated with internal failure.	Repair or replace unit as necessary.
Problems associated with air turbine starters		
1. Engine does not rotate when the start switch is closed		
a. Malfunctioning APU or GPU	Check for presence of air in starting manifold (monitor the cockpit gauge).	Correct as necessary.
b. Malfunctioning starter air valve	a) Check for proper solenoid operation. b) Determine whether ice or corrosion prevents valve from operating.	Repair or replace air valve. Cycle with manual override or apply heat.
c. Defective starter	Inspect drive shaft to determine if it is sheared.	Replace shaft or starter.
2. Starter does not rotate to normal cutoff speed		
a. Malfunctioning APU or GPU	Check for low air supply.	Repair or replace air unit.
b. Starter	Check the setting of the centrifugal flyweight switch cutout.	Adjust setting or replace starter.
c. Starter Air Valve	Bench check valve for proper opening.	Replace valve.
3. Starter does not cut off		
See 2a or 2c above.		
4. Metal particles found on magnetic drain plug		
Internal starter malfunction	Evaluate size and texture of particles.	Small fuzzy particles are considered normal; chips or slivers indicate damage that requires starter replacement.

QUESTIONS:

1. Where is a turbine engine starter normally mounted?
2. What starter clutch feature prevents the engine from driving the starter to burst speed?
3. Which type of starter remains completely engaged to the engine during engine operation?
4. Which unit controls airflow to the pneumatic (air turbine) starter?
5. From which three sources does the pneumatic (air turbine) starter receive its air supply?
6. Does the pneumatic starter create engine rotation by introducing mechanical energy to the compressor or by introducing air into the inlet to rotate the compressor?
7. Which unit in a FADEC system creates the signal to initiate airflow to the starter pressure regulating and shutoff valve?
8. Does a high-low pressure type starter "produce" or "receive" high or low air pressure to initiate engine start?

CHAPTER 11
Ignition Systems

A gas turbine ignition system contains three major components: a high-voltage exciter, a high-voltage transmission lead, and an igniter plug. The exciter, which is powered by the aircraft electrical system (either DC or AC) or a dedicated permanent-magnet alternator (PMA), produces a high-voltage pulse through the igniter lead to the plug. Then, at the tip of the igniter plug, the current arcs—that is, it bridges a gap, creating a spark that ignites the fuel/air mixture in the combustion chamber.

Modern gas turbine ignition systems are high-intensity, capacitor discharge systems with either intermittent duty or extended duty cycles. Intermittent duty systems draw sufficiently high current to overheat their units, so they have a restricted duty cycle based on operating time, followed by a cooling off period. Extended duty systems have long duty cycles; in fact, some systems are rated for continuous duty with no time limits.

After a normal start, the flame within the combustor acts as the ignition source for continuous combustion. Because an external ignition source is no longer needed, the ignition system is deactivated.

The two common classifications of capacitor discharge ignition systems are the high-tension system and the low-tension system. In each of these systems, two igniter plugs are usually placed in the engine combustor at approximately the four o'clock and eight o'clock positions. The typical system also consists of two exciter units (or channels) and two high-tension leads that attach to the igniter plugs. The two exciter channels might be housed separately or integrated into a single unit. [Figure 11-1]

MAIN IGNITION SYSTEM

The main ignition system is used primarily during ground starting. A secondary function of this system is to provide a standby protection against in-flight flameout, which might occur at takeoff or landing, during bad weather operations, or when operating in anti-ice bleed air mode.

If an extended duty main system is installed, operators can select full ignition to either or both plugs at their discretion (for example, when considering the service life of the igniter plug).

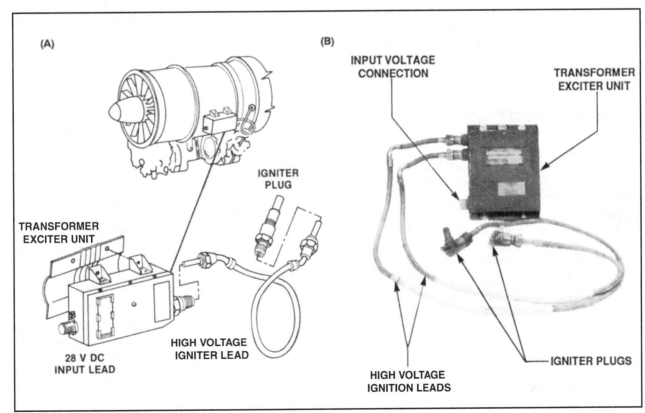

Figure 11-1A. One side of a dual, main ignition system
Figure 11-1B. Dual, main ignition system

When the operator turns the flight deck start and ignition selector switch shown in Figure 11-2A to the ground start position (GRD START) the starter air valve opens (indicated by the "Start Valve Open" light) and the ignition system begins its operation. The specific igniter plug that fires is determined by the position of the IGN L-**BOTH**-IGN R (L-**B**-R) toggle switch. In the present position shown, only the left igniter plug will fire. After engine start, the selector switch is either manually turned from GRD START to the OFF position, or it automatically returns to the OFF position.

The start panel shown in Figure 11-2A represents an aircraft with an air turbine starter. If the aircraft has a flat-panel display (glass cockpit) for the engine instruments, the "valve open" indication would appear on the display rather than an individual indicator light turning on.

The flight position (FLT START) is used to relight the engine after an engine shutdown or an engine flameout. It typically provides ignition to both igniter plugs, regardless of the position of the L-B-R selector switch, but generally does not provide air to the starter. Engine rotation for in-flight starting is normally accomplished by engine windmilling from ram air within the engine inlet. If assistance from the starter is needed, then a ground start procedure is initiated, or in the case of a FADEC-controlled engine, the electronic engine control (EEC) automatically brings the starter online.

On older aircraft, the main ignition system might be an intermittent duty system with an operation time limit. Intermittent duty is characteristic of high-tension systems in which excessive heat can build up and damage the exciter units. A typical time limit is two minutes on, three minutes off. If a second two-minute-on interval is needed, a 20-minute cooling period would typically be required.

CONTINUOUS DUTY

The CONT switch position in Figure 11-2A is used during takeoff and landing and when flying in bad weather or during icing conditions. With the switch in this position, ignition is continuously on for the igniter plugs selected by the L-B-R switch, which helps prevent engine flameout.

In recent years, the majority of new ignition exciter designs have incorporated extended- or continuous-duty circuits. This has driven the designs to store lower energies and incorporate as many system efficiencies as possible in the exciter circuitry, ignition leads, and igniter plugs. Nonetheless, to avoid premature failure of the ignition components, the ignition system should not be left on for the entire flight.

If the main system is intermittent duty, a second, low-energy (low joule) system called a continuous duty circuit might be incorporated within the ignition exciter to provide stand-by protection against flameout at critical times. This circuit is considered to have no time limit. Figure 11-3 illustrates a dual unit that can be operated on either the intermittent or the continuous duty circuit. If an engine relight in flight becomes necessary and continuous ignition does not create sufficient spark energy to initiate combustion, the main system is then used, but must be operated within its duty constraints.

AUTO-IGNITION

Many turbine-powered aircraft have an auto-ignition circuit installed. It is designed primarily to ensure instantaneous ignition if an engine begins to lose power from loss of inlet airflow. Any inlet obstruction to airflow, such as inlet icing and inlet damage, can cause the engine to flame out. When the engine start panel switch is in the AUTO position, electrical power is supplied to a sensor on the engine that, if alerted, reacts by signaling the ignition circuit to fire one or both igniter plugs. In most auto-ignition configurations, both igniter plugs are fired. [Figure 11-2A]

Three common engine-sensing systems that detect engine power loss, illuminate warning lights, and initiate auto-ignition are:

- Sensors that detect the loss of engine speed in turbojet and turbofan engines.
- Sensors that detect the loss of compressor discharge pressure in turbojet and turbofan engines.
- Sensors that detect the loss of torque oil pressure in turboshaft and turboprop engines.

The most current generation of aircraft have an automatic ignition feature that does not require an arming switch labeled AUTO. When engines are controlled by electronic engine control (EEC) components of a FADEC system, the OFF position on the start panel often serves as the automatic position as well. Figure 11-2B shows a system in which the EEC is interfaced with the engine start levers, the start panel, and the ignition exciters. In this system, after the engine has started successfully, the ground start selector switch automatically returns to the OFF position. Even though the switch is off, the EEC will initiate ignition if any of the engine sensors indicate that the engine is at risk of flaming out.

The EEC automatically initiates ignition when the following conditions are met:

- The start lever is in the engine run position.
- The core (N_2) speed is above a threshold limit, indicating that the engine is in normal operational mode.
- The EEC senses an engine deceleration, without command, greater than the normal schedule.

Other alert signals that can cause the ignition to turn on automatically include loss of compressor discharge pressure or compressor speed in a turbofan engine and loss of torque oil pressure in a turboprop or turboshaft engine.

The switch positions shown in Figure 11-2B, in conjunction with the EEC, correspond to the following conditions:

Ignition Systems

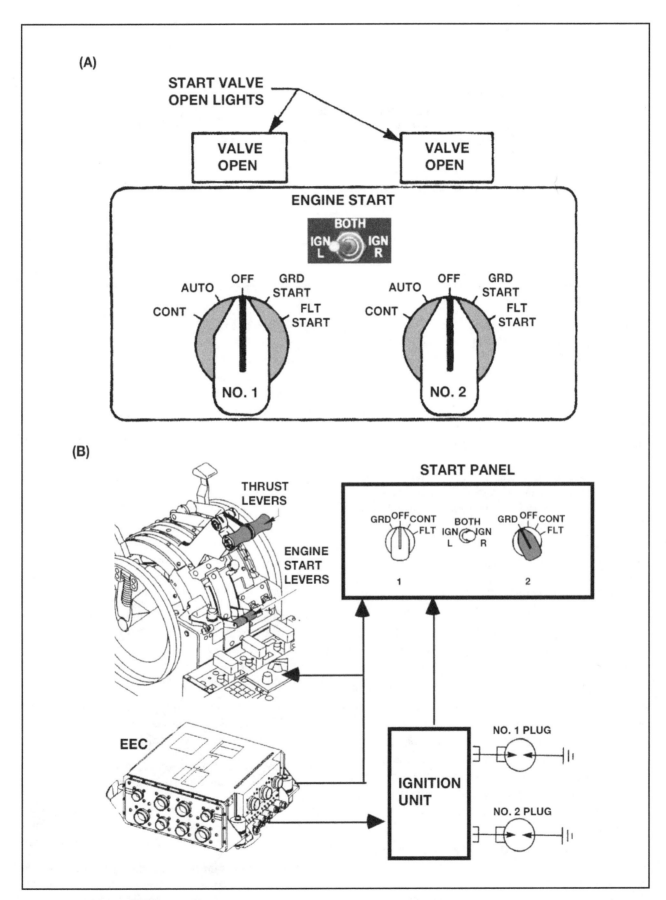

Figure 11-2A. Flight deck start and ignition switch
Figure 11-2B. FADEC ignition interface

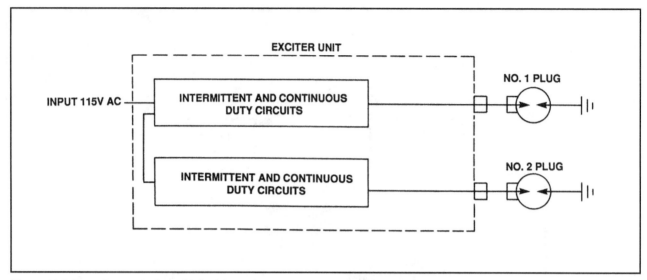

Figure 11-3. Transformer exciter with both intermittent- and continuous-duty circuits

GRD — This position is used for normal starting of the engine on the ground. Moving the switch to this position energizes the starter and turns on the ignition, firing the selected igniter plugs. After a successful start, the system automatically returns the switch to the OFF position.

CONT — This position is used during takeoff, landing, and bad weather operation as a safety measure against flameout. In this switch position, the starter is de-energized, but ignition is energized, with one plug or both plugs active, depending on the position of the ignition selector switch and what the EEC has commanded. The flight crew must manually return the switch to the OFF position.

FLT — This position is used to restart the engine if it flames out in flight. Both igniter plugs are fired, regardless of which igniter plugs are selected by the switch, but the starter is not energized unless the EEC senses that it is needed to assist the engine in the relight attempt.

OFF — This position turns off the starter and ignition, and also acts as the automatic position for the ignition system.

IGN L, BOTH, IGN R — This switch controls which igniter plugs are fired during a ground start procedure. For ground starting, it is common practice to use only one igniter plug, and to alternate plugs from one flight leg to the next. This procedure reduces wear on the ignition system, and it also helps to isolate a malfunction of one of the systems. In the FLT or OFF positions, the EEC controls which igniter plugs fire regardless of the position of this switch.

Some airplanes with FADEC-controlled engines (such as the Boeing 777) do not have a dedicated switch for selecting the individual igniter plugs. For example, on the Boeing 777, the EEC determines which igniter plugs fire during various operating conditions.

SPECIAL HANDLING

In ignition systems, the term *high intensity* infers that a lethal charge is present and that the system requires special maintenance and handling as prescribed by the manufacturer. The following procedures are typical of high-intensity systems:

- Ensure that the ignition switch is turned off before performing any maintenance on the system.

- To remove an igniter plug, disconnect the exciter input lead and wait for the time prescribed by the manufacturer to pass (usually one to five minutes). Doing so permits any residual stored energy to dissipate through the internal safety resistors. Then disconnect the igniter lead and ground the center electrode to the engine, to ensure that the exciter has no remaining charge. The igniter plug is now safe to remove.

- Exercise great caution when handling damaged, hermetically sealed exciter units. Some contain a small amount of radioactive material within the air gap tubes. This material is used to calibrate and stabilize the discharge point to a preset voltage.

- Ensure that you properly dispose of unserviceable igniter plugs. Some plugs contain aluminum oxide or beryllium oxide, both of which are toxic.

- Before testing igniters, ensure that the combustor is not fuel-wetted to avoid a fire or explosion.

- Do not energize the system for troubleshooting when the igniter plugs are removed. When the system is energized, high voltage is present at the igniter leads.

- Discard any igniter plugs that you drop because internal damage, such as cracked ceramic insulators, can occur that might not be detectable by testing or examination.

- Always use a new gasket when reinstalling an igniter plug. The gasket is necessary not only to ensure an adequate seal against escaping hot gases, but also to provide a good conductive current path to ground.

JOULE RATINGS

Turbine ignition systems carry a joule rating. A joule is defined as power (watts) multiplied by time (seconds), whereby one joule equals one watt per second. The time interval for plug firing is very short, in the millionths of a second. Ignition of atomized fuel occurs very rapidly, also in milliseconds, so a long spark duration is not necessary.

For example, consider a turbine-engine ignition system with a stored voltage of 2,000 VDC and an ionizing voltage at the plug of 500 VDC. The current in the system is 200 amps, and the spark jumps the igniter plug gap in 40 millionths of a second (0.000040 sec.). With this information, you can determine the joule rating on this ignition system as follows.

$$\text{Watts} = \text{Volts} \times \text{Amps}$$
$$\text{Watts} = 500 \times 200$$
$$\text{Watts} = 100{,}000$$

$$\text{Joules} = \text{Watts} \times \text{Time}$$
$$\text{Joules} = 100{,}000 \times 0.000040$$
$$\text{Joules} = 4$$

NOTE: The higher stored voltage (compared to the ionizing voltage) ensures that the ionizing voltage at the igniter plug is sufficient, taking into account the voltage drop that occurs due to long igniter leads and the fact that, as the electrodes in the igniter plug wear away, additional voltage is necessary to bridge the gradually increasing gap.

Some high-energy ignition systems are rated as high as 20 joules, with 2,000 amps output. This power is possible because of the short amount of time required to cause flashover at the igniter plug gap.

As a general rule of thumb, the stored energy of large main engine turbine ignition exciters is between 4 and 20 joules. Stored energy for small main engine exciters is 1 to 4 joules, and the exciters within auxiliary power units can store between 0.75 and 4.0 joules. The actual energy delivered to the spark event at the end of the igniter plug is typically on the order of 20 to 30 percent of the stored energy and is typically delivered at a minimum of 1 to 2 spark events per second.

The output voltage of the ignition exciter can be completely independent of the stored energy. That is, a one-joule ignition exciter could be a high-tension (high-voltage) unit capable of 24 kilovolt output.

TYPES OF IGNITION SYSTEMS

Both low- and high-tension ignition systems are in general use, and, depending on their configuration, they are powered either by direct current or alternating current.

Systems powered by DC receive their power from the battery bus; and AC systems are powered from the aircraft AC bus or by a dedicated permanent magnet alternator (PMA). PMAs can serve as a power supply to an ignition system that stores between one and four joules of energy. They are designed to produce sufficient current during the low cranking speeds associated with starting.

INTERMITTENT DUTY, LOW-TENSION IGNITION SYSTEM WITH DC VOLTAGE INPUT

The output voltage of a low-tension ignition system ranges from two to ten kilovolts. Figure 11-4 depicts a low-tension, DC-input system typically used in business jet applications. Systems such as this typically store from one to four joules of energy. Note that only one igniter plug is fired by each exciter channel. Therefore, the engine will have either two identical circuits in a single exciter unit or two separate exciter units to supply power to its two igniter plugs.

The following specifications apply to the ignition system in Figure 11-4:

Input voltage — 24 to 28 VDC

Operational limit — 10 to 30 volts

Input current — 3 amps

Stored energy — 4.0 joules

Output voltage — 3,000 to 10,000 volts

Output current — 133 amps at 3,000 volts

Output power — 400,000 watts

Spark rate (sparks per second) — 4 at 14 volts
                                                            8 at 30 volts

Time for spark to jump gap — 0.000010 seconds
                                          (10 millionths of a second)

SEQUENCE OF EVENTS OF A DC EXCITER SYSTEM

The following sequence of events occurs during the operation of the ignition system from the time the cockpit switch is selected to the flashover at the igniter plug:

1. When the cockpit switch is open, the permanent magnet holds the points closed by attraction of the point armature, which supplies power to the ignition exciter circuitry.

2. When the switch is closed, current flows from the battery negative side, through the primary coil, across the points, and to the battery positive terminal.

3. As electromagnetic force builds, the points are pulled open, momentarily stopping current flow. This action

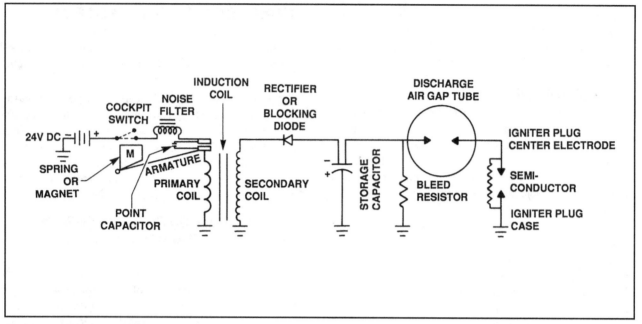

Figure 11-4. Low-tension (2 to 7 KV) intermittent duty ignition system showing one side of a dual system

occurs approximately 200 times per second. As the points open, the current has a tendency to arc across the gap between the points. A "point" capacitor within the point circuitry prevents arcing by offering a path of least resistance for this current flow.

4. When current first flows through the closed points, bottom to top of the primary coil, it produces a pulse in the secondary coil. This pulse attempts to flow in the opposite direction, from ground, through the storage capacitor, to the positive side of the secondary coil. However, the rectifier (or blocking diode) blocks current flow in this direction. The current path is also blocked by the discharge tube, which is open at this time.

5. A second pulse, stronger than the first, occurs when the points open and the primary field collapses into the secondary, creating a voltage of greatly increased value. Secondary current flows in the opposite direction, from the top of the coil and through the rectifier, to permit electrons to collect on the top plate of the storage capacitor. The current path is completed as free electrons are pushed from the bottom plate of the capacitor, out of the ground, to the bottom side of the secondary coil. The half-wave rectifier or blocking diode is present to change secondary coil induced alternating current to pulsating direct current.

6. After repeated cycles, a charge builds on the negative (or top) side of the storage capacitor, ultimately becoming sufficient to overcome the air gap in the discharge tube. The initial current surge ionizes (makes conductive) this air gap and permits the capacitor to discharge fully to the igniter plug.

7. In a low-tension system, the igniter plug is referred to as a self-ionizing or shunted-gap plug. The firing end of the plug contains a semiconductor material that initially provides a highly conductive path by bridging the gap between the center electrode and the ground electrode (provided by the igniter plug outer casing). The plug fires when the current flows from the storage capacitor through the center electrode, the semiconductor, the outer casing, and then back to the lower positive plate of the capacitor. As current flows initially through the semiconductor, heat builds up, which creates increased resistance to current flow. When the semiconductor reaches an incandescent state, the air gap heats sufficiently to ionize and the current takes the path of least resistance across the ionized gap, fully discharging the capacitor and creating a high-energy capacitive discharge spark.

Note: A bleed resistor is placed in the circuit to act as a safety device to provide overload- overheat protection to the circuit. It accomplishes this by:

- *Dissipating excess voltage beyond what the plug requires to fire. Plugs fire at the minimum required voltage, and the bleed resistor releases the remainder.*

- *Dissipating the capacitor discharge if the voltage required to fire a worn plug is greater than the voltage available.*

- *Providing a discharge path for capacitor energy if the system is fired when no igniter plug is installed.*

- *Bleeding off the capacitor charge when the system is de-energized.*

INTERMITTENT DUTY, HIGH-TENSION WITH AC VOLTAGE INPUT

The combustors in some modern large gas turbine engines need a higher intensity flashover at the igniter plug; these engines use a high-tension system, typically 14 to 28 kilovolts, with an alternating current input voltage. The following specifications apply to the ignition system in Figure 11-5:

Input voltages — 105V to 122V

Frequency — 380Hz to 420Hz

Input power/current — 0.65 amps max at 115V, 400Hz

Stored energy — 16 joules

Output voltage — 20 KV (at lead output conductor)

Output current — 200 amps at 20,000 volts

Spark rate (sparks per second) — 1.0 at 105V and 380Hz
2.0 at 115V and 400Hz
3.0 at 122V and 420Hz

Time for spark to jump gap — 0.000004 sec.
(4 millionths of a second)

SEQUENCE OF EVENTS FOR AN AC EXCITER SYSTEM

The following sequence of events occurs during the operation of the ignition system from the time the cockpit switch is selected to the flashover at the igniter plug:

1. Alternating current at 115 volts, 400 cycles is supplied to the primary coil of the power transformer. Note the absence of the vibrator point system, which is unnecessary with an AC input system. In some DC systems, the points were a common source of malfunction, and the AC system was developed to counteract this problem.

2. During the first half cycle, the primary coil produces approximately 2,000 volts in the secondary coil and current flows from the bottom (negative) end of the coil and out at the ground. Current then flows into the ground at rectifier tube A through resistor R1, through the doubler capacitor, and back to the top (positive) end of the secondary coil. This leaves the left side of the doubler capacitor charged at 2,000 volts. Rectifier tube B blocks any other current path during the first half-cycle current flow.

3. During the second half cycle, the primary coil produces another 2,000 volts in the secondary coil and current flows from the top end of the coil, which is now the negative end, through the doubler capacitor, where it now has a total of 4000 volts, through resistor R2, through Rectifier Tube B, through the storage capacitor, out of the ground, and returning to the bottom (positive) end of the secondary coil. Note that the presence of resistor R1 and the air gap discharge tube cause current to seek the path of least resistance, which is directly back to the secondary coil. Rectifier tube A also blocks current flow from the doubler capacitor and R1 to ground, which ensures current flow to the storage capacitor.

4. Repeated pulses charge the top (negative) side of the storage capacitor top at 4,000 volts to a point at which the air gap in the discharge tube ionizes. When this

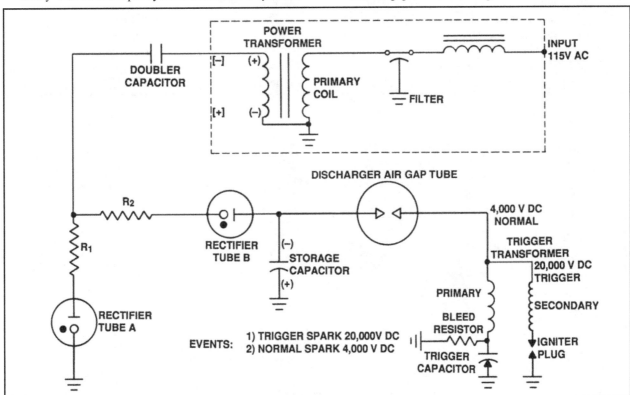

Figure 11-5. High-tension ignition system—20 joule, 28,000 volts

occurs, current flows through the trigger transformer primary coil, the trigger capacitor, the ground, and back to the bottom (negative) side of the storage capacitor.

5. This action induces voltage into the secondary coil of the trigger transformer, at approximately 20,000 volts, sufficient to ionize the igniter plug air gap and complete a path back to the storage capacitor. The trigger spark, which occurs by action of the trigger transformer and capacitor, creates a low resistance path and permits both the trigger capacitor and the storage capacitor to fully discharge at the igniter plug, creating a second high-intensity spark.

The high-tension spark created by this type system is needed to vaporize fuel globules at the firing end sufficiently to ignite the air-fuel mixture in the combustor either on the ground or in flight. The high-energy spark also helps to blast carbon deposits from the igniter plug electrodes and preserves the quality of the flashover.

SOLID-STATE CIRCUITRY IGNITION SYSTEMS

Most modern gas turbine engines use solid-state ignition systems. Solid-state circuitry produces less heat, weighs less, and is designed so that the firing interval at the igniter plug is constant regardless of input voltage. This enhances system reliability and extends the service life of the unit.

Current solid-state low-tension systems have little or no duty-cycle restrictions and can be operated with full rated power supplied to both igniter plugs. Transistors replace the mechanical points in the primary circuit, and other low-heat-generating circuit designs account for the change in duty cycle times.

The extended-duty units typically have a maximum four joules output with no time restriction to their operation or a maximum of eight joules with a typical cycle time of 30 minutes on, 30 minutes off. In solid-state systems, the operational time consideration is made by the pilot to increase the service life of the igniter plug rather than for the transformer units, bearing in mind that the exciter unit has an expected service life of thousands of hours, but the expected service life of the typical igniter plug is much less.

Some extended-duty systems on very large aircraft have as high as 16 joules of stored energy available in their capacitors, but they are still considered to be of low tension because the energy needed by a new igniter plug to fire correctly is only approximately two joules. As the plug wears out, though, the full stored energy is available to continue to fire the plug until the energy required to fire the plug exceeds the capacity of the transformer.

Extended-duty systems are designed for either DC input or AC input voltage and use semiconductor (shunted-gap) igniter plugs previously mentioned.

Figure 11-6 shows a schematic of a 24 VDC solid-state circuit ignition exciter. The following specifications apply to this ignition system:

Input voltage — 14 to 32 VDC (24 VDC nominal)

Input current — 4.0 amps DC maximum

Stored energy — 4.0 joules

Spark rate (sparks per second) — 1 at 14 VDC
                                                              10 at 32 VDC

Output voltage — 21,000 volts nominal (21 KV)

SEQUENCE OF EVENTS FOR A SOLID-STATE IGNITION SYSTEM

The following sequence of events (based on a Unison Corporation unit) occurs during the operation of a solid-state ignition. [Figure 11-6] The explanation of events follows conventional current flow theory, from positive to negative.

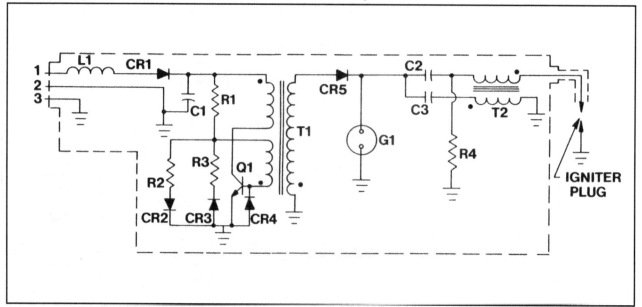

Figure 11-6. DC-powered, solid state, high-tension ignition system

1. When 24 VDC power is applied across input terminal pins 1 and 2 of the exciter, current initially flows through coil L1, reverse polarity protection diode CR1, starting resistor R1, base resistor R2, and diode CR2 to the negative side of the power supply. The current parameters, the value of resistors and the characteristics of the diodes are such that the voltage developed at the junction of R1 and R2 is always greater than the base to emitter voltage of transistor Q1. This voltage causes transistor Q1 to turn on.

2. Current flows through the primary winding of transformer T1 and the collector-emitter junction of the transistor to ground. Current through the primary winding induces a tertiary voltage, the polarity of which increases the forward-bias on transistor Q1. The tertiary voltage causes the transistor to conduct additional current. Due to this regenerative action, transistor Q1 quickly goes into saturation.

3. During the "on" period of the cycle, a relatively constant voltage (approximately equal to the supply voltage) appears across the primary of transformer T1. Because the polarity of the secondary voltage does not permit high-voltage rectifier CR5 to conduct during the transistor's on period, the secondary circuit is open with no energy being transferred at this instant of the cycle.

4. The relatively constant voltage induced on the tertiary winding produces a constant base current, which determines the maximum (peak) collector current. The linearly rising collector (primary) current reaches a maximum value determined by beta XIb, where beta is the current gain of the transistor and Ib is the base current. The path for the base current during the conduction period is from base to emitter junction of the transistor, diode CR3, base resistor R3, and back to the base of the transistor through the tertiary winding. The amplitude of the base current is controlled by the base resistor R3. When the maximum current point is reached, transistor Q1 moves out of saturation. At this instant, the induced voltage in the tertiary of transformer T1 drops to near zero. This drop in induced voltage initiates a regenerative action that drives the transistor into the cut-off region. As the primary current drops, the induced voltage in the secondary winding is reversed, which permits high-voltage rectifier CR5 to conduct, enabling the energy in the core of the transformer to be transferred to storage capacitor C2 and high-frequency capacitor C3. As long as the voltages across capacitors C2 and C3 and rectifier CR5 anode cause CR5 to be forward-biased, energy is transferred to C2 and C3.

5. As the current flowing through the primary winding of transformer T1 decreases, the voltage induced in the tertiary winding is also reversed. This voltage reversal in the tertiary winding holds the transistor in the non-conducting (off) state. The reverse-voltage condition in the tertiary winding remains until the energy in the core of transformer T1 is transferred to capacitors C2 and C3.

6. When all energy is transferred to tank capacitor C2 and high-frequency capacitor C3, the current in the secondary winding of transformer T1 goes to zero. The voltages induced in the secondary and tertiary winding are reversed, preventing high voltage on rectifier CR5 from flowing. The polarity of induced voltages on primary and tertiary windings are such that the switching transistor is forward-biased and turns on. The converted circuit is restored to its initial condition and the on/off cycle is repeated.

7. The gap between the electrodes of spark gap tube G1 is set to break down (ionize) between 2900 and 3200 volts. When the charge across capacitor C2 reaches this value, the spark gap ionizes. This completes a path from capacitor C3 through the primary of transformer T2 to ground and back to C3 through the spark gap G1. The current flow through this path is a high-frequency, oscillating current caused by the combination of capacitor C3 and the primary winding of transformer T2. This high-frequency current induces a high voltage in the secondary winding of transformer T2.

8. With the high-voltage pulse present, the igniter plug is ionized and the current starts to flow from the storage capacitor C2 through transformer T2 and the igniter plug.

9. Safety resistor R4, in parallel with the igniter plug, provides an alternate path for discharging capacitor C2 whenever the ignition exciter is operated inadvertently with the igniter plug removed (open-circuited) or whenever the igniter plug becomes open-circuited by an eroded or heat damaged gap that is too wide for the current to flow.

AC VERSUS DC SYSTEMS

The AC input system is more reliable in extreme climate conditions than the older DC input systems, which depends on the aircraft battery for its input. The AC system receives its power from the aircraft auxiliary power unit generator, from the aircraft inverters, or from its own dedicated permanent magnet alternator.

The operational cycle of a typical intermittent duty exciter powered by AC is 10 minutes on, 10 to 20 minutes off (for cooling). The older DC main system heats up more rapidly, and a typical operational cycle of a system with the same joule rating as the AC system might be 2 minutes on, 3 to 20 minutes off. The newer solid state DC or AC systems generally have no duty restrictions.

NOTE: If it becomes necessary to operate beyond the time limit, a special inspection is required after landing.

In flight, both AC and DC main systems can be switched from one igniter plug to the other. This procedure can be repeated as long as in-flight ignition is required.

If a low-joule AC, continuous ignition system is installed to supplement an intermittent duty system, there is usually no time limit imposed—that is, the system can run continuously with no cool-down period.

The DC system remains in popular use, especially when the aircraft is not equipped with an auxiliary power unit and a battery is the only power source available for starting.

On larger aircraft, the APU has a battery DC input ignition, and the main engines use the alternator output from the APU to power the AC input system.

HIGH-TENSION VERSUS LOW-TENSION SYSTEMS

Engines in which carbon has a tendency to accumulate on the firing tip of the igniter plug, high-tension systems better counteract the buildup. In addition, some engines require a high blast effect to better vaporize fuel droplets during starting—especially for reliable high-altitude relight capability.

The lower energy of a low-tension system might be less effective from this standpoint but low-tension systems are nevertheless widely used in engines where carbon buildup and high altitude problems are not present. Low-tension systems are typically less expensive, and their design is simpler due to the absence of a trigger transformer and capacitor circuit employed to create the high-voltage output.

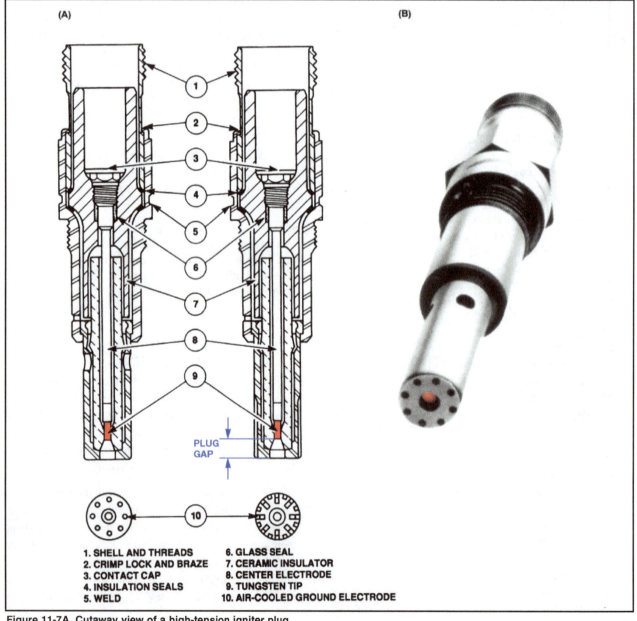

Figure 11-7A. Cutaway view of a high-tension igniter plug
Figure 11-7B. High-tension igniter plug

IGNITER PLUGS

Recall that under most conditions, combustion in a gas turbine engine, once initiated, is self-sustaining (except for abnormal events such as a flameout). However, some mechanism within the combustor must initiate the combustion process, and this is the job of the igniter plug. Igniter plugs are of two types: the spark igniter and the glow plug.

SPARK IGNITERS

Though conceptually similar, spark igniters differ considerably from spark plugs used in reciprocating engines. The gap at the igniter plug tip is much wider and the electrode is designed to withstand a much higher-intensity spark. [Figure 11-7] The igniter plug is also less susceptible to fouling because the high-energy spark removes carbon and other deposits each time the plug fires. The construction material is also different—for example, the igniter plug shell is made of a very high quality, nickel-chromium alloy and the center electrode is of tungsten or iridium, materials that are all highly resistant to wear. The threads at the terminal end in many cases are also silver-plated to prevent seizing. For all of these reasons, spark igniters are considerably more expensive than spark plugs.

The shell at the hot end of the igniter plug might be air cooled to keep it 500°F to 600°F cooler than the surrounding gas temperature. This helps prevent hot corro-

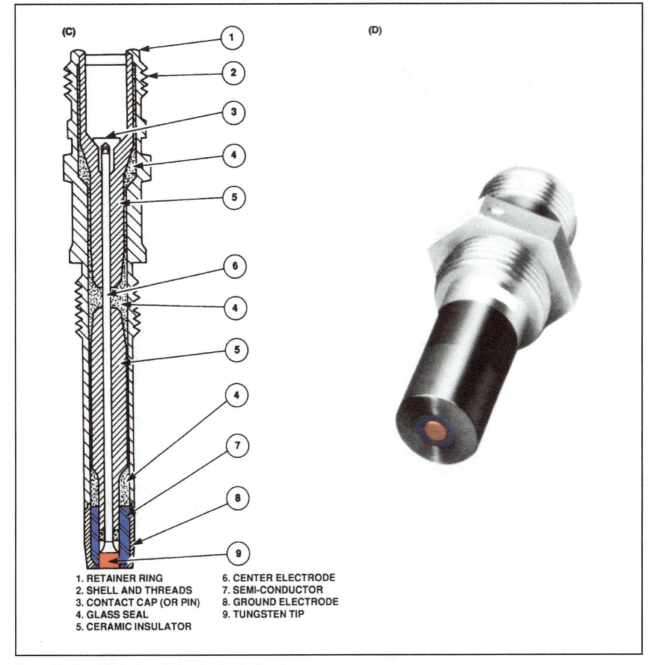

Figure 11-7C. Cutaway view of a low-tension igniter plug
Figure 11-7D. Low-tension igniter plug

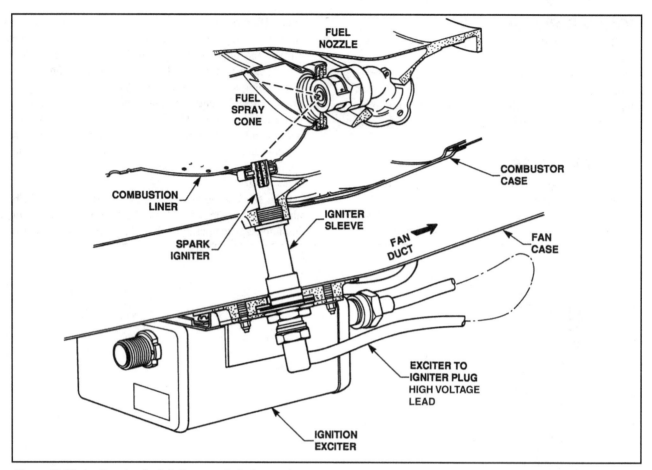

Figure 11-8A. Igniter plug installation on a turbofan engine

sion and erosion. Cooling air is pulled inward through the cooling holes by the pressure differential, which exists between combustor primary and secondary airflow.

Many varieties of igniter plugs are available, but usually only one will suit the needs of a particular engine. The igniter plug tip must protrude properly into the combustor in each installation and, on some fully ducted fan engines, must be long enough to mount on the outer case, pass through the fan duct, and penetrate into the combustor liner. [Figure 11-8A]

Igniters for high- and low-tension systems are not interchangeable, and care should be taken to ensure that the manufacturer's recommended igniter plug is used. In addition, it is important to select the correct gasket to ensure the position of the firing tip in the combustion liner. If the tip penetrates too deeply into the liner, the resulting increase in tip temperature can cause the plug to fail. [Figure 11-8B]

GLOW PLUG IGNITERS

Some smaller engines incorporate a glow plug igniter rather than a spark igniter. A glow plug is a resistance coil of very high heat value that is designed for extreme low-temperature starting. [Figure 11-9] A typical glow plug system is used in some models of the Pratt & Whitney PT6 turboprop engine.

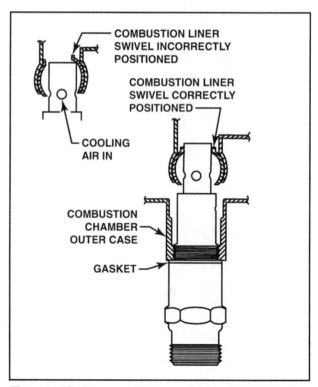

Figure 11-8B. Correct and incorrect installation of igniter into liner

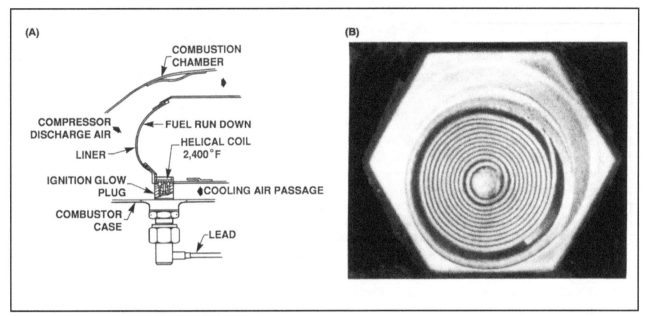

Figure 11-9A. Glow plug igniter installation
Figure 11-9B. Glow plug coil

The glow plug is powered by 28VDC at approximately 10 amps to heat the coil to a yellow hot condition. The coil is similar in appearance to an automobile cigarette lighter. Air directed up through the coil mixes with fuel running down from the main fuel nozzle. This is designed to occur at low flow conditions during engine starting when the main nozzle is not completely atomizing its discharge. The influence of the airflow on the fuel acts to create a hot streak or blow-torch-like ignition. After fuel is terminated, the air source then cools the igniter coil during normal engine operation.

HIGH-TENSION IGNITER PLUG CLEANING AND INSPECTION

Igniter plug removal for cleaning and inspecting is a routine maintenance task performed at specific intervals and whenever the engine is experiencing ground starting difficulties, in-flight restart difficulties, or flameouts when in the auto-ignition relight mode.

CLEANING THE IGNITER PLUG

Recall that turbine ignition systems can deliver a potentially lethal shock if contacted at the high-voltage end of the circuit. To remove an igniter plug, first remove the power input lead to the exciter. Next, disconnect the high-tension lead from the output of the ignition exciter. The last step is to disconnect the high-tension lead from the igniter plug and remove the plug.

Clean the outer case and the terminal end of high-tension igniter plugs (such as the one shown in Figure 11-10) with a soft brush and approved solvent. Clean the ceramic insert at the terminal end with a felt swab and approved solvent. Black flashover marks on the ceramic portions, which are caused by air gaps or contaminants, must be completely removed because they can cause the plug to misfire. This ceramic insulator on some igniters can also be cleaned with light abrasive materials to remove stubborn stains. Inspect and clean the igniter lead connector to prevent recurrence of flashover. The firing electrode tip is usually cleaned with solvent, a soft non-metallic brush and a light abrasive. Abrasive grit-blast cleaning, such as that used on spark plugs for reciprocating engines, is never permitted because the ceramic insulator across the gap between the center electrode and the case would be damaged. After cleaning, use compressed air to blow off the remaining solvent and ready the plug for inspection.

INSPECTION AND OPERATIONAL CHECKS

Inspecting high-voltage igniter plugs generally consists of a visual inspection and a measurement check of the spark gap with a mechanic's scale and a suitable depth micrometer to determine the center electrode depth from the shell electrode. [Figure 11-11]

After visual inspection, perform an operational check. A typical operational check might include connecting the conditioned plug to its circuit lead, with the plug positioned outside of the engine and firing it for 20 to 30 seconds to compare its spark intensity with that of a new plug. During this check, take extreme care when dissipating the capacitor's charge before handling the center electrode.

Another check typical of installed igniters is to fire the plugs one at a time. Do this by using the aircraft cockpit switches and listening near the tailpipe for the sharp snapping noise associated with good ignition spark. The spark rate, typically from 0.5 to 2.0 sparks per second, can also be timed during this check. Maintenance manuals specify the exact rate for each particular system. To avoid the possibility of an explosive fire, exercise caution when performing these procedures to ensure that no fuel vapors are present in the combustor during the check.

CHANGE INTERVALS, HIGH-TENSION IGNITER PLUGS

Change high-tension igniter plugs at intervals prescribed by the manufacturer. These intervals are established based on trend analysis of igniter usage. For example, an aircraft on a long route schedule with little igniter use might establish an 800- to 1,200-hour interval between changes, based on estimated igniter use during that engine operating time. Conversely, a short-haul operator might have a 200- to 300-hour interval in a similar type aircraft because that aircraft undergoes more igniter operation due to more frequent takeoffs and landings.

LOW-TENSION IGNITER PLUG CLEANING AND INSPECTION

Cleaning and inspecting low-tension igniter plugs is a routine maintenance task accomplished as scheduled or unscheduled maintenance just as for high-tension igniter plugs. However, the cleaning and inspection procedures are substantially different.

CLEANING THE IGNITER PLUG

As a general rule, clean the low-tension, self-ionizing igniter plug only on its outer casing and at the terminal end as for high-tension plugs. The semiconductor material at the firing end is easily damaged, and most manufacturers do not permit cleaning, regardless of the carbon buildup, except during reconditioning at the factory. [Figure 11-10]

INSPECTION AND OPERATIONAL CHECKS

Inspection checks do not include measurement checks because no cleaning is allowed at the firing tip. It is too difficult to measure gap clearances accurately when a carbon buildup is present. [Figure 11-10] The generally accepted inspection method for these plugs is to inspect the terminal end insulator and outer casing for cracks and damage. Then inspect the firing tip visually and compare the plug's condition against a drawing provided by the manufacturer. [Figure 11-12] The operational checks mentioned for high-voltage plugs are also applicable inspection criteria for low-tension igniter plugs. Therefore, without being able to clean and measure the firing end of the plugs, the visual and operational checks are the only means of determining a plug's serviceability.

GAP DESCRIPTION	TYPICAL FIRING END CONFIGURATION	CLEAN FIRING END
HIGH VOLTAGE AIR SURFACE GAP	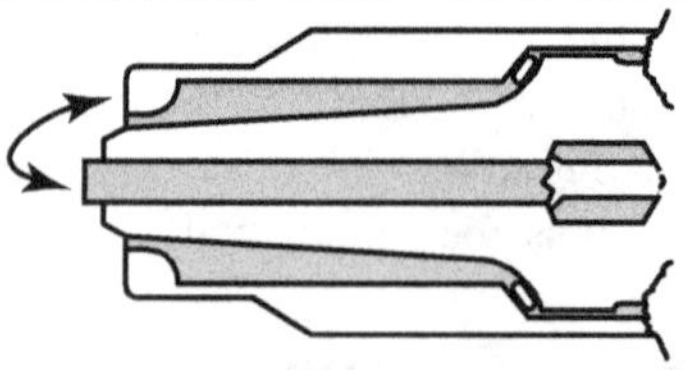	YES
HIGH VOLTAGE SURFACE GAP	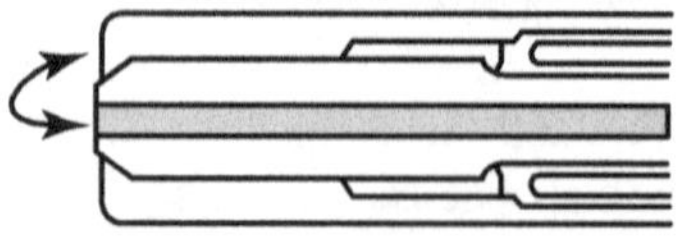	YES
HIGH VOLTAGE RECESSED SURFACE GAP	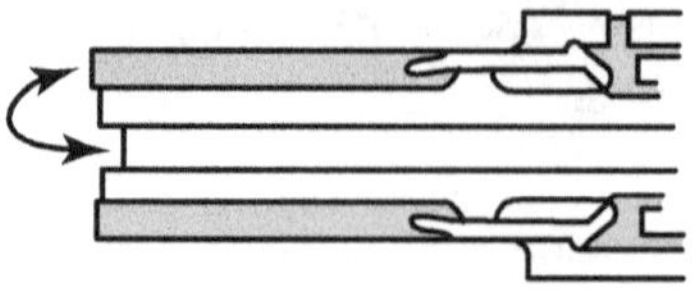	YES
LOW VOLTAGE SHUNTED SURFACE GAP (SELF IONIZING)	SEMI-CONDUCTOR 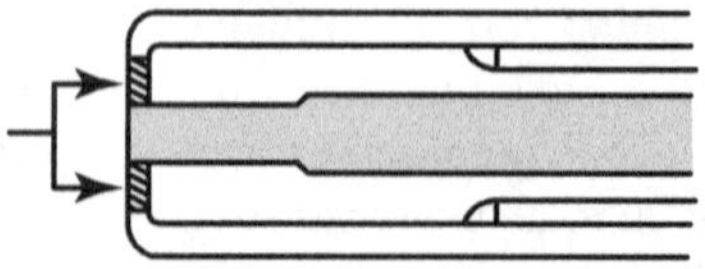	SELDOM
LOW VOLTAGE GLOW COIL ELEMENT		YES

Figure 11-10. Common types of ignition plug firing ends

Ignition Systems

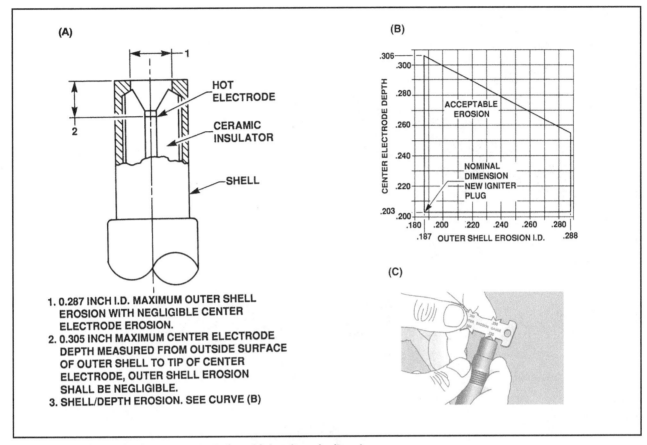

Figure 11-11A. Wear check measurements for a high-voltage igniter plug
Figure 11-11B. Example of a wear check chart for high-tension igniter plugs
Figure 11-11C. Special tool for wear measurement checks

CHANGE INTERVALS FOR LOW-TENSION IGNITER PLUGS

Change low-tension igniter plugs based on an interval system similar to high-tension plugs mentioned earlier. Older style plugs, both those with center electrodes made from tungsten and those with a semiconductor coating on a base material, typically have a 400- to 500-hour change interval. Newer plugs with iridium center electrodes and what is called a solid pellet semiconductor have an 800- to 1,200-hour service life. Iridium, a metallic element found in platinum, is one of the few materials that can withstand the high-temperature environment at the tip of the igniter plug in modern gas turbine engines.

GLOW PLUG CLEANING AND OPERATIONAL CHECKS

Inspect the glow plug heater coils for evidence of carbon buildup that appears to fuse the coils together. If necessary, immerse the coil end in carbon remover solution to soften the carbon. Then remove the loosened carbon with a soft, nonmetallic brush such as nylon or fiber. Avoid using metal of any kind, which can damage the insulation on the coils. Finally, rinse the coil in warm water and dry it with compressed air. The maximum acceptable fusing of coils that is acceptable is small—typically one coil fused to another, eliminating the space between individual coils. The maximum thickness of fused coils can be no more than one-eighth inch.

Carbon can build up early on glow plugs for the following reasons:

- The pilot inadvertently initiates fuel flow before the coil heats up adequately.
- Low voltage provided to the coil by a component malfunction prevents it from heating up adequately.
- Loose connections in system wiring prevent the coil from heating up adequately.

INSPECTION

Operationally check the plug after it passes the visual test by attaching the plug to its engine ignition lead and checking for a bright yellow glow within a prescribed time limit, generally 20 to 30 seconds.

SPECIAL TEST EQUIPMENT

If the igniters fail an operational check, test the wiring for opens and shorts with a traditional volt-ohmmeter. Special test units, such as the one shown in Figure 11-13, are designed to perform additional tests on this system. Examples include tests for input voltage, output voltage, insulation breakdown, input amperage, output amperage, and spark rate per input voltage.

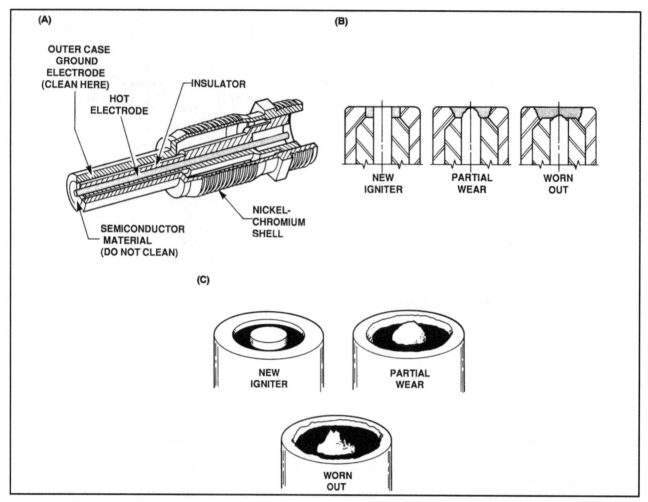

Figure 11-12A. Cutaway view of a low-tension igniter plug
Figure 11-12B. Side view of erosion of firing end seen during visual inspection
Figure 11-12C. End view of firing tip erosion

COMPLETE ENGINE IGNITION SYSTEM — GE/SNECMA CFM56

As shown in Figure 11-14, the ignition system of the GE/Snecma CFM56 engine is located on the right-hand side of the fan containment case at the five o'clock position. The ignition system has two independent circuits consisting of two high-tension ignition exciters, two ignition lead assemblies, and two igniter plugs.

POWER SUPPLY

The ignition system receives its electrical power from the aircraft AC bus by way of the two separate channels (A and B) within the electronic engine control (EEC). The ignition exciters are powered by 115 VAC at 400 Hz. Each channel of the EEC is able to control both ignition exciters, thereby providing redundancy in the system.

IGNITER SELECTION

The EEC selects (or enables) the left, right, or both igniter plugs based on the position of the flight-compartment ignition selector switch. The standard operating procedure calls for the flight crew to change the ignition selection manually on successive engine starts from ignition left to ignition right. By following this procedure, each igniter plug receives approximately the same operating time, and if a fault occurs in the ignition system, its presence is more quickly detectable, given the equal distribution between the use of the left and the right system. [Figure 11-15]

The engine start panel, as used on a Boeing 737, has two engine start switches and one ignition selector switch. Each of the engine start switches (engine 1 and 2) has four positions, as follows:

Off — The starter is de-energized and ignition is de-energized, except in the case of an engine flameout, in which case the ignition turns on automatically.

Ground — The starter is energized and ignition is energized, with one plug or both plugs firing depending on the position of the ignition selector switch.

Continuous — The starter is de-energized and the ignition is energized, with one plug or both plugs firing depending on the ignition selector switch position and what the EEC has commanded.

Ignition Systems

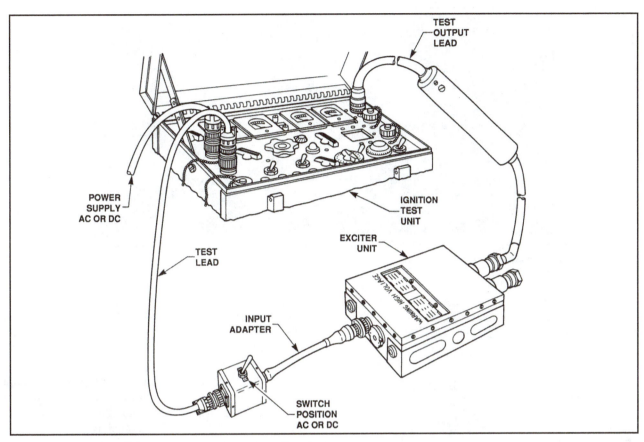

Figure 11-13. Ignition system spark rate and output voltage tester

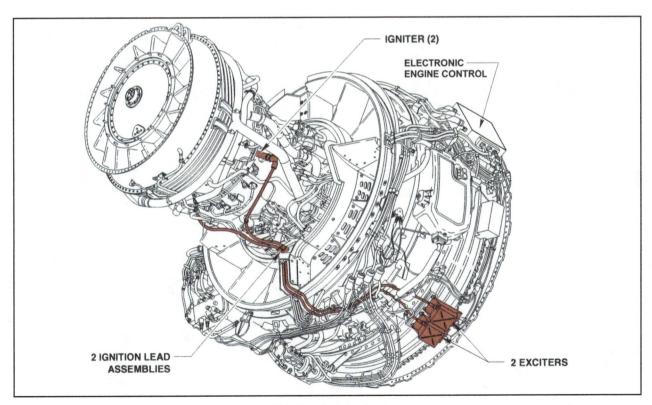

Figure 11-14. Ignition system layout—G.E./Snecma CFM56 turbofan

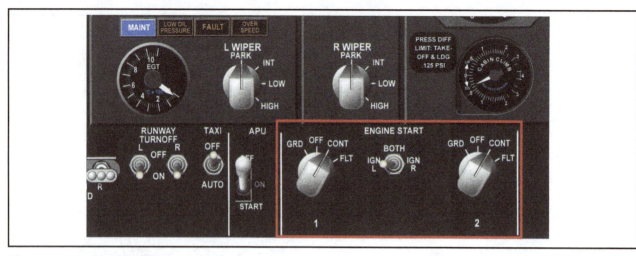

Figure 11-15. Ignition and start panel—Boeing 737-800

Flight — The starter is de-energized and both igniter plugs are energized regardless of the ignition selector switch position.

The ignition selector switch has three positions:
- Ignition Left
- Ignition Right
- Both

SYSTEM OPERATION

The ignition exciters use 115 VAC to produce a 14,000 to 18,000 VDC output at the rate of approximately one pulse per second to the igniter plugs. The exciters transform, rectify, and store energy in a capacitor at an energy level of 14.5 to 16 joules. The exciter housings are hermetically sealed, and the interior components are secured mechanically or with silicon cement for protection against engine vibration.

From the ignition exciters, two ignition leads carry the electrical energy to the two igniter plugs located at four and eight o'clock in the combustor. The ignition leads on this engine are identical and interchangeable. The portion of the igniter lead that passes along the core engine, as well as the outer portion of the igniter, is cooled by booster discharge air. The igniter leads consist of 14-gauge stranded copper conductors with silicone rubber insulation within a tinned copper braid and nickel outer braid.

The igniter plugs have a recessed gap. Their center electrode is insulated from the outer shell by aluminum oxide. The plugs thread into an igniter bushing, which threads into the combustion case. [Figure 11-16]

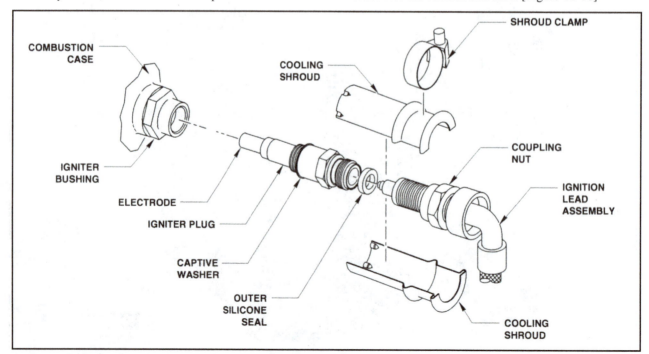

Figure 11-16. Ignition lead and igniter plug assembly—Boeing 737-800

TROUBLESHOOTING THE IGNITION SYSTEM

PROBLEM/POSSIBLE CAUSE	CHECK PROCEDURE	REMEDY
1. No igniter spark with the system turned on		
a. Faulty ignition relay	Determine if power is available at the relay unit.	Correct relay problems (refer to the starter-generator circuit).
b. Faulty exciter unit	Test to verify whether the exciter unit generates the correct power output.	Remove exciter for bench check or replace unit.
c. Damaged high-tension lead	Use an ohmmeter and a megger test unit to check for continuity or high-resistance shorts.	Replace lead.
d. Damaged igniter plug	1. Inspect for damaged contact cap and insulator or damaged semiconductor.	Replace plug.
	2. Inspect center electrode for erosion.	Replace plug.
2. Long interval between sparks		
Inadequate power supply	Test battery.	Recharge battery.
3. Weak (low-intensity) spark		
Faulty igniter plug	Inspect terminal end for contamination or damage.	Replace plug.

QUESTIONS:

1. What purpose does the half-wave rectifier have in a turbine engine ignition system?

2. What is the main difference between the ignition spark of a reciprocating engine and that of a turbine engine?

3. Is the high voltage present in the primary or the secondary circuit of a turbine ignition system?

4. What construction material makes the turbine igniter more expensive than a spark plug?

5. Which switch position causes the ignition to initiate when a loss of compressor speed is sensed?

6. What unit in a FADEC system supervises the ignition system?

7. On a turboprop engine, the loss of which engine parameter will cause the ignition to initiate during flight?

8. How many igniter plugs are present in a typical gas turbine engine?

CHAPTER 12
Engine Instrument Systems

Engine instruments in the cockpit (or flight deck in larger gas turbine aircraft) are of two primary categories—performance indicators and engine condition indicators. Performance indicators consist of the thrust-indicating instruments such as engine pressure ratio (EPR) and fan speed (N_1) and power-indicating instruments such as torque oil pressure or torque percent. Instruments that monitor engine conditions include exhaust gas temperature (EGT), fuel flow, compressor speed, oil pressure, and various temperature gauges are described as engine condition monitoring instruments.

Condition indicators show how hard the engine is working to produce the power reported by the performance indicators. If some portion of the engine is working too hard, it will show up as high exhaust gas temperature, high r.p.m., and so on. Pilots must then take the necessary action to reduce power, shut down the engine, or whatever action is appropriate to ensure safe operation of the aircraft.

The photographs in Figure 12-1 show two types of instrument panels—the conventional panel with typical gauge displays and the newer "glass cockpit" with cathode ray tube (CRT), liquid crystal (LCD), or light emitting diode (LED) displays. Both types of panels provide essentially the same information to the pilot. The newer flight decks, however, can display more fault isolation information about the instrument package and the engine. For example, many glass cockpit readouts turn red when the maximum engine operating limits are reached. At that time, the instrument values and the duration times are recorded automatically in the aircraft computers.

The following briefly describes each of the gauges included in Figure 12-2. Most of the associated indicating systems are discussed in greater detail later in the chapter.

Engine pressure ratio (EPR) — Receives inputs from two pressure sources—one located in the engine inlet at station 2 (Pt_2) and one located at the high-pressure (HP) turbine discharge at Station 5.4. ($Pt_{5.4}$). The gauge has both a pointer and a digital display. In older aircraft, EPR was traditionally a ratio of Pt_7 to Pt_2, with Pt_7 reflecting the total pressure at the exit of the low-pressure (LP) turbine (as shown in Figure 12-13B). With newer high-temperature materials, the total pressure probes are placed in higher pressure/temperature locations to provide more accurate readings. That accounts for why EPR is shown as $Pt_{5.4}$ compared to Pt_2 in Figure 12-2.

Oil pressure — Taken from an external oil line at the accessories gearbox.

Oil temperature — Taken by a sensor in an external line at the accessory gearbox.

Oil quantity — Taken at the oil tank.

Fuel pressure — Taken at the metered pressure line from the fuel control.

N_1 tach — Receives a signal from an electronic generating device in the fan case as an indication of fan (LP compressor) speed and turbine speed. The gauge has both numerical and pointer readouts.

ITT (interstage turbine temperature) gauge — Receives electrical impulses from a set of averaging thermocouple probes located in the HP turbine discharge airflow. The gauge has both a pointer and a digital display.

N_2 tach — Receives a signal from an electric tachometer generator in the accessory gearbox to indicate HP compressor and turbine speed. The gauge has both a pointer and a digital display.

FF gauge — Receives a signal from a fuel flow transmitter. The gauge has both a pointer and a digital display.

Engine vibration — The monitor interprets the signal from the transducers and sends the data to the gauge. The test button, when depressed, causes the pointers to move to full scale. When the button is released, the pointers

Figure 12-1A. Conventional flight deck
Figure 12-1B. Newer "glass cockpit"

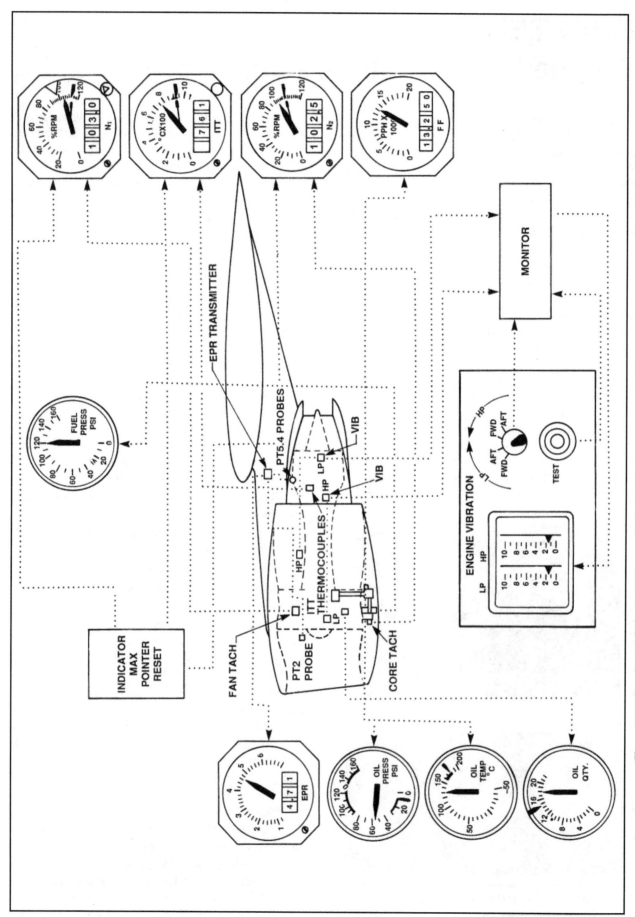

Figure 12-2. Functional diagram of large engine indicating systems — General Electric CF-6 Turbofan, DC-10 aircraft

return to zero to indicate that the gauge is on line. The vibration level is expressed in mils (thousandths) of an inch at four locations: two on the LP system at the fan and turbine, and two on the HP system at the N_2 compressor and turbine. Four mils is the approximate allowable maximum vibration at any location.

Engine indicator maximum pointer reset — Resets the maximum indicator pointer when actuated. Three critical gauges are configured with a second pointer, which locks in overshoot values of N_1, N_2, and the temperature at the turbine (ITT).

The following briefly describes the electronic engine gauges shown in Figure 12-3. The display includes primary and secondary engine instruments. This combination digital and analog gauge display would have the following color scheme:

- White changes to gray with a black pointer for the current readout.
- Gray changes to amber when the readout is in the cautionary range.
- Amber changes to red when the readout exceeds the limit (red line).
- The shaded area changes to red when the limit is exceeded.
- Red reverts to gray when a normal reading returns.
- When a limit has been exceeded, the frame border on the digital display turns red and remains so even if the reading returns to normal.

These instruments typically appear on two separate screens. Figure 12-3 shows a variety of possible instrument indications to illustrate a number of different engine

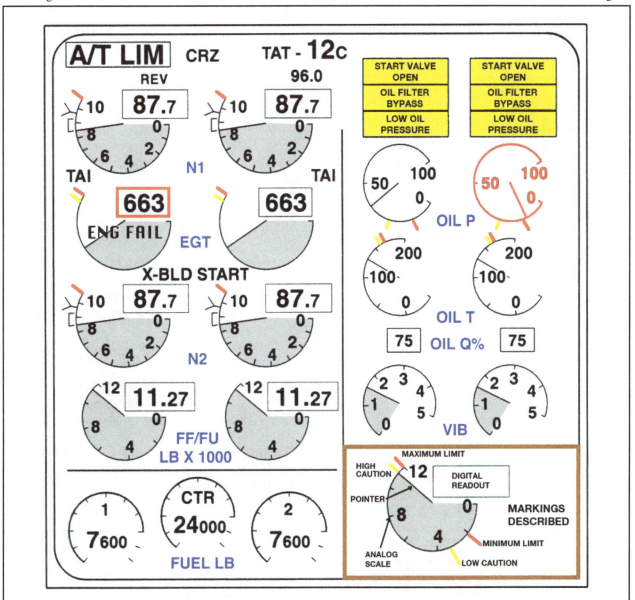

Figure 12-3. Primary and secondary engine instruments displayed on a CRT

conditions. Some of the readings shown here would not be expected to exist at the same time—for example, the left engine is shown in reverse thrust and the right engine in forward thrust, and the EGT reading indicates that the left engine has failed, even though other instruments indicate that it is running.

The following indications appear on the left side of the display:

A/T LIM — Illuminates when the auto throttle limit is active.

CRZ — Illuminates when the thrust mode for the engines is cruise.

TAT - 12c — Illuminates to show the total air temperature is 12 degrees Celsius.

REV — Illuminates when the left engine is in reverse thrust. (Reverse thrust is not operational in flight.)

96.0 — Indicates that the takeoff N_1 reference is 96 percent (fan speed). The Y-shaped symbol on the analog scale also shows 96 percent as the value desired by the pilot.

N_1 — Indicates both engines are operating and have an N_1 (fan speed) of 87.7 percent. The scale and pointer turn amber in cautionary range and red at maximum limit.

TAI — Illuminates when thermal anti-ice is turned on.

EGT — Indicates by the shaded area that both engines are operating at an EGT of 663 degrees Celsius. As a separate possible indication, it shows that the left engine has failed. Assuming that it failed because the EGT exceeded its limit explains why the border around the number is red.

X-BLD START — Illuminates when a cross-bleed engine start is taking place.

N_2 — Indicates both engines have an N_2 (high-speed compressor) of 87.7 percent. The scale and pointer turn amber in the cautionary range and red at the maximum limit.

FF/FU — Indicates fuel flow for both engines is 11,270 pounds per hour. The operator toggles a switch to display the fuel used (FU) rather than fuel flow.

FUEL LB — Indicates the fuel level in three separate tanks, expressed in pounds. The rim of the gauge moves as an analog display in unison with the digital display.

The following indications appear on the right side of the display:

The top advisory lights are for the left and right engine start valves, oil filter bypass, and low oil pressure. When they are illuminated, as shown, the start valve is open, the oil filter is bypassing, and the oil pressure is low.

OIL P — Oil pressure on the left engine is approximately 40 p.s.i. The scale remains white in the normal range with the pointer in black. In the low cautionary range, the scale and pointer turn amber, and at the minimum limit (red line) the scale and pointer turn red (the low oil pressure advisory also lights up). In Figure 12-3, the right engine oil pressure is below the minimum limit and the display has turned red.

OIL T — Oil temperature on the left engine is approximately 120 degrees Celsius. The scale remains white in the normal range with the pointer in black. The scale and pointer turn red at the maximum limit (red line).

OIL Q% — The left engine oil tank is 75 percent full (digital readout only).

VIB — Vibration on the left engine is approximately 1.6 mils (.0016"). The scale is shaded when operating (analog readout only).

The legend in the lower right portion of Figure 12-3 describes the various gauge markings: it is not part of the engine instrumentation.

Although many slight variations in gauge configurations and color markings (such as black backgrounds, colored gauge rims, and movable and stationary colored pointers) are used on aircraft flight decks, all configurations must meet the FAA requirements. [Figure 12-27]

EXHAUST TEMPERATURE INDICATING SYSTEMS

The temperature of the exhaust gases is always monitored closely during engine operation, especially during the starting cycle, when the engine is most susceptible to damage from excessive EGT. Hot section temperature is considered one of the most critical of all engine operating parameters because an out-of-limits condition can render an engine unairworthy in a matter of seconds. The three common cockpit EGT indications are as follows:

- **Turbine inlet temperature (TIT)** — Temperature is monitored forward of the turbine wheels.
- **Interstage turbine temperature (ITT)** — Temperature is monitored at some intermediate position between multiple turbine wheels.
- **Exhaust gas temperature (EGT)** — Temperature is monitored aft of the turbine wheels. EGT is sometimes referred to as turbine outlet temperature.

Regardless of the actual monitoring position, the most significant consideration is the temperature at the turbine inlet (TIT) just forward of the first stage turbine nozzle. However, it is not always possible to monitor temperature at this point in the engine because the high heat sometimes degrades the service life of the temperature-sensing probe. To compensate, manufacturers typically provide a comparison value between TIT temperature and temperature at other points within the engine where actual monitoring can take place. Although the temperatures are lower at these points, the combination of values still provides the necessary temperature indications to reflect the engine's internal condition. However, when an accurate turbine inlet temperature is an essential factor for fuel scheduling, as with an electronic engine control (EEC), a photoelectric cell might also be used to provide a TIT value to protect against over-temperature conditions that could damage the engine.

Several total temperature probes, called thermocouples, are positioned around the engine on pads that permit one end, referred to as the hot junction, to penetrate into the hot gas path. When all thermocouples are connected in a parallel electrical circuit, the system indicates the average of all the thermocouple temperatures on a cockpit gauge. [Figure 12-4]

The thermocouple system, more so than any other engine instrument system, indicates the integrity of the turbine components. For instance, inefficiencies due to damaged or missing turbine blades often result in a high

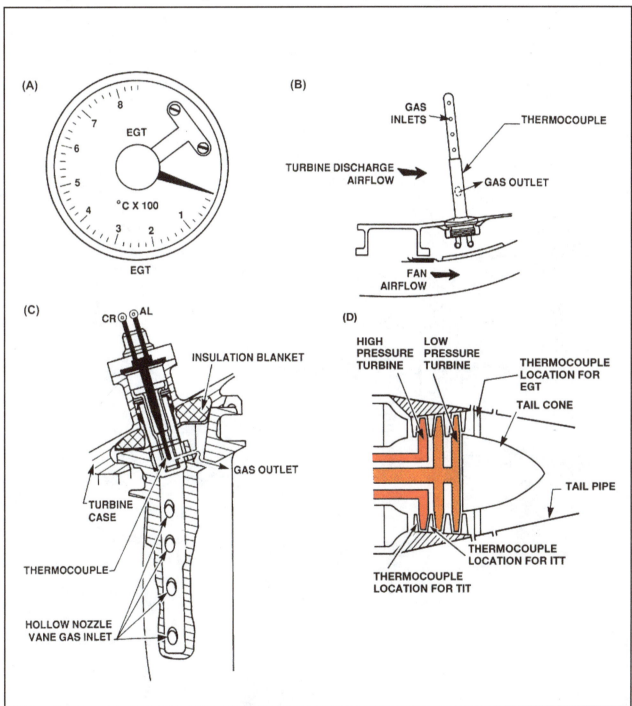

Figure 12-4A. Cockpit exhaust gas temperature gauge
Figure 12-4B. Thermocouple in a fully ducted turbofan
Figure 12-4C. ITT thermocouple located in a hollow turbine nozzle vane
Figure 12-4D. Thermocouple location with respect to Hp and Lp turbines

temperature indication because the hot gases reach the thermocouples quicker.

SYSTEM COMPONENTS

Figure 12-5 shows a typical exhaust gas temperature circuit made up of eight thermocouples, each containing chromel and alumel conductor wires. Thermocouples, which are placed in a thermo-electric circuit, operate under the principle by which electric current is generated proportional to the temperature of the heat applied. Other components in the circuit include the circuit leads, a variable calibrating resistor, and an indicator.

Chromel is a nonferrous nickel chromium alloy. It is nonmagnetic, has positive electrical potential, and is color-coded white. Its terminal connector is often the smaller of the two and has 8-32 threads. Alumel is a ferrous alloy of nickel aluminum. It is magnetic, has negative potential, and is color-coded green. Its terminal connector is often the larger of the two and has 10-32 threads. These characteristics make it easier to identify the leads, which sometimes become discolored from extended use in heated areas outside of the engine.

Gas turbine engine temperature systems contain thermocouples known as K-type. The chromel and alumel materials they use are suitable for temperatures up to 1,200 degrees Celsius. Copper and constantan wire are used in portions of the thermocouple circuit where temperatures do not exceed 300 degrees Celsius. [Figure 12-5]

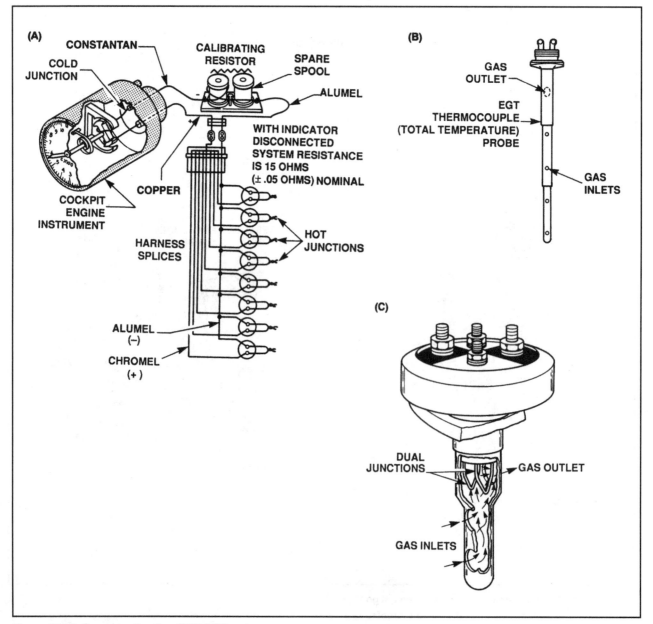

Figure 12-5A. Components of an OHM EGT system

Figure 12-5B. Single hot junction thermocouple probe

Figure 12-5C. Dual hot junction thermocouple probe

The K-type thermocouple generates 40 millionths of a volt per degree Celsius of heat applied. Because chromel-alumel wire has a relatively high resistance per foot, it is used only from the thermocouple harness to the engine terminal block. From the terminal block, copper-constantan wire completes the circuit to the indicator on the flight deck. The indicator is a d'Arsonval meter, which also serves as a cold junction in the circuit. D'Arsonval is a commonly used sensing mechanism used in DC ammeters.

The calibrating resistor enables the system to be calibrated to the specific total resistance required. A typical circuit is either 8, 15, or 22 ohms, depending on the distance from the thermocouple harness on the engine to the indicator in the cockpit; the longer the length, the higher the resistance. Without the means to calibrate the system to a specific resistance, the larger wire diameter required to keep resistance low would be prohibitively heavy.

Some newer systems are alternating or direct current powered and differ from the traditional self-generating system mentioned here. One type uses a nonintrusive pyrometer to monitor optical and infrared emissions.

THERMOCOUPLES

Themocouples can have either a single, dual, or triple element, meaning that they can have one, two, or three hot junctions. The single type, shown in Figure 12-5B, powers only a temperature indicator. The dual type, shown in Figure 12-5C, provides an additional identical hot junction, which can give a signal to an electronic fuel control for scheduling purposes, or it can be used as a test connection for calibrating the exhaust gas temperature circuit.

In both single and multiple hot junction types of thermocouples, hot gases impact the outer surface with some gas entering the inlet holes. The gas then passes over the hot junctions on its way to the outlet holes and back to the gas path. This method enables the total temperature of the exhaust gases to be measured. When dual or triple element thermocouples are used, they can be of different lengths to acquire temperatures at additional locations, which enables the system to better average the temperature of the gas flow within the exhaust path.

SYSTEM OPERATION

Each hot junction is a pair of dissimilar metallic electrical conductors. When connected in a closed-loop parallel circuit, the conductors change resistance at a known rate when heated and produce an average current flow proportional to the heat applied. Each thermocouple, when heated to 1,000 degrees Celsius higher temperature than the cold junction, produces approximately 0.04 volts. The chromel lead contains a deficiency of free electrons. The alumel lead contains an excess of free electrons.

When heated, the free electrons in the negative lead move from the hot junction, through the cold junction, and back to the positive hot junction lead. The indicator monitors current flow.

The function of the cold junction is easily understood in terms of the electron theory. If the same heat were to be applied at the gauge end (the cold junction) as at the thermocouple end (the hot junction), the negative alumel lead at the hot end would try to flow electrons at the same rate as the gauge end. Because electron flow is proportional to heat applied, one flow would cancel out the other. With no current flow, no reading would appear on the gauge.

A reading can normally be observed on an EGT gauge when the engine is not operating and cooled down to ambient temperature. This is because a compensating coil within the gauge creates an indication of ambient temperature, which in turn provides the operator with an exhaust gas temperature reading corrected for ambient temperature.

The thermocouple in use in this example is referred to as a total temperature type because it measures both static temperature and temperature rise due to ram effect, which represents the actual heat loading on the internal parts of the engine. Ram effect can be calculated by using the formula for Tt/Ts in Appendix 8.

For example, assume that the exhaust gas temperature (Tt_7) is 1,600°R and the Mach number of gas flow is 0.9. Use the formula to calculate the Tt/Ts ratio and the temperature due to ram effect.

$$\frac{Tt}{Ts} = 1 + \left[\frac{\gamma - 1}{2} \times M^2\right]$$

$$\frac{1,600}{Ts} = 1 + \left[\frac{1.4 - 1}{2} \times 0.9^2\right]$$

$$\frac{1,600}{Ts} = 1 + (0.20 \times 0.81)$$

$$Ts = \frac{1,600}{1.162}$$

$$Ts = 1,376.9°R$$

The amount of heat rise due to ram effect is 1,600 minus 1,376.9, or 223.1°F.

EGT LIMITS

Every engine design has strict internal temperature limits. Figures 12-6A and 12-6B show a set of typical EGT limits for a small gas turbine engine. In these charts, note that the normal operating mode temperature limits are more lenient than the starting mode limits. This is a design feature of more contemporary engines. Research indicates that engine service life is greatly reduced by high starting temperatures; thus, newer engines are designed to maintain the lowest possible temperatures during the starting cycle. On many older engine designs,

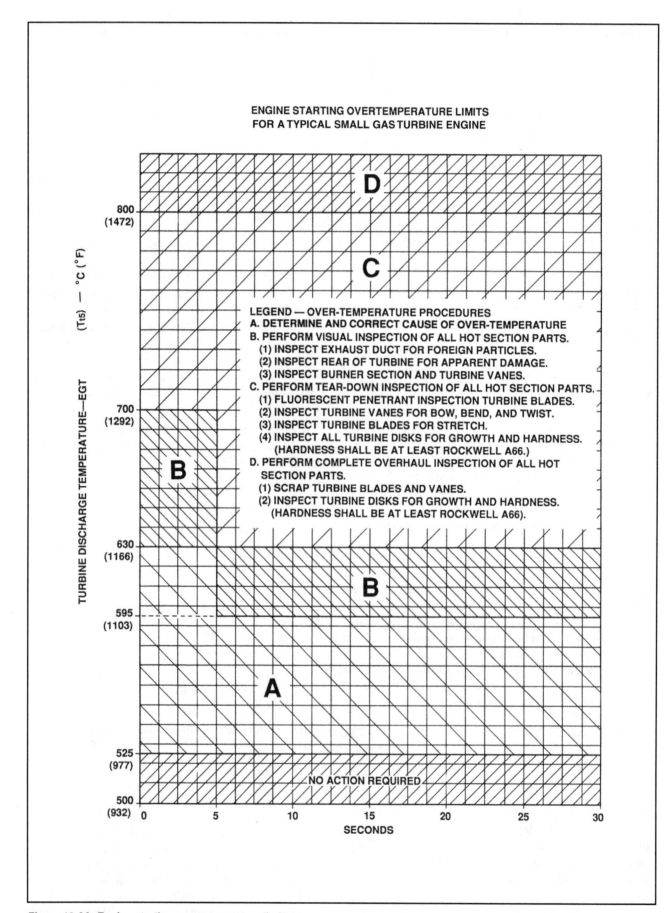

Figure 12-6A. Engine starting over-temperature limits

the lack of cooling air caused excessively high starting temperatures, which in turn adversely affected hot-end service life.

Note that the time limits in the table are very short—typically expressed in seconds. Not only are the temperature limits themselves critical, but also the length of time that components endure excessive heat is also critical, and can also precipitate the premature failure of hot-end parts. During the construction process, turbine disks with a Rockwell hardness of A66 are sudden-quench hardened after being heated to their critical temperature. During an engine over-temperature condition, the unit cools slowly to ambient temperature, which leaves it in a lower state of hardness.

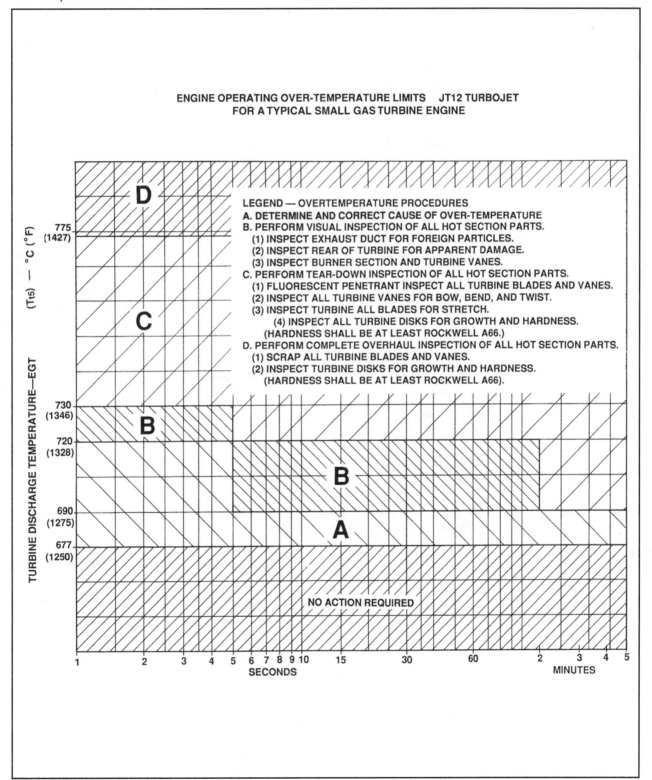

Figure 12-6B. Engine operating over-temperature limits

JETCAL ANALYZER

Before maintenance personnel perform engine inspections for evidence of over-temperature, they must first establish that the cockpit instrument is indicating accurately. One device used to determine the reliability of the exhaust gas temperature indicating system is the Jetcal Analyzer, a device used to test EGT and engine speed. [Figure 12-7A and 12-7B] A Jetcal Analyzer can:

- Check the aircraft EGT system without running the engine.
- Check the aircraft EGT system during engine run-up.
- Check continuity and resistance of the EGT circuit. For example, the typical circuit tolerance might be 8 ohms ± 0.05 ohms.
- Check individual thermocouple output with the engine either static or operating.
- Check the aircraft percent r.p.m. system during engine run-up.

Figure 12-7C and 12-7D show a maintenance technician installing Jetcal heaters on the thermocouples within the tailpipe. The unit heats the thermocouples and accurately registers the temperature on both the Jetcal indicator panel and the cockpit exhaust gas temperature indicator. The cockpit indicator is then checked against the standard temperature on the Jetcal analyzer.

OTHER EGT SYSTEM CHECKS

If a thermocouple bulb or harness is suspect and special test equipment is unavailable, the system can still be checked out with a good quality multimeter or a wheatstone bridge as follows:

1. Check the resistance of each thermocouple bulb against manufacturer's specifications. (The typical resistance is 0.10 ohm ± 0.01 ohm.)
2. Attach the test equipment to a known good thermocouple bulb and the suspect bulb and place both in an oven to compare readings.
3. If the bulbs are not detachable from the harness, check the combined resistance of the bulb and harness. (The typical resistance is 3.0 ohms ± 0.02 ohms.)
4. Check for breakdown between the hot junction and the outer harness covering (typically a minimum of 50,000 ohms resistance).

Systems such as TIT and ITT also have special test units for system checkout. These units are usually supplied as special test equipment by the manufacturer of the engine or the aircraft.

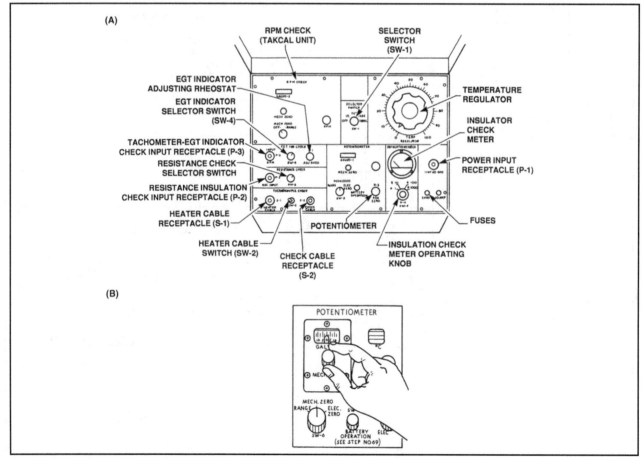

Figure 12-7A. Jetcal analyzer control panel
Figure 12-7B. Setting the heater probe temperature

TROUBLESHOOTING THE EGT/ITT INDICATING SYSTEM

PROBLEM/POSSIBLE CAUSE	CHECK PROCEDURE	REMEDY
1. False low EGT/ITT indication at all power settings		
a. Damaged thermocouple leads	1. Inspect for shorting together outside the engine, which causes a low average reading.	Repair and relocate leads.
	2. Inspect for broken thermocouple lead.	Repair as necessary.
b. Damaged thermocouple	Determine if hot junction is burned off (open), which causes total circuit resistance to increase.	Replace thermocouple.
c. High circuit resistance	1. Check for corroded terminals.	Clean or repair terminals as necessary.
	2. Determine whether wire had been lengthened during repair.	Replace leads as necessary.
	3. Perform a system calibration using a Jetcal or similar test unit.	Adjust or replace calibrating resistor.
2. False high EGT/ITT reading at all power settings		
Low circuit resistance	Determine whether wire had been shortened during repair. Check resistance with an accurate ohmmeter, Wheatstone bridge, Jetcal analyzer, or similar unit.	Recalibrate circuit.
3. Fluctuating EGT/ITT		
a. Improperly connected circuit leads	Inspect for loose connections.	Tighten any loose connections.
b. Faulty indicator	Exchange indicator connections or slave in another indicator.	Replace indicator.

TROUBLESHOOTING THE ENGINE WITH THE EGT/ITT INDICATING SYSTEM

PROBLEM/POSSIBLE CAUSE	CHECK PROCEDURE	REMEDY
1. High EGT/ITT throughout power lever range		
a. Turbine wheel distress	Check for damage visually through tailpipe or with a borescope.	Repair or replace affected turbine wheel.
b. Damaged turbine vanes	Check vanes visually through tailpipe or with a borescope.	Repair or replace affected turbine vanes.
c. Compressor contamination or damage	Check for contamination or foreign object damage, which can cause increased fuel flow and EGT.	Field-clean to remove contaminants. Repair or replace compressor.
d. Engine bleeds open	Check for inadvertently open anti-stall, anti-ice, or customer bleed air, which can cause increased fuel flow and EGT.	Correct as necessary.
e. Fuel control sensors (Ps_4 or Pb) sending incorrect signals or no signals at all	Check for loose connections and signal loss.	Tighten any loose sensor connections or replace connectors.
f. EPR indicating system reading false low, requiring power lever advancement to achieve correct thrust	1. Verify whether EPR system is calibrated correctly.	Calibrate system.
	2. Check for loose pressure lines to transmitter.	Tighten pressure lines.

TACHOMETER PERCENT RPM INDICATING SYSTEMS

Gas turbine engine speed is measured in percent of compressor speed, expressed in r.p.m. The number of compressors generally determines the number of percent RPM indicators present in the cockpit. All aircraft cockpits are required by 14 CFR Part 33 to have a tachometer indicating system.

Because no two engines and no two compressors operate at the same speed, percent RPM is used rather than actual RPM to simplify the cockpit indication.

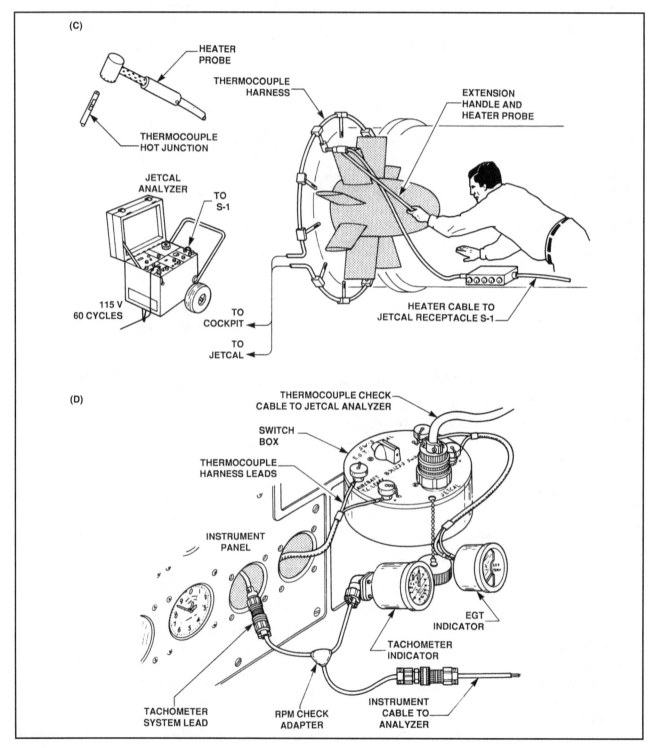

Figure 12-7C. Jetcal heater probe installation

Figure 12-7D. Switch box and RPM check adapter connections

PERCENT RPM INDICATOR

The percent RPM indicator is used to:

- Monitor speed during the starting sequence. N_1 speed is monitored in a single-spool engine, N_2 in a dual-spool engine, and N_3 in a triple-spool engine.
- Monitor speed in case of over-speeding. This applies to all tach indicators installed.
- Indicate both compressor speed and thrust on centrifugal-flow engines and some single-spool axial-flow engines.
- Indicate both compressor speed and thrust on some turbofan engines; monitors N_1 fan speed.
- Check operating schedules of engine support systems such as bleed valves, variable vanes, and so on.
- Check engine speed during in-flight shutdown and windmilling.

Several types of percent RPM indicating systems are currently in use. The two most common types are the three-phase generator percent RPM system and the magnetic pickup percent RPM system.

THREE-PHASE GENERATOR PERCENT RPM SYSTEM

In the three-phase generator percent RPM system, the tachometer is an independent electrical device, consisting of an engine-driven, three-phase AC generator and a synchronous motor-driven indicator. Most manufacturers set the gearbox tachometer drive ratio to compressor speed, so that at 100 percent compressor speed the tachometer drive output is 4,200 r.p.m. This facilitates interchangeability of system components, making it possible to interchange the tach generator from one engine to another. [Figure 12-8]

Referring to Figure 12-9, the tachometer generator sends a low-voltage signal (approximately 20 VAC) to the synchronous motor field in the indicator. Because the motor magnet is designed to remain in synchronization with the generator magnet, frequency (in cycles per second) is the critical factor, not voltage. No physical connection exists between the pointer yoke and the flux coupler magnet. The pointer yoke turns the pointer on the indicator dial through induced eddy current.

MAGNETIC PICKUP PERCENT RPM SYSTEM

The magnetic pickup percent RPM system is a system developed after the three-phase generator for measuring fan percent speed. It employs a magnetic sensor mounted in the fan case adjacent to the path of fan blade rotation. The sensor counts the number of blades passing by and converts this to a signal, which is interpreted by the indicator on the flight deck to show percent RPM.

EXAMPLE PERCENT RPM INDICATING SYSTEM (GENERAL ELECTRIC CF-6)

In some General Electric CF-6 engine installations, the fan tips pass through the magnetic field of the sensor

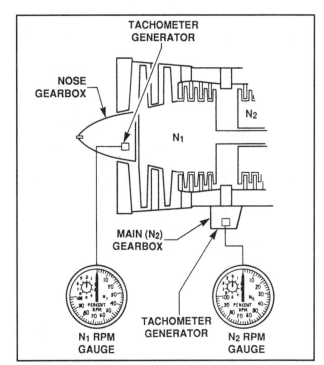

Figure 12-8. Location of tachometer generators for low- and high-pressure compressors

head, which induces an eddy current. [Figure 12-10A] The conditioner unit rectifies the AC current to DC and amplifies the signal to the percent tachometer indicator. On this installation, the fan speed has a direct relationship to thrust and the manufacturer has chosen the N_1 tach as the pilot's primary thrust indicator. This engine also uses an engine pressure ratio (EPR) system as the cockpit backup thrust indicator.

ELECTRONIC GEARBOX-MOUNTED N_2 SPEED SENSOR

Another system for measuring N_2 percent speed uses a sensor mounted in the main accessory gearbox. The sensor head is fitted close to a rotating gear, which has a special ferrous material on one of its teeth. As the lines of flux are broken by the ferrous gear tooth, the sensor unit electronically counts the gear revolutions based on the number of times per minute that the ferrous tooth passes the sensor. [Figure 12-10B]

N_1 INDICATION AND SPEED SENSING FOR FADEC SYSTEMS

Figure 12-11A shows a typical N_1 tach indicator as it would appear in a glass flight deck. This is the same indicator shown in the overall display in Figure 12-3, and is part of the engine indication for a FADEC system. The information shown on this indicator, counterclockwise from top right, is as follows:

- 87.0 indicates the current speed, in percent, of the N_1 system.
- 96.0 indicates the N_1 percent which has been called for by the auto throttle system or by the N_1 set controls on the flight deck. The N_1 reference can be manually

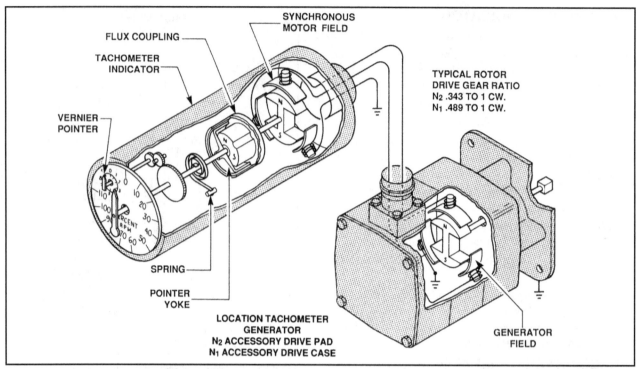

Figure 12-9. Engine tachometer indicating system for low-pressure compressor (N_1) and high-pressure compressor (N_2)

set by the pilot based on the engine performance chart. In autothrottle mode, it is set automatically.

- The N_1 redline is the maximum speed allowed.

- The N_1 reference bug corresponds to the 96 percent of RPM, which has been set either by the autothrottle system or by the pilot.

- The N_1 command reflects the current throttle position.

- The N_1 command sector shows the difference between the commanded thrust and the actual thrust.

- The N_1 pointer is an analog representation of the current percent of RPM, and it matches the 87 percent digital readout.

Figure 12-11B shows the N_1 speed sensor, which provides the signal for the indication shown in Figure 12-11A. As shown in the figure, this sensor is mounted on the side of the fan case and has three sensing elements at its tip. The three sensing elements provide the output signals shown at the end of the sensor. One of the outputs is routed to the display electronics unit (DEU) and the airborne vibration monitoring (AVM) system, and the other two are routed to the two separate channels of the electronic engine control (EEC).

TYPICAL RPM LIMITS

As with exhaust gas temperature parameters, manufacturers prescribe RPM operating parameters. The following table provides a typical set of percent RPM limits and actions required:

PERCENT RPM LIMITS	INDICATED PERCENT RPM	ACTION REQUIRED
1. 104.2 to 106.2 percent	Example: 105 percent	Special inspection—inspect the compressor and turbine sections for rubbing after shutdown.
2. 106.3 percent and over	Example: 106.3 percent	Overhaul the engine.
NOTES: 1. Manufacturers sometimes specify a time limit for overspeed conditions. 2. Centrifugal loading on rotating components varies with the square of the speed—a fact made particularly significant in overspeed conditions. For example, an overspeed from the normal 104.1 percent limit to 110.1 percent, a 6 percent increase in speed, results in a 36 percent increase in centrifugal loading.		

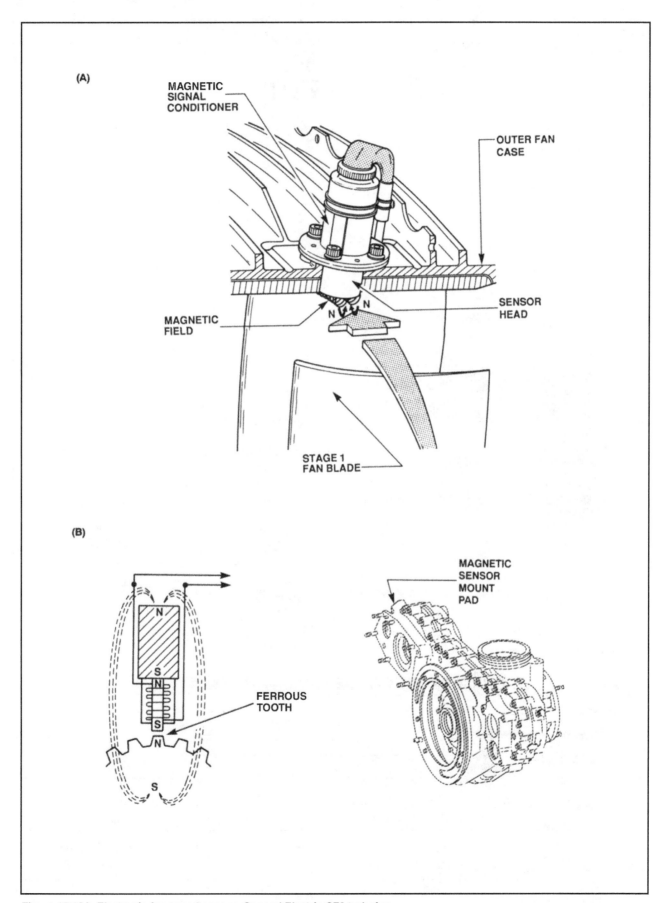

Figure 12-10A. Electronic fan speed sensor, General Electric CF6 turbofan

Figure 12-10B. Electronic, gearbox-mounted, N_2 speed sensor

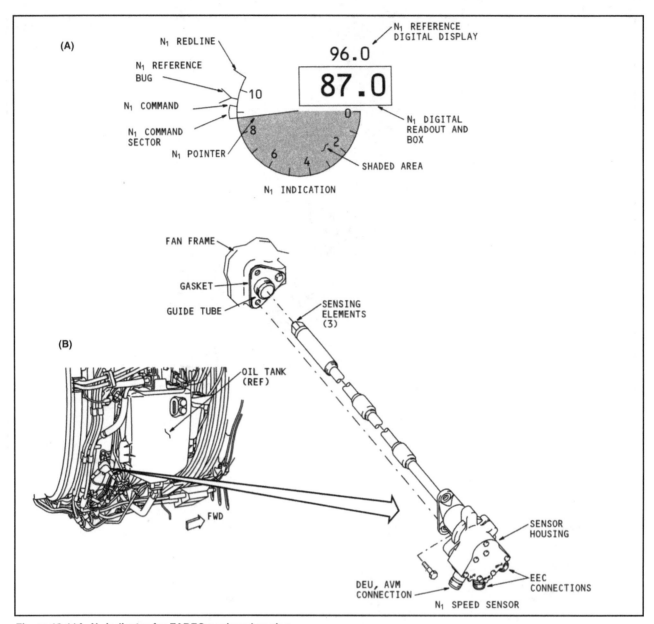

Figure 12-11A. N_1 indicator for FADEC-equipped engine

Figure 12-11B. N_1 speed sensor for FADEC-equipped engine

TROUBLESHOOTING THE TACHOMETER PERCENT RPM INDICATING SYSTEM

PROBLEM/POSSIBLE CAUSE	CHECK PROCEDURE	REMEDY
1. No percent RPM indication or fluctuating indication		
a. Faulty tach indicator	Check for proper operation by interchanging with a known good indicator.	Replace the indicator.
b. Faulty circuit wiring	Inspect for loose leads, proper connections, and circuit continuity.	Tighten or repair connections and wiring as necessary.
c. Faulty tach generator	Test for proper output voltage with meter or slave in another generator.	Replace tach generator.

Engine Instrument Systems

TROUBLESHOOTING THE ENGINE WITH THE TACHOMETER PERCENT RPM INDICATING SYSTEM

PROBLEM/POSSIBLE CAUSE	CHECK PROCEDURE	REMEDY
1. No percent RPM indication on start		
a. Faulty starter	Listen for audible indications of malfunction. Refer to Chapter 10, starter troubleshooting.	Isolate problem, change starter shaft or starter.
b. Damaged compressor	Determine whether compressor is seizing. Attempt to turn by hand. Wait for cooldown and check for rotation. Attempt a restart.	Depending on severity of problem, engine teardown might be necessary.
c. Accessories restricting engine's ability to turn.	Determine whether any accessories are seizing by removing one accessory at a time and attempting to turn engine over through the drive pad.	Repair as necessary.
2. RPM at limit before target EPR is reached		
Faulty internal engine components	Perform a visual inlet and tailpipe check for damage to compressor or turbine. Borescope engine for evidence of damage to the compressor or turbine sections.	Repairs vary depending on fault.

ENGINE PRESSURE RATIO SYSTEM

The engine pressure ratio (EPR) system is a widely used thrust indicating system for aircraft cockpits. As noted elsewhere, EPR is used as a performance (thrust) setting instrument on many flight decks and also as a back-up thrust instrument on some fan-speed-rated engines that use N_1 speed as their primary performance instrument parameter.

THE EPR FORMULA

For discussion purposes, EPR is expressed in absolute values. In flight conditions, EPR undergoes changes due to ram compression; therefore values are given in Pt (pressure total units).

EPR is a ratio of two engine pressures: turbine discharge total pressure and compressor inlet total pressure. Each manufacturer uses a slightly different station numbering system, and engine stations are a means of identifying tap-off points for determining EPR. For example, the Pratt & Whitney Company uses Station (2), Pt_2, and Station (5), Pt_5, to identify the EPR tap-off points of single-spool engines. They use Station (2), Pt_2, and Station (7), Pt_7, to identify the EPR tap-off points of dual-spool engines. The following example applies to the EPR cockpit indication for a Pratt & Whitney single-spool engine. Assuming a turbine discharge pressure of 28.52 p.s.i.a. and a compressor inlet pressure of 14.7 p.s.i.a., the EPR would be as follows:

$$EPR = \frac{Pt_5}{Pt_2}$$

$$EPR = \frac{28.52}{14.7}$$

$$EPR = 1.94$$

To understand how EPR can be used to measure thrust, recall that a gas turbine engine increases potential energy in the form of high-pressure gas, and then converts this pressure to kinetic energy in the form of a high-velocity jet of gases. The gases exiting the engine tailpipe create a reacting force referred to as thrust.

Recall from Chapter 2 that total pressure in the tailpipe represents the force necessary to completely stop the flow of gases. Given the large exit flow area and high velocities in the tailpipe, it is easy to understand how gas under relatively low pressure (1.94 times ambient) can provide significant thrust.

THE COCKPIT EPR GAUGE IN ACTION

To better understand how the cockpit EPR gauge functions, examine the following operational procedure:

1. Using a performance chart, the operator first determines that takeoff EPR is 1.94. As shown in Figure 12-12A, the operator has set the engine pressure ratio reminder to display that value.

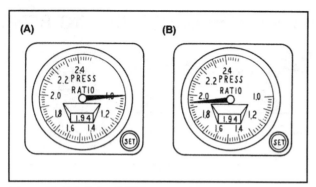

Figure 12-12A. Takeoff EPR set at 1.94; engine not running

Figure 12-12B. Engine running at takeoff power (1.94 EPR)

2. After starting the engine, the operator accelerates the engine to 1.94 EPR in preparation for takeoff. [Figure 12-12B]
3. During flight, the operator resets the display for climb EPR, and then again for cruise EPR, and adjusts the engine speed accordingly. This is necessary because the EPR value changes (decreases) during flight conditions due to the rise in Pt_2 pressure from the effect of ram compression.

EXAMPLE EPR SYSTEM (PRATT & WHITNEY DUAL-SPOOL ENGINE)

The EPR indicating system shown in Figure 12-13 consists of a set of Pt_7 probes, a Pt_2 probe, a manifold, an Autosyn transmitter, and a cockpit indicator. The single Pt_2 probe senses compressor inlet pressure (either suction at high ground-level compressor speeds or pressure above ambient in flight) and sends a signal to the Autosyn transmitter. The set of Pt_7 probes sends a signal of turbine discharge pressure to the transmitter via the manifold. The two signals combine to provide an EPR indication in the cockpit.

The indication of 1.8 for the engine pressure ratio means that turbine discharge pressure (Pt_7) is 1.8 times greater than compressor inlet pressure (Pt_2). Unlike the overlimit values for exhaust gas temperature and speed, EPR has no overlimit value. After the engine reaches the target takeoff value of 1.8, it does not exceed that value except in emergencies, in which case the exhaust gas temperature limits or speed limits (or both) prevail.

Engine power management is discussed in detail in Chapter 7.

TROUBLESHOOTING THE EPR INDICATING SYSTEM

PROBLEM/POSSIBLE CAUSE	CHECK PROCEDURE	REMEDY
1. No EPR reading in the cockpit		
a. Circuit breakers open	Verify whether circuit breakers have been tripped.	Reset circuit breakers.
b. No power to circuit	Check voltage and continuity.	Repair as necessary.
c. Faulty indicator	Interchange instruments to verify proper operation.	Replace indicator.
d. Faulty transmitter	Verify proper operation by slaving in another unit.	Replace transmitter.
2. False low EPR at takeoff power lever setting (ground and flight)		
a. Low turbine discharge pressure	Check for loose connections or obstructions to flow.	Tighten pressure line connections or clear line and Pt probes of obstructions.
b. Same as 1c or 1d.		
3. False high cockpit indication (in flight)		
a. Pt_2 probe or line loose or obstructed	Check for obstructions and loose connections.	Tighten pressure line connections or clear line and Pt probe of obstructions.
b. Leaks at the indicator or transmitter	Check for leakage or loose connections.	Tighten connections.

Engine Instrument Systems 12-19

PROBLEM/POSSIBLE CAUSE	CHECK PROCEDURE	REMEDY
4. EPR normal but high EGT, RPM, and fuel flow indications (ground and in flight)		
a. Loose or leaking lines in EPR system	Verify whether any system lines—particularly the turbine discharge pressure lines—are loose.	Tighten pressure line connections.
5. EPR false high when EGT, RPM, fuel flow all low indications (in flight)		
a. Icing in EPR system	Check for ice in inlet pressure lines.	Isolate and eliminate the cause of icing.

TROUBLESHOOTING THE ENGINE WITH THE EPR INDICATING SYSTEM

PROBLEM/POSSIBLE CAUSE	CHECK PROCEDURE	REMEDY
1. EPR normal at all power settings, but EGT, fuel flow, and RPM indications are high		
a. Contaminated or damaged compressor	Examine compressor for contamination or damage. (Refer to cold section inspection and repair.)	Clean or repair as necessary.
b. Damaged hot section parts	Inspect the hot section for damage (Refer to hot section inspection and repair.)	Repair as necessary.
c. Compression loss due to external air leaks	Determine the source of any external air leaks.	Isolate leaks at compressor cases and split-lines and repair as necessary.
d. Air bleeds open (anti-ice, bleed band, customer service air, and so on)	Determine whether any air bleed sources are unnecessarily open, or whether their respective circuits are leak-free.	Close all bleeds, isolate leaks, and repair as necessary.
2. EPR for one engine registers either high or low when power lever is aligned with another engine		
a. Fuel control trim	Determine whether fuel control is out of adjustment.	Retrim problem engine. Repair or replace fuel control.
b. Rigging problem	Determine if linkage is out of rig.	Rerig linkage between fuel control and cockpit controls.
3. EPR high or low when power lever is at part-power trim stop (also covered in Chapter 7, Fuel Systems)		
Engine out of trim due to faulty fuel control or out of adjustment.	Consult trim charts.	Perform trim run adjust or replace fuel control.
4. Unable to attain takeoff power (EPR) before EGT or RPM reaches its limit		
Same as number 1 above		

TORQUE INDICATING SYSTEM

Federal regulations require torque indicating systems on all torque-producing, turbine-powered engines such as turboprops and turboshafts. The torque indicating system is the primary performance instrument in the cockpit.

The torque indicator receives its input from a torque sensing system on the engine. The cockpit torque reading provides a continuous indication of the power output of the engine.

Torque is displayed in various ways in the cockpit. The most common are torque oil pressure expressed in pounds per square inch (p.s.i.), torque oil pressure expressed in foot-pounds (ft. lbs.), torque percent, and sometimes a direct horsepower read-out.

The two torque sensing systems most widely used are the "balanced oil piston" hydromechanical system, which converts engine oil pressure to a torque signal, and an electronic "phase shift" system, which converts the twist of the power output shaft into a torque signal.

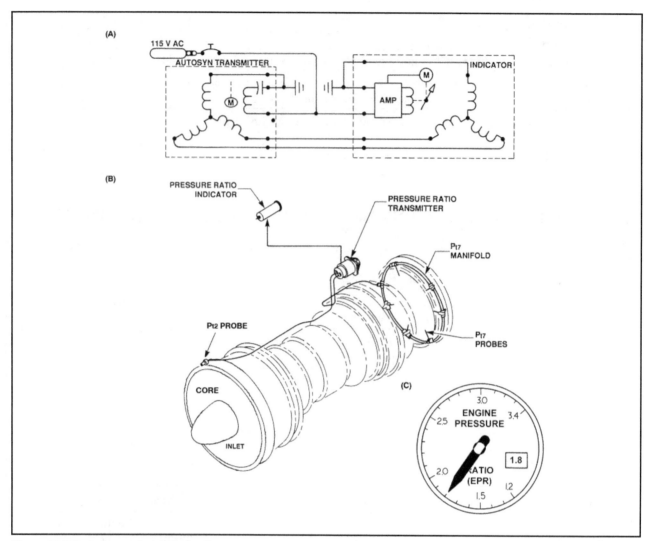

Figure 12-13A. Autosyn electrical circuit
Figure 12-13B. Typical EPR system arrangement
Figure 12-13C. Cockpit instrument displaying takeoff EPR

HYDROMECHANICAL TORQUE INDICATING SYSTEM

The torque sensing system in Figure 12-14 includes a cockpit gauge, an electrical transmitter, a hydromechanical sensor mechanism, and drive gears for the main shaft and the torsion shaft. The illustration includes both the fixed turbine design and the free turbine design. Recall that in a fixed turbine, the turbines and compressor are mechanically coupled and rotate as one unit, and that the free turbine rotates independently of the compressor system.

In the systems shown, both the main and the torsion shafts rotate at the same speed as the turbines that drive them. However, the torsion shaft is subjected to the majority of the load on the turbines from the output shaft. The main shaft provides a reference point.

The torque sensing mechanism illustrated in Figure 12-15 is a hydromechanical unit that contains a pilot valve that is under almost no load at zero torque. In zero-torque conditions, engine oil pressure in both oil lines to the differential pressure gauge is the same, which results in a zero gauge reading.

When the output shaft exerts a load on the torsion gear and forces the outer helical gear to the right, additional load is applied to the pilot valve spring. The additional load moves the pilot valve closer to the closed position, which reduces case pressure. The reduced case pressure causes a differential pressure within the torque pressure gauge, which in turn causes the torque pressure gauge to rise. The pressure drop between calibrated engine oil pressure and case oil pressure is proportional to the torque load applied; thus the torque oil pressure signal to the gauge is proportional to engine torque.

SYSTEM OPERATION

When the system experiences an increase in torque from either an increase in engine speed or an increase in propeller pitch, the sequence of events that cause the

Engine Instrument Systems

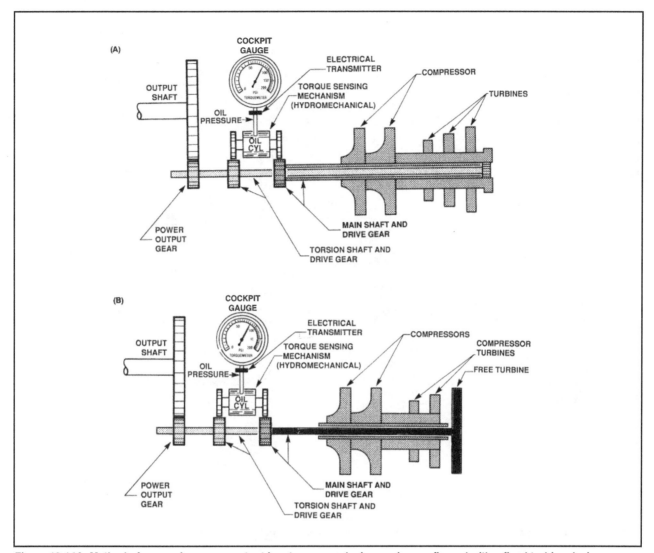

Figure 12-14A. Method of measuring power output in a torque producing engine configured with a fixed turbine design

Figure 12-14B. Method of measuring power output in a torque producing engine configured with a free power turbine design

cockpit torque gauge to rise in response is as follows: [Figures 12-14 and 12-15]

1. The main shaft and drive gear rotate clockwise.

2. The torsion shaft and drive gear also rotate clockwise.

3. The power output gear moves clockwise, overcoming the resistance of the output shaft and propeller drag.

4. The output shaft moves counterclockwise.

5. Both the outer and inner helical gears move counterclockwise. However, the inner gear turns slightly more than the outer gear and screws inward toward the inner gear (because of a left-hand thread that pulls the outer gear laterally and to the right). That is, when the torsion shaft moves under a load, its gear lags in angular movement because its drive shaft is less rigid. If the angular difference did not occur, the outer gear would not move to the right and the torque oil pressure would not change.

6. When the outer helical gear is pulled to the right by the inner helical gear (acting as a threaded nut), it pushes the pilot valve along with it and to the right. This overcomes the opposing oil force acting on the surface of the pilot valve.

7. When the pilot valve moves to the right and further compresses the pilot valve spring, the valve moves towards its seat.

8. As the pilot valve moves toward its seat, it restricts oil flow to the case, which causes the case pressure to decrease.

9. The torque gauge takes the differential pressure into account and registers a pressure increase, which is expressed as torque p.s.i.

When the torque load on the system decreases, the helical gear set moves the pilot valve back to the left, increasing case pressure and decreasing the torque oil pressure reading.

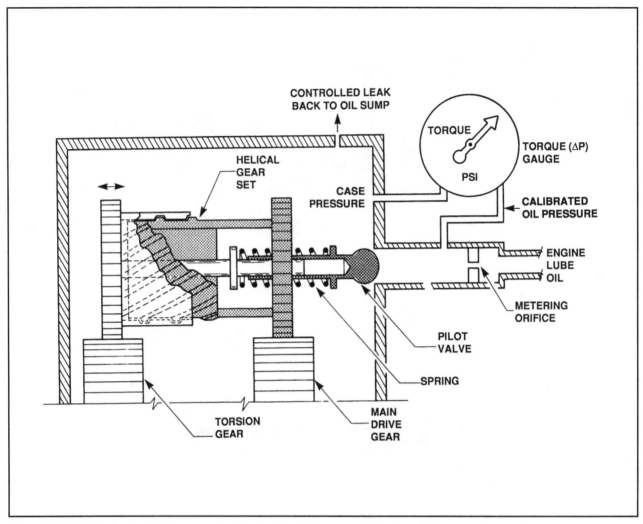

Figure 12-15. Hydromechanical torque sensor (main drive shaft moves clockwise with increase in r.p.m.)

ELECTRONIC TORQUE INDICATING SYSTEM

The electronic torque indicating system shown in Figure 12-16 includes a cockpit indicator, a torque signal transmitter or pickup, and an inner and outer drive shaft.

Both the inner and outer drive shafts rotate at the same speed as the engine turbines, which are mechanically coupled to them. However, only the inner shaft is subjected to the majority of the load on the turbines from the power output shaft. The outer shaft is used as a reference point.

Under a zero-torque condition, the teeth machined on the front end of both shafts are aligned. When a load is applied to the inner shaft, the machined teeth move out of alignment with the teeth on the outer shaft, causing it to deflect. The deflection or twist, when applied to the torque sensor circuit, converts this angular deflection to a voltage output, which powers the cockpit gauge.

TORQUE LIMITS

The torque load that can be applied to the power reduction gearbox is limited and overtorque is prevented by the operator by closely monitoring the torque gauge during engine operation.

In Figure 12-17, note that the torque limits are influenced by time. For example, the engine can operate to 5,900 foot-pounds of torque for up to 15 seconds with no maintenance action required. However, if either the torque limit or the 15-second limit is exceeded, the reduction gearbox in this example must be removed for overhaul.

Engine Instrument Systems

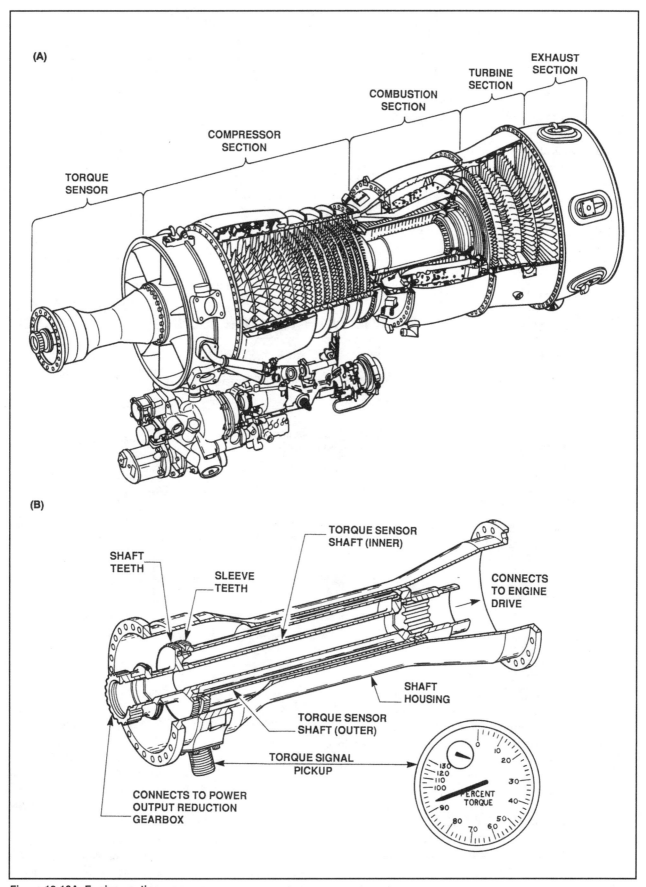

Figure 12-16A. Engine sections

Figure 12-16B. Torque sensor shaft

TROUBLESHOOTING THE TORQUE INDICATING SYSTEM

PROBLEM/POSSIBLE CAUSE	CHECK PROCEDURE	REMEDY
1. No torque reading in the cockpit		
a. Circuit breakers	Verify whether circuit breakers have been tripped.	Reset circuit breakers.
b. No power to circuit	Check for proper voltage and continuity.	Repair as necessary to restore power.
c. Faulty indicator	Determine proper operation by interchanging indicators.	Replace indicator.
d. Faulty transmitter	Determine proper operation by slaving in another unit.	Replace transmitter.
2. Low torque indication at all settings		
a. Faulty indicator	Interchange indicators or slave in another indicator.	Replace indicator.
b. Faulty transmitter	Determine proper operation by slaving in another unit.	Replace transmitter.
c. Torque pressure lines	Check for loose connections or obstructions to flow.	Tighten connections; clean and flush system.

TROUBLESHOOTING THE ENGINE WITH THE TORQUE INDICATING SYSTEM

PROBLEM/POSSIBLE CAUSE	CHECK PROCEDURE	REMEDY
1. Low or normal torque indication, but high EGT, speed and fuel flow indications		
a. Faulty torque sensing system	Check for correct torque output signal at engine.	Repair as necessary.
b. Improperly adjusted fuel control linkage to propeller governor	Check linkage adjustment, which might by causing a low blade angle.	Rerig as necessary.
c. Faulty fuel control or fuel governor	Check for internal malfunctions that cause low blade angle.	Replace faulty units.
d. Improper propeller or rotor blade angle	Check for low blade angle.	Adjust angle.
e. Malfunctioning engine bleed system	Check for open bleeds (anti-stall, anti-ice, customer service air, and so on).	Adjust or repair.
f. Internal engine faults	1. Inspect compressor for contamination or damage.	Clean or repair as necessary.
	2. Inspect hot section for damage.	Repair as necessary.
2. Unable to attain takeoff power before reaching EGT or RPM limits		
Same as number 1 above		

FUEL FLOW INDICATING SYSTEM

The fuel flow indicating system for turbine engines measures fuel consumption in pounds per hour (PPH). This indicating system is typically powered by either 26 VAC or 115 VAC from the aircraft bus. There are three primary types of fuel flow indicating systems, two of which are motor-driven, and one that uses no motor.

VANE FLOWMETER SYSTEM

The vane flowmeter is an older system and is designed to measure volume of flow. The system consists of a flowmeter transmitter (generally located in the engine fuel line to the combustor) and an indicator located in the cockpit.

Figure 12-18 shows the circuit arrangement. The loop circuit contains the delta windings of both the transmitter and indicator, connected in parallel. The transmitter and indicator magnets are in a 26 VAC, 400 cycle circuit. As the vane is moved against its restraining spring by volume of flow, the transmitter magnet moves along with the vane. The magnet in the indicator to which the pointer is attached tracks with the transmitter magnet and provides the fuel flow reading to the pilot.

SYNCHRONOUS MASS FLOW

The synchronous mass flow measures mass flow rather than volume. Developed after the vane flowmeter, it provides greater accuracy by compensating for fuel temperature.

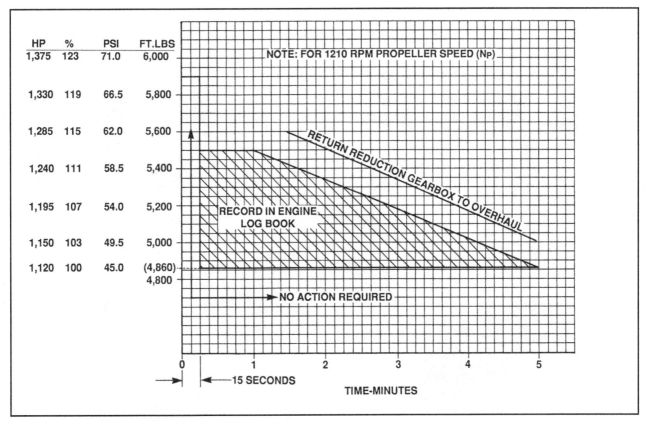

Figure 12-17. Typical torque limits (all conditions of engine operation)

The components in the system in Figure 12-19 are located similarly to the vane type system. Fuel enters the transmitter impeller, which is rotated at a constant 60 revolutions per minute by the synchronous impeller motor. The temperature of the fuel determines its volume and the amount of force to be created by the action of the impeller. The turbine twists against its restraining spring by the mass flow force created by impeller movement. The mass flow electrical transmitter arrangement is similar to the vane type system.

MOTORLESS MASS FLOWMETER SYSTEM

The solid-state, motorless flowmeter is the most current fuel measuring system. Despite its small size, it can account for variables such as fuel temperatures and specific gravity with an accuracy of ±1 percent as opposed to approximately 2 percent for motor driven flow meters. Almost all large turbine-powered aircraft are configured with the motorless fuel flowmeter system. The system provides a digital display rather than the traditional gauge and pointer.

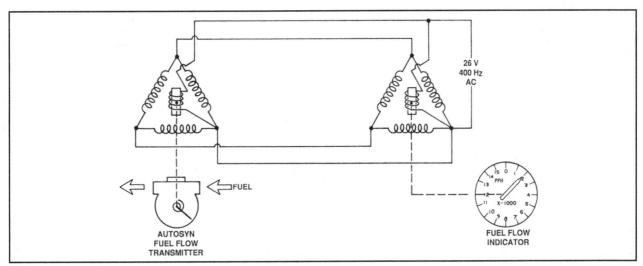

Figure 12-18. Vane-type fuel flowmeter indicating system

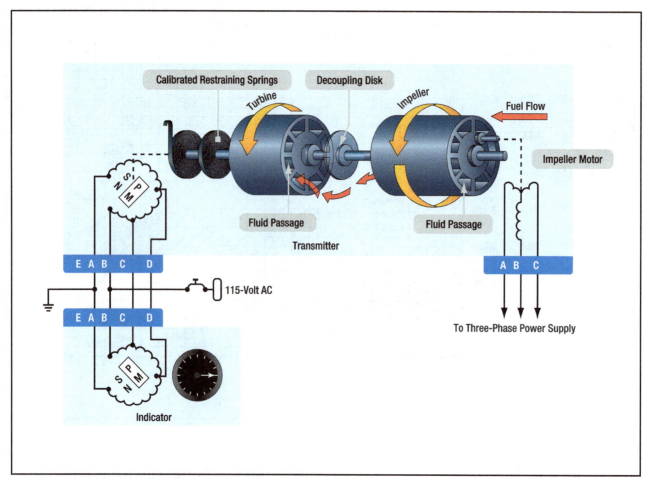

Figure 12-19. Synchronous mass flow-type fuel flowmeter system

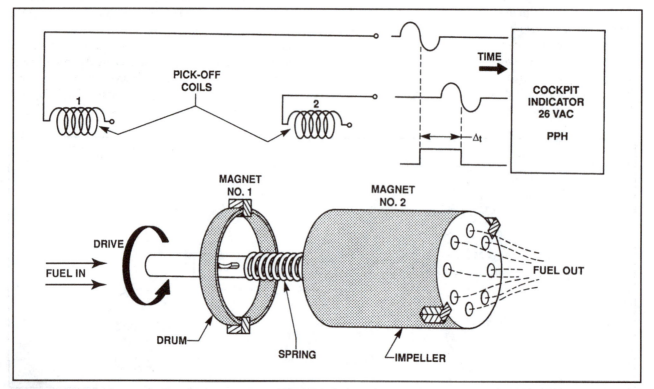

Figure 12-20. Motorless mass flow flowmeter system (EDEC Corp)

Engine Instrument Systems

The flowmeter transmitter converts flow rate into two electronic signals. The signals are created as the flowing fuel imparts an angular displacement to two continuously rotating magnets. The magnets induce electronic impulses into stationary coils and the time difference is used as a measure of mass flow rate.

To understand where the time difference originates, refer to Figure 12-20. Note that fuel enters from the drive end and rotates the drum containing magnet number 1 and the drive shaft. The spring connects the drive shaft to the impeller that connects magnet number 2. As the magnets rotate, the pick-off coils receive current pulses, the first pulse occurring at pick-off coil number 1. Then as the spring deflects in proportion to fuel flow, the number 2 magnet turns with the impeller and induces a current pulse with a time lag into pick-off coil number 2. The greater the mass flow, the greater the spring deflection and angular difference between the magnets. The time displacement that results is directly proportional to mass flow rate in this design.

The 26 VAC cockpit indicator contains electronics that convert the time difference to pounds per hour.

TROUBLESHOOTING THE FUEL FLOW INDICATING SYSTEM

PROBLEM/POSSIBLE CAUSE	CHECK PROCEDURE	REMEDY
No fuel flow indication or fluctuating indication		
a. Faulty circuit wiring	Check for loose connections and circuit continuity.	Tighten or repair connections as necessary.
b. Faulty fuel flow indicator	Check for proper indication by interchanging indicators.	Replace indicator.
c. Faulty fuel flow transmitter	Verify the correct input voltage. Check for proper operation by slaving in another transmitter.	Correct circuit problem or replace transmitter.

TROUBLESHOOTING THE ENGINE WITH THE FUEL FLOW INDICATING SYSTEM

PROBLEM/POSSIBLE CAUSE	CHECK PROCEDURE	REMEDY
High fuel flow indication at all power settings		
a. Fuel system malfunction	Refer to fuel system troubleshooting.	
b. Damaged turbine wheel or stator vanes	1. Inspect components using a borescope or by directing a strong light through the tailpipe. 2. Check for other high cockpit indications—high fuel flow usually occurs with other abnormal indicator readings.	Possible engine teardown for turbine section repair.
c. Compressor	1. Inspect for foreign object damage.	Possible engine teardown for compressor repair.
	2. Inspect for contamination.	Field-clean. (See Chapter 5.)

OIL SYSTEM INDICATORS

Oil system indicators generally consist of oil temperature, oil pressure, and oil quantity instruments. [Figure 12-21] Many cockpits also include warning lights for low oil pressure and for filter bypass. Only oil temperature and pressure are discussed here. The remaining oil system indicating systems are discussed in Chapter 6.

OIL TEMPERATURE INDICATING SYSTEMS

The oil temperature indicating system provides the operator with critical information about the engine's condition. The system depends on reliable temperature sensors that are precisely located.

At first glance, the location of the temperature sensor in the lubrication system seems to be of little significance. Manufacturers place the sensor in either the pressure subsystem or the scavenge subsystem. This is possible because gas turbine engine oil systems have a high flow rate, circulating at the rate of two to five times the oil tank capacity per minute. This rapid circulation rate causes temperatures to stabilize throughout the entire lube system rapidly and provide a quick and reliable oil temperature indication.

Some manufacturers place the sensor in the scavenge subsystem on the theory that it gives a slightly quicker indication of high friction heat buildup from failing parts such as bearings and gears. The more common location, however, is in the pressure subsystem to show the temperature of the oil as it enters the engine. Temperature sensors are of two types—the resistance bulb and the thermocouple.

RESISTANCE BULB

The resistance bulb oil temperature indicating system consists of a resistance bulb and an indicator in a 28-VDC-powered circuit. The bulb contains a temperature-sensitive, pure-nickel wire wound around a mica core contained in a steel outer casing. The bulb is installed in an oil line with the tip of the bulb protruding into the oil stream. [Figure 12-22]

In Figure 12-23, the circuit shows the resistance bulb as the variable resistor in a wheatstone bridge circuit. Bulb resistance increases when heated; as this occurs, more and more current flows from point A to point B. This milliampere current flow gives an indication of oil temperature in the cockpit.

THERMOCOUPLE

The thermocouple oil temperature indicating system is not powered by the aircraft bus. It is a self-contained and self-generating circuit. It derives its power from a pair of dissimilar metals, iron and constantan, which, when heated at the hot junction, produce a millivoltage and

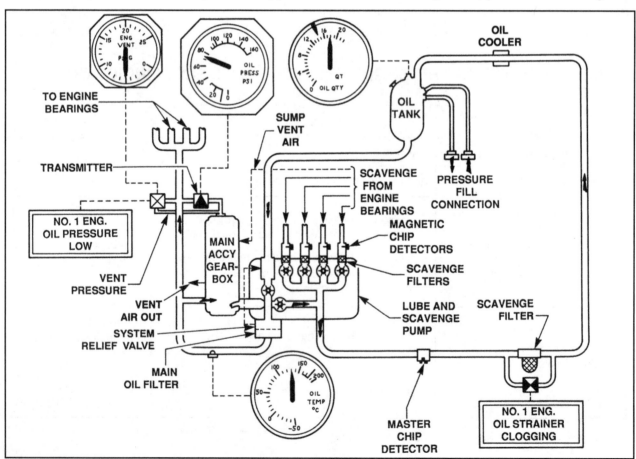

Figure 12-21. Engine oil system indicators (positive sump vent system)

Engine Instrument Systems

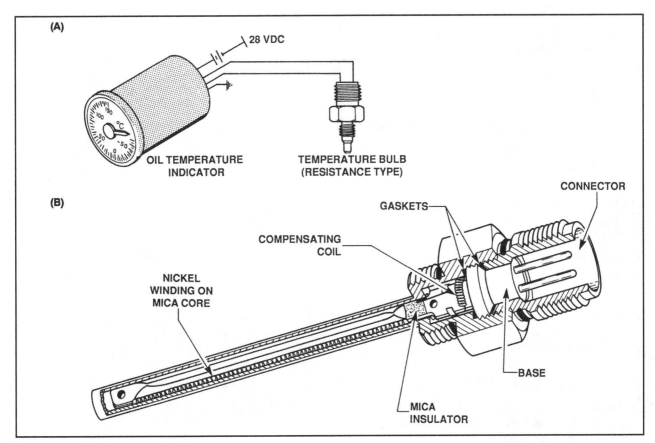

Figure 12-22A. Resistance bulb and gauge
Figure 12-22B. Cutaway view of resistance bulb

cause current to flow through a cockpit indicator. This circuit is similar to the exhaust temperature indicating system except that the hot junction in this thermocouple system is in the oil stream. [Figure 12-24]

OIL PRESSURE INDICATING SYSTEM

The oil pressure indicating system is an Autosyn design, powered by either 26 VAC or 115 VAC from the aircraft bus. [Figure 12-25] In the example system, the transmitter receives two input pressure signals, engine vent subsystem pressure and engine oil pressure subsystem pressure. The signals apply pressure to a pair of opposing bourdon tubes that are linked mechanically to an electromagnet in a coil. When the magnet rotates within its electrical field, the indicator magnet also rotates because it is in a similar coil connected in parallel with the transmitter coil.

By using two pressure inputs, this system algebraically subtracts vent pressure from the pressure subsystem fluid pressure to provide a differential oil pressure indication in the cockpit. This is required on many engines to give an accurate cockpit indication of the actual oil flow through the engine.

Two conditions can occur in bearing sumps in the area of the oil jets. In some engines, pressure builds up from gas path air bleeding inward through bearing seals. On other engines, tight sealing arrangements permit the scavenge pumps to create a negative pressure in the sumps. In either case, the vent pressure influence at the oil jet affects oil flow.

If higher than normal positive pressure is present, it can retard the normal oil flow to a point where insufficient lubrication takes place. The same conditions can take place in a negative sump system. Negative vent pressures are generally in the range of 2 to 6 p.s.i.g. below ambient at cruise power, and this vent pressure is designed to generate a designated oil flow in conjunction with the oil pumping system. If bearing seals leak excessive amounts of air into the sumps, the negative pressure rises, moving toward zero gauge pressure or ambient. The back pressure that occurs will retard normal oil flow from the oil jets.

Negative sump systems are stabilized by connecting part of the system to ambient pressure or by letting engine bleed air enter the system at some point to pressurize the return of vent air and contaminants to the atmosphere.

An example of this concept follows for both a negative sump pressure and a positive sump pressure. Negative sump pressure occurs from scavenge pump suction being greater than the seal leakage air entering the bearing sump.

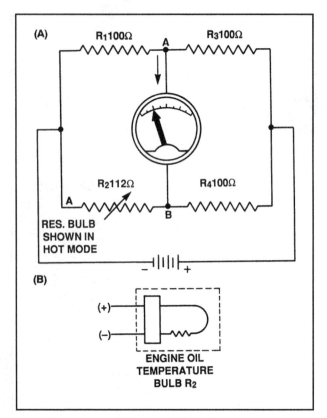

Figure 12-23A. Bridge circuit for a resistance bulb-type oil temperature indicating system

Figure 12-23B. Resistance bulb shown as a variable resistor

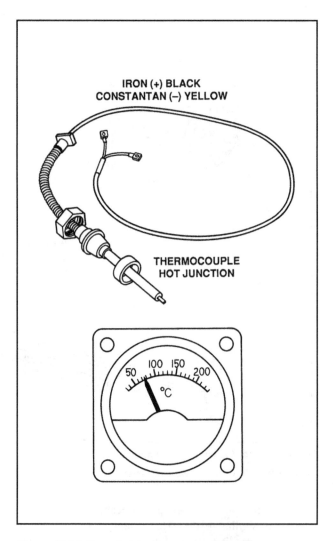

Figure 12-24. Temperature thermocouple and gauge

Example—positive sump pressure:

80.0 p.s.i.g. oil pressure
−(+5.0) p.s.i.g. vent pressure
75.0 p.s.i.g. corrected oil pressure

Example—negative sump pressure:

80.0 p.s.i.g. oil pressure
−(−5.0) p.s.i.g. vent pressure
85.0 p.s.i.g. corrected oil pressure

In the example positive sump pressure, 5 p.s.i.g. back pressure at the oil jet results in a net differential 75 p.s.i.g. actual oil pressure, which in effect represents a calibrated amount of oil flow in gallons per minute.

In the negative sump example, a negative condition is present at the oil jet, which permits more oil to flow. The negative 5 p.s.i.g., when subtracted algebraically, results in an 85 p.s.i.g. corrected oil pressure, which results in more oil flow than if the sump were of positive pressure.

This is an important consideration for maintenance personnel to keep in mind when diagnosing a low or high oil pressure indication with a direct oil pressure test gauge. Two gauges must be used to measure both the oil pressure and the vent pressure to calculate the corrected (differential) oil pressure. For example, high vent pressure from a damaged carbon seal at a main bearing location can cause a low-pressure indication in the cockpit. Careful troubleshooting and knowledge of system design reveals the source of this problem to be an internal engine condition rather than a fault in the indicating system or in the oil pressure subsystem. [Figure 12-26]

Engine Instrument Systems

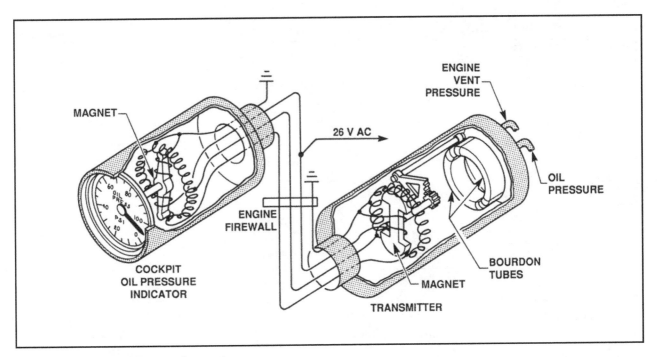

Figure 12-25. Oil pressure transmitter and gauge

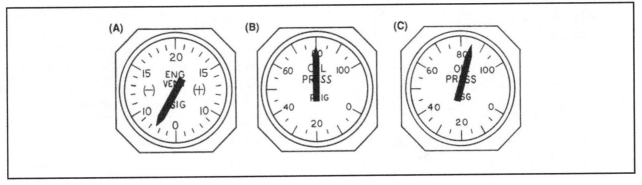

Figure 12-26A. Vent pressure test-gauge reading
Figure 12-26B. Oil pressure test-gauge reading
Figure 12-26C. Cockpit gauge reading in corrected units

TROUBLESHOOTING THE OIL INDICATING SYSTEM

PROBLEM/POSSIBLE CAUSE	CHECK PROCEDURE	REMEDY
1. No oil temperature indication in the cockpit		
a. Resistance bulb circuit 1. Tripped circuit breaker	Check circuit breaker position.	Reset circuit breaker.
2. Lack of continuity and power	Check for loose connections or an open circuit.	Tighten or repair as necessary.
3. Defective indicator	Test for defective indicator by interchanging indicators.	Replace indicator.
4. Defective resistance bulb	Test for defective bulb by slaving in another bulb.	Replace bulb.

PROBLEM/POSSIBLE CAUSE	CHECK PROCEDURE	REMEDY
b. Thermocouple circuit		
1. Lack of continuity	Check for loose connections or an open circuit.	Tighten or repair as necessary.
2. Defective thermocouple bulb	Test for defective bulb by slaving in another bulb.	Replace bulb.
3. Defective indicator	Test for defective indicator by interchanging indicators.	Replace indicator.
2. Oil temperature fluctuates in either the resistance bulb or the thermocouple bulb circuit		
a. Loose connections	Check for loose connections.	Tighten as necessary.
b. Faulty indicator	Test for defective indicator by interchanging indicators.	Replace indicator.
c. Defective bulb	Test for defective bulb by slaving in another bulb.	Replace bulb.
3. High oil temperature indication		
a. Faulty indicator	Same as item 2b.	

TROUBLESHOOTING THE ENGINE WITH OIL SYSTEM INDICATORS

PROBLEM/POSSIBLE CAUSE	CHECK PROCEDURE	REMEDY
1. High oil temperature indication		
a. Low oil level	Verify oil level.	Add oil if necessary.
b. Faulty fuel-oil cooler	Determine if thermo-valve is sticking open by checking bypass valve pressure drop across the cooler with direct gauges.	Replace cooler.
c. Worn or damaged main engine bearing	Check for metal contamination at chip detectors and filters.	Possible engine teardown.
2. Oil pressure high, low, or fluctuating		
Refer to oil system troubleshooting, Chapter 6		

MARKING OF POWERPLANT INSTRUMENTS

The following guidelines from FAA circular AC 20-88 offer acceptable, but not exclusive, methods of compliance with dial face markings for gas turbine powerplant instruments. [Figures 12-27A and 12-27B]

- FUEL PRESSURE
  - Red radial at maximum or minimum (or both) permissible pressures established as engine operating limitations.
  - Green arc at normal operating range.
  - Yellow/amber arc at cautionary ranges indicating any potential hazard in the fuel system such as malfunctions, icing, and so on.
- OIL PRESSURE
  - Red radial at maximum or minimum (or both) permissible pressures established as engine operating limitations.
  - Green arc at normal operating range.
  - Yellow/amber arc at cautionary ranges indicating any potential hazard due to overpressure during cold start, low-pressure during idle, and so on.

- OIL TEMPERATURE
  - Red radial at maximum or minimum (or both) permissible temperatures established as engine operating limitations.
  - Green arc at normal operating range.
  - Yellow/amber arc at cautionary ranges indicating any potential hazard due to overheating, high viscosity at low temperature, and so on.
- TORQUE INDICATOR
  - Red radial at maximum permissible torque pressure for dry or wet operation, whichever is greater.
  - Green arc from maximum torque pressure for continuous operation to minimum torque pressure recommended.
  - Yellow/amber arc from maximum torque pressure for continuous operation to maximum permissible torque pressure.
- EXHAUST GAS TEMPERATURE
  - Red radial at maximum permissible gas temperature for wet or dry operation, whichever is greater.
  - Green arc from maximum permissible temperature for continuous operation to minimum recommended by the engine manufacturer.
  - Yellow/amber arc from maximum temperature for continuous operation to maximum permissible gas temperature.
- TACHOMETER
  - Red radial at maximum permissible rotational speed (RPM).
  - Green arc from maximum rotational speed for continuous operation to minimum rotational speed recommended for continuous operation.
  - Yellow/amber arc from maximum rotational speed for continuous operation to maximum rotational speed.
- DUAL TACHOMETER (HELICOPTER)
  - Red radial on a dual tachometer (Engine) at maximum permissible rotational speed.
  - Dual tachometer (rotor) at maximum and minimum rotor speed for power "OFF" operational condition.
  - Green arc on a dual tachometer (engine) from maximum rotational speed for continuous operation to minimum recommended for continuous operating power (except in the restricted ranges, if any).
  - Dual tachometer (rotor) from maximum to minimum normal operating range.
  - Yellow/amber arc, dual tachometer (engine) precautionary ranges such as altitude limits.
- GAS PRODUCER (N_1) TACHOMETER (TURBOSHAFT HELICOPTER)
  - Red radial at maximum permissible rotational speed.

THRUST INDICATOR (TURBOJET, TURBOFAN)

This indicator has no markings because values vary considerably with temperature and altitude operating conditions. Limiting gauge markings cannot be established for all such conditions. It is necessary to refer to thrust setting charts (EPR or N_1 fan speed) for the acceptable values.

FAA SUGGESTED METHODS OF MARKING POWERPLANT INSTRUMENTS

To satisfy the requirement for clearly visible markings for low light conditions at a viewing distance of 28 inches, a hypothetical instrument dial and vertical tape instrument are shown. These markings are intended as a guide only. Some instruments need only a few of these markings. [Figure 12-27A and 12-27B]

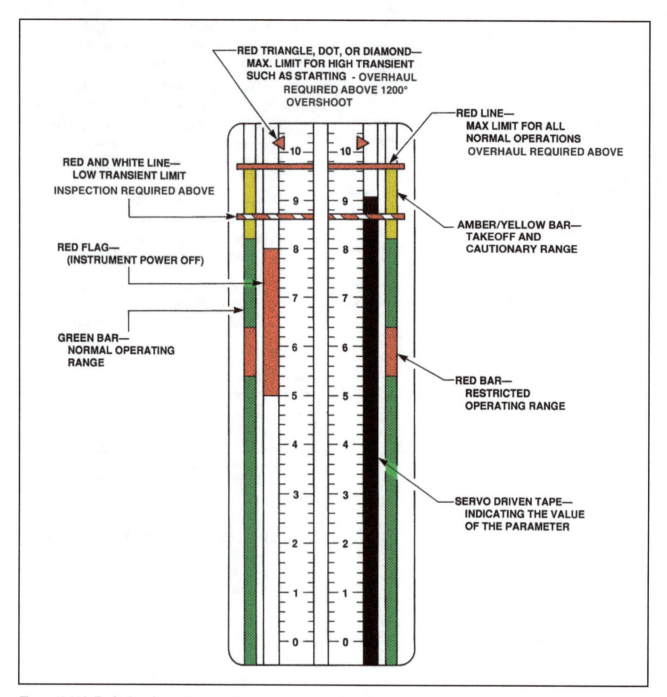

Figure 12-27A. Typical engine vertical-type instrument markings (twin-engine aircraft)

Engine Instrument Systems

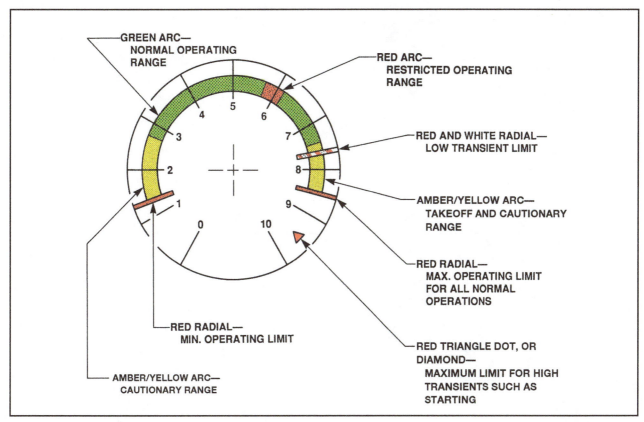

Figure 12-27B. Typical engine dial type instrument markings.

QUESTIONS:

1. Temperature taken forward of the turbine wheels is known by what name?

2. Which cockpit indicator is most likely to show an elevated reading if the turbine wheel becomes damaged?

3. What is the name of the exhaust temperature analyzer unit that is used on gas turbine engines?

4. What are two of the main functions of a tachometer indicator on an EPR-rated, axial flow engine?

5. If the aircraft loses its electrical generating power, will the tachometer system continue to function?

6. Does an indication of 100 percent engine speed on a single-spool turbojet engine mean that 100 percent thrust is also available?

7. Is there both an EPR indicator and a thrust indicator in the cockpit of a typical turbine engine aircraft?

8. Does a speed-rated fan engine use an EPR system as a primary thrust indicator?

9. Is the fuel flow indicating system powered by the AC or the DC aircraft bus?

10. How is the rate of turbine engine fuel flow expressed?

11. Where is the flow-meter transmitter usually located?

12. Which of the two oil temperature systems—resistance bulb or thermocouple—is an independent electrical circuit?

13. Which oil indicating system transmitter is vented to the engine gearbox?

14. What does a red arc on an engine indicator signify?

15. What does a red radial on an engine indicator signify?

CHAPTER 13
Fire/Overheat Detection and Extinguishing Systems for Turbine Engines

The turbine engine (or the cowlings adjacent to the engine) contains fire detection devices that illuminate a warning light in the cockpit if a fire or serious overheating occurs. Quite often the engine's hot and cold sections are divided into two distinct fire zones, each with its own detection devices set to alarm according to the operating temperature of that zone. For example, the device in the cold section might trigger the alarm at 200 to 300°F, but the device in the hot section might not trigger the alarm until temperatures reach as high as 300 to 1,200°F. The temperatures are set at the factory and generally cannot be changed in the field.

Several varieties of fire surveillance systems are available, the most common of which are the single-wire thermal switch, the two-wire thermal switch, the continuous loop, and the pneumatic loop.

SINGLE-WIRE THERMAL FIRE/OVERHEAT DETECTION SWITCH

The single-wire thermal switch system features several heat-sensitive thermal switches that contain a pair of open contacts that close when the temperature reaches a preset value. As shown in Figure 13-1A, when the switch heats up, the heat-sensitive arms to which the contacts are attached expand in the direction opposite the electrical terminal. This completes an electrical circuit to a warning indicator in the cockpit. This system automatically resets itself when cool.

As shown in Figure 13-1B, 28 VDC is applied to both paths of the thermal switch loop. If a fire or overheating occurs and any of the switches close, the closed switch completes a path to ground. With this loop arrangement, if one circuit remains open, the system still provides protection at all of the fire surveillance points. The test switch tests the entire loop and indicates whether an open circuit is present. A short circuit in the loop will cause a false fire warning indication.

The dimming relay provides low voltage to the light for night operation.

TWO-WIRE THERMAL FIRE/OVERHEAT DETECTION SWITCH

The two-wire thermal switch is designed so that the circuit can remain functional with an open circuit or a

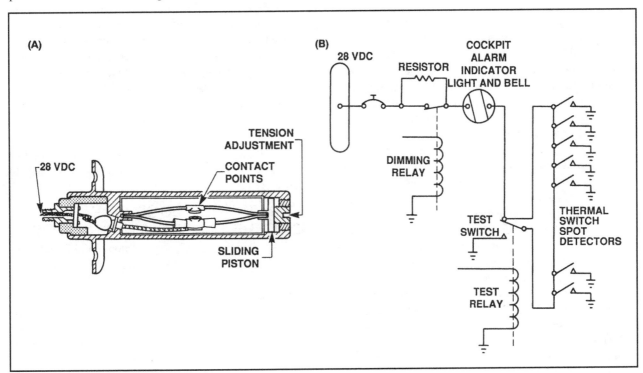

Figure 13-1A. Fenwal bimetallic thermal switch
Figure 13-1B. Single-wire, thermal switch fire/overheat detector circuit

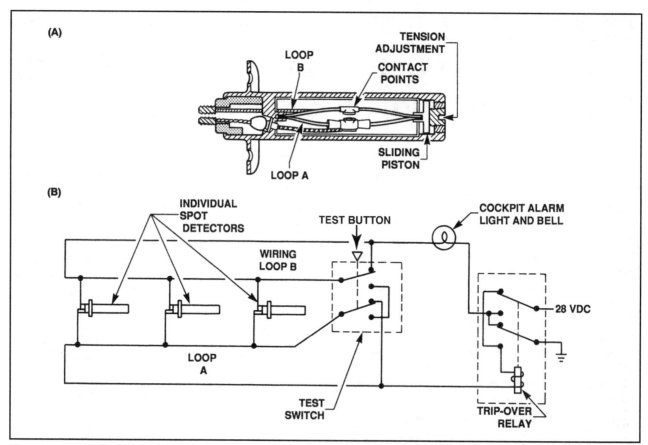

Figure 13-2A. Bimetallic thermal switch
Figure 13-2B. Two-wire, thermal switch fire/overheat detector circuit

short. During operation and testing of the circuit shown in Figure 13-2A and 13-2B, the following sequence of events occurs:

1. **Normal operation** — With the trip-over relay in the normal position, 28 VDC is supplied to Loop A from both ends. If a fire/overheat occurs or if the test button is pressed, current will flow through Loop B and illuminate the warning light. The trip-over relay will remain in this position due to the low current draw present in the normal mode of operation.
2. **Operation with a short in Loop A** — A high current draw with a short in this loop is sufficient to cause the trip-over relay to actuate. If this occurs, the reset button on the relay casing pops out and remains out until reset by hand. Loop B now receives the 28 VDC power to protect the engine and Loop A provides the ground circuit. If a serious overheat or a fire occurs or if the test button is pressed, the warning light illuminates. A short in Loop A is detectable only by observing the popped reset button.
3. **Operation with a short in Loop B** — If a fire/overheat occurs or if the test button is pressed, a high current draw sufficient to cause trip-over will be present. After trip-over, the alarm light illuminates and remains on, giving an indication that Loop B is shorted.
4. **Operation with an open in Loop A** — This loop is powered from both ends and provides protection similar to the single-wire system. If an open circuit is present in the loop, power is still available to each thermal switch. Pressing the test button reveals this condition because for current to flow and the light to illuminate, the entire loop has to be secure. The light will not illuminate with an open circuit in this loop.
5. **Operation with an open in Loop B** — The system still provides fire protection with one or more open circuits in this loop. If the alarm light does not illuminate after pressing the test button, there is an open circuit in Loop B.

As in the single-wire system, after cooling, the two-wire system automatically resets itself and is ready for reuse.

CONTINUOUS LOOP FIRE/OVERHEAT DETECTION SYSTEM

Two types of electrical continuous loop fire/overheat detection systems are in common use today, the single loop with a single-wire core and the single loop with a two-wire core. Both are designed for use on larger engines. These systems are discrete in that they are independent of surrounding engine bay temperatures; they trigger the alarm only when a temperature rise occurs that is above the average engine bay temperature.

In the single-wire system, the Inconel® outer case provides the ground potential. In the two-wire system, the second wire performs this function. In each case, the hot lead is insulated from ground—one uses ceramic beads coated with a substance called eutectic salt, the other uses a thermistor-type material. Each loses its electrical resistance as melting occurs when heated. The composition of the insulator material determines the temperature at which the system triggers the alarm.

In addition to being available in single- or two-wire cores, as shown in Figures 13-3 and 13-4A, continuous loop systems are also available in single- and dual-loop configurations. The dual loop shown in Figure 13-4B offers a backup capability if one loop fails.

Normally, both loops are set at the same alarm temperature. In the Fenwal system, if different alarm temperatures are required, sensing loop segments set at different alarm temperatures can be connected in series in one continuous loop. Each segment will trigger the alarm at its own preset temperature without an averaging effect. The older Kidde systems cannot connect different temperature loops in series, but the newer Kidde systems can.

In the circuit diagram shown in Figure 13-3, 28 VDC is supplied to the hot lead through an alarm relay coil. When cool, the insulation material does not permit current to flow between ground and the hot lead. When a fire or overheating occurs, however, the insulator material heats and loses enough resistance to complete a path to ground. The relay coil is energized by this current flow and the alarm light illuminates in the cockpit. This system, like the thermal switch systems, automatically resets itself when cooled.

The continuous loop installation drawing in Figure 13-4B shows two separate loops, one for the cold section and one for the hot section. The figure also shows the fire extinguishing system components that are completely independent of the detection circuit. The loop system incorporates control circuits that automatically compensate for operational heat in the engine compartment.

Figure 13-5 shows a continuous loop testing device, the Jetcal Analyzer unit, which was described in Chapter 7 for calibrating the exhaust gas temperature (EGT) system. The heater probe applies a prescribed heat value to the continuous loop. The heat value appears on the Jetcal control panel's potentiometer. When the alarm temperature is reached, the cockpit warning light illuminates. If the light illuminates before the prescribed temperature setting, the entire loop should be inspected for dents, kinks, or other damage that could reduce the normal spacing between the power lead and ground potential of the loop.

PNEUMATIC FIRE/OVERHEAT DETECTION SYSTEM

The pneumatic fire protection system is another type of fire/overheat surveillance system. It is produced in various sensor tube lengths and features several preset alarm temperatures that are nonadjustable.

The tube contains an inert gas that expands when heated. When the trigger temperature is reached, the gas pressure is sufficient enough to overcome the check valve, and gas flows into the diaphragm. [Figure 13-6] This gas flow forces the diaphragm contacts to move and come into contact with the alarm contactors, which triggers the alarm circuit.

After the heat source is removed, the gas cools and the pressure drops. The diaphragm then forces the gas back into the tube, ready for another operation.

To provide spot protection as well as area protection, the loop also contains a small core of special solid material, that, when heated, releases a secondary gas. This secondary gas pressurizes the detector loop and actuates the responder in the same way that the inert gas pressure unseats the check valve and shifts the diaphragm.

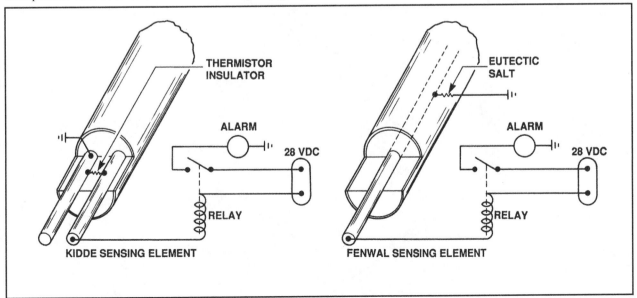

Figure 13-3. Continuous loop detector fire/overheat detector system

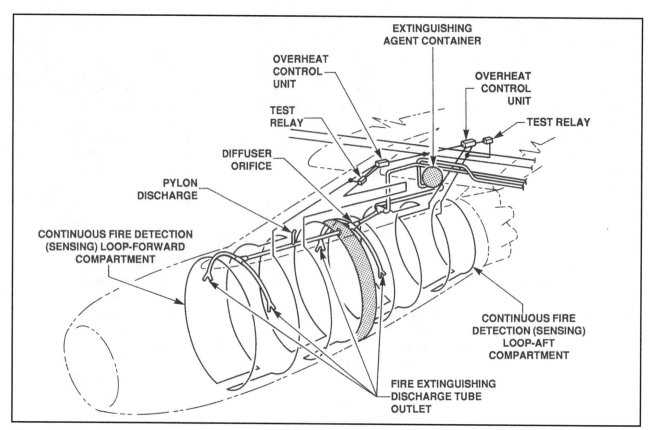

Figure 13-4A. Typical pod and pylon continuous loop fire/overheat detection installation

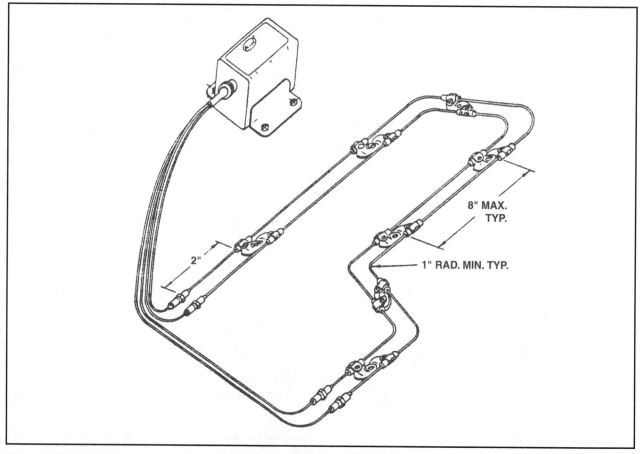

Figure 13-4B. Typical dual loop fire detection system

Fire/Overheat Detection and Extinguishing Systems

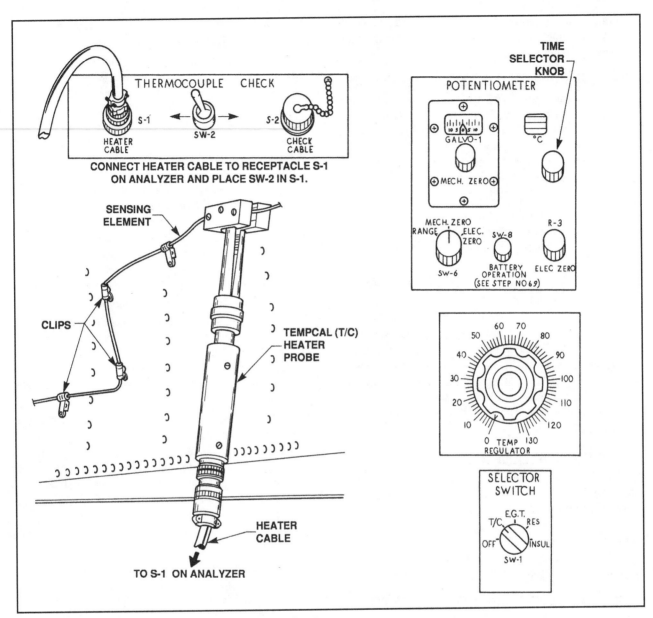

Figure 13-5. Jetcal analyzer testing of continuous loop fire detector

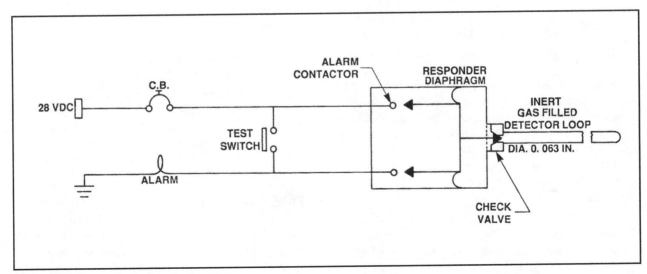

Figure 13-6. Pneumatic fire/overheat system

For additional information, refer to Figure 13-8, which shows a commercial aircraft dual-loop pneumatic fire/overheat protection system.

OTHER FIRE DETECTION SYSTEMS

A system that gives fire protection without offering overheat detection is the flame detector system. It uses infrared detectors to receive direct or reflected rays from a flame source. The detectors are located in the engine nacelle and send a signal to an amplifier that powers an alarm circuit in the cockpit.

Another similar circuit is the smoke detector, which uses photoelectric cells and a beam of light. If enough smoke is present, the reference beam refracts light and directs it to the photoelectric cells, which triggers the alarm.

Both of these circuits and the overheat detectors self-reset to the standby state. The photoelectric sensor is not widely used for turbine engine application because it cannot detect hot air leaks. Such leaks are a common malfunction of the gas turbine engine that can cause a fire if hot air is directed toward an oil or fuel line. Some systems have a discrete function, meaning that they can distinguish between an overheat condition due to a hot air leak and an actual fire. Details of this circuitry are beyond the scope of this text.

FIRE EXTINGUISHING

The fire extinguishing system includes a cockpit control switch, fire extinguishing agent containers, and an agent distribution system. The engine fire extinguishing system is part of the larger aircraft fire extinguishing system. Extinguishing agents are not generally introduced into the internal parts of the engine but rather into the engine nacelle surrounding the exterior of the engine.

THE FIRE EXTINGUISHING SYSTEM FOR THE ENGINE NACELLE

Figure 13-7A shows a typical container that houses the extinguishing agent. An engine might be protected with one bottle or by a cross-feed system with multiple bottles.

The bottle, pressurized between 500 and 600 p.s.i.g., includes a gauge that indicates the current charge as well as what the charge should be. The relief valve is a fusible disk that ruptures if the bottle overheats. To discharge the bottle from the cockpit, the operator toggles the discharge switch shown in Figure 13-8, which applies an electrical current to the contactor that detonates an explosive cartridge known as a squib. The squib shatters a disk located in the bottle outlet, which permits the agent to flow to the engine.

Figure 13-7B illustrates a twin engine extinguisher system with a cross-feed. With this distribution system, the number one and the number two extinguishing bottles can be used on a fire in either of the two engines.

COMMON EXTINGUISHING AGENTS FOR GAS TURBINE ENGINES

Several common extinguishing agents are used for gas turbine engines. Carbon dioxide (CO_2) is the oldest type of agent used in aviation. It is noncorrosive to metal parts, but it can cause thermal, low-temperature shock to hot running parts of the engine if used in great quantity.

A number of halogenated hydrocarbons (Freon products) have also been used, but only a few are still in use today:

- **Carbon Tetrachloride (Halon 104) (CCl_4)** — Poisonous and toxic. Hydrochloric acid vapor, chlorine, and phosgene gas are produced whenever carbon tetrachloride is used on ordinary fires. The amount of phosgene gas increases whenever carbon tetrachloride directly contacts with hot metal, certain chemicals, or continuing electrical arcs. It is no longer approved for any fire extinguishing use.

- **Methyl Bromide (Halon 1001) (CH_3Br)** — Lighter in weight than carbon dioxide but more toxic and highly corrosive to nonferrous alloys. Contaminated areas must be washed down immediately per manufacturer's instructions. Not generally recommended for aircraft use.

- **Chlorobromomethane (Halon 1011) (CH_2ClBr)** — CB, as it is called, is a more effective agent than CO_2 or CH_3Br, and it is less toxic. However, it is corrosive to both ferrous and nonferrous metals, and contaminated parts must be immediately washed down. Not recommended for aircraft use.

- **Dibromodifluoromethane (Halon 1202) (CBr_2F_2)** — An expensive, nontoxic, noncorrosive agent. Not recommended for aircraft use.

- **Bromochlorodifluoromethane (Halon 1211) ($CBrClF_2$)** — Colorless and noncorrosive, it evaporates rapidly, leaving no residue. It does not freeze or cause cold burns, and it does not harm fabrics, metals, or other materials it contacts. Halon 1211 acts rapidly on fires by producing a heavy blanketing mist that eliminates air from the fire source; more importantly, it interferes chemically with the combustion process. It has outstanding properties in preventing reflash after the fire has been extinguished.

- **Bromotrifluoromethane (Halon 1301) (CF_3Br)** — An expensive, nontoxic, noncorrosive agent that is very effective on engine fires. It is considered one of the safest agents when considering toxicity and corrosion. Halon 1301 has all of the characteristics of Halon 1211, but it is less toxic.

FIRE EXTINGUISHING (ENGINE GASPATH)

If a fire occurs on startup and a dry chemical powder, ground-based, fire extinguishing agent is used by the ground crew or flight crew, the starter should continue to motor the compressor so that the observed engine

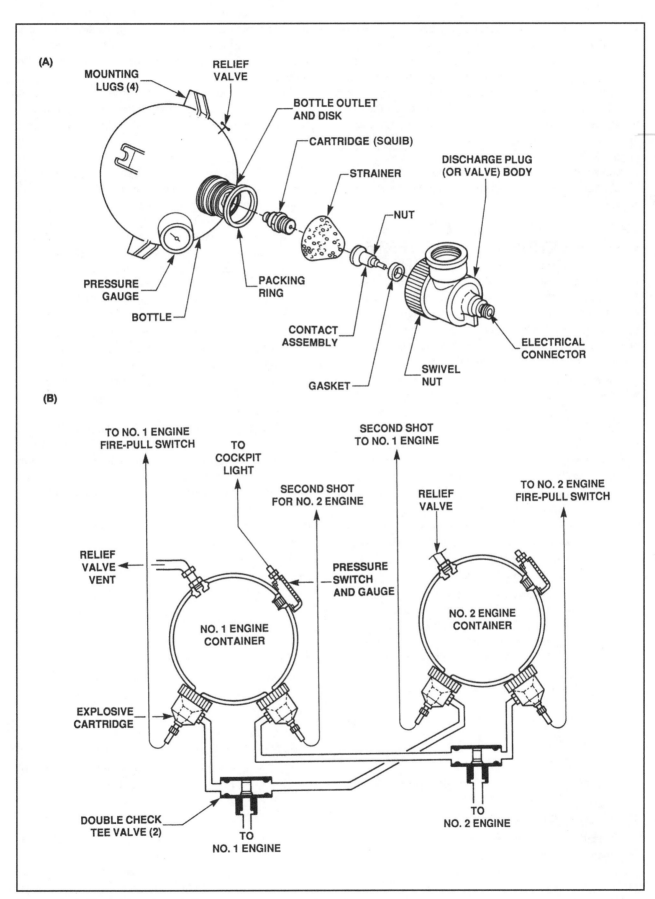

Figure 13-7A. Fire bottle components
Figure 13-7B. Fire extinguishing system for twin-engine aircraft

gas temperature can be lowered as rapidly as possible to below 500°C.

After the fire is out and the engine has cooled sufficiently to reduce the likelihood of thermal shock to hot section parts, wash the engine gas path down by introducing wash solution through the inlet and through the exhaust section. Hot water is most effective, if available, and the washing operation should be done while the engine is being "motored over," if possible.

Immediately thereafter, dry the engine by operating at idle speeds or by introducing heat from an external source.

CLEANING THE ENGINE AFTER USE OF EXTINGUISHING AGENTS

Using chemically corrosive fire extinguishing agents in gas turbine engines can be harmful to the engine. When corrosive fire extinguishing agents are introduced onto the exterior of the engine or into the engine gas path, such agents may cause severe corrosive damage to the engine compressor section and turbine area parts. They can also contaminate the engine oil system.

It is extremely important that such dry chemical agents be neutralized and completely removed from all engine parts as soon as possible because most dry chemical powder fire extinguishing agents contain a sodium or potassium bicarbonate base that is particularly corrosive to most engine metal parts. The wash solution typically includes a water and chloride mixture.

Exposure to dry chemical agents can cause extreme corrosion damage, especially in the rear portions of the gas turbine engine. When internal engine parts are exposed to sodium or potassium bicarbonate-based agents in temperature environments exceeding 500°C, corrosion can occur in a matter of a few hours.

As soon as possible, the engine should be processed through normal shop cleaning. Pay close attention to the inspection of all parts exposed to the fire extinguishing chemicals to detect and evaluate evidence of possible corrosive attack. Pay particular attention to parts with protective coatings to assure that they have not been adversely affected. Refer to the manufacturer's manual for all prescribed procedures to follow. Following the washing procedure, a common practice is to spray an approved preservative into the gas path while motoring the engine.

PNEUMATIC FIRE/OVERHEAT DETECTION AND FIRE EXTINGUISHING SYSTEM

Typically, a twin-engine commercial aircraft uses the pneumatic fire/overheat detection and fire extinguishing system. [Figure 13-8] The overheat/fire detection portion of this system is similar to the more basic system shown in Figure 13-6 in that gas in a sealed tube expands as it heats up. When the temperature and pressure rise to the first alarm level, an open path to ground closes and an overheat warning light illuminates in the cockpit. If the temperature rises to the second alarm level, a fire warning light illuminates.

The dual loop provides dual protection to the areas under surveillance. The fire detection control module that is connected to the loop's detector system provides a means of identifying faults in all areas of the dual loop system.

Figure 13-8 also shows the flight deck panels, which would be typical of a modern twin engine commercial airplane. The top right portion of the figure shows the fire/overheat detector loop system, which has four detectors incorporated into each of the two loops. The gas pressure in the continuous loop acts on the three system switches located within each of the detectors in three ways:

- If the gas is at normal pressure, one of the three switches is activated, enabling a test to confirm a correctly functioning system.
- If an engine overheat occurs, the gas pressure rises and activates a second switch, which illuminates the engine overheat light.
- If an engine fire occurs, the pressure rises even higher and activates the third switch, which illuminates the fire warning light.

The bottom right portion of the figure shows the fire and overheat detection control module. This component monitors the detectors in the two loops and sends out the appropriate signal to the overheat/fire protection panel in the event of an overheat, a fire, or a fault. This module incorporates built-in test equipment (BITE), which enables technicians to evaluate and troubleshoot system faults.

The bottom left portion of the figure shows the overheat/fire protection panel. This panel would be located right behind the throttle quadrant. The layout of the panel, from left to right, is as follows:

- The OVHT DET switch enables the A or B loop to be separately selected, or if it is in the normal position, to have both selected.
- ENG 1 OVERHEAT is the amber advisory light that illuminates when engine number 1 is experiencing an overheat condition.
- The TEST switch enables the fault detection circuit and the overheat/fire circuit to be tested.
- The number 1 engine T-handle incorporates the red fire light. In the event of a fire, the operator pulls out the T-handle to shut off the flow of engine fluids, and then rotates it left or right to discharge a fire bottle.
- Next to the T-handle are four advisory lights. The top light is red and signals a wheel-well fire. The second light is amber and indicates an engine detector fault. The third light is amber and signals an inoperative detector at the APU. The fourth light is amber and identifies a discharged APU fire bottle.

Fire/Overheat Detection and Extinguishing Systems

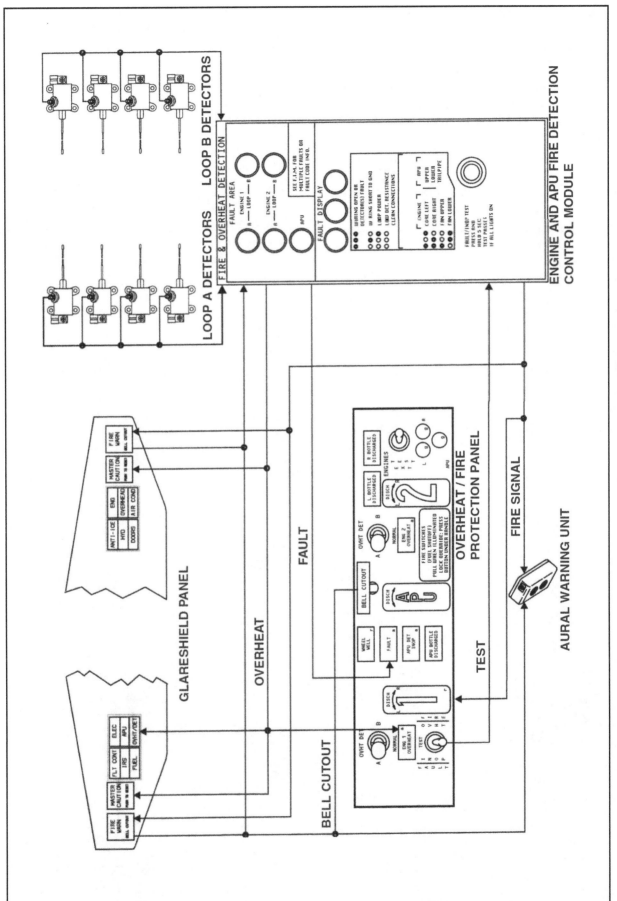

Figure 13-8. Twin-engine pneumatic dual loop, overheat/fire protection system

- Adjacent to the four advisory lights is the T-handle for the APU.
- Next are the switch and light for the number 2 engine.
- On the far right side of the panel is a test switch for checking the squibs at each of the three fire bottles. Below the test switch are three green lights that show the results of the test.
- Above the test switch for the fire bottle squibs are two amber advisory lights. These lights indicate when the left or right fire bottles have been discharged.

The top left portion of the figure shows the glareshield panel, where the master caution and fire warning lights are located. This panel is in the line of sight for the flight crew. If an engine fire were to occur, the master caution and fire warning lights would both illuminate. The flight crew would then look at the overheat/fire protection panel to determine the severity of the problem.

QUESTIONS:

1. Do any of the fire detection circuits used for turbine engines need power from the aircraft bus?

2. Which of the fire detection circuits contains a switching circuit to provide fire protection to the engine if a short appears in one of its loops?

3. Does the continuous loop fire/overheat detection system contain individual heat sensors?

4. Does the pneumatic fire/overheat detection system receive air from an engine pneumatic air source?

5. What is the purpose of a squib located at the fire bottle discharge port?

CHAPTER 14
Engine Operation

There are many instances when ground personnel other than pilots are required to operate a gas turbine engine. For example, they might need to:

- Duplicate a flight-crew-reported discrepancy for troubleshooting.
- Perform a basic engine checkout or an engine system checkout after maintenance.
- Move an aircraft from one maintenance location to another.
- Taxi-check an aircraft system.

SAFETY PRECAUTIONS

The engine operator must be thoroughly familiar with the flight line safety precautions for engine operation, including the use of hearing protection, awareness of inlet and exhaust area hazards for protection of both personnel and equipment, and knowledge of adverse weather restrictions that, if neglected, could result in poor engine performance or possible engine damage. Complete familiarity with the manufacturer's checklists and maintenance manuals is a must for safe and accurate performance testing.

TURBOJET AND TURBOFAN ENGINE RUN-UP

Runup of a gas turbine engine is performed only by flight crews and maintenance personnel who have specific training and authorization. These personnel must ensure that the logbook or other similar documents attest to the fact that all of the systems are secure and that the aircraft is safe to operate.

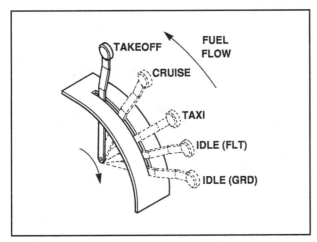

Figure 14-1. Power lever (throttle) connects to fuel control

NORMAL OPERATING PROCEDURES

All aircraft have a specific checklist, provided by the manufacturer, for engine runup. The general procedures for operating a turbine engine include, but are not necessarily limited to, the following items.

PRIOR TO ENGINE OPERATION

Before turning on the engine:

1. Remove the inlet and exhaust covers (where applicable).
2. Clear the inlet and exhaust areas of personnel and equipment.
3. Clear the ramp of debris that could cause foreign object damage to the engine.
4. Perform a walk-around inspection of the aircraft to ensure complete security of necessary aircraft and engine systems.
5. Ensure that the servicing of fuel and oil is adequate for the intended runup.
6. Connect the ground power unit to the aircraft, if required.

WHEN FIRST ENTERING THE AIRCRAFT

After entering the aircraft, check that the instruments are in the appropriate positions:

1. The master switch is turned off.
2. The landing gear handle is in the wheels-down position.
3. Seat pedals and brake pedals are properly adjusted.
4. Generator switches are off.
5. The power lever or the fuel control shutoff (or both if applicable) is off (engines with thrust reversers require a separate shutoff control).
6. The starter and ignition switches are off.
7. All aircraft systems are safe for operation.

ENGINE START

To start the engine:

1. Turn on the master switch.
2. Select battery or external power.
3. Select the necessary aircraft fuel valves.
4. Turn on the aircraft fuel boost pumps.
5. Turn on the engine starter switch.

6. Turn on the engine ignition system, typically between 5 and 10 percent compressor r.p.m.

NOTE: The starter and ignition are often time-sequenced after actuation of only the starter switch.

7. Move the fuel shutoff lever to open if the power lever's full rearward position is the idle position, or move the power lever to idle if it has a dual function as the fuel shutoff. Allow 10 to 20 seconds to light-off. If necessary, abort the start at the light-off time limit. [Figure 14-1]

8. Turn off the ignition and starter at the required time below idle speed.

9. Turn on the engine-driven generating system.

INSTRUMENT CHECKS ON START CYCLE

When on the start cycle:

1. Ensure that the exhaust temperature starting peak and stabilized limits are not exceeded.

2. Check that the engine oil pressure is in the correct range of operation.

3. On dual-compressor engines, ensure that a positive N_1 indication is present when 20 percent N_2 speed is reached.

INSTRUMENT CHECKS STABILIZED AT IDLE

While at idle, check these instruments to ensure that readouts are within limits:

- Percent r.p.m. (generally between 40 and 60 percent)
- Exhaust temperature (EGT, TIT, or ITT)
- Fuel flow
- Fuel manifold pressure
- Oil temperature
- Fuel temperature
- Oil pressure
- Vibration amplitude (large aircraft)

TYPICAL HIGH POWER CHECKS

When starting an engine, also perform these high power checks:

- Engine trim check (EPR, fan speed, or engine torque)
- Acceleration and deceleration time check
- Compressor bleed valve and variable vane schedule checks

TAXI PROCEDURE

Release the brakes and move the power lever forward as required for r.p.m., thrust, and ground speed. Communication with the airport control tower is often required before taxiing.

NORMAL SHUTDOWN PROCEDURE

When shutting down the engine, operate the engine at the prescribed speed for the recommended time interval—usually idle or slightly above idle, for 20 to 30 seconds. This stabilizes component temperatures, prevents engine distortion, prevents coking of oil on extremely hot surfaces, and properly scavenges the oil back to the oil tank. Then follow these steps:

1. Move the power lever or the fuel lever (or both if applicable) to the OFF position with a quick motion to the stop.

2. Turn off the fuel boost.

3. Turn off the fuel valves.

4. Turn off the generator, battery, and external power.

5. Turn off the master switch.

ENGINE OPERATION WITH FADEC CAPABILITIES

The Full Authority Digital Engine Control (FADEC) system both receives and delivers signals from the aircraft and the engine to provide an oversight for proper, safe, and economical engine operation.

GROUND STARTING

In aircraft with a FADEC system and electronic engine control (EEC) capability, as shown in Figure 14-2, an electronic oversight controls many of these procedures for manually starting a gas turbine engine. Several safety features go into effect after the start lever is moved from cutoff to idle and the controlling EEC channel is online. The system:

- Automatically terminates the engine starter and ignition if the EGT does not increase in the prescribed time and with the prescribed initial temperature rise.

- Automatically terminates the starter and ignition if the EGT attempts to overshoot the high (hot-start) limit.

- Commands the fuel metering valve to close, preventing a fuel over-scheduling.

- Produces a flashing light and a message on a flight deck display that describes any malfunction, such as low oil pressure.

- Protects against an N_2 r.p.m. rollback from idle speed that could create a low compressor air supply and a possible engine over-temperature.

- Provides a starter cut-out at the prescribed rotor speed—typically 55 to 60 percent N_2—by turning off the starter air supply valve.

Engine Operation

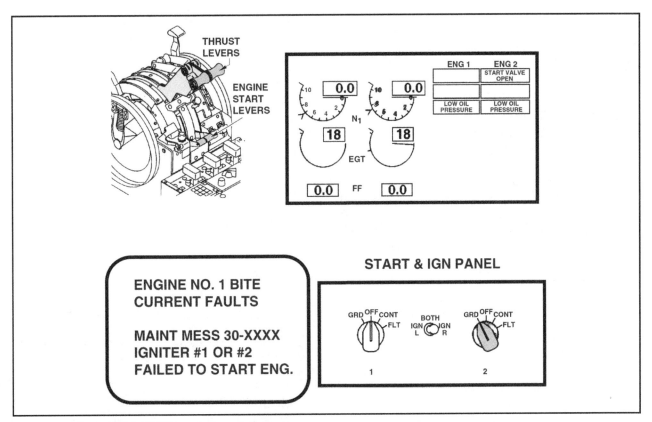

Figure 14-2. Cockpit with FADEC controls and display

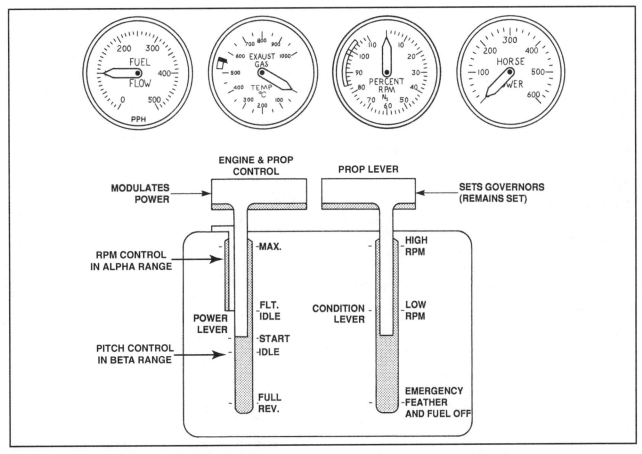

Figure 14-3. Cockpit controls and instruments, Honeywell - Garrett TPE-331 turboprop (fixed turbine)

The FADEC system interface is also discussed in the engine starting section of Chapter 10, and in Chapter 11, "Ignition Systems," which describes the switch positions in detail.

IN-FLIGHT STARTING PROTECTION, CREW-INITIATED RELIGHT

If an engine flames out in flight and it is safe to attempt a relight, the flight crew will manually place the start switch in the FLT position. In this position, the ignition system turns on but the starter does not typically energize because the engine is already wind-milling. If the EEC senses that the engine is not turning at a high enough speed to accomplish a successful relight, it automatically energizes the starter to assist in the engine start.

IN-FLIGHT STARTING PROTECTION, EEC-INITIATED RELIGHT

If the EEC detects an eminent in-flight engine shutdown, the ignition system turns on the engine igniters for engine relight, provided the following conditions are met:

- The start lever is in the idle position.
- N_2 is above the prescribed limit, typically 50 percent.
- The EEC has not received a distress signal that prevents a relight. For example, the EEC senses that the engine is experiencing an over-temperature, which causes it to shut off the fuel supply.

AUTO-THROTTLE

When the auto-throttle is installed, the EEC and several other computer devices automatically handle full range throttle lever positioning during all flight modes. Refer to Chapter 7 for details of how an auto-throttle system functions.

NOTE: Chapter 11 describes the "Cont" switch position (continuous ignition) shown in Figure 14-2.

EMERGENCY OPERATING PROCEDURES

Flight crews and ground runup crews must be fully aware of all aircraft systems and also of all the normal and emergency operating procedures. Without complete training in this area, many hazards might be overlooked, presenting a great danger to personnel and equipment.

ENGINE TAILPIPE FIRE DURING GROUND START

If fire erupts in the engine tailpipe during ground startup, follow these steps to extinguish it:

1. Turn the power lever or the fuel lever (or both if applicable) to the OFF position.
2. Continue cranking the starter in an attempt to blow out the fire.
3. Turn on the fire extinguisher if the fire is still active.

NOTE: A Freon-based or carbon dioxide extinguisher is preferred to avoid engine contamination.

4. Turn off the master switch.
5. Turn off all other switches.

After you have extinguished the fire and turned everything off, troubleshoot the cause of the fire.

HOT START

To prevent a hot start:

1. If the temperature is nearing the "do not exceed" temperature limit, turn the power lever or the fuel lever (or both if applicable) to the OFF position.
2. Turn off the master switch.
3. Check for normal rotation on engine coast-down and listen for unusual noises.
4. Inspect the inlet and tailpipe for signs of damage.
5. Troubleshoot the fuel system for fuel scheduling problems that are causing the over-temperature condition.

FAILURE TO START

If normal combustion does not occur within the required time period, usually 10 to 20 seconds after fuel is introduced to the engine, move the power lever or the fuel lever (or both if applicable) to the OFF position. Then troubleshoot the cause of the failure.

NOTE: If the engine fails to start because the fuel flow was terminated inadvertently, do not reopen the fuel lever; doing so would most likely result in a hot start. Let 30 to 60 seconds elapse for fuel to drain from the combustor. If necessary, perform an engine purging procedure to clear the engine of trapped fuel vapors.

ENGINE PURGING PROCEDURE (DRY MOTORING)

Engine purging is a common practice by which the rotation of the compressor rids the gas path of dangerous fuel vapor. For instance, vapors often accumulate when the engine fails to start. To purge the engine of fuel vapors:

1. Turn on the aircraft electrical power.
2. Move the power lever or the fuel lever (or both if applicable) to the OFF position.
3. Turn off the ignition, and pull the circuit breaker if necessary.
4. Turn on the starter (usually 15-20 seconds) to motor the engine over.
5. Turn off starter and wait for starter cool down before attempting another engine start.

EMERGENCY SHUTDOWN PROCEDURE

If the engine continues to operate when the power lever or fuel lever is moved to OFF, turn off the fuel boost and the aircraft fuel valves. Fuel starvation will force the engine to shut down within 30 to 60 seconds. This is an emergency procedure because lubrication of the fuel wetted components will cease and repeated shutdowns in this fashion reduce fuel system service life.

EMERGENCY IN-FLIGHT RAM-AIR STARTING PROCEDURE

If an in-flight flameout occurs, move the starter switch to the FLT START position. This bypasses the engine starter and allows only ignition to occur. Except at low airspeeds, the engine motors over sufficiently from ram-air entering the engine inlet, and the electrical ignition relights the mixture when fuel is reintroduced into the combustor. If airspeed is too low for a successful ram-air start, also called a windmilling start, the starter can be used in what is called a starter assisted ram-air start. Manufacturers stipulate the cautions involved in this procedure.

When a flight manual sets a high altitude limit for an attempted in-flight relight, however, it might be necessary to descend into a denser atmosphere before attempting any type of relight to prevent a hot start. The hot start could result from a mismatch of the fuel-to-air mixture in the combustor.

ENGINE RUNUP OF TURBOPROP ENGINES (FIXED TURBINE ENGINE)

Turboprop engine-powered aircraft are generally configured with at least two engine controls on the flight deck. The power lever, also called throttle, controls the engine, and the prop lever controls the propeller. Sometimes one or the other controls both the propeller and the engine fuel scheduling at different power settings.

For example, the Garrett TPE-331 engine is a fixed-turbine design with a Hartzell propeller. The power lever controls both the fuel control and the propeller pitch setting in the low speed (beta) range. The second lever controls the propeller r.p.m. at higher speeds in what is known as the (alpha) range. [Figure 14-3]

The following sequences of operation are typical of the TPE-331 turboprop engine:

GROUND STARTING PROCEDURE

To start the TPE-331 turboprop engine:

1. Complete the prestart checks (similar to turbojet/turbofan checks).
2. Turn on the aircraft electrical power.
3. Turn on the aircraft fuel valve and boost pump.
4. Move the power lever to the START GROUND IDLE position (beta range).
5. Move the condition lever to LOW RPM.
6. Turn on the battery or the external power selector.
7. Turn on the starter.
8. Observe cockpit indicators to ensure that ignition and fuel turn on automatically at 10 percent compressor speed.
9. Observe cockpit indicators to ensure that ignition and starter automatically turn off at 50 percent compressor speed.
10. Monitor all other engine instruments closely, as per the operator's manual.
11. Observe whether the idle speed has automatically been achieved at 65 percent compressor speed.
12. Reset the under-speed governor by moving the condition lever to HIGH RPM.

TAXI PROCEDURE

When taxiing:

1. Move the condition lever to the HIGH RPM position (the low blade angle position).
2. Move the power lever forward, toward or past the flight idle position, or alpha range, as necessary for the required thrust and ground speed.

NOTE: For takeoff and flight, movement of the power lever sets the engine power at a predetermined horsepower or torque value. The condition lever sets engine speed by changing the propeller blade angle. During flight, this lever usually remains at its set position with the engine running at a constant speed. When power changes are required, adjust the power lever position. Procedures for starting pneumatic (air turbine) engines are discussed in detail in Chapter 10.

PT6 TURBOPROP OPERATION (FREE TURBINE ENGINE)

The Pratt & Whitney Canada PT6 turboprop engine is a free turbine design, configured with either three or four engine control levers in the cockpit. [Figure 14-4]

- **Power control lever** — Attaches to the fuel control. Serves to moderate engine power (torque) from full reverse thrust and idle speed to takeoff.

- **Propeller control lever** — Attaches to the propeller governor to request blade angle and maintain r.p.m. In the maximum decrease position it feathers the propeller.

- **Start control lever** (condition lever) — Attaches to the fuel control and the fuel system shutoff valve. It has three positions: cut-off, low idle (run), and high idle.

- **Emergency power lever** — Used to directly control the engine power if the pneumatic side of the fuel control fails. Not all PT-6-powered aircraft have this lever.

GROUND OPERATIONS

Aircraft manufacturers that use the PT6 will adapt the following procedures to their particular Airplane Flight Manual. This procedure covers the typical requirements of a fixed-wing installation.

PRESTARTING

Before starting the engine:

1. Move the power control lever to IDLE.
2. Move the propeller control lever to any position in the operating range.
3. Move the starting control lever to the CUT-OFF position.
4. Turn on the master switch.
5. Open the fuel system shutoff valve.
6. Turn on the fuel boost pump.

ENGINE START

To start the PT6 engine:

1. Turn the engine ignition switch and the engine starter switch to the ON position. The minimum speed for obtaining a satisfactory light is 4,500 r.p.m. (12 percent Ng tachometer indication).
2. After attaining a stabilized gas generator speed, move the starting control lever to the RUN position.
3. Observe whether the engine accelerates normally to idle r.p.m. and that the maximum allowable inter-turbine temperature starting limit is not exceeded.

CAUTION: Whenever EGT fails to indicate light-off within ten seconds after moving the starting control lever to the RUN position, cut off the fuel and turn off the starter and ignition. Let the fuel drain for 30 seconds, and then perform a dry motoring run for 15 seconds before attempting another start. If a starting attempt is discontinued, let the engine come to a complete stop before implementing a dry motoring run. Repeat the starting sequence, being sure to observe the starter limits. (Refer to the applicable starter manufacturer's manual for more information.)

4. When the engine attains idle r.p.m., turn the engine starter switch and the ignition switch to the OFF position.

GROUND RUNUP

Before proceeding with a ground runup, ensure that the propeller control system is purged. To do so, feather the propeller once or twice with the power control lever in the IDLE position.

AIRCRAFT GROUND HANDLING

The low range of the power control lever can be used for taxiing.

ENGINE PURGING PROCEDURE (DRY MOTORING)

Air passing through the engine serves to purge raw fuel, fuel vapor, or fire from the combustion section, gas generator turbine, power turbine, and exhaust system. To clear an engine at any time of internally trapped fuel and vapor, or if there is evidence of an engine fire:

1. Move the starting control lever to the CUT-OFF position.
2. Turn off the ignition switch.
3. Turn on the switch to supply current for the engine starter.
4. Open the fuel system shutoff valve.
5. Turn on the fuel boost pump to provide lubrication for the engine-driven fuel pumping elements.
6. Turn on the engine starter switch.

WARNING: If the fire persists, as indicated by sustained inter-turbine temperature, close the fuel system shutoff valve and continue motoring.

7. Maintain the starter operation for the desired duration, being sure to observe the starter limits in the applicable manufacturer's manual.
8. Turn off the engine starter switch.
9. Turn off the fuel boost pump.
10. Close the fuel system shutoff valve.

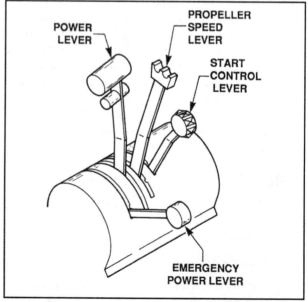

Figure 14-4. Engine controls, pilot's pedestal, Pratt & Whitney PT6 turboprop (free turbine)

11. Let the starter cool for the required cooling period before attempting any further starting operation.

ENGINE SHUTDOWN

To shut down the engine:

1. Move the power control lever to the IDLE position.

   NOTE: Let the engine stabilize for a minimum of one minute at the minimum obtainable ITT.

2. Move the propeller control lever to the FEATHER position.

3. Move the starting control lever to the CUT-OFF position.

4. Turn off the fuel boost pump.

5. Close the fuel system shutoff switch.

   NOTE: During the shutdown, ensure that the compressor decelerates freely.

   <u>WARNING: If there is any evidence of fire within the engine after shutdown, immediately perform a dry motoring run.</u>

PROPELLER WINDMILLING

While the aircraft is unattended, ensure that the propeller is tied down to prevent windmilling with zero oil pressure.

FLIGHT OPERATIONS

The following procedures are general in nature and are not applicable to any particular aircraft. They do, however, represent the typical procedures for setting the engine power factors to attain takeoff, climb, and cruise under normal flight operations.

TAKEOFF POWER SETTING

Before setting takeoff power:

1. Observe the corrected outside air temperature (OAT).

2. Observe the barometric pressure.

3. Enter the applicable takeoff power-setting torque curve (or torque computer) with the OAT and barometric readings and note the takeoff torque value required.

4. If it was not already done during the runup, purge the propeller control system.

To set takeoff power:

1. Move the propeller control lever to the applicable r.p.m. position.

2. Advance the power control lever to attain the required torque pressure.

3. Monitor the inter-turbine temperature to ensure that it has not exceeded limits.

4. Note any increase in Ng and Np speeds above the maximum limits.

NOTE: As the aircraft gains airspeed during takeoff, an increase in torque pressure at a fixed power control lever position is normal and should be retained as long as limiting torque pressure is not exceeded.

CLIMB SETTING

Because of the rapidly varying conditions during climb, power can be set by indicated ITT, using the nominal climb ITT value.

To carry out the climb using a lower rating, set power to a lower indicated ITT or use the torque setting method.

CRUISE SETTING

Use the torque indicating system to set the cruise power because it is the only parameter common to both aircraft performance and engine operating condition. Reference the torquemeter at regular intervals to ensure that it is reading the pressure required for a particular flight condition. Doing so aids in troubleshooting instrument or engine malfunctions and can be used to identify increased aircraft drag.

EMERGENCIES

Follow these general procedures when addressing emergencies involving the engine.

GROUND ENGINE FIRE

Perform a dry motoring run as described in "Ground Operations."

IN-FLIGHT ENGINE FIRE

If an engine fire occurs while in flight:

1. Move the prop control lever to the FEATHER position.

2. Move the starting control lever to the CUT-OFF position.

3. Turn off the fuel boost pump.

4. Close the fuel system shutoff valve.

5. Turn off the engine master.

6. Move the power control lever to IDLE.

7. Shut off all equipment operated by engine bleed air.

8. Carry out the in-flight engine fire procedure recommended in the Aircraft Flight Manual.

ENGINE FAILURE

If the engine fails:

1. Move the propeller control lever to the FEATHER position.

2. Move the starting control lever to the CUT-OFF position.

3. Turn off the fuel boost pump.

4. Close the fuel system shutoff valve.

5. Turn off the engine power switch.

6. Move the power control lever to the IDLE position.

WARNING: To avoid shutting down an engine unnecessarily, exercise caution during a suspected engine failure on takeoff or landing. Do not attempt to restart an engine when the flight crew determines that the engine has definitely failed.

ENGINE FLAMEOUT

The symptoms of an engine flameout are the same as those of an engine failure. A flameout creates a drop in inter-turbine temperature, torquemeter pressure, and r.p.m. Flameouts might result from lack of fuel or unstable engine operation. When the fuel supply has been restored to the engine or the cause of the unstable operations is eliminated, restart the engine in the manner described in the topic "Air Starts."

CAUTION: Do not attempt a relight of the engine if the Ng tachometer indicates zero r.p.m.

AIR STARTS

The most common air start technique is to initiate a windmilling relight procedure immediately after a flameout, provided that the flameout did not result from a malfunction that would make it dangerous to attempt a relight. Successful air starts can be achieved at all normal altitudes and airspeeds. However, above 14,000 feet, or with gas generator r.p.m. below 10 percent, starting temperatures tend to be higher and caution is required.

IMMEDIATE RELIGHTS

The engine might light up successfully as soon as the ignition is turned on. In an emergency, turn on the ignition as soon as possible after flameout, provided the gas generator speed has not dropped below 50 percent. It is not necessary to cut off the fuel or feather the propeller. The power control lever, however, should be retarded to IDLE.

NOTE: Propeller feathering is dependent on circumstances and is at the discretion of the pilot. However, a minimum engine oil pressure of 15 p.s.i.g. should be recorded if the propeller continues to windmill.

AIR STARTS — COMPRESSOR RPM BELOW TEN PERCENT NG WITH STARTER ASSISTANCE

Before attempting to perform an air start:

1. Move the prop control lever to any position in the operating range.

    NOTE: Propeller feathering is dependent on circumstances and is at the pilot's discretion. Fine pitch selection (prop lever forward) provides increased gas generator windmilling speed for emergency starts if the starter fails.

2. Move the power control lever to the IDLE position.

3. Turn on the engine master.

4. Open the fuel system shutoff valve.

5. Move the starting control lever to the CUT-OFF position.

6. Turn on the fuel boost pump.

7. Ensure that the fuel inlet pressure indicator shows a reading of at least 5 p.s.i.g..

To perform an air start:

1. Turn on the engine ignition and the engine starter. The minimum gas generator r.p.m. to obtain a satisfactory light is 4,500 (12 percent Ng). A windmill air start without electrical starter assistance is more difficult on free turbine engines because the windmilling propeller is not driving the engine's compressor (Ng).

2. Move the starting control lever to the RUN position after approximately five seconds of stabilized gas generator speed.

NOTE: A relight normally should be obtained within ten seconds and is evidenced first by a rise in gas generator (Ng) r.p.m. A rise in inter-turbine temperature will also occur.

When the engine attains idle r.p.m.:

1. Turn off the engine starter and the ignition (if there is no automatic cut-off).

2. Move the prop control lever into the operating range.

3. Move the power control lever to the desired position.

4. Check that the engine operating limits are not exceeded. If a satisfactory start is not obtained, discontinue the air start. Repeat the engine air start procedure if necessary.

AIR STARTS — COMPRESSOR RPM BELOW 10 PERCENT NG WITHOUT STARTER ASSISTANCE

To perform an air start below 10 percent Ng without assistance from the starter:

1. Move the propeller control lever to a fine pitch position (full forward).

2. Move the power control lever to the IDLE position.

3. Move the starting control lever to the CUT-OFF position.

4. Turn on the fuel boost pump.

5. Turn on the ignition.

6. Advance the starting control lever to the RUN position and monitor ITT. If over-temperature tendencies are encountered, move the starting control lever to the OFF position periodically during acceleration to idle.

7. Ensure that 50 percent gas generator r.p.m. has been attained before advancing the power control lever to the desired power setting.

FAA ENGINE POWER RATINGS

Turbine engines, both turbojet and turbofan, are thrust-rated in terms of either engine pressure ratio or fan speed; and turboshaft/turboprop engines are rated in terms of shaft horsepower (SHP) in the following categories:

- Takeoff
- Maximum continuous
- Maximum climb
- Maximum cruise
- Idle

For certification purposes, the manufacturer demonstrates to the FAA that the engine will perform at certain thrust or shaft horsepower levels for specified time intervals and still maintain its airworthiness and service life. These ratings can usually be found on the engine Type Certificate Data Sheets:

- Takeoff wet thrust/SHP — This time-limited rating represents the maximum power available while in water injection mode. It is used only during takeoff operation. Engines are trimmed to this rating.

- Takeoff dry thrust/SHP — Limits on this rating are the same as takeoff wet but without water injection. Engines are trimmed to this rating.

- Maximum continuous thrust/SHP — This rating has no time limit but is used only during emergency situations at the discretion of the pilot, such as during cruise operation with an inoperative engine. For example, maximum continuous thrust on a B737 occurs at the amber high cautionary marking on the EPR (thrust) indicator.

- Maximum climb thrust/SHP — Maximum climb power settings are not time-limited. They are used for normal climb, to cruising altitude, or when changing altitudes. This rating is sometimes the same as maximum continuous.

- Maximum cruise thrust/SHP — This rating is used at any time period during normal cruise at the discretion of the pilot.

- Idle speed — This power setting is not actually a power rating, but is the lowest usable thrust setting for either ground or flight operations.

Figure 14-5 shows an airliner flight envelope with a ceiling at 45,000 feet. It also shows limits of airspeed and altitude between which the pilot must remain during climb, at maximum climb, or maximum continuous power ratings.

TYPICAL OPERATING CAUTIONS FOR ALL TURBINE-POWERED AIRCRAFT

STARTING

Poor starting technique undoubtedly contributes to hot-section deterioration. Good starting requires adequate power supplied to the starter and correct fuel flow to the engine. Ensure that the power source (APU, GPU, battery truck, or aircraft battery) is well-maintained and that the output meets the requirements of the aircraft manual.

Monitor the exhaust gas temperature during the start cycle and if the exhaust gas temperature rises rapidly, reduce the fuel flow by retarding the power lever or shutoff lever, whichever is applicable. The aim is to minimize peak exhaust gas temperatures without reducing the acceleration time of the engine.

To minimize thermal gradients within the engine, avoid increasing the fuel too early in the start cycle and avoid opening the power lever (throttle) to taxi until idle r.p.m. has stabilized.

TAKEOFF

Prior to takeoff, obtain accurate pressure altitude and outside air temperature values to ensure the correct takeoff power setting of engine torque, pressure ratio (EPR), or fan speed. Smoothly open the throttles to the takeoff position and keep in mind that rapid power lever movements lead to accelerated deterioration of the hot-end components. Where conditions permit, carry out a rolling takeoff.

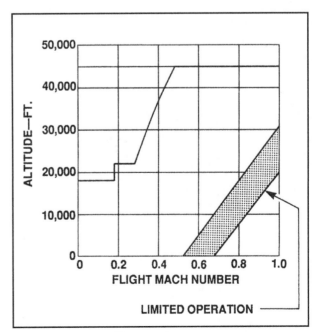

Figure 14-5. Airliner flight envelope

When you can choose between a dry or a wet takeoff, perform a dry takeoff. Doing so reduces water mixture costs and possibly lowers future parts replacement costs.

On either wet or dry takeoff, reduce speed to the climb setting as soon as possible, staying within aircraft safety requirements.

MAXIMUM CONTINUOUS RATING

Use the maximum continuous rating when one of the engines has failed in flight or has been shutdown in flight.

The remaining engines can be held at this power setting at the discretion of the pilot.

MAXIMUM CRUISE RATING

Use the maximum cruise rating when conditions require more than normal climb and cruise power but less than maximum continuous. Use this rating:

- When severe turbulence exists at the normal flight altitude and additional altitude is required.
- When additional power is required for high terrain clearance.
- When ATC requirements dictate a faster rate of climb.
- After an engine failure, when using maximum continuous power is not required.

CLIMB AND CRUISE

After takeoff, select a climb power (EPR, torque, or fan speed) as soon as possible. Where possible, use the alternate (lower) power setting for climb. Monitor exhaust gas temperature during climb and adjust the power lever as required. Most fuel controls are designed with sensors that reduce fuel flow to maintain a constant engine gas temperature with increasing altitude. Variations from the standard lapse rate and tolerances on fuel control calibration and trimming can cause changes in exhaust gas temperature to which the operator might have to react.

DESCENT AND APPROACH

To perform a descent and approach, ensure that the power lever is set no lower than flight idle position.

LANDING

For landing, move the power lever to ground idle position. Apply brakes and thrust reverse as applicable to runway conditions, normally 75 percent N_2 maximum, or 100 percent N_2 in emergencies.

SHUTDOWN

When shutting down the engine, ensure that the power lever is in the manufacturer's recommended shutdown position, wait until the r.p.m. has stabilized, and then close the fuel system shutoff valve. Failure to observe this procedure will result in uneven cooling of the engine hot section, which can cause turbine seal rub. In addition, a rapid shutdown can lead to incorrect oil consumption figures due to variable oil tank levels that result from poor scavenging.

Appendix 1

DEPARTMENT OF TRANSPORTATION
FEDERAL AVIATION ADMINISTRATION

E1GL
ALLISON
250-C28

April 28, 1976

TYPE CERTIFICATE DATA SHEET NO. E1GL

Engines of models described herein conforming with this data sheet (which is part of type certificate No. E1GL) and other approved data on file with the Federal Aviation Administration, meet the minimum standards for use in certificated aircraft in accordance with pertinent aircraft data sheets and applicable portions of the Federal Aviation Regulations provided they are installed, operated and maintained as prescribed by the FAA approved manufacturer's manuals and other FAA approved instructions.

Type Certificate Holder	Detroit Diesel Allison Division of General Motors Corporation Indianapolis, Indiana 46206
Model	250-C28
Type	Free turbine turboshaft 1 stage centrifugal flow gas producer compressor 2 stage gas producer turbine 2 stage power turbine Single combustion chamber with pre-chamber
Shaft ratio	5.55:1

Ratings (see NOTE 3)
  Max. continuous
    s. hp. at sea level   478
    Gas producer r.p.m.   50193
    Output shaft r.p.m.   6016
    Measured rated gas temp.   1392° F (755° C)

  Takeoff s. hp.
    5 min. at sea level   500
    Gas producer r.p.m.   51005
    Output shaft r.p.m.   6016
    Measured rated gas temp.   1430° F (777° C)

  30 Minute power,
    s. hp. at sea level   500
    Gas producer r.p.m.   51005
    Output shaft r.p.m.   6016
    Measured rated gas temp.   1430° F (777° C)

Output shaft	Internal spline
Control system	Bendix gas producer fuel control DP-T1 Bendix power turbine governor AL-AC1 Pneumatic accumulators and check valves or orifices (see NOTE 10)
Electronic Power Turbine Overspeed Control System	N2 Overspeed Control, P/N 6893-63 Overspeed Solenoid Valve, Valcor V5000-125 Power Turbine Speed Pickup P/N 6894602

E1GL

Fuel pump	Single element fuel pump Sundstrand Model 500950 or TRW model 388100
Fuel	MIL-T-5624, Grade JP-4 or JP-5; Aviation Turbine Fuels ASTM-D1655 Jet A or A-1 or Jet B; (for other fuel and limitations see NOTE 9).
Lubricating oil	MIL-L-23699 and subsequent revisions
Principal dimensions:	
Length overall, in.	43.000
Width, in.	21.940
Height, in.	25.130
C.G. location, aft of side mount pad centerline, in.	5.73
C.G. location, above side mount pad, centerline, in.	3.23
C.G. location, left side of engine cenerline looking forward, in.	.02
Weight (dry), lb. Includes basic engine, fuel pump, ignition and fuel control systems	219
Ignition system (see NOTE 12)	Low tension capacitor discharge exciter. Simmonds Precision P/N 43754 or Bendix Scintilla P/N 10-387150-1 Shunted surface gap spark igniter. Champion P/N CH34078 or AC P/N 8990157
Certification basis	Part 33 of the Federal Aviation Regulations effective February 1, 1965, and Amendments 33-2, 33-3, and 33-4, and Exemption No. 2087 from FAR 33.69, Regulatory Docket No. 13294 issued February 24, 1975. Application for Type Certificate dated October 2, 1973.
Production basis	Production Certificate No. 310

NOTE 1.   Maximum permissible temperatures:

    Measured gas temperature

Takeoff and 30 minute power	1450° F (787° C)
Maximum continuous	1430° F (777° C)
Maximum transients (not to exceed 6 seconds)	1450° F (787° C) to 1600° F (872° C)
Starting (not to exceed 10 seconds)	1450° F (787° C) to 1600° F (872° C)
Oil inlet temperatures	Minus 65° F (-55° C) to 225° F (107° C)

E1GL

NOTE 2. Fuel inlet and oil pressure limits:

    Fuel: Applicable to MIL-T-5624 and ASTM-D1655 Jet A or A-1 minimum at fuel connection to engine: not less than ambient pressure minus 9 in. Hg at sea level; ambient minus 5.5 in. Hg at 6000 ft.; ambient minus 3.5 in. Hg at 10,000 ft.; ambient minus 1.0 in. Hg at 15,000 ft.; and ambient plus 1.5 in. Hg at 20,000 ft. altitude. Maximum pressure 25 p.s.i.g No inlet depression permitted with MIL-G-5572 fuel.

    Oil: Operating gauge pressures:

48,000 rpm (94.2 percent) gas generator speed and above	115 to 130 p.s.i.g.
40,000 rmp (78.5 percent) to 48,000 rpm (94.2 percent)	90 to 130 p.s.i.g.
Below 40,000 rpm (78.5 percent)	50 to 130 p.s.i.g.
Oil pump inlet pressure:	5 in. Hg absolute minimum.

NOTE 3. The engine ratings, unless otherwise specified, are based on static sea level standard conditions. Compressor inlet air (dry) 59° F, 29.92 in. Hg. Compressor inlet bell attached to provide suitable air approach conditions. No external accessory loads and no air bleed.

Measured rated gas temperature as indicated by average of the 4 gas temperature thermocouples.

NOTE 4. The following accessory drive mounting provisions are available:

	*Direction of Rotation	Speed Ratio To turbine	Max. Torque (in-lb) Continuous	Max. Torque (in-lb) Static	Max. Overhung Moment (in-lb)
Driven by Gas Producer Turbine					
Tachometer	CC	0.0825	7	50	4
Starter-Generator	C	0.2351	**550	1100	150
Driven by Power Turbine					
Tachometer	CC	0.1257	7	50	4
Power Take-off	C	0.180	***5556	10,000	100
Spare	C	0.3600	79	395	150

*   C - Clockwise viewing drive pad: CC - Counterclockwise

**   The maximum generator load is 12 horsepower.

*** The sum of the torques extracted in any combination from the front and rear power output drives shall not exceed the torque values specified in NOTE 7. The value given in the above table represents the 30 minute limited maximum total torque.

NOTE 5. External air bleed may not exceed 4.5 percent.

NOTE 6. There are no engine equipment items which are aircraft mounted.

E1GL

NOTE 7. The maximum allowable torque as measured by the torquemeter for below standard inlet air temperature and/or ram conditions is 463 lb-ft for takeoff and 30 minute power, 417 lb-ft for maximum continuous and 480 lb-ft for 10 seconds.

NOTE 8. The maximum output shaft speed for momentary transients (up to 15 seconds) varies linearly from 113 percent at flight autorotation to 105 percent at takeoff. The maximum output shaft speed limit for sustained periods varies linearly from 108% at flight autorotation to 103 percent at takeoff. Gas producer speeds are permissible up to 105 percent for 10 seconds and up to 104 percent for sustained periods. 100 percent output shaft speed is defined as 6016 r.p.m. and 100 percent gas producer speed is defined as 50940 r.p.m.

NOTE 9. Emergency use of aviation gasoline MIL-G-5572, all grades, is limited to the amount of fuel required to operate the engine for not over 6 hours during any overhaul period except that a mixture consisting of 1/3 by volume of aviation gasoline MIL-G-5572, grade 80/87 and 2/3 by volume MIL-T-5624, grade JP-5, or aviation turbine fuels ASTM-D1655, Jet A or A-1 may be used for unrestricted periods of time. A mixture consisting of 1/3 by volume of aviation gasoline MIL-G-5572, grade 100/130 with a maximum of 2.0 mi./gal. lead content and 2/3 by volume of MIL-T-5624, grade J-5, or aviation turbine fuels ASTM-D1655 Jet A or A-1 may be used for not over 300 hours during any overhaul period. It is not necessary to purge the unused fuel from the system before refueling with different type fuels. No fuel control adjustment is required when switching these type fuels. Fuels containing Tri-Cresyl-Phosphate additives shall not be used. Anti-icing additives conforming to MIL-I-27686 are approved for use in fuels in amounts not to exceed 0.15 percent by volume. Shell anti-static additive is approved for use at a concentration that will not exceed fuel conductivity of 300 picomhos per meter.

NOTE 10. A pneumatic accumulator(s), double check valve(s) or other attentuating devices can be incorporated for compatability with the rotor system of the particular model helicopter in which the engine is to be installed.

NOTE 11. A magnetic oil drain plug indicator lamp is an installation requirement.

NOTE 12. Engines produced under the terms of this type certificate having single ignition systems, are limited to installation in rotorcraft certificated in accordance with FAR 27 or FAR 29 Category B. The engine is not eligible for installation in transport Category A rotorcraft certificated under FAR 29.

NOTE 13. Life limits established for critical rotating components are published in Detroit Diesel Allison Commercial Service Letter No. 250-C28 2005.

NOTE 14. Engine produced under this type certificate require inlet protection, not having been tested by ingestion of Group II foreign objects.

Appendix 2

```
                                    E23EA-4
                            GENERAL ELECTRIC
                                    CF6-6D
                                    CF6-6D1
                                    CF6-6H
                                    CF6-50A
                                    CF6-50C
                                    CF6-50D
                                    CF6-50E
                                    CF6-50H

                            December 15, 1974
```

DEPARTMENT OF TRANSPORTATION

FEDERAL AVIATION ADMINISTRATION

TYPE CERTIFICATE DATA SHEET NO. E23EA

PART B – CF6 – SERIES

Engines of models described herein conforming with this data sheet (which is part of type certificate No. E23EA) and other approved data on file with the Federal Aviation Administration, meet the minimum standards for use in certificated aircraft in accordance with pertinent aircraft data sheets and applicable portions of the Federal Aviation Regulations provided they are installed, operated and maintained as prescribed by the approved manufacturer's manuals and other approved instructions.

Type Certificate Holder	General Electric Company Aircraft Engine Group Cincinnati, Ohio 45215					
Model	CF6-50A	CF6-50C	CF6-50D	CF6-50E	CF6-50H	
Type	High bypass turbofan: Coaxial front fan driven by multi-stage low pressure turbine, multi-stage compressor with two stage turbine and annular combustor					
Rating Maximum continuous at sea level, static thrust, lb.	46,300	---	---	---	---	
Takeoff (5 min.) at sea level, static thrust, lb.	48,400	50,400	---	51,800	50,400	
Alternate takeoff (5 min.) at sea level, static thrust, lb.	---	---	---	---	48,400	
Flat rating ambient temperature						
Takeoff	87°F (30.5°C)	86°F (30.0°C)	77°F (25°C)	78°F (25.5°C)	86°F (30.0°C)	
Alternate takeoff	86°F (30.0°C)	---	---	---	87°F (30.5°C)	
Maximum continuous					---	

"---" indicates "same as preceding model"
"——" indicates "does not apply"

E23EA-4
Part B
CF6-50 Series

	CF6-50A	CF6-50C	CF6-50D	CF6-50E	CF6-50H
Fuel					
Fuel control, Woodward, GE P/N	9070M55	--	9148M33	--	9070M55
CIT sensor, Woodward, GE P/N	9069M91	--	--	--	--
Fuel pump, GE P/N	9039M45 single-element gear type pump	--	--	--	--
Fuel	Conforming to GE Specification D50TF2 (see Note 7)	--	--	--	--
Oil	Synthetic type conforming to GE Specification D50TF1, Classes A or B. GE Service Bulletin 79-1 lists approved brand oils.				
Ignition System	Two ignition units, GE P/N 910lM52; Two igniter plugs, GE P/N 910lM37	--	--	--	--
Starting					
Starter	AiResearch Model ATS100-350, GE P/N 9014M18	--	--	--	--
Starter valve	AiResearch, GE P/N 9033M46	--	--	--	--
Principle dimensions:					
Length, in. (fan spinner to LPT aft flange fact)	183	--	--	--	--
Width, in. (maximum envelope)	94	--	--	--	--
Height, in. (maximum envelope)	105	--	--	--	--
Weight (dry), lb. (includes basic engine accessories and optional equipment as listed in Manufacturer's engine specification, including condition monitoring instrumentation sensors per GE Specification, GEK 9251	8560	--	8625	--	--
Center of Gravity Location:					
Station, in. (engine only)	223.0 ± 2.0	--	--	--	--
Waterline, in. (engine only)	98.1 ± 1.0	--	--	--	--
Notes	1 through 12	--	--	--	--

```
E23EA-4
Part B
CF6-50 Series
```

	CF6-50A	CF6-50C	CF6-50D	CF6-50E	CF6-50H
Certification basis: FAR33 effective February 1, 1965 as amended by 33-1, 33-2, 33-3, and Special Conditions No. 33-36-EA-9					
Date of Application	5 Sept 1969	9 July 1971	--	2 April 1973	21 Aug 1973
Date T.C. E23EA issued/revised	23 Mar 1972	20 Nov 1973	27 Nov 1972	20 Nov 1973	7 Sept 1973
Production Basis: Production Certificate No. 108	--	--	--	--	--

Import Requirements:

Licensing agreement dated 2 December 1970, revised 8 January 1971, effective 17 June 1971 between General Electric, Cincinnati, Ohio and SNECMA, France, identified as "Production Agreement for CF6-50 Engine for A300B Airbus between General Electric Technical Services Co. Inc. and Societe Nationale d'Etude et de Construction de moteurs d'Aviation" and Licensing agreement dated 20 January 1971, revised 29 January 1971, effective 17 June 1971 between General Electric, Cincinnati, Ohio and M.T.U., Germany, identified as "Production Agreement for CF6-50 Engine for A300B Airbus between General Electric Technical Services Co. Inc. and Motoren and Turbinen Union, Munchen, GMBH" for the production of the General Electric model CF6-50 series turbofan engines and parts in Europe. The engines produced in accordance with these agreements conform to type certificate E23EA, are in condition for safe operation, and have been subjected to a final operational check.

Engine identification plates shall be marked as follows:

1. Manufactured by SNECMA, France.
2. Model CF6-50A or CF6-50C
3. Serial Numbers 455-701 and up
4. Type Certificate Number E23EA
5. Established Rating

CF6-50A	CF6-50C
48,400 TO	50,400 TO
46,300 MC	46,300 MC

For parts, assemblies, or modules produced by SNECMA, France and/or MTU, Germany for use in certificated aircraft, they must be accompanied by a French (if produced by SNECMA) or German (if produced by MTU) certificate containing the following statement and signatures.

This certifies that engine (parts, assemblies, modules, etc.) manufactured by (name and address) and listed here are made to Type Certificate E23EA type design and quality control data accepted by the United States Federal Aviation Administration.

(List articles and serial numbers covered and affix thereto the dated signature of responsible employee of supplier for Director of Quality Control and that of the authorized representative of Airworthiness Authority of Country of Manufacture.)

	CF6-50A	CF6-50C	CF6-50D	CF6-50E	CF6-50H
NOTE 1. Maximum permissible engine rotor speeds:					
Low pressure rotor (N₁), r.p.m.	3982 (116%)	--	--	3999 (116.5%)	3982 (116%)
High pressure rotor (N₂), r.p.m.	10,613 (108%)	--	--	--	--
NOTE 2. Maximum permissible temperatures:					
Turbine exhaust gas temperatures (T5.4): Takeoff (5 min.)	1679°F (915°C)	1715°F (935°C)	1679°F (915°C)	1715°F (935°C)	1679°F (915°C)
Maximum continuous	1607°F (875°C)	--	--	--	--
Maximum for acceleration (2 min.)	1706°F (930°C)	1742°F (950°C)	1706°F (930°C)	1742°F (950°C)	1706°F (930°C)
Starting (max. transient for 10 sec.)	1598°F (870°C)	--	--	--	--
(Additional 10 sec. or total of 20)	1382°F (750°C)	--	--	--	--
(Additional 20 sec. or total of 40)	1247°F (675°C)	--	--	--	--
Refer to CF6 Operating Instructions for time temperature envelope	GEK 28467	--	--	--	--
Oil outlet: Continuous operation	320°F (160°C)	--	--	--	--
Transient operation (Transient operation is limited to 15 minutes)	347°F (175°C)	--	--	--	--

E23EA-4
Part B
CF6-50 Series

	CF6-50A	CF6-50C	CF6-50D	CF6-50E	CF6-50H

NOTE 3. Fuel and oil pressure limits:
Fuel: Minimum at engine pump inlet; 3.5 p.s.i. above absolute fuel vapor pressure, with maximum of 50 p.s.i. above absolute ambient atmospheric pressure.
Oil: At idle, 10 p.s.i.g. minimum. Operating range, 30 to 90 p.s.i.g.
Operating
Instruc-
tions
range
limits   GEK 28467   --   --   --   --

NOTE 4. Accessory drive provisions:

Drive Pad	Rotation	Gear Ratio to Core Speed CF6-50 Series	Torque (in.-lb.) Cont.	Torque (in.-lb.) Static	Static Overhung Moment (in.-lb.)
Starter	CC	0.956	10,800	19,200	400
CSD	CC	0.832	(250 h.p.)	17,400	900
Alternator*	C	-----	-----	-----	1,000
Tachometer (core)**	C	0.409	7	540	3
Hydraulic pump	CC	0.350	(85 h.p.)	7,400	500
Hydraulic pump	CC	0.350	(85 h.p.)	7,400	500

C = Clockwise; CC = Counter-clockwise
* = Alternator DRiven by CSD
** = Tachometer Mounted on and Driven Through Main Lube & Scavenge Pump

NOTE 5. Engine ratings are based on calibrated stand performance under the following conditions:
Fan inlet air at 59°F and 29.92 in. Hg.
GE bellmouth air inlet per GE Drawing 4013106-124, or 4013070-409 (light weight)
No external air bleed or accessory drive power for aircraft accessories.
Fan nozzle configuration defined by GE Drawing 4013157-495.
Jet nozzle configuration defined by GE drawing 4013156-186.
Turbine temperature and engine rotor speed limits not exceeded.
Core engine acceptance test cowling defined by GE Drawing 4013124-021.
Pylon configuration acceptance test cowling defined by GE Drawing 4013124-091.
Stand thrust adjusted for scrubbing drag per Figure A-11 of CF6 Installation Manual GEK 9286.
Engine performance deck R71AEG135 is the prime source of engine performance data throughout the flight envelope.

E23EA-4
Part B
CF6-50 Series

NOTE 6. Maximum permissible air bleed extraction is as follows:

Bleed location	CF6-50A	CF6-50C	CF6-50D	CF6-50E	CF6-50H
Stage 8, Compressor airflow % (normal)	5	--	--	--	--
Stage 8, compressor airflow % (intermittent)*	5.75	--	--	--	--
Compressor discharge					
Steady state at takeoff rating	5	--	--	--	--
Steady state between 80% N_2 and maximum continuous	10	--	--	--	--
During acceleration above 80% N_2	7	--	--	--	--
Operation at 80% N_2 or below	12.5	--	--	--	--
Stage 10	2	--	--	--	--

*The engine manufacturer is to be consulted regarding conditions, number of occurrences and duration of each occurrence within the limitations of: average of 2×10^{-3} occurrences per engine operating hour and a maximum of .5 hour duration per occurrence (cumulative total of 50 hours). Intermittent operation is defined as "dispatch with a bleed system inoperative, or bleed system or engine failure in flight" and should be confined to the physical core speed (N_2) range of 81.5 to 98.5 r.p.m.

NOTE 7. a) Approved fuel conforming to GE Specification D50TF2. MIL-T-5624H, Grades JP-4 or JP-5, ASTM D 1655-65T, Jet A, A1 and B, and ASTM ES-2-74 are consistent with this General Electric Specification. Primary fuel is Jet A, with other fuels listed being acceptable alternates. No fuel control adjustment is required when changing from primary to alternate fuels. A fuel control specific gravity adjustment is required when operating with Avgas to provide proper engine starting characteristics. Consult the Operating Manual for other restrictions when using Avgas.

b) Use of aviation gasoline under emergency conditions is restricted to 3 hours continuous operation at any one time, not to exceed 10 hours total cumulative time during any one hot section inspection period.

NOTE 8. Life limits established for critical rotating components are published in the CF6 Shop Manual, Inspection Section.

```
E23EA-4
PART B
CF6-50 SERIES
```

NOTE 9. Power setting, power checks and control of engine thrust output in all operations is to be based on GE engine charts referring to Fan Speed (N_1). Speed sensors are included in the engine assembly for this purpose.

NOTE 10. The following thrust reverser models are approved in accordance with FAR 33.97 for incorporation on CF6 engine models:

	CF6-50A	CF6-50C	CF6-50D	CF6-50E	CF6-50H
Fan Reverser Model No.	TR-CF6-F3	--	TR-CF6-F6	--	TR-CF6-F3
Turbine Reverser Model No.	TR-CF6-5	--	TR-CF6-7	--	TR-CF6-5

NOTE 11: British Civil Aviation Authority validation of FAA type certification of engine model CF6-50A as detailed herein granted 31 May 1972.

NOTE 12: The following models incorporate the following general characteristics:

CF6-50 Series	Characteristics
-50A	Basic model
-50C	Same as -50A except takeoff rating increased to 50,400 lbs, flat rated to 86°F ambient temperature sea level static and with improved engine parts.
-50D	Same as -50A except the engine is operated to an increased takeoff thrust of 50,400 lbs at a lower flat rated ambient temperature of 77°F sea level static.
-50E	Same as -50C except the engine is operated to increased thrust of 51,800 lbs. at a lower flat rated ambient temperature of 78°F sea level static.
-50H	Same as -50A except takeoff rating increased to 50,400 lbs flat rated to 86°F ambient temperature sea level static with an alternate takeoff rating of 48,400 lbs at a flat rated ambient temperature of 87°F with improved engine parts.

...END...

Appendix 3

Decimal Equivalents

Inch Fraction	Decimal	mm	Inch Fraction	Decimal	mm	Inch Fraction	Decimal	mm
1/64	0.0156	0.397	23/64	0.3594	9.128	45/64	0.7301	17.859
1/32	0.0312	0.794	3/8	0.3750	9.525	23/32	0.7187	18.256
3/64	0.0469	1.191	25/64	0.3906	9.922	47/64	0.7344	18.653
1/16	0.0625	1.587	13/32	0.4062	10.319	3/4	0.7500	19.050
5/64	0.0781	1.984	27/64	0.4219	10.716	49/64	0.7656	19.447
3/32	0.0937	2.381	7/16	0.4375	11.112	25/32	0.7812	19.844
7/64	0.1094	2.778	29/64	0.4531	11.509	51/64	0.7969	20.241
1/8	0.1250	3.175	15/32	0.4687	11.906	13/16	0.8125	20.637
9/64	0.1406	3.572	31/64	0.4844	12.303	53/64	0.8281	21.034
5/32	0.1562	3.969	1/2	0.5000	12.700	27/32	0.8437	21.431
11/64	0.1719	4.366	33/64	0.5156	13.097	55/64	0.8594	21.828
3/16	0.1875	4.762	17/32	0.5312	13.494	7/8	0.8750	22.225
13/64	0.2031	5.159	35/64	0.5469	13.891	57/64	0.8906	22.622
7/32	0.2187	5.556	9/16	0.5625	14.288	29/32	0.9062	23.019
15/64	0.2344	5.953	37/64	0.5781	14.686	59/64	0.9219	23.416
1/4	0.2500	6.350	19/32	0.5937	15.081	15/16	0.9375	23.812
17/64	0.2656	6.747	39/64	0.6094	15.478	61/64	0.9531	24.209
9/32	0.2812	7.144	5/8	0.6250	15.875	31/32	0.9687	24.606
19/64	0.2969	7.540	41/64	0.6406	16.272	63/64	0.9844	25.003
5/16	0.3125	7.937	21/32	0.6562	16.669	1	1.0000	25.400
21/64	0.3281	8.334	43/64	0.6719	17.065			
11/32	0.3437	8.731	11/16	0.6875	17.462			

Drill Sizes/Decimal Equivalents

Drill No.	Dia. In.	Drill No.	Dia. In.	Drill No.	Dia. In.	Drill No.	Dia. In.	Drill No.	Dia. In.
A	0.234	G	0.261	L	0.290	Q	0.332	V	0.377
B	0.238	H	0.266	M	0.295	R	0.339	W	0.386
C	0.242	I	0.272	N	0.302	S	0.348	X	0.397
D	0.246	J	0.277	O	0.316	T	0.358	Y	0.404
E	0.250	K	0.281	P	0.323	U	0.368	Z	0.413
F	0.257								

Drill No.	Dia. In.	Drill No.	Dia. In.	Drill No.	Dia. In.	Drill No.	Dia. In.	Drill No.	Dia. In.
1	0.2280	17	0.1730	33	0.1130	49	0.0730	65	0.0350
2	0.2210	18	0.1695	34	0.1110	50	0.0700	66	0.0330
3	0.2130	19	0.1660	35	0.1100	51	0.0670	67	0.0320
4	0.2090	20	0.1610	36	0.1065	52	0.0635	68	0.0310
5	0.2055	21	0.1590	37	0.1040	53	0.0595	69	0.0292
6	0.2040	22	0.1570	38	0.1015	54	0.0550	70	0.0280
7	0.2010	23	0.1540	39	0.0995	55	0.0520	71	0.0260
8	0.1990	24	0.1520	40	0.0980	56	0.0465	72	0.0250
9	0.1960	25	0.1495	41	0.0960	57	0.0430	73	0.0240
10	0.1935	26	0.1470	42	0.0935	58	0.0420	74	0.0225
11	0.1910	27	0.1440	43	0.0890	59	0.0410	75	0.0210
12	0.1890	28	0.1405	44	0.0860	60	0.0400	76	0.0200
13	0.1850	29	0.1360	45	0.0820	61	0.0390	77	0.0180
14	0.1820	30	0.1285	46	0.0810	62	0.0380	78	0.0160
15	0.1800	31	0.1200	47	0.0785	63	0.0370	79	0.0145
16	0.1770	32	0.1160	48	0.0760	64	0.0360	80	0.0135

Screw Dia. = (Screw No. × 0.013) + 0.060

Temperature Conversions — Fahrenheit to Celsius

Degrees Fahrenheit to Degrees Celsius*		°C = [5/9 (°F + 40)] – 40
Values for Interpolation in the Following Table		
Degrees Fahrenheit — 1 2 3 4 5 6 7 8 9		
Degrees Celsius — 0.56 1.11 1.67 2.22 2.78 3.33 3.89 4.44 5.00		
*All decimals in the tables are repeating decimals — 37.78 is actually 37.777 ...		

°F	°C	°F	°C	°F	°C	°F	°C	°F	°C	°F	°C	°F	°C
−40	−40.00	25	−3.89	70	21.11	175	79.44	400	204.44	650	343.33	1,500	815.56
−38	−38.89	26	−3.33	71	21.67	180	82.22	405	207.22	660	348.89	1,550	843.33
−36	−37.78	27	−2.78	72	22.22	185	85.00	410	210.00	670	354.44	1,600	871.11
−34	−36.67	28	−2.22	73	22.78	190	87.78	415	212.78	680	360.00	1,650	898.89
−32	−35.56	29	−1.67	74	23.33	195	90.55	420	215.56	690	365.56	1,700	926.67
−30	−34.44	30	−1.11	75	23.89	200	93.33	425	218.33	700	371.11	1,750	954.44
−28	−33.33	31	−0.56	76	24.44	205	96.11	430	221.11	710	376.67	1,800	982.22
−26	−32.22	32	0.00	77	25.00	210	98.89	435	223.89	720	382.22	1,850	1,010.00
−24	−31.11	33	+0.56	78	25.56	215	101.67	440	226.67	730	387.78	1,900	1,037.78
−22	−30.00	34	1.11	79	26.11	220	104.44	445	229.44	740	393.33	1,950	1,065.56
−20	−28.89	35	1.67	80	26.67	225	107.22	450	232.22	750	398.89	2,000	1,093.33
−18	−27.78	36	2.22	81	27.22	230	110.00	455	235.00	760	404.44	2,050	1,121.11
−16	−26.67	37	2.78	82	27.78	235	112.78	460	237.78	770	410.00	2,100	1,148.89
−14	−25.56	38	3.33	83	28.33	240	115.56	465	240.55	780	415.56	2,150	1,176.67
−12	−24.44	39	3.89	84	28.89	245	118.33	470	243.33	790	421.11	2,200	1,204.44
−10	−23.33	40	4.44	85	29.44	250	121.11	475	246.11	800	426.67	2,250	1,232.22
−8	−22.22	41	5.00	86	30.00	255	123.89	480	248.89	810	432.22	2,300	1,260.00
−6	−21.11	42	5.56	87	30.56	260	126.67	485	251.67	820	437.78	2,350	1,287.78
−4	−20.00	43	6.11	88	31.11	265	129.44	490	254.44	830	443.33	2,400	1,315.56
−2	−18.89	44	6.67	89	31.67	270	132.22	495	257.22	840	448.89	2,450	1,343.33
0	−17.78	45	7.22	90	32.22	275	135.00	500	260.00	850	454.44	2,500	1,371.11
+1	−17.22	46	7.78	91	32.78	280	137.78	505	262.78	860	460.00	2,550	1,398.89
2	−16.67	47	8.33	92	33.33	285	140.55	510	265.56	870	465.56	2,600	1,426.67
3	−16.11	48	8.89	93	33.89	290	143.33	515	268.33	880	471.11	2,650	1,454.44
4	−15.56	49	9.44	94	34.44	295	146.11	520	271.11	890	476.67	2,700	1,482.22
5	−15.00	50	10.00	95	35.00	300	148.89	525	273.89	900	482.22	2,750	1,510.00
6	−14.44	51	10.56	96	35.56	305	151.67	530	276.67	910	487.78	2,800	1,537.78
7	−13.89	52	11.11	97	36.11	310	154.44	535	279.44	920	493.33	2,850	1,565.59
8	−13.33	53	11.67	98	36.67	315	157.22	540	282.22	930	498.89	2,900	1,593.33
9	−12.78	54	12.22	99	37.22	320	160.00	545	285.00	940	504.44	2,950	1,621.11
10	−12.22	55	12.78	100	37.78	325	162.78	550	287.78	905	510.00		
11	−11.67	56	13.33	105	40.55	330	165.56	555	290.55	960	516.56		
12	−11.11	57	13.89	110	43.33	335	168.33	560	293.33	970	521.11		
13	−10.56	58	14.44	115	46.11	340	171.11	565	296.11	980	526.67		
14	−10.00	59	15.00	120	48.89	345	173.89	570	298.89	990	532.22		
15	−9.44	60	15.56	125	51.67	350	176.67	575	301.67	1,000	537.78		
16	−8.89	61	16.11	130	54.44	355	179.44	580	304.44	1,050	565.56		
17	−8.33	62	16.67	135	57.22	360	182.22	585	307.22	1,100	593.33		
18	−7.78	63	17.22	140	60.00	365	185.00	590	310.00	1,150	621.11		
19	−7.22	64	17.78	145	62.78	370	187.78	595	312.78	1,200	648.89		
20	−6.67	65	18.33	150	65.56	375	190.55	600	315.56	1,250	676.67		
21	−6.11	66	18.89	155	68.33	380	193.33	610	321.11	1,300	704.44		
22	−5.56	67	19.44	160	71.11	385	196.11	620	326.67	1,350	732.22		
23	−5.00	68	20.00	165	73.89	390	198.89	630	332.22	1,400	760.00		
24	−4.44	69	20.56	170	76.67	395	201.67	640	337.78	1,450	787.78		

Temperature Conversions — Celsius to Fahrenheit

Degrees Celsius to Degrees Fahrenheit				°F = [9/5 (°C + 40)] − 40			
Values for Interpolation in the Following Table							
Degrees Celsius — 1 2 3 4 5 6 7 8 9							
Degrees Fahrenheit — 1.8 3.6 5.4 7.2 9.0 10.8 12.6 14.4 16.2							

°C	°F	°C	°F	°C	°F	°C	°F	°C	°F	°C	°F	°C	°F
−40	−40.0	0	32.0	30	86.0	100	212	250	482	400	752	1,000	1,832
−38	−36.4	+1	33.8	31	87.8	105	221	255	491	405	761	1,050	1,922
−36	−32.8	2	35.6	32	89.6	110	230	260	500	410	770	1,100	2,012
−34	−29.2	3	37.4	33	91.4	115	239	265	509	415	779	1,150	2,101
−32	−25.6	4	39.2	34	93.2	120	248	270	518	420	788	1,200	2,192
−30	−22.0	5	41.0	35	95.0	125	257	275	527	425	797	1,250	2,282
−28	−18.4	6	42.8	36	96.8	130	266	280	536	430	806	1,300	2,373
−26	−14.8	7	44.6	37	98.6	135	275	285	545	435	815	1,350	2,462
−24	−11.2	8	46.4	38	100.4	140	284	290	554	440	824	1,400	2,552
−22	−7.6	9	48.2	39	102.2	145	293	295	563	445	833	1,450	2,642
−20	−4.0	10	50.0	40	104.0	150	302	300	572	450	842	1,500	2,732
−19	−2.2	11	51.8	41	105.8	155	311	305	581	455	851	1,550	2,822
−18	−0.4	12	53.6	42	107.6	160	320	310	590	460	860	1,600	2,912
−17	+1.4	13	55.4	43	109.4	165	329	315	599	465	869	1,650	3,002
−16	3.2	14	57.2	44	111.2	170	338	320	608	470	878	1,700	3,092
−15	5.0	15	59.0	45	113.0	175	347	325	617	475	887	1,750	3,182
−14	6.8	16	60.8	46	114.8	180	356	330	626	480	896	1,800	3,272
−13	8.6	17	62.6	47	116.6	185	365	335	635	485	905	1,850	3,362
−12	10.4	18	64.4	48	118.4	190	374	340	644	490	914	1,900	3,452
−11	12.2	19	66.2	49	120.2	195	383	345	653	495	923	1,950	3,542
−10	14.0	20	68.0	50	122.0	200	392	350	662	500	932	2,000	3,632
−9	15.8	21	69.8	55	131.0	205	401	355	671	550	1,022	2,050	3,722
−8	17.6	22	71.6	60	140.0	210	410	360	680	600	1,112	2,100	3,812
−7	19.4	23	73.4	65	149.0	215	419	365	689	650	1,202	2,150	3,902
−6	21.2	24	75.2	70	158.0	220	428	370	698	700	1,292	2,200	3,992
−5	23.0	25	77.0	75	167.0	225	437	375	707	750	1,382	2,250	4,082
−4	24.8	26	78.8	80	176.0	230	446	380	716	800	1,472	2,300	4,172
−3	26.6	27	80.6	85	185.0	235	455	385	725	850	1,562	2,350	4,262
−2	28.4	28	82.4	90	194.0	240	464	390	734	900	1,652	2,400	4,352
−1	30.2	29	84.2	95	203.0	245	473	395	743	950	1,742	2,450	4,442

Conversion Factors

Multiply	By	To Obtain	Multiply	By	To Obtain
Amperes	1.04×10^{-5}	Faradays/Sec.	Grams/Liter	0.122	Ounces/Gallon (Troy)
Amperes/Sq. Ft.	0.00108	Amperes/Sq. Cm.	Grams/Liter	0.134	Ounces/Gallon (Avdp)
Ampere-hours	3,600	Coulombs	Grams/Liter	1,000	Parts Per Million
Amperes/Sq. Cm.	929	Amperes/Sq. Ft.	Grams/Liter	2.44	Pennyweights/Gallon
Angstrom Units	3.94×10^{-9}	Inches	Inches	2.54	Centimeters
Angstrom Units	1×10^{-10}	Meters	Inches	1/12	Feet
Angstrom Units	1×10^{-4}	Microns	Inches	1,000	Mils
Centimeters	0.394	Inches	Kilograms	15,432.4	Grains
Centimeters	393.7	Mils	Kilograms	1,000	Grams
Centimeters	0.0328	Feet	Kilograms	35.27	Ounces (Avdp)
Circular Mils	5.07×10^{-6}	Sq. Centimeters	Kilograms	32.15	Ounces (Troy)
Circular Mils	7.85×10^{-7}	Sq. Inches	Kilograms	643.01	Pennyweights
Cubic Centimeters	3.53×10^{-5}	Cubic Feet	Kilograms	2.205	Pounds (Avdp)
Cubic Centimeters	0.061	Cubic Inches	Kilograms	2.679	Pounds (Troy)
Cubic Centimeters	2.64×10^{-4}	Gallons	Liters	1,000.027	Cubic Centimeters
Cubic Centimeters	9.9997×10^{-4}	Liters	Liters	0.035	Cubic Feet
Cubic Centimeters	0.0338	Ounces (Fluid)	Liters	61.025	Cubic Inches
Cubic Centimeters	0.0021	Pints	Liters	0.264	Gallons
Cubic Centimeters	0.0011	Quarts (Liquid)	Liters	33.81	Ounces (Fluid)
Cubic Feet	28.317	Cubic Centimeters	Liters	2.11	Pints
Cubic Feet	1.728	Cubic Inches	Liters	1.057	Quarts (Liquid)
Cubic Feet	7.48	Gallons	Meters	100	Centimeters
Cubic Feet	28.32	Liters	Meters	3.281	Feet
Cubic Feet	29.92	Quarts	Meters	39.37	Inches
Cubic Feet of Water 60°F (16°C)	62.37	Pounds	Meters	0.001	Kilometers
			Meters	1.094	Yards
Cubic Inches	16.39	Cubic Centimeters	Microhms	1×10^{-12}	Megohms
Cubic Inches	0.0043	Ounces (Fluid)	Microhms	1×10^{-6}	Ohms
Cubic Inches	0.0173	Quarts (Liquid)	Microns	3.9×10^{-5}	Inches
Faradays	9.65×10^{-4}	Coulombs	Microns	0.001	Millimeters
Faradays/Second	96,500	Amperes	Mile	1.15	Knots
Feet	30.48	Centimeters	Miles per hour (mph)	1.467	Feet/Second
Feet	12	Inches	Milligrams	0.0154	Grains
Feet	0.3048	Meters	Milligrams	0.001	Grams
Feet/Second	0.6817	Miles Per Hour	Milligrams	1×10^{-6}	Kilograms
Gallons	4	Quarts (Liquid)	Milligrams	3.5×10^{-5}	Ounces (Avdp)
Gallons	3,785.4	Cubic Centimeters	Milligrams	3.215×10^{-5}	Ounces (Troy)
Gallons	0.1337	Cubic Feet	Milligrams	6.43×10^{-4}	Pennyweights
Gallons	231	Cubic Inches	Milligrams	2.21×10^{-6}	Pounds (Avdp)
Gallons	3,785	Liters	Milligrams	2.68×10^{-6}	Pounds (Troy)
Gallons	128	Ounces (Fluid)	Milligrams/Liter	1.0	Parts Per Million
Gallons (Imperial)	1.201	Gallons	Milliliters	1.000027	Cubic Centimeters
Gallons	0.8327	Gallons (Imperial)	Milliliters	0.061	Cubic Inches
Gallons	8	Pints	Milliliters	0.001	Liters
Gallons	8.31	Pounds (Avdp of Water at 62°F (17°C))	Milliliters	0.034	Ounces (Fluid)
			Millimeters	0.1	Centimeters
Grains	0.0648	Grams	Millimeters	0.039	Inches
Grains	0.0023	Ounces (Avdp)	Millimeters	0.001	Meters
Grains	0.0021	Ounces (Troy)	Millimeters	1,000	Microns
Grains	0.0417	Pennyweights (Troy)	Mils	0.0025	Centimeters
Grains	1/7,000	Pounds (Avdp)	Mils	0.001	Inches
Grains	1/5,760	Pounds (Troy)	Mils	25.4	Microns
Grams	15.43	Grains	Ounces (Avdp)	437.5	Grains
Grams	1,000	Milligrams	Ounces (Avdp)	28.35	Grams
Grams	0.0353	Ounces (Avdp)	Ounces (Avdp)	0.911	Ounces (Troy)
Grams	0.0321	Ounces (Troy)	Ounces (Avdp)	18.23	Pennyweights
Grams	0.643	Pennyweights	Ounces (Avdp)	1/16	Pounds (Avdp)
Grams	0.0022	Pounds (Avdp)	Ounces (Avdp)	0.076	Pounds (Troy)
Grams	0.0027	Pounds (Troy)	Ounces/Gallon (Avdp)	7.5	Grams/Liter

Conversion Factors, cont'd.

Multiply	By	To Obtain	Multiply	By	To Obtain
Ounces (Troy)	480	Grains	Pounds (Avdp)	14.58	Ounces (Troy)
Ounces (Troy)	31.1	Grams	Pounds (Avdp)	291.67	Pennyweights
Ounces (Troy)	31,103.5	Milligrams	Pounds (Avdp)	1.215	Pounds (Troy)
Ounces (Troy)	1.097	Ounces (Avdp)	Pounds (Troy)	5,760	Grains
Ounces (Troy)	20	Pennyweights	Pounds (Troy)	373.24	Grams
Ounces (Troy)	0.069	Pounds (Avdp)	Pounds (Troy)	0.373	Kilograms
Ounces (Troy)	1/12	Pounds (Troy)	Pounds (Troy)	13.17	Ounces (Avdp)
Ounces/Gallon (Troy)	8.2	Grams/Liter	Pounds (Troy)	12	Ounces (Troy)
Ounces (Fluid)	29.57	Cubic Centimeters	Pounds (Troy)	240	Pennyweights
Ounces (Fluid)	1.80	Cubic Inches	Pounds (Troy)	0.823	Pounds (Avdp)
Ounces (Fluid)	1/128	Gallons	Pounds of Water 62°F (17°C)	0.016	Cubic Feet
Ounces (Fluid)	0.0296	Liters	Pounds of Water 62°F (17°C)	27.68	Cubic Inches
Ounces (Fluid)	29.57	Milliliters			
Ounces (Fluid)	1/16	Pints	Pounds of Water 62°F (17°)	0.1198	Gallons
Ounces (Fluid)	0.031	Quarts			
Ounces/Gallon (Fluid)	7.7	CC/Liter	Quarts (Liquid)	946.4	Cubic Centimeters
Pennyweights	24	Grains	Quarts (Liquid)	57.75	Cubic Inches
Pennyweights	1.56	Grams	Quarts (Liquid)	0.033	Cubic Feet
Pennyweights	1,555	Milligrams	Quarts (Liquid)	0.25	Gallons
Pennyweights	0.0549	Ounces (Avdp)	Quarts (Liquid)	0.946	Liters
Pennyweights	0.05	Ounces (Troy)	Quarts (Liquid)	32	Ounces (Fluid)
Pennyweights	0.0034	Pounds (Avdp)	Quarts (Liquid)	2	Pints
Pennyweights	0.0042	Pounds (Troy)	Square Centimeters	127.32	Circular Millimeters
Pennyweights/Gallon	0.41	Grams/Liter	Square Centimeters	197,350	Circular Mils
Pints	473.2	Cubic Centimeters	Square Centimeters	0.001	Square Feet
Pints	0.017	Cubic Feet	Square Centimeters	0.155	Square Inches
Pints	28.88	Cubic Inches	Square Centimeters	100	Square Millimeters
Pints	0.125	Gallons	Square Feet	929.03	Square Centimeters
Pints	0.473	Liters	Square Feet	144	Square Inches
Pints	16	Ounces (Fluid)	Square Inches	1.2732	Circular Mils
Pints	0.5	Quarts	Square Inches	6.45	Square Centimeters
Pounds (Avdp)	7,000	Grains	Square Inches	1/144	Square Feet
Pounds (Avdp)	453.6	Grams	Square Inches	1×10^{-6}	Square Mils
Pounds (Avdp)	0.454	Kilograms	Square Inches	1/1,296	Square Yards
Pounds (Avdp)	16	Ounces (Avdp)			

Appendix 4

Gas Turbine-Powered Aircraft Familiarization

The civil aircraft included in this appendix have been selected because they are among the most common in commercial and general aviation. Although some of the aircraft included are no longer in production, many remain in service for an extended time. Other aircraft are re-engined with newer models from time to time, so the information in the listing changes slightly over time. A space is provided at the end of the appendix for new entries.

Note: A key to the abbreviations appears near the end of this appendix.

Fixed Wing Aircraft

* Indicates an alternate engine for the same aircraft

AIRCRAFT MANUFACTURER	ENGINE MANUFACTURER	DESIGNATION	NUMBER AND TYPE OF ENGINES
Aerospatiale/BAC			
Concorde	Rolls Royce/SNECMA	Olympus 593	4 (TJ)
Airbus Industries (EADS), France			
A300	General Electric	CF6	(2) TF
	*Pratt & Whitney	PW4000	(2) TF
A310	General Electric	CF6	(2) TF
	*Pratt & Whitney	PW4000	(2) TF
A318	CFM International	CFM56	(2) TF
	*Pratt & Whitney	PW6000	(2) TF
A319	Int'l Aero Engines	V2500	(2) TF
	*General Electric	CFM56	(2) TF
A320/321	CFM International	CFM56	(2) TF
	*Int'l Aero Engines	V2500	(2) TF
A330	General Electric	CF6	(2) TF
	*Pratt & Whitney	PW4000	(2) TF
	*Rolls-Royce	Trent 700	(2) TF
A340	CFM International	CFM56	(4) TF
	*Rolls-Royce	Trent 500	(4) TF
A380	G.E. & P&W	GP7000	(4) TF
	*Rolls-Royce	Trent 900	(4) TF
Antonov Aero Corporation, Russia			
An-70	Progressive	D-27	(4) PF
An-218	Progressive	D-18	(2) TF
An-225	Progressive	D-18T	(6) TF
Avions de Transport Regional (ATR), France			
ATR 42, 52	Pratt & Whitney (Canada)	PW121/127	(2) TP
ATR 72	Pratt & Whitney (Canada)	PW124/127	(2) TP
ATR 82	Rolls-Royce	AE2100	(2) TP

AIRCRAFT MANUFACTURER	ENGINE MANUFACTURER	DESIGNATION	NUMBER AND TYPE OF ENGINES
Beriev Aircraft Company, Russia			
Be-32	Pratt & Whitney (Canada)	PKGA	(2) TP
Be-200	Progress	D-436	(2) TP
Boeing Company, Renton WA, USA			
707 early models	Pratt & Whitney	JT3C & JT4C	(4) TJ
707	Pratt & Whitney	JT3D	(4) TF
717	Rolls-Royce/BMW	BR715	(2) TF
727	Pratt & Whitney	JT8D	(3) TF
737	Pratt & Whitney	JT8D	(2) TF
	*CFM International	CFM56	(2) TF
747	Pratt & Whitney	JT9D/PW4000	(4) TF
	*General Electric	CF6	(4) TF
	*General Electric	GEnx	(4) TF
	*Rolls-Royce	RB211/Trent	(4) TF
757	Pratt & Whitney	PW2000	(2) TF
	*Rolls-Royce	RB211	(2) TF
767	Pratt & Whitney	JT9D/PW4000	(2) TF
	*General Electric	CF6	(2) TF
	*Rolls-Royce	RB211	(2) TF
	*Rolls-Royce	Trent 800	(2) TF
777	Pratt & Whitney	PW4000	(2) TF
	*Rolls-Royce	Trent 800	(2) TF
	*General Electric	GE-90	(2) TF
787	General Electric	GEnx	(2) TF
	*Rolls-Royce	Trent 1000	(2) TF
Boeing Business Jet 1,2,3	CFM Int'l	CFM56	(2) TF
Boeing Corp. (Longbeach), USA			
DC-8	Pratt & Whitney	JT3D	(4) TF
	*CFM International	CFM56	(4) TF
DC-9	Pratt & Whitney	JT8D	(2) TF
DC-10	General Electric	CF6	(3) TF
	*Pratt & Whitney	JT9D	(3) TF
MD-11	Pratt & Whitney	PW4000	(3) TF
	*General Electric	CF6	(3) TF
MD-80 to MD-88	Pratt & Whitney	JT8D	(2) TF
MD-90	Int'l Aero Engines	V2500	(2) TF

AIRCRAFT MANUFACTURER	ENGINE MANUFACTURER	DESIGNATION	NUMBER AND TYPE OF ENGINES
Bombardier Aerospace Corporation, Canada			
Bombardier 415	Pratt & Whitney (Canada)	PW123	(2) TP
C110	General Electric	CF34	(2) TF
C130	General Electric	CF34	(2) TF
CRJ200	General Electric	CF34	(2) TF
CRJ700	General Electric	CF34	(2) TF
CRJ900	General Electric	CF34	(2) TF
CRJ1000	General Electric	CF34	(2) TF
Dash-6	Pratt & Whitney (Canada)	PT6A	(2) TP
Dash-7	Pratt & Whitney (Canada)	PT6A	(4) TP
Q100, Q200, Q 300), Dash-8	Pratt & Whitney (Canada)	PW123	(4) TP
Q400, Dash-8	Pratt & Whitney (Canada)	PW150	(4) TP
Bombardier Aerospace (Shorts)			
SD3	Pratt & Whitney (Canada)	PT6A	(2) TP
Bombardier Aerospace, USA			
Learjet 24 to 29	General Electric	CJ-610	(2) TJ
Learjet 35 to 56	Honeywell	TFE731	(2) TF
Learjet 60	Pratt & Whitney (Canada)	PW305	(2) TF
Learjet 85	Pratt & Whitney (Canada)	PW307	(2) TF
Bombardier (Canadair) Corporation (Canada)			
Challenger 300	Honeywell	HFT 7000	(2) TF
Challenger 600	Honeywell	ALF-502	(2) TF
Challenger 601	General Electric	CF34	(2) TF
Challenger 604	General Electric	CF34	(2) TF
Challenger 605	General Electric	CF34	(2) TF
Challenger 800 series	General Electric	CF34	(2) TF
Corporate Jetliner	General Electric	CF34	(2) TF
CRJ200	General Electric	CF34	(2) TF
CRJ700	General Electric	CF34	(2) TF
CRJ900	General Electric	CF34	(2) TF
CRJ1000	General Electric	CF34	(2) TF
Global 5000	Rolls-Royce	BR710	(2) TF
Global Express	Rolls-Royce	BR710	(2) TF

AIRCRAFT MANUFACTURER	ENGINE MANUFACTURER	DESIGNATION	NUMBER AND TYPE OF ENGINES
British Aerospace Corporation, UK			
ATP	Pratt & Whitney (Canada)	PW120	(2) TP
Avro RJ70	Honeywell	LF507	(4) TF
Avro RJ85	Honeywell	LF507	(4) TF
Avro RJ100	Honeywell	LF507	(4) TF
BAC-111	Rolls-Royce	Spey	(2) TF
BAe 125	Honeywell	TFE731	(2) TF
BAe 146	Honeywell	ALF 502	(4) TF
HS 748	Rolls-Royce	Dart	(2) TP
Jetstream 31,32,41	Honeywell	TPE331	(2) TP
CASA Corporation (EADS), Spain			
C212	Honeywell	TPE331	(2) TP
CN235	General Electric	CT7	(2) TP
Cessna Corporation, USA			
Citation CJ1/2/3/4	Williams-R/R	FJ44	(2) TF
Citation Columbus	Pratt & Whitney (Canada)	PW810	(2) TF
Citation X	Rolls-Royce	AE3007	(2) TF
Citation XLS	Pratt & Whitney (Canada)	PW545	(2) TF
Citation Bravo	Pratt & Whitney (Canada)	PW530	(2) TF
Citation Encore	Pratt & Whitney (Canada)	PW535	(2) TF
Citation Excel	Pratt & Whitney (Canada)	PW545	(2) TF
Citation Jet (CJ1,CJ2)	Williams Int'l.	FJ44	(2) TF
Citation Mustang	Pratt & Whitney (Canada)	PW615	(2) TF
Citation Ultra	Pratt & Whitney (Canada)	JT15D	(2) TF
Citation Sovereign	Pratt & Whitney (Canada)	PW306	(2) TF
Caravan Series	Pratt & Whitney (Canada)	PT6A	(1) TP
Cirrus Design Corporation, USA			
Cirrus Vision SJ50	Williams	FJ33	(2) TF
Convair Corporation			
Convair 540	Rolls-Royce	501D	(2) TP
Daimler-Chrysler Corp., Germany			
DO 128	Pratt & Whitney (Canada)	PT6A	(2) TP
DO 228	Honeywell	TPE331	(2) TP
DO 328	Pratt & Whitney (Canada)	PW119	(2) TP

AIRCRAFT MANUFACTURER	ENGINE MANUFACTURER	DESIGNATION	NUMBER AND TYPE OF ENGINES
Dassault Corporation, France			
Falcon 7X	Pratt & Whitney (Canada)	PW307	(3) TF
Falcon 10	Honeywell	TFE731	(2) TF
Falcon 20F	General Electric	CF-700	(2) TF
Falcon 50 /100	Honeywell	TFE731	(2) TF
Falcon 900	Honeywell	TFE731	(3) TF
Falcon 2000	LHTEC	CFE738	(2) TF
	*Pratt & Whitney (Canada)	PW308	(2) TF
Diamond Aircraft, Canada			
D-Jet	Williams	FJ33	(2) TF
Eclipse Aviation, USA			
Eclipse 400	Pratt & Whitney (Canada)	PW615	(2) TF
Eclipse 500	Pratt & Whitney (Canada)	PW615	(2) TF
Embraer Corporation, Brazil			
EMB 110/111/121	Pratt & Whitney (Canada)	PT6A	(2) TP
EMB 120	Pratt & Whitney (Canada)	PW118	(2) TP
EMB 170	General Electric	CF34	(2) TF
EMB 190	General Electric	CF34	(2) TF
EMB 195	General Electric	CF34	(2) TF
ERJ 135	Rolls-Royce	AE3000	(2) TF
ERJ 140	Rolls-Royce	AE3000	(2) TF
ERJ 145	Rolls-Royce	AE3000	(2) TF
Legacy 450	Honeywell	HTF7500	(2) TF
Legacy 500	Honeywell	HTF7500	(2) TF
Legacy 600	Rolls-Royce	AE3007	(2) TF
Legacy Shuttle	Rolls-Royce	AE3007	(2) TF
Phenam 100	Pratt & Whitney (Canada)	PW617	(2) TF
Phenam 300	Pratt & Whitney (Canada)	PW535	(2) TF
Emivest Aerospace Corp., USA			
SJ 30	Williams-R/R	FJ44	(2) TF

AIRCRAFT MANUFACTURER	ENGINE MANUFACTURER	DESIGNATION	NUMBER AND TYPE OF ENGINES
Fairchild Dornier Industries, Germany			
Dornier 328	Pratt & Whitney (Canada)	PW119	(2) TP
Envoy 3	Pratt & Whitney (Canada)	PW306	(2) TF
Envoy 7	General Electric	CF34	(2) TF
FH 227	Rolls-Royce	Dart	(2) TP
Fairchild USA Industries, USA			
Merlin 23	Honeywell	TPE331	(2) TP
Metro 3, 23	Honeywell	TPE331	(2) TP
Fokker Corporation, Netherlands			
Fokker F27	Rolls-Royce	Dart	(2) TP
Fokker F50	Pratt & Whitney (Canada)	PW125/127	(2) TP
Fokker F60	Pratt & Whitney (Canada)	PW127	(2) TP
Fokker 70	Rolls-Royce	TAY	(2) TF
Fokker 100	Rolls-Royce	TAY	(2) TF
Grob Aerospace, Germany			
G 140	Rolls-Royce	RR 250	(1) TP
Grob SP	Williams	FJ44	(2) TF
General Dynamics Gulfstream, USA			
Gulfstream I	Rolls-Royce	Dart	(2) TP
Gulfstream II, III	Rolls-Royce	Spey	(2) TF
G150	Honeywell	HTF7500	(2) TF
G200	Pratt & Whitney	PW306	(2) TF
G250	Honeywell	HTF7500	(2) TF
G350	Rolls-Royce	TAY	(2) TF
G450	Rolls-Royce	TAY	(2) TF
G500	Rolls-Royce	BR710	(2) TF
G550	Rolls-Royce	BR710	(2) TF
G650	Rolls-Royce	BR725	(2) TF
Hawker Beech Aircraft, USA			
Beech 1900	Pratt & Whitney (Canada)	PT6A	(2) TP

AIRCRAFT MANUFACTURER	ENGINE MANUFACTURER	DESIGNATION	NUMBER AND TYPE OF ENGINES
Hawker (Beechcraft) Corporation, USA			
B-99	Pratt & Whitney (Canada)	PT6A	(2) TP
Beech 1900	Pratt & Whitney (Canada)	PT6A	(2) TP
Hawker 400	Pratt & Whitney (Canada)	JT15	(2) TF
Hawker 750	Honeywell	TFE731	(2) TF
Hawker 800	Honeywell	TFE731	(2) TF
Hawker 850	Honeywell	TFE731	(2) TF
Hawker 900	Honeywell	TFE 731	(2) TF
Hawker 4000	Pratt & Whitney (Canada)	PW308	(2) TF
KingAir 350	Pratt & Whitney (Canada)	PT6A	(2) TP
KingAir B200	Pratt & Whitney (Canada)	PT6A	(2) TP
KingAir C90	Pratt & Whitney (Canada)	PT6A	(2) TP
Premier I and II	Williams	FJ44	(2) TF
Super King 300	Pratt & Whitney (Canada)	PT6A	(2) TP
Honda Aircraft, USA			
Honda Jet	GE/Honda	HF120	(2) TF
Ilyushin Corporation, Russia			
IL 96	Perm	PS-90	(4) TF
	*Pratt & Whitney	PW2000	(4) TF
IL 114	Klimov	TV117	(2) TP
Indonesian Aerospace, Indonesia			
N250	Rolls-Royce	AE2100	(2) TP
Lockheed Corporation, USA			
Jetstar I	Pratt & Whitney	JT12	(4) TJ
Jetstar II	Honeywell	TFE731	(4) TF
Hercules (C-130)	Rolls-Royce	T-56	(4) TP
Hercules II	Rolls-Royce	AE2100	(4) TP
Tristar L1011	Rolls-Royce	RB211	(3) TF
Mitsubishi Corporation, Japan			
MRJ70	Pratt & Whitney (Canada)	PW121	(2) TP
MRJ90	Pratt & Whitney (Canada)	PW121	(2) TP
MU-2	Honeywell	TPE331	(2) TP

AIRCRAFT MANUFACTURER	ENGINE MANUFACTURER	DESIGNATION	NUMBER AND TYPE OF ENGINES
Nextant Aerospace, USA			
400 NXT	Williams	FJ44	(2) TF
People's Republic of China			
Xinzhou-60	Pratt & Whitney (Canada)	PW127	(2) TP
Yun-12	Pratt & Whitney (Canada)	PT6A	(2) TP
Piaggio Aero Industries, Italy			
P166	Pratt & Whitney (Canada)	PT6A	(2) TP
P180	Pratt & Whitney (Canada)	PT6A	(2) TP
Pilatus Corporation, Switzerland			
PC-6	Pratt & Whitney (Canada)	PT6A	(2) TP
PC-12	Pratt & Whitney (Canada)	PT6A	(1) TP
Piper Aircraft, USA			
Piper Jet	Williams	FJ44	(2) TF
Piper Corporation, USA			
Cheyenne I, II, III	Pratt & Whitney (Canada)	PT6A	(2) TP
Cheyenne 400	Honeywell	TPE331	(2) TP
Meridian PA-46	Pratt & Whitney	PT6A	(2) TP
Turbine Malibu	Pratt & Whitney (Canada)	PT6A	(2) TP
Reims Aviation, USA			
Cessna F406 (Caravan)	Pratt & Whitney (Canada)	PT6A	(2) TP
Saab Corporation, Sweden			
Saab 340	General Electric	CT7	(2) TP
Saab 2000	Allison, R/R	AE2100	(2) TP
Sabreliner Corporation, USA			
Sabreliner 40/65	Honeywell	TFE731	(2) TF
Sabreliner 60	Pratt & Whitney (Canada)	JT12	(2) TJ
Sabreliner 75/85	General Electric	CF700	(2) TF
Socata (EADS), France			
TBM 700	Pratt & Whitney (Canada)	PT6A	(1) TP
TBM 850	Pratt & Whitney (Canada)	PT6A	(1) TP

AIRCRAFT MANUFACTURER	ENGINE MANUFACTURER	DESIGNATION	NUMBER AND TYPE OF ENGINES
Spectrum Aeronautical, USA			
S.33	Williams	FJ33	(2) TF
S.40	GE/Honda	HF120	(2) TF
Sukhoi Design Bureau, Russia			
Superjet 100	SM Corp.	SM146	(2) TF
Tupolev Corporation, Russia			
TU-204	Perm	PS90	(2) TF
TU-334	Progress	D-436	(2) TF
Vulcanair Corporation, Italy			
A-Viator	Rolls-Royce	RR 250	(2) TP
SF 600	Rolls-Royce	RR 250	(2) TP
Yakovlev Corporation, Russia			
Yak-40	Saturn	AI-25	(3) TF
Yak-242	Saturn	PS-90	(2) TF

Rotary Wing Aircraft

AIRCRAFT MANUFACTURER	ENGINE MANUFACTURER	DESIGNATION	NUMBER AND TYPE OF ENGINES
Agusta-Westland, Italy			
A109	Rolls-Royce	RR 250	(2) TS
	*Pratt & Whitney (Canada)	PT6T	(2) TS
A119	Pratt & Whitney (Canada)	PT6T	(1) TS
A129 (Mongoose)	Rolls-Royce	GEM 1004	(2) TS
AB205	Honeywell	T53	(1) TS
AB206	Rolls-Royce	RR 250	(1) TS
AB212	Pratt & Whitney (Canada)	PT6T	(2) TS
AB412	Pratt & Whitney (Canada)	PT6T	(2) TS
AW129 (Mangusta)	Rolls-Royce	GEM 42	(2) TS
AW139	Pratt & Whitney (Canada)	PT6C	(2) TS
Agusta-Westland, UK			
AW101	(Merlin) General Electric	T700	(2) TS
Super Lynx 100	Rolls-Royce	GEM 42	(2) TS
Super Lynx 300	LHTEC	CTS800	(2) TS
WAH 64 (Apache)	Rolls-Royce	RTM322	(2) TS

AIRCRAFT MANUFACTURER	ENGINE MANUFACTURER	DESIGNATION	NUMBER AND TYPE OF ENGINES
Bell Corporation, USA			
Bell 205	Honeywell	T53	(1) TS
Bell 206	Rolls-Royce	RR 250	(2) TS
Bell 209	General Electric	700	(2) TS
Bell 212	Pratt & Whitney (Canada)	PT6T	(2) TS
Bell 214	Honeywell	T53	(2) TS
Bell 230	Rolls-Royce	RR 250	(2) TS
Bell 406/407	Rolls-Royce	RR 250	(2) TS
Bell 412	Pratt & Whitney (Canada)	PT6T	(2) TS
Bell 430	Rolls-Royce	RR 250	(2) TS
V-22 (Bell/Boeing)	Rolls-Royce	T406	(2) TS
Bell Helicopter Textron, USA			
AH-1	General Electric	T700	(2) TS
BA609 (Tilt Rotor)	Pratt & Whitney (Canada)	PT6C	(2) TS
OH-58	General Electric	T700	(2) TS
TH-56/57 (Sea Ranger)	Rolls-Royce	RR250	(1) TS
UH-1 (Huey)	Honeywell	T53	(1) TS
V-22 (Osprey)	Rolls-Royce	AE1107	(2) TS
206 (Jet Ranger)	Rolls-Royce	RR 250	(1) TS
206L (Long Ranger)	Rolls-Royce	RR 250	(2) TS
407	Rolls-Royce	RR 250	(2) TS
412	Pratt & Whitney (Canada)	PT6T	(2) TS
427	Pratt & Whitney (Canada)	PW207	(2) TS
429	Pratt & Whitney (Canada)	PW207	(2) TS
430	Rolls-Royce	RR 250	(2) TS
Boeing Company, USA			
234	Honeywell	AL5512	(2) TS
414	Honeywell	T55	(2) TS
AH-64 (Apache)	General Electric	T700	(2) TS
CH-46	General Electric	T58	(2) TS
CH-46E (Sea Knight)	General Electric	T58	(2) TS
CH-47 (Chinook)	Honeywell	T55	(2) TS
MH-47 (Chinook)	Honeywell	T55	(2) TS

AIRCRAFT MANUFACTURER	ENGINE MANUFACTURER	DESIGNATION	NUMBER AND TYPE OF ENGINES
Boeing (McDonnell) Helicopter Company			
MD 500	Rolls-Royce	RR 250	(1) TS
MD 520, 530	Rolls-Royce	RR 250	(1) TS
MD 600	Rolls-Royce	RR 250	(1) TS
MD 900/901/902	Pratt & Whitney (Canada)	PW206	(2) TS
Denel Group, South Africa			
CSH-2	Turbomeca	Makila 1	(2) TS
EH Industries LTD (Great Britain)			
EH101	Turbomeca	RTM 322	(3) TS
	*General Electric	CT7	(3) TS
Endstrom Helicopter Corporation, USA			
480	Rolls-Royce	RR 250	(1) TS
Ericson Air Crane Inc., USA			
SH-64	Pratt & Whitney, USA	JFTD12	(2) TS
Eurocopter Company, (EADS), France			
AS330 (Puma)			
AS332 (Super Puma)	Turbomeca	Makila	(2) TS
AS350 (Astor)	Turbomeca	Makila	(1) TS
AS350 (Ecureuil)	Rolls-Royce	RR 250	(1) TS
AS355	Rolls-Royce	RR 250	(2) TS
AS365 (Dauphin)	Turbomeca	Arriel	(2) TS
AS532 (Cougar)	Turbomeca	Makila	(2) TS
AS550	Pratt & Whitney (Canada)	PW206	(2) TS
AS555 (Fennec)	Turbomeca	Makila	(2) TS
AS565 (Panther)	Turbomeca	Arrius	(2) TS
AS635	Turbomeca	Arrius	(2) TS
BK 117	Honeywell	LTS11	(2) TS
Bo 105	Rolls-Royce	RR 250	(2) TS
EA 135	Pratt & Whitney (Canada)	PW206	(2) TS
EA 145	Turbomeca	Arrius	(2) TS
EC120 (Calibri)	Turbomeca	Arrius	(1) TS
EC130	Turbomeca	Arriel	(1) TS
EC135	Pratt & Whitney (Canada)	PW206	(2) TS
EC145	Turbomeca	Arriel	(2) TS
EC155	Turbomeca	Arriel	(2) TS

(Continued on next page)

AIRCRAFT MANUFACTURER	ENGINE MANUFACTURER	DESIGNATION	NUMBER AND TYPE OF ENGINES
Eurocopter Company, (EADS) Continued			
EC175	Pratt & Whitney (Canada)	PW206	(2) TS
EC225	Turbomeca	Makila	(2) TS
EC655 (Tiger)	Turbomeca	Arriel	(2) TS
EC725	Turbomeca	Makila	(2) TS
NH90	Turbomeca	RTM 322	(2) TS
SA 315, 318 (Lama)	Turbomeca	Artouse	(1) TS
SA 365 (Dauphin)	Turbomeca	Arriel	(2) TS
Hiller Aircraft Corp., USA			
UH-12	Rolls-Royce	RR 250	(1) TS
Kaman Aerospace, USA			
K-1200	Honeywell	T53	(1) TS
SH-2G	General Electric	T700	(2) TS
Kamov Co., Russia			
Ka-27 (Helix-D)	Kamov	TV3-117	(2) TS
Ka-29 (Helix-A)	Kamov	TV3-117	(2) TS
Ka-31 (Helix-B)	Kamov	TV3-117	(2) TS
Ka-32 (Fire)	Kamov	TV3-117	(2) TS
Ka-50 (Black Shark)	Kamov	TV3-117	(2) TS
Ka-52 (Alligator)	Kamov	TV3-117	(2) TS
Ka-60 (Kasatka)	Rybinsk	RD-600	(2) TS
Ka-226 (Seregi)	Rolls-Royce	RR 250	(2) TS
Kawasaki Industries, Japan			
BK 117	Honeywell	LTS101	(2) TS
CH-47	Honeywell	T55	(2) TS
HK-500	Rolls-Royce	RR 250	(2) TS
KV-107	IHI	CT58	(2) TS
OH-6	Rolls-Royce	RR 250	(1) TS
MD Helicopters, Inc., USA			
MD 500	Rolls-Royce	RR 250	(1) TS
MD 520	Rolls-Royce	RR 250	(1) TS
MD 530	Rolls-Royce	RR 250	(1) TS
MD 600	Rolls-Royce	RR 250	(1) TS
MD Explorer	Pratt & Whitney (Canada)	PW207	(1) TS

AIRCRAFT MANUFACTURER	ENGINE MANUFACTURER	DESIGNATION	NUMBER AND TYPE OF ENGINES
Mil Co., Russia			
Mi-8 (Hip)	Klimov	TB2-117	(2) TS
Mi-10 (Harka)	Progress	D-25	(2) TS
Mi-14 (Haze)	Klimov	TV3-117	(2) TS
Mi-17 (Hip-H)	Klimov	TV3-117	(2) TS
Mi-26 (Halo)	Klimov	TV3-117	(2) TS
Mi-34 (Hermit)	Progress	D136	(2) TS
Mi-38	Pratt & Whitlelly (Canada)	PW127T	(2) TS
Mi-171A, 172A	Klimov	TV3-117	(2) TS
Mitsubishi Technologies Corporation, Japan			
SH-60	IHI Corp.	T700-IHI	(2) TS
UH-60	IHI Corp.	T700-IHI	(2) TS
NH Industries, France			
NH90	General Electric	T700	(2) TS
People's Republic of China			
Zhi-8(Z8)	Zhanghou	WZ-6	(3) TS
Zhi-9(Z9)	Turbomeca	Arriel	(2) TS
Zhi-11(Z-11)	Zhanghou	WZ-8	(1) TS
Rogerson Helicopter Co.			
H-1100	Rolls-Royce	RR 250	(1) TS
Schweizer Aircraft Corporation, USA			
333	Rolls-Royce	RR 250	(1) TS
Sikorsky (United Technologies), USA			
S-61, S-62	General Electric	CT58	(2) TS
S-64	General Electric	CT64	(2) TS
S-65 (H-53)	General Electric	CT64	(2) TS
S-70	General Electric	CT7	(2) TS
S-76	Rolls-Royce	RR 250	(2) TS
S-92	General Electric	CT7	(2) TS

AIRCRAFT MANUFACTURER	ENGINE MANUFACTURER	DESIGNATION	NUMBER AND TYPE OF ENGINES
United Technologies Corporation, USA			
CH-53	General Electric	T64	(2) TS
HH-53	General Electric	T64	(2) TS
MH-53	General Electric	T64	(3) TS
MH-60	General Electric	T700	(2) TS
S-70	General Electric	T700	(2) TS
S-76	Rolls-Royce	RR 250	(2) TS
SH-3	General Electric	T58	(2) TS
SH-60	General Electric	T700	(2) TS
S-92/H-92	General Electric	CT7	(2) TS
UH-60	General Electric	T700	(2) TS
Vulcanair Spa, Italy			
Aviator (APG8),	Rolls-Royce	RR 250	(2) TS
SF 600 (Canguro)	Rolls-Royce	RR 250	(2) TS
Westland Helicopters LTD, (Great Britain)			
Lynx	Rolls-Royce	GEM	(2) TS
Lynx 800	LHTEC	CTS800	(2) TS
W30	Rolls-Royce	GEM	(2) TS
W30-200, 300	General Electric	CT7	(2) TS
Wessex	Rolls-Royce	Gazelle	(2) TS

Type Engine Abbreviations:

PF = Propfan

TF = Turbofan

TJ = Turbojet

TP = Turboprop

TS = Turboshaft

Manufacturer's Abbreviations:

CASA – Constructiones Aeronauticas, Spain

EADS – European Aeronautic Defense and Space Co.(France, Germany, Spain)

G.E. – General Electric, USA

IHI – Ishikawajima-Harima Heavy Industries

LHTEC – Light Helicopter Turbine Engine Co., USA

MHI – Mitsubishi Heavy Industries

Appendix 5
Common Hand Signals

EMERGENCY SIGNALS

PERSONNEL IN DANGER (for any reason) REDUCE THRUST AND SHUT DOWN ENGINE(S).
(A) Draw right forefinger across throat. When necessary for multi-engine aircraft. Use a numerical finger signal (or point) with the left hand to designate which engine should be shut down.
(B) As soon as the signal is observed, cross both arms high above the face. The sequence of signals may be reversed, if more expedient.

FIRE IN TAILPIPE. TURN ENGINE OVER WITH STARTER.
(A) With the fingers of both hands curled and both thumbs extended up, make a gesture pointing upward.
(B) As soon as the signal is observed, use circular motion with right hand and arm extended over the head (as for an engine start). When necessary for multi-engine aircraft, use a numerical finger signal (or point) with the left hand to designate the affected engine.

FIRE IN ACCESSORY SECTION. SHUT DOWN ENGINE AND EVACUATE AIRCRAFT.
(A) Draw right forefinger across throat. When necessary for multi-engine aircraft, use a numerical finger signal (or point) with the left hand to designate which engine should be shut down.
(B) As soon as the signal is observed, extend both thumbs upward, then out. Repeat, if necessary.

GENERAL SIGNALS

AFFIRMATIVE CONDITION SATISFACTORY OK, TRIM GOOD, ETC.

Hold up thumb and forefinger, touching at the tips to form the letter "O".

NEGATIVE CONDITION UNSATISFACTORY NO GOOD, ETC.

With the finger curled and thumb extended, point thumb downward toward the ground.

ADJUST UP (higher)

With the fingers extended and palm facing up, move hand up (and down), vertically, as if coaxing upward.

ADJUST DOWN (lower)

With the fingers extended and palm facing down, move hand down (and up), vertically, as if coaxing downward.

SLIGHT ADJUSTMENT

Hold up thumb and forefinger, slightly apart (either simultaneously) with the other hand when calling for an up or down adjustment, or with the same hand, immediately following the adjustment signal.)

SHORTEN ADJUSTMENT (as when adjusting linkage)

Hold up thumb and forefinger somewhat apart (other fingers curled), then bring thumb and forefinger together in a slow, closing motion.

LENGTHEN ADJUSTMENT (as when adjusting a linkage)

Hold up thumb and forefinger pressed together (other fingers curled), then separate thumb and forefinger in a slow, opening motion.

NUMERICAL READING (of any instrument or to report a numerical value of any type)

Hold up appropriate number of fingers of either one or both hands, as necessary, in numerical sequence (i.e., 5, then 7 = 57).

ENGINE OPERATING SIGNALS

CONNECT EXTERNAL POWER SOURCE.

Insert extended forefinger of right hand into cupped fist of left hand.

DISCONNECT EXTERNAL POWER SOURCE

Withdraw extended forefinger of right hand from cupped fist of left hand.

START ENGINE

Circular motion with right hand and arm extended over the head. When necessary for multi-engine aircraft, use a numerical finger signal (or point) with the left hand to designate which engine should be started.*

*NOTE: To use as an "ALL CLEAR TO START" signal, pilot, or engine operator initiates the signal from the aircraft cockpit. Ground crewman repeats the signal to indicate "ALL CLEAR TO START ENGINE."

Appendix 6

Local Speed Of Sound (Cs) Chart

°F	200	180	160	140	120	100	80	60	40	20	0	–20	–40	–60	–80	–100
ft/sec	1260	1240	1220	1200	1180	1160	1140	1120	1100	1075	1051	1028	1004	980	955	930
mph	860	845	830	818	804	790	776	762	747	732	716	700	684	668	650	635

1. C_S = THE TERMINAL VELOCITY °F SOUND WAVES IN AIR AT A SPECIFIED TEMPERATURE.

2. C_S = 1116.8 FPS AT SEA LEVEL, STANDARD TEMPERATURE 59° F, WITH A CHANGE OF 1.1 FPS FOR EACH DEGREE FAHRENHEIT INCREASE.

3. $C_S = 49.022 \sqrt{°R}$ and $°R = °F + 460$

4. MACH NO. = VELOCITY (FPS) ÷ C_S (FPS)

Appendix 7

U.S. Standard Atmosphere, 1962 (Geopotential Altitude)

Altitude feet	Temperature			British Units Pressure		Sonic Velocity		ft.³/lb.	lb./ft³
	°F	°R	°C	psia	in. Hg	ft./sec.	kts.		
-2000	66.1	525.8	19.0	15.79	32.15	1124.	666.0		
-1000	62.5	522.2	17.0	15.23	31.02	1120.2	663.7		
0	59.0	518.7	15.0	14.70	29.92	1116.8	661.5	13.1	.076474
1000	55.4	515.1	13.0	14.17	28.86	1112.6	659.2		
2000	51.9	511.6	11.0	13.66	27.82	1108.7	656.9		
3000	48.3	508.0	9.1	13.17	26.82	1104.9	654.6		
4000	44.7	504.4	7.1	12.69	25.84	1101.0	652.3		
5000	41.2	500.9	5.1	12.23	24.90	1097.1	650.0	15.2	.065896
6000	37.6	497.3	3.1	11.78	23.98	1093.2	647.7		
7000	34.0	493.7	1.1	11.34	23.09	1089.2	645.4		
8000	30.5	490.2	-0.8	10.92	22.23	1085.3	643.0		
9000	26.9	486.6	-2.8	10.50	21.39	1081.3	640.7		
10000	23.3	483.0	-4.8	10.11	20.58	1077.4	638.3	17.7	.056475
11000	19.8	479.5	-6.8	9.720	19.79	1073.4	636.0		
12000	16.2	475.9	-8.8	9.346	19.03	1069.4	633.6		
13000	12.6	472.3	-10.7	8.984	18.29	1065.4	631.2		
14000	91.0	468.8	-12.7	8.633	17.58	1061.3	628.8		
15000	5.5	465.2	-14.7	8.294	16.89	1057.3	626.4	20.8	.048117
16000	1.9	461.6	-16.7	7.965	16.22	1053.2	624.0		
17000	-1.6	458.1	-18.7	7.647	15.57	1049.2	621.6		
18000	-5.2	454.5	-20.7	7.339	14.94	1045.1	619.2		
19000	-8.8	450.9	-22.6	7.041	14.34	1041.0	616.7		
20000	-12.3	447.4	-24.6	6.754	13.75	1036.8	614.3	24.5	.040745
21000	-15.9	443.8	-26.6	6.475	13.18	1032.7	611.9		
22000	-19.5	440.2	-28.6	6.207	12.64	1028.5	609.4		
23000	-23.0	436.7	-30.6	5.947	12.11	1024.4	606.9		
24000	-26.6	433.1	-32.5	5.696	11.60	1020.2	604.4		
25000	-30.2	429.5	-34.5	5.454	11.10	1016.0	601.9	29.2	.034267
26000	-33.7	426.0	-36.5	5.220	10.63	1011.7	599.4		
27000	-37.3	422.4	-38.5	4.994	10.17	1007.5	596.9		
28000	-40.9	418.8	-40.5	4.777	9.725	1003.2	594.4		
29000	-44.4	415.3	-42.4	4.567	9.298	988.9	591.9		
30000	-48.0	411.7	-44.4	4.364	8.886	994.6	589.3	35.0	.028608
31000	-51.6	408.1	-46.4	4.169	8.489	990.3	586.8		
32000	-55.1	404.6	-48.4	3.981	8.106	986.0	584.2		
33000	-58.7	401.0	-50.4	3.800	7.737	981.6	581.6		
34000	-62.3	397.4	-52.4	3.626	7.383	977.3	579.0		
35000	-65.8	393.9	-54.3	3.458	7.041	972.9	576.4	42.2	.023699
36000	-69.4	390.3	-56.3	3.297	6.712	968.5	573.8		
*36089	-69.7	390.0	-56.5	3.282	6.683	968.1	573.6	44.0	.022798
37000	-69.7	390.0	-56.5	3.142	6.397	968.1	573.6		
38000	-69.7	390.0	-56.5	2.994	6.097	968.1	573.6		
39000	-69.7	390.0	-56.5	2.854	5.811	968.1	573.6	50.7	.019735
40000	-69.7	390.0	-56.5	2.720	5.538	968.1	573.6		
41000	-69.7	390.0	-56.5	2.592	5.278	968.1	573.6		
42000	-69.7	390.0	-56.5	2.471	5.030	968.1	573.6		
43000	-69.7	390.0	-56.5	2.335	4.794	968.1	573.6		
44000	-69.7	390.0	-56.5	2.244	4.569	968.1	573.6	64.4	.015531
45000	-69.7	390.0	-56.5	2.139	4.335	968.1	573.6		
46000	-69.7	390.0	-56.5	2.039	4.151	968.1	573.6		
47000	-69.7	390.0	-56.5	1.943	3.956	968.1	573.6		
48000	-69.7	390.0	-56.5	1.852	3.770	968.1	573.6		
49000	-69.7	390.0	-56.5	1.75	3.953	968.1	573.6	81.8	.012213
50000	-67.9	390.0	-56.5	1.682	3.425	968.1	573.6		
51000	-69.7	390.0	-56.5	1.603	3.264	968.1	573.6		

Altitude feet	Temperature			British Units Pressure		Sonic Velocity		ft.³/lb.	lb./ft.³
	°F	°R	°C	psia	in. Hg	ft./sec.	kts.		
52000	-69.7	390.0	-56.5	1.528	3.111	968.1	573.6		
53000	-69.7	390.0	-56.5	1.456	2.965	968.1	573.6		
54000	-69.7	390.0	-56.5	1.388	2.826	968.1	573.6	104.1	.009605
55000	-69.7	390.0	-56.5	1.323	2.693	968.1	573.6		
56000	-69.7	390.0	-56.5	1.261	2.567	968.1	573.6		
57000	-69.7	390.0	-56.5	1.201	2.446	968.1	573.6		
58000	-69.7	380.0	-56.5	1.145	2.321	968.1	573.6		
59000	-69.7	390.0	-56.5	1.091	2.222	968.1	573.6	132.4	.007553
60000	-69.7	390.0	-56.5	1.040	2.118	968.1	573.6		
61000	-69.7	390.0	-56.5	.9913	2.018	968.1	573.6		
62000	-69.7	390.0	-56.5	.9448	1.924	968.1	573.6		
63000	-69.7	390.0	-56.5	.9005	1.833	968.1	573.6		
64000	-69.7	390.0	-56.5	.8582	1.747	968.1	573.6		
65000	-69.7	390.0	-56.5	.8179	1.665	968.1	573.6	176.7	.005660
*65617	-69.7	390.0	-56.5	.7941	1.617	968.1	573.6		
70000	-67.3	392.4	-55.2	.6437	1.311	971.0	575.3		
75000	-64.6	395.1	-53.6	.5073	1.0333	974.4	577.3		
80000	-61.8	397.9	-52.1	.4005	.8155	977.8	579.3		
85000	-59.1	400.6	-50.6	.3167	.6449	981.2	581.3		
90000	-56.3	403.4	-49.1	.2509	.5108	984.5	583.3		
95000	-53.6	406.1	-47.5	.1990	.4052	987.9	585.3		
100000	-50.8	408.9	-46.0	.1581	.3220	991.2	587.3		
*104987	-48.1	411.6	-44.5	.1259	.2563	994.5	589.2		
150000	21.0	480.7	-6.1	.01893	.03854	1074.8	636.8		
*154199	27.5	487.2	-2.5	.01609	.03275	1082.0	641.1		
*170604	27.5	487.2	-2.5	.00557	.01742	1082.0	641.1		
200000	-5.1	454.9	-20.4	.02655	.005406	1045.5	619.5		
*200131	-5.2	454.8	-20.5	.02641	.005377	1045.4	619.4		

*Boundary between atmosphere layers of constant thermal gradient.

Note: The ICAO atmosphere is identical to the U.S. Standard Atmosphere for altitudes below 65,617 ft.

Adiabatic Lapse Rates: 1. Temperature 3.57°F per 1,000 ft.
2. Pressure 0.934 in. Hg. per 1,000 ft.

Appendix 8
Other Useful Formulae and Standard Information

1. Specific heat at Constant Volume $C_v = 0.1715$ Btu/lb. °F

2. Specific heat at Constant Pressure $C_p = 0.24$ Btu/lb. °F

3. 1 Btu = 778 ft. lbs.

4. Ratio of specific heat $(C_p/C_v)\ \gamma = 1.4$

5. $778 \times (C_p - C_v) = 53.3$ ft. lb.

6. F_g Afterburning vs. Non–afterburning $= \sqrt{T_a}$
    Where: Temperature Ratio $(T_a) = \dfrac{\text{°R with A/B}}{\text{°R without A/B}}$

7. To calculate T_S if T_T and M are known: $T_T/T_S = 1 + \left[\dfrac{\gamma - 1}{2}\right] \times M^2$
    Where: T = °R
    M = Mach number

8. C_S (mph) $= 33.42\ \sqrt{\text{°R}}$

9. C_S (kts) $= 29.04\ \sqrt{\text{°R}}$

10. $\text{ESHP}_{(FLT)} = \text{SHP} + \dfrac{F_n \times V_1\ (\text{fps})}{550 \times \text{propeller eff. (\%)}}$ $\text{ESHP}_{(GROUND)} = \text{SHP} + \text{JET HP}$

11. Horsepower to drive the compressor
    $$hp = \dfrac{.24 \times T_r \times m_s \times 778}{550}$$
    Where: T_r = Temperature rise above ambient at compressor discharge(°F)
    m_s = lb./sec. mass airflow
    $.24 = C_p$ (Btu/lb.°F)
    550 = conversion to hp

12. Weight of air at 59°F (std. day) = 0.07647 lb./ft.^{3}
    or = 13.1 ft.^{3}/lbs.

13. Specific Weight and Density Explained:
    Specific Weight = lb./ft.^{3}
    Density = lb./ft.^{3}/g or lb. sec.^{2}/ft.^{4}

14. To calculate Total Pressure if Density and Velocity are known:
    $P_t = (½\rho V^2) + P$
    $P_t = $ lb. sec.^{2}/ft.^{4} $\times$ ft.^{2}/sec.^{2} + P
    Where: P_t = Kinetic + Static
    ρ = Density
    P = Static Pressure

15. To calculate Ram Pressure if P_t and M are known:
    $$\dfrac{Q}{P_t} = ½\,\gamma M^2 \left[1 + \dfrac{\gamma - 1}{2} \times M^2\right]^{\tfrac{\gamma}{1-\gamma}}$$
    Where: Q = Ram pressure
    P_t = Total Pressure
    M = Any Subsonic Velocity

16. To calculate Total Pressure (P_t) or Static Pressure (P_s) if Mach number (M) is known:
    $$\dfrac{P_t}{P_s} = \left[1 + \left(\dfrac{\gamma - 1}{2} \times M^2\right)\right]^{\tfrac{\gamma}{\gamma - 1}}$$

Appendix 9

Table 1 — Pressure Correction Factors

$$\text{DELTA}(\delta) = \frac{P}{P_o} = \frac{P}{29.92}$$

P IN. HG. ABS	δ	P IN. HG. ABS	δ	P IN. HG. ABS	δ	P IN. HG. ABS	δ
39.9	1.334	35.4	1.183	30.9	1.033	26.4	0.8823
39.8	1.330	35.3	1.180	30.8	1.029	26.3	0.8790
39.7	1.327	35.2	1.176	30.7	1.026	26.2	0.8757
39.6	1.324	35.1	1.173	30.6	1.023	26.1	0.8723
39.5	1.320	35.0	1.170	30.5	1.019	26.0	0.8690
39.4	1.317	34.9	1.166	30.4	1.016	25.9	0.8656
39.3	1.313	34.8	1.163	30.3	1.013	25.8	0.8623
39.2	1.310	34.7	1.160	30.2	1.009	25.7	0.8586
39.1	1.307	34.6	1.156	30.1	1.006	25.6	0.8556
39.0	1.303	34.5	1.153	30.0	1.003	25.5	0.8523
38.9	1.300	34.4	1.150	29.9	0.9993	25.4	0.8489
38.8	1.297	34.3	1.146	29.8	0.9960	25.3	0.8456
38.7	1.293	34.2	1.143	29.7	0.9926	25.2	0.8422
38.6	1.290	34.1	1.140	29.6	0.9893	25.1	0.8389
38.5	1.287	34.0	1.136	29.5	0.9859	25.0	0.8356
38.4	1.283	33.9	1.133	29.4	0.9826	24.9	0.8322
38.3	1.280	33.8	1.130	29.3	0.9793	24.8	0.8289
38.2	1.277	33.7	1.126	29.2	0.9759	24.7	0.8255
38.1	1.273	33.6	1.123	29.1	0.9726	24.6	0.8222
38.0	1.270	33.5	1.120	29.0	0.9692	24.5	0.8188
37.9	1.267	33.4	1.116	28.9	0.9659	24.4	0.8155
37.8	1.263	33.3	1.113	28.8	0.9626	24.3	0.8122
37.7	1.260	33.2	1.110	28.7	0.9592	24.2	0.8088
37.6	1.257	33.1	1.106	28.6	0.9559	24.1	0.8055
37.5	1.253	33.0	1.103	28.5	0.9525	24.0	0.8021
37.4	1.250	32.9	1.100	28.4	0.9492	23.9	0.7988
37.3	1.247	32.8	1.096	28.3	0.9458	23.8	0.7954
37.2	1.243	32.7	1.093	28.2	0.9425	23.7	0.7921
37.1	1.240	32.6	1.090	28.1	0.9392	23.6	0.7888
37.0	1.237	32.5	1.086	28.0	0.9358	23.5	0.7854
36.9	1.233	32.4	1.083	27.9	0.9325	23.4	0.7821
36.8	1.230	32.3	1.080	27.8	0.9291	23.3	0.7787
36.7	1.227	32.2	1.076	27.7	0.9258	23.2	0.7754
36.6	1.223	32.1	1.073	27.6	0.9224	23.1	0.7720
36.5	1.220	32.0	1.070	27.5	0.9191	23.0	0.7687
36.4	1.217	31.9	1.066	27.4	0.9158	22.9	0.7654
36.3	1.213	31.8	1.063	27.3	0.9124	22.8	0.7620
36.2	1.210	31.7	1.059	27.2	0.9091	22.7	0.7587
36.1	1.207	31.6	1.056	27.1	0.9057	22.6	0.7553
36.0	1.203	31.5	1.053	27.0	0.9024	22.5	0.7520
35.9	1.200	31.4	1.049	26.9	0.8990	22.4	0.7487
35.8	1.196	31.3	1.046	26.8	0.8957	22.3	0.7453
35.7	1.193	31.2	1.043	26.7	0.8924	22.2	0.7420
35.6	1.190	31.1	1.039	26.6	0.8890	22.1	0.7386
35.5	1.186	31.0	1.036	26.5	0.8857	22.0	0.7353

P IN. HG. ABS	δ	P IN. HG. ABS	δ	P IN. HG. ABS	δ	P IN. HG. ABS	δ
21.9	0.7319	19.4	0.64684	16.9	0.5648	14.4	0.4813
21.8	0.7286	19.3	0.6450	16.8	0.5615	14.3	0.4779
21.7	0.7253	19.2	0.6417	16.7	0.5581	14.2	0.4746
21.6	0.7219	19.1	0.6384	16.6	0.5548	14.1	0.4713
21.5	0.7186	19.0	0.6350	16.5	0.5515	14.0	0.4679
21.4	0.7152	18.9	0.6317	16.4	0.5481	13.9	0.4646
21.3	0.7119	18.8	0.6283	16.3	0.5448	13.8	0.4612
21.2	0.7085	18.7	0.6250	16.2	0.5415	13.7	0.4579
21.1	0.7052	18.6	0.6216	16.1	0.5381	13.6	0.4545
21.0	0.7019	18.5	0.6183	16.0	0.5348	13.5	0.4512
20.9	0.6985	18.4	0.6150	15.9	0.5314	13.4	0.4479
20.8	0.6952	18.3	0.6116	15.8	0.5281	13.3	0.4445
20.7	0.6918	18.2	0.6083	15.7	0.5147	13.2	0.4412
20.6	0.6885	18.1	0.6050	15.6	0.5214	13.1	0.4378
20.5	0.6852	18.0	0.6016	15.5	0.5180	13.0	0.4345
20.4	0.6818	17.9	0.5983	15.4	0.5147	12.9	0.4311
20.3	0.6785	17.8	0.5949	15.3	0.5114	12.8	0.4278
20.2	0.6751	17.7	0.5916	15.2	0.5080	12.7	0.4245
20.1	0.6718	17.6	0.5882	15.1	0.5047	12.6	0.4211
20.0	0.6684	17.5	0.5849	15.0	0.5013	12.5	0.4178
19.9	0.6651	17.4	0.5815	14.9	0.4780	12.4	0.4144
19.8	0.6618	17.3	0.5782	14.8	0.4946	12.3	0.4111
19.7	0.6584	17.2	0.5749	14.7	0.4913	12.2	0.4077
19.6	0.6551	17.1	0.5715	14.6	0.4880	12.1	0.4044
19.5	0.6517	17.0	0.5682	14.5	0.4846	12.0	0.4011

Temperature Correction Factors

$°F = \frac{9}{5}(°C + 32)$

$°F = °R + 460$

$°C = \frac{5}{9}(°F - 32)$

$C = °K + 273$

THETA $(\theta) = \frac{T}{T_0} = \frac{T}{519}$

FOR INTERPOLATION, 1° C = 1.8° F

T (°F)	θ	√θ	T (°F)	θ	√θ	T (°F)	θ	√θ	T (°F)	θ	√θ
200	1.272	1.128	160	1.195	1.093	120	1.118	1.057	80	1.041	1.020
199	1.270	1.127	159	1.193	1.092	119	1.116	1.0566	79	1.039	1.019
198	1.269	1.126	158	1.191	1.091	118	1.114	1.055	78	1.037	1.018
197	1.267	1.125	157	1.189	1.090	117	1.112	1.054	77	1.035	1.017
196	1.265	1.124	156	1.187	1.089	116	1.110	1.054	76	1.033	1.016
195	1.263	1.123	155	1.185	1.089	115	1.108	1.053	75	1.031	1.015
194	1.261	1.123	154	1.183	1.088	114	1.106	1.052	74	1.029	1.014
193	1.259	1.122	153	1.181	1.087	113	1.104	1.051	73	1.028	1.013
192	1.257	1.121	152	1.179	1.086	112	1.102	1.050	72	1.026	1.012
191	1.255	1.120	151	1.177	1.085	111	1.100	1.049	71	1.024	1.012
190	1.253	1.119	150	1.176	1.084	110	1.098	1.048	70	1.022	1.011
189	1.251	1.118	149	1.174	1.083	109	1.096	1.047	69	1.020	1.010
188	1.249	1.117	148	1.172	1.082	108	1.095	1.046	68	1.018	1.009
187	1.247	1.117	147	1.170	1.082	107	1.093	1.045	67	1.016	1.008
186	1.245	1.116	146	1.168	1.081	106	1.191	1.044	66	1.014	1.007
185	1.243	1.115	145	1.166	1.080	105	1.089	1.043	65	1.012	1.006
184	1.242	1.114	144	1.164	1.079	104	1.187	1.042	64	1.010	1.005
183	1.240	1.113	143	1.162	1.078	103	1.085	1.041	63	1.008	1.004
182	1.238	1.112	142	1.160	1.077	102	1.083	1.041	62	1.006	1.003
181	1.236	1.111	141	1.158	1.076	101	1.082	1.040	61	1.004	1.002
180	1.234	1.111	140	1.156	1.075	100	1.080	1.039	60	1.002	1.001
179	1.232	1.110	139	1.154	1.074	99	1.078	1.038	59	1.000	1.000
178	1.230	1.109	138	1.152	1.073	98	1.076	1.037	58	0.999	0.999
177	1.228	1.108	137	1.150	1.073	97	1.074	1.036	57	0.997	0.998
176	1.226	1.107	136	1.149	1.072	96	1.072	1.035	56	0.995	0.997
175	1.224	1.106	135	1.147	1.071	95	1.070	1.034	55	0.993	0.996
174	1.222	1.105	134	1.145	1.070	94	1.068	1.033	54	0.991	0.995
173	1.220	1.104	133	1.143	1.069	93	1.066	1.032	53	0.989	0.994
172	1.218	1.104	132	1.141	1.068	92	1.064	1.031	52	0.988	0.993
171	1.216	1.103	131	1.139	1.067	91	1.062	1.030	51	0.986	0.992
170	1.214	1.102	130	1.137	1.066	90	1.060	1.029	50	0.984	0.991
169	1.212	1.101	129	1.135	1.065	89	1.058	1.029	49	0.982	0.990
168	1.210	1.100	128	1.133	1.064	88	1.056	1.028	48	0.980	0.989
167	1.208	1.099	127	1.131	1.064	87	1.055	1.027	47	0.978	0.988
166	1.206	1.098	126	1.129	1.063	86	1.053	1.026	46	0.976	0.987
165	1.204	1.097	125	1.127	1.062	85	1.051	1.025	45	0.974	0.986
164	1.202	1.096	124	1.125	1.061	84	1.049	1.024	44	0.972	0.985
163	1.200	1.095	123	1.123	1.060	83	1.047	1.023	43	0.970	0.984
162	1.199	1.095	122	1.122	1.059	82	1.045	1.022	42	0.968	0.984
161	1.197	1.094	121	1.120	1.058	81	1.043	1.021	41	0.966	0.983

T (°F)	θ	√θ	T (°F)	θ	√θ	T (°F)	θ	√θ	T (°F)	θ	√θ
40	0.964	0.982	10	0.907	0.952	−20	0.848	0.921	−50	0.790	0.889
39	0.962	0.981	9	0.905	0.951	−21	0.846	0.920	−51	0.788	0.888
38	0.960	0.980	8	0.903	0.950	−22	0.844	0.919	−52	0.786	0.887
37	0.959	0.979	7	0.901	0.949	−23	0.842	0.918	−53	0.784	0.886
36	0.957	0.978	6	0.899	0.948	−24	0.840	0.917	−54	0.782	0.885
35	0.955	0.977	5	0.897	0.947	−25	0.838	0.916	−55	0.780	0.883
34	0.953	0.976	4	0.895	0.946	−26	0.836	0.914	−56	0.778	0.882
33	0.951	0.975	3	0.893	0.945	−27	0.834	0.913	−57	0.777	0.881
32	0.949	0.974	2	0.891	0.944	−28	0.832	0.912	−58	0.775	0.880
31	0.947	0.973	1	0.889	0.943	−29	0.831	0.911	−59	0.773	0.879
30	0.945	0.972	0	0.887	0.942	−30	0.829	0.910	−60	0.771	0.878
29	0.943	0.971	−1	0.884	0.940	−31	0.827	0.909	−61	0.769	0.877
28	0.941	0.970	−2	0.883	0.939	−32	0.825	0.908	−62	0.767	0.876
27	0.939	0.969	−3	0.881	0.938	−33	0.823	0.907	−63	0.765	0.875
26	0.937	0.968	−4	0.879	0.937	−34	0.821	0.906	−64	0.763	0.874
25	0.935	0.967	−5	0.877	0.936	−35	0.819	0.905	−65	0.761	0.872
24	0.934	0.966	−6	0.875	0.935	−36	0.817	0.904	−66	0.759	0.871
23	0.932	0.965	−7	0.873	0.934	−37	0.815	0.903	−67	0.757	0.870
22	0.930	0.964	−8	0.871	0.933	−38	0.813	0.902	−68	0.755	0.869
21	0.928	0.963	−9	0.869	0.932	−39	0.811	0.901	−69	0.753	0.868
20	0.926	0.962	−10	0.867	0.931	−40	0.809	0.900	−70	0.751	0.867
19	0.924	0.961	−11	0.865	0.930	−41	0.807	0.899	−71	0.750	0.866
18	0.922	0.960	−12	0.863	0.929	−42	0.805	0.897	−72	0.748	0.865
17	0.920	0.959	−13	0.861	0.928	−43	0.804	0.896	−73	0.746	0.864
16	0.918	0.958	−14	0.859	0.927	−44	0.802	0.895	−74	0.744	0.862
15	0.916	0.957	−15	0.857	0.926	−45	0.800	0.894	−75	0.742	0.861
14	0.914	0.956	−16	0.856	0.925	−46	0.798	0.893	−76	0.740	0.860
13	0.912	0.955	−17	0.854	0.924	−47	0.796	0.892	−77	0.738	0.859
12	0.910	0.954	−18	0.852	0.923	−48	0.794	0.891	−78	0.736	0.858
11	0.908	0.953	−19	0.850	0.922	−49	0.792	0.890	−79	0.734	0.857

Appendix 10

Ground Vs. Flight Performance Data

	Operation at Sea Level	Operation at Mach 0.8 at 36,089 feet	Data Source
1. Ambient Pressure (P_{am})	30.0 in. Hg	6.7 in. Hg	measured
2. Ambient Temperature (T_{am})	535 °R	390 °R	measured
3. Ram Pressure Ratio ($\frac{P_{t_2}}{P_{am}}$)	1.0	1.524	measured
4. Ram Temperature Ratio ($\frac{T_{t_2}}{T_{am}}$)	1.0	1.135	measured
5. Engine Inlet Total Pressure (P_{t_2})	30.0 in. Hg	10.2 in. Hg	1 × 3
6. Engine Inlet Total Temperature (T_{t_2})	535 °R	443 °R	2 × 4
7. Pressure Correction Factor (δ_{t_2})	1.003	0.341	$\frac{5}{29.92}$
8. Temperature Correction Factor (θ_{t_2})	1.031	0.854	$\frac{6}{519}$
9. Square Root of θ_{t_2}	1.015	0.924	$\sqrt{8}$
10. Net Thrust (F_n)	7,000 lbs.	3,000 lbs.	measured
11. Corrected Net Thrust ($\frac{F_n}{\delta_{t_2}}$)	6,979 lbs.	8,798 lbs.	$\frac{10}{7}$
12. Fuel Flow (W_t)	4,600 pph	3,100 pph	measured
13. Corrected Fuel Flow ($\frac{W_t}{\delta_{t_1}\sqrt{\theta_{t_2}}\,0.5}$)	4,569 pph	9,272 pph	$\frac{12}{7 \times 9}$
14. Exhaust Gas Temperature (T_{t_5})	1,400 °R	1,500 °R	measured
15. Corrected EGT ($\frac{T_{t_5}}{\theta_{t_2}}$)	1,358 °R	1,756 °R	$\frac{14}{8}$
16. Compressor Speed (rpm)	9,000	9,100	measured
17. Corrected Compressor Speed ($\frac{rpm}{\sqrt{\theta_{t_2}}}$)	8,867	9,848	$\frac{16}{9}$

Glossary

This glossary is provided as a ready reference of terms as used in this text. These definitions may differ from those of standard dictionaries, but are more common in reference to the gas turbine engine.

aborted start — Termination of the engine starting cycle when combustion (light-off) does not occur within a prescribed time limit.

acceleration due to gravity — The acceleration of a free-falling body due to the attraction of gravity, expressed as the rate of increase of velocity per unit of time. In a vacuum, the rate is 32.2 feet per second per second near sea level.

abradable shroud ring (turbine) — A shroud ring constructed of sintered metal or honeycomb metal that will wear (abrade) away upon contact with a turbine blade tip. The abradable shroud protects against blade length reduction and reduced blade efficiency.

Example—Abradable shroud ring location on a two-stage turbine:

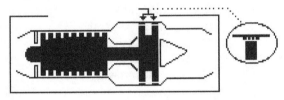

absolute pressure — Pressure above zero pressure as read on a barometer-type instrument. For example, Standard Day, 14.7 p.s.i.a.

accessory drive gearbox — A gearbox that provides mounting space for engine accessories. Also referred to as the main gearbox.

accessory drive gearbox (ADG) — The main unit of the accessory section. The ADG provides mounting points for accessories.

Example—ADG driven from rear of compressor:

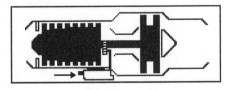

afterburner — A tubular combustion chamber with a variable-size exhaust outlet attached to the rear of a gas turbine engine into which fuel is injected through a set of spray bars. Burning of fuel in the exhaust supplements the normal thrust of the engine by increasing the acceleration of the air mass through an additional temperature rise.

aft-fan (turbofan engine) — An older turbofan engine design in which the fan is an extension of the power turbine blades rather than an extension of the compressor blades as is the case with forward-fan turbofan engines.

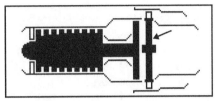

airfoil — Any surface designed to obtain a useful reaction upon its surfaces from the air through which it moves. Velocity increases over the cambered side, which produces lift on the underside.

air, ambient — The atmospheric air surrounding all sides of the aircraft or engine. Expressed in units of lbs./sq. inch or in. Hg.

annular combustor — A cylindrical, one-piece combustion chamber, sometimes referred to as a single-basket-type combustor.

anti-stall system — an engine system designed to aid in preventing compressor stalls and surges.

auto-throttle — An electronic system designed to provide automatic throttle positioning of the flight deck throttle levers after receiving commands from aircraft flight monitoring systems.

auxiliary drive gearbox — A small gearbox driven by the main rotor shaft by a beveled gear system and a radial shaft. The auxiliary gearbox, which is used to drive the accessory drive gearbox via a horizontal drive shaft, is used when a direct drive to the accessory drive gearbox is not desired.

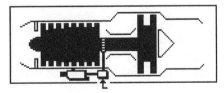

auxiliary power unit (APU) — A type of gas turbine, usually located in the aircraft fuselage, whose purpose is to provide either electrical power, air pressure for starting main engines, or both. It is similar in design to ground power units.

axial — 1. Motion along a real or imaginary straight line about which an object supposedly or actually rotates. 2. The engine centerline.

axial flow compressor — A compressor with airflow parallel to the axis of the engine. The numerous compressor stages raise pressure of air but essentially make no change in direction of airflow.

Bernoulli's Principle — A principle stating that static pressure and velocity (RAM) pressure of a gas or fluid passing through a duct (at constant subsonic flow rate) are inversely proportional—that is, total pressure does not change.

blade — A rotating airfoil used in a compressor as a means of compressing air or in a turbine for extracting energy from the flowing gases.

Brayton cycle — A thermodynamic cycle of operation that underlies the operating principles of the gas turbine engine. It is sometimes referred to as the continuous combustion, or constant pressure cycle.

British thermal unit (BTU) — A unit of heat. One BTU equals the heat energy required to raise one pound of water one degree Fahrenheit (for example, one pound of jet fuel contains approximately 18,600 BTU).

bucket — An informal term for turbine blade.

bypass duct — The cold airstream duct of a turbofan engine.

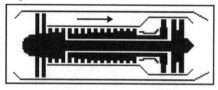

can-annular combustor — A set, generally of 6 to 10 liners within one outer annulus (combustor outer case).

carbon oil seal (bearing) — Single or multiple rings of carbon material that are spring-loaded onto a highly polished metal surface. Carbon seals are used at main bearing locations to prevent leakage of engine lubricating oil into the gas-path.

Centistoke (cSt) — One-hundredth of a stoke. A measurement unit of kinematic viscosity (resistance to flow), to describe the thickness of synthetic turbine oils.

centrifugal flow compressor (single-stage) — An impeller rotor and housing designed to draw in air at its center (the inducer section) and accelerate that air outward into a diffuser manifold to increase air pressure.

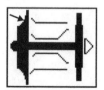

centrifugal flow compressor (dual entry) — A compressor design that uses back-to-back impellers. This arrangement effectively doubles the mass airflow of the engine as it takes in air simultaneously at both impeller faces. This arrangement does not, however, increase the compressor pressure ratio.

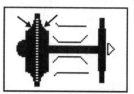

centrifugal flow compressor (two stage) — A compressor containing two single-sided impellers in series for the purpose of enhancing compressor pressure ratio. The newer types contain dual, independently rotating impellers. The older types were fixed and rotates as a single unit.

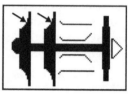

choked airflow — An airflow condition from a convergent shaped nozzle in which the gas is traveling at the speed of sound and cannot be further accelerated. Any increase in internal pressure passes through the nozzle in the form of pressure.

cold section — A typical reference to the air inlet and compression sections of the engine. The cold section starts at the engine inlet case and ends at the rear flange of the diffuser case.

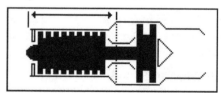

combination flow compressor (engine) — A compressor design that uses both an axial and a centrifugal compressor in combination, with the axial section serving as the front stages and the centrifugal section as the last stage. In most engines, the two sections are fitted together to form one rotor. In some newer engines, the axial and centrifugal compressors are split and rotate independently.

combustion chamber — The area in a gas turbine engine where fuel in introduced and combustion of fuel and air occurs. The combustion chamber consists of an inner liner and an outer case.

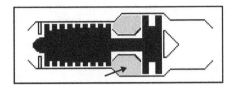

combustor — The section of the engine into which fuel is injected and burned to create gas expansion.

compressor — An impeller or a multibladed rotor assembly. The compressor is driven by a turbine rotor to compress incoming air.

compressor inlet guide vane — An engine system typically located within the inlet case. A set of stator vanes positioned in front of the compressor first stage rotor blades to direct airflow at the optimum angle into the blades, thereby reducing aerodynamic drag. Air is angled in the blade direction of rotation and the approach speed is reduced, creating a desirable angle-of-attack. The angle of the guide vanes can be fixed or variable.

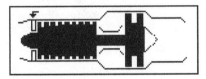

compressor pressure ratio — Compressor discharge pressure divided by compressor inlet pressure. For example, a large turbofan might have a compressor pressure ratio of 40:1.

compressor stage (axial compressor) — A rotor blade set followed by a stator vane set. The rotating airfoils (blades) on the rotor accelerate air velocity, which changes to a static pressure rise in the diverging passageways formed by the stator vanes. Stages are numbered front to back. Stage one is generally the first fan of a turbofan engine or the first compressor stage of a turbojet, turboprop and turboshaft engine.

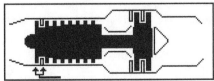

compressor stall — A condition in an axial-flow compressor in which one or more stages of rotor blades fail to pass air smoothly to the succeeding stages. A stall condition is caused by a pressure ratio that is incompatible with engine speed. A compressor stall is indicated by a rise in exhaust temperature or a fluctuation in engine speed, and if permitted to continue, can result in flameout and damage to the engine.

compressor stator vanes — Stationary airfoils placed to the rear of the rotor blades to form a stage of compression.

convergent-divergent inlet duct (C-D) — A nacelle component. A supersonic aircraft inlet duct of either fixed (C-D) geometry or of variable (C-D) geometry. Its forward inlet section is convergent to reduce air velocity from supersonic speed to sonic speed (Mach 1.0) and thereby increase static pressure. The aft section is divergent (acting as a subsonic diffuser) to increase air pressure still further and slow airflow to approximately Mach 0.5 before it enters the engine.

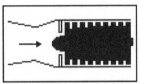

convergent duct — A cone-shaped passage or channel (sometimes referred to as nozzle shaped) in which a gas is made to flow from its largest area to its smallest area, resulting in an increase in velocity and a decrease in pressure. In those conditions, the weight of airflow remains constant.

diffuser — The divergent section of the engine, which is used to convert the velocity energy in the compressor discharge air to pressure energy. Aircraft inlet ducts and compressor stator vanes are also described as diffusers due to their effect in raising air pressure.

directional reference — An industry standard to describe engine locations. The orientation is to look from the rear towards the front of the engine and use standard twelve hour clock reference points. Right side and left side are also determined in this manner.

divergent duct — A cone-shaped passage or channel in which a gas is made to flow from its smallest to its largest area resulting in an increase in pressure and a decrease in velocity. In those conditions, the weight of airflow remains constant—for example, within the engine diffuser.

dual-spool compressor — A design that uses two independently rotating axial flow compressors. The front compressor is referred to as the low pressure (LP) Compressor and the rear one is referred to as the high pressure (HP) compressor.

electronic engine control (EEC) — An electronic system designed to perform engine control calculations necessary to monitor engine operating conditions.

energy — Inherent power or the capacity for performing work. When a portion of matter is stationary, it often has engine energy due to its position in relation to other portions of matter. This is called potential energy. If the matter is moving, it is said to have kinetic energy, or energy due to motion.

engine cycle — An instance of one takeoff and landing. Engine cycles are used to compute time between overhaul of engines and components where operating hours are not used.

engine pressure ratio (EPR) — The ratio of turbine discharge pressure divided by compressor inlet pressure and displayed in the cockpit as an indication of engine thrust.

engine stations (physical) — Reference points on an engine along its horizontal center-line. Two commonly used systems are aerodynamic engine stations and inch station numbering. Aerodynamic engine station numbering identifies locations along the engine gas path from the first station at the inlet to the final station at the exhaust. Inch station numbering identifies inch locations along the engine's physical horizontal length.

Example—Aerodynamic engine stations:

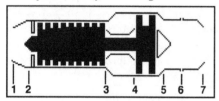

exhaust gas temperature (EGT) — The temperature of the gases taken at the turbine exit. Often referred to as Tt7.

exhaust nozzle — In a strict sense, the final opening at the rear of a core engine tailpipe or fan exhaust duct, but commonly used to mean the exhaust duct itself. Also referred to as the jet nozzle.

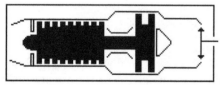

FADEC — See Full Authority Digital Engine Control.

fixed turbine — A turbine rotor in a turboprop or turboshaft engine that is mechanically attached to drive both a compressor rotor and an output reduction gearbox. The fixed turbine in this sense is directly attached to the propeller of a turboprop engine or to the transmission drive of a turboshaft engine.

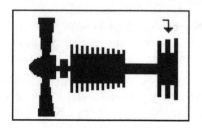

flame out — An unintentional extinction of combustion due to a blowout (too much fuel) or die-out (too little fuel).

foreign object damage (FOD) — Damage to the engine (primarily to the compressor) from ingestion of foreign objects into the engine inlet. FOD also refers to damage resulting from objects being dropped into the compressor or other internal engine parts.

free power turbine — A turbine wheel that drives an output reduction gearbox of a turboshaft or turboprop engine rather than an engine compressor. The free turbine engine design permits two operating conditions: Variable gearbox speed output at constant core engine speed and constant gearbox speed output over a range of core engine speeds.

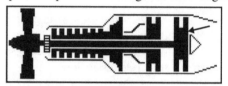

fuel control unit — The main fuel scheduling device, which receives a mechanical input signal from the power lever and various other signals, such as Pt2, Tt2, etc. These signals provide for automatic scheduling of fuel at all ambient conditions of ground and flight operation.

fuel flow — Rate at which fuel is consumed by the engine, typically expressed in pounds per hour (pph).

fuel nozzle — The unit that introduces fuel into the combustion liner. The three most common fuel nozzle types are the aerating type, which creates a fine spray under low delivery pressure; the pressure atomizing type, which creates a fine spray under high delivery pressure; and the fuel vaporizing type, which creates a fine spray under a high heat condition.

Full Authority Digital Engine Control (FADEC) — An electronic system designed to take complete command of the engine control systems in response to command inputs from the aircraft into an Electronic Engine Control unit.

gas generator turbine — The high-pressure turbine wheels that drive the compressor of a turboshaft or turboprop engine.

gas turbine — An engine that consists of a compressor, combustor and turbine, using a gaseous fluid as a working medium, and producing either shaft horsepower, jet thrust, or both. The four common types of gas turbine engines are the turbojet, the turbofan, the turboprop, and the turboshaft.

geared turbofan — A turbofan engine with a geared-down fan rotor. A reduction gearing is interposed between the fan and the compressor to permit the compressor to rotate at a higher speed than the fan. This provides higher compressor tip speeds, greater pressure ratio of the compressor, and improved cycle efficiency. The geared fan reduces the number of turbine wheels required and thus provides for a shorter engine length than the ungeared type turbofan engine.

Example—Two-stage geared-fan design:

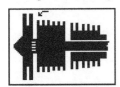

ground power unit (GPU) — A type of small gas turbine whose purpose is to provide either electrical power, air pressure for starting aircraft engines, or both. A ground power unit is connected to the aircraft when needed. The GPU operates similarly to an aircraft-installed auxiliary power unit.

high-bypass turbofan engine — Turbofan engines whose bypass ration (BPR) is approximately 4:1 to 9:1are considered high-bypass engines. BPR is the ratio of fan airflow to core engine airflow. For example, an engine with 1,500 lbs./sec. total mass airflow, in which 1,250 lbs./sec. flows through the fan and 250 lbs./sec. simultaneously flows through the core has a BPR of 5:1. A BPR of 10:1 and higher is considered an ultra-high-bypass turbofan engine.

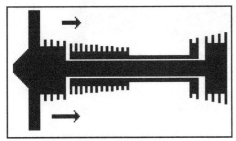

high pressure compressor (HPC) — The rear section of a dual-spool (or split-spool) compressor. The HPC is used in conjunction with a low pressure compressor (LPC) to deliver air under pressure to the diffuser and the combustor. The high pressure compressor might also be referred to as the HP compressor, the N_2 compressor, or the high speed compressor.

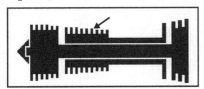

high pressure turbine (HPT) — The forward most turbine wheels of a dual- or triple-spool axial flow turbine engine that are mechanically attached to and drive the high pressure compressor. The HPT is named as such because it receives the highest gas pressure of all the turbines. The HPT might also be referred to as the HP turbine, the N_2 turbine in a dual-spool configuration, the N_3 turbine in a triple-spool configuration, or the high speed turbine.

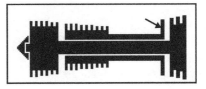

horsepower — A unit of power equal to 33,000 foot-pounds of work per minute, 550-foot pounds per second, or 375 mile pounds per hour.

hot section (engine) — A typical reference to the combustion through exhaust sections of an engine. The hot section starts at the combustor front flange and ends at the exhaust nozzle and is sometimes referred to as the hot end.

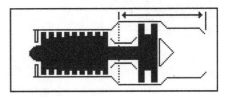

Hot start — A starting condition that occurs with normal engine rotation, but exhaust temperature exceeds prescribed limits. Hot starts are usually caused by an excessively rich mixture in the combustor. Fuel flow to the engine must be terminated immediately to prevent engine damage.

Hot tank oil system — An engine main lubrication system wherein the oil cooler is located in the pressure oil subsystem. Oil returns uncooled to the oil tank and is then cooled before it reenters the engine.

hung start — A condition of normal lightoff but with engine speed remaining at some low value rather than increasing to the normal idle speed. Hung starts are often the result of insufficient power to the engine from the starter. In the event of a hung start, the engine should be shut down.

hydromechanical fuel control — A primary fuel-scheduling device that uses hydraulic servos in combination with mechanical linkages to operate its mechanisms. Hydromechanical fuel controls are one of several types of fuel controls used on gas turbine engines.

idle — A percent r.p.m. setting, the value of which changes from engine to engine. Idle speed is the lowest engine operating speed authorized.

igniter plug — An electrical sparking device used to start the burning of the fuel-air mixture in a combustor.

impeller — The name given to the centrifugal flow compressor rotor.

inlet duct — The ambient air entrance duct, which directs air into the engine.

inlet guide vane — A component with stationary airfoils (called guide vanes) that precede the first stage compressor rotor blades. These guide vanes direct air onto the blades at the optimum angle.

inlet section (aircraft) — The portion of an aircraft in which ambient air is allowed to decrease in velocity and increase in pressure before entering the engine inlet. The inlet section is also called the flight inlet.

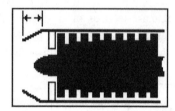

inlet section (engine) — The portion of a turbine engine where air enters from the flight inlet. This section often houses inlet guide vanes, which optimize the flow angle of air entering the first stage of compression. On large turbofan engines, inlet guide vanes are not used and inlet section air flows directly into the fan rotor.

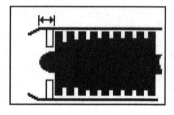

intermediate-pressure compressor (IPC) — The middle (IPC) compressor of a triple-spool axial flow engine. Its function is to receive air under pressure from the LP compressor and deliver an even higher pressure to the HP compressor. The IPC might also be referred to as the IP compressor or the N_2 compressor when the high-pressure compressor is referred to as the N_3 compressor.

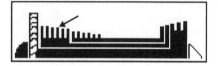

jet engine — A reaction engine that derives its thrust from the acceleration of an air mass through an orifice. The four common types are rocket, ramjet, pulsejet, and turbojet.

kinetic energy — Energy due to motion.

labyrinth oil seal — A soft metal main bearing oil seal, consisting of a rotor and a stator.

low-pressure compressor (LPC) — The front compression section of a dual- or triple-spool, axial-flow compressor. On many turbofan engines, the LPC consists of only a fan rotor; on others the fan might be followed by one or more compression stages. The LPC might also be the front compression section of a dual, combination axial-centrifugal compressor. The LPC might also be referred to as the LP compressor, the N_1 compressor, or the low-speed compressor.

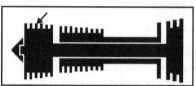

low-pressure turbine (LPT) — The rear turbine section of a dual- or triple-spool axial-flow turbine engine. The LPT mechanically attaches to and drives the low-pressure compressor. It is so named because it receives the lowest gas pressure of all the turbines. LPT functions include driving the fan rotor on the triple-spool turbofan engine, driving the fan rotor on a dual-spool turbofan engine, and driving the front compressor on a dual-spool turbojet, turboprop or turboshaft engine.

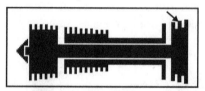

mach number — The ratio of the speed of the airplane to the speed of sound (at the temperature in which the airplane is operating.)

mass — A basic property of matter. Mass is referred to as weight when in a gravitational field such as that of the earth.

N_1 compressor — Depending on the type of engine, the following designations apply: 1) the low-pressure compressor of a dual-spool axial flow engine; 2) the compressor of a single-spool axial flow engine; and 3) the compressor of a centrifugal flow engine.

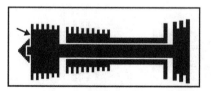

N_2 compressor — Depending on the type of engine, the following N_2 compressor designations apply: 1) the high pressure compressor of a dual-spool axial flow engine; 2) the intermediate compressor of a triple-spool axial flow engine; and 3) the second impeller of a dual-impeller, centrifugal flow engine.

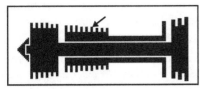

N₃ compressor — The high pressure compressor of a triple-spool, axial flow turbofan engine.

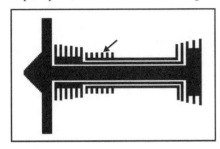

oil jet — A small nozzle (flow orifice) that directs a calibrated stream of oil onto a point to be lubricated such as bearings, carbon seals, gears, and so on.

oil pressure subsystem — The oil supply side of the engine lubrication system. It is one of three subsystems in the lubrication system. The oil pressure subsystem delivers pressurized oil to the oil jets.

oil scavenge system — The return side of the engine lubrication system. The scavenge subsystem transports oil back to the oil tank under pressure from the bearing sumps and gearboxes.

oil vent system — A system of interconnecting air passageways between oil sumps that directs unwanted air back to the atmosphere.

on-condition maintenance — A concept under which many engine accessories and components are maintained. Refers to engine parts with no life-limiting requirements. During inspection, if the part shows no defects, it is said to be in satisfactory condition to remain in service.

output reduction gearbox — A reduction gearbox on a turboshaft engine that converts a high speed, low torque input from a turbine shaft into low speed, high torque via the reduction gearing mechanism. The gearbox in turn powers the output drive shaft.

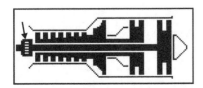

overtemperature — Any condition in which exhaust gas temperature exceeds the maximum allowable limits.

potential energy — Energy due to position.

power lever — The cockpit lever that connects to the fuel control unit and schedules fuel flow to the combustor. The power lever is also referred to as the power control lever or the throttle.

power turbine — A turbine rotor connected to an output reduction gearbox. Also referred to as a free power turbine.

pressure, static — The pressure measured in a duct containing air, a gas or a liquid, in which no velocity (ram) pressure is allowed to enter the measuring device. Symbol (Ps).

pressure, total — Static pressure plus ram pressure. Total pressure can be measured by use of a specially shaped probe that stops a small portion of the gas or liquid flowing in a duct, thereby changing velocity (ram) energy to pressure energy. Symbol (Pt).

probe — A sensing device that extends into the airstream or gas stream for measuring pressure, velocity or temperature.

propeller reduction gearbox (turboprop) — A reduction gearbox on a turboprop engine that converts a high speed, low torque input from a turbine wheel into low speed, high torque to a propeller shaft. This gearbox is generally a two-stage planetary gear system and described as a very heavily loaded engine component. In some cases, the reduction ratio is as high as 30:1.

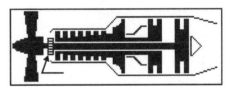

propulsive efficiency — The external efficiency of an engine expressed as a percentage.

ram pressure rise — Pressure rise in the inlet due to the forward speed of the aircraft. For example, at M = .85, a pressure of 1.6 times above ambient typically occurs.

rotor — A rotating disk or drum to which a series of blades are attached.

shock stall — Turbulent airflow on an airfoil that occurs when the speed of sound is reached. The shock wave distorts the aerodynamic airflow, causing a stall and loss of lift.

shroud — A cover or housing used to aid in confining an air or gas flow to a desired path.

single-spool compressor — A single axial flow compressor design, typically with eight or more stages.

speed of sound — The terminal velocity of sound waves in air at a specific air temperature and typically referred to as Mach one. Symbol (M).

SYMBOLS

A — Acceleration

A_j — Area of jet nozzle

C_p — specific heat

C_s — local speed of sound

F_g — static or gross thrust

F_n — net thrust

g — gravity

Ke — Kinetic energy

m — mass airflow

M — mach number

N_c — speed, single compressor

N_1 — speed, low pressure compressor

N_2 — speed, high pressure compressor

N_f — speed, free turbine

N_g — speed, gas producer turbine

P_{am} — pressure, ambient

P_b — pressure, burner

P_j — pressure at jet nozzle

P_s — pressure, static

P_t — pressure, total

T_c — temperature, total

V_1 — velocity of aircraft

V_2 — velocity, jet nozzle

W_f — weight of fuel

γ — Gamma, ratio of specific heats (Cp/Cv)

η — Eta, efficiency

ρ — Rho, density

thermal efficiency — Internal engine efficiency or fuel energy available versus work produced; expressed as a percentage.

thrust — A pushing force exerted by one mass against another, which tends to produce motion. In jet propulsion, thrust is the forward force in the direction of motion caused by the pressure forces acting on the inner surfaces of the engine—in other words, it is the reaction to the exhaust gases exiting the nozzle. Thrust force is typically measured in pounds or kilograms.

thrust, gross — The force that the engine exerts against its mounts while it is operating but not moving. Gross thrust is also referred to as static thrust. Symbol (Fg).

thrust, net — The effective thrust developed by the engine during flight, taking into consideration the initial momentum of the air mass prior to entering the influence of the engine. Symbol (Fn).

thrust reverser (aerodynamic blockage type) — A device attached to a turbine engine tailpipe that reverses the exhaust gas flow before it reaches the exhaust nozzle. Aerodynamic reversers are referred to pre-exit reversers. Reversers assist aircraft brakes and provide aircraft control during landing and during rejected takeoffs.

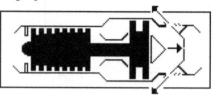

thrust reverser (mechanical blockage type) — A device that changes the direction of rearward thrust by means of a mechanical obstruction. The two most common types are the clamshell design and the target-bucket design. The clamshell reverser is so named because of its two rounded and ribbed shape sections. The target-bucket design uses two or more rectangular reverser panels. Both types of reversers are located in core (hot) exhausts and mixed exhausts of turbofan engines and referred to as a post-exit reverser. Reversers assist aircraft brakes and provide aircraft control during landing and during rejected takeoffs.

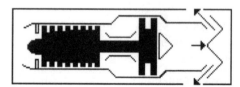

thrust-specific fuel consumption (TSFC) — An equation: TSFC = Wf /Fg where Wf is fuel flow in pounds per hour, and Fn is net thrust in pounds; used to calculate fuel consumed and as a means of comparison between engines.

time between overhaul (TBO) — The time in hours or engine cycles that the manufacturer recommends as the service life of an engine or engine component, from new to overhaul, or from one overhaul to the next.

torque — A force multiplied by its lever arm, acting at right angles to an axis.

torquemeter indicator — A turboprop or turboshaft cockpit instrument used to indicate engine power output. The propeller or rotor inputs a twisting force to an electronic or oil-operated torquemeter, which sends a signal to the indicator.

translating cowl (thrust reverser) — A component part of an engine nacelle. A movable portion of the engine cowling. When actuated, the translating cowl forms both the fan and hot exhaust nozzles, uncovering turning vanes that redirect the discharge gases forward to create reverse thrust.
Example—High bypass turbofan with fan and hot exhaust reversers deployed:

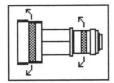

turbine nozzle guide vane assembly — A ring of stationary airfoils located directly in front of each turbine wheel. The function of the assembly is to increase gas velocity and to direct the gases into the turbine blades at the optimum angle.
Example—Two stage turbine with view of 1st and 2nd stage guide vanes:

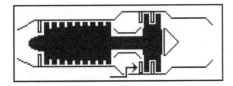

turbine rotor assembly — The complete rotating assembly of a turbine system, including the turbine wheel and its drive shaft.

turbine stage — A stage of turbine consists of a turbine nozzle vane assembly positioned in front of a turbine wheel assembly. Gases directed through the turbine nozzle guide vanes experience a change in direction and an increase in velocity in order to impinge on the turbine rotor at the optimum angle and with maximum energy.
Example—Single spool turbojet engine with two stage turbine:

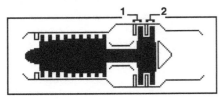

turbine wheel — A rotating device actuated either by reaction, by impulse, or by a combination of both, and used to transform some of the kinetic energy of the exhaust gases into shaft horsepower to drive the compressors and accessories.

turbofan engine (full bypass duct) — A simple turbojet core with the addition of a fan. The fan is typically located in front of the engine compressor and serves as a ducted, fixed-pitch propeller to create a pressurized bypass airflow and to aid in core compression.
Example—Fully ducted, dual spool turbofan engine with a three stage turbine:

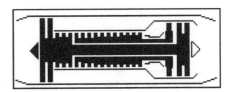

turbofan engine (short ducted) — An engine design wherein the fan exhaust duct does not extend to the rear of the engine. In this design, the fan discharges its air at a forward location in relation to the core-engine exhaust.

Example—Short ducted, dual-spool turbofan engine with a three-stage turbine:

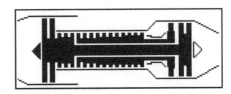

turbofan engine (ultra-high-bypass) — A turbofan engine with a BPR of 10:1 or higher.

turbojet engine — A basic gas turbine engine design with inlet, compressor, combustor, turbine and exhaust sections. The turbojet was the original gas turbine engine.

Example—Nine stage, single spool, axial flow compressor with two stage turbine:

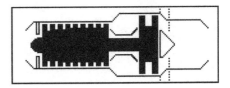

turboprop engine — A type of gas turbine engine. A simple turbojet core with the addition of a propeller

output reduction gearbox and a propeller shaft.
Example—Combination-centrifugal-flow, single-spool compressor with four stage turbine:

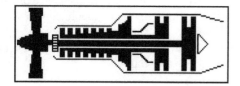

turboshaft engine — A gas turbine engine designed for rotary-wing aircraft. The turboshaft engine has a simple turbojet as its core, as do all current types of gas turbines. Turboshaft engines are similar to turboprop engines except that they provide power to a transmission unit connected to a shaft that typically powers a rotor rather than driving a propeller.
Example—Combination centrifugal flow, single-spool compressor with four-stage turbine:

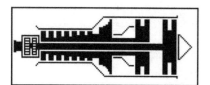

vector — A line that, by scaled length, indicates magnitude, and whose arrow point represents direction of action.

velocity — The actual change of distance with respect to time. The average velocity is equal to total distance divided by total time and is usually expressed in miles per hour or feet per second.

viscocity (oil) — The cohesive force between molecules of an oil (the fluid resistance to flow).

weight of fuel (Wf) — Refers to the fact that in a gas turbine engine, fuel is scheduled by weight via a fuel control to the engine combustor. Scheduling by weight is more accurate than by volume because the fuel's BTU value is constant per unit weight.

x-ray inspection — A nondestructive inspection method in which X-rays are used to locate discontinuities in a structure, either on or beneath its surface. X-ray inspection is especially effective when inspecting irregularly shaped parts.

zero balance mark — A type of matchmark. A "0" mark stamped or etched on two adjacent rotating parts. Zero balance marks are used as a reference for alignment purposes to ensure that the unit retains its balance when rotating.

Answers to Study Questions

CHAPTER 1

1. Hero's aeolipile, 100-200 B.C.
2. Sir Frank Whittle
3. The German Heinkel 178
4. The Boeing 707
5. The Anglo-French Concorde
6. To drive the compressor
7. A turboprop
8. ME-262
9. The Airacomet
10. Tupolev (TU) 144

CHAPTER 2

1. Turbofan
2. Turboshaft
3. Centrifugal impeller
4. Turboprop
5. Kinetic energy
6. Power, velocity, acceleration
7. Newton's third law
8. Continuous combustion cycle
9. An inverse proportion
10. Net
11. Thrust
12. Ambient temperature, altitude, and airspeed
13. E.S.H.P.
14. Tip, shock stall
15. Compression ratio

CHAPTER 3

1. Divergent
2. To increase static pressure
3. Turboshaft
4. To control the direction of the air to each stage
5. A profile or squealer
6. High peak efficiency and pressure ratio
7. The diffuser section
8. 25 to 35 percent
9. Cooling of the liner and gases
10. Because of its shorter length and lighter weight
11. The shrouded tip
12. At the base
13. Nickel alloy
14. Exhaust or jet nozzle
15. Mechanical and aerodynamic blockage
16. The turbofan has lower exhaust velocity.

CHAPTER 4

Chapter 4 contains no study questions.

CHAPTER 5

1. Field cleaning.
2. No, overhaul
3. Thermal cracking
4. Across the leading and trailing edges of turbine blades
5. To maintain turbine wheel balance
6. The trailing edge is thinner, and converging cracks will more easily cause loss of material.
7. Malfunctioning fuel nozzle
8. Both axial and radial loads
9. They offer little rotational resistance.
10. Nondestructive inspection
11. To rebuild a worn surface
12. For internal engine inspections
13. Mils
14. To provide a substitute load
15. To measure a twisting force on a metal fastener

CHAPTER 6

1. Little change in viscosity
2. Higher
3. The word *oil*
4. Turbine oils have a naturally low pour point.
5. The pressurization check valve
6. Between the pump and the internal system
7. To compensate for entrained air in the oil
8. Fuel-cooled and air-cooled types
9. The pressure subsystem
10. Specific volume (displacement)

CHAPTER 7

1. The fuel control
2. The power lever or throttle lever
3. No. The mixture control lever is a reciprocating-engine control lever.
4. Burner can pressure
5. Demineralized or distilled water (sometimes a water/alcohol mixture)

6. Takeoff
7. Trimming
8. To assure that maximum rated thrust is being developed
9. Engine thrust
10. No wind and low humidity
11. The gear type
12. At the filter screens
13. Engine starting and idle speed
14. To act as a flow divider and to dump fuel from the manifold on shutdown
15. Combustor gas pressure
16. To control all engine systems
17. To control fuel scheduling
18. To detect both internal and external faults in engine systems
19. It automatically positions the throttle levers to maintain engine thrust requirements.
20. On the flight deck

CHAPTER 8

1. To reduce the engine's tendency to stall on acceleration or deceleration at low or intermediate speed
2. All
3. RPM effect on airflow
4. Yes
5. Overboard
6. System maladjustment
7. The electronic engine control (EEC)
8. The N_1 low-pressure compressor

CHAPTER 9

1. No. It is designed to prevent ice formation
2. No. It is controlled by a bimetallic spring.
3. Airflow is blocked or distorted into the compressor.
4. The compressor
5. With the engine running

CHAPTER 10

1. On the engine accessory gearbox
2. The overrunning clutch assembly
3. The starter-generator
4. The starter pressure regulating and shutoff valve
5. APU, GPU, or engine cross bleed air
6. Mechanical energy

7. Electronic engine control (EEC)
8. Receive

CHAPTER 11

1. To change AC to DC
2. The turbine engine has a much higher intensity spark.
3. Secondary
4. Nickel-chromium alloy
5. Auto-position or continuous position
6. The EEU unit
7. Torque oil pressure
8. Two

CHAPTER 12

1. Turbine inlet temperature (TIT)
2. The EGT or ITT indicator
3. Jetcal analyzer
4. To monitor engine speed during start and for over-speed
5. Yes. It operates as an independent electrical system.
6. No. On a very warm day, thrust is necessarily well below 100 percent.
7. No. EPR is the thrust indicator on an EPR-rated engine.
8. No. The tachometer indicator is the thrust indicator on a speed-rated turbofan engine.
9. The AC bus
10. Pounds per hour (pph)
11. In the engine fuel line to the combustor
12. The thermocouple
13. The oil pressure transmitter
14. An operating range
15. An operating limit

CHAPTER 13

1. Yes. All of them do.
2. The two-wire thermal switch
3. No
4. No. It has self-contained air.
5. To explode when heated and permit the extinguishing agent to flow

CHAPTER 14

Chapter 14 contains no study questions.

Index

A

abrasion, defined, 5-39, 5-58
abrasive grit process, 5-6
absolute pressure, 3-29
acceleration
    calculation, 2-13 to 2-14
    defined, 2-13
    hydropneumatic fuel control system, 7-14
acceleration checks, 7-31
accessory drive gearbox, 6-9, 6-37
accessory unit
    crash engagement damage, 10-8
    design and construction, 3-6 to 3-9
    GE/Snecma CFM56 turbofan, 4-47 to 4-48
    Pratt & Whitney JT8D turbofan, 4-9
    Pratt & Whitney PT6 turboprop, 4-34
    Rolls-Royce Allison 250 turboshaft, 4-22
AC exciter systems
    vs. DC systems, 11-9 to 11-10
    high-tension ignition systems, 11-7 to 11-8
ACMS (Aircraft Condition Monitoring System), 5-8
active clearance control
    compressors, 3-28
    turbines, 3-44
additives, fuel, 7-3
aeolipile, 1-1
aerodynamic blockage thrust reversers, 3-51 to 3-52
affordable jets, 1-8
afterburners, 3-50 to 3-51
aft-fan system, 2-8
air, weight of, A8-1
air balance chamber, 5-34
air blast simplex fuel nozzles, 7-58 to 7-59
Airbus A300, 3-55
Airbus A400 military transport, 2-8
Airbus Industries (EADS), A4-1
Aircraft Condition Monitoring System (ACMS), 5-8
aircraft manufacturers list, A4-1 to A4-14
airfoil, centrifugal compressor inspection criteria, 5-24
air-fuel ratio, 7-7 to 7-8
air speed
    record, 1-4
    thrust impact, 2-35 to 2-36
air starts, 14-5, 14-8 to 14-9
air temperature, Mach number impact, 2-38. *See also* temperature
Air Transport Association of America (ATA), technical data standards, 5-60
air turbine starters. *See* pneumatic starters
Allison 250 turboshaft engine. *See* Rolls-Royce Allison 250 turboshaft engine
altitude, thrust impact, 2-35
altitude compensation, 7-14
alumel, 12-6
ambient temperature. *See* temperature
American Society of Testing Materials (ASTM), viscosity index, 6-2
aneroid shutoff valve, 6-31

angle of attack (AOA)
    compressor anti-stall systems, 8-1 to 8-6
    compressor pressure ratio influence, 3-24
    compressor stall, 3-24 to 3-25
    control over, 3-22
annular combustors, 3-32 to 3-34, 7-57 to 7-58
annular reverse-flow combustors, 3-34
anti-icing systems, 9-1 to 9-6
antileakage valve, GE/Snecma CFM56 turbofan, 6-37
anti-stall systems, 8-1 to 8-15
    bleed systems, 8-6 to 8-14
    introduction, 8-1
    variable vane systems, 8-1 to 8-6
Antonov Aero Corporation, A4-1
AOA. *See* angle of attack (AOA)
approach procedures, 14-10
APU. *See* auxiliary power unit (APU)
Arnold, H.H. Hap, 1-6
ASM (auto-throttle servo mechanisms), GE/Snecma CFM56 turbofan, 7-27
ASTM (American Society of Testing Materials), viscosity index, 6-2
ATA (Air Transport Association of America), technical data standards, 5-60
athodyd (aero-thermodynamic duct), 2-1 to 2-2
A/T systems. *See* auto-throttle (A/T) systems
Augusta-Westland, A4-9
auto-ignition circuits, 11-2 to 11-4
auto throttle limit indicator, 12-4
auto-throttle servo mechanisms (ASM), GE/Snecma CFM56 turbofan, 7-27
auto-throttle (A/T) systems
    function and operation, 7-27 to 7-28, 14-4
    GE/Snecma CFM56 turbofan, 7-27
auxiliary power unit (APU)
    electric starters, 10-3
    fuel controlling systems, 7-28 to 7-30
    pneumatic starting systems, 10-10
    starting power source, 10-6
Avions de Transport Regional (ATR), A4-1
axial flow compressors and fans
    advantages and disadvantages, 3-21
    blade replacement, 5-22 to 5-23
    blade tip clearance, 5-22
    cascade effect, 3-23
    components, 3-14 to 3-17
    compressor pressure ratio, 3-17 to 3-18
    cycle pressure ratio, 3-19
    fan bypass ratio, 3-20
    fan pressure ratio, 3-19
    inspection and repairs, 5-20 to 5-23
    lift, 3-21
    pressure rise per stage, 3-18 to 3-19
    r.p.m. limitations, 2-37 to 2-38
    taper design, 3-23 to 3-24
    types, 3-12 to 3-14
axial turbine construction, 3-41 to 3-44, 4-8

B

"balanced oil piston" hydromechanical indicating system, 12-19, 12-20 to 12-21
ball bearings, 5-33 to 5-34
band system, bleed anti-stall systems, 8-7 to 8-10

BCF (Bromochlorodifluoromethane), 13-6
bearings
    distress terms, 5-39 to 5-42
    GE/Snecma CFM56 turbofan, 4-37, 4-39 to 4-40
    inspection and repairs, 5-33 to 5-42
    installation, 5-39
    Pratt & Whitney JT8D turbofan, 4-10 to 4-12
    Pratt & Whitney PT6 turboprop, 4-37
    Rolls-Royce Allison 250 turboshaft, 4-22 to 4-24
    types, 5-33
bearing seals, inspection and repairs, 5-34 to 5-37
bearing support sub-module, GE/Snecma CFM56 turbofan, 4-39
Bell Corporation
    aircraft product list, A4-10
    history, 1-6
Bell Helicopter Textron, A4-10
bellmouth compressor inlets, 3-5
bellows assembly, 7-13
Bendix fuel control
    DP-L2®, 7-16 to 7-18
    Pratt & Whitney PT6 turboprop, 7-11 to 7-16
Beriev Aircraft Company, A4-2
Bernoulli's principle, 2-14 to 2-16
bhp (brake horsepower), 2-4
Biojet fuel, 7-2
BITE. *See* built-in-test-equipment (BITE)
blades
    compressors, 3-14 to 3-17, 3-23 to 3-24, 3-28, 5-24
    turbines, 3-41 to 3-44
    See also fan blades
bleed air
    anti-icing systems, 9-1, 9-3
    bearing pressurization, 4-10
    compressor role, 3-9
    control valve, 4-17
    control with seals, 3-38
    extraction through diffuser case, 4-4
    high-pressure compressors, 4-42
    high-pressure turbines, 4-45
    starter systems, 10-3, 10-10
    water-injection systems, 7-46
bleed anti-stall systems, 8-6 to 8-14
    band system, 8-7 to 8-10
    introduction, 8-6 to 8-7
    operation, 8-7
    valve system, 8-10 to 8-11
    variable and transient bleed valve systems, 8-13 to 8-14
blisk, 3-29, 3-38
blisters, defined, 5-58
blow-away jets, 3-6
BMW, 1-5
Boeing
    aircraft product list, A4-2, A4-10 to A4-11
    history, 1-6 to 1-7
Boeing 707, 1-7, 7-45
Boeing 727, 1-8, 3-55, 3-57, 4-1, 7-65
Boeing 737, 4-1, 4-34, 9-2, 10-6, 11-16 to 11-18

Boeing 737-100, 3-55
Boeing 737-200, 3-57
Boeing 747, 2-5
Boeing 757, 6-13
Boeing 777, 11-4
Boeing 787, 3-9, 10-5 to 10-6
Boeing 2707, 1-7
Boeing KC-135, 4-34
Bombardier Aerospace Corporation, A4-3
borescoping, 5-12, 5-25
bowing, defined, 5-58
brake horsepower (bhp), 2-4
braking systems, 3-51 to 3-54
Branca's turbine device, 1-1
Brayton cycle, 2-16 to 2-18
Brazil, aircraft manufacturers, A4-5
brinelling, defined, 5-39
British Aerospace Corporation, A4-4
Bromochlorodifluoromethane (Halon 1211—CBrClF2), 13-6
Bromotrifluoromethane (Halon 1301—CF3Br), 13-6
brush bearing seals, 5-35 to 5-37
buckets. *See* turbine blades
buckling, defined, 5-58
built-in-test-equipment (BITE)
    advantages, 5-53
    function in FADEC system, 7-22
    pneumatic fire/overheat detection and fire extinguishing system, 13-8
burner can pressure, 7-8
"burner-can shift" inspection, 5-25
burners. *See* combustors
burning, defined, 5-39
burnishing, defined, 5-39
burns, defined, 5-58
burrs, defined, 5-40, 5-58
business jets
    combination compressors, 3-21
    compressor pressure ratio, 3-18
    drag chutes, 3-54
    fan bypass ratio, 3-20
    fuel systems, 7-28 to 7-29
    gas turbine engine use, 1-8
    scheduled line maintenance inspections, 5-7
    tail cone, 3-46
butyl rubber o-ring seals, 5-46
bypass ducts, 2-16

C

Campini, Secundo, 1-5 to 1-6
Canada, aircraft manufacturers, A4-3, A4-5
can-annular combustors, 3-31 to 3-32, 4-5 to 4-6
capacitor discharge ignition systems, 11-1
Caproni Company, 1-5 to 1-6
Carboblast grit cleaning procedure, 5-6
carbon dioxide (CO_2), 13-6
carbon oil bearing seals, 5-35
carbon tetrachloride (Halon 104—CCL4), 13-6
cartridge-pneumatic starters, 10-14
CASA Corporation, A4-4
cascade effect, 3-23
C-D (convergent-divergent) inlets, 3-4
CDU. *See* control display unit (CDU)
Celsius, conversions from/to Fahrenheit, A3-2 to A3-3

centistoke values, 6-2 to 6-3
centrifugal flow compressors
    advantages, 3-12
    components and operation, 3-9 to 3-12
    inspection and repairs, 5-23 to 5-24
    lift, 3-21
    r.p.m. limitations, 2-38
Cessna Corporation, A4-4
CF6 turbofan engine. *See* General Electric CF6 turbofan engine
CFM56 turbofan engine. *See* General Electric/Snecma CFM56 turbofan engine
chafing, defined, 5-40
Chinese aircraft manufacturers, A4-8, A4-13
Chinese rocket, 1-1
chip detectors, 6-29
chipping, defined, 5-40
chlorobromomethane (Halon 1011—CH2ClBr), 13-6
choked exhaust nozzles, 2-22 to 2-23, 3-46 to 3-48
chromel, 12-6
Cirrus Design Corporation, A4-4
CIT (compressor inlet temperature) sensors, 8-2
civil aviation kerosene, 7-1
CJ610 turbojet engine, 6-23 to 6-31
cleaning
    after extinguishing agent use, 13-8
    fluid cleaning procedure, 5-4 to 5-6
    turbine blades and vanes, 5-6
climb setting, 14-7, 14-10
clutch assemblies, 10-3, 10-6
CM (condition monitoring) maintenance, 5-51
CO_2 (carbon dioxide), 13-6
coatings. *See* plasma sprays or coatings
cockpit indicating system. *See* instrument systems
Code of Federal Regulations (CFR)
    lubrication system requirements, 6-1
    noise standards, 3-55
coking, 6-30
cold section
    compressors (*See* compressors)
    diagram, 5-13
    disassembly, 5-17
    inspection and repairs, 5-17 to 5-24, 5-33
    materials, 3-59 to 3-60
    Pratt & Whitney JT8D turbofan, 4-3
cold tank oil systems
    GE/Snecma CFM56 turbofan, 6-35 to 6-38
    vs. hot tank systems, 6-38 to 6-39
    Pratt & Whitney PT6 turboprop, 6-31 to 6-33
combination flow compressors, 3-21, 4-17 to 4-18
combustion chamber
    afterburners, 3-50 to 3-51
    design and construction, 4-5
    detachment, 5-56 to 5-58
    early designs, 1-2, 1-3
    function, 3-30
    GE/Snecma CFM56 turbofan, 4-35, 4-43 to 4-44
    inspection points, 5-26
    V-1 engines, 2-2
    See also combustors

combustion liners
    annular combustors, 3-32
    annular reverse-flow combustors, 3-34
    borescope inspections, 5-25
    fuel nozzles, 7-54 to 7-59
    functions, 3-30, 4-18
    inspections and maintenance, 5-25
    location, 4-5
    materials, 3-60
    Pratt & Whitney JT8D, 4-5
    Pratt & Whitney PT6 turboprop, 4-24, 4-30
    Rolls Royce Allison, 4-18
combustor drain valves, 7-61
combustors
    annular combustors, 3-32 to 3-34, 7-57 to 7-58
    annular reverse-flow combustors, 3-34
    can-annular combustors, 3-31 to 3-32, 4-5 to 4-6
    components, 3-29
    configurations, 3-29 to 3-30
    construction materials, 3-60
    efficiency, 3-31
    emissions, 3-34 to 3-36
    flameout, 3-30 to 3-31
    function, 3-29
    GE/Snecma CFM56 turbofan, 4-43 to 4-44
    inspection and repairs, 5-25
    malfunction, 5-55 to 5-58
    multiple-can combustors, 3-31
    new designs, 3-34
    operation, 3-30 to 3-31
    Pratt & Whitney JT8D turbofan, 4-5 to 4-6
    Pratt & Whitney PT6 turboprop, 4-30
    Rolls-Royce Allison 250 turboshaft, 4-18
commercial aircraft
    fuel systems, 7-29 to 7-30
    history, 1-6 to 1-8
    scheduled line maintenance inspections, 5-7
    time between overhaul, 5-51
commuter aircraft
    fan bypass ratio, 3-20
    fuel systems, 7-28 to 7-29
    gas turbine engine use, 1-8
    scheduled line maintenance inspections, 5-7
composite materials, 3-60
compressor bleeds, 7-26
compressor cases
    active clearance control, 3-28
    components, 4-17
    construction materials, 3-59
    high-pressure compressors, 4-41
    inspection and repairs, 5-24
compressor-diffuser section, 3-29
compressor discharge pressure, 7-8
compressor inlet area thrust, 2-24
compressor inlet guide vanes, 3-17, 3-22
compressor inlet screens, 3-5
compressor inlet temperature (CIT) sensors, 8-2
compressor outlet area thrust, 2-23 to 2-24
compressor pressure ratio
    angle of attack impact, 3-24
    calculation, 3-18
    centrifugal flow compressors, 3-10
    cycle pressure ratio, 3-19

design considerations, 3-17 to 3-18
dual-spool axial compressors, 3-18 to 3-19
fan pressure ratio, 3-19 to 3-20
mass airflow impact, 3-25 to 3-26
Pratt & Whitney JT8D turbofan, 4-3, 4-4
Pratt & Whitney PT6 turboprop, 4-24
rated compressor pressure ratio, 7-8
rise per stage, 3-18 to 3-19
Rolls-Royce Allison 250 turboshaft, 4-12
stalls, 8-2
thermal efficiency impact, 2-33 to 2-34
compressors
  anti-stall systems (*See* anti-stall systems)
  axial flow compressors and fans (*See* axial flow compressors and fans)
  blade damage, 5-3 to 5-4
  bleed air distribution, 3-9
  bleed systems, 8-6 to 8-14
  cascade effect, 3-23
  centrifugal flow compressors (*See* centrifugal flow compressors)
  combination compressors, 3-21
  construction materials, 3-61 to 3-62
  design advances, 3-28 to 3-29
  efficiency, 2-33 to 2-34, 3-9
  function, 3-9
  GE/Snecma CFM56 turbofan, 4-41 to 4-42
  horsepower requirement, 2-28 to 2-29
  inspection and repairs, 5-17 to 5-24
  interstage airflow, 3-21 to 3-22
  lift, 3-21
  maintenance, 5-3 to 5-6
  malfunction, 5-54 to 5-55
  mixed-flow compressors, 3-28 to 3-29
  operation, 3-9
  Pratt & Whitney JT8D turbofan, 4-1 to 4-4
  Pratt & Whitney PT6 turboprop, 4-24, 4-29 to 4-30
  Rolls-Royce Allison 250 turboshaft, 4-17 to 4-18
  stalls, 3-24 to 3-29, 8-2
  starter systems, 10-1 to 10-3
  taper design, 3-23 to 3-24
compressor stator vanes
  axial flow compressors, 3-14
  blisks, 3-29
  GE/Snecma CFM56 turbofan, 4-42
  inspection and repairs, 5-24
  interstage compressor airflow, 3-22
  Pratt & Whitney JT8D turbofan, 4-4
  Pratt & Whitney PT6 turboprop, 4-29
  Rolls-Royce Allison 250 turboshaft, 4-17
  types, 3-17
  variable angle compressor stator vane systems, 8-1 to 8-5, 8-6
computing section of fuel control
  hydromechanical system, 7-10
  hydropneumatic system, 7-11 to 7-13
Concorde, 1-7
condition levers, 14-5
condition monitoring (CM) maintenance, 5-51
construction features. *See* design and construction features
contaminants, in oil system, 6-16
continuous duty circuits, 11-2

continuous loop fire/overheat detection system, 13-2 to 13-3
control display unit (CDU)
  EEC output, 7-23
  GE/Snecma CFM56 turbofan, 7-67, 8-5
Convair Corporation, A4-4
convergent "choked" nozzle theory, 3-46 to 3-48
convergent-divergent exhaust ducts, 3-48 to 3-49
convergent-divergent (C-D) inlets, 3-4
convergent ducts, 2-16, 3-47
converging, defined, 5-58
conversions
  measurement, A3-4 to A3-5
  temperature, A3-2 to A3-3
cooling
  electronic engine control, 3-44
  engine compartment ventilation and cooling, 3-58
  turbine blades and vanes, 3-42 to 3-44
core engine module, GE/Snecma CFM56 turbofan, 4-41 to 4-45
corrected exhaust gas temperature, 5-50
corrected fuel flow, 5-50
corrected mass airflow, 5-50
corrected revolutions per minute, 5-50
corrosion, defined, 5-40, 5-58
cowl thermal anti-icing (CTAI), 7-26
cracks
  combustion section, 5-25
  defined, 5-58
  turbine section, 5-26 to 5-27, 5-29 to 5-33
crash engagement, 10-8
crazing, defined, 5-58
creep, 5-27
critical area, centrifugal compressor inspection criteria, 5-23
cross-bleed engine start indicator, 12-4
cross-bleed starting, 10-11 to 10-13
cruise indicator, 12-4
cruise setting, 14-7, 14-10
CTAI (cowl thermal anti-icing), 7-26
cushion checks, 7-31
cycle counters, 5-51
cycle pressure ratio, 3-19

D

DAC (dual annular combustors), 3-33, 4-43 to 4-44
Daimler-Chrysler Corp., A4-4
d'Arsonval meter, 12-7
Dart turboprop engine, 3-31
Dassault Corporation, A4-5
data plate speed check, 7-36
DC-8, 3-57, 4-34, 7-45
DC-9, 3-55, 4-1
DC-10, 12-2
DC exciter systems
  vs. AC systems, 11-9 to 11-10
  low-tension ignition systems, 11-5 to 11-6
deceleration, hydropneumatic fuel control system, 7-14 to 7-16
decimal equivalents, A3-1
deformation, defined, 5-58
DeHavilland Comet, 1-6
deicers, 7-50 to 7-52
Denel Group, A4-11
density, 2-10

dents, defined, 5-58
descent procedures, 14-10
design and construction features, 3-1 to 3-63
  accessory unit, 3-6 to 3-9
  bearings (*See* bearings)
  combustion section (*See* combustors)
  compressor-diffuser section, 3-29
  compressor section (*See* compressors)
  construction materials, 3-58 to 3-63
  directional references, 3-63
  engine compartment ventilation and cooling, 3-58
  engine mounts, 3-58
  engine station numbers, 3-63
  entrance ducts, 3-1 to 3-6
  exhaust section (*See* exhaust section)
  noise suppression, 3-54 to 3-58
  overview, 3-1
  thrust reversers, 3-51 to 3-54
  turbine section (*See* turbines)
DFCS (digital flight control system), 7-27. *See also* full authority digital engine control (FADEC)
Diamond Aircraft, A4-5
dibromodifluoromethane (Halon 1202—CBr_2F_2), 13-6
differential metering head regulator, 7-16
differential pressure, 12-29 to 12-30
  indicating light, 6-21
diffuser inlets, 3-4 to 3-5
diffusers
  centrifugal flow compressors, 3-10
  Pratt & Whitney JT8D turbofan, 4-4 to 4-5
  Pratt & Whitney PT6 turboprop, 4-29 to 4-30
  pressure, 3-29
  Rolls-Royce Allison 250 turboshaft, 4-18
digital flight control system (DFCS), 7-27. *See also* full authority digital engine control (FADEC)
directional references, 3-63, 4-13
disassembly of powerplant, 5-11
distortion, defined, 5-58
distress, defined, 5-58
divergent ducts, 2-24, 3-10
domestic object damage, 5-4
drag chutes, 3-54
drain tanks, 7-61
drill sizes, A3-1
drip valves, 7-61
drive shafts, 3-41
dry motoring, 14-4, 14-6 to 14-7
dry sump lubrication systems, 6-9 to 6-23
  component overview, 6-9 to 6-10, 6-23
  differential pressure light, 6-21
  dual-pressure indicating system, 6-21
  filter bypass warning light, 6-20 to 6-21
  filter pop-out warning, 6-22
  GE CJ610 turbojet, 6-23 to 6-31
  low oil pressure procedures, 6-22
  low oil pressure warning light, 6-19 to 6-20
  oil filters, 6-15 to 6-19
  oil pumps, 6-11 to 6-15
  oil tanks, 6-10 to 6-11
  Pratt & Whitney JT8D turbofan, 6-33 to 6-35
  Pratt & Whitney PT6 turboprop, 6-31 to 6-33

dual annular combustors (DAC), 3-33, 4-43 to 4-44
dual-line duplex fuel nozzles, 7-58
dual-pressure indicating system, 6-21
dual-spool axial compressors
    advantages, 3-13 to 3-14
    compressor pressure ratio, 3-18 to 3-19
    Pratt & Whitney JT8D turbofan, 4-1 to 4-4
    starting procedure, 10-10 to 10-11
ducted ultra high-bypass engines, 2-8
dump valves, 7-61
duplex fuel nozzles, 7-55 to 7-56, 7-58 to 7-59
duty cycle, air starters, 10-13
dye-penetrant method, 5-15
dynamometers, 2-27, 2-29, 5-47

E

EADS (Eurocopter Company), A4-11 to A4-12
ear protection, 7-37
Eclipse Aviation, A4-5
eddy current method, 5-16 to 5-17
EEC. *See* electronic engine control (EEC)
effective perceived noise decibels (EPNdB), 3-55
efficiency
    combustors, 3-31
    overall efficiency, 2-33
    propulsive efficiency, 2-29 to 2-32
    thermal efficiency, 2-32 to 2-34
EGT. *See* exhaust gas temperature (EGT) indicating system
EH Industries LTD, A4-11
electric starters, 10-3
electron beam welding, 5-20, 5-29 to 5-31
electronic engine control (EEC)
    anti-icing system, 9-5
    cooling, 3-44
    engine operation procedures, 14-2 to 14-5
    FADEC interfaces, 7-22
    fuel control, 7-8
    fuel scheduling systems, 7-18 to 7-25
    function, 7-22
    GE/Snecma CFM56 turbofan, 7-22 to 7-27, 8-13 to 8-14, 11-16
    ignition systems, 11-2 to 11-4
    starter systems, 10-6, 10-13 to 10-14
    variable angle compressor stator vane systems, 8-4 to 8-5
electronic fuel scheduling systems, 7-18 to 7-25
electronic gearbox-mounted N2 speed sensor, 12-13
electronic torque indicating system, 12-19, 12-22
electro-thermal anti-icing systems, 9-5
Embraer Corporation, A4-5
emergencies
    hand signals, A5-1
    operating procedures, 14-4 to 14-5, 14-7
emergency power levers, 14-6
emissions, from combustors, 3-34 to 3-36
Emivest Aerospace Corp., A4-5
Empressa Brasillira, A4-5
Endstrom Helicopter Corporation, A4-11
energy, defined, 2-14
engine compartment ventilation and cooling, 3-58

engine condition indicators, 12-1
engine cycle, 5-27, 6-17
engine data sheets, 4-48 to 4-56
engine failure
    causes, 3-24, 3-25, 5-3
    Pratt & Whitney PT6 turboprop, 14-7 to 14-8
engine indicator maximum pointer reset gauge, 12-3
engine instrument systems. *See* instrument systems
engine mounts, 3-58
engine operation, 14-1 to 14-10
    cautions, 14-9 to 14-10
    emergency operating procedures, 14-4 to 14-5
    FAA engine power ratings, 14-9
    FADEC system, 14-2 to 14-5
    by ground personnel, 14-1
    hand signals, A5-1
    run-up procedures, 14-1 to 14-4
    safety precautions, 14-1
    turboprop engines, 14-5 to 14-9
engine overhauls, 5-50 to 5-51
engine pressure ratio (EPR), 12-17 to 12-19
    EPR formula, 12-17
    function, 12-17
    gauge, 12-17 to 12-18
    input sources, 12-1
    Pratt & Whitney dual-spool engine example, 12-18
    Pt_2 probes, 9-3
    thrust indication, 7-31
    trimming procedure for EPR-rated engines, 7-32 to 7-36
engine purging procedure, 14-4, 14-6 to 14-7
engine rating identification plug, GE/Snecma CFM56 turbofan, 7-24 to 7-25
engine sensors, GE/Snecma CFM56 turbofan, 7-25
engine shutdown
    emergency procedure, 14-5
    hydropneumatic fuel control system, 7-16
    pneumatic starter cautions, 10-6
    Pratt & Whitney PT6 turboprop engine, 14-7
    procedures, 14-2, 14-10
engine speed signal, 7-8
engine stations
    Pratt & Whitney JT8D turbofan, 4-12
    Pratt & Whitney PT6 turboprop, 4-24
    purpose, 3-63
engine symbols, 3-63
engine test-run worksheet, Pratt & Whitney JT8D turbofan, 4-15
engine vibration gauge, 12-1 to 12-3
enrichment valves, 7-16
entrance ducts, 3-1 to 3-6
Environmental Protection Agency (EPA), 1-7, 3-34, 3-36
EPNdB (effective perceived noise decibels), 3-55
epoxy-resin materials, 3-60
EPR. *See* engine pressure ratio (EPR)
equivalent shaft horsepower (Eshp), 2-27 to 2-28, A8-1
Erickson Air Crane Inc., A4-11
erosion
    defined, 5-26, 5-58

material loss problem, 5-4
Eshp (equivalent shaft horsepower), 2-27 to 2-28, A8-1
ethylene propylene o-ring seals, 5-46
Eurocopter Company (EADS), A4-11 to A4-12
Europrop International Corporation TP 400, 1-7
exciters
    AC exciter systems, 11-7 to 11-8
    DC exciter systems, 11-5 to 11-6
    function, 11-1
exhaust cone outlet area thrust, 2-24
exhaust cones, 3-45 to 3-46
exhaust gas temperature (EGT) indicating system
    checks, 12-10
    components, 12-5 to 12-7
    instrument markings, 12-4, 12-33
    limits, 12-7 to 12-9
    operation, 12-7
    Tt_7 probes, 4-10
    turbine inlet temperature, 12-4 to 12-5
    types, 12-4
exhaust section
    afterburners, 3-50 to 3-51
    components and operation, 3-45 to 3-48
    convergent-divergent exhaust system, 3-48 to 3-49
    inspection and repairs, 5-33
    Pratt & Whitney JT8D turbofan, 4-10
    Pratt & Whitney PT6 turboprop, 4-33
    variable area exhaust nozzles, 3-51
exhaust temperature indicating systems, 12-4 to 12-10
extended-duty ignition systems, 11-1, 11-8 to 11-9

F

FAA. *See* Federal Aviation Administration (FAA)
FADEC. *See* full authority digital engine control (FADEC)
Fahrenheit, conversions from/to Celsius, A3-2 to A3-3
failure, engine. *See* engine failure
Fairchild Dornier Industries, Germany, A4-6
Fairchild USA Industries, A4-6
fan and booster sub-module, GE/Snecma CFM56 turbofan, 4-36 to 4-38
fan blades
    construction materials, 3-59 to 3-60
    damage limits, 5-17 to 5-19
    design features, 3-15 to 3-16
    efficiency, 7-6
    inspections and maintenance, 5-20, 5-23
    tips and roots, 3-16 to 3-17
fan blisk, 3-29
fan bypass ratio, 3-20
fan engine thrust, 2-25
fan frame sub-module, GE/Snecma CFM56 turbofan, 4-39 to 4-41
fan module, GE/Snecma CFM56 turbofan, 4-35 to 4-41
fan pressure ratio, 3-19 to 3-20
fan speed trims, 7-32 to 7-36
FARs (Federal Aviation Regulations). *See* Code of Federal Regulations (CFR)
fasteners, locking methods, 5-44 to 5-46
FCU (fuel control unit), 7-11 to 7-14

Federal Aviation Administration (FAA)
    dial face markings for instruments, 12-32 to 12-33
    engine power ratings, 14-9
    Form 337, 5-9, 5-11
    noise and exhaust pollution regulation, 1-7
    noise level measurement, 3-55
    shop maintenance requirements, 5-8
    type certificate data sheets
        No. E23EA (GE CF6 turbofan), A2-1 to A2-7
        No. EIGL (Allison 250-C28), A1-1 to A1-4
Federal Aviation Regulations (FARs). See Code of Federal Regulations (CFR)
filter bypass warning light, 6-20 to 6-21
filters
    fuel filters, 7-16, 7-52 to 7-53
    oil filters (See oil filters)
fire extinguishing systems, 13-6 to 13-8
fire/overheat detection and extinguishing systems, 13-1 to 13-10
    continuous loop fire/overheat detection system, 13-2 to 13-3
    fire extinguishing systems, 13-6 to 13-8
    flame detector system, 13-6
    introduction, 13-1
    photoelectric sensors, 13-6
    pneumatic fire/overheat detection system, 13-3 to 13-6, 13-8 to 13-10
    single-wire thermal overheat detection switch, 13-1
    smoke detectors, 13-6
    two-wire overheat detection switch, 13-1 to 13-2
fires
    during ground starts, 14-4, 14-7
    in-flight, 14-7
flaking, defined, 5-58
flame detector system, 13-6
flameout
    causes, 3-30 to 3-31, 7-50
    emergency in-flight ram-air starting procedure, 14-5
    main ignition's role in prevention, 11-1, 11-2, 11-14
    Pratt & Whitney PT6 turboprop, 14-8
    relights, 14-4, 14-8
flat rating, 7-37 to 7-38
flight inlet ducts, 3-1 to 3-6
flight management computers (FMC), GE/Snecma CFM56 turbofan, 7-27
flowmeters, 12-24 to 12-27
fluid cleaning procedure, 5-4 to 5-6
fluids, 7-44. See also lubrication systems
fluorocarbon o-ring seals, 5-46
FMC (flight management computers), GE/Snecma CFM56 turbofan, 7-27
FOD (foreign object damage), 5-3 to 5-4
Fokker Corporation, A4-6
force, 2-12
foreign object damage (FOD), 5-3 to 5-4
formulae, A8-1
France
    aircraft manufacturers, A4-1, A4-5, A4-8, A4-11 to A4-12, A4-13
    supersonic aircraft, 1-7
free power turbines, 2-6 to 2-7, 3-42
Freon fire extinguishing agents, 13-6
frequency tuning, 3-16 to 3-17

fretting, defined, 5-40
frosting, defined, 5-58
fuel additives, 7-3
fuel-air combustion starters, 10-14
fuel consumption and efficiency
    thrust specific fuel consumption, 7-3 to 7-7
    turbofan engines, 2-38 to 2-39
    turbojet engines, 1-5
fuel control unit (FCU), 7-11 to 7-14
fuel distributors, 7-54 to 7-59
fuel efficiency. See fuel consumption and efficiency
fuel filters, 7-16, 7-52 to 7-53
fuel filter warning switches, 7-52
fuel flow indicating systems, 12-1, 12-4, 12-24 to 12-27
fuel heaters, 7-50 to 7-52
fuel inlet, 7-16
fuel level by weight indicator, 12-4
fuel metering section, 7-8 to 7-10, 7-11
fuel nozzles, 7-54 to 7-59
fuel pressure gauge, 12-1, 12-32
fuel pressurizing and dump (P & D) valves, 7-59 to 7-61
fuel pumps
    functions, 7-48 to 7-50
    hydromechanical systems, 7-8 to 7-10
    Pratt & Whitney PT6 turboprop, 7-11
    types, 7-48
fuel scheduling
    electronic systems, 7-18 to 7-25
    fuel control unit, 7-11 to 7-14
fuel systems, 7-1 to 7-69
    adjustments on main engines, 7-30 to 7-43
        data plate speed check, 7-36
        engine pressure ratio and speed trims, 7-31 to 7-36
        flat rating, 7-37 to 7-38
        part power trim, 7-31
        performance checks, 7-30 to 7-31, 7-38 to 7-43
        safety precautions, 7-37
        specific gravity adjustment, 7-30
        trim restrictions, 7-36 to 7-37
    air-fuel ratio, 7-7 to 7-8
    auxiliary power unit fuel controlling systems, 7-28 to 7-30
    basic schematic, 7-63
    combustor drain valves, 7-61
    drain tanks, 7-61
    dump valves, 7-61
    electronic fuel scheduling systems, 7-18 to 7-25
    fuel additives, 7-3
    fuel control, 7-1, 7-7 to 7-10
    fuel filters, 7-52 to 7-53
    fuel handling and safety, 7-2 to 7-3
    fuel heaters, 7-50 to 7-52
    fuel nozzles, 7-54 to 7-59
    fuel pressurizing and dump valves, 7-59 to 7-61
    fuel pumps (See fuel pumps)
    fuel quantity in pounds indicator, 12-4
    fuel types, 7-1 to 7-2
    functions, 7-1, 7-7
    GE/Snecma CFM56 turbofan, 7-20 to 7-28, 7-65 to 7-67
    hydromechanical systems, 7-8 to 7-10

    hydropneumatic systems, 7-11 to 7-18
    icing, 7-50
    power management and fuel scheduling, 7-25 to 7-28
    Pratt & Whitney JT8D turbofan, 7-64, 7-65
    signals, 7-8
    thrust specific fuel consumption, 7-3 to 7-7
    troubleshooting, 7-68 to 7-69
    water detection in fuels, 7-3
    water injection thrust augmentation, 7-43 to 7-47
fuel temperature bi-metallic disks, 7-16
fuel to airspeed comparison, 2-5
fuel used indicator, 12-4
full authority digital engine control (FADEC)
    anti-icing system, 9-5
    components, 7-22
    design, 7-22
    engine operation procedures, 14-2 to 14-5
    functions, 5-53 to 5-54, 7-20 to 7-21
    GE/Snecma CFM56 turbofan, 7-20 to 7-25
    ignition systems, 11-2 to 11-4
    interfaces, 7-22
    quantitative debris monitor, 6-29
    speed sensing, 12-13 to 12-14
    starter systems, 10-6, 10-13 to 10-14
    tip clearance control, 3-44
    trim procedures, 7-34 to 7-36
    variable and transient bleed valve systems, 8-13 to 8-14
    variable angle compressor stator vane systems, 8-4 to 8-5
full power checks, 7-32
full reversing propellers, 3-54

G

galling, defined, 5-40, 5-58
Garrett TFE-731 turbofan. See Honeywell TFE-731 turbofan engine
gas generator turbines, 2-6
gas path
    domestic object damage, 5-4
    erosion, 5-4
    Pratt & Whitney PT6 turboprop, 4-24
    Rolls-Royce Allison 250 turboshaft, 4-12
gas producer turbine (N1)
    Pratt & Whitney PT6 turboprop, 4-30
    Rolls-Royce Allison 250 turboshaft, 4-18 to 4-20
gas turbine engines
    anti-icing systems (See anti-icing systems)
    anti-stall systems (See anti-stall systems)
    components, 2-2
    cost, 5-51
    design and construction (See design and construction features)
    engine operation (See engine operation)
    fire/overheat detection and extinguishing systems (See fire/overheat detection and extinguishing systems)
    fuel systems (See fuel systems)
    history, 1-1 to 1-9
    ignition systems (See ignition systems)
    inspections and maintenance (See

inspections and maintenance)
instrument systems (*See* instrument systems)
jet propulsion theory (*See* jet propulsion theory and principles)
lubrication systems (*See* lubrication systems)
vs. piston engines, 2-4 to 2-5
power output ratings, 2-3 to 2-4
powerplant selection, 2-2 to 2-5
starter systems (*See* starter systems)
See also specific types of engines
gearboxes, 3-6 to 3-9. *See also* accessory unit
gear fuel pumps, 7-48
gear pumps, 6-15, 7-16
gear ratios, 3-7
General Dynamics Gulfstream, A4-6
General Electric
annular combustors, 3-33 to 3-34
counter-rotating turbines, 3-42
history, 1-6
unducted fan engines, 1-7, 1-8
See also specific engines
General Electric 90-115 turbofan engine, 4-54
General Electric CF6 turbofan engine
borescope locations, 5-13
engine instrument system, 12-2
indicating system, 12-13
inlet and exhaust wake danger areas, 5-39
thrust specific fuel consumption, 7-4, 7-6
type certificate data sheet, A2-1 to A2-7
variable angle compressor stator vane systems, 8-2
General Electric CJ610 turbojet engine, 6-23 to 6-31
General Electric GE4 turbojet engine, 1-7
General Electric I-A turbojet engine, 1-6
General Electric/Snecma CFM56 turbofan engine, 4-34 to 4-48
accessory drive module, 4-47 to 4-48
anti-stall system, 8-13 to 8-14
control display unit, 8-5
core engine module, 4-41 to 4-45
data sheet, 4-53
fan module, 4-35 to 4-41
fuel system, 7-20 to 7-28, 7-65 to 7-67
ignition system, 11-16 to 11-18
low-pressure turbine module, 4-45 to 4-47
lubrication system, 6-35 to 6-38
oil sump design, 6-10
on-condition maintenance monitoring, 5-52
overview, 4-34 to 4-35
starting system, 10-6
thrust ratings, 5-53
variable angle compressor stator vane systems, 8-4 to 8-5
Germany
aircraft manufacturers, A4-4, A4-6
gas turbine engine development, 1-5
V-1 rocket jet, 2-2
V-2 rocket jet, 2-1
gerotor pumps, 6-12 to 6-14
G-force, 3-37
Gloster Aircraft Company, 1-3
glow plug igniters, 11-12 to 11-13, 11-15
gouging, defined, 5-40, 5-58

governing, 7-14
GPU. *See* ground power units (GPU)
Gravensade, 1-2
Great Britain
aircraft manufacturers, A4-4, A4-9, A4-11, A4-14
commercial aircraft development, 1-6
supersonic aircraft, 1-7
turbojet engine development, 1-2 to 1-5
Grob Aerospace, A4-6
grooving, defined, 5-40, 5-58
gross thrust, 2-20 to 2-21
ground power units (GPU)
APU starting power, 10-6
electric starters, 10-3
pneumatic starting systems, 10-10
ground starts, 14-2 to 14-5
GTP-30 engine, 7-28 to 7-29
guttering, defined, 5-40

H

half-wave rectifiers, 11-6
halogenated hydrocarbon (Halon) fire extinguishing agents, 13-6
hand signals, A5-1
hard rubs, 3-60
hard time (HT) maintenance, 5-51
harmonics, defined, 5-49
Hawker Beechcraft, A4-6, A4-7
Heinkel Company, 1-5
Heinkel He-178, 1-5
heli-arc method, 5-29
helicopters
combination compressors, 3-21
tachometer marking guidelines, 12-33
turboshaft engines, 2-2, 2-6, 4-12
Hero's aeolipile, 1-1
high-bypass turbofan engines
advantages, 2-9 to 2-10
fan pressure ratios, 3-19
GE/Snecma CFM56 turbofan (*See* General Electric/Snecma CFM56 turbofan engine)
propulsive efficiency, 2-29 to 2-30
subsonic flight inlet ducts, 3-2
high-intensity ignition systems, 11-4 to 11-5
high-low pressure pneumatic starters, 10-14
high power checks, 14-2
high-pressure compressors (HPC), 4-4, 4-41 to 4-42
high-pressure turbines (HPT), 4-8, 4-44 to 4-45
high rotor governor, 7-16
high-tension ignition systems
inspections and maintenance, 11-14
vs. low-tension systems, 11-10
specifications and operation, 11-7 to 11-8
Hiller Aircraft Corp., A4-12
Honda Aircraft, A4-7
Honeywell GTP-30 engine, 7-28 to 7-29
Honeywell T-53 turboshaft engine, 3-34
Honeywell T-55 turboshaft engine, 2-2
Honeywell TFE-731 turbofan engine
combustors, 3-34
compressors, 3-13
fuel system, 7-20
thrust specific fuel consumption, 7-6
Honeywell TPE 331 turboprop
cockpit controls and instruments, 14-3

run-up procedures, 14-5
specifications, 2-3
horizontal drive shaft, GE/Snecma CFM56 turbofan, 4-48
horsepower
brake horsepower, 2-4
compressor requirement, 2-28 to 2-29, A8-1
equivalent shaft horsepower, 2-27 to 2-28, A8-1
formula, 2-12 to 2-13
isentropic gas horsepower, 2-29
ram shaft horsepower, 2-29
shaft horsepower (*See* shaft horsepower (Shp))
thermodynamic horsepower, 2-29
thrust horsepower, 2-25 to 2-26
hot section
combustors (*See* combustors)
diagram, 5-13
inspection and repairs, 5-25 to 5-33
materials, 3-60 to 3-61
Pratt & Whitney JT8D turbofan, 4-3
turbines (*See* turbines)
hot spots, 5-25, 5-26
hot starts, 10-2, 14-4
hot streaking, 5-26
hot tank oil systems
vs. cold tank oil systems, 6-38 to 6-39
GE CJ610 turbojet, 6-23 to 6-31
lubrication system, 6-33 to 6-35
HPC (high-pressure compressors), 4-4, 4-41 to 4-42
HPT (high-pressure turbines), 4-8, 4-44 to 4-45
HT (hard time) maintenance, 5-51
humidity, thrust impact, 2-25
hung stalls, 3-24
hung starts, 7-61, 10-2
hydraulic pressure indicator, 12-4
hydraulic quantity percent indicator, 12-4
hydraulic starters, 10-14
HYDROKIT®, 7-3
hydromechanical fuel control, 7-8 to 7-10
hydromechanical torque indicating system, 12-19, 12-20 to 12-21
hydropneumatic fuel control systems, 7-11 to 7-16
hypersonic engines, 2-1 to 2-2

I

icing
anti-icing systems, 9-1 to 9-6
conditions conducive to, 9-1 to 9-2
icy landing conditions, 3-52
igniter plugs, 11-11 to 11-15
ignition systems, 11-1 to 11-19
AC vs. DC systems, 11-9 to 11-10
components, 11-1
GE/Snecma CFM56 turbofan, 11-16 to 11-18
high-intensity systems, 11-4 to 11-5
high-tension vs. low-tension systems, 11-10
igniter plugs, 11-11 to 11-15
inspections and maintenance, 11-13 to 11-15
joule ratings, 11-5
main ignition systems, 11-1 to 11-4
troubleshooting, 11-19
types, 11-5 to 11-10

Ilysushin Corporation, A4-7
impellers, 3-10, 5-23 to 5-24
impulse-reaction blades, 3-38 to 3-41
inclusion, defined, 5-42, 5-58
indicating systems. *See* instrument systems
Indonesia, aircraft manufacturers, A4-7
Indonesian Aerospace, A4-7
in-flight data analysis, 5-54 to 5-58
inlet gearbox, GE/Snecma CFM56 turbofan, 4-47
inlet guide vanes, 3-17, 3-22
inlet pressure, 7-8
inlet section (aircraft), 3-1 to 3-6
inlet section (engine), 5-17
inlet temperature, 7-8
inspections and maintenance, 5-1 to 5-61
    component expected service life, 5-51, 5-53
    EGT system, 12-10
    engine cleaning after extinguishing agent use, 13-8
    engine time change and on-condition maintenance concepts, 5-50 to 5-51
    igniter plugs, 11-13 to 11-15
    Jetcal Analyzer, 12-10
    line maintenance (*See* line maintenance)
    locking methods for fasteners, 5-44 to 5-46
    lubrication systems, 6-7 to 6-8
    maintenance program methods, 5-51
    major vs. minor repairs, 5-10, 5-11
    nondestructive inspections (NDI) (*See* nondestructive inspections (NDI))
    oil pressure, 12-30
    shop maintenance (*See* shop maintenance)
    technical data standards, 5-60
    terms, 5-58 to 5-60
    test cell maintenance, 5-46 to 5-50
    torque wrenches, 5-42 to 5-44
    troubleshooting (*See* troubleshooting)
instrument panels, types, 12-1
instrument systems, 12-1 to 12-35
    anti-icing system, 9-4 to 9-5
    categories, 12-1
    dial face marking guidelines, 12-32 to 12-33
    engine pressure ratio system (*See* engine pressure ratio (EPR))
    exhaust temperature indicating systems, 4-10, 12-4 to 12-11, 12-33
    fuel flow indicating systems, 12-24 to 12-27
    gauge overview, 12-1 to 12-4
    Honeywell TPE 331 turboprop, 14-3
    introduction, 12-1 to 12-4
    lubrication system, 6-19 to 6-21
    oil system indicators, 12-28 to 12-32
    pressure-regulating and shutoff valve, 10-9
    run-up checks, 14-2
    tachometer percent RPM indicating systems, 12-12 to 12-17
    torque indicating systems, 12-19 to 12-24
    troubleshooting, 12-11
    See also specific indicators and gauges
integrity checks, 5-46 to 5-48
intermediate-bypass turbofan engines, 2-9
intermittent duty ignition systems, 11-1, 11-5 to 11-8
International Standard Day (ISD), 5-50
interstage compressor airflow, 3-21 to 3-22
interstage turbine temperature (ITT), 12-1, 12-4, 12-11
ISD (International Standard Day), 5-50
isentropic gas horsepower, 2-29
Italy
    aircraft manufacturers, A4-8, A4-9, A4-14
    gas turbine engine development, 1-5 to 1-6
ITT (interstage turbine temperature), 12-1, 12-4, 12-11

J

Japan, aircraft manufacturers, A4-7, A4-12, A4-13
Jet A-1 fuel, 7-1
Jet-A fuel, 7-1
Jet B fuel, 7-2
Jetcal Analyzer, 12-10, 13-3
jet fuels, 7-1 to 7-3. *See also* fuel systems
jet nozzles, thrust calculation, 2-22 to 2-23
jet propulsion theory and principles, 2-1 to 2-40
    Bernoulli's principle, 2-14 to 2-16
    Brayton cycle, 2-16 to 2-18
    defined, 2-1
    early devices, 1-2
    efficiency, 2-29 to 2-34
    horsepower (*See* horsepower)
    kinetic energy, 2-14
    Newton's laws, 2-18 to 2-20
    physics principles, 2-10 to 2-14
    potential, 2-14
    r.p.m. limits, 2-37 to 2-38
    thrust (*See* thrust)
joule ratings, ignition systems, 11-5
JP-5 fuel, 7-2
JT8D turbofan engine. *See* Pratt & Whitney JT8D turbofan engine
JT9D engine, 2-5
JT15D turbofan engine. *See* Pratt & Whitney JT15D turbofan engine
Junker Company, 1-5

K

Kaman Aerospace, A4-12
Kamov Co., A4-12
Kawasaki Industries, A4-12
kinematics, 6-2
kinetic energy, 2-14
knife-edge seals, 3-41 to 3-42
K-type thermocouples, 12-6 to 12-7

L

labyrinth bearing seals, 5-34 to 5-35
landing procedures, 14-10
laser beam welding method, 5-29 to 5-31
last chance filters, 6-29
leading edge, centrifugal compressor inspection criteria, 5-23
lean die-out, 7-1
life limited cycle time maintenance, 5-51
lift, axial vs. centrifugal compressors, 3-21
limited heavy maintenance, 5-8
line maintenance, 5-1 to 5-8
    defined, 5-1
    fluid cleaning procedure, 5-4 to 5-6
    foreign object damage, 5-3 to 5-4
    locking methods for fasteners, 5-44 to 5-46
    modular maintenance, 5-1, 5-8 to 5-11, 5-50
    scheduled maintenance inspections, 5-6 to 5-7
    scheduled maintenance repairs, 5-8
    tools, 5-2 to 5-3
    torque wrenches, 5-42 to 5-44
    troubleshooting (*See* troubleshooting)
    unscheduled maintenance, 5-8
Lockheed Corporation, A4-7
locking methods for fasteners, 5-44 to 5-46
lock washers and tabs, 5-46
lockwiring, 5-44 to 5-46
lost-wax casting, 3-61 to 3-63
low-bypass fans, fan pressure ratios, 3-19
low-bypass turbofan engines, 2-9, 3-2
low oil pressure procedures, 6-22
low oil pressure warning light, 6-19 to 6-20
low-pressure compressors (LPC), 4-3 to 4-4
low-pressure turbines (LPT), 4-45 to 4-47
low-tension ignition systems
    vs. high-tension systems, 11-10
    inspections and maintenance, 11-14 to 11-15
    specifications and operation, 11-5 to 11-6
LPC (low-pressure compressors), 4-3 to 4-4
LPT (low-pressure turbines), 4-45 to 4-47
lubrication systems, 6-1 to 6-41
    dry sump systems (*See* dry sump lubrication systems)
    GE CJ610 turbojet, 6-23 to 6-31
    GE/Snecma CFM56 turbofan, 6-35 to 6-38
    inadvertent mixing of lubricants, 6-7 to 6-8
    lubricant requirements, 6-1 to 6-3
    lubricant storage, 6-8
    Pratt & Whitney JT8D turbofan, 6-33 to 6-35
    Pratt & Whitney PT6 turboprop, 6-31 to 6-33
    principles, 6-1
    Rolls-Royce Allison 250 turboshaft, 4-24
    safety, 6-7, 6-8
    sampling, 6-3 to 6-5
    servicing, 6-7 to 6-8
    troubleshooting, 6-39 to 6-41
    types, 6-1
    wet sump systems, 6-8 to 6-9
lubrication unit, GE/Snecma CFM56 turbofan, 6-37

M

Mach number
    air temperature impact, 2-38
    ram compression ratio, 3-3
    r.p.m. limits imposed on turbine engines, 2-37
magnetic particle method, 5-13 to 5-15
magnetic pickup percent RPM system, 12-13
magnetism checks, 5-38 to 5-39, 6-29
main bearings. *See* bearings
maintenance. *See* inspections and maintenance
manufacturers list, A4-1 to A4-14
markings
    instruments, 12-32 to 12-34

procedures, 5-33
mass, 2-12
mass airflow
    compressor pressure ratio impact, 3-25 to 3-26
    Rolls-Royce Allison 250 turboshaft, 4-12
maximum continuous rating, 14-10
maximum flow stop adjustment, 7-16
MD-80, 3-55, 4-1
MD Helicopters, Inc., A4-12
Me-262 aircraft, 1-5
measurement conversion factors, A3-4 to A3-5
mechanical blockage thrust reversers, 3-51 to 3-52
mechanical monitoring, 5-54
medium-bypass turbofan engines
    features, 2-9
    subsonic flight inlet ducts, 3-2
metal contaminants, 6-3 to 6-5, 6-16, 6-29
metallization, defined, 5-58
metering valves, Bendix DP-L2® fuel control, 7-16
methyl bromide (Halon 1001—CH3Br), 13-6
micron ratings, 6-16, 7-52
Mil Co., A4-13
military aircraft
    drag chutes, 3-54
    fuel, 7-2
    history, 1-2 to 1-6
    supersonic aircraft, 2-3, 2-26, 3-4
    vectoring exhaust nozzles, 3-50 to 3-51
minimum flow adjustment, Bendix DP-L2® fuel control, 7-16
Mitsubishi Corporation, A4-7
Mitsubishi Technologies Corporation, A4-13
mixed-flow compressors, 3-28 to 3-29
modular engines. *See* General Electric/Snecma CFM56 turbofan engine
modular maintenance
    maintenance category, 5-1
    purpose, 5-8
    remanufacturing facilities, 5-11
    time between overhaul, 5-50
    types, 5-8 to 5-9
Moss, Sanford A., 1-2
motorless mass flowmeter system, 12-25 to 12-27
movable wedge inlets, 3-5
multigrade lubricants, 6-2
multiple-can combustors, 3-31

N

N_1 compressor, 3-13
N_1 fan speed indicator, 12-4, 12-13 to 12-14
N_1 indicator, 12-4
N_1 tach gauge, 12-1
N_2 compressor, 3-13
N_2 indicator, 12-4
N_2 tach gauge, 12-1
N_2 turbine, 3-41
N_3 compressor, 3-13
natural frequency of vibration, defined, 5-49
NDI. *See* nondestructive inspections (NDI)
Netherlands, aircraft manufacturers, A4-6
net thrust, 2-21 to 2-22
Newton's horseless carriage, 1-2
Newton's laws of motion, 1-2, 1-19, 2-18, 2-20
Nextant Aerospace, A4-8

NH Industries, A4-13
nickel-base alloys, 3-60
nicks, defined, 5-42, 5-58
nitrile o-ring seals, 5-46
noise protection, 7-37
noise suppression, 3-54 to 3-58
nondestructive inspections (NDI), 5-12 to 5-33
    borescoping, 5-12, 5-25
    cold section, 5-17 to 5-24
    defined, 5-12 to 5-13
    dye-penetrant method, 5-15
    eddy current method, 5-16 to 5-17
    hot section, 5-25 to 5-33
    magnetic particle method, 5-13 to 5-15
    marking parts, 5-33
    radiographic method, 5-15 to 5-16
    ultrasonic method, 5-17
nonpetroleum fuels, 7-2
nozzles
    exhaust nozzles, 2-22 to 2-23, 3-46 to 3-48, 3-51
    fuel nozzles, 7-54 to 7-59
    oil nozzles (jets), 6-27 to 6-29
    turbine nozzles, 4-6 to 4-8, 4-46

O

OC (on-condition) maintenance, 5-51
Ohain, Hans Von, 1-5
oil consumption, 6-1, 6-8. *See also* lubrication systems
oil coolers, 6-24 to 6-27
oil filler openings
    flapper seals, 6-11
    markings required by federal regulations, 6-1
    removal of cap during remote pressure fill, 6-10
    safety, 6-8
    securing cap, 6-8
oil filters, 6-15 to 6-23
    assembly, 6-17 to 6-18
    contaminants, 6-16
    differential pressure light, 6-21
    dual-pressure indicating system, 6-21
    filter bypass warning light, 6-20 to 6-21
    filter pop-out warning, 6-22, 6-37
    forces acting on, 6-16 to 6-17
    function, 6-15
    last chance filters, 6-29
    low oil pressure warning light, 6-19 to 6-20
    microns, 6-16
    oil pressure relief valve interaction, 6-18 to 6-19
    types, 6-17
oil jets (nozzles), 6-27 to 6-29
oil pressure indicating system
    design, 12-29 to 12-31
    dial face markings, 12-32
    gauge, 12-1, 12-4
    troubleshooting engine with, 12-32
oil pressure relief valves
    GE CJ610 turbojet, 6-24
    GE/Snecma CFM56 turbofan, 6-37
    location, 6-18 to 6-19
oil pressure subsystem. *See* pressure lubrication subsystems
oil pumps, 6-11 to 6-15
oil quantity gauge, 12-1
oil quantity indicator, 12-4

oil scavenge system. *See* scavenge lubrication subsystem
oil supply circuit, GE/Snecma CFM56 turbofan, 6-35 to 6-37
oil system indicators, 12-28 to 12-32
oil tanks
    design and construction, 6-10 to 6-11
    GE/Snecma CFM56 turbofan, 6-35
    hot vs. cold tank systems, 6-38 to 6-39
oil temperature indicating systems
    design, 12-28 to 12-29
    dial face markings, 12-33
    gauges, 12-1, 12-4
oil vent system. *See* vent lubrication subsystems
Olympus turbojet engine, 1-7
on-condition (OC) maintenance, 5-51
"one-in, one-out" theory, 2-20
open-tip blades, 3-41
operating procedures. *See* engine operation
o-ring seals, 5-46
output reduction gearbox, 2-7
overall efficiency, 2-33
overhauls, engine, 5-50 to 5-51
overheat detection. *See* fire/overheat detection and extinguishing systems
overrunning clutch, 10-3, 10-6
over-speed condition, 7-10
overtemperature, 5-27, 7-30

P

part power trims, 7-31, 7-36
peening, defined, 5-42, 5-58
People's Republic of China, aircraft manufacturers, A4-8, A4-13
percent RPM indicating systems, 12-12 to 12-17
performance checks
    turbojet and turbofan engines, 7-30 to 7-31
    turboprop and turboshaft engines, 7-38 to 7-43
performance data, ground vs. flight, A10-1
performance indicators and monitoring, types, 5-54, 12-1
performance ratings, Rolls-Royce Allison 250 turboshaft, 4-25
permanent magnet alternators (PMA), 11-5
petroleum lubricants, 6-2. *See also* lubrication systems
"phase shift" electronic indicating system, 12-19, 12-22
photoelectric sensors, 13-6
Piaggio Aero Industries, A4-8
Pilatus Corporation, A4-8
Piper Aircraft, A4-8
Piper Corporation, A4-8
piston engines, vs. turbine engines, 2-4 to 2-5
pitting, defined, 5-42, 5-58
plain bearings (bushings), 5-33
plasma sprays or coatings
    cold section parts, 3-60
    procedures, 5-21 to 5-22
    turbine case repairs, 5-29
PMA (permanent magnet alternators), 11-5
pneumatic computing section, hydropneumatic fuel control system, 7-11 to 7-13
pneumatic fire/overheat detection system, 13-3 to 13-6, 13-8 to 13-10

pneumatic starters, 10-6 to 10-14
    air supply, 10-10
    crash engagement, 10-8
    duty cycle, 10-13
    FADEC interface, 10-13 to 10-14
    introduction, 10-6 to 10-8
    oil supply, 10-6
    operating procedure, 10-10 to 10-14
polyacrylate o-ring seals, 5-46
potential energy, 2-14
powder metallurgy, 3-60
power, defined, 2-12
power and accessory unit, Rolls-Royce Allison 250 turboshaft, 4-22
power back operation, 3-54
power checks, 7-31
Power Jets, Ltd., 1-2
power levers
    Bendix DP-L2® fuel control, 7-16
    movement, 7-10
    Pratt & Whitney PT6 turboprop engine, 14-5
    See also trimming
power management, 7-25 to 7-28
power output ratings, 2-3 to 2-4
powerplant removal and disassembly, 5-11
powerplant selection, 2-2 to 2-5
power turbines
    hydropneumatic fuel control system, 7-13, 7-14 to 7-16
    Pratt & Whitney PT6 turboprop, 4-32 to 4-33, 7-13, 7-16
    Rolls-Royce Allison 250 turboshaft, 4-20 to 4-22
Pratt & Whitney, can-annular combustor use, 3-31 to 3-32
Pratt & Whitney 100 series turboprop engine, 3-10
Pratt & Whitney 4090 turbofan engine, 4-55
Pratt & Whitney JT8D turbofan engine, 4-1 to 4-12
    accessory unit, 4-9
    anti-stall system, 8-10 to 8-11
    bearings, 4-10 to 4-12, 5-40
    combustors, 4-5 to 4-6
    compressors, 4-3 to 4-5
    data sheet, 4-50
    design feature overview, 4-1 to 4-3
    diffuser case, 4-4 to 4-5
    directional references, 4-13
    engine section overview, 4-3
    exhaust section, 4-10
    fuel system, 7-64, 7-65
    identification of cases, flanges, and materials, 4-13
    lubrication system, 6-33 to 6-35
    overview, 4-1
    station locations, 4-12
    takeoff EPR setting, 4-14
    takeoff values, 4-15
    test-run worksheet, 4-15
    thrust according to runway altitude, 4-14
    turbines, 4-6 to 4-9
Pratt & Whitney JT9D engine, 2-5
Pratt & Whitney JT15D turbofan engine
    combustors, 3-34
    cost, 5-51
    fuel system, 7-16 to 7-18
    inlet and exhaust jet wake danger areas, 7-38
    line maintenance tools, 5-2 to 5-3
Pratt & Whitney PT6 turboprop engine, 4-24 to 4-34
    accessory unit, 4-34
    bearings, 4-37, 5-36
    combustors, 3-34, 4-30
    compressors, 4-24, 4-29 to 4-30
    data sheet, 4-52
    engine leading particulars, 4-38
    engine section overview, 4-24
    exhaust section, 4-33
    fluid cleaning procedure, 5-5
    fuel system, 7-11 to 7-16
    gas path, 4-24
    ignition system, 11-12
    lubrication system, 6-31 to 6-33
    operating conditions and limits, 4-38
    overview, 4-24
    propeller reduction gearbox, 4-33 to 4-34
    run-up procedures, 14-5 to 14-9
    station numbers, 4-24
    turbines, 4-30 to 4-33
Pratt & Whitney PW4000 engine, 2-9
Pratt & Whitney R-4360 engine, 2-5
precombustor chambers, 3-34
pressure
    Bernoulli's principle, 2-14 to 2-16
    Brayton cycle, 2-16 to 2-18
    defined, 2-12
pressure, static (P_s), 2-15, 3-29
pressure, total. *See* total pressure (P_t)
pressure-atomizing fuel nozzles, 7-54 to 7-59
pressure correction factors, A9-1 to A9-2
pressure lubrication subsystems
    GE CJ610 turbojet, 6-23 to 6-29
    GE/Snecma CFM56 turbofan, 6-35 to 6-37
    Pratt & Whitney JT8D turbofan, 6-33
    Pratt & Whitney PT6 turboprop, 6-31 to 6-33
pressure-regulated oil systems
    GE/Snecma CFM56 turbofan, 6-35 to 6-38
    Pratt & Whitney JT8D turbofan, 6-33 to 6-35
    Pratt & Whitney PT6 turboprop, 6-31 to 6-33
pressurization, of oil tanks, 6-10
pressurizing and dump (P & D) valves, 7-59 to 7-61
PRIST®, 7-3
propeller control levers, 14-5
propeller reduction gearbox, 4-33 to 4-34
propeller thrust (F_p), 2-26 to 2-27
propeller windmilling, 14-7
propfan engines
    design, 2-7 to 2-8
    early development, 1-8
    fan bypass ratio, 3-20
propulsive efficiency, 2-29 to 2-32
Pt_2 probes, 9-3, 12-18
PT6 turboprop engine. *See* Pratt & Whitney PT6 turboprop engine
Pt_7 probes, 4-10, 9-3, 12-18
pulsejet, 2-2
purging procedure, 14-4, 14-6 to 14-7
PW4000 engine, 2-9

Q
quantitative debris monitor (QDM), 6-29

R
R-4360 engine, 2-5
radial drive shaft, GE/Snecma CFM56 turbofan, 4-47
radial inflow turbines, 3-45
radial outflow compressors. *See* centrifugal flow compressors
radiographic method, 5-15 to 5-16
ram-air starting procedure, 14-5
RAM drag, 3-50
ramjet, 2-1 to 2-2
ram pressure, 2-16, A8-1
ram pressure recovery, 3-2 to 3-4
ram shaft horsepower, 2-29
rated compressor pressure ratio (Cr), 7-8
rathode filter spectroscopy (RFT), 6-5
RB-211 turbofan engine, 7-18 to 7-20
reaction principle, 1-1
reciprocating engines
    advantages and disadvantages, 2-2, 2-5
    power output, 2-4
reduced smoke combustors, 3-30, 3-34 to 3-36
regional aircraft. *See* commuter aircraft
regulator valves, 9-3
Reims Aviation, A4-8
relief valves, Bendix DP-L2® fuel control, 7-16
relights, 14-4, 14-8
remanufacturing facilities, 5-11
removal of powerplant, 5-11
repairs. *See* inspections and maintenance
resistance bulb oil temperature indicating system, 12-28
resonance, defined, 5-49
reverse flow annular combustors, 3-30
reverse thrust indicator, 12-4
reversing propellers, 3-54
RFT (rathode filter spectroscopy), 6-5
rich blowout, 7-1
rocket jets, 2-1
Rogerson Helicopter Co., A4-13
roller bearings, 5-33 to 5-34
Rolls-Royce Allison 250 turboshaft engine, 4-12 to 4-24
    bearings and lubrication system, 4-22 to 4-24
    combustors, 4-18
    compressors, 4-17 to 4-18
    cost, 5-51
    data sheet, 4-51
    engine section overview, 4-15 to 4-17
    gas path, 4-12
    overview, 4-12
    performance ratings, 4-25
    power and accessory unit, 4-22
    turbines, 4-18 to 4-22
    type certificate data sheet, A1-1 to A1-4
    water injection system, 7-47
Rolls-Royce Dart turboprop engine, 3-31
Rolls-Royce Olympus turbojet engine, 1-7
Rolls-Royce RB-211 turbofan engine, 7-18 to 7-20
Rolls-Royce Tay engine, 7-61
Rolls-Royce TRENT 895 turbofan engine, 4-56, 5-51

rotary air-oil separators, 6-31
rotors
    compressors, 3-14, 3-28, 3-29
    oil pumps, 6-12 to 6-14
    turbines, 3-37
r.p.m.
    converting percent r.p.m. to actual r.p.m., 7-42
    limits, 2-37 to 2-38, 12-14
    percent RPM indicating systems, 12-12 to 12-17
    thrust impact, 2-36 to 2-37
run-up
    procedures, 14-1 to 14-5
    turboprop engines, 14-5 to 14-9
Russia
    aircraft manufacturers, A4-1, A4-2, A4-7, A4-9, A4-12, A4-13
    supersonic passenger liner, 1-8

S

Saab Corporation, A4-8
Sabreliner Corporation, A4-8
SAC (single annular combustors), 3-33, 4-43 to 4-44
SAE (Society of Automotive Engineers), lubricant ratings, 6-2
safety precautions
    ear protection, 7-37
    engine operation, 14-1
    fuel handling, 7-2 to 7-3
    ground starts, 14-4 to 14-5
    high-intensity ignition systems, 11-4 to 11-5
    starter system features, 10-6
    trimming, 7-37
sand and ice separators, 3-5 to 3-6
Saybolt-Universal Seconds (SUS) viscosimeter, 6-2
scavenge lubrication subsystem
    GE CJ610 turbojet, 6-29
    GE/Snecma CFM56 turbofan, 6-37 to 6-38
    Pratt & Whitney JT8D turbofan, 6-35
    Pratt & Whitney PT6 turboprop, 6-33
Schweizer Aircraft Corporation, A4-13
scoring, defined, 5-42, 5-58
scramjet, 2-1 to 2-2
scratches, defined, 5-58
scuffing, defined, 5-58
seal drains, 3-7
secondary air combustion section, 3-30
seizure, defined, 5-58
service life of components, 5-51, 5-53
SFC (specific fuel consumption), 7-6 to 7-7
shaft horsepower (Shp)
    calculation from cockpit reading, 7-42 to 7-43
    calculations, 2-26 to 2-28, 7-40 to 7-42
    FAA engine power ratings, 14-9
    water-alcohol injection impact, 7-48
shock stalls, 2-30, 2-37
shock wave inlets, 3-4 to 3-5
shop maintenance, 5-8 to 5-11
    categories, 5-8
    locking methods for fasteners, 5-44 to 5-46
    modular maintenance, 5-1, 5-8 to 5-11, 5-50
    test cell maintenance, 5-46 to 5-50
    torque wrenches, 5-42 to 5-44

troubleshooting (See troubleshooting)
Shp. See shaft horsepower (Shp)
shroud ring, 3-38
shrouds, 3-41 to 3-42
shutdown, engine. See engine shutdown
Sikorsky (United Technologies), A4-13
silicone o-ring seals, 5-46
simplex fuel nozzles, 7-54 to 7-55
single annular combustors (SAC), 3-33, 4-43 to 4-44
single-crystal casting, 3-60, 3-63
single-line duplex fuel nozzles, 7-55 to 7-56
single loop continuous loop fire/overheat detection system, 13-2 to 13-3
single-spool axial compressors, 3-13
single-wire core continuous loop fire/overheat detection system, 13-2 to 13-3
single-wire thermal overheat detection switch, 13-1
sliding vane fuel pumps, 7-48
smoke detectors, 13-6
smokeless combustors, 3-30, 3-34 to 3-36
Snecma CFM56 turbofan engine. See General Electric/Snecma CFM56 turbofan engine
Socata (EADS), A4-8
Society of Automotive Engineers (SAE), lubricant ratings, 6-2
solid-state circuitry ignition systems, 11-8 to 11-9
South Africa, aircraft manufacturers, A4-11
space shuttle, 2-1
Spain, aircraft manufacturers, A4-4
spalling, defined, 5-42, 5-58
spark igniters, 11-11 to 11-12
specific gravity adjustment, 7-30
specific heat, A8-1
spectrometric (spectrographic) oil analysis, 6-3 to 6-5
Spectrum Aeronautical, A4-9
speed of sound
    chart, A6-1 to A6-2
    r.p.m. limitations, 2-38
speed-rated fan engines
    engine pressure ratio system, 12-17
    flat rating, 7-37
    trimming procedure, 7-31, 7-32
    trim restrictions, 7-37
spinner front cones, 4-36 to 4-37
spools, 3-12 to 3-14
sprag clutch assemblies, 10-6
squealer tips, 3-16 to 3-17
squibs, 13-6, 13-10
staged fuel nozzles, 7-56 to 7-58
stall margin graph, 3-26 to 3-27
stalls
    compressor stalls, 3-24 to 3-29, 8-2
    shock stalls, 2-30, 2-37
    See also anti-stall systems
standard atmosphere chart, A7-1
standard day conditions, 5-49 to 5-50
start control levers, 14-5
starter-generators, 10-3 to 10-6
starter systems, 10-1 to 10-19
    alternative systems, 10-14
    cautions, 14-9
    electric starters, 10-3
    FADEC capabilities, 14-2 to 14-4
    fires during startup, 13-6 to 13-8
    ground starts, 14-2 to 14-5
    hydropneumatic fuel control system, 7-14

in-flight ram-air procedure, 14-5
location, 10-1
operating procedures, 14-1 to 14-2
pneumatic starters, 10-6 to 10-14
Pratt & Whitney PT6 turboprop engine, 14-6
pressure-regulating and shutoff valve, 10-9
starter-generators, 10-3 to 10-6
starting process, 10-1 to 10-3
troubleshooting, 10-18
static pressure (Ps), 2-15, 3-29
station numbers
    Pratt & Whitney JT8D turbofan, 4-12
    Pratt & Whitney PT6 turboprop, 4-24
    purpose, 3-63
stators
    compressors (See compressor stator vanes)
    inspection and repairs, 5-24
    turbines, 3-37 to 3-38
straight-through combustors, 3-29
stress, defined, 5-58
subsonic aircraft
    convergent-divergent exhaust ducts, 3-48 to 3-49
    flight inlet ducts, 3-2
    propulsive efficiency, 2-29 to 2-30
    tail cone, 3-46
    variable area exhaust nozzles, 3-51
Sukhoi Design Bureau, A4-9
super alloys, 3-60
supersonic aircraft
    convergent-divergent exhaust ducts, 3-48 to 3-49
    history, 1-7, 1-8
    inlet ducts, 3-4 to 3-5
    propulsive efficiency, 2-29 to 2-30
    thrust specific fuel consumption, 7-6
surge margin graph, 3-26 to 3-27
surges, defined, 3-26
SUS (Saybolt-Universal Seconds) viscosimeter, 6-2
Sweden, aircraft manufacturers, A4-8
Switzerland, aircraft manufacturers, A4-8
synchronous mass flow system, 12-24 to 12-25
synthetic lubricants
    characteristics, 6-1, 6-5
    discoloration, 6-5 to 6-7
    properties, 6-7
    safety, 6-7
    types, 6-5, 6-7
    viscosity, 6-2
    See also lubrication systems

T

T-53 turboshaft engine, 3-34
T-55 turboshaft engine, 2-2
tachometer percent RPM indicating systems, 12-12 to 12-17
tachometers, marking guidelines, 12-33
tail cones, 3-46
tailpipe area thrust, 2-24 to 2-25
tailpipes, 3-46, 14-4
takeoff cautions, 14-9 to 14-10
takeoff values and settings
    charts, 7-42
    Pratt & Whitney JT8D turbofan, 4-14, 4-15
    Pratt & Whitney PT6 turboprop, 14-7

TAPS (Twin Annular Premixing Swirler)® combustor, 3-33 to 3-34, 7-57 to 7-58
taxi procedure, 14-2, 14-5
Tay engine, 7-61
TBO (time between overhaul), 5-50 to 5-51
TBV (transient bleed valve), 8-13 to 8-14
tears, defined, 5-58
technical data standards, 5-60
temperature
    axial flow compressor impact, 3-14
    conversions, A3-2 to A3-3
    correction factors, A9-3 to A9-4
    defined, 2-12
    flat rating, 7-37 to 7-38
    Mach number impact, 2-38
    thrust impact, 2-34 to 2-35
    turbine inlet temperature, 2-33 to 2-34
temperature sensors, Bendix DP-L2® fuel control, 7-16
test cell maintenance, 5-46 to 5-50
TFE-731 turbofan engine. See Honeywell TFE-731 turbofan engine
T-handles, manual operation with, 10-9
thermal anti-ice indicator, 12-4
thermal efficiency, 2-32 to 2-34
Thermatic Compressor Rotor®, 3-28
thermocouple oil temperature indicating system, 12-28 to 12-29
thermocouples, 12-5 to 12-7
thermodynamic horsepower, 2-29
Thp (thrust horsepower), calculation, 2-25 to 2-26
three-phase generator percent RPM system, 12-13
throttle lever, GE/Snecma CFM56 turbofan, 7-26
throttle spring-back checks, 7-31
through-flow combustors, 3-29
thrust
    afterburners, 3-50 to 3-51
    altitude impact, 2-5, 2-35
    calculations, 2-20 to 2-27
    distribution, 2-23 to 2-25
    factors, 2-34 to 2-37
    gross thrust, 2-20 to 2-21
    and humidity, 2-25
    net thrust, 2-21 to 2-22
    Pratt & Whitney JT8D turbofan, 4-14
    propeller vs. jet, 2-18 to 2-20
    ratings, 2-3 to 2-4
    water injection thrust augmentation, 7-43 to 7-47
thrust control operating modes, GE/Snecma CFM56 turbofan, 7-26 to 7-27
thrust horsepower (Thp), calculation, 2-25 to 2-26
thrust horsepower specific fuel consumption, 7-6 to 7-7
thrust indicators, 12-33
thrust lever, GE/Snecma CFM56 turbofan, 7-26
thrust reversers, 3-51 to 3-54
thrust specific fuel consumption (TSFC), 7-3 to 7-7
thrust spoilers, 3-54
time between overhaul (TBO), 5-50 to 5-51
tip design, compressor blades, 3-16 to 3-17
tip speed (Ts), 2-37 to 2-38
TIT (turbine inlet temperature), 2-33 to 2-34, 12-4 to 12-5
titanium, 3-59 to 3-60

torque
    calculations and conversions, 7-42
    limits, 12-22
torque indicating systems, 12-19 to 12-24, 12-33
torquemeters, 4-33 to 4-34
torque wrenches, 5-42 to 5-44
total air temperature (TAT) indicator, 12-4
total pressure (Pt)
    calculations, A8-1
    compressor-diffuser section, 3-29
    measurement, 2-15 to 2-16
trailing edge, centrifugal compressor inspection criteria, 5-23 to 5-24
transfer gearbox, GE/Snecma CFM56 turbofan, 4-48
transient bleed valve (TBV) systems, 8-13 to 8-14
transient stalls, 3-24
transonic compressor blades, 3-28
trend analysis, 5-54
TRENT 895 turbofan engine, 4-56, 5-51
trimming, 7-30 to 7-37
    defined, 7-30
    engine pressure ratio trims, 7-31 to 7-36
    FADEC controlled engines, 7-34 to 7-36
    fan speed trims, 7-32 to 7-36
    guidelines, 7-30 to 7-31
    part power trim, 7-31
    restrictions, 7-36 to 7-37
    safety, 7-37
triple-spool axial compressors, 3-13 to 3-14
troubleshooting, 5-51 to 5-60
    anti-icing systems, 9-5
    compressor bleed anti-stall systems, 8-14
    EGT/ITT indicating systems, 12-11
    engines using
        EGT/ITT indicating system, 12-11
        EPR indicating system, 12-19
        fuel flow indicating system, 12-27
        oil indicating system, 12-32
        tachometer percent RPM indicating system, 12-17
        torque indicating system, 12-24
    EPR system, 12-18 to 12-19
    FADEC, 5-53 to 5-54
    fuel flow indicating systems, 12-27
    fuel system, 7-68 to 7-69
    guidelines, 5-51 to 5-52
    ignition systems, 11-19
    in-flight data analysis, 5-54 to 5-58
    lubrication systems, 6-39 to 6-41
    oil indicating systems, 12-31 to 12-32
    starter systems, 10-18
    tachometer percent RPM indicating system, 12-16
    terms, 5-58 to 5-60
    torque indicating systems, 12-24
    variable vane anti-stall systems, 8-6
TSFC (thrust specific fuel consumption), 7-3 to 7-7
Tupolev Corporation, A4-9
turbine blades
    active clearance control, 3-44
    cleaning, 5-6
    creep, 5-27
    inspection and repairs, 5-27 to 5-29
    low-pressure turbine modules, 4-46

    replacement, 5-27
    stress rupture cracks, 5-27
turbine cases
    active clearance control, 3-44
    design and construction, 3-60, 4-46
    inspection and repairs, 5-29 to 5-33
turbine exhaust collectors, 3-45 to 3-46
turbine impingement starters, 10-14
turbine inlet temperature (TIT), 2-33 to 2-34, 12-4 to 12-5
turbine nozzle guide vane assembly, 3-37
turbine nozzles
    low-pressure turbine modules, 4-46
    Pratt & Whitney JT8D turbofan, 4-6 to 4-8
turbine outlet area thrust, 2-24
turbine rotor assembly, 3-39, 3-41
turbines
    axial construction, 3-41 to 3-44
    components and operation, 3-36 to 3-38
    construction materials, 3-60 to 3-62
    counter-rotating turbines, 3-42
    efficiency, 2-34, 3-42
    function, 3-36
    GE/Snecma CFM56 turbofan, 4-44 to 4-47
    G-force on blade, 3-37
    impulse-reaction blades, 3-38 to 3-41
    inspection and repairs, 5-25 to 5-33
    malfunctions, 5-58
    Pratt & Whitney JT8D turbofan, 4-6 to 4-9
    Pratt & Whitney PT6 turboprop, 4-30 to 4-33
    radial inflow turbines, 3-45
    Rolls-Royce Allison 250 turboshaft, 4-18 to 4-22
    serial numbers, 5-34
turbine stages, 2-7, 3-37
turbine vanes
    axial turbines, 3-42 to 3-44
    cleaning, 5-6
    design and construction, 3-61
    inspection and repairs, 5-29 to 5-33
    untwist, 5-29
turbine wheels
    history, 1-2
    indicating systems, 12-4
    inspection and repairs, 5-26 to 5-27
    location, 3-36
    turbofan engines, 2-8
    turbojet engines, 2-6
turbofan engines
    advantages, 2-3, 2-38 to 2-39
    components and operation, 2-8 to 2-10
    fan installation, 2-8
    igniter plug installation, 11-12
    noise suppression, 3-56 to 3-57
    performance checks, 7-30 to 7-31
    power output, 2-4
    propulsive efficiency, 2-29 to 2-30
    run-up, 14-1 to 14-2
    starter-generators, 10-3 to 10-4
    thrust horsepower, 2-25 to 2-26
    thrust indicators, 12-33
    thrust specific fuel consumption, 7-3 to 7-4
    types, 2-9 to 2-10
    ultra high-bypass turbofan engines, 2-9 to 2-10, 2-29 to 2-30, 3-20
    See also specific engine names

turbojet engines
    advantages and disadvantages, 2-3, 2-38 to 2-39
    components and operation, 2-5 to 2-6
    history, 1-2 to 1-5
    performance checks, 7-30 to 7-31
    power output, 2-4
    propulsive efficiency, 2-29 to 2-30
    run-up, 14-1 to 14-2
    starter-generators, 10-3 to 10-4
    thrust horsepower, 2-25 to 2-26
    thrust indicators, 12-33
    See also specific engine names
turboprop engines
    advantages, 2-2 to 2-3
    components and operation, 2-6 to 2-8
    equivalent shaft horsepower, 2-27 to 2-28
    fixed vs. free power turbine, 2-6 to 2-7
    full reversing propellers, 3-54
    performance checks, 7-38 to 7-43
    power output, 2-4, 2-7
    run-up procedures, 14-5 to 14-9
    starter-generators, 10-3 to 10-4
    thrust, 2-26 to 2-27
    See also specific engine names
turboshaft engines
    advantages, 2-2
    components and operation, 2-6
    performance checks, 7-38 to 7-43
    starter-generators, 10-3 to 10-4
    See also specific engine names
turbo-supercharger, 1-2
Twin Annular Premixing Swirler (TAPS)® combustor, 3-33 to 3-34, 7-57 to 7-58
two-wire overheat detection switch, 13-1 to 13-2
type certificate data sheets
    No. E23EA (GE CF6 turbofan), A2-1 to A2-7
    No. E1GL (Allison 250-C28), A1-1 to A1-4

U

UDF (unducted fan) engines, 1-7, 1-8, 2-7 to 2-8
ultra high-bypass turbofan engines
    fan bypass ratio, 3-20
    features, 2-9 to 2-10
    propulsive efficiency, 2-29 to 2-30

ultra low-bypass turbofan engines, 2-9
ultrasonic method, 5-17
unbalanced condition, defined, 5-58
under-speed condition, 7-10
unducted fan engines (UDF), 1-7, 1-8, 2-7 to 2-8
United States, gas turbine engine development, 1-6
United Technologies, A4-13 to A4-14
unlimited heavy maintenance, 5-8
unmixed exhaust thrust, 2-25
untwist, 5-29
USSR TU-144, 1-8

V

V-1/V-2 rocket jet, 2-2
valve systems, bleed anti-stall systems, 8-10 to 8-14
vane flowmeter system, 12-24
vane oil pumps, 6-11 to 6-12
vanes. *See* compressor stator vanes; turbine vanes
vaporizing fuel nozzles, 7-59
variable angle compressor stator vane systems, 8-1 to 8-5, 8-6
variable angle inlet guide vane systems, 8-5 to 8-6
variable area exhaust nozzles, 3-51
variable bleed valve systems, 8-13 to 8-14
variable pitch turbofan engines, 2-10
variable-pressure lubrication system, GE CJ610 turbojet, 6-23 to 6-31
variable stator vane (VSV) system, 8-4 to 8-5
vectoring exhaust nozzles, 3-50 to 3-51
vectors
    defined, 3-22
    interstage compressor airflow, 3-22
velocity
    Bernoulli's principle, 2-16
    calculation, 2-13
vent lubrication subsystems
    GE CJ610 turbojet, 6-29 to 6-31
    GE/Snecma CFM56 turbofan, 6-37 to 6-38
    Pratt & Whitney JT8D turbofan, 6-35
    Pratt & Whitney PT6 turboprop, 6-33
very light jets (VLJs), 1-8
vibration analysis, 5-46 to 5-49
vibration indicator, 12-4

Vickers Viscount, 1-6, 1-8
viscosity, 6-1 to 6-3
VLJs (very light jets), 1-8
Von Ohain, Hans, 1-5
vortex dissipators, 3-6
V-STOL aircraft, 3-51
VSV (variable stator vane) system, 8-4 to 8-5
Vulcanair Corporation, A4-9
Vulcanair Spa, A4-14

W

water detection in fuels, 7-3
water injection thrust augmentation, 7-43 to 7-47
water washes, 5-4 to 5-6
wear, defined, 5-60
weather conditions
    icing, 9-1 to 9-2
    trim restrictions, 7-36 to 7-37
    wet landings, 3-52
weight, 2-10
weight of fuel, 7-3, 7-8
Westland Helicopter LTD, A4-14
wet landing conditions, thrust reversers, 3-52
wet sump lubrication systems, 6-8 to 6-9
Whittle, Frank, 1-2 to 1-5, 2-5
Whittle W-1/W-2, 1-3
wind conditions, trim restrictions, 7-36 to 7-37
work, 2-12

X

x-ray inspections, 5-15 to 5-16

Y

Yakovlev Corporation, A4-9